D0001628

THE LETTERS OF
Jessie Benton Frémont

THE LETTERS OF
Jessie Benton Frémont

EDITED BY

PAMELA HERR AND MARY LEE SPENCE

UNIVERSITY OF ILLINOIS PRESS
Urbana and Chicago

Frontispiece: Jessie Benton Frémont. From the portrait by T. Buchanan Read in 1856 (Courtesy of the Southwest Museum, Los Angeles)

© 1993 by the Board of Trustees of the University of Illinois
Manufactured in the United States of America
C 5 4 3 2 1

This book is printed on acid-free paper.

Library of Congress Cataloging-in-Publication Data

Frémont, Jessie Benton, 1824–1902.
  [Correspondence. Selections]
  The letters of Jessie Benton Frémont / edited by Pamela Herr and
Mary Lee Spence.
      p.   cm.
  Includes bibliographical references and index.
  ISBN 0-252-01942-3 (cl)
  1. Frémont, Jessie Benton, 1824–1902—Correspondence. 2. Frémont,
John Charles, 1813–1890. 3. Pioneers—United States—
Correspondence. 4. Women pioneers—United States—Correspondence.
I. Herr, Pamela. II. Spence, Mary Lee. III. Title.
E415.9.F79F74   1993
973.6′092—dc20
  [B]   92-5871
                                                                   CIP

CONTENTS

Illustrations follow pages 100 and 416

ACKNOWLEDGMENTS

Many scholars, librarians, and institutions have assisted in the preparation of this volume. While it is impossible to list all by name, we are profoundly grateful to them. At the institutional level, we single out three for special thanks: the National Historical Publications and Records Commission for its financial support and the unflagging cooperation of its staff; the University of Illinois Press, our publisher, for its sustained interest in the project; the Research Board of the University of Illinois for the purchase of a computer.

At the personal level, we wish to thank Anthony Shipps, Indiana University, for help in ferreting out obscure literary quotations and University of Illinois professors Stanley Shinall, for assistance with French translations, Robert Johannsen and John Hoffman, for advice on the Civil War period, and Clark C. Spence, for solving computer problems. Virginia J. Laas, the editor of *Wartime Washington: The Civil War Letters of Elizabeth Blair Lee,* answered knotty questions about the Blairs. Barton J. Bernstein of Stanford commented perceptively on several of the essays and gave his steady encouragement to the entire project, as did Edith Gelles of the Stanford Institute for Research on Women and Gender. Members of the Stanford Biographer's Seminar insightfully discussed the 1856 election essay and letter selection.

We are also grateful to Paula Frémont Cummings, of Boulder, Colorado, the great-great-granddaughter of Jessie Benton Frémont, for representing the family in granting us permission to use certain papers not in government repositories.

The editors have shared equally in the work on the volume.

Jessie Benton Frémont:
AN OVERVIEW

The correspondence of Jessie Benton Frémont forms a remarkable portrait of a woman, a marriage, and an age. Clever, bold, and ambitious, she was one of the most famous and controversial women in Victorian America. As the favorite child of powerful Senator Thomas Hart Benton of Missouri and as the wife of John Charles Frémont, explorer, gold-rush millionaire, presidential candidate, and Civil War general, she not only witnessed but also attempted to influence many of the major events and movements of her time. Although as a woman she was severely restricted in the part she could play, she managed to carve out a significant role for herself as a writer, a dedicated abolitionist, and as "secretary and other self"[1] to her ambitious and mercurial husband.

At seventeen, she defied her family to elope with the dashing young explorer who was born illegitimate. As a young bride, she collaborated with him on the accounts of his exploring expeditions that made him famous and persuaded thousands to head west. Journeying to California herself in 1849, and again in 1851 and 1858, she came to know the rough cosmopolitanism of San Francisco and the primitive isolation of Bear Valley in the Sierra Nevada foothills, where their Las Mariposas mines brought them a fortune in gold. During these years, she also bore five children, two of whom died in infancy.

In 1856, when John Frémont ran for the presidency as the first candidate of the newly formed Republican party, she served as a behind-the-scenes aide in what became known as the "Frémont and Jessie" campaign. "What a shame that *women* can't vote!" exclaimed abolitionist Lydia Maria Child. "We'd carry 'our Jessie' into the White House on our shoulders, *would n't* we."[2]

In the early months of the Civil War, when John Frémont was appointed major general with headquarters in rebel-threatened St. Louis, she was branded "General Jessie" for her role as his chief aide and confidant. When he was dismissed by Abraham Lincoln, in part because he had issued an unauthorized emancipation proclamation freeing the slaves of Missouri rebels, Jessie became an outspoken critic of the president's "tenderness toward slavery."[3]

After the Civil War, John was irresistibly drawn into dubious business schemes that tarnished his reputation and dissipated their fortune. By the mid-1870s, the Frémonts were living in genteel poverty, and Jessie began to write professionally, turning out reminiscences and children's stories to augment the family income.

Charming, imperious, outspoken, and original, she evoked controversy all her life. Meeting her in 1859 when the Frémont family was living in isolated Bear Valley, California, writer Richard Henry Dana pronounced her "a heroine equal to either fortune, the salons of Paris and the drawing-rooms of New York and Washington, or the roughest life of the remote and wild . . . Mariposa."[4] A politically sympathetic journalist who knew her in St. Louis during the Civil War was dazzled by her "great intellectual power" and "quick feminine intuitions." He described her as "an uncompromising friend and a 'good hater'; an enthusiastic believer in the destiny of her husband, an invaluable assistant in his arduous labors, yet full of wifely and motherly tenderness." She was, he concluded expansively, not only a "historic woman, but the greatest woman in America."[5] To many others, however, her active if half-concealed role was a flagrant violation of woman's proper sphere. Typical was the two-edged remark of a man who met the Frémonts in San Francisco in 1849 and pronounced her "the better man of the two."[6] To another, commenting on her attempt to spare a black man the death penalty, she was a "fighting cuss."[7]

Women tended to be more sympathetic. Rebecca Harding Davis remembered her "keen intellect" and "magnetic charm."[8] Although conservative New Yorker Maria Daly, who met her during the Civil War, expected to dislike her, she found her brilliant and accustomed to rule, yet without hypocrisy. "I'm afraid she is too positive and truthful to be popular in New York. Nobody likes so much fresh breeze and so much sunlight."[9]

To the outside world Jessie Frémont could appear bold and out-spoken, yet her letters often reveal ambivalence and confusion about woman's role. Enmeshed in a culture in which women were expected to be pious, passive, and domestic, she struggled, both as a writer and in her own life, to conceal her natural temperament behind charm, indirection, and anecdote. "Feminine courtesy, and deference, are the crutches the public expects a woman to use," she explained, acknowledging the handicaps of her gender.[10] She came to be so firmly wedded to the paths of indirection that in 1866, when Elizabeth Cady Stanton asked her to sign a petition for woman's suffrage, she refused, explaining that "women in their present position manage men better." More ambivalent than her words conveyed, several months later she sent money for the cause.[11]

We have located more than 800 of Jessie Frémont's letters, of which 271, including several miscellaneous documents, have been selected for this volume. Many more, particularly early family letters, were burned in the fire that swept Thomas Hart Benton's Washington, D.C., home in 1855. Others were doubtless lost in the numerous moves of the Frémonts' peripatetic lives. After her parents' deaths, the Frémonts' daughter, Lily, destroyed additional letters to prevent them from falling into the "wrong hands."[12] Despite all this, a remarkable number have survived. Spanning the Victorian age, they range from the high-spirited letter of a fifteen-year-old boarding-school girl in 1839 to a gallant note to Theodore Roosevelt from a proud widow, living on charity in turn-of-the-century Los Angeles.

In selecting letters for this volume, we have attempted to choose not only those of historical significance but also those most characteristically revealing, or representative, of Jessie Frémont and of her times. Because occasional gaps occur, we have included a few excerpts from other documents, including her unpublished 1901–2 "Memoirs." Our volume is divided into seven sections, corresponding to the major periods of Jessie Frémont's life. Each section is preceded by an introductory essay providing general biographical information about her life during that period. In many cases, the notes to individual letters add specific details about particular episodes and events.

We have not included any of the numerous letters, signed by John Frémont, that are actually in Jessie's handwriting. Soon after her marriage in October 1841, she assumed what would be a lifelong task of collaboration—not only in her husband's correspondence but also in the widely heralded reports of his exploring expeditions, and, years later, in his *Memoirs*. Thus as early as April 1842, when John Frémont submitted a long overdue report to the Bureau of Topographical Engineers, describing a six-week reconnaissance of the Des Moines River region that he had made the previous summer, the report was in the handwriting of his young bride.

In this volume, however, we have included only correspondence and other material actually signed as well as composed by Jessie, among these many letters written on her husband's behalf, although not always with his knowledge or approval. During the antebellum years, when a respectable woman was mentioned publicly only at her marriage and death, Jessie accepted the role of anonymous partner; in fact, only late in life did she admit her role in writing the celebrated expedition reports. Similarly, in 1847, when she wrote a newspaper article about Kit Carson, which along with the Frémont reports brought the modest scout his first fame, she did it anonymously, although her friend, Elizabeth Blair Lee, suspected her part. "I have my reasons for thinking that 'tis written by Jessie," she confided to her husband. "She is a smart woman."[13]

What we have sought in this volume, then, is Jessie's own voice. At times it is a voice difficult to locate even in her own letters. Like her life, her correspondence is skewed by the restrictions on women and by the censorship she imposed on herself. Despite such obstacles, her energy, her natural activism, her true self come through, creating a vital counterpoint to the diversionary rhetoric of compliance.

It is certainly Jessie's own young voice, naive and optimistic, that emerges in the early series of letters to Adelaide Talbot, the widowed mother of a young lieutenant who was a member of John Frémont's second expedition. Written from St. Louis in 1843–44, while the expedition made its perilous way across the northwest to Oregon and California, they reveal an ardent young woman longing for her absent husband. Though Jessie's first letters to the widow Talbot are deferential and restrained, they grow more open and frank as her concern for her long-overdue husband grows. The letters also suggest many of the themes that would dominate her life: John's absence, a pattern begun during these first exploring expeditions and continued throughout his life; her own frustration, more an undercurrent than an expressed thought, at the passive role she was forced to assume as she waited for his return; her pride in and identification with his successes; and her ardor in defending him against all attacks.

In 1847, this last theme emerged more strongly when John Frémont, in the first of the many controversies of his turbulent career, was caught in a dispute between feuding military officers during the conquest of California and was threatened with court-martial. Jessie did not hesitate to call on President James Polk, with Kit Carson in her wake, to present her husband's case, or, several months later, to write Polk directly concerning the court-martial. "Do not suppose Sir, that I lightly interfere in a matter properly belonging to men," she justified her presumption, "but in the absence of Mr. Frémont I attend to his affairs at his request."[14] Jessie was of course not alone in such acts: countless nineteenth-century women appealed behind the scenes for their husbands, brothers, and sons. But Jessie practiced this far more boldly than most. As a senator's daughter, she had learned early that her name gave privilege. As John Frémont became famous, she acquired a kind of double power, although she was reluctant to accept that for her, a woman, it would always be borrowed and fickle. Throughout her life, she would write men of influence on behalf of her husband, and, in later years, her two sons. She was also generous in helping others with less access than she. Among the first of many was young Charles Taplin, a member of her husband's second expedition, for whom, on February 16, 1847, she wrote Polk requesting a second lieutenant's commission in the war with Mexico.

Two months later, Jessie began a quite different kind of communication when she wrote the first of some eighty-five letters to Elizabeth Blair Lee, launching what would become the most important and revealing group of letters in her large correspondence. "I never said so much about myself to anyone but you before," she confided to the woman who would be her closest friend for the next fifteen years.[15]

Lizzie Lee was in many ways an ideal confidant. A distant cousin, she, like Jessie, had been raised in the heady political atmosphere of the nation's capital, where her father, former Washington *Globe* editor Francis Preston Blair, was Thomas Hart Benton's closest political ally. Both women were intelligent and well educated, although Lizzie was significantly more gentle, reserved, and conventional. Six years older than Jessie, she at first found her exuberant, frank, and impulsive friend "very amusing and bright witted," though at times "very wanting in taste."[16] While Jessie had defied her family to marry John Charles

Frémont, Lizzie waited nearly four years to secure her parents' reluctant consent before marrying naval officer Samuel Phillips Lee. While Jessie would travel constantly in the wake of her restless husband, Lizzie, childless until she was thirty-seven and often in poor health, remained rooted in the Washington area. Even after her marriage, she continued to live for many years at Silver Spring, the Blair family estate outside Washington, since her husband was frequently at sea.

The letters to Lizzie Lee cover a range of national and personal events as Jessie changed from a willful and irreverent young girl to a mature woman, stepping beyond her proper sphere to intervene actively in Civil War political and military affairs. It was to Lizzie, when fire swept the Frémonts' San Francisco home in 1851, that Jessie confessed, "I really have something like the blues."[17] And it was to Lizzie, writing again from San Francisco nine years later, that Jessie rejoiced over her husband's new (and temporary) domesticity. "No 'wild turkey' left," she wrote. "You need no telling how satisfied my craving heart is."[18] Most especially, it is the large group of letters written during the 1856 election campaign that comprise the most intense and intimate correspondence between the two women.

Jessie's letters to Lizzie during this period, a time when Francis Blair was one of John's most important political advisors, suggest some of the early planning and orchestration that went into the Frémont nomination as well as Jessie's own behind-the-scenes work as campaign aide. Most personally and poignantly, they reveal the depth of the split between John Frémont and Thomas Hart Benton, who refused to leave the Democratic party to support his son-in-law. For Jessie, the rift was deeply painful. Caught between husband and father, she struggled to avoid a permanent break. In letters to Lizzie she expressed her anguish. "I am all dammed up—for want of sympathizing ears. Most about Father," she wrote in one letter before pouring out her troubles in another the next day.[19]

The 1856 election, one of the most impassioned in American history, has been generally neglected by historians. Moreover, its significance in women's history, as the first time women participated in a national campaign, is scarcely known. By 1856 attitudes toward women were changing. The 1848 woman's rights declaration at Seneca Falls, the participation of women in the abolitionist movement, and the emergence of professional women writers—the "scribbling women" whom Nathaniel Hawthorne so abhorred—all prepared the way for Jessie, as the wife of the dashing candidate of a new political party, to achieve a recognition that no woman had gained before. To advocates of woman's rights, she represented a new kind of woman, praised not for her modesty and purity but for her spunk, her wit, and her dedication to the antislavery cause. Still, the pro-Frémont press was careful to stress her domestic virtues as well. Significantly, in her 1856 letter on slavery to New England reformer Lydia Maria Child, Jessie herself emphasized its damage in the domestic sphere. "I would as soon place my children in the midst of small pox, as rear them under the influences of slavery," she wrote.[20] Nonetheless, the opposition exploited her prominence to condemn the participation of women in the Republican campaign, snidely suggesting that she was the "real candidate."[21]

"Write me a wommanish letter next time," Jessie wrote Lizzie in the midst of the campaign, "You have belonged to mannish ideas lately."[22] Despite her political interests, Jessie's letters to Lizzie were more often personal than political and frequently expressed the traditional concerns of women. Thus Jessie recorded her fears of childbirth, and her views on breast feeding and child-rearing. She announced that daughter Lily "has been womanly for four months now,"[23] and in an undated note, probably written in January 1857, thirty-two-year-old Jessie asked Lizzie to secure a midwife for her because "familiar symptoms" made her think she was pregnant again. "I dread the ordeal," she confided.

The correspondence between the two women forms a story in itself, one suddenly ruptured during the first year of the Civil War when Lizzie's brothers and father feuded with the Frémonts over John's role as Union general in St. Louis. For the two women, it meant a virtual severing of ties. Over the next twenty years, they kept in touch only indirectly. Not until 1883 did they meet again when Lizzie, learning of Jessie's financial problems, unexpectedly paid her a visit in New York City. Afterward, Jessie wrote a last poignant letter to her old friend. Recalling the long ago death of her own infant daughter, Jessie wrote bitterly of woman's lot: "I knew it, dimly, then—I know it surely now, that for the death of a baby girl there should be no sorrow for life is hard on women."[24] By then, Lizzie Lee had come to view John Frémont as morally shabby and financially irresponsible, a man who could "gamble away his own & her children's bread over & over again . . . and he too faithless even to pretend to live with her." To her, Jessie's loyalty seemed excessive: "She belongs to him body & soul &

he does with [her] as he pleases as much as he does with his own right hand."[25]

Closer observers might have said it was not that simple. Only a small group of letters from Jessie to her husband survive, but they provide vital glimpses of the Frémonts' marriage at important points in their lives. The first of these, written in 1846 when John was in California on his third expedition, displays both the innocence of her early letters to the widow Talbot and a pride in his accomplishments that would, all his life, be a spur, a burden, and a solace. Three letters also survive from the postelection period, when the Frémont marriage was under strain. Rumors were circulating that John had seduced a household maid, and in June 1857, Jessie chose to go to France with the children, while John journeyed to California to superintend his Las Mariposas mines. Whatever unease she may have felt, her letters from France are those of a vulnerable and deeply devoted wife. "Love me in memory of the old times when I was so dear to you," she wrote. "I love you now much more than I did then."[26]

The Frémonts' marriage was a complex relationship between two very different individuals. John Frémont was a loner: taciturn, courteous, and remote. His illegitimacy and early poverty made him an outsider, skeptical of rules and authority, reluctant to expose his feelings, and eager to prove himself. While Jessie was as ambitious as her husband and could be as contemptuous of authority, she was both more secure and more emotionally expressive. John's response to adversity was often silence and retreat; hers was more typically anger and action. Warm and affectionate, protective and maternal, she longed for intimacy but came to accept her husband as "the most reserved and shy nature I ever met."[27] Bold and visionary in the wilderness, John Frémont was at his best leading mountain men and *voyageurs,* restless men like himself, into the frontier West. A dreamer longing for a vague glory, he lacked political savvy, administrative skills, and the discipline to write. While admirers lauded his courage and eagle eye, over the years others came to question his competence and integrity. Inevitably, many who met both Frémonts rated Jessie's abilities far higher.

She could scarcely explain, and friends like Lizzie Lee could not understand, her enduring attachment. "My life from my fifteenth year was the General's," she wrote near the end of her life.[28] Unable to act directly, she dedicated her considerable talents to her husband's career. As he encountered criticism and difficulties, she became increasingly protective. When his name was damaged by his failures as a general and political leader during the Civil War, and by business scandals after the war, it was she who felt compelled to restore his image — an image that had become hers as well.

No single correspondent ever replaced Lizzie Lee. The letters of Jessie Frémont's middle years, especially the Civil War period when she was at her most vigorous, are addressed to a wide variety of individuals, ranging from Abraham Lincoln to the poet John Greenleaf Whittier. Her correspondence during the dramatic hundred days when John served as military commander of the Western Department with headquarters in St. Louis forms an important body of material on the episode and also provides a fascinating glimpse of a formidable woman at the height of her powers, yet unable to act directly and freely. Her celebrated 1861 interview with Lincoln, when he contemptuously called her "a female politician," is only the most vivid example of the frustration she faced.[29]

After Lincoln dismissed John Frémont from his St. Louis post and in mid-1862 virtually forced his resignation from a second command in West Virginia, John became the symbolic leader of abolitionist and radical Republican forces impatient with Lincoln's slowness to emancipate the slaves. By then, Jessie's own antislavery convictions and her dreams for her husband had become so interwined that it was impossible to separate idealism from ambition. To sympathetic friends like the Unitarian minister Thomas Starr King, whom she had known in San Francisco, and committed abolitionists like journalist Sydney Gay, Congressman George Julian, and educator Elizabeth Palmer Peabody, she vented her bitterness at the "Pontius Pilate of the slaves," as she called the president.[30] In her many letters to *Atlantic Monthly* editor James T. Fields, however, she found a more constructive outlet for her anger in arranging for the publication of her first book, *The Story of the Guard,* a skillfully indirect defense of her husband's Missouri command.

In 1865, as John abandoned his political ambitions and turned to assorted business ventures, Jessie's public correspondence dropped precipitously. As the war drew to a close, she turned inward toward her children and household affairs. She retreated to Pocaho, the Frémont estate on the Hudson River, where her main correspondent was young Nelly Haskell Browne, the daughter of one of John's most loyal and longtime aides. Her letters to Nelly are warmly maternal, occasionally charming, and minor. At times she also wrote to promote a cause or help a friend. Possibly Jessie would have remained quiescent as she grew older, if everything had not begun to unravel. In 1873, as their fortune and John's reputation were battered by the collapse of his scandal-ridden Memphis and El Paso Railroad, Jessie acted to defend his image and, more immediately, to provide money for the family. Her desperate letters to her lawyer, Jeremiah Black, former U. S. attorney general and shrewd Washington insider, trace the loss of Pocaho and, bit by bit, their remaining wealth.

Her letters to William King Rogers, personal aide to President Rutherford B. Hayes, are equally sad and revealing. In 1878, when President Hayes appointed John governor of Arizona Territory, the Frémonts traveled west, openly eager to profit from the office. To a young friend, Dr. William Morton, Jessie confided her hopes for a restored fortune through mining investments. In her letters to Rogers, who became financially involved with the Frémonts in various Arizona mining ventures, she showed herself to be a determined, at times unscrupulous woman, seeking some financial security for her family. It is a tawdry yet poignant chapter in Jessie Frémont's turbulent life.

Her letters from Los Angeles, where the Frémonts moved in late 1887, sound a different note. When John died in 1890, Jessie, stricken, continued her efforts to restore his good name. Yet expressions of lyric pleasure also punctuate her Los Angeles correspondence, an appreciation of sea and sky and blossoming orchard. As she recovered from her husband's death in this benign setting, she began to find an enriched personal life within a flourishing regional culture. In her many letters to the young sculptor John Gutzon Borglum, she became again the supportive advisor; inspiring, cajoling, encouraging, just as she had been for her husband and other talented men like Thomas Starr King, Bret Harte, and William Morton, prodding them to aspire to heights that she, a woman, could never reach.

Jessie Frémont's correspondence suggests several themes that relate specifically to women in nineteenth-century America. While she clearly chafed at confinement in the domestic sphere, she was also nourished by its values. Despite her attraction to the male world of political action, she had grown up in a family of sisters, with two, much younger brothers. Although she subconsciously, if not overtly, rejected her mother's exclusively domestic role, again and again in later life, she sought support and comfort in her friendships with women and in family life. Her friendship with Lizzie Lee, and in later years with other women like suffrage leader Caroline Severance in Los Angeles, as well as with her own daughter, who never married, underscore the importance of supportive female friendship for women of this era. And on one great nineteenth-century issue, slavery, it was quite specifically her Virginia-born mother's domestic values that shaped Jessie's, as well as Thomas Benton's opposition to the institution. An intelligent, pious, and conservative woman, Elizabeth Benton opposed slavery on religious grounds and because she believed that slavery was profoundly damaging to family life. In Jessie's 1856 letter on slavery to Lydia Maria Child, it is her mother's view that she cites, both because she sensed it would be more acceptable in a semipublic letter and because it influenced her so deeply as a child.

While Jessie was in many ways ambivalent toward woman's separate sphere, both constrained and nourished by it, she was also conflicted about the direct use of power by women, perhaps because, even in her years of financial anxiety, she retained at least tangential access to power. Yet her correspondence suggests that she was well aware that most women were far less privileged. In an 1856 letter to Lizzie Lee, she wrote sympathetically of a friend, a young widow with children to support, who had managed to find work as a copyist at the Patent Office but received only $50 a month. A year later, during the depression of 1857, Jessie was disturbed by the plight of thousands of New York City seamstresses who could get no work.

Throughout her life, she attempted to help less privileged women on a personal level, persuading a publisher to read a friend's manuscript or writing on behalf of a black woman hoping to purchase a house in Washington, D.C. Although Jessie originally relied on traditional charitable activities, in the 1860s she began to favor mechanisms by which women as a group could help themselves. In 1864 she supported the idea of a woman's work exchange, as she did again in Los Angeles in the 1890s. Her own loss of money and consequent experience as a professional writer made her more understanding of the economic problems many women faced. Although she never outlined a coherent solution, she did write enthusiastically, in a surprising 1890 article for the magazine *Wide Awake,* about a large and successful cooperative jam-making business, founded and run by a woman who shared the profits with her all-female staff.[31] In this modest article, written in her usual disarming and discursive style and based on the actual experience of a friend, she suggested a way in which the female world of friendship and mutual support could interact successfully with the male world of success and profit. Just as her mother's domestic values fueled her early opposition to slavery, the female values of cooperation and friendship underlaid her support for this cooperative business.

Jessie was less able to demand direct political power for women. As the movement for woman's suffrage grew in the late nineteenth century, she remained ambivalent. Consumed by her struggle to restore the Frémont name and fortune, her relative powerlessness caused her at times to view woman's place with bitterness. Yet she found it difficult to admit or assert her own or other women's need for or enjoyment of direct power. Talented and ambitious, she tried to legitimize her energy and drive—and hide them even from herself—by channeling them into her husband's glittering and turbulent career. The result was a life-long oscillation between her active, assertive temperament and the more domestic role she found both comforting and confining.

As a child, Jessie was deeply influenced by her father's philosophic optimism. Virtually a self-made man, Benton believed he had succeeded by his own energy and will. Describing his recovery from tuberculosis after a vigorous regime of exercise and outdoor work, Jessie explained that he had found an "ally within himself on which he could surely rely—his own will."[32] Although she possessed her father's energy and buoyant temperament, she discovered that as a woman, her will was less effective than a man's. She had exercised her own passionate preference in marrying John Charles Frémont, but she soon learned that she had far less control over the subsequent course of her life. In later years, she quoted Tennyson's lines, "For man is man and master of his fate," then added bluntly, "That is poetry. When one is not man but woman, you follow in the wake of both man and fate, and the prose of life proves one does not so easily be 'master' of fate."[33]

As she recognized her own vulnerability, she sought patience, pasting Whittier's "Angel of Patience" in her prayer book when she was in her early twenties. The 1856 election defeat, the disappointments of the Civil War, the loss of their fortune in the 1870s, all pushed her toward a religion of resignation. "Thy will, not mine, be done," she repeated.[34] Despite this overt belief, her temperament remained un-tamed: optimistic, energetic, and assertive. Even as she preached res-ignation to herself in the hope of ultimate justice in the afterlife, she found it irresistible to continue the struggle to restore reputation and family fortune. Even in her last years in Los Angeles, where she flowered in a wise acceptance of the injustices and disappointments of life, her letters show that she could could never entirely give up the struggle. Yet more than any other aspect of her character, it is this ebullience, this brave vigor, this gallantry, that touches us most deeply.

Notes

1. PICKARD, 2:462.
2. L. M. CHILD, 291.
3. To Thomas Starr King, Dec. 29, 1861, below.
4. DANA, 453.
5. New York *Tribune,* Oct. 11, 1861.
6. CROSBY, 35.
7. Calvin Park to Trenor W. Park, March 2, 1861 (Park-McCullough House Archives).
8. DAVIS, 116.
9. DALY, 321.
10. To William Carey Jones, Jr., Oct. 28, 1890, below.
11. STANTON, 2:112; STANTON ET AL., 2:911.
12. To Sarah Preston McDowell, Aug. 6, 1907 (KyU—Preston Family Papers).
13. June 16, 1847 (NjP—Blair-Lee Papers).
14. Sept. 21, 1847, below.
15. Apr. 15, 1847, below.
16. To S. Phillips Lee, July 20, 1846 (NjP—Blair-Lee Papers).
17. Aug. 14, 1851, below.
18. June 2, 1860, below.
19. Apr. 17, 1856, below.
20. [Late July/Aug. 1856], below.
21. Washington *Union,* July 12, 1856.
22. [Dec.] 14 [1855], below.
23. [Spring 1854?], below.
24. July 29 [1883], below.
25. To S. Phillips Lee, July 21, 1883 (NjP—Blair-Lee Papers).
26. July 29 [1857], below.
27. To John Greenleaf Whittier, [Jan. 21–22, 1880], below.
28. To William Carey Jones, Jr., Oct. 28, 1890, below.
29. See the Lincoln Interview, Excerpt from "Great Events," below.
30. To Elizabeth Palmer Peabody, Feb. 14 [1864], below.

31. "Play and Work," *Wide Awake,* 30 (Apr. 1890): 336–39.
32. MEMOIRS, 13.
33. To William J. Morton, Christmas [1881] (CU-B—Morton Papers).
34. To Nelly Haskell, Nov. 1 [1864], below.

EDITORIAL PROCEDURES

The Documents

In editing the letters of Jessie Benton Frémont, we have followed the procedures and style established by Donald Jackson and Mary Lee Spence in *The Expeditions of John Charles Frémont* (Urbana: University of Illinois Press, 1970–84). The manuscript text is followed as closely as the demands of typography will permit. In the matter of capitalization the original is followed, unless Jessie Benton Frémont's intention is not clear, in which case we resort to modern practice. Occasionally, in the interests of clarity, a long, involved sentence is broken into two sentences but this is rare, as our author was a clear, straightforward writer. Missing periods at the ends of sentences are supplied, dashes terminating sentences are supplanted by periods, and superfluous dashes after periods are omitted. In abbreviations, raised letters are brought down and a period supplied if modern usage calls for one. Words underscored in manuscripts are italicized. Punctuation in datelines and salutations follows the manuscript, but the complimentary closing is run in with the preceding paragraph and a comma is used if no other end punctuation is present. The acute accent mark on the *e* in Frémont is supplied when it appears in the document and omitted where it does not appear, but it is used in all of our own references to Jessie Frémont. Procedures for dealing with missing or illegible words, conjectural readings, and other items are shown in the list of symbols, pp. xxxiii–xxxvi. When in doubt as to how to proceed in a trivial matter, modern practice is silently followed; if the question is more important, the situation is explained in a note.

Jessie Frémont was inconsistent in the use of the apostrophe to indicate the possessive case. Where she failed to supply it, we have done so. "Show" is often written as "shew," and so it has been transcribed.

The Notes

If endorsements or addresses on the letters contribute useful information, they are quoted in full.

The very few letters that are taken from printed texts are so indicated (printed, STANTON ET AL.), but no attempt is made to record other printed versions.

Recipients and persons referred to in the letters are briefly identified at first mention. For recipients, this identification is made in the first paragraph of the notes, and no reference number is used. The reader can usually find the identification of an individual by locating in the index the page on which he or she is first mentioned.

No source is cited for the kind of biographical information to be found in standard directories, genealogies, and similar aids. Where it has been difficult to identify a person, however, the source is cited.

Names of authors in SMALL CAPITALS are citations to sources listed in the bibliography on pp. 559–74. This device enables us to keep many long titles and other impedimenta out of the notes. In the case of two or more works by the same author, a number is assigned, as in NEVINS [1]. When a published work is discussed, not merely cited, we often list it fully by author and title in the notes.

To avoid the constant repetition of the Frémont names, we have freely used the initials JCF and JBF for John Charles and Jessie Benton.

SYMBOLS

Libraries and Archives, as Designated
by the *National Union Catalog*
of the Library of Congress

AzHi	Arizona Historical Society, Tucson
AzTeS	Arizona State University, Tempe
C	California State Library, Sacramento
CLjC	Copley Library, La Jolla
CLSM	Southwest Museum, Los Angeles
CLU	University of California, Los Angeles
CSfCP	Society of California Pioneers, San Francisco
CSmH	Henry E. Huntington Library, San Marino
CSt	Stanford University, Stanford
CtY	Yale University, New Haven
CU-B	Bancroft Library, University of California, Berkeley
DeWint	Henry Francis DuPont Winterthur Museum, Winterthur
DLC	Library of Congress, Washington, D.C.
IaHi	State Historical Society of Iowa, Iowa City
ICHi	Chicago Historical Society, Chicago
ICN	Newberry Library, Chicago
IGK	Knox College, Galesburg

IHi	Illinois State Historical Society, Springfield
KHi	Kansas Historical Society, Topeka
KyLoF	Filson Club, Louisville
KyU	University of Kentucky, Lexington
MB	Boston Public Library
MCR	Radcliffe College, Cambridge
MdBJ	Johns Hopkins University, Baltimore
MeB	Bowdoin College, Brunswick
MeHi	Maine Historical Society, Portland
MH	Harvard University, Cambridge
MHi	Massachusetts Historical Society, Boston
MiMtpT	Central Michigan University, Mount Pleasant
MiU-C	Clements Library, University of Michigan, Ann Arbor
MoSHi	Missouri Historical Society, St. Louis
MoSW	Washington University, St. Louis
NAll	Albany Institute of History and Art
NhHi	New Hampshire Historical Society, Concord
NHi	New-York Historical Society, New York
NIC	Cornell University, Ithaca
NjHi	New Jersey Historical Society, Newark
NjP	Princeton University, Princeton
NjR	Rutgers University, New Brunswick
NN	New York Public Library, New York
NNBG	New York Botanical Garden, Bronx Park
NNC	Columbia University, New York
NNPM	Pierpont Morgan Library, New York
NPV	Vassar College, Poughkeepsie
NSyU	Syracuse University, Syracuse
OFH	Hayes Presidential Center, Fremont
PHi	Historical Society of Pennsylvania, Philadelphia

RPB	Brown University, Providence
TxU	University of Texas, Austin
UHi	Utah State Historical Society, Salt Lake City
WHi	State Historical Society of Wisconsin, Madison

Collections without a Designated Symbol

Billings Mansion Archives, Woodstock, Vermont

Mariposa County Historical Society, Mariposa, California

Park-McCullough House Archives, North Bennington, Vermont

National Archives Record Groups

DNA-15	Records of the Veterans Administration
DNA-24	Records of the Bureau of Naval Personnel
DNA-48	Records of the Office of the Secretary of Interior
DNA-49	Records of the Bureau of Land Management — General Land Office
DNA-75	Records of the Bureau of Indian Affairs
DNA-77	Records of the Office of Chief of Engineers
DNA-92	Records of the Office of the Quartermaster General
DNA-94	Records of the Adjutant General's Office, 1780s–1917
DNA-153	Records of the Office of the Judge Advocate General (Army)

Other Symbols and Editorial Aids

AD	Autograph document
ADS	Autograph document, signed
AL	Autograph letter

ALS	Autograph letter, signed
D	Document
DS	Document, signed
JBF	Jessie Benton Frémont
JCF	John Charles Frémont
Lbk	Letterbook
NHPRC	National Historical Publications and Records Commission
RG	Record Group
[ ]	Word or phrase supplied to clarify, correct, or translate.
[?]	Conjectural reading or conjectural identification of an addressee.
[. . .]	A word or two missing or illegible.
⟨ ⟩	Word or phrase deleted from manuscript by the sender. The words are set in italics.

THE LETTERS OF

Jessie Benton Frémont

CREATING NATIONAL REPUTATIONS

"We had three homes," Jessie Benton Frémont remembered the locales of her childhood. "That in Washington was, so to speak, the official residence, while the Saint Louis home to which the long travel of that day made it too far for going except on alternate years—after the short session—had spacious grounds, and trees, and much gay young French companionship. But *the* home was my grandfather's place in Virginia. There was real country. Far as the eye could see all was ours and there we had been born."[1]

Jessie's maternal grandfather, James McDowell, was the descendant of a Scotch-Irish family who had emigrated to America in the early eighteenth century, and his estate, worked by slaves, was Cherry Grove in Rockbridge County in the Blue Ridge Mountains of Virginia. His daughter, Elizabeth, gentle, brown-haired, and deeply religious, was twenty-seven when, after a long courtship, she married Thomas Hart Benton, who was already representing the new state of Missouri in the U.S. Senate.

The son of land speculator Jesse Benton and his wife, Ann Gooch, Thomas Hart Benton had spent his youth in North Carolina, studied law and entered politics in Tennessee, and then after a notorious brawl with Andrew Jackson, moved on to St. Louis where he built a reputation as a lawyer and newspaper editor. Missourians would reelect him to the Senate until 1850 and then in 1852 give him a term in the House of Representatives. Consequently, the family's official and permanent home became Washington, but Benton often returned to Missouri, frequently with family in tow, to mend political fences and campaign for reelection.

Jessie Ann, the second of four sisters and two much younger brothers, was born on May 31, 1824, and quickly became her father's favorite. Possessed of spirit, bold intellect, and imagination, she was given "the place a son would have had" in his heart.[2]

We have found two letters written by her as a girl and print the more important one. Consequently, we must rely on Jessie's published writings and unpublished "Memoirs," written in two drafts at the end of her life, for information about her early years. Nostalgically, she recalled how her father took her with him to the White House to visit President Jackson, with whom he had made peace and a political alliance, or deposited her in the Library of Congress under the watchful eye of the librarian while he went on to the Senate. "While reading was still a little difficult, the books of glorious pictures were mine to pasture in—Audubon's birds—the Louvre gallery—fine French engravings of many others . . . I, sitting entranced took in visions of art and beauty that must have molded my thought and life."[3]

When she and her older sister Eliza (later called Liz) reached school age, Benton employed a series of tutors, but Jessie seized every opportunity to escape to her father's library, where she cajoled Benton into correcting her exercises and supervising her reading. As the references and quotations in her letters indicate, she acquired a broad knowledge of classical and European history and literature. Increasingly, as she grew into her teens, she became her father's secretary and confidante, and in the process, she was educated by a master craftsman in Washington politics and personalities, who was also one of the West's leading spokesmen.

She met politicians, diplomats, scientists, scholars, and rough westerners at the dinner table in the various boardinghouses where the Bentons resided or, in later years, in their permanent home on C Street. Trips by coach and steamboat to St. Louis, her father's political base and the residence of his widowed mother, reinforced her interest in the West. Here, as in Washington, Jessie absorbed much talk about the need to acquire new territory and to open new routes to tap frontier resources.

At fourteen, she, with Eliza, was sent as a boarder to Miss English's Female Seminary in Georgetown. It was a favorite place for the daughters of congressmen and military officers, but Jessie thoroughly despised it, calling it a "Society school." On a visit home, the willful brown-eyed girl seized the scissors, cut her wavy auburn hair, and announced to her father that she would not return. "I meant to study and be his friend and companion," she explained, "as Mdme. de Staël had been to her Father, for I wanted no more 'Society.' " Benton was thoroughly displeased, but she never went back to school.[4] She had already met her future husband, John Charles Frémont, but would not see him again for many months.

John Charles Frémont was born in Savannah, Georgia, on January 21, 1813, the illegitimate first child of an itinerant Frenchmen, Charles Fremon, who had enticed Anne Beverley Whiting Pryor to leave the bed and board of her elderly husband, Major John Pryor of Richmond, Virginia.[5] The parents lived as a couple but were never able to obtain a legal divorce, and John would bear the stigma of bastardy all of his life, especially during the presidential campaign of 1856. Fremon died in 1818, leaving Anne living in poverty with three small children (a fourth had died). By 1823 the little family had become residents of Charleston.

As a teenager, John went to work in the law office of John W. Mitchell and also studied with Dr. John Roberton, a distinguished Edinburgh scholar, who prepared boys for the College of Charleston, which John entered as a member of the junior class in May 1829. He was in the Scientific Department when he was dismissed in February 1831 for "habitual irregularity and incorrigible negligence."[6] In his *Memoirs,* John explained that he had fallen in love with Cecilia, the raven-haired daughter of a Creole family who had escaped from Santa Domingo, and spent too much time with her and her brothers and sisters, picnicking in the woods or sailing the bay.

His family's poverty would not permit John too long a holiday. Fortunately, his charm and intelligence caught the eye of Joel Poinsett, an influential politician in South Carolina, who had also been minister to Mexico. He helped him obtain a civilian post as a teacher of mathematics on board the USS *Natchez,* bound for a two-year cruise in South American waters. When John returned, Poinsett arranged for him to become a member of the crew surveying the route for the projected Charleston, Louisville, and Cincinnati Railroad. After the work on the railroad survey was suspended, he became an assistant engineer in the survey of the Cherokee Indian lands in Georgia, Tennessee, and North Carolina.

By then, John had found his occupation, and in December 1837, he applied for a commission in the U.S. Corps of Topographical Engineers.

Now secretary of war in the Martin Van Buren administration, Poinsett had the French-speaking young man assigned as a civilian assistant to the distinguished French scientist-explorer, Joseph N. Nicollet, who had been employed by the Topographical Corps to survey and map the region between the upper Mississippi and Missouri rivers. Within a short time John received his army commission.

The Corps of Topographical Engineers was a separate unit from the Corps of Engineers, with its own chief but likewise under the secretary of war. It had been officially created in 1838 and only seventy-two officers would serve between that date and its termination in 1863. And of these seventy-two, all but eight had been graduated from the military academy at West Point. John was among the eight, and Jessie and Thomas Benton would become convinced that he had encountered prejudice and paid a heavy penalty for not having entered the Corps through the gates of the academy. His army critics were equally convinced that his rapid advancement was due to his political connections.

During the Minnesota reconnaissance, Nicollet treated his assistant with fatherly affection and was pleased with how quickly he absorbed the details of survey work and the management of an expedition. When the field work was over, John came to Washington to help Nicollet prepare the great map that would display the results of their explorations. Benton sometimes dropped by to observe the work and was soon inviting Nicollet and Frémont to informal evenings at his home, where the conversation often centered on the need to explore the lands west of the Missouri River to the Rocky Mountains and even beyond to the Pacific. However, it was at a school concert at Miss English's seminary, where John had gone with Eliza Benton, that he met Jessie for the first time. Many years later he recalled: "She was then in the bloom of her girlish beauty, and perfect health effervesced in bright talk which the pleasure of seeing her sister drew out. Naturally I was attracted. She made the effect that a rose of rare color or a beautiful picture would have done."[7] After she left school, he began to see her at the Benton home.

Jessie's parents became alarmed at the attention John was paying their daughter. She was very young, and he lacked money and family background. Nonetheless, "there was no room for reason" in their romance. John was sent off on what the couple always believed was a trumped up six-week survey of the Des Moines River. "We were married soon after," Jessie records, " 'for was it not written?' "[8] Never—

not even during the campaign of 1856—did she give many details about her elopement, which had occurred on October 19, 1841, the day Benton left on a trip to Kentucky and St. Louis. After the secret marriage, she returned to the Benton home, but the news soon leaked out, tongues wagged, and Elizabeth Benton rushed word of the crisis to her husband in Kentucky. He canceled plans to go on to St. Louis and hurried back to Washington. One relative reported that the irate Benton would not let Jessie remain in his house. The marriage was published, and John took his wife to his lodgings. At Elizabeth Benton's request, a Preston family member got the senator to "treat them with passing civility."⁹ By the end of the year, however, Benton was reconciled to the marriage. The couple moved into the Benton home, and the senator, as chairman of the Senate Committee on Military Affairs, used his influence to support the career of his son-in-law and to fulfill his own dreams about the West.

On New Year's Day, 1842, Frémont, almost twenty-nine, learned that he would have the command of an expedition to the Rocky Mountains, which would draw all eyes to the promise of the West. Originally Benton and his western colleagues in Congress had hoped that Nicollet would lead the expedition, with John as his assistant, but the poor health of the scientist made that an impossibility. Jessie was several months pregnant when John left Washington on May 2 for St. Louis to complete preparations for the survey, which would take him to South Pass on the Continental Divide and into the Wind River Mountains. When the expedition left the frontier some four hundred miles beyond St. Louis, it included as topographer the German Charles Preuss and as guide Christopher (Kit) Carson, a veteran of the Rocky Mountain fur trade and well known among his fellow trappers. The next year, John was ordered to connect his 1842 survey with the Pacific Coast surveys of naval commander Charles Wilkes. He again included Preuss and Carson in his expedition, which lasted fourteen months and made a virtual circuit of the entire West.

With the help of Jessie, John wrote lively, readable reports of these two expeditions. Together they were able to capture his love of adventure and his enthusiasm for the natural environment and to involve readers vicariously in the shooting of the canyons of the Sweetwater, the navigation of the Great Salt Lake in an eighteen-foot India rubber boat, and the month-long battle with snow in crossing the Sierra Nevada in mid-January. The reports were filled with human touches, even

frontier gossip, and provided curious Americans with a wealth of miscellaneous information about the West: the superiority of Indian buf-
falo-skin lodges to American tents, the appearance of Sutter's Fort on
the Sacramento River, the size of the redwoods, and the importance
of the acorns in the diet of the California Indians. More important,
to the increasing number of western settlers, the reports gave utilitarian
information about terrain, campsites, water, vegetation, wildlife, and
weather; emigrants were able to travel by the maps, which Preuss helped
draw. The reports and maps were ordered published by Congress, and
subsequently a number of commercial editions appeared at home and
abroad. John became a national hero, was breveted captain, and then
while he was away on his third expedition (1845–47), which took him
into California again, he was commissioned a lieutenant colonel in the
Mounted Rifles. In eight short years he had advanced from an unknown
second lieutenant to one of the most admired and talked-of lieutenant
colonels in the army. Jessie jubilantly wrote to him that he was ranked
with Daniel Defoe. "They say that as *Robinson Crusoe* is the most
natural and interesting fiction of travel, so Frémont's report is the most
romantically truthful."[10]

During his third expedition, John Frémont became involved with
the Americans in the Bear Flag rebellion against Mexico. His battalion
of volunteers, composed of *voyageurs* from his topographical party and
American settlers in California, served under the command of Robert
F. Stockton, who became chief of naval and land operations on the
Pacific Coast and who later appointed Frémont governor of the conquered territory. The arrival in California of Brigadier General Stephen
Watts Kearny created problems for John. In the power struggle between
Kearny and Stockton, he chose the wrong side, and Kearny sent him
home to face a court-martial for mutiny and disobedience. Jessie marshaled all her love, sympathy, and tact to support him through the
ordeal. She acted as secretary and copyist for her father and brother-
in-law, William Carey Jones, who prepared his defense. John was convicted, and, although President James Polk remitted the penalty and
ordered him to duty again, he resigned from the army, unwilling to
admit in any way the justice of the decision. Rather than tarnishing
Frémont's national reputation, the court-martial actually added to it,
and the trial wrote indelibly into the public mind the fact — or fiction,
as some historians would have it — that he had played a daring role in
the acquisition of California.

With Jessie's assistance again, John completed a *Geographical Memoir upon Upper California* and prepared for a fourth expedition. It would be a winter expedition, financed by Benton and his St. Louis friends, and its purpose would be to determine the feasibility of a railroad along the thirty-eighth parallel. It was hoped that he would win new laurels and wipe out the sting of the court-martial. Since he and Jessie planned to settle in California, where he was the claimant to a vast property, Las Mariposas, which as yet had no set boundaries or confirmed title, she would travel west by sea and the Isthmus of Panama to meet him in San Francisco.

Jessie, with daughter Lily, was actually en route in the spring of 1849 when she received news that John's expedition had met disaster (with ten men dead and all the supplies and mules gone) in the rugged mountains of southern Colorado and that he was proceeding to California by a more southern route.

The family was reunited in San Francisco in June and scarcely six months later was on the way back to Washington. John had been elected a California senator, although a political opponent asked why anyone who "has any interest in California would like to see it represented in the Senate by Col. Benton & Mrs. Fremont?"[11] Jessie was doubtless disappointed when, upon the admission of California to the Union, her husband drew the short term, forcing them to return to California to campaign for his reelection in the winter of 1850–51. When, after 142 ballots, the election of a senator was carried over to the next term, John gave up on politics and turned his attention to developing his properties, especially the rich gold-bearing quartz veins on Las Mariposas. To raise capital to develop these mines, he and his family went to Europe in 1852.

When Benton wrote them in Paris that Congress had authorized several western surveys to determine the best route for a transcontinental railroad, John, through his father-in-law, became an applicant for one of the commands and returned to the United States. Jessie with Lily, two-year-old Charley, and tiny baby Anne, followed shortly. Although John was not selected to head one of the official surveys, he launched his fifth and final expedition. In spite of his growing reservations about his son-in-law, Benton backed him financially, as he wished to see established the viability of the central route in all weather. While the results did not win John new laurels, neither did they damage his popularity. To many Americans, including his ambitious and devoted wife, he was still the dashing explorer of the *Reports,* the conqueror of California.[12]

Notes

1. JBF, "Memoirs," 15.
2. J. B. FRÉMONT [3], 25.
3. JBF, "Memoirs," 24.
4. Ibid., 31.
5. JCF's mother's name has been spelled variously: Ann, Anne, Anna. In the notes, JBF made for John Bigelow with respect to Frémont's ancestry, she spells it Anne.
6. For JCF's school and college experience, see JACKSON & SPENCE, xxv.
7. MEMOIRS, 66.
8. JBF, "Memoirs," 47 [first draft].
9. See JBF to Charles W. Upham, May 31, 1856, and JBF to Elizabeth Blair Lee, July 23 [1856], both below. Benton had his editor friend, Francis P. Blair, publish a curt announcement of the marriage in the Washington *Globe,* Nov. 27, 1841. Sarah Simpson (Hart) Thompson gives some details of the Bentons' reactions in her letter to Nathaniel Hart, Jan. 19, 1842 (KyLoF—Edmund T. Halsey Collection).
10. June 18, 1846, below.
11. The brother of the marine who had delivered despatches to JCF in the Oregon wilderness in 1846, Charles V. Gillespie, was an ardent political foe of JCF. See his letters to Archibald Gillespie, Sept. l, 15, 28, Oct. 31, Dec. 31, 1849 (CLU—Gillespie Papers).
12. The foregoing summary of JBF's and JCF's early years is not intended as a complete biography. For more detailed accounts of their lives, see HERR and NEVINS [1]. The three volumes of documents edited by JACKSON and/or SPENCE give many details relating to JCF's five western expeditions. CHAMBERS and E. B. SMITH [2] are helpful for understanding Benton and the politics of his day.

To Susanna Smith McDowell

Georgetown Hotel   August 9th 1839

My dear Aunt,

We will be down upon you, "horse, foot, & dragoon" for as Father returned yesterday we will leave about the middle of next week & bring Mary in tow. So prepare yourself to meet a second invasion of the Goths — "be armed with Christian fortitude to bear with us awhile." Sally gave us a most ludicrous account of Ran's & William's ineffectual attempts at picking their ears with their elbows.[1] Ask them if they can bite their own backs & let them practise until we arrive. Grandmother[2] will be more alarmed than ever. Sally wrote to Mother, that Grandma never left her seat without saying how infirm she was & Mother has become very anxious to see her. How is Aunt Taylor? & Benton?[3] The last accounts we had they were both quite sick. I do most truly hope that your headaches if not entirely destroyed by your visit to the Springs are at least banished for a long time. Mother says she will send us to the Alum Springs[4] when we go to Lexington, to remove the tan from our skins, for we can scarcely be distinguished from our Pottowatamee & Pawnee friends in the West.

We will I think leave here Wednesday or Thursday & go to Fredericksburg & there take the cars as far as they go & the rest of the road we will go in stages. Mary has given up hopes of being sent for & we will make her one of us with your consent. Mother is very very busy, & you may imagine how hurried she is when *I* am called into help. As I have nothing but school news to tell you I will have to stop as I know it is not interesting to you to hear who will be back next term & what new teachers & girls are expected &c. All send their love to you, Sally & all. Tell Ran he must have his face washed and head smooth when we come. Your affectionate niece,

Jessie A. Benton

ALS (NNC—Nevins Papers). Addressed to "Mrs. James McDowell, Lexington, Rockbridge Co., Vir." and franked by "Thomas H. Benton, U.S. Senate." Susanna Smith McDowell (1800–1847) was the wife of James McDowell, Jr. (1795–1851), brother of JBF's mother. Their ten children included Sally Campbell Preston McDowell (d. 1895), who had been at Miss English's Female Seminary in Georgetown, and Mary B. McDowell (b. c. 1824), who was currently JBF's schoolmate at the same school. James McDowell, Jr., would be elected governor of Virginia in 1842 (DORMAN, 226–33).

1. "Ran" was John Randolph, JBF's brother, born Nov. 11, 1829 (DORMAN, 226); William was the son of Susan Preston McDowell (1793–1849), sister of JBF's mother, and her husband William Taylor (1788–1846), who was elected as a Democrat to Congress in 1843 (DORMAN, 220–21). The young William Taylor would become a successful lawyer in California.
2. Sarah Preston McDowell (1767–1841).
3. A reference to Susan Preston McDowell Taylor, mentioned above, and to a second son, Thomas Benton Taylor (b. 1832).
4. The Alum Springs were seventeen miles west of Lexington, Va., on the road to the warm and hot springs of Bath County (HOWE, 450).

Excerpt from "Memoirs"

[c. 1901–2]

My splendid health never failed me though when Mr. Frémont got home in November [of 1842 from his first western expedition] he only arrived a few days before the birth of my first child.[1] Spreading over me a wind-whipt flag, he said, "This flag was raised on the summit peak of the highest point of the Rocky Mountains. I brought it to you."[2] I have it now—1842 to 1902—a long story it tells me.

The horseback life, the sleep in the open air, had unfitted Mr. Frémont for the indoor work of writing—and second lieutenants cannot indulge in secretaries. After a series of hemorhages from the nose and head had convinced him he must give up trying to write his report, I was let to try, and thus slid into my most happy life work.

This was no holiday work. Every morning at nine I took my seat at the writing table and left it at one. Mr. Frémont had his notes all ready and dictated as he moved about the room. I soon learned that I could not make a restless motion—he was (at first) constantly afraid of the motionless calm for me—it was hard—but that was lost in the great joy of my being so useful to him, and so, swiftly, the report of the First Expedition was written. Then followed the proof correcting, and this too I mastered; all the queer little signs that must be accurate and behold! Mr. Frémont's first book was finished.[3]

Typescript, JBF, "Memoirs," 41–42.

1. Elizabeth Benton Frémont (1841–1919) or Lily as she was familiarly called.
2. For a description of the flag, see JBF to Thomas Starr King, [early 1861], below. PHILLIPS, 68, writes that JCF gave the flag to Jessie shortly after the birth of Lily, apparently to console her for not having produced a boy.

3. The surviving manuscript of JCF's printed report (DNA-77) indicates that at least this final draft was less of a joint effort than she remembered. The first nineteen sheets are in JBF's hand and the remainder in JCF's, with some corrections and refinements in her hand. Without a doubt, she increasingly served as her husband's amanuensis, sometimes composing letters and boldly signing his name.

To Adelaide Talbot

Saint Louis,   Sep. 16th. 1843.

My dear Madam,

Knowing the anxiety you must feel on account of your son, I take great pleasure in sending you the news which we received a few days since from the party. They had gotten on very prosperously as late as the 26th of June, at which time Mr. Frémont found an opportunity to write by two Indians who brought the letter in. Twenty five of the party were to take one route while the remaining fifteen crossed through the Mexican territory. He does not say in which division your son has been placed, but I assume he is with Mr. Frémont himself, as, knowing him to be an only son he was very anxious to bring him home to you in safety. By the middle or end of December they expect to be in this place & at the New Year's rejoicings Mr. Talbot will I hope be again with you. There are no means of communication with the party & I have therefore retained all the letters for Mr. Talbot which I will give to him on his return. If you see our friend Dr. Martin[1] will you tell him that you heard from us & that all the family beg to be remembered to him?

Should any other intelligence be had of our voyageurs I will do myself the pleasure of communicating it to you instantly. Very respectfully yours,

Jessie B. Frémont

ALS (DLC—Talbot Papers).

Addressed, "Mrs. Talbot, F. Street Washington City D.C." Adelaide Talbot, the widow of Isham Talbot, who had served as U.S. senator from Kentucky, 1815–25, was the mother of young Theodore Talbot (1825–62), who was accompanying JCF as an aide on this expedition (TALBOT, xi–xx). The expedition was designed to connect JCF's 1841 survey with that made of the northwest coast by Charles Wilkes (see J. J. Abert to JCF, Mar. 10, 1843, printed in JACKSON & SPENCE, 160–61). Young Talbot would also go on JCF's third expedition, which became embroiled in the Bear Flag revolt and the conquest of California from Mexico.

1. Dr. J. L. Martin was a physician, a Democratic party activist, and longtime friend of the Benton family. He had authored the article, "Political Parties with Pen and Pencil" in *U.S. Magazine and Democratic Review,* 2 (May 1838), and would be employed for a brief time in translating and preparing for the press Joseph N. Nicollet's unfinished notes on Indian matters (see J. J. Abert to Martin, Oct. 17, 1843, Lbk, DNA-77, 6:463; Abert to Martin, Apr. 27, 1844, and Abert to P. Wagner, Apr. 27, 1844, 7:224–25). More than any other person, the French scientist Nicollet (1786–1843) was responsible for educating Frémont in the sophisticated methods of geodetic surveying, including using the barometer to measure altitude. Before his marriage, JCF had accompanied him on two U.S. government–supported reconnaissances of the Minnesota country. Martin was with Nicollet near his death in Sept. 1843. Martin's own death occurred in Rome in 1848 while he was serving as chargé d'affaires there. For a biographical sketch of Nicollet, see BRAY.

To Mr. Claiborne

St. Louis Mri.   October 30th 1843

As Mr. Frémont is at present in Oregon Territory where not even the voice of Fame can reach him, Mr. Claiborne must permit me to make him the acknowledgements due for his flattering notice of the Report of last year's exploration; rendered doubly gratifying by coming from such a source, as it is to me a very great pleasure to find my husband holding so high a stand in the good opinion of my Father's friends. The wish you express for the continuance of the survey is already fulfilled as Mr. Frémont left here the first of May to join his survey which terminated at the South Pass, to that of Lieut. Wilkes[1] which reached two or three hundred miles up the Columbia river. He expected to return about Christmas & when the Report on this last exploration shall be completed I will do myself the pleasure of sending you a copy, and as the ground passed over is so much more interesting this year than the last, it will I hope confirm your opinion of his abilities.

Father tells me to join his respect to mine & send you his kindest remembrances, he has such a press of business, as he leaves tomorrow that he could not write himself. Respectfully yours,

Jessie Benton Frémont

ALS (CtY—Western Americana Collection, Beinecke Rare Book and Manuscript Library). "Mr. Claiborne" is probably the voluminous writer, John Francis Hamtramck Claiborne (1809–84), who had been a member of the House of

Representatives between 1835 and 1838. In 1843 he was editing the *Fair Trader* in Natchez; the next year he moved to New Orleans where he continued in journalism.

1. Charles Wilkes (1798–1877), naval officer and explorer, had just completed a long voyage, begun in Aug. 1838, that had taken him to the Antarctic, certain islands of the Pacific, and the northwest coast of North America. As noted earlier, J. J. Abert, the chief of the Bureau of Topographical Engineers, had ordered JCF to connect his survey with that of Wilkes.

To Adelaide Talbot

St. Louis Mri.   Dec. 3d. 1843.

My dear Madam,

When I wrote to you a few days since I had not anticipated having the pleasure of sending you any news of our travellers until their arrival here; but last night I saw one of the party who had left them at Fort Hall on the 27th of September. He had a packet of letters and among them one for yourself but in swimming a river they were lost & consequently the gratification of getting news from Mr. Talbot will be denied you. The man gave me many details of the Summer's campaign & a particular account of your son's health. He says he is "fat stout & all the time in a good humour"—and has not been sick an hour since they left the settlements. Mr. Frémont would have accomplished his survey in a week after Lee[1] left, & by the middle of October, would be making his way homeward, and in a letter received by Mr. Campbell[2] of this place, Mr. Frémont says that early in January 1844, he will be here. They had had perfect success in all their undertakings but when they arrived at Fort Hall Mr. Frémont found he could not procure provisions enough & therefore gave permission to ten of the least useful of the party to return—to one of these ten our letters were given & by him lost—one or two others were entrusted to a different man & by him brought in safely.[3] You will feel their loss more than I for I have seen the living witness who testified to their health & good progress—but I hope it will be a comfort to you even though it comes at a second hand. Very respectfully yours,

Jessie B. Frémont

ALS (DLC—Talbot Papers).

1. Henry Lee was in charge of the *voyageurs* who were detached from the main exploring party at Fort Hall and sent home because of the difficulty of rationing a large party in the field. JCF also seems to have concluded that some of the men were not fit for the laborious service that would be required if he decided to make a winter survey into California (JACKSON & SPENCE, 355n, 519).

2. Robert Campbell (1804–79) of St. Louis was one of the chief suppliers of cash and equipment for JCF's second and third expeditions (SCHARF [2], 1:369–72). He had once been very active in the fur trade and, as JBF notes, had made many trips west.

3. Mrs. Talbot had or would read in the *National Intelligencer,* Dec. 15, 1843, which cited the St. Louis *Gazette,* that the Lee party had brought in a "very unfavorable account of their expedition, having been compelled for a portion of the time to subsist on horseflesh."

To Adelaide Talbot

Saint Louis   Feby. 1st 1844.

Your letter has remained unanswered my dear Mrs. Talbot because it found me prostrated by sick headaches occasioned as you will at once conceive by "the sickness of the heart." It made me sorry to see the note to your son for he is not here yet—and I knew that little note contained the welcome home. If our sorrows could be alleviated by knowing that others had as great, yours my dear madam would not seem so insupportable—for although Theodore is an only son yet you have another child[1] & she is with you—whilst my poor mother in law[2] has but one living thing to love. She says "Charles is all that the grave has left me"—and should anything happen to him how utterly desolate must she be; for your own heart would tell you that no daughter in law could replace your son, however much she might love you—and Mr. Frémont's mother has not even the comfort of having me with her so you are not the worst off, although I will admit that you have grief & anxiety enough, & the absence of an only son is cause sufficient for it. My own Mother says I am too young & too perfectly healthy to know all the miseries that attend a separation, & that if I were older and in a nervous state of health this incessant disappointment would wear me out. It is very fortunate for us all that I have elastic spirits for being here I hold a very responsible place & the letters I write my Mother & yourself are I know guides to your thoughts & exert an influence over your feelings.

For the last two weeks I had become so excited & unhappy for every day every hour indeed brought a fresh disappointment, that not then would I have written to you. But last night Mr. Campbell, who has been to Oregon himself twenty years ago nearly, when every difficulty was greater than now, traced out on the map Mr. Frémont's route & gave me the date of his probable arrival at each place, and satisfied me that he would be here in February. As Mr. Campbell says, "They may have a *tedious* journey but I assure *not a dangerous* one." If you knew Mr. Campbell you would feel as quiet as I do—for he is an honest man one who in word nor deed *is* untrue. Ma says, I believe, because it is what I want to hear, and although I do not think so yet perhaps it is the case. I do not tell you then my dear Mrs. Talbot to believe as I do in Mr. Campbell, but it would be a very happy thing for you if you could—it is so pleasant to rely implicitly on anyone, especially if they tell you what you love to hear. So this morning I resolved to write and tell you all he had said & hope it would have its influence in tranquilizing your feelings. You only look for your son at regular periods of the day—you cannot estimate that comfort until you are situated as I am. Mr. Frémont may come in any conveyance but a steam car & from the moment I open my eyes in the morning until I am asleep again I look for him. I hurry home from a visit and from church & the first question is "Has he come?" Judge then how the ever recurring *"no"* jars on my ear—it is worse I assure you than it can be to you to see "They have not arrived yet" in the beginning of every letter from me. Still I have the hope that very soon I shall be able to efface all those feelings by telling you "they are here safe and well" and in that little sentence will be healing for every pain.

If it is not asking too much, will you write to me again? but do not tell me I do so much for you—indeed it gratifies me to write much more than it can you to receive them and if I give you an hour of comfort I feel more than compensated. Mother desires me to give her kindest regards to you and I add mine for your daughter whose health is I hope restored. For yourself believe me dear Madam, most sincerely your friend,

Jessie A. B. Frémont

ALS (DLC—Talbot Papers).

1. Mrs. Talbot had a daughter, Mary.
2. At this time, JCF's mother, Anne B. Hale, was probably residing in Aiken, S.C. Her third husband was dead, and JCF was the only one of her four children who was living. See JBF's notes on the Frémont family background [July 1856], below, for the scandal she created when she ran away from her first husband with Frémont's father.

To Adelaide Talbot

Saint Louis   March 3d. 1844.

I have been obliged to leave your letter unanswered for some days
my dear Mrs. Talbot for Mother had a return of her fall attack of
chills & fever & for ten days has needed such constant attention that
I have had no time for writing except to give Father a daily bulletin.[1]
My letter giving you the news of the finding of Mr. Frémont's [. . .]
has reached you by this time & has I hope given you the same certainty
that it has me — that is, that with his jaded animals he has not ventured
to travel in the winter but made a comfortable camp in the buffalo
country & gotten through the worse of the winter without exposure.
Consequently he cannot be here until the middle of April. I *have*
sympathized in your anxieties for your son more than I had expressed
for I was aware before they left the frontier, of Mr. Talbot's delicate
health. Mr. Frémont sent for Sir William Stuart's [Stewart's] physician,
Dr. Tighlman [Tilghman], to attend Mr. Talbot & kept him for that
purpose until Sir Wm.'s party left.[2] I know my husband would have
mentioned in his letter from Oregon, any sickness of your son's for
every one written from the frontier expressed anxiety as to the result
of the experiment — for such he felt it — & the responsibility was greater
as the Government allows no physician — they are to do or die. The
appropriations are doled out from the Department with a view to the
praise of Congress for their economy & not with any regard to the
comfort of the party. From 10 to 11 thousand was all Col. Abert
allowed for this expedition — an expedition to consist of thirty men
& last for nine months & to go through the heart of a hostile country,
for after the Sioux & Blackfeet are passed they have to encounter the
British occupants of Oregon & only those who will not be convinced
refuse to believe that they are treacherous and would willingly assist
the Indians in case of difficulty. And yet Mr. Frémont has been censured
by Col. Abert,[3] Col. Totten & the Secretary at War, separately &
collectively for obtaining arms from the arsenal to defend himself, and
the arms charged to his private account.[4] Col. Kearny[5] who acted like
a generous soldier & gentleman, and ordered their issue has also been
censured by Mr. Porter, who I am rejoiced to see was rejected contemptuously by the Senate.[6] I am doing what you apologized for my
dear Madam but when I think of the injustice done my husband I

have no longer patience with those who have behaved so unjustly towards him. It is hard for a man to leave a family to tremble for him daily, & receiving no reward for his exertions & encounters with danger, but the approval of his Colonel, to be met on his return by a letter equally wounding to him & disgraceful to the writer. It makes me sick to think of its effect upon Mr. Frémont for the bitterest lesson in life is to meet with such miserable behaviour from those who professed friendship. You must pardon me for occupying your time with my own affairs dear Mrs. Talbot but I wish you who have shewn such a kind interest in me to know the truth when you will hear Mr. F. blamed for being displeased with his Colonel. As it is a private affair I have no right perhaps to speak of it, but it will be public when he returns. Will you make my kindest regards to your daughter. I hope to have the pleasure of making her acquaintance in six weeks. As for yourself I feel as if I knew you well already. My poor baby has taken the whooping cough & will need all my time but I will find an opportunity to answer all your letters for they are a great pleasure to me. Very sincerely yours,

Jessie A. B. Frémont

ALS (DLC—Talbot Papers).

1. Benton had returned to Washington to attend the congressional session. Elizabeth Benton, whose paralytic stroke in the summer or fall of 1842 left her brain-damaged and subject to seizures, remained in St. Louis (HERR, 76–77).

2. Dr. Stedman Richard Tilghman, a recent graduate of the Baltimore Medical School, was traveling with the Scottish baron, Sir William Drummond Stewart (1796–1871), on his purely adventurous expedition to the Wind River Mountains (PORTER & DAVENPORT, 218).

3. The chief of the Topographical Bureau, Col. John J. Abert (1788–1863), was responsible for the extensive surveys made of the West in the pre–Civil War period. On hearing that JCF had taken a twelve-pound howitzer on his expedition, he wrote to him asking what authority he had to make the requisition and telling him that if he believed that the Indians and the condition of the country would not permit the peaceful accomplishment of the scientific goals of the mission, he should desist (Abert to JCF, May 22, 1843, DNA-77, Lbk 6:279–80). JBF claimed, however, that Abert had ordered the expedition cancelled and that she had suppressed the order and sent a message to her husband to hurry west. Over the years, she and JCF gave several versions of the incident: MEMOIRS, 167–68; JBF, "The Origin of the Frémont Explorations," *Century*, 41 (Mar. 1891): 768–69; JBF, "Memoirs," 55–59).

4. Joseph Gilbert Totten (1788–1864), chief engineer and also Abert's superior officer, seems not to have sent a separate letter of censure to JCF, but Acting Secretary of War James Madison Porter (1793–1862) called JCF's requisition of the howitzer irregular and noted that he had not sanctioned the proceeding (see JACKSON [1] and Senate Doc. 14, 28th Cong., 1st sess., serial 432).

5. Stephen Watts Kearny (1794–1848) was then commanding the Third Military Department, which had its headquarters at Jefferson Barracks near St. Louis. On the outbreak of war with Mexico in 1846, he was ordered to occupy Santa Fe and strike for California. It was in California that JCF became trapped in a quarrel between naval commodore Robert Stockton and Kearny over the supremacy of comand. Kearny filed charges against JCF, and a bitter enmity developed between the two men.

6. Because of Porter's censure of JCF, Benton, as chairman of the Military Affairs Committee, may have blocked his confirmation as secretary of war.

To Adelaide Talbot

Saint Louis   March 24th 1844.

It is so long since I received your kind letter of congratulation on Father's escape my dear Mrs. Talbot, that I feel ashamed not to have answered it.[1] But in that time I have had a little battle in my mind and it has not been decided until a day or two since. You know I had made my plans to go on with Mother, but as the time drew near to leave St. Louis I felt my resolution leaving me & at last the temptation to remain became so great that like many a better & wiser person I fell before its force. So that I shall not have the pleasure of seeing you as soon as I had supposed but then I shall see your son the sooner & give him your letters & tell him that you have been well during the winter. All the mountaineers agree upon the last of April as the earliest date at which Mr. Frémont can be here, as he can then come swiftly & pleasantly by water.

After Mother leaves I shall be very lonely here and will depend upon you dear Madam for letters to shorten the time of waiting for I shall feel like a sentinel on the look out until Mr. Frémont returns—and then I can give pleasure to you in return for your kindness to me. Then too I can make my letters more agreeable but now I do believe I have but a single idea. Our friend Dr. Martin has a great many & if he were a good Christian he would feel it a charitable act to write to such an unfortunate forlorn person as I will soon be; I think I shall have to resort to some desperate remedy such as plain sewing to relieve the nervous state I shall fall into.

You see Mrs. Talbot I have written you a letter about myself & you must answer in the same way, telling how you feel & think also. There cannot be two more charm[ing] subjects although it might be more selon les règles [according to the rules] to leave such speeches to others.

Make mine & Mother's kindest regards to your daughter & receive for yourself Mother's warmest thanks for your remembrance of & feeling for her. As she leaves in three days she has no time to write but desires me to say for her that she was much gratified by your writing so kindly.[2] Yours most sincerely,

Jessie A. B. Frémont

ALS (DLC—Talbot Papers).

1. Benton was one of the dignitaries aboard the USS *Princeton*, commanded by Robert F. Stockton, which took a Sunday excursion down the Potomac on Feb. 28, 1844. There was exhibition firing of a new cannon, which exploded into its audience, killing Secretary of the Navy Thomas Gilmer and Secretary of State Abel Upshur. Benton, who only a few seconds earlier had moved from the ranks of those hit by flying metal, suffered heavy shock and a ruptured eardrum (CHAMBERS, 272).

2. Elizabeth Benton was returning to Washington.

To Adelaide Talbot

Saint Louis   April 21st, 1844.

A trading party came in from Fort Laramie last week and I had hoped to give you news of Theodore my dear Mrs. Talbot but they knew nothing of our party later than ourselves; still as their arrival shews the country to be in travelling order it has been a pleasure to me. The wise in such matters tell me that Mr. Frémont has either camped immediately at the foot of the mountains on this side or that very probably he did not cross at all but wintered in Oregon—in that event he will not be here until the middle of May—so you see dear Mrs. Talbot I can say nothing to comfort you—but only repeat—patience patience. The advancing season cannot fail to bring them. The locust trees by my windows are covered with white blossoms. They look as if they had come forth to meet a bridegroom. I am sure I feel more like a bride than I ever expected to do again only Lilly[1] makes an unusual addition to a wedding party.

When I think of their coming and the joy I shall have, I check myself & feel reproached that I should be so happy when Mr. Frémont's mother & yourself will have to wait so long before you see your sons. I will do as you ask me, & try to make Theodore as you tell me to call him, feel that he has friends here although that will be but very insufficient to satisfy his heart after such an absence from home. Your consideration about his expenses shews your refined feelings but you had no need to have disquieted yourself on that account. Each one renders to another the services in their power, without money and without price when they are freed from the cities & get on the broad prairies. I will however do as you request & shew your letter to Mr. Frémont. It is very flattering to see him remembered and praised as he has been although I am so unreasonable I constantly want to hear more. I will not apologize my dear Madam for filling my letter with such entirely personal topics for you feel as forcibly as I do that where such a strong feeling takes possession of the mind it is vain to attempt writing of anything else—and my anxiety about Mother & Mr. Frémont exclude all other thoughts. I hope Ma is now in Washington as I think the comforts of home will be of much service in reestablishing her health. Still home will not be home to her. There are four there & four here—the youngest & most helpless & then Mr. Frémont is a source of anxiety to all. How long they have been gone Mrs. Talbot— in ten days it will be a year since you saw Theodore—the 13 of May they left here together—by the 13th of this May I hope perhaps in vain—that I may write to you that they are here with me well & safe; twenty days yet—it is not impossible & how glad it would make my heart to be able to say so. As there is so much uncertainty in sending letters about the upper country I have kept all your son's and will give them to him when he comes. In the letters which I have written to Mr. Frémont at Fort Leavenworth & Westport I have always given the last news I had from you & explained why I did not send his letters.

Do write to me again Mrs. Talbot—your letters are a great pleasure & I need all the love & friendship that persons can find to give me.

With kindest regards to your daughter I am most sincerely yours,

Jessie Benton Frémont

ALS (DLC—Talbot Papers).

1. By 1851, JBF was spelling her daughter's name "Lily."

To Adelaide Talbot

Saint Louis, June 15, 1844.

You must think it very strange dear Mrs. Talbot that I have not yet answered your two kind letters but since they arrived my little Lilly has been very sick, and I myself have had incessant headaches for the last three weeks. And you know with the headache and a sick child nothing can be done. Lilly is well again now & although I have my usual pain in the head I will no longer defer thanking you for your kindness in writing so often & more especially for the copy of the remarks in the English work you mentioned. Mr. Frémont will be doubly gratified when he reads them for neither of us had any claim to the kindnesses you have shewn us. In return for your attention I can tell you some little news of our party. A Mr. Glasgow has just arrived from California.[1] He saw Mr. Fremont early in November & learned from him that he was to winter at Fort Hall. As Mr. Glasgow came in by the Southern route he of course arrived sooner than our party could as it was probably to return by the Yellowstone.[2] We know that the snows in the mountains are breaking up, for the rivers above are all rising & if after so many disappointments you can still hope, then look for their being here the first of July. How sorry I do feel that neither Mr. Frémont's mother nor yourself can have the certainty of restored happiness as soon as I. It will seem wrong to be so very happy whilst you are still in trembling anxiety. I wish I had Morse's telegraph for that once—it would surely be a better use than disappointing Presidential candidates, and bothering the country about the Texas Treaty.

Nothing but the wish that you might not think harshly of me for not having written before, would have made me write this morning, for I am sure my dear Mrs. Talbot that you will find difficulty in reading my short letter & nothing to reward your trouble when it is read. Remember however that it is a hot Saint Louis day. I have the headache & to add to my troubles my pen is very contrary & refuses to write as I wish it. I will make a second & hope more creditable effort next week & perhaps I may by that time have some news from the mountains. With kindest regards to your daughter I am dear Madam very sincerely yours,

Jessie B. Frémont

I find I have omitted what I principally wished to say—that at Fort Hall our friends would have every comfort that fire food & shelter could give. So you need be under no apprehensions as to Theodore's health during the winter for I am sure Mr. Frémont would not let him expose himself.[3]

ALS (DLC—Talbot Papers).

1. Possibly Edward J. Glasgow (1820–1908), who had been in business at Mazatlan with his uncle, James Glasgow. This JBF letter implies that Glasgow had seen JCF at Fort Vancouver before returning to St. Louis to engage in the Santa Fe trade.

2. This refers to the river and not the famous steamship *Yellow Stone*, which became lost to history after 1837. For a colorful account of the vessel, see JACKSON [2].

3. JCF and his party finally arrived at St. Louis on Aug. 6, 1844, in the steamer *Iatan* (*National Intelligencer*, Aug. 17, 1844).

To John Charles Frémont

Washington City   June 18th 1846.

A Mr. Magoffin[1] says he will be at Bent's Fort a month from to-morrow, and that he will leave a letter for you, so I write, dearest husband, to tell you how happy we have been made by hearing of you up to the 31st of March, through Mr. O'Larkin.[2] Only the day before, I had received the Mexican account of your being besieged by Gen. Castro,[3] and I was much relieved by what Mr. O'Larkin says—that you could present yourself in Monterey, alone, if you wished, & not be harmed. But I hope that as I write, you are rapidly nearing home, and that early in September there will be an end to our anxieties. In your dear letter[4] you tell me that *le bon temps viendra* [the good time will come], and my faith in you is such that I believe it will come: and it will come to all you love, for during your long absence God has been good to us and kept in health your mother & all you love best.

This opportunity of writing only presented itself last night, so that there is not time for a letter from your mother herself, but I had one from her two days ago in which she tells me that during the warm weather she will remain at a place about ten miles from the city called Mount Pleasant [in South Carolina]. Her stay in the country did her health much good last fall & indeed it has been good generally through-out the winter. Her heart has been made glad by your brilliant success, and your late promotion, although it distressed her to anticipate more separations, could not but be most gratifying in many respects. You must let me make you my heartiest congratulations. I am sorry that I could not be the first to call you Colonel. It will please you the more as it was entirely a free will offering of the President's, neither father nor I nor anyone for us having asked or said we would like it.

So your merit has advanced you in eight years from an unknown 2d. Lieut. to the most talked of and admired Lieut. Col. in the army. Almost all of the old officers called to congratulate me upon it, the Aberts among them, & I have heard of no envy except from some of the lower order of Whig papers who only see as you as Col. Benton's son-in-law. As for your Report, its popularity astonished even me, your most confirmed & oldest worshipper. Lilly has it read to her (the stories, of course) as a reward for good behavior. She asked Preuss[5] the other day if it was true that he caught ants on his hands and eat them—he was so much amazed that he could not answer her, & she said, "I read it in papa's lepote [report]; it was when you were lost in California." Father absolutely idolizes Lilly; she is so good and intelligent that I do not wonder at it. And then you should see his pride in you.

Mother's health has been worse than ever during the winter, but the force of the disease seems now to have expended itself, and she is quite well again. That gave me a reason for staying at home quietly as I wished, and I have read so much that is improving that you will be very pleased with me. Your mother was kind enough to send me your daguerreotype, & it hangs over the head of my bed & is my guardian angel, for I could not waste time or do anything you did not like with that beloved face looking so kindly and earnestly at me. I opened a new history of Louisiana, a week or two ago, and it commenced with the Spanish discoveries on the southern part of the continent. I was by myself, Lilly asleep, and reading by our lamp, when I came to De Soto's search for the fountain of youth. I stopped, for it seemed as if pleasant old days had returned; and then I remembered so well what you once wrote to me that I could not help bursting into tears. Do you remember, darling? It was soon after we were married, & you wrote me, "Fear not for our happiness; if the hope for it be not something wilder than the Spaniards' search for the fountain in Florida, we will find it yet." I remembered it word for word, although it was so long since I read it. Dear, dear husband, you do not know how proud & grateful I am that you love me. We have found the fountain of eternal youth for love, & I believe there are few others who can say so. I try very hard to be worthy of your love.

I had meant to tell you of many things which might interest, but it would take a day to choose out from the year's accumulation. The road you have discovered is spoken of as giving you more distinction than any thing you have yet done. I had to publish almost all your letter, and like everything you write it has been reprinted all over the country. I have some beautiful poetry to shew you on our hopeful motto *le bon temps viendra*. Editors have written to me for your biography & likeness, but I had no orders from you & then you know it would look odd to leave out your age, & you never told me how old you were yet.

How old are you? You might tell me now I am a Col.'s wife—won't you, old papa? Poor papa, it made tears come to find you had begun to turn gray. You must have suffered much & been very anxious, "but all that must pass." I am very sorry you did not get our letters. Yours gave so much happiness that I grieved you could not have had as much from ours. You will of course come on here as soon as you get back. I wanted to go to St. Louis to meet you, but Father says I had better not, as it will be very uncomfortable and even dangerous to go out in the worst of the season, & I don't want to be sick, for I am not going to let you write anything but your name when you get home. And then we will probably have to be at Jefferson Barracks during the winter and until the new regiment is ready for the field. Father says you are to accept the appointment as it was given, with the understanding that you were to be kept on scientific duty under the direction of the Senate. Mr. [Daniel] Webster says it would be too great a loss to the science of the country if you were stopped in your onward course. If I begin telling you the sincere compliments from people whose names are known in Europe as well as America I would need a day.

You must have a few to think of, however. Edward Everett, Mr. Gallatin, Stevens (Central America), Davis, the author of "Jack Downing," a Dr. Barrett of Conn., a botanist who sent me his herbarium of American grasses (for which he wants the buffalo and bunch grasses) are among the northern men.[6] The South Carolinians claim you bodily, and Dr. Grayson[7] of Charleston wrote one of the most beautiful of all the notices I saw. Your early & steady friends, Mr. McCrady[8] & Mr. Poinsett,[9] were the first to whom I sent well-bound copies of your book. You are ranked with [Daniel] DeFoe. They say that as *Robinson Crusoe* is the most natural and interesting fiction of travel, so Frémont's report is the most romantically truthful. I have a letter from the President of the Royal Geographical Society, Lord Chichester [Colchester],[10] who says he could not help preparing a paper on your travels to be read at their meeting—& more & more and many more of the same.

Mr. Magoffin has come for the letter & I must stop. I have not had so much pleasure in a very great while as today. The thought that you may hear from us & know that all are well & that I can tell you again how dearly I love you makes me as happy as I can be while you are away.

All Jacob's[11] relations are well. I see Mrs. Talbot and her daughter constantly. They are so grateful to you for your mention of Theodore.

Farewell, dear, dear husband. In a few months we shall not know what sorrow means. At least, I humbly hope & pray so. Your own affectionate and devoted wife,

Jessie B. Frémont

ALS (NNC—Nevins Papers). In the previous summer, JCF had mounted his third government expedition, which took him into California, where he became involved in the Bear Flag revolt and the subsequent war with Mexico.

1. James Wiley Magoffin (1799–1868), a native of Kentucky, had long been interested in trade with Santa Fe and Chihuahua. He had resided within Mexican territory for some nineteen years, spoke Spanish fluently, and knew many influential Mexicans. Benton introduced him to Polk, and when Magoffin sped west to Bent's Fort, a trading post on the Arkansas River, with JBF's letter, he had special presidential instructions concerning the peaceful occupation of New Mexico by American forces. A secret conference with Governor Manuel Armijo, a cousin of Magoffin's wife, preceded Stephen Watts Kearny's resistance-free occupation of Santa Fe. Bribery was suspected, especially when Benton, after the war, steered a bill through Congress awarding Magoffin $30,000 for "secret services" to the American government. See Benton, 2:682–84.

2. Thomas O. Larkin (1802–58) was U.S. consul at Monterey and working very hard peacefully to separate California from Mexico in furtherance of President Polk's expansionist policy.

3. The Mexican officials were wary of American intentions in California, but seem to have granted JCF permission to winter there and purchase supplies for his forces. His movement in early spring toward the coastal towns, rather than toward Oregon, alarmed them, and General José Castro (c. 1810–60) ordered JCF to leave California. Instead of complying, the explorer retired to a peak in the Gabilan Mountains and erected a log fort with the intention of fighting to the last man if attacked, or so he wrote Larkin. Castro collected a large force, and Larkin sent word that an attack was about to begin. JCF reflected on the awkwardness of his position, and, when the pole bearing the American flag fell down, he told his men it was time to move camp. They set out for Oregon, slowly and defiantly. For documents, notes, and historians' speculations relating to JCF's intentions, see SPENCE & JACKSON, 63–86.

4. JCF's letter of Jan. 24, 1846, from Yerba Buena, printed in SPENCE & JACKSON, 46–48.

5. Charles Preuss (1803–54), a fine German cartographer, had been with JCF on his first and second expeditions. His diaries indicate that he was not always a happy traveler and that he was frequently critical of JCF's abilities and personality. Erwin G. and Elisabeth K. Gudde give a lengthy biographical sketch in PREUSS.

6. Most of the "northern men" mentioned by JBF had national reputations. Edward Everett (1794–1865), Unitarian clergyman and statesman, had been the U.S. minister to Great Britain; at the time of JBF's letter he was president of Harvard University. Albert Gallatin (1781–1849), former secretary of the treasury in both Thomas Jefferson's and James Madison's administrations, would seek information from JCF when the latter returned from his third expedition. Noted for the study of Mayan civilization and for volumes on his travels in Central America and the Yucatan, John Lloyd Stephens (1805–52) would initiate the building of the Panama Railroad. Various letter writers used the pseudonym "Major Jack Downing," which had been originated by Seba Smith, but New York businessman Charles Augustus Davis (1795–1867) was the most popular to do so. At least eight printings of his *Letters of J. Downing, Major, Downingville Militia, Second Brigade, to His Old Friend, Mr. Dwight, of the New-York Daily Advertiser* were issued in 1834. Although both JBF and an obituary in the New York *Times* (Jan. 27, 1882) give Barrett as the name of the Connecticut physician, botanist, and mineralogist, this was actually the English-born Joseph Barratt.

7. Not a doctor but a lawyer, William John Grayson (1788–1863) was a member of an old South Carolina family. He had been in Congress in the 1830s, but at the time of JBF's letter he was collector of the port of Charleston. In the fifties he turned poet, both for self-expression and as an apologist for the South, with *The Hireling and the Slave,* his best-known poem.

8. Although the Charleston lawyer, Edward McCrady (1802–92), was some eleven years older than the explorer, JCF claimed him as a friend and named a stream in California and Oregon after him (MEMOIRS, 483). In 1856, politics and the publication of an old private letter brought a rift in the friendship ("Great Events," 198).

9. The former U.S. minister to Mexico, Joel Poinsett (1779–1851), had taken an early interest in JCF's career. It was while he was secretary of war that JCF obtained his appointment to the Corps of Topographical Engineers.

10. Charles Abbot (1798–1867), Lord Colchester, an officer in the Royal Navy, was president of the society from 1845 to 1847.

11. Jacob Dodson, a free black from the Benton household, was making his third expedition with JCF as his personal servant. Later he served as a messenger in the U.S. Senate (*National Intelligencer,* Mar. 30, 1849).

To Thomas Oliver Larkin

Washington City   July 24th 1846

My Dear Sir

I am very happy that a safe opportunity has presented itself, for sending you my warmest thanks for your hospitality and kindness to Mr. Frémont. Mr. Buchanan[1] sent me all your private despatches, which shew me how much you risked in your generous kindness to him. It is hardly possible to tell you with how much gratitude his family & mine especially my Father and myself we think and speak of you. We are daily looking for some news of him although we cannot expect his return until September; and as the new duties which his promotion will bring him, may again carry him into Oregon, I hope that I may succeed in my intention of going also, & then I shall assuredly extend the journey a little and make a visit to Monterey, that I may thank you in person.

That you may not forget Mr. Frémont in the meantime, I send you a copy of his report on the past Expeditions, which have made me very anxious to see the beautiful country lying around you, although I am not brave enough to risk as much as he did in reaching it. With sincere thanks for your kindness to my husband I am very truly yours,

Jessie Benton Frémont

Printed in LARKIN, 5:166

1. James Buchanan (1791–1868), the secretary of state and later JCF's opponent in the presidential campaign of 1856.

To James K. Polk

[Feb. 16 (1847)]

My Dear Sir,

There is a very brave young man named Charles Taplin,[1] of education & respectable family, who was with Mr. Frémont throughout his second expedition & only returned from the present one when there was nothing left to be done. He is very anxious to go to Mexico and a 2d Lieutenancy would not only gratify him, but both Mr. Frémont & myself extremely. Father told me he intended asking for it for him, but he is so busy that I am afraid you will say "too late" when he gets leisure to think of him. Mr. Westcott[2] says patronage is only used for bribery but with me you can be purely disinterested as my good wishes are all I have to give in return & they are already yours. Unlike other applicants I shall not entertain much hope of succeeding & disappointments of many kinds are familiar to me. Still I hope to succeed. Very truly & respectfully yours,

Jessie Benton Frémont

To his Excellency The President
Tuesday 16th February

ALS (CLjC).

1. A St. Louisan, Charles Van Linneus Taplin (c. 1818–c. 1855) did receive the commission, but resigned it just a week after JCF submitted his own resignation following the verdict in his court-martial.

2. Democratic senator James Diament Westcott, Jr. (1802–80) of Florida.

To John Torrey

Washington City   March 21st 1847.

My Dear Sir,

The marriage of my sister[1] prevented my writing last week and giving you an answer in regard to the time of Mr. Frémont's return. I am half ashamed to say that the Fremontia reached here last summer— but if you can excuse my neglect for that once I will promise never to do so again. For once Mr. Cave Johnson[2] is not to blame, but in another case I think he is. Before Mr. Frémont left I sent to your daughter,[3] who pressed some of his plants, a card case of Chinese manufacture brought to me from Canton, which is I expect in the dead letter office. The uncertainty of trusting to a third party on the prairies as well as here, will I think deter Mr. Frémont from sending in his plants in advance of his party; and for his own arrival we cannot reasonably look until May or June if indeed then. This war has interfered badly with his original intentions. Our own letters from him date no later than the first of October. Despatches from the fleet & Comre. Stockton[4] are here dated the 25th of November, but as Mr. Fremont was several hundred miles in the interior he was not aware of the chance for writing. Capt. Stockton's letters are vexatious—because they require more assistance from Mr. Frémont. I am in hopes that the dragoon force under Genl. Kearny & the New York regiment, will procure his release for as you may perceive I have no sympathy for the war, nor has Mr. Frémont. Fighting is not his aim & though he threw all his energy into the affair last July & August yet it was as if revenging a private insult for he knew nothing of the war.[5] Of course as an officer, real insults to the country would be felt, & met by him in the same manner, but in my private opinion, there was no necessity for blood to wipe out the insult offered by Mexico. I have let myself go from the point, but you will see that it is uncertain when Mr. Frémont can leave California. Genl. Kearny carries him his Lieut. Col.'s commission & discretionary orders, to stay or return as he thinks fit.

I know what he would wish, but one's feelings cannot always be allowed to direct. So you can see I can only say that I know nothing. I hope that we shall soon hear—perhaps by May even he may arrive at St. Louis, but now it is impossible to decide. Should I hear, I will lose no time in giving you the news. At all events some good will result from the year in California for Mr. Frémont has been able to collect through all the seasons, & get plants in all stages.

Young Abert's[6] report accompanies this—perhaps it may be of some interest although he seems unskilled in explorations.

I am sorry to say farewell to the Fremontia for it was a sort of flower child from its name, but the other as you say is more characteristic as it comes from California.

Mr. Frémont was forbidden to write on account of pain in his chest, whilst at home the last time, and as I was his amanuensis, it seems that you are an old correspondent of mine, which must be my apology for giving you so long a letter but I knew it was a subject on which you felt really much interest. With much respect I am very truly yours,

Jessie Benton Frémont

ALS (NNBG-Torrey Correspondence). Torrey (1796–1873), professor of chemistry at Columbia and Princeton, was a pioneer taxonomic botanist, who described and classified many of the plants JCF brought back from his western expeditions. For biographies of Torrey, see RODGERS and ROBBINS.

1. Eliza (Liz) Preston Carrington Benton (1822–95) married William Carey Jones (1814–67), a former New Orleans editor, on Mar. 18, 1847, during a period of rapprochement when Benton and President Polk were cooperating on the Mexican War; hence, Polk escorted the bride to the supper table (Washington *Union,* Mar. 19, 1847; POLK, Mar. 18, 29, 1847). Jones was also an attorney who assisted Frémont in his court-martial trial. Later he was sent as a special agent to California to examine land titles at which time he also became interested in acquiring large tracts of land for himself (GATES and Jones's obituary, *Alta California,* Nov. 8, 1867).

2. Cave Johnson (1793–1866), the postmaster general.

3. Probably Margaret, the youngest of Torrey's three daughters. See letter of Dec. 8, 1848, below.

4. Commodore Robert F. Stockton (1795–1866) and JCF had cooperated in taking California for the United States. An influential businessman and and wealthy landowner from New Jersey, Stockton had a reputation for flamboyant, unconventional, and adventurous action. In a sense he was the prototype of the aggressive American nationalist of the 1830s and 1840s.

5. "The affair of last July and August" refers to the conquest of California. By her assertion that JCF knew nothing of the war, JBF seems to refer to the events connected with the Bear Flag revolt of June 1846. In early July, JCF was officially notified of the existence of war between Mexico and the United States (see John B. Montgomery to

JCF, July 9, 1846, printed in SPENCE & JACKSON, 166–67). Her assertion that he had "little sympathy for the war" is in contrast to his own actions in California and to her later statement to Josiah Royce that her father and husband had "earnestly planned, discussed and *intended*" the acquisition of California (J. Royce notes on Frémont interview [winter 1884–85] with JBF marginalia, CU-B—Oak Papers). See also her 1884 "Statement," below, in which she expresses doubts that Larkin had had a secret mission and that he would have been able to avail "against well known English intentions and Californian preferences."

6. The son of the chief of the Topographical Engineers, young James W. Abert (1820–97) had been a member of JCF's third expedition as far as Bent's Fort, where he was detached to survey the Canadian River from its source to its junction with the Arkansas. His report was published as Senate Exec. Doc. 438, 29th Cong., 1st sess., serial 477.

To Elizabeth Blair Lee

Washington City   April 15th 1847.

There are such encouraging accounts from Lizzy Woodbury[1] to night that I must write to tell you dear Lizzie how much I thought of & felt for you for many reasons of late; & each reason the strongest in its turn although now that we know Frank[2] is safe & Lizzy [Minna] out of danger, Mr. Lee's absence is the worst misfortune.[3] The castle[4] is taken & the vomito[5] never goes to sea so there are two consolations at once—but I don't know of any others for to be honest dear Lizzie there are some things for which we may (in secret) mourn as Rachel did for her children "without comfort."[6] Your kind and good mother is right, as she always is, in not letting you come home to the doubt & anxiety of an illness, even when there is no danger, as there is not now in Mrs. Blair's case. I am sorry for her disappointment, but that is not an irreparable loss & you know children are not necessary to happiness. It was wise in you not to let her remain in St. Louis for I begin to think there is something fatal in the climate for that situation. Pink Selden has just died in her confinement—she was so gay & thoughtless a person that her death saddens me—in fact it has dwelt in my mind so much that I have written you a raven's letter in place of the comfort I mean to administer for your loneliness. We have been out to Silver Spring twice in the past week. Your mother was looking very well and very busy getting the flowers into spring training. Mrs. Maury's book on the statesmen of America furnished us all, your Father most, with some of the heartiest laughs I have heard for some time.[7]

I didn't much like to come away. It would have been much more agreeable to me to have gone to *my own* room up stairs & stayed there quietly than to have returned to the one here which always reminds me that it was not always mine alone. Is there anything as selfish as grief dear Lizzie. You feel nothing so much as Mr. Lee's absence & here I am lamenting to you Mr. Frémont's when I pity you more than myself. I am so much healthier for one thing & then it is with me a sort of penance to wipe out the past—but you are delicate and with you there is no atonement to make—you have been good always—it is so hard for you poor Lizzie—it makes me very sorry for you—but every day lessens the absence & the sea voyage will do Mr. Lee good—nursing you so much was making him delicate too.

I never said so much about myself to any one but you before & I am beginning to be ashamed but you have more cause for sympathy & fellow feeling for me than any person I ever knew so you will forgive the selfishness that makes me yield for the second time in six years to the relief of sympathy; & feel why it is I want to give you what comfort I can. But I will not write any longer now for I feel decidedly that I am not cheerful. Most affectionately your friend & cousin,[8]

Jessie B. Frémont

ALS (DLC—Blair Papers). The daughter of Francis Preston Blair (1791–1876) and Eliza Violet Gist Blair (1794–1877) of Silver Spring, Md., Elizabeth (1818–1906), who was married to Samuel Philips Lee (1812–97), a naval officer, was JBF's dearest friend and confidant until the Civil War disrupted their relationship. Many details about Lizzie's life are given in CORNISH & LAAS. Although in 1847 her father no longer edited the Washington *Globe* and had never held or would hold political office, he was very much a force in national affairs and would be quite influential with Presidents Abraham Lincoln and Andrew Johnson as he had been with Andrew Jackson and Martin Van Buren. Furthermore, he was a longtime friend of the Benton family, and at first the Frémonts would benefit from his support and later suffer from his opposition. For a biography of Blair, see E. B. SMITH [1]; for a history of the Blair family in politics, see W. E. SMITH.

1. "Lizzy" or Elizabeth Woodbury was the sister of Mary Elizabeth Woodbury (1821–87), better known as "Minna." Minna was the second wife to Montgomery Blair, the brother of Elizabeth Blair Lee. Montgomery Blair's first wife had died in childbirth, and Minna has just undergone a painful delivery at the home of Francis Preston Blair, Sr., in Silver Spring. On the same day that JBF wrote to Lizzie Lee, Elizabeth Woodbury described the horrors of Minna's travail to her mother: "I have been waiting a few days for Minna to gain a little in strength before I wrote you that her confinement had taken place—a week ago last Sunday I came out to make her a little visit of a few days—most unexpectedly to us all about 4 o'clock the following

morning she was seized with severe pain. The Physician was immediately sent for. She continued night and day in severe and agonizing pain for eight days, having the Physician & nurse with her the whole time. The infant was taken with instruments, after such protracted suffering on the *eight*[*h*] day. Her strength at last gave out, & she was sustained by brandy & water. A few hours after her confinement, her physician said her symptoms were unfavorable, & she was sinking rapidly. Another Physician was called in & gave us more hope, tho's considered her situation doubtful, as they feared an internal rupture had occurred" (DLC—Blair Papers). Minna Blair recovered; her baby died.

2. Francis Preston Blair, Jr. (1821–75), Lizzie's brother, a young lawyer, was in Santa Fe at the time of the final Mexican uprising there (E. B. SMITH [1], 188). Fiery, hard-drinking, and generous, he was the youngest Blair son and the family's political hope.

3. Lee was heading for the war zone. His brig *Washington* had cleared the Navy Yard on Apr. 7 and on May 4 made Anton Lizardo, just south of Vera Cruz (CORNISH & LAAS, 65–66).

4. The "castle" is no doubt a reference to the fortress San Juan de Ulloa that guarded the entrance to the port of Vera Cruz. The terms of surrender for Vera Cruz had been agreed upon on Mar. 27, and the news reached New York on Apr. 10 (JOHANNSEN, 102, 106).

5. "Vomito" was a Spanish term for yellow fever. JBF is trying to reassure Lizzie that Lee would not get yellow fever because he was on a ship.

6. Matthew 2:18 and Jeremiah 31:15.

7. Mrs. Sarah Mytton (Hughs) Maury (1803–49) was the author of *The Statesmen of America in 1846* (London, 1847). In it she describes Thomas Hart Benton as "of robust and muscular frame, somewhat inclined to corpulence" (p. 96). JCF is described as "able and spirited" (p. 98). JBF had been introduced to Mrs. Maury by William Seward in 1846.

8. The Blairs and Bentons were related by both their Hart and Preston connections. Francis Preston Blair, Sr.'s mother, Elizabeth Smith, was a granddaughter of John Preston, as was JBF's maternal grandmother, Sarah Preston McDowell. A second connection was a Blair cousin married to the sister of Henry Clay; Clay, in turn, was married to Lucretia Hart, daughter of Thomas Hart, whose ward and niece was THB's mother, Ann (Gooch) Benton. See W. E. SMITH, 1:15; CHAMBERS; 26, and DORMAN, 11, 22, 24.

To Edward F. Beale

Washington City,   Sepr. 20th 1847.

My Dear Sir,

I heard this evening that you asked for orders for the Pacific, which is I hope a mistake—for a selfish reason I wish your stay a little longer in the country. Mr. Frémont's trial will take place in a month & I think he wishes you as a witness to some facts.[1] More positively I cannot speak for he is in Charleston[2] & not until I hear from him in answer to a letter I shall write tonight, can I give you a decided reason for postponing your departure. I hear with great pleasure of your improved health & if you can render Mr. Frémont the service of remaining a month longer on land I hope to judge of your improvement myself. Very truly yours,

Jessie Benton Frémont

ALS (DCL—Beale Papers). Edward Fitzgerald Beale (1822–93), a young naval officer with distinguished naval forebearers, had met JCF during the military operations in California, and throughout the balance of their lives there would be many contacts between Beale and the Frémonts. As did JCF, Beale made several transcontinental journeys, on one of them carrying the first official news of California gold to Washington, and on another encountering JBF in the city of Panama in 1849 as she made her way to California. He left the Navy in 1851 to accept an appointment as superintendent of Indian Affairs in California and Nevada and began acquiring large tracts of land, which were to make up fabulous El Tejon Rancho in southern California. "The cattle on a thousand hills" was his (JBF to Isaac Sherman, Nov. 1865, copy in editors' possession). In 1861, he was appointed surveyor general of California and Nevada, and in 1876, minister to Austria-Hungary. On his death, JBF would remember him as an "eccentric and witty man," who on her plea had given Bret Harte a position in his surveyor's office (to M. H. de Young, Oct. 10, 1893, DLC—Borglum Papers). For additional biographical details, see G. THOMPSON.

1. JCF was being tried for his refusal to surrender the military governorship of California to Gen. Stephen Watts Kearny the previous winter. The charges were mutiny, disobedience of the lawful command of his superior officer, and conduct to the prejudice of good order and military discipline. If called as a witness, JBF expected Beale's testimony to be favorable to her husband. The proceedings of the court-martial may be found in SPENCE & JACKSON, Vol. 2 Supplement.

2. Because of the serious illness of his mother, Anne B. Hale, JCF had gone to South Carolina. She died before he could reach Aiken, and he took the body to Charleston for internment (BARTRAM, 75).

To James K. Polk

[Sept. 21, 1847]

To the President,
Sir,

I enclose you this notice from the St. Louis Whig paper, the Republican,[1] and after reading it you will see the manifest injustice to Mr. Frémont of letting his accusers escape from the investigation of the charges they have made against him. There is an impression prevalent that Genl. Kearny also is to obtain orders for Mexico, at once.

You have the power to do justice & I ask it of you that Mr. Frémont be permitted to make his accusers stand the trial as well as himself. Do not suppose Sir, that I lightly interfere in a matter properly belonging to men, but in the absence of Mr. Frémont I attend to his affairs at his request. I trust he will be returned in a week, when agreeably to your request he will have the honor of calling on you. The precarious situation of his mother & my own want of health are I hope a sufficient apology for not having presented myself to Mrs. Polk. Very respectfully yours,

Jessie Benton Frémont

Tuesday evening
Sepr. 21st 1847.

ALS (DLC—Polk Papers).

1. The notice that JBF enclosed must have been from the *Missouri Republican*, Sept. 13, 1847, whose editors understood that orders had been received from Washington directing Capt. Henry S. Turner to proceed to Santa Fe and Maj. Philip St. George Cooke to Mexico. The journal noted, "These gentlemen have just returned from California, and the sudden order to proceed upon such distant service, looks as if the President did not intend to be in a hurry about ordering a Court Martial to investigate the charges against Col. Fremont." The Frémonts and Benton feared that if the court-martial were delayed, JCF would be tried in the press. But they also feared a trial based largely on documents, thereby losing the right to cross-examine witnesses. Both Turner and Cooke had been critical of JCF's role in California, and the defense wished to expose their prejudices and impeach their credibility through cross-examination.

The trial began on Nov. 2 at the Washington Arsenal, with Jessie frequently present. On Jan. 31, 1848, the court found JCF guilty on all charges and sentenced him to dismissal from the service. Seven members of the court-martial board recommended him to the clemency of the president. After reading the case and consulting with his cabinet, Polk decided to approve the sentence but remit the penalty. He was not satisfied that mutiny had been proven, but he did see proof of disobedience of orders and conduct prejudicial to good order and military discipline. The adjutant general ordered JCF to join his regiment in Mexico. Rather than accept the president's clemency and admit in any way the justice of the court's findings, the explorer resigned from the army.

To John Torrey

Washington City   May 29th 1848.

My Dear Sir,

Mr. Frémont is so pressed to finish his little memoir for the Senate, that he has asked me to send you the enclosed remnants of plants.[1]

They are the earliest flowering plants of the Joaquin valley (Cal.) and he would be much obliged if you could send him very soon, their names.

Mr. Trécul,[2] the French botanist, made Mr. Frémont a visit in which he talked over his intended explorations, so he has seen him.

As he will have to go to the North Mr. Frémont hopes to see you before leaving for California, which he trusts will be in the coming month.

Your wishes for my successful journey are a little premature. I shall go by the isthmus after the steamers commence running, a much less interesting, but shorter & safer way for women & children.[3] I should have written to your daughter some time since in answer to her kind message but for some months I have been unwell & since the last of April I have not left my room, but have had a battle with a violent bilious fever, which like Bunyan's fight with Apollyon was the dreadfullest fight I ever had.[4] Like him, however I have gained the victory & I am more than willing not even to remember it. Very truly yours,

Jessie Benton Frémont

ALS (NNBG—Torrey Correspondence).

1. JCF was writing an essay to accompany the map of Oregon and California, which his cartographer, Charles Preuss, was preparing. The geographical memoir and map may be found in Senate Misc. Doc. 148, 30th Cong., 1st sess., serial 511.

2. The French botanist Auguste A. L. Trécul (1818–96) was on his way to Kansas to collect specimens for the Muséum National d'Histoire Naturelle in Paris. By September he was working on the Arkansas and Little Arkansas (MCKELVEY, 1048–52).

3. Frémont planned to lead an expedition to California (it would be his fourth western expedition) and in so doing ascertain the practicality of a central railroad route, especially in winter. JBF would travel by sea, with an isthmus crossing, and meet him in San Francisco.

4. The strain of the court-martial trial with its harsh verdict, hard work with JCF on the geographical memoir, her advanced pregnancy, and concern about the future all had caused JBF to collapse. She likens her wrestle with the demon of despair to Christian's battle with the fiend Apollyon in the Valley of Humiliation in *Pilgrim's Progress* by John Bunyan.

To John Torrey

Washington City—December 8th. 1848.

My Dear Sir,

Mr. Frémont left me a list of plants to copy out for you, but until now I have had neither the quiet nor the strength to do it.[1] A few days will bring it to a close, and you may derive fresh interest for examining those from Feather river by reading the accounts of the great wealth of that region. Are there any flowers or plants peculiar to a gold region? One flower, 209, which Mr. Frémont supposes may be the "Cumas" may be belonging to that kind of earth. I have as you know very vague botanical ideas. Your daughter [Margaret] would laugh at me, but Mr. Frémont encourages my questionings and I am a sort of privileged person in the family which must excuse my questioning you also.

By some Indians who are to be sent back from Bent's Fort I shall get letters from Mr. Frémont before the New Year. Then, or at any time you wish to know anything I can inform you of, I hope you will let me have the pleasure of doing so. Father reserves for his part the sending of documents—none of any interest are out yet, but Mr. Frémont's memoir is just coming in from the last session, and shall be sent to you. Very respectfully yours,

Jessie Benton Frémont

Dr. John Torrey

ALS (NHi—Misc. Jessie Benton Frémont).

1. In the six months between this and the previous letter, JBF had given birth to a little boy, Benton (July 24, 1848), who died on the Missouri River, Oct. 6, as she traveled with her husband to the frontier town of Westport to see him off on his fourth expedition. The men left on Oct. 20.

To John Torrey

Washington City,   February 21, 1849.

My dear Sir,

I have been so continuously out of health since the beginning of the year that your letter and the list have had to lie by until now— my eyes being somewhat affected by general weakness I would not use them. Long hopeful letters from Mr. Frémont and the knowledge of his being in safety up to the 1st of December have had their share in making me feel better, and although I leave now in a fortnight[1] I shall send you the finished list. I think the drawings made on the last expedition must have been carried along to be put with those now being made—I cannot find the one you speak of. Mr. Frémont shewed it to me & I remember it well. If you have a proof can you let me have one to take to Mr. Frémont? I shall be in New York for two or three days before we sail—about the 6th or 7th of March. If you are in the city at that time I shall hope to see you. At all events I expect to carry Mr. Frémont a long letter from you.

From this Congress Mr. Frémont will not allow anything to be asked—they have but twelve days to live and we hope for a better set.[2] This expedition will do something for geography but the snows are too deep for botanizing. I send you the papers which contain as much of his letters as answer the kind inquiries of his friends. Very respectfully yours,

Jessie Benton Frémont

Dr. John Torrey
New York

ALS (NNBG—Torrey Correspondence).

1. JBF and Lily would leave for California via the isthmus on the steamer *Crescent City* on Mar. 15, 1849 (HERR, 186).
2. Benton had been defeated not only in his attempts to have Congress appropriate funds for the expedition, but also to get JCF the post of naval agent in California, supplanting Larkin (M. L. SPENCE [2], xxi–xxiii).

Elizabeth Benton Frémont to Thomas Hart Benton

Panama, April 27, 1849

My dear Grandfather,

I liked it very well traveling over the Isthmus. I came in a canoe first, then on a bony cavallo [horse],—the road was part high & part low with mud places about—narrow so all the horses had to follow mine.

I've been saying a Spanish lesson and a reading lesson every day since we came to the new house.[1] From here I see the jail and the government house and the water carts and the little indians flocking about—(tell Grandfather they have no clothes at all.)

I see horses coming along with water. I saw a plenty processions and one the man that led it was dressed all in gold cloth that shined like the sun; we saw the prisoners marching with dirt on their shoulders and chains around their waists and one of the guard masters with a gun on his shoulder to make them march about.

We went to Taboga[2]—we were two hours on the way and all of it seemed very pretty—but, and, I meant to say, we eat pine apples—a man there said it would [make me] sick, but it did not. But the second day coming back from Taboga wasn't as pleasant as the first for the boatman would not row—but the patron was very good, and there was one man that put up the sail all the time & wouldn't let it come down; and we were out a day and a night without any provisions only a plum cake and some olives which Mr. Weller[3] was made sick by eating. Mother was sick all the way out & I not at all and all the way back I was sick & not Mother.

I was so hungry I couldn't eat nothing at all when we got home. It was from nine o'clock until one o'clock at night we were out on the ocean.

AL in JBF's hand (NNC—Nevins Papers). The letter was dictated by six-year-old Lily, who, with her mother, was in Panama City after a twenty-one mile journey across the isthmus, mostly by muleback. They had not yet heard of the disaster that had overcome JCF's overland expedition. The men lost their way in the rugged San Juan Mountains, and heavy snow, knife-sharp winds honed by subzero temperatures, and failing supplies forced them to retreat. But before they could get out, ten men and 120 mules perished. JCF refitted and with a majority of the survivors went on to California by a more southern route than the thirty-eighth parallel.

1. JBF and Lily had been invited to move from one of the hotels and share the home of Señora Arcé y Zimena, aunt of the Panamanian ambassador in Washington (HERR, 190).
2. JBF describes the harrowing Taboga incident in "A Picnic Near the Equator," *Wide Awake,* 30 (Mar. 1890): 266–71.
3. A former member of Congress, John B. Weller (1812–75) was going to California as head of the commission to mark the new boundary between the United States and Mexico. His third wife, Susan McDowell Taylor, a cousin of JBF's, had died a few months earlier. Weller was governor of California during the Mariposas mine crisis in July 1858 (see MELENDY & GILBERT, 81–90; JBF to Francis Preston Blair, July 16, 1858, below).

To Evey Heap

[Mar. 14 (1851)]

Dear Evey,

I was grieved to hear from Mr. Beale that you had met with so painful a loss as that of your little daughter. I know that the sympathy of friends can do very little in such an affliction but I cannot refrain from expressing mine to you. I remember so well how hard it seemed to me to see you and your baby & then to go home to Liz with hers & remember that I too so lately had had one which I should never see again.[1] I did not envy either of you but I thought you were very happy. Before this reaches you I shall have another,[2] and my health has been so good that I have all reason to believe it will not have the fate of my dear little boy.

Mr. Heap stayed with us a little while about Christmas and was most usefully kind & attentive.[3] I found him as Mother used to think you a very agreeable person to stay in one's house. Mr. Frémont went up to the Mariposas a week ago.[4] Mr. Beale was with him. We heard from these [them] not long since & Mr. Heap was entirely well. His box by the White Squall went up last week under Mr. Edwards care.[5] I send you his last letters that have come down and dear Evey a great deal of love from your affectionate friend,

Jessie B. Frémont

March 14th

ALS (CLU—Department of Special Collections, Main Library). Addressed to "Mrs. G. H. Heap Chester, Delaware." Evey's formal name was Evelina Porter (d. 1863). She was a sister of Admiral David D. Porter and was married to her cousin Gwinn Harris Heap, who was also a cousin of Edward F. Beale (HAFEN & HAFEN, 22–23).

Almost two years had passed since Lily and JBF had written to Benton from the little city of Panama. The Frémonts had been reunited in San Francisco in June 1849 but had returned to Washington the following year when JCF was elected to the Senate. On the admission of California to the Union, he had the misfortune to draw the short term, and, taking his family with him, he returned to the Pacific Coast to campaign for reelection. The legislature dissolved without settling on a candidate, and by the next term, perhaps sensing failure, he decided that politics was "too costly an amusement" and was not a contender.

1. A reference to the baby Benton. See JBF to John Torrey, Dec. 8, 1848, note 1, above.

2. The baby was born on Apr. 19, 1851, and named John Charles after his father (HERR, 221).

3. Gwinn Harris Heap (1817–87) had gone to California with William Carey Jones in 1850 when he became JCF's resident agent on Las Mariposas, the estate described in the note below. He went with the Frémonts to England in 1852, and he was the diarist for Beale when the latter went overland in 1853 to take up his superintendency of the California Indians. The friendship between the Heaps and the Frémonts soured; Heap brought suit against JCF for money owed to him and wrote to his wife on Dec.

1, 1856: "if Fremont would be honest for once and pay me, what a fortunate thing it would be . . . but we can not expect to make a silk purse out of a sows ear, or to milk from a turnip" (AzHi—Camels in Western America Collection).

4. Located not far from Yosemite Valley, Las Mariposas was a vast grant of land that had been purchased by Larkin for Frémont in February 1847. It was a "floating grant," with no set boundaries, and the vendor, Juan B. Alvarado, did not have absolute title. Because of the Indian menace, JCF had been unable to comply with the Mexican government's provisions for survey and settlement; in addition, one of the terms of the grant had forbidden the sale or alienation of the property. The legal problems were further complicated by the discovery of gold in 1849. It was not until Feb. 19, 1856, that JCF received a U.S. patent, but his problems with the 44,386.83–acre tract did not end there, as later letters indicate.

5. Henry B. Edwards (c. 1826–c. 1892), Beale's brother-in-law, had traveled to California with Heap and Jones. He did some business on his own account on the Mariposas and later assisted JCF in the delivery of cattle to the Indians under the 1851 contract that the explorer obtained from Indian Commissioner George W. Barbour. He was the first postmaster at Mariposa and later the farming agent for the Indians in the southern part of the San Joaquin Valley (M. L. SPENCE [2], 144n–45n, 237–39, 260–62).

To Francis Preston Blair

San Francisco,   April 11th 1851.

My dear Mr. Blair,

Mr. Frémont has excited himself on the subject of hedges to that point that he can no longer rest without such a one of Osage orange as you described to him. To gratify that wish he begs that the next time you go into town you will turn Quaker[1] within a square of her usual stopping place and ask at the Patent Office that they will repeat a former attention & send him some of that as well as other seed. Adam's Express will relieve you of any farther charge & deliver them within six weeks to him at this place. When I look up at the length of my sentence I feel that I have yielded to the Spanish influence of this coast, but I wrote as I would have talked, until my breath gave out. Good seeds, of any kind, are hard to obtain and would be very acceptable to us here. We are just about going on a rancho[2] & from this time forward will be gathering all that we can in the way of fruit & vegetable seed, as Mr. Frémont is going largely into farming and I hope we shall make you a very good report of our success. I intend to rise early every day—not Saturdays only as some amateur farmers of my acquaintance do.

Mr. Frémont says I must tell you something of the place we shall be upon to interest you in it—after we are there he will make you a topographical report of it himself. For one item, horses & cattle both included there are over six thousand head. It is soft enough in climate for olives figs & grapes, as well as peaches & apricots to be now growing there. The Mariposas is no place for me—Indians, bears & miners have made it lose its good qualities as a country place & it is very out of the way.

Mrs. Blair[3] and I live opposite each other. Vivy[4] often calls to me from her mother's balcony. Mammy takes Lily out with Violet constantly for a walk as that young lady won't go alone always—never if she sees "Lilly Cemont."

She is greatly improved and is a very sweet child. Mrs. Blair is still confined to her room. I have not seen her for some days, although I keep well posted as to her need of assistance. But she is most comfortably situated in all respects, and has even many acquaintances here whom she likes.

I am looking for Liz by the steamer of the 22d. It will be a great pleasure to have her & dear little Betty here.[5] Lily has been my scholar this winter and you can realize her progress when I tell you that she sits in the hammock with her doll in her lap, reading for amusement Hood's poems.[6] She has learned, because it remained in her memory, & not as a task, "The song of the Irish" & "I remember" as well as many verses of Miss Kilmansegg. Mr. Frémont has with him here a very fine horse which she feeds with great care and affection. A hen & nine chickens of her own complete her list of pets—with a little bed of parsley radishes &c. which have grown finely much to her surprise. She is looking fat & really handsome from good health & an actively employed mind.

Her messages to you all are so numerous I will put them in a separate letter from herself. I wish that I may not be entirely forgotten among you. Neither Mrs. Blair nor yourself will I expect a letter from, but Lizzie is a regular scribe and can transmit long messages in those which I most certainly expect from her. In the meantime you see me connect you with our visions of a beautiful home—which I hope you will some day see in its realization. With love to all from Mr. Frémont & Lil I am sincerely & affectionately yours,

Jessie Benton Frémont

ALS (NjP—Blair-Lee Papers).

1. Quaker was a Blair horse.

2. The rancho seems to have been Los Alamitos, one side of which bordered the Pacific Ocean, south of present-day Long Beach. JCF tried unsuccessfully to buy it from Abel Stearns for $300,000 (M. L. SPENCE [2], 229).

3. In the previous fall, the Frémonts had escorted Mary Serena (Jesup) Blair (1826–1914), the wife of James L. Blair (1819–52), and her daughter "Vivy," to San Francisco for a reunion with the husband and father, who was operating a steamship line on the Sacramento River. Two years later, James Blair sent his little family back to the "Moorings," a cottage on the Silver Spring estate. His death a year later in California of a ruptured aorta was a shock to all the Blairs (E. B. SMITH [1], 186–87).

4. Violet Blair (1848–1933) would spend most of her life in Lafayette Square near the White House except for brief periods in New Orleans following her marriage to attorney Albert Covington Janin. Janin became the manager of Mammoth Cave Estate in Kentucky.

5. Betty was JBF's niece, the daughter of Eliza Benton Jones ("Liz").

6. The Hood here is Thomas Hood (1799–1845), English poet and humorist. *Miss Kilmansegg* was one of his comic poems.

To Charles F. Mayer

San Francisco,   Augt. 1, 1851

My dear Sir:

Will you please write to Mr. Hoffman[1] who will I fear think Mr. Frémont a myth and let him know that letters to him have been mailed by Mr. Frémont as late as the 15th May. In the fire of the 21 June, I amongst others, had my home destroyed, but as I had some half hour's time all Mr. Frémont's papers as well as the most valuable things in the house were saved.[2] In the flutter of such a sudden removal I did not think to do what I hope is not now too late & write telling Mr. Hoffman of the safe arrival of several contracts and many letters. All that has been done Mr. Frémont approves of entirely. He will be here, I think, certainly before the Steamer of the 15th & having been now some time (since 14th May) in the Mariposa in the Mining Country to the South will be able to write very fully.

The papers of this place give generally as much reliable information as exists about the mining in operation throughout the Country. The only drawback is the want of Capital without which at the start the other expenditures are useless.

But that too will be alleviated by the consolidation of individual efforts & several companies and from what I was told by two very dispassionate and reliable persons a few days ago the results even this summer from Quartz mining will be very immense.

Mr. Frémont will answer to all the points on which Mr. Hoffman asked information. I merely write to let him know the safety of his letters and the fact of their having been in part answered although from my having been ill at that time I heard no particulars. With respects, I am, yours truly,

Jessie Benton Frémont

Copy, p. 55 in Chancery Brief, Frémont *v.* Hoffman (NHi—J. C. Frémont-David Hoffman Papers). An attorney in Baltimore, Charles F. Mayer (1797–1864) was acting as JCF's American solicitor in the attempt to raise capital for the mines of the Mariposas, especially from foreign sources. He and his better known brother, Brantz, were lifelong friends of David Hoffman. See SCHARF [1] for biographical details on the Mayers.

1. David Hoffman (1784–1854), a former professor of law at the University of Maryland, had been living in London since 1847, where he sometimes promoted land and emigration companies. He and JCF were casual acquaintances of long standing, having been introduced by Joseph N. Nicollet. JCF had given him authority to grant leases and organize mining companies to work on the Mariposas. Relations between him and the explorer became very abrasive, as M. L. SPENCE [1] indicates.
2. The first San Francisco fire had been on May 3, 1851, about two weeks after the birth of Charley. The flames came so close to the Frémont house that its painted walls were scorched, and the grass shriveled and died. The next fire, JBF's "last," occurred on June 22—not June 21—and burned her out as she indicates in the letter.

To Francis Preston Blair

San Francisco,   August 14th 1851.

My dear Mr. Blair,

Knowing how the editorials for the Globe were written I most fully appreciate your immediate answer to my letter and shew my sense of the unusual exertion by this prompt acknowledgement. But do not feel obliged to make a game of battledore of it & send me letter for letter although I need not say how much pleasure it would give me to have frequent gossips from your fire side to mine.

Literally a fire side with me even in this month of August, for as our season of fogs is not over we need bright fires morning & night although the sun is hot at midday. I am writing now at our tea table (a match in size to yours). Mr. Frémont who is just now at home after an overland journey to & back from Los Angeles, sits nearest the fire being the thinnest & most cold blooded of the two. We have been drinking some real China tea and altogether with late magazines, Soyer's menagère[1] (by which I made a cake today, and very well too) and many household gods about, little Charley in his basket at the head, it has very much the look of a home in an old country.

I shall be on the Mariposas in the planting season and will look with eagerness for the seed. My own hands will plant them and if a decently honest commission come to decide our land titles, my own hands will gather the fruits.

Be that as it may there will be much pleasure and health to be had in the planting and the future may take care of itself.

I have asked Mr. Frémont for a message and he says I must tell you to prepare yourself for a Whig Senator in his place, politics being too costly an amusement in this country just now, but that he will come to it with renewed vigor by the next election. The state is decidedly Whig—partly I suppose from the great commercial interests involved, but more from the misrule of those who have had the state government in their hands and who but used it for private ends. As they were nominally Democrats we the genuines must suffer for their sins.

Major Redding [Reading], the Whig Candidate, will be almost unanimously elected.[2] He was as you may remember a warm personal friend of Mr. Frémont's. He is unaltered and as we are here steadily now, Mr. Frémont will have more influence on the state government than under a democratic governor. The one most serious question for us, is the keeping order among the Indians, but we hope our frontier will not go through the bloody baptism of the other states. As Major Redding's own property is surrounded by Indian villages, in the same manner as the Mariposas, you will see how fortunate it is for our interests that he should be in power.

I am coming home next spring. It will always be home to me where Father and Mother are, so I may say it. This is a residence—a "location" anything you like but I shall always feel the house on C. street as my home. Then, I trust I shall be able to shew you my dear little boy of whom you say such kind things. Mr. Frémont was greatly pleased at your way of putting his title claims and Mrs. Frémont was greatly pleased too at your praise of her.

One day, in Father's office, nearly five years ago, both yourself and Father gave me some commendation for behaving properly. No doubt you have forgotten it and the occasion but it has since been of more use to me than you know of, in aiding me to do what at first seemed difficult. In this case any loss of comfort or risk from traveling has been a thousand fold repaid to me. My baby has not had a moment's pain [yet?] in his little life of now near four months and I myself am in perfect health. A more thankful heart than mine does not beat. Mr. Frémont has had heavy losses in his gold experiments, but his energy and real "Bentonian industry" have brought him out of them. His health is again firm and with health, happiness and good friends I don't know what more life can give. I trust we may never lose sight of the source from which all our good gifts have been granted us. The evil coming first has made us more sensible of the contrast.

Your own life was much the same in its chief points and you will pardon my presumption in putting myself in the same chapter, but there is a strong bond in similarity of misfortunes, and although I am still very young "by the calendar" as Father says, still I am old enough in experience of the world learned in my military academy (I hope John Lee[3] isn't spending the day with you) to feel self justified in taking quite a familiar tone not only to you but to Mrs. Blair, whom I regard with more awe, for she is not so easy to please as yourself. I shall have Mrs. Blair's good word for being a really good mother to the baby. He has no nurse at all but myself, and yet I teach Lily and sew (but I hate that) and keep house and all quite easily and pleasantly. As these last are merits hitherto unsuspected in me, even by myself, I glorify myself not a little. But you will think me a perfect Mr. Ritchie[4] if I never quit speaking of what I did & what I do & what I can shall will or may do.

I can't tell you anything much of Vivy as Mrs. Greenhough[5] has succeeded in establishing herself a la Hetzel[6] with Mrs. Blair and I am in disgrace—I suppose in consequence of the alliance but I have really been too busy and too happy to think or ask why Mrs. Blair's door is closed to me.

My dear Mr. Blair I have written you the letter of a boarding school girl but we depend on Lizzie for all our little home details and so feeling, I have written of mine. I will give her a separate letter of thanks for the great satisfaction her letters give Liz and I. Liz is just now at Santa Clara—merely to see the country. Betty & herself are both very well. We are all together and it is very homelike. Lily can ride very well now. Dr. Bowie[7] often takes her out. Mr. Holmes, Robert McLane,

& Mr. Blunt were here together Sunday, so you can see I sometimes have old surroundings.[8] I hope before this time next year to have told all my travellers' stories over to you in your hospitable house near which I pray no cares may come. Most truly yours,

Jessie Benton Frémont.

ALS (NjP—Blair-Lee Papers).

1. Alexis Benoît Soyer was the French chef of the Reform Club in London. His culinary publications became extremely popular and went through many editions in both England and the United States. The one JBF notices here is *The Modern housewife, or Menagère. Comprising nearly one thousand receipts for the economic and judicious preparation of every meal of the day, and those for the nursery and sick room; and minute directions for family management in all its branches,* first published in 1849. Soyer had a varied career: erecting soup kitchens in Ireland during the famine and cooking for the fourth division of the army during the Crimean War.

2. Pierson B. Reading (1816–68), with property in Shasta County, had been paymaster of the California Battalion, commanded by JCF in 1846 (PIONEER REGISTER, 689). JCF was supporting him for the governorship of California and T. Butler King for his old seat in the U.S. Senate, but both men failed of election.

3. Career army officer John Fitzgerald Lee (1813–84) had been the judge advocate or prosecuting attorney for the army in JCF's court-martial in 1848. He was the brother of Lizzie Blair's husband, Samuel Phillips Lee.

4. Mr. Ritchie is Thomas Ritchie (1778–1854), who became editor of the Washington *Globe* after President Polk dismissed Blair.

5. Mrs. Greenhough is Rose O'Neal Greenhow (c. 1815–64), who had a sharp wit, dynamic manner, and many political friends. She and her husband, Robert Greenhow, a former State Department official, had been on the same steamer that brought the Frémonts from Panama City to San Francisco in November 1850. The Greenhows went to California to help the French speculator José Limantour press his dubious claims to San Francisco real estate in what would later be branded the largest land fraud scheme in the state's history. The antagonism between the two women had been long term, and JBF suggests here that Rose Greenhow promoted ill feeling with the Blairs, but see E. B. SMITH [1] 186–87, which describes a quarrel caused when James Blair refused to sign a second loan for JCF. Years later, JBF insisted to Josiah Royce that in the 1840s, she, Benton, and Secretary of State Buchanan had known that Rose passed information to the British (Statement Concerning Secret Affairs Relating to the Mexican War, [late Dec. 1884], below). She was often engaged in intrigues and during the Civil War became a spy for the Confederacy.

6. Probably Margaretta R. Hetzel, who had lived in the vicinity of the Bentons in Washington, D.C. She was an occasional correspondent of Elizabeth Blair Lee and in 1890 served with her as secretary of the Mary Washington Memorial Association.

7. The Frémonts' physician, Augustus J. Bowie (1815–87) was a cultivated man with a large library whose attractive house, prefabricated and shipped around the Horn, was a gathering place for intellectual Californians in the 1850s. He had served in the navy between 1837 and 1852 and had been a groomsman at the Lee-Blair wedding in 1843 (C. COLLINS, 147, and CORNISH & LAAS, 53, 201n).

8. The editors are unable to identify Holmes, but Blunt may have been Simon

Fraser Blunt (d. 1854), who was married to Ellen Lloyd Key, the daughter of Francis Scott Key. For his marriage and death, see *National Intelligencer,* Jan. 29, 1846, May 1, 1854. Without specific dates, BOSQUI, 59–62, indicates that Blunt had been engaged in the geodetic survey of the coasts of Oregon and California and that he was also the commander of the Pacific Mail Steamship Company's *Winfield Scott* when it was wrecked in Dec. 1853. Robert McLane (1815–98) was the brother of Louis McLane, a passed midshipman of the *Savannah,* who had commanded the artillery in the California Battalion. They were both sons of Louis McLane, secretary of the treasury and then of state under President Andrew Jackson. Robert McLane, a West Point graduate who had served a term in Congress, had come out to California in 1851 to serve as an attorney on the New Almaden quicksilver mine case, which was beginning to interest the wealthy Rothschilds in Europe (MCLANE, 23).

To Elizabeth Blair Lee

San Francisco,   August 14, 1851.

I wrote a long letter to your Father last night and ought properly to have deferred yours my dear Lizzie until another time. But I don't think you will find it unwelcome if I may judge by the pleasure with which I received yours. You write so sensibly for a long distance. Like DeFoe's ghost story,[1] we must have all the accessories of time place & circumstance to make things real at this great distance and Susy[2] has not your experience of an absence from home to make her know how much value we attach to the most trifling home details.

Your letter to me came just after the last fire—after the excitement was over and I was left unintruded upon to feel as strange and lonely as I well could endure, in my new ugly house in place of the pretty cottage where I had been so happy and where little Charley was born. I really had something like the blues. It is more disagreeable than you can realize without the experience to be burnt out, and although I saved almost everything, or rather many kind hands cared for me, (Mr. Frémont & Mr. Jones, even Mr. Beale being absent) still the new house was a sudden unchosen place and I felt shipwrecked. Wasn't it odd, or is it in character, that Mary Blair should have given no evidence of knowing I had been burnt out? She called on Liz after she had been here five weeks, and was quite decided in her tone of coldness to me. Taking that in connection with her not receiving me when I made my first visit after Charley's birth, I suppose I may consider myself cut. Mrs. Greenhough [Greenhow] I think is the motive power but I really have not time for such investigations. Only never think me lacking in good will or courtesy to any member of your family, as you might if you heard I had not been there for some months.

15th

I had begun this for a long letter dear Lizzie but was interrupted and close it now suddenly with la suite au prochain numéro [more in the next edition]. Yours affectionately,

                                                J. B. Frémont

ALS (NjP—Blair-Lee Papers).

1. JBF has reference to Daniel Defoe's "A True Relation of the Apparition of Mrs. Veal, the Next Day After Her Death, to One Mrs. Bargrave, at Canterbury, the 8th of September, 1705," first published in 1706.

2. Susy was JBF's youngest sister, Susan Virginia (1833–74). See DORMAN, 226.

To Elizabeth Blair Lee

                              San Francisco,   November 14, 1851.

Dear Lizzie,

I wish I could hear from you once a month. Your letters take the place of Eliza's which gave me every detail of home. So please write as often as you find it convenient & be sure we will thank you very much for your kindness. Mr. Jones & Mr. Frémont are absent for a few weeks & Liz & Betty are with me until their return. My other household charm of whom you as yet know nothing personally, makes with the other two children quite a noisy set & with our home servants, who are steady & true, we have an enviable home for this place. In fact we have all such good health & so much good fortune of every kind that everything is very well with us. I don't like to make a plan for fear I may in some way have to break it & so give disappointment instead of pleasure, but as far as I can see I shall be in Washington next May. Even if Mother is in Misouri she will not stay there through the hot weather, and I never mean to expose myself to heat when it can be avoided. I hope I will find all the flowers of my own state blooming around you at that time. Perhaps Mrs. Blair may like the new clover, as it is acid I should think cattle would like it in warm weather. The Calycanthus is five times the size of ours & a brighter red with great fragrance.

May I trouble you to give the enclosed piece of money to the mother of my nurse Catherine. "Her name is Emily Stewart & she lives by the Jesups' back gate."[1] (Condensed & deduced from Catherine's topographical report.)

Tomorrow is Lily's birthday[2] and I have not as much time as I had wished to write you in. If Mother does not go to the West please write often to me about her & when you are in town see her in our place. You are very amiable to speak as you do of Susan. I think it will not end in a marriage and if my representations to both herself & Father avail it is quite ended. If not I have a sister the less unless she become as is most probable an object of compassion.

Mrs. Blair has paid me a visit, which I returned for your sake, & because I hate a fuss & talk about such small things. I suppose I owe the returning notice to Mrs. Greenhow's absence as she was really the spiritual director there. But as you say we forgive her that grudge & all others. It is too small a thing to notice in a little letter that has to travel six thousand miles were it not that she might contrive to annoy you by something of the same kind now she is again in Washington. I never spoke to her after we left the ship or visited her which piqued her very much. But that is too much of her.

I hope you all keep well. I shall expect to find all as I left it with you the next strawberry season. Have my place ready and make room in your hearts for my beautiful baby. He has six teeth and keeps well. I hope Mary Riggs' baby will be as healthy.[3] Remember me kindly to her and with more than that to your Mother. Tell your Father that I almost hesitated about shewing his little note on the envelope to Mr. Fremont. Such words might have fatal consequences. But I will only exact a letter in explanation of such enthusiasm. The only politics we hear come from you & that is as much as we want. We are living so peacefully I don't care to trouble it with outer world jars. I hope Lizzie Woodbury was not hurt by her Father's death.[4] With her affectionate nature it will cast a sad shadow over her.

I feel you a regularly [entered?] correspondent now and as I don't write for the eyes of the public or even for a select circle of friends I write very disjointedly but always hope to hear more in detail from you who has no baby (mores the pity) or big girl to sew for, or little housework to see after. Yours affectionately,

Jessie Benton Frémont

Write all your lamentations to me about your separation from Mr.

Lee.[5] I should dissolve the Union sooner than let Mr. Frémont go away a year to Congress.

ALS (NjP — Blair-Lee Papers).

1. "The Jesups" were probably Gen. Thomas Jesup, quartermaster general of the army, and his wife. They were the parents of Mary Serena Blair.
2. PHILLIPS, 353, gives Lily's birthday as Nov. 13, 1842, but this letter and a letter of Lily's to Nelly Haskell Browne, Nov. 16, 1876 (CuB — Frémont Papers), cite it as Nov. 15.
3. Mary Boswell Riggs was the adopted daughter of Benjamin Gratz, a Blair relative. She was courted by both Frank and James Blair, but married banker Elisha Riggs, Jr. (1826–81) (CORNISH & LAAS, 57, 202n; E. B. SMITH [1], 183–84, 190).
4. Called the "rock of New England democracy" by Benton, Levi Woodbury (1789–1851) had served his state of New Hampshire in the U.S. Senate and Presidents Jackson and Van Buren in various cabinet posts. At the time of his death on Sept. 4, he was an associate justice of the U.S. Supreme Court and, according to Montgomery Blair, would have been the next Democratic nominee for the presidency.
5. Lee, commanding the brig *Dolphin,* was away on an eight months' cruise in the Atlantic, making hydrographic and meteorological observations (CORNISH & LAAS, 73–78).

To David Hoffman

8th April/52
Clarendon

Mr. Hoffman need not trouble himself to take the long drive into the City as Mr. Frémont has no longer any need of assistance. Mr. Wright[1] went at once last night to Mr. Peabody, whom he found but after some delay. Mr. Frémont knew nothing of Mrs. Frémont's application to Mr. Hoffman [for bail money] and disapproves of it, knowing it was useless!

AL (NHi — J. C. Frémont–David Hoffman Papers). This is the only surviving fragment of a JBF letter written during her first residence in Europe, although her book *Souvenirs of My Time,* published in 1887, contains several chapters describing the splendor of the Frémonts' social engagements and the prestige of their hosts in both England and France. With their daughter, infant son, and Gwinn Harris Heap, JCF and JBF, now reputedly to be millionaires, had arrived in England on Mar. 22, 1852, and settled into a magnificent suite of rooms at the Clarendon Hotel in London.

Approximately two weeks later, on Apr. 7, just as the Frémonts were entering a carriage for a glittering evening out, the explorer was arrested for nonpayments of drafts he had drawn upon the secretary of state while governor of California. The drafts had subsequently passed into the hands of Anthony Gibbs and Sons of London, who instituted the charges. Frantically JBF sought out Heap and together they went to the residence of Hoffman, with whom JCF had just quarreled, to find bail money. Hoffman had retired for the night, but, on being awakened by his servant, he gave them an interview. On telling JBF that he had not money for bail, either from his own funds or Mariposas agency funds, JBF berated him, "You are a great rascal—my father says so." For an account of the late night interview, see Hoffman's copy of his Apr. 29, 1852, letter to JCF (NHi—J. C. Frémont-David Hoffman Papers); for full details of JCF's quarrel with Hoffman, see M. L. SPENCE [1].

JCF spent the night in Sloman's Lock-up on Cursitor Street, Chancery Lane. Overnight, the American investment banker George Peabody (1795–1869) came to his financial rescue and JBF penned the note above.

1. George W. Wright (1816–85), a business partner of JCF, was urging him to break off with Hoffman. Wright had been one of California's first representatives in Congress and was a member of the California banking firm of Palmer, Cook and Company. For a biographical sketch, see M. L. SPENCE [3].

To Elizabeth Blair Lee

Saint Louis, October 14th [1853]

Liz told me my dear Lizzie of yours and Mr. Lee's kind feelings about me & of Mr. Lee's wishing he could have accompanied me. You will before this have had the real pleasure which I know all in your friendly home shared with us of finding Mr. Frémont's illness lessened — to your Father who felt so much the greatness of the work it will be also very agreeable to know that it will not fail. Mr. Frémont has prevailed upon Dr. Ebers[1] to go with him & with his care & skill he is, he thinks, quite safe for the exposure. Dr. Ebers has the further advantage of having seen real service in 1828 — he was in the Russian army in its war upon the Turks. So that he is no novice in field life & Mr. Frémont likes him & has confidence in him. Certain it is that where our good friend Dr. Bowie failed even to give temporary relief, Dr. Ebers has soothed the pain, uprooted the inflammation & Mr. Frémont though greatly shaken is again literally "on his legs." Since he was attacked this time, the pain being chiefly in the upper part of his left leg & from there hits the breast & even at one time the throat & head, he was kept still with his feet up. He does not quite like its being said that he carries a homeopathic physician with him for he thinks Dr. Ebers's skill in his case is owing to his knowledge of surgery & experience in similar cases at Graffenberg (I don't think I know how to spell it) the great water cure place in Germany—he recommends Mr. Frémont's going there which he will do next year. All the rheumatic generals & sciatic naval men of distinction in Great Britain & Europe have been there nearly—and it has been decided that cold water is the surest of remedies for all such complaints.

I can't say I am satisfied, but it is such a relief from the undefined dread of all that long journey that I hardly dare argue against it. I am what your Mother called me a poor mean-spirited woman & she will be the first in her heart to justify my meanness. I would rather have Mr. Frémont at the fireside taking care of himself—writing out what he has done & enjoying the repose and happiness of our quiet home, than getting all the stupid laurels that ever grew. I think he has done enough—but he does not. If this ends well, I shall be glad for his sake it was done for he would have always regretted it—but nothing it can ever bring can reward either of us for its cost in suffering to him & anxieties to me.

However, we agree so well in all those points that it is only tiring you to tell them over & for those who think differently (because their hearts are not concerned) no amount of talking will bring them to agree with me—so enough of myself.

I shall see Sarah after I come down the river.[2] She is in a very strange state. I hope I may be of some service to her in determining her to take good advice about herself. I shall be here only a day or two on my return—I hope to get home the end of this month. Mr. Frémont, his surgeon, & I leave here tomorrow for Independence. His party is at the Smoky Hills among the Buffalo—everything going on well. His servant & an Indian[3] are at Westport waiting him—they are just in from the main party (so the servant telegraphed this morning—very sensibly.)

Mr. Frémont tells me to say for him to your Father & Mother as well as Mr. Lee & yourself all kind remembrances. The chronometer works finely. Thank Mr. Lee for his kind wish to help me—he need do nothing more for me to make me feel him a friend. Give my especial love to your Mother & Father & for yourself dear Lizzie the warmest love of your affectionate,

Jessie B. Frémont

ALS (NjP—Blair-Lee Papers). In the eighteen months that had elapsed since JBF penned the above note to Hoffman, the Frémonts had returned to the United States, and JCF prepared for his fifth and final geographical survey. The expedition was privately financed, and its purpose was to prove the feasibility of constructing a railroad to the Pacific along a central route, that is, between the 38th and 39th parallels of latitude, a route long advocated by Benton.

JBF did not accompany her husband to the frontier but remained in Washington in a house just a few doors from her parents. A few miles out of Westport, JCF became ill with inflammatory rheumatism in his leg, frostbitten during his disastrous fourth expedition, and turned back to St. Louis for medical treatment. When he telegraphed JBF of his illness, she hurried west by train.

1. The editors know little about Ebers beyond that contained in JBF's letter. MON-TAGUE lists an A. Ebers, homeopathic physician at 160 Market (between Sixth and Seventh) in St. Louis.

2. JBF planned to accompany her husband up the Missouri River to Independence and then see her sister Sarah (1826–63) when she returned to St. Louis. Sarah was married to Richard Taylor Jacob (1825–1903), a well-to-do Kentuckian who had served in JCF's California Battalion.

3. The servant was a mulatto, Albert Lea, who also served as cook; the Indian was Solomon, who had been on JCF's third expedition and who claimed to be a Delaware chief.

To John Torrey

[fall 1853?]

Those include all the material necessary I think my dear Sir. The selection I leave to your judgment. The letter from which I quote first, was prepared by Mr. Frémont for publication but the reason for its not appearing although sufficient at the moment, was so only for the moment, and Mr. Fremont asked of me to watch for the right time and have it published, as all the reasons which induced him to publish it, only became the more forcible with time.[1] The name of the person to whom the letter was addressed, is not I presume material at this time—if needed it can always be *given*. It tells the [whole?] reasons of his journey so clearly and at the same time with such characteristic modesty that I am glad it is to come out. I think everything contained in it Mr. Frémont had already told to you when we met you in New York this summer. You should have had this the day following my seeing you but I have been really ill & only this morning am able to be up again.

If it is too late for Sillimans[2] journal will you please return it to me as in that case I will try to find some other paper equally creditable abroad, as one strong motive in publishing it is to give Baron Humboldt[3] & others who take interest in such matters, a proper idea of what Mr. Frémont is doing.

Perhaps the best and most admirable part of his journey was the fortitude with which he returned to it after being worn down with incessant pain for weeks. In my position of wife I am denied the utterance of such sentiments, but when I saw him rise from his suffering and resolutely abandon the care and comfort so grateful to him, to follow out his work at every risk, I honored him more than words.

AL fragment (NNBG—Torrey Correspondence).

1. Part of JCF's letter outlining the geographical objectives of his journey was printed in the *American Journal of Science and Arts,* 2d ser., 17 (May 1854), and later reprinted in M. L. SPENCE [2], 379–81.

2. *The American Journal of Science and Arts* was often referred to as "Sillimans journal," after its founder, Yale chemist Benjamin Silliman, Sr. (1779–1864).

3. JCF was a great admirer of Baron Alexander von Humboldt (1769–1859), the world-renowned German naturalist, traveler, and statesman, and patterned his explorations of the American West after his by combining mapmaking with the objectives of a naturalist.

To Francis Preston Blair

[winter 1853–54]

My dear Mr. Blair. You will be glad to know the letters have come at last and many good things in them. Mr. Frémont found his mules all weak & some lame when he returned to his party so that he was long in getting to Bents' upper fort[1]—some 800 miles out as I understand—10 to 12 miles a day were all he could make the party gradually getting on foot & losing in different ways fifteen animals. The weather too was very cold.

That is the end of the bad news for at Bents he bought fifteen other mules, the weather had become very mild and his own health was perfectly restored. The party worked well. The Daguerre failed at first but the artist put his heart in his work, & each day Mr. Frémont writes surpassed the work of the day previous.[2] So that he will have faultless illustrations. There is good coal there in great beds—it is burned there & proves to be good. Father is very much pleased with that.

In all, it comes to a wintering in the mountains to use Mr. Frémont's own words—and he does not think of reaching San Francisco until in February. After ourselves here none will feel so much interest in all this as you and your household who have been so kind to me in so many ways. I hope soon we may get the final report of his good success throughout, and from himself.

Mr. Lee is making a statue for himself of the love of the children for he takes Lil & Nina[3] to see the Yankee actress tonight. I only wish I could have had more of you under my roof. With love to Lizzie Yours most truly,

Jessie Frémont

ALS (NjP—Blair-Lee Papers).

1. Bent's upper fort stood on the north bank of the Arkansas River, about thirty-eight miles downstream from the Old Fort, where for so many years travelers and expeditions had stopped and resupplied. The new fort had just been completed when JCF's expedition arrived and probably furnished a better site for trade than the old location. See LAVENDER for a history of the fort.

2. Frémont made arrangements with Solomon Nunes Carvalho (1815–97) to accompany him as artist and daguerreotypist. Carvalho had already won notice for his technique of protecting daguerreotypes from abrasion by the application of a thin coating of varnish or enamel that made it unnecessary to enclose them in cases and cover them with glass. When John Bigelow collected materials for his campaign biography of Frémont in 1856, it was Carvalho who provided the information about the journey, reconstructing the details from "letters," he maintained, but perhaps from a journal he may have kept secretly. A few months later his own book, *Incidents of Travel and Adventure in the Far West; with Col. Frémont's Last Expedition across the Rocky Mountains: Including Three Months' Residence in Utah and a Perilous Trip across the Great American Desert to the Pacific*, was released first in England, then in the United States. Ironically, Carvalho's illustrations do not appear in his own book, but in Frémont's *Memoirs*. For a biography of Carvalho, see STURHAHN; for details on the publication of his book, see M. L. SPENCE [2], 403n.

3. Named Frances Anne Cornelia at her birth on Aug. 18, 1838, Nina was the daughter of JCF's dead brother, Horatio Francis. After her grandmother's death in 1847, she lived off and on with JCF, her guardian, and JBF, who, as later letters indicate often found her a burden—frivolous, moody, and easily bored. Nina married Maj. H. M. Porter, the assistant provost marshall of New Orleans, on July 18, 1864 (TRAPIER, 99; *The Era* [New Orleans], July 29, 1864). She died in virtual poverty on Apr. 13, 1903 (Elizabeth Benton Fremont to Nelly Haskell Browne, May 4, 1903, CU-B—Fremont Papers).

To Elizabeth Blair Lee

[spring 1854?]

My dear Lizzie, little Lily has been womanly for four months past—
this was not quite her time but I suppose her unusual exercise made
something of a return. I am much obliged for yours and your Mother's
kind offer of giving her the exercise she needs, and which is the true
reason of her horseback lessons, and will let her go this Friday and
every other Friday until I take her to the seaside.

I hope soon to feel well myself. When I have no more anxious
thoughts pressing on my heart it will not ache but until Mr. Frémont
gets home I must rely on Dr. Ebers's "ten globules" to give me the
rest I need.

I have no uneasiness for Lily for in her precocity she is my true
child—only I was even younger. Very affectionately yours,

J. B. Frémont
Monday mg.

Father is very happy in seeing his book, bound & all ready to read.[1]

ALS (NjP—Blair-Lee Papers). Envelope addressed to: "Mrs. S. P. Lee, Silver
Spring."

1. A reference to vol. 1 of Thomas Hart Benton's *Thirty Years' View; or, A History
of the Working of the American Government for Thirty Years, from 1820 to 1850,*
which was published in the spring of 1854.

To Francis Preston Blair

[(Apr.) 13 (1854)]

My dear Mr. Blair

Will Mr. Lee and yourself dine with me on Saturday to meet Mr.
Babbitt[1]—if you will forget he has lots of wives and look upon him
only as I do in his last character as friend & banker to Mr. Frémont.[2]

I make the hour early to suit your return—will five o'clock suit
you? Very truly yours,

Jessie B. Frémont

Thursday the 13th.

ALS (NjP—Blair-Lee Papers).

1. En route east, by way of San Francisco, the Mormon Almon W. Babbitt had met JCF's fifth expedition, battered by the winter weather, in Parowan, Utah. He not only carried letters to Washington for the men, but he also arranged for JCF to be furnished horses and mules out of the Mormon tithing money. In return, JCF arranged to have San Francisco bankers compensate Gov. Brigham Young of Utah (San Francisco *Herald,* Mar. 15, 1854).

2. Babbitt seems to have had only one wife, Julia Ann Hills Johnson, whom he had married on Nov. 23, 1833 (RIDD, 2).

To Elizabeth Blair Lee

[after May 17, 1855]

Dear Lizzie,

I send Margaret for some of the Blackberry root medicine your Mother makes. I wish I could see her too again. Perhaps you know the shades of using it. I think opiates are so sickening I want to be done with them.

I am going to be well again soon. I have no fever at all. Yours affcty,

Jessie

The baby can see & laugh. He examined one wall yesterday & gave a pretty bright smile.[1]

ALS (NjP—Blair-Lee Papers). Addressed to "Mrs. S. P. Lee at Judge Blair's." The year had been a sad one for JBF. Her mother died on Sept. 10, 1854, and fire destroyed Benton's home on Feb. 27, 1855.

1. Francis Preston Frémont, named for Francis Preston, Blair, Sr., and called Frank, was born on May 17, 1855.

To Elizabeth Blair Lee

Siasconset,   17th August [1855].

Dear Lizzie,

Tell your Father I opened his letter as Mr. Frémont is not here yet.[1] I look for him to-morrow and hope he may be here then or else it would be Tuesday before I could even hear again, there being no Sunday boat. I shall not begin to tell you how forlornly lonesome this island is — my ship is burnt so I shall not sit on the beach and lament especially as the air here is really strengthening me. I am quite dethroned now. I think even my temporary reign has passed from the memory of all as not even old Harriet[2] has any prudent changes to make now. Lamb[3] was quite right about it.

Travelling does in our day what misery did when the proverb was made. We had here for some days a really charming Quaker family from Philadelphia — a girl of sixteen and a boy a year younger made Lily's half and I had for mine the parents — well educated & travelled, abroad as well as in our country, but their charm was in their quiet sincere affection for each other.[4] I never saw such loving gentle obedience and good will between parents & children & from the children to each other — and they were all as full of life and fun as of thee's and thy's. Lily is in love with them all and I have promised them a day or two on my return home. The point of the whole is their name — they are the daughter and grandchildren of Lucretia Mott. Badly as she thinks of southern people I always thought worse of a "strong-minded" speech making woman, but these all live with her and "by their fruits & -"

I hope to be in Washington for perhaps a week before we leave finally — but when that will be is not yet decided. It will be the 20th of September or the 5th of October — hardly later. Mr. Frémont has so much to do in New York & Philadelphia that we shall go to New York at the end of this month & remain there, at the Clarendon, until the time of sailing. Union Park is just by that hotel and that provides the necessary outlet for Charley.

Mr. Lee would feel Charley his godson[5] by new ties if he were to see how he has adopted the style of the village which is made up of old sailors and whaling captains (I ought to have put them first but they are the least amusing) and a little crowd of boys who will inevitably go whaling in their turn. Until that comes they go off with the shark boats, and one of my days was given to watching the landing of enormous sharks eight nine and ten feet long — they get some oil from them but they are hideous objects as they lie on the beach. I sat apart on the edge of a dry boat but Charley was with the thick of it and ended by begging a grappling iron and pitching into a dead shark. He imitates the walk of the men and goes barefoot with his drawers rolled up and practices climbing on all possible places.

One big wave cooled forever his love for his pretty bathing dress and all belonging to it, but Lily takes her place at the end of the rope daily and enjoys the beating of the waves. You have the family history now except that of little Frank who is really loveable now. He looks so fat and contented and makes quite sensible faces and noises. The nurse No. 3, as I call her is a fine cow[6] — patient and silly and as submissive as even Marie's despotism requires. Marie[7] is disgusted with the want of fashion or style here but partially consoles herself by jerking out french sentences to bewilder the rustics, and by dressing her hair in such complicated ways as must drive them to despair before they can imitate it. The anteroom looks up to her with awe.

Give my love to your Mother if she has returned, & to your Father and with kindest regards to Mr. Lee I am affectionately yours,

Jessie Frémont

ALS (NjP — Blair-Lee Papers).

1. JBF had taken the children to Nantucket while JCF tended to business in Washington, Philadelphia, and New York. They planned to go to California in the fall.

2. Old Harriet was a free black woman who worked for the Benton and then the Frémont family as head nurse. In *Year of American Travel*, 11, JBF refers to a "young Harriot" [*sic*] as her maid, whose fiancé persuaded her not to accompny JBF to California in 1849. In 1871, JBF would try to help the younger Harriet, by then a seamstress, buy a house in Washington. See JBF to Oliver Otis Howard, Sept. 7 [1871], below.

3. Charles Lamb (1775–1834), English essayist and critic.

4. This was the Edward M. Davis family from Philadelphia. Davis (1811–87), a Quaker merchant and strong abolitionist, was also a friend of George W. Wright, JCF's business partner in many California ventures. Davis became an ardent supporter of the Frémonts for the White House. Naming JBF a "real heroine," he told her and Wendell Phillips he would "rather see her there than any other woman" he knew "except Mrs. Chapman [abolitionist Maria Weston Chapman]" (Davis to Phillips, July 16, 1856, MH — Phillips Papers). In 1861, Davis would seek, unsuccessfully, the treasureship of the U.S. Mint in Philadelphia, and still later become assistant quartermaster in JCF's Civil War command in St. Louis. His wife Maria (1811–97) was the second daughter of Lucretia Coffin Mott (1793–1880), the Quaker minister, abolitionist, and pioneer in the movement for women's rights. Lucretia Mott had been born on Nantucket and lived there until 1804. For information on Edward M. Davis, see HALLOWELL; correspondence in the Wendell Phillips Papers, MH; scattered items in the George W. Wright Papers, Chevy Chase, Md.; and Frederick Billings to T. W. Park, Oct. 1, 1861, Park-McCullough House Archives.

5. Charley (John Charles Frémont, Jr.) was baptized Dec. 28, 1853, by the Rev.

John W. French at Washington's Episcopal Church of the Epiphany with Lizzie and S. Phillips Lee as godparents (BIGELOW [1], 27).

6. JBF had nursed Charley, but she hired wet nurses for Frank.

7. Marie was one of the two maids JBF had brought back from France.

THE 1856 PRESIDENTIAL CAMPAIGN

Jessie, languishing on the beach at Siasconset in August 1855, as she slowly recuperated from childbirth, expected that the family would soon leave for California, where John would manage his Mariposas gold mines. But that month another possibility emerged that would put their California plans in abeyance. The newly formed Republican party was looking for its first presidential candidate: among the names bandied about was that of the dashing western explorer and gold-rush millionaire John Charles Frémont.

The Republican party had been created in 1854–55 by Whig and Democratic dissidents impatient with their parties' tolerance of slavery expansion into the new western territories. The issue had come to a head with the question of statehood for Kansas and Nebraska. Both territories lay north of the line between free and slave states drawn in the Missouri Compromise of 1820; but in the winter of 1853–54, Senator Stephen A. Douglas of Illinois had reopened the issue when he proposed the Kansas-Nebraska Act, legislation that would repeal the ban on slavery north of the line and allow the two territories to decide by vote whether they wanted to be slave or free. President Franklin Pierce, anxious to retain southern support, endorsed the measure.

In the North there were mass protests against what many saw as a devious scheme to smuggle slavery into the new territories. Thomas Hart Benton, who had entered the Senate at the time of the Missouri Compromise, condemned this violation of its intent, while Jessie herself did not hesitate to express her opposition in sympathetic company. When antislavery senator William Seward of New York paid a call that winter, he found her in strong agreement with his views. "She is a noble-spirited woman. Has much character," he reported enthusiastically to his wife, Frances, herself a dedicated abolitionist. "I am sure you would like her. She is very outspoken."[1]

In the spring of 1854, when the Kansas-Nebraska Act passed a fiercely divided Congress, opponents of the measure, such as former Washington *Globe* editor Francis P. Blair, New York *Tribune* editor Horace Greeley, politicians Nathaniel Banks and Charles Sumner of Massachusetts and Salmon P. Chase of Ohio, and, somewhat later, Abraham Lincoln and William Seward, began to talk of creating a new political party that clearly opposed the extension of slavery.[2] By the summer of 1855, such men, not all of whom yet called themselves Republicans, were looking for a presidential candiate to represent their views.

That August at Siasconset, the Frémonts talked over their options. John had received an offer from a contingent of moderate southern Democrats, who included several of Jessie's politically prominent relatives. This group proposed to back him for the presidency if he endorsed the Kansas-Nebraska Act.[3] The offer was tempting. Since the Whig party was hopelessly split over slavery and the Republicans too new and disorganized to have a wide following, the Democratic candidate could be expected to win the presidency. In contrast, pursuing the Republican nomination would mean the severing of strong ties with Jessie's close-knit southern family. Even more disturbing was the possibility of a break with Thomas Benton, who vigorously claimed he would never desert the Democratic party. But in the end, their antislavery convictions prevailed. "There was only one decision possible," Jessie recalled.[4]

Jessie's hostility to slavery was rooted in childhood experiences. Her maternal grandfather, James McDowell of Rockbridge County, Virginia, had owned forty slaves worth $13,000 when he died in 1835,[5] and during her many childhood visits to his prosperous estate, she gained firsthand knowledge of the system. In reality, however, this patrician Virginia family was deeply conflicted about slavery. In 1831, when Jessie was eight, her uncle, the young Princeton-educated politician James McDowell, Jr., spoke out against slavery in the Virginia legislature and argued for a system of gradual emancipation.[6] Jessie's mother, Elizabeth McDowell Benton, who had taught family slaves to read, supported her brother's stand. But as McDowell's political ambitions grew, his nerve failed. Elected governor in 1842 and congressman in 1846, he came to accept slavery as an "indispensable institution" in the South, taking refuge, Jessie explained to Lydia Maria Child, "in fine sentences about his native State and Northern aggression." Her mother, she added, "was of a more enduring nature." When Elizabeth Benton inherited slaves from her father, she freed them "because of her conscientious feeling on the subject [and] maintained them and their children until they were self-supporting."[7]

Like Frances Seward, Elizabeth Benton was clearly key in her husband's steadily growing opposition to slavery. Although Thomas Benton represented a slave state in the Senate, he, too, came to see slavery as a moral evil and to oppose its extension into the new western territories. "I am Southern by my birth; Southern in my affections, interest, and connections," he stated in a crucial senate speech in 1844, but "I will not engage in schemes for [slavery] *extension* into regions where . . . a slave's face was never seen." Benton's support in Missouri slipped dangerously as his antagonism to slavery grew, but he continued to proclaim his views: "I despise the bubble popularity," he announced in his usual grandiose style.[8] In 1851, after thirty years in the Senate, he lost his seat to a proslavery candidate of his own party.

The following year, with the support of Francis Blair's sons Montgomery and Frank, who had both read law in Benton's Missouri firm, he managed to win a congressional seat from the St. Louis area, where the growing German immigrant population was strongly antislavery. Defeated for a second term in 1854 and despondent over his wife's death the same year, Benton might be expected to find a new vitality in supporting his son-in-law's ambitions. Thus in August 1855, contemplating her husband's political prospects, Thomas Benton's favorite daughter had reason to hope that her father could be persuaded to back both the Republican party and her husband's presidential candidacy.

Behind the scenes, Jessie acted quickly on their decision to pursue the Republican nomination. As in the past, her connections proved vital to her husband's career. On August 27, 1855, she wrote a crucial letter to Francis Preston Blair, requesting that he meet with John in Washington to give him "friendly advice and counsel" on an "important step" John was considering. Deliberately indirect in its language, the letter was nonetheless a shrewd bid for support from the man who would become John's most influential backer for the nomination. Although Francis Blair was Thomas Benton's closest friend and political ally, Jessie knew not only that Blair had become involved in the formation of the new antislavery party and the search for a first presidential candidate, but also that he was already partial to John. "I think of Frémont *as a new man*," Blair would explain several months later to Martin Van Buren. "He is brave, firm, has a history of romantic heroism . . . & has no bad political connections—never had—no tail of hungry, corrupt hangers on like Buchanan who will I think be the [Democratic] candidate."[9]

John's talk with Blair was a success, as was a second meeting that included powerful Massachusetts congressman Nathanial Banks. By early October 1855, the Frémonts had cancelled their California plans and settled temporarily in New York City, where Jessie began the spirited personal-political correspondence with the Blairs that forms the bulk of letters for this period. Most of these letters are addressed to Elizabeth Blair Lee, who was also engaged in "clerking it for the Heads of the People," as Jessie irreverently described their more than secretarial labors.[10] It was to Lizzie that Jessie wrote about the tensions and problems of the campaign and, most agonizingly, about the rift with her beloved father.

For Thomas Benton proved recalcitrant. Although both the Blairs and Frémonts at first believed they could convince him to support John's candidacy, the crusty old politician remained stubbornly opposed. Twice during November 1855, Francis Blair visited his old friend, hoping to persuade him to back his son-in-law. Benton, however, remained convinced that a new party supported by only one section of the country would split the Union irrevocably and bring civil war. More personally, he had come to distrust his son-in-law's judgment, in part because of disagreements over John's management of the Mariposas gold mines.[11] Lizzie Lee also detected an element of rivalry in Benton's opposition; the former senator, she suspected, still had presidential ambitions himself.[12]

Despite Benton's damaging opposition, the Frémont candidacy prospered. Blair paved the way in late December 1855 when he hosted a dinner for Republican leaders at Silver Spring, where he and Banks broached the name of Frémont. In February 1856, when Banks was elected Speaker of the House of Representatives and Blair was chosen president of a preliminary Republican planning convention, Frémont's chances surged. By spring he was the dominant candidate. While possible nominees like William Seward and Salmon Chase were more politically experienced, their extreme antislavery views alarmed many potential Republican converts. Frémont, a national hero with fewer political entanglements and less publicly known views on slavery, seemed the shrewder choice. Two weeks before the national nominating convention, when Greeley's powerful New York *Tribune* endorsed Frémont, his prospects were assured. At the June 17 convention in Philadelphia, a thousand cheering, stomping supporters nominated John Charles Frémont on the first ballot.

The campaign that followed was one of the most fervent in American history. To many northerners the "Frémont and Jessie" campaign, as it soon became known, was a great moral crusade against slavery. In New England, New York, and the upper Midwest, their support was massive. The enthusiasm for Jessie was unprecedented. Never before had a woman been featured in a political campaign. Republicans sang songs like "Oh, Jessie Is a Sweet Bright Lady" (to the tune of "Comin' through the Rye") and wore ribbons proclaiming "Frémont and Our Jessie" or "Jessie's Choice."

Inspired by her prominence, American women for the first time became involved in a national political campaign. At a Buffalo, New York, rally, for example, a reporter noted "a new feature — four hundred ladies" among the cheering throng. A mass meeting of thirty thousand in Needham, Massachusetts, included "a multitude of the sisters of Jessie, who, by their presence, inaugurated a new and happy era in the history of out-door political meetings in this section."[13] Woman's suffrage leaders, including Elizabeth Cady Stanton, Susan B. Anthony, and Lucretia Mott, were enthusiastic about the Frémont candidacy.

Although Jessie tried to maintain a discreet public image, she worked tirelessly behind the scenes, supervising John's voluminous correspondence and several campaign biographies. She traveled to Virginia to gather information about his family background for New York *Evening Post* editor John Bigelow's biography and, in the chapter she subsequently furnished him, neatly papered over her husband's illegitimacy while emphasizing a distant kinship with George Washington. Opponents were quick to exploit her unusual role. "At a Fremont meeting in New Hampshire," reported the hostile Washington *Union* on July 31, "one of the banners bore the inscription 'John and Jessie' and another ignored poor John altogether by the inscription 'Jessie for the White House.' It is evident that our opponent fully sympathizes with the woman's rights movement."

In the South the campaign against Frémont was brutal. The opposition branded him a "Frenchman's bastard" and spread stories of rumored love affairs and purported secret Catholicism. Even more painful for Jessie, Thomas Benton campaigned actively for the Democratic candidate, James Buchanan. "I am above family and above self when the good of the Union is concerned," he proclaimed.[14]

Amid the campaign frenzy, Jessie continued to supervise her large household, which included baby Frank, one year old in the summer of 1856, Charley, five, and Lily, nearly fourteen, as well as John's niece Nina, a frivolous and moody eighteen-year-old whom Jessie found particularly exasperating. Buttressed by her two capable and loyal French servants, she managed her household with considerable "executive faculty," as Greeley admiringly called her managerial skill,[15] finding time between campaign correspondence and a stream of visitors to plan and supervise her children's schoolwork, visit the Blairs' niece Betty at boarding school in Tarrytown, and even shop for Lizzie Lee's clothing needs in New York's fashionable millinery and dry goods stores.

Jessie's letters to the Blairs during this time depict a woman caught in a mesh of conflicting obligations. Deeply loyal and fiercely protective of her husband, she nonetheless struggled to maintain ties with her father, despite his damaging political opposition. Both ambitious and maternal, she found herself pulled from an exhausting night with a teething baby to a long day at campaign headquarters. A week before the election, however, she temporarily lost all interest in the campaign when baby Frank fell dangerously ill.

The election on November 4, 1856, was surprisingly close. Frémont swept New England, New York, and the upper Midwest. But his drive faltered in the pivotal states of Pennsylvania, Illinois, and Indiana. Overall the Democratic compromise candidate, James Buchanan, "a Northern man with Southern principles,"[16] won 1.8 million votes; Frémont garnered 1.4 million.

Despite the defeat, leaders of the Republican party were elated by the vote: more than a million Americans had deserted traditional parties to vote Republican. Suffragists were also heartened by the campaign, during which "women were urged to attend political meetings and a woman's name was made the rallying cry of the party of progress."[17]

Although Jessie was bitterly disappointed by their loss, she maintained a gallant public image. But over the next months her letters to Lizzie Lee suggest a prolonged depression that may have been caused as much by personal as political events. There is some evidence that Jessie suffered a miscarriage in early 1857, but the main cause may have been her marriage itself.

Shortly after the election, Bigelow, who had worked closely with Jessie during the campaign, became convinced that John Frémont had "debauched" a maid in the Frémont household.[18] It is impossible to say whether Jessie believed or even heard the story, but her letters suggest a persistent malaise. Her old rapport with her father had been shaken, and her relationship with her husband had changed as well. After fifteen years of marriage, the passionate intensity had seeped away. John was by nature a reticent, even taciturn man, and the acrimony of the campaign had heightened his reserve. In the early summer of 1857, when John journeyed to California to attend to Las Mariposas, Jessie chose to go to Europe with the children instead.

The separation, whatever her original intent, reaffirmed her attachment. Jessie's letters to John from France, which are among the few from her to him that have survived, reflect her continuing love for a man she more and more saw as isolated, lonely, and vulnerable.

Jessie hurried back to New York in November when she learned that her father was seriously ill. John, back from California, urged that the whole family go with him to live at remote Las Mariposas. Although Jessie was unenthusiastic about the "primitive life" and reluctant to leave her ailing father, she was determined to follow her husband. On March 20, 1858, Jessie, with her husband, three children, and niece Nina, boarded the Panama-bound steamer *Star of the West* for the first leg of yet another long, rough journey to California.[19]

Notes

1. SEWARD, 216–17.

2. For a detailed account of the formation of the Republican party, see GIENAPP.

3. See MEMOIRS, 192–204; New York *Herald*, Aug. 30, 1856; New York *Tribune*, Sept. 13, 1856.

4. "Great Events," 204.

5. Ms. inventory of James McDowell estate, Nov. 9–10, 1835 (WHi— McCormick Papers).

6. See ROBERT on McDowell's early opposition to slavery.

7. McDowell quoted in S. MILLER, 182–85; JBF to Child, [late July/Aug. 1856], below; J. B. FRÉMONT [3], 92–93.

8. CHAMBERS, 276, 372.

9. Jan. 25, 1856 (DLC—Van Buren Papers).

10. To Elizabeth Blair Lee, Dec. 7 [1855], below.

11. See JBF to Elizabeth Blair Lee, Apr. 18 [1856], below. For earlier evidence of Benton's coolness toward JCF, see Montgomery Blair to Minna Blair, May 10, 1854 (DLC—Blair Papers).

12. To S. Phillips Lee, May 12, 1856 (NjP—Blair-Lee Papers).

13. New York *Tribune,* July 11, 1856; *Liberator,* Aug. 29, 1856.

14. New York *Tribune,* June 27, 1856.

15. "Great Events," 214.

16. HALSTEAD, 35.

17. Lucy Stone quoted in STANTON ET AL., 1:633.

18. For speculation on the rumored affair, see Preston King to Gideon Welles, Mar. 3, Apr. 9, 21, 1860 (DLC—Welles Papers); Welles to Francis Preston Blair, April 9, 1860 (DLC—Blair Papers).

19. New York *Herald,* Mar. 20, 1858.

To Francis Preston Blair

Siasconset
Monday [Aug.] 27th [1855]

My dear Mr. Blair,

Mr. Frémont has under consideration so important a step, that before taking it he wishes for the advice and friendly counsel which have heretofore proved so full of sagacity and led to such success. In talking of it together I offered to ask it from you again, and my own little judgment being favorable I almost ventured to promise your assistance.[1] The wish was parent to that thought. It is not alone for your great experience and insight that Mr. Frémont refers to you, but for the exquisite good taste that is so grateful to his own nature, and assures him from the shocks that Father with his different organization is dangerously apt to give.[2]

I wish I could have gone on with Mr. Frémont at this time but I cannot risk my newly acquired strength in Washington until the end of September. But as the world will move on regardless of my convenience I must let this note replace me in asking your most favorable consideration of this matter and in doing so I am sure I do not presume too far on the affectionate indulgence you always shew me.

Silver Spring will not send me away again on my return for I gain only health from the waters that surround us here and half my days and some time into the night have been passed on the sounding shore. I shall be glad to have my old place among you again although it must be for so short a time. Give my kindest love to Mrs. Blair and Lizzie and for yourself the affectionate regards of your old friend's daughter,

Jessie.

F. P. Blair, Esqre.
Silver Spring.

ALS (NjP—Blair-Lee Papers).

1. Blair responded favorably to this indirect bid for his support by drafting a Sept. 16, 1855, letter in JCF's name, which outlined a political platform for the incipient candidate. While endorsing the Missouri Compromise and condemning the proslavery regime in Kansas, it was more conciliatory toward slavery than later JCF statements. Two drafts of the letter exist in the Blair Papers, DLC, including one in Elizabeth Blair Lee's hand, with corrections by Francis Preston Blair. The letter was evidently never used. See GIENAPP, 321-22.

2. In unusually convoluted prose, JBF suggests that her reserved, unfailingly courteous husband shrank from discussing his political plans with his flamboyant father-
in-law, whose vehement and earthy opposition they both anticipated and feared.

To Francis Preston Blair

Clarendon Hotel
October 21st [1855]

My dear Mr. Blair,

Mr. Frémont wants me to tell you that the result of Mr. B's[1] intervening was all that could be wished and more than he had looked for.
Everything is working well—in Quakerdom the spirit moves them in
the right direction.[2] The Post Office is so tricky that Mr. Frémont
reserves all particulars until he sees you which will be quite soon again,
but with your wisdom less than a half word will suffice.

Rachel[3] is to give a week in Washington in December about the end
of the month. I should like to be there then and bespeak a seat between
yourself and Father. She played her last here last night. A driving rain
storm made no difference in our getting there. As the old song says

> "Through rain and snow
> Through mud and mire
> I'd trudge to meet my heart's desire."

And Rachel is my condensation of theatricals.

Tell Lizzie that Mr. Frémont growls daily because we cannot have
ochra soup—it is past here. He relies on her promise to include me
among the deer in the gleanings of the ochra bed.[4] We will go into
our house this week I think. People are slow in moving—or we are
impatient of delay.

Mr. Frémont is out at a second council composed of all who were
to have met in Washington.

Susan has been here all week—we met nightly at the theatre and
she dines with us today. It had quite a home feeling to exchange looks
three boxes off when the same thing pleased us. She has been enjoying
her new position a little in visiting a french war steamer where a salute
was fired & some of those little nonsenses that the wisest women are
weak enough to be gratified at receiving.[5] Only a sentence here & there
is yours, the rest is Lizzie's also and if Mrs. Blair will listen hers also.

Give her my kindest love and tell her I take good care of her little godson[6] who is going to be something worth noticing. Yours affectionately,

Jessie B. Frémont

ALS (NjP—Blair-Lee Papers).

1. Both JBF and the Blairs suspected that their mail was opened by the Democratic-controlled post office, so they at times disguised names in a secret code. "Mr. B" was Nathaniel Banks (1816–94), an ambitious Massachusetts Know-Nothing congressman with free-soil convictions who, with Francis Blair, was one of JCF's first supporters. In the summer of 1855, Banks had been present when JCF received a southern offer of support for the presidency, which both rejected ("Great Events," 193–94).

2. JBF is probably referring to efforts by her Siasconset neighbor, Philadelphia Quaker Edward M. Davis, who in the summer of 1855 had been among a group meeting at the Philadelphia home of Morton McMichael, editor of the *North American*, to consider possible Republican candidates; Davis had suggested JCF (CRANDALL, 161; BARTLETT, 15; on Edward Davis's early support for JCF also see William M. Davis to Elizabeth Davis, Sept. 17, 1861, DLC—Henry Kirke Brown Papers). Later JCF would call Davis "a strong worker in the campaign" (to Francis Preston Blair, Willards, Monday morning, 6 o'clock, [n.d.], NjP—Blair-Lee Papers).

3. Rachel (Élisa Félix) (1821–58), the great French tragedienne, had just completed a seven-week engagement at New York's Metropolitan Theatre with an Oct. 20 performance of Corneille's *Les Horaces* before a packed house. The New York *Herald* pronounced her "transcendently grand," despite the fact that much of the audience had to follow the play in translation amid constant rustling of pages (Oct. 21, 1855). JBF, whose French was fluent, doubtless had no need of such props.

4. An accomplished gentleman-farmer after his retirement from the *Globe*, Francis Blair was famous for his bountiful table of home-grown fruits and vegetables, including okra.

5. JBF's youngest sister, Susan, had married the French diplomat Baron Gauldrée de Boilleau in Washington, D.C., on June 2 (CHAMBERS, 415–16). The French war steamer was doubtless the *Grondeur*, which had reached New York on Oct. 8 for a four-week stay (New York *Herald*, Oct. 10, 1855). JBF and Susan may have been among the audience at the Metropolitan Theatre the following night when Rachel, in honor of the visiting French ship, recited "The Marseilles" before a cheering French-American crowd. "French patriotism is really very nice—on the stage," the New York *Herald* commented dryly (Oct. 9, 1855).

6. Francis Preston and Eliza (Gist) Blair had become godparents to Francis Preston Frémont in a ceremony conducted by the Rev. John W. French on Aug. 1, 1855, at Washington's Episcopal Church of the Epiphany (JBF to Elizabeth Blair Lee, Saturday morning [July 1855], NjP—Blair-Lee Papers; BIGELOW [1], 27).

To Francis Preston Blair

Clarendon Hotel.
Saturday 3d November [1855].

My dear Mr. Blair,

The Mr. B. to whom I referred in my note to Lizzie, was our northern friend, and not Rip Van Winkle. The Turkey is getting restless and will make his next flight to the pines of Silver Spring—where he will be found the middle of next week.[1]

We go into our house this morning—176, 2d avenue. It was impossible to get one which gratified our taste in every way, for less than a year, so I was prudence for the family and took one for six months, as that is the longest time for which I think we should make a decided move. It is very comfortable and we have everything we need in the house—water, fire and gas, all over it, and a fine wide street, with an excellent neighborhood. Hamilton Fish has quite a palace just by us— and the new Historical society raises its grey stone towers next door but one.[2]

We have two "guest chambers"—after leaving to each one a separate room and to Mr. Frémont a working place. It is bright and pretty within and without and Mr. Frémont says Lizzie must come back with him and occupy it. She has been so unremittingly at home that a change of scene will be of service. I have secured places for Rachel's next two weeks here and that is (to me) the first inducement that can be made. She satisfies my brain.

If your own house were not so charming and filled with comforts I would try to tempt you with Rachel, but I don't like to make failures.

We are living just as though we were in a foreign country. I make no visits and don't intend to go into that weary round, except of course in some few cases where there have been previous reasons. But once in our own house we are entrenched and Mr. Frémont begins his work and the children their lessons and we will have all the benefits of a great city together with its perfect liberty of being let alone.

Mr. Frémont encloses to you a note from Mr. J[3] (it seems half foolish to be using initials only) which will let you see he is working actively.

With love to Mrs. Blair and Lizzie I am always yours affectionately,

Jessie Benton Frémont

ALS (NjP—Blair-Lee Papers).

1. No note to Lizzie Lee has been found, but JBF may be recalling her Oct. 21 letter to Francis Preston Blair, in which she mentions "Mr. B." (Nathaniel Banks). In the Frémont/Blair code, JCF was the "wild turkey." "Rip Van Winkle" has not been identified.

2. The Frémonts' house was located between 10th and 11th streets directly across from St. Mark's Church in the Bowery. The New-York Historical Society was under construction on the corner of 11th Street and Second Avenue (LAMB, 1:188; 2:508n). New York senator Hamilton Fish (1808–93) had lived at 138 Second Avenue near 9th

Street until 1851, when he erected a lavishly ornate high Victorian mansion at the corner of Second Avenue and 17th Street (NEVINS [2], 21, 35; FISH, 49). Fish, a loyal Whig, would dally until September to endorse JCF (New York *Tribune*, Sept. 26, 1856). He would later serve as Ulysses S. Grant's secretary of state.

3. "Mr. J." was probably Charles James (1817–1901), a lawyer from Albion, N.Y., who was a political associate of Nathaniel Banks. James would become a valued campaign aide, later work for the Frémonts at Las Mariposas, and serve as collector of the port of San Francisco during the Civil War. JBF found him "witty and clear sighted," although there is some evidence he was "slippery" (Washington *Post*, Oct. 27, 1901; "Great Events," 205; HARRINGTON, 35; GIENAPP, 376–77).

To Francis Preston Blair

Sunday morning—18th Nov. [1855]
176 Second Avenue.

My dear Mr. Blair,

I am told to say to you that satisfactory intelligence has been brought in from the east & the west—the details are to be given you in your own library. Mr. Frémont writes today to ask the Judge[1] if his presence will be of advantage to the Mariposas, during the coming week. If not, he will not go on until Monday week. Mr. Frémont is anxious to consult with you before the opening of Congress.

I see Mr. Crittenden is already there. Col. Hays (Jack Hays) of California is also there.

Mr. Frémont saw him on his way through. Col. Hays was already & always friendly to Mr. Frémont. Just now, he is threatened with the loss of his surveyor generalship for making the survey differently from what was desired by the district attorney.[2] I hope the Judge will see him—& yourself if it comes in your way. He told Mr. Frémont there were not five men on the Mariposas who would resist his taking possession—that all the real settlers wished him to have it & to hold under his title.[3] I think Mr. Crittenden should see him.

Mr. Frémont is making out his calculations for his map,[4] & he will take some on to Mr. Hubbard at the Observatory[5] if he is not needed now in Washington but if you think so, he will put them aside & come on immediately.

I have volumes to tell about Rachel but I can't mix my talk with all these hard subjects, and as my coming on is not for just now I must write again about her. With love to all. Yours affcty,

Jessie.

ALS (NjP—Blair-Lee Papers).

1. "The Judge" was Frances Preston Blair's oldest son, Montgomery (1813–83), who along with Kentucky senator and former attorney general John J. Crittenden (1787–1863) was assisting JCF in his Mariposas case. After graduation from West Point, Blair had practiced law in Thomas Benton's St. Louis office before returning to Washington in 1853. Dour, earnest, and scholarly, he was dubbed "the Judge" by the family more because it fit his somber character than because he had briefly served as presiding judge in the St. Louis Court of Common Pleas (W. E. SMITH, 1:286, 290).

2. JCF's shaky title to Las Mariposas had been confirmed by the California Land Commission in Dec. 1852, declared invalid by the District Court of Northern California in Jan. 1854, and reconfirmed by the U.S. Supreme Court on Mar. 10, 1855. The Supreme Court ordered a survey of the property, and it was at this point that the famed "Indian fighter" and Mexican War hero Col. John ("Jack") C. Hays (1817–83), who in 1853 had become the U.S. surveyor general for California, proved "friendly," allowing JCF to manipulate the boundaries of his grant to include rich mines claimed and worked by others. Meanwhile, the U.S. attorney in California, Samuel W. Inge (1817–68), a Pierce-appointed southerner who later viewed JCF's inflated boundaries as "monstrous pretensions" (*Alta California,* June 23, 1857), had appealed the case again to the Supreme Court, probably at the instigation of the administration. It was this appeal that Blair and Crittenden were preparing to rebut. Although the administration evidently attempted to delay a final decision for another year by claiming that Inge had not filed the appropriate papers in time, the Supreme Court would reject this argument and on Feb. 17, 1856, deny the appeal. For a detailed discussion of the legal problems of Las Mariposas, see M. L. SPENCE [2], lix–lxx. For charges of Pierce administration meddling, see the *Missouri Democrat,* Jan. 25, 1856, reprinted in the New York *Evening Post,* Jan. 30, 1856.

3. Hays was either disingenous or misinformed, for there was substantial local opposition to JCF's claims. Discontent was so widespread that in the 1856 presidential election, JCF would win a meager 6 percent of the vote in Mariposa County and no votes in some mining precincts (GATES, 38). JBF would personally experience this hostility in July 1858, when a group of dissident miners blockaded one of the disputed mines.

4. JCF was evidently working on a map of his expeditions, probably for inclusion in a general account that he planned to write. However, no such volume would appear until his 1887 *Memoirs.* See M. L. SPENCE [2], xxxi–xxxii, for a discussion of this map, which was probably the one ultimately published in his *Memoirs.*

5. Yale-trained astronomer Joseph Hubbard (1823–63) had been doing map calculations for JCF since 1844. In part due to JCF's influence, Hubbard was appointed professor of mathematics at the Naval Observatory in 1845.

To Elizabeth Blair Lee

1.
Wednesday morning
New York, 21st November [1855]

Dear Lizzie,

I answer your last letter immediately, and can assure you of the safety of the first which we read yesterday with all the pleasure you intended to give. I think Sidney's shade hovered about you Sunday.[1] I will be sure to examine the squirrel[2] and I will furthermore number my letters that we may acknowledge them without trouble.

Mr. Frémont says, that as Montgomery [Blair] has written to him that Mr. Crittenden is not there, and that he is not needed until the opening of the session, he will not come on until then.[3]

"In the mean time," I am told to say, "everything is working out remarkably well." Our only regret is the want of trust in the Washington Post Office which forbids our sending you agreeable intelligence as we receive it. All your suggestions about Father shall be observed.[4]

Susan writes me that Father goes on horseback daily and is very well. I am going to send Lily to see him when her Father goes on. It is a break upon Lily's lessons, but no accomplishment she can acquire will give any one such happiness as her simple presence does to that lonely old man. For he is lonesome Lizzie. He misses Mother, her voiceless form was more to him than the eloquence of others—it is not the head but the heart that hungers and thirsts for home life.

Liz is not fitted to supply that want. You know I do feel for her although she would repel the idea of needing sympathy—but she has let her domestic trials harden her and make her insensible to those of others.[5]

Sarah would suit Father a thousand times more[6]—I know I would do best of all—but how reconcile opposite duties.

I never indulge in these thoughts but to you for we have them in common only you can put yours into action and I cannot.

Did you get a joint prayer from Mr. Frémont & I that you would come here and get yourself well? Mr. Frémont was to bring you on and Mr. Lee was to take you back. And my part was to take you to

see Rachel. I think you must have failed to get it. It will not be too
late when they go on now for we always want you. Love to all,

                                                                    J.B.F.

Can I do any bonnet or dress work for you?

AL initialed (NjP—Blair-Lee Papers).

1. JBF is suggesting that Lizzie Lee's praise-filled letter was influenced by the ghost
of Sydney Smith (1771–1845), the English clergyman and satirical writer who commented in *Lady Holland's Memoirs,* chap. 9, "Praise is the best diet for us, after all!"
JBF refers again to the remark in her Mar. 7 [1856] letter to Lizzie Lee, below.
2. Lizzie Lee used a stamp that imprinted a picture of a squirrel in the wax she
used to seal letters. Thus, by examining the squirrel, JBF could tell if the letter had
been tampered with.
3. The Supreme Court session opened on Dec. 3, 1855 (Washington *Globe,* Dec.
4, 1855).
4. The Blairs and Frémonts still hoped to persuade Thomas Benton to support his
son-in-law for the presidency. Francis Blair had broached the subject in mid-November,
but Benton responded that JCF lacked political experience. Blair would again introduce
the theme on Nov. 30, but Benton would remain stubbornly opposed. The conversations
are reported in Elizabeth Blair Lee to S. Phillips Lee, Nov. 17, 30, 1855 (NjP—Blair-
Lee Papers).
5. By 1855, JBF's relationship with her sister, Liz Benton Jones, had soured, in part
because of William Carey Jones's drinking. In May, JCF business partner Joseph Palmer
had written Montgomery Blair of Jones: "his head is as thick, as a pumpkin, and his
skin is continually soaked with rum" (May 31, 1855, DLC—Blair Papers). The Joneses
opposed JCF's presidential bid, and the antagonism between the two families would
grow as the campaign intensified.
6. JBF's sister Sarah and her husband, Richard Taylor Jacob, had recently moved
to Kentucky.

To Elizabeth Blair Lee

                                        Tuesday 27th November [1855].

My dear Lizzie,

Our northern ally who was with us at your Father's is among the
most prominent of the candidates for Speaker.[1] If your Father thinks
with Mr. F. that it would be a point attained to have him in that place,
he may perhaps like to know of the intended movement in time to
give his aid.

Mrs. Fish called just now to take her farewell & say she would see
my people in a few days.[2] I will come some time this winter—not yet.

We are all at work now. The children study well with me. Even Charley is doing something. He is learning his letters & how to make straggling roman capitals on the slate—and in one of Foster's copybooks[3] he is making his traceries of straight lines. He is very apt and very good. He, as well as Lily go to dancing school and little Frank goes with the whole at one o'clock to the park near by where they have a good play.

I know you will have your hands full now with visiting in addition to other things but send me if only ten lines at a time, to keep Mr. Fremont from doubting himself. Yours affectionately,

J.B.F.

AL initialed (NjP—Blair-Lee Papers).

1. JBF is alerting Blair to the fact that Nathaniel Banks was a candidate for Speaker of the House. On Feb. 2, after a bitter nine-week struggle that pitted slavery against antislavery forces, Banks would emerge the victor. While the Frémont campaign received an important boost, the fact that Banks was the first Speaker ever elected without a single southern vote was an ominous sign of the depth of national divisions (HARRINGTON, 28–31).

2. Mrs. Julia (Kean) Fish (1816–87), the patrician wife of Senator Hamilton Fish, was about to set off for Washington, where the Fish family would live during the congressional session that began Dec. 3 (FISH, 77; Washington *Globe*, Dec. 4, 1855).

3. Benjamin Franklin Foster, a penmanship teacher, had developed a rapid, unified system of script that was taught in his copybooks (C. CARPENTER, 184).

To Elizabeth Blair Lee

No. 2
Friday evening
December 7th [1855]

Dear Lizzie,

If I had not been subdued for several days by one of my old ill turns, your responsive No. 1, should have had an immediate answer. Mr. Frémont's being there will have given you all a great talk together and settled many open questions. Mrs. Crittenden[1] came to see me to-day—two weeks after my call—very condescending and affable and with more attempt at dignity than I had ever seen before. Altogether I think coming events seem certain enough to her to cast their shadow upon her.

Please look at Susy's hat and see if it suits you enough to order one like it. As Susy is such a reformed sinner in the way of expenditures for dressing I sent her an economical present in her present style & from necessity mine too just now. It was only twelve dollars, and I had the children really pretty hats made at the same place for seven. Do encourage my newborn efforts at shopping. Do you believe that I take five cent drives in horsedrawn cars?[2] and that I take the copper in change — (I let it fall into my purse — I don't touch it) — and that I have only two long dresses. All the rest are as short as yours. After you believe these marvels I will tell you some more — about breakfast at nine — & getting up at seven, but for one time you have trial enough of your credulity.

The flounced dress is a step in the right direction but I will not be satisfied with less than seven flounces and a quarter of a yard longer than your other skirts.

Isn't it charming to relapse into small talk after clerking it for the Heads of the People. I feel like a horse set free from harness in writing all by myself just such stuff as comes uppermost although a more willing horse than myself I don't know — unless it be yourself. The Congressional harness seems to be very weak & not able to bear any strain — when the different men have had their vanity sufficiently put down I suppose two real candidates only will remain. I hope Mr. Banks will be elected. You must be lonely all this time constantly expecting Mr. Lee and being disappointed.[3] I have had so much of that in my time that I felt sorry to read your "fire and water are both against me." Don't get discouraged. Votre bon temps reviendra [your good time will return] and very soon I hope and then everything will be the pleasanter from your long Lent — a true "fast of St. Phillip" which lasts six weeks in the Greek Church. I am very glad of the *carpets & curtains* especially the curtains. To give me home details makes me feel you love me.

JBF.

AL initialed (NjP — Blair-Lee Papers).

1. Elizabeth (Moss) Wilcox Ashley (1805–73), the attractive and wealthy widow of the renowned fur trader and Missouri congressman William H. Ashley, had married twice-widowed John J. Crittenden in 1853. The seeming coolness between JBF and the new Mrs. Crittenden may have stemmed, in part, from the fact that William Ashley and Thomas Hart Benton had been political opponents (L. COLLINS, 1:240; KIRWIN, 282–83; CHAMBERS, 217). Moreover, JBF had apparently been close to Crittenden's

second wife, Maria, who, according to one account, had encouraged the forbidden romance between Jessie and John, and even allowed their secret marriage ceremony to be performed in her home (PHILLIPS, 57).

2. In the 1850s, in what was a revolution in urban transport, horse-drawn streetcars, seating forty passengers and running on smooth metal tracks, began to replace smaller, slower, bumpier and more expensive horse-drawn coaches in New York and other large cities (G. TAYLOR, 39–47).

3. In mid-September, S. Phillips Lee had gone west to attend to family business, including real estate investments in St. Louis. He returned to Washington in early December, about the time JBF wrote Lizzie Lee (CORNISH & LAAS, 79–81).

To Elizabeth Blair Lee

No. 3
Friday, [Dec.] 14th [1855]
New York. 176 Second Avenue.

I put the heading dear Lizzie—only to find if you hear from me, but not for any secrets this time. Mr. Frémont told me your Father had taken cold & was when he left, ill from its effects.

Let me hear from yourself how he is and take care of yourself, for I know in your double care for your Mother & Father you will do imprudent things and Mr. Lee is not there to look a remonstrance even.

My Father writes that he is wonderfully well. The children go to him next week. And if you should see in him at any time a need for me, you will let me know.[1] Perhaps Father may feel the loss of his winter's occupation for so long and the want of its excitement may make time drag notwithstanding his book. If he can accustom himself to it, I think the standing aloof from violent scenes better befits his past dignities and present age, than mingling in them.[2]

Give my most affectionate remembrances to your Mother and tell her that her little godson has four teeth, with two more on their way, & neither fever nor fretfulness from them. He testifies in his whole plump body and cheerful temper, to the even quiet temper of his nurse, who is like a great child with a doll, in regard to him. He is her perpetual admiration and having no set ways, and nursery ideas, Frank is as much a child of nature in most things as a young Indian. A regulation Mother would have nervous attacks at the state he gets his gowns into rolling on the carpet. He has a large sunny room—two windows looking on the old Stuyvesant burial ground (long disused) where there are superb old trees, an open fire, no furnace except in the halls, his bed, chair and little bath tub, the only things in the room. Charley has the front room, as that gives him the street to watch and his taste for horses is as great as Lily's.

Lil is very well—and gay as a bird singing all the time and looking resolutely away from all but the bright side of everything. Marie says "On vivra toujours en paix avec Mlle. Lily" [One will always live in peace with Miss Lily]. I am glad my little leopard has such spots and I hope it will be a great while before they dim—change, I realize by myself does not come to them—but they may get less bright.

Write me a womanish letter next time. You have belonged to mannish ideas lately, and much as those interest us all—deeper and most lasting of all is our interest in those whose friendly hearts and clear heads gave rise to them.

Mr. Frémont joins me in love to you all. Yours affectionately,

Jessie Frémont

ALS (NjP—Blair-Lee Papers).

1. At the last minute, JBF accompanied the children to Washington for a short, strained visit with her father. When she returned to New York, she left Lily and John's niece Nina for a longer stay.

2. Benton's usual winter occupation was, of course, politics, but in 1851, he had been defeated for a sixth Senate term, in part, because of his opposition to the extension of slavery. Refusing to retire, he won a congressional seat in 1852 but was not reelected. During 1855, Benton was rewriting the second volume of his monumental memoir, *Thirty Years' View,* since the original manuscript had been destroyed when his house burned down in February. The volume would be published in May 1856 by D. Appleton. Despite JBF's hopes for a dignified retirement, during the summer of 1856, Benton would launch a strenuous but unsuccessful campaign for the governorship of Missouri as a Democrat opposed to slavery extension (CHAMBERS, 374–75, 387, 417–24).

To Elizabeth Blair Lee

No. 1 (1856)
Saturday evening—12th Jany.

Dear Lizzie,

Mr. Frémont thought to have passed this evening and to-morrow morning with you—I, giving him the invitation. But he came back from Philadelphia after waiting in vain for a train to start in time for the Supreme Court on Friday. The telegraph says "Major Reading's case was confirmed on the same ground as the Frémont case" and then goes on, "that Mr. Cushing opposed Mr. Crittenden's motion for dismissing the appeal in Mr. Frémont's case." And I don't see how we shall know anything more unless Mr. Frémont goes on to find out. For Mr. Crittenden is lazy, Mr. Jones is away (and of no use when there) Judge Bibb is in his dotage and there our informants end.[1] Unless you find something more and write me. Or our new ally Mr. James, your brother Frank's friend. He is the double of Warrington in Pendennis—but you don't read Thackeray.[2] He is a very clear headed man and has his head crammed with an unassorted mass of literary gatherings which come spilling out in the quaintest and aptest quotations—not much polish but very fine raw material. I have no doubt an excellent political aid and manager. He wants to see and talk with your Father. Mr. [Freeman?][3] has not appeared yet. But another six footer with a letter of introduction (on the same errand) made us a visit today. Col. Barnes[4] of Boston. You know of him through the Woodbury's. Mr. Frémont says, "all these tall men will think I am too short."

Sun. mg.

Rain and sleet all night have kept me in doors although our church[5] is within a stone's throw but there are two feet of "slush" in the street. Mr. Frémont is working away up stairs and as I sometimes speak before I remember that calculations must not be interfered with, I keep out of harm's way by staying down in my own domain where a cannel coal fire[6] and primroses in bloom make the outside weather forgotten. My garden however is like Adam's—a solitude. Frank is asleep and Charley prefers running his "Belocipede" (as he calls it) up and down the basement story to being company up stairs. I have written to Lily and now I inflict myself on you. The weather has been such since my return that I have left the house but once. Friday was a sunny day and I was in the carriage for a drive when I met Mr. Frémont who had had to return from Philadelphia—so I came back into the house to play black woman to his Mungo Park.[7]

I wish I could go on in February but even my modified form of housekeeping needs my presence. Mr. Frémont says I must go too. But I am not enough used to that word to mind it. Frank goes on cutting teeth without fever or crying—six fully out, and two shinning through his gums. He is superbly well made—even better than Charley, although he may like Charley take a Frémont turn about the legs when he grows older. But no more eyes look like Charley's. He has his fine color again and his great brown eyes sparkle with fun and good health. I think I love him better than I ever can Frank, for he is my own nurseling and has a hundred faults that came with his Mother's milk— all of which he atones for to me by his loving nature. If your godson ever comes to your care have patience with him for I think he has the capacity to repent, if he does try one by his little sins. I am not a fair judge for him, for I realize it is almost excusing my own self, so alike are we in temper.

I wrote to your Father on the 8th because Genl. Jackson looked at me to remind me it was his day, and since your gifts of the horse & his rider yours and mine too.[8] I always feel too that that day you all dined with me ended one part of your life.[9] After death has once broken the home circle a shadow rests there forever. Time dims our grief—sometimes I think even the habit of enduring hardens the heart, but things are never the same again. Mrs. Talbot used to say to me— "It is not the old who are most to be pitied when grief falls upon them—they know they can bear again what they have borne before— but pity the young in their first grief when they believe they must die, and find they live to be more wretched than they could have imagined— live to suffer on again and again until a dull apathetic silence takes the place of their useless tears and cries." I used to think her views colored by her own sad experience but now that I am old enough to look back and see how much of it is true of my own life I give all my pity to the young—and all my care to the old who are calm because they know the end is near. In middle life men, women too, busy themselves in other pursuits and forget for the time. And I believe ambition, and activity in domestic life—in charity—in every channel where we find them absorbed—have their rise in a sore heart which cannot be listened to but must be silenced by the outer world. "From the troubled waters healing comes."[10] There is my text at the end of my sermon which was written before I intended to make it. You once promised me the hymn which should close it "Earth has no sorrow that Heaven cannot cure"[11] but you never gave it. I know the air but not all the words.

Whilst you are failing in your attempt at imitating me in my long gowns I am succeeding in getting used to your style. I am thin enough now to wear them—and in other things I hope to grow more like you.

If Maretzek[12] took his full orchestra you had some delicious music— I regret its lose to us. Madame La Grange[13] has nothing touching in her voice—she gave me no pleasure.

You must have noticed the beautiful aptness of the Shakespearian quotations applied to public men that were given in Saturday's Post. Was not the one for Father perfect. "He was the noblest Roman of them all."[14]

The girls write me that he enjoys his rides with them—they ought to come home but I am not sorry that the bad travelling forces a little detention. Still Nina is at a bad age for idling. One thinks directly of love in idleness, and she is too young in everything but years for that yet. Help to start them back to me when the time comes. Father has great deference for your opinions—and I would rather not take it all on myself. You see every letter asks a fresh service of you. Do write whenever you find a little time to give me. Mr. Frémont always asks me to read your letters to him, and says "Read the whole. I like Lizzie's way of writing." So with Mr. Lee's permission write for both of us. Love to all from yours affcty,

Jessie.

ALS (NjP—Blair-Lee Papers).

1. Frémont ally Pierson B. Reading's claim to the Buena Ventura Ranch in Shasta County, Calif., was sustained by the U.S. Supreme Court on Jan. 12, "affirming the principle established in the Frémont case." That same day, Frémont lawyer George M. Bibb (1772–1859), a former Kentucky senator and state chief justice, introduced a motion to dismiss the government's appeal of the Mar. 10, 1855, Supreme Court decision granting JCF title to Las Mariposas (see JBF to Francis Preston Blair, Nov. 18 [1855], note 2, above). Crittenden spoke in favor of Bibb's motion, and U.S. Attorney General Caleb Cushing (1800–1879) opposed it (New York *Times*, Jan. 12, 1856).

2. William Makepeace Thackeray (1811–63) describes George Warrington, a character in his novel Pendennis (1848–50), as a rough diamond. A tall, black-bearded, pipe-smoking man of frank, idealistic temperament, Warrington is outspoken, good-humored, and down-to-earth.

3. Possibly Blair family friend William Grigsby Freemen (1814–66), a West Pointer who would resign from the army in Mar. 1856.

4. Col. Barnes may be James Barnes (1801–69), a native of Boston who graduated from West Point, resigned his commission as first lieutenant (not colonel) in 1836, and became a successful builder of railroads. At the outbreak of the Civil War, he was appointed colonel of the Eighteenth Massachusetts Volunteers. He was wounded at the battle of Gettysburg. James Barnes is the only Barnes listed in HEITMAN who reasonably fits JBF's description.

5. St. Mark's (Episcopal) Church in the Bowery (E. B. FRÉMONT, 76).

6. Cannel coal contains much volatile material, which causes it to burn with unusual brightness.

7. In his *Travels in Africa*, Scottish explorer Mungo Park (1771–1806) describes an occasion when he was starving and an African woman gave him food. JBF thus means that she fed her husband.

8. No letter of Jan. 8, 1856, has been found. It was the anniversary of the Battle of New Orleans, Gen. Andrew Jackson's greatest military victory in the War of 1812. Yearly on this date, the president placed a wreath at the base of the Jackson equestrian statue in Lafayette Square, in front of Blair House and across from the White House. Blair had been instrumental in raising money to erect the statue, and Lizzie may have given JBF a miniature replica of it (W. E. SMITH, 1:198).

9. JBF refers to the unexpected death of James Blair in San Francisco on Dec. 15, 1853. The news evidently reached the Blair family in Washington about Jan. 8, a day they dined with JBF (Washington *Globe*, Jan. 11, 1854; JBF to Elizabeth Blair Lee, New Year's Day, 1854, NjP—Blair-Lee Papers).

10. See John 5:4.

11. JBF refers to the hymn "Come, Ye Disconsolate" by Irish poet Thomas Moore (1779–1852), in which each verse ends with the refrain, "Earth has no sorrow that Heaven cannot heal."

12. During the 1850s, Czechoslovakian-born composer, conductor, and opera impressario Max Maretzek (1821–97) permanently established Italian opera in New York City. In the fall of 1855, his company performed for forty nights at New York's Academy of Music on 14th Street. Maretzek and "the entire opera troupe" also presented Verdi's *Il Trovatore* in Washington on Jan. 9 (New York *Herald*, Jan. 14, 1856).

13. Anna de La Grange (1825–1905), the French coloratura soprano, appeared with Maretzek's company in New York City in 1855 and 1856 (O. THOMPSON, 1203).

14. New York *Evening Post,* Sat., Jan. 12, 1856, quoting from *Julius Caesar,* act 5, sc. 5.

To Elizabeth Blair Lee

[Jan./Feb. 1856]

I come to you for help dear Lizzie. Father has so many prejudices and Liz is so indifferent, that I rely on you to see with me and to help me.

The flattery to Nina from the French attaché (I do not know the name) is quite enough for me of that kind of thing. Nina is hopelessly sentimental—not romantic or impulsive or enthusiastic—but simply and [miserably?] sentimental and would enjoy of all things a "persecution." If that man, or any other fancied she was an heiress and would be a "good catch" she has no more powers of discernment than one of your barn yard family. From the long apprenticeship I served under Sarah and Susan I consider myself now graduated and so come to decisions like Cuvier[1] did from seeing only the smallest bone of the animal. One such compliment is as good proof for me as if I heard all the rest. Without wounding Susan's feelings I can't well tell her Nina will not receive any fortune at all if she marries a foreigner and yet such is her uncle's fixed determination and written & recorded will — and Nina knows it — and gave occasion for the clause, in Paris. Boilleau's is an exceptional case. I believe that he really loves Susan but we all remember how more than doubtful his attentions to her were — no one could fail to see it was not a marrying matter with him in the beginning. And to us all it was an unlooked for blessing that it ended so.[2] Susan has qualities and attractions to justify a real attachment — and indeed Nina has not — she is shallow in everything, even her beauty is of the kind that will not last at all. So that to any frenchman — the keenest nation living for a matrimonial bargain — it is the idea of fortune that would make them think of a marriage. I think Nina married to a sensible man — one rather given to social observances — with a fixed society and routine life would make a very successful voyage through life. She needs money a great deal — without it she would be peevish and envious — with it gentle and charitable. You see I am daring to tell you my true opinion because I know you will not think wrong of me. You may think me mistaken, but not intentionally unjust or fault seeing. I do not think I am even mistaken. Properly controlled Nina will dwell in decencies forever and be "such a sweet feminine woman" but without such control she cannot guide herself, but would take any impression that a stronger will chose to give her. All this means that it is easy to stop a thing in the beginning and impossible when it has taken root — and that therefore Nina must come back to her Duenna and not left to negligence from Liz and temptations from Susan, and you must get her back.

I am not sound in health as I was. Every anxiety or distress brings those spasms at the heart — and my longer or shorter life is dependent on my freedom from cares. That is a fact now that no one who has been with me in the past year doubts. Mr. Frémont was slow to realize it but this fall convinced him. It is no part of my plans to wear myself out for Nina when Lily remains to be cared for so I will begin at the beginning and not let the evil grow. Your good Father took my part years ago when my Father called me suspicious. He said it was not that — it was more like prophetic foresight. And with his authority to sustain mine, I hope you will see nothing croaking in this but look upon it only as a setting forth of the whole subject in an unvarnished (a very unvarnished) light and help me to keep free from both mental and physical sufferings. Your affectionate Cassandra.

I think if Father has any memory for private affairs, it would be enough if you would tell him Nina has an admirer in the French Legation. This is a secret diplomatic service I ask of you. I will help kill off any man you don't like about Betty[3] when her time comes.

I get all your letters safely. Please answer this soon and don't think it over-anxious or harsh to Nina. I wouldn't say so much to any one but yourself and you will please tell Father as much as may be needed. Liz would not take interest enough to do it, and of course Susan can't be applied to, so I rely on you dear Lizzie. Father knows you of old and relies on your judgment in such matters. There is to my thinking no such thing as cure — only prevention.

AL (NjP — Blair-Lee Papers).

1. A reference to the French naturalist Georges Cuvier (1769–1832), whose *Studies of Fossil Bones* was the earliest systematic account of vertebrate paleontology.

2. Boilleau may have been reluctant to marry Susan Benton because he feared it would damage his diplomatic career. Evidently it did, for in 1857 Senator Charles Sumner of Massachusetts, who admired Boilleau as a man of "talents and learning," was informed by the French foreign minister, Count Alexandre Walewski, that Boilleau's marriage to "a person without fortune" had barred him from high diplomatic positions. "Thus," Sumner reported, "is the romance of that marriage crowned by his renunciation of most distinguished prospects in the diplomatic service" (Sumner to Henry Wadsworth Longfellow, Apr. 2, 1857, quoted in LONGFELLOW, 4:28n).

3. Elizabeth (Betty) Blair (1841–72), daughter of Montgomery Blair and of his first wife, Caroline Buckner, lived with Francis and Eliza Blair after her mother's death during childbirth in 1844 and was adopted by them when Montgomery remarried in 1846. In 1869 she married Cyrus Ballou Comstock, a career army officer; she herself died in childbirth in 1872 (W. E. SMITH, 2:596; E. B. SMITH [1], 178, 431–32).

To Elizabeth Blair Lee

[Feb. 1856]

Dear Lizzie,

Mr. Frémont and Lily came in Sunday evening having been stopped in Philadelphia where they dined with the [James and Lucretia] Motts and so made the little journey in comfort. Mr. Frémont goes back either Saturday or Monday. The past teaches him suspicion, and he is going to watch the wording of the Patent lest they introduce some "rascality" as Father phrases it.[1] He said he wished to say as much to Mr. Crittenden, but feared it would look unnecessary to him—as he (Mr. Crittenden) had not felt all the causes which led to such distrust.

I have exactly the same reason to give you for your dissent from my opinion of Nina. I kept my letter a day and a half after writing it because I felt you would think me harsh and you are one of the very few—the number grows less lately—whose good opinion I would grieve to lose. But I could write nothing different if I wrote at all. Susan, who knew why I was so positive, was not in the right position to help me and Liz cares for no one enough to take the trouble necessary to get Father to abandon an idea. But I saw with pain that you thought me unjust to Nina. If you ever happen to know her well you will do me justice—until then I shall have to be Cassandra. If Nina were capable of a real heartfelt love I would not disturb it without serious cause—for I believe in love. But as three sentimental attachments have already faded from the wax of her nature I have no compunctions in arranging the duration of a fourth (should it arise) to suit myself. Miss Hayne's school[2] for a reality and the White House for a castle in the air, will keep her out of nonsense until next year when I shall have to let her take her chances. I hope an early and good marriage may be hers. I think then her good traits of character may become more fixed and a routine established which may keep her from outside influences. Who the man is I have no idea yet—but the crisis will bring them. I know this is contrary to your doctrine of free will—but I prescribe for a very different case from yours or mine—and I know my flock.

Dr. Hodge[3] would not recommend hum drum to me in everything. I do lead a very simple and regulated life and I have been reading some very useful books—but my illness, or rather the cause for illness, will not go so easily—but I can keep it down. I believe my heart—my physical heart, the organ, I mean—has been so often overtried, in the last eight years that its strength is in some way diminished. I do not understand my form of disease there—in fact I know nothing of any form of ill health except an accouchement in which branch I have taken my degree—but from my own unaided observations in many a return of these spasms, I feel that the heart gets overfilled—it literally swells with pain. If there is such a thing, it is like an apoplexy of the heart. Sometimes I am so exhausted that a sudden sleep falls on me like a fainting fit—it always tires me. The absence of annoyance or excitement in the last month has made me look well again, but I was worn out the week I was in Washington. One might as well die of that as of anything else and with all the chances that rise against life I don't see that it makes any difference to have one of the chances fixed within one. It does not even determine the manner much less the time of one's death. I only avoid all causes which may rouse it for I have a certainty of pain and of feeling good for nothing the next day. I did not mean to be like a representative and weary you with such a long "personal explanation" but it made itself.

I see on reading it over that I have not made myself very clear but I have left your letter so long unacknowledged that I will not delay longer. After this I will not intrude myself again, but go back to my secretaryship.

Frank crowed over his cup and his little nurse joins me in gratified pleasure at your Father's remembrance of him. He is becoming a large and very beautiful child. My darling Charley is getting to be a little musician—ask Mr. Frémont about him.

AL (NjP—Blair-Lee Papers).

1. JCF's Mariposas title was definitively settled on Feb. 17, 1856, when the Supreme Court dismissed the government's appeal. Two days later, JCF visited Franklin Pierce at the White House and received the patent, personally signed by the president (M. L. SPENCE [2], lxiii).

2. JBF probably refers to the nearby private school (10 Gramercy Park at 20th Street) of Miss Henrietta B. Haines, whose discreet advertisements occasionally appeared in New York newspapers (see, for example, New York *Tribune,* Aug. 28, 1856). Later both Lizzie Lee's niece Betty Blair and JBF's young friend Nelly Haskell would attend the school.

3. Dr. Hugh Lenox Hodge (1796–1873) was a noted Philadelphia gynecologist and University of Pennsylvania professor of obstetrics, whom JBF had evidently consulted about her poor health after the birth of Frank. Hodge may have been recommended by Lizzie Lee, who in 1846, after four years of marriage, had gone to Hodge when she could not conceive. Hodge had diagnosed a displaced uterus and attempted to reposition it with a pessary he had designed. Like many Victorian women, she was mortified by the physical examination, possibly the first she had experienced: "a horrible ordeal" about which she felt "a miserable sense of humiliation & a chilly shuddering at the thoughts of what I have endured" (CORNISH & LAAS, 64).

To Elizabeth Blair Lee

Friday evening
March 7th [1856].

Mr. Frémont is with you so much dear Lizzie that my occupation's
gone and in your pleasantly occupied life my tame personality can
hardly catch your attention. Mr. Bigelow (the Evening Post)[1] made me
some comments on yourself and Mr. Lee, in a visit I had from him
tonight, which carried my mind back to your hospitable home and I
cannot go to bed until I have obeyed the spirit that moves me to send
you a gossiping good night.

I shall not repeat Mr. Bigelow's opinion of you—you have heard
the same from so many sources that it is not new but I know you will
always listen with fresh interest to agreeable things about Mr. Lee. To
begin, he thought him strikingly handsome and as he understands the
cruise of the Dolphin[2] better than I could with all my efforts, he finds
him very distinguished in his profession also. "I was very much impressed by him altogether." When you remember that Mr. Bigelow is
a natural critic it is quite something to attract only favorable notice
from him.

I think Sidney Smith would consider I had kept his rule towards
you tonight.[3]

While I am remembering about naval officers I want to ask your
compassion and care for a most forlorn old lady now quite alone with
only one son—an idiot—remaining of her family, two of whom were
in the Navy—one a Captain, the other a Lieutenant. Her name is
Weaver[4] and she is now on Massachusetts Avenue. Betsy (cook) at my
Father's will know her exact address. I am afraid she misses me very
much. I have looked after her for a year past and Nina kept it up for
me, but Liz forgets. Some of the many comforts that are wasted in
our homes make her old days less hard if one only remembered to
take them to her but she is very old—over 80 and cannot go to remind.
I think she is in a special manner your charge from her sons having
been in Mr. Lee's profession. A little wine is a great medicine for her.
I left her some but it is long since I could see to her.

My other naval widow Ellen Blunt[5] is also an object of true interest.
We did her great injustice about the writing. She did not let me know
until I had a letter from her (within the month) telling me she had

done it since April last year—at first at the Patent Office—oh Lizzie how hard that must have been to her—then at her own house all for *fifty dollars* a month. Is not that bitter.

> "She, has her bread in sorrow ate—
> She, through the lonely midnight hours
> Weeping upon her bed has sate"[6]

Your last letter gave me something to think of. I had thought better of myself than to suppose poverty and sorrow would make me hard. We are so much more lenient in judging ourselves than others can be. I think I have been tried somewhat but I did not know it had had such a result—until you know you cannot judge how much of humility and dread of exposure of feeling comes upon one in such trials and they may seem hardness. But just now we are in one of the lulls in our agitated life and I will not recall old things. Mr. Frémont is very gay and pleased & all his plans seem prospering. He will tell you how yours and your Father's little boys thrive. Frank is beautiful. My Charley is my darling however. Be very sure he does not forget either of you nor does your affectionate

Jessie

ALS (NjP—Blair-Lee Papers).

1. John Bigelow (1817–1911), the energetic and skilled partner and coeditor (with William Cullen Bryant) of the New York *Evening Post,* had been converted to the Frémont cause by Nathaniel Banks. Bigelow would work closely with JBF during the campaign, finding her "a remarkably capable and accomplished woman." During this visit, he probably discussed his projected campaign biography. JBF furnished Bigelow with an outline (now in NN—Bigelow Papers) and volunteered to write the ticklish first chapter about JCF's family background (BIGELOW [2], 1:141–44). A Bigelow excerpt would appear in the *Evening Post* on May 19 with others following at intervals during the campaign. The 480-page biography, *Memoir of the Life and Public Services of John Charles Fremont,* was published on Aug. 6 (New York *Evening Post,* Aug. 6, 1856).

2. In 1851–52, S. Phillips Lee had commanded the brig *Dolphin* during an eight-month scientific cruise in the Atlantic to make hydrographic and meteorological observations for the Navy (see CORNISH & LAAS, 73–78).

3. JBF again refers to Sydney Smith's "rule": "Praise is the best diet for us, after all!" See JBF to Elizabeth Blair Lee, Nov. 21 [1855], above.

4. Mrs. Weaver may have been Catherine Weaver, for whom a private bill for a naval pension was adversely reported from the Congressional Committee on Pensions on Jan. 12, 1854 (*Congressional Globe,* 33rd Cong., 1st sess., p. 159). One of her sons may have been William H. Weaver, an 1841 graduate of the Naval Academy, who died Sept. 24, 1851 (CALLAHAN, 574).

5. Ellen Lloyd Blunt (1821–86), a daughter of Francis Scott Key, was the young widow of naval lieutenant Simon Fraser Blunt. To support herself and her children, she was working as a copyist for the U.S. Patent Office, where, by 1855, Patent Commissioner Charles Mason was employing four women clerks, including Clara Barton, who later founded the American Red Cross. In mid-1855, however, when Mason resigned, the women were forced to work at home because Secretary of the Interior Robert McClelland, who had assumed supervision of the Patent Office, objected to "the obvious impropriety in the mixing of the two sexes within the walls of a public office." Their pay was reduced to the piecework rate of ten cents per hundred words, and during some of the following months, they were given little or no work at all (PRYOR, 56–61). For JBF's attempt to help Ellen Blunt, see JBF to George W. Blunt, [winter 1857–58?], below.

6. JBF is loosely quoting the opening motto from Longfellow's *Hyperion* (1839), in turn derived from Goethe's *William Meister's Apprenticeship*, bk. 2, chap. 13. She also quotes it in J. B. FRÉMONT [2], 170.

To Elizabeth Blair Lee

Saturday morning
8th March [1856]

Our letters crossed each other my dear Lizzie—yours of Thursday came to me just after I had sent one to the office for you.

Yours and your Father's kind interest will be made known to the responsible person who is again with you, and who is always only too well pleased to have your Father's advice and opinions.

I did not know Mr. Frémont had such a pleasure in view for me as a visit to Silver Spring. Whenever he gives me the word I am ready. I'll go my chief. I can not forgive Mr. Lee's spoiling that ballad. Nina cried out against him at the time for pointing out in the most matter of fact manner that Campbell made them continue to row the boat after she was stove in—a purely professional view of the case leaving no excuse for a poet's license.[1] It would be a real pleasure to me to make you a visit. Such a different sort of people I meet here—I had rather not go out at all than be so bored. I was at a party this week where it was so dull that I absolutely had to rub my eyelids to keep them open. The party was given to me but in place of taking me in to supper himself the master of the house chose out a man who had written a book (Botta, we know him as "Otis' Botta")[2] as a fitting match for the wife of a book maker and daughter of an historian. He told me that in a sentence that would be three inches long in type.

The man was an Italian & literary, and never saw that I had a bunch of violets in my belt & another in my hand, but discoursed excitedly on the oddness of my not eating oysters, and ate so many himself as to release me from all trouble of entertaining him.

Mr. Frémont was even worse off for he was put up as a mark in the centre of the room and a number of authoresses fired at him with brilliant sentences, evidently prepared after their invitation to meet him. He said as we drove home he would much rather have fought a duel than have gone through that evening.

Ask Mr. Frémont to tell you of the Wadsworth dinner.[3] I find myself rambling on in the most indefinite manner when I begin writing to you. You are really the only person I ever write to now. I have had one note from Liz in five months—none from Susan. I don't mind that much for she is new to her occupations this winter and I am very glad she is happy enough to do without me, but old Jones (bad luck to him) has completely chilled Father's family. I can see his traces in many things—Liz is irretrievably alienated. But so far I have given no sign of noticing it and with his low tastes she will need us all so that I shall not be the one to put obstacles in the way of her return when she feels inclined to us. The dropping of water wears away stone[4] and I think the constant dropping of insinuations by Mr. Jones has worn away much of Father's remaining regard for Mr. Frémont. If *he* ever makes the chance, I will get him apart from Liz and "blow him sky high"—and I know all his vulnerable points.

I hope your Father's hoarseness will be nursed away—the spring will soon be with us now and I think the breath of the pines is almost life giving then.

I hoped your Father might have had to come here on his way from Pittsburgh[5] this is such a meeting ground for conspirators. I hoped I might get my part in the pleasure of seeing his kind and friendly face again. I wish you had something to bring you here. Next to that are your letters. You have always something to say but I have only myself to speak of and sometimes I have a fit of humility and don't feel myself worth mentioning. The girls are just now at dancing school. Charley is the happy owner of a new drum which is waking all the echoes in the house. Frank is worth shewing—he is royally beautiful and as healthy as is possible. Give my kindest love and remembrance to your Mother & tell her I want her to see the baby for she would appreciate him. Do write often and if my letters go back too often in answer, don't open them. Yours affectionately,

Jessie Frémont.

ALS (NjP—Blair-Lee Papers).

1. In "Lord Ullin's Daughter" by Scottish poet Thomas Campbell (1777–1844), a highland chieftain and Lord Ullin's daughter have eloped and must cross a stormy sea to escape her father's wrath. A boatman, asked to row them across, responds, "I'll go, my chief! I'm ready." Lee objected to the subsequent description of their fate: "The boat has left a stormy land,/ A stormy sea before her,—/ When, oh! too strong for human hand,/ The tempest gathered o'er her./ And still they rowed amidst the roar/ Of waters fast prevailing."

2. In 1853, Italian scholar Vincenzo Botta (1818–94) emigrated to the United States; two years later he married poet Anne Charlotte Lynch (1815–91), whose salon was a popular gathering place for New York literati. In 1858 he became professor of Italian languages and literature at the University of the City of New York (now New York University).

3. James S. Wadsworth (1807–64) was a wealthy and influential New York Republican and abolitionist. Named a brigadier general during the Civil War, he would command divisions at Fredericksburg and Gettysburg, and die heroically during the battle of the Wilderness.

4. Job 14:19.

5. Francis Blair had attended a preliminary convention of several hundred Republican leaders at Pittsburgh on Feb. 22 to organize a national party and plan a presidential nominating convention. When Blair was enthusiastically elected permanent president of the Pittsburgh meeting, JCF's prospects soared. For convention details see W. E. SMITH, 1:327–31; E. B. SMITH [1], 220–21; and GIENAPP, 254–59.

To Elizabeth Blair Lee

Thursday 1 'oclock
April 17/ 56

Dear Lizzie,

I return you the letter which came to me some days since. Mr. Frémont has been using it.[1] Your Father will have been pleased to find his idea carried out so promptly. I do not have your doubts of the good faith of Mr. Banks[2]—to speak plainly—but if it should be so we must all put our shoulders to our own wheel and roll it ahead for I think, partiality apart Mr. Frémont would get the largest popular vote.

I am tired & not over well so I put off a longer note until after our dinner at Mr. Butler's to-day where we are to meet Mr. Van Buren.[3]

Thank you for the [. . .] finding out Mrs. Weaver—her frail tottering walk was so like Mother's that my heart ached when I first saw her— it was in the fall just after—I cannot do more than give money at this distance but she needs care. If she gets ill it will be her last illness & perhaps at the Hospital under Dr. May's[4] care her life would end less painfully than in her own poor home with chance attendance. She is Catholic & might like the Sisters nursing her. If you could find the time, or Liz either. I am so glad Liz has begun to look in the right path for relief of mind from her own sorrows. Would you see if she would go to the Hospital. I would pay for the room—her son is the only obstacle—she would not separate from him.

If Mr. Lee does go west ask him to come this way. I so wish to see a home face again. I hope you will find you can come too if only for a little while. I would hurt your health talking to you for I am all dammed up—for want of sympathizing ears. Most about Father. Yours most affcty,

Jessie.

ALS (NjP—Blair-Lee Papers).

1. Both JCF and Blair were writing public letters, JCF's to be read at an Apr. 29 Republican mass meeting at the New York Tabernacle, and Blair's "A Voice from the Grave of Jackson!" for publication at about the same time. See JBF to Elizabeth Blair Lee, Apr. 29 [1856], notes 1–2, below, for details.

2. Lizzie Lee evidently feared that Nathaniel Banks was wavering in his support of JCF: there were rumors that Banks, known as both shrewd and ambitious, hoped to be the Republican nominee himself or that he would support William Seward if Seward could be elected (GIENAPP, 310, 332–33).

3. Benjamin F. Butler (1795–1858) of New York had been former president Martin Van Buren's law partner and remained a trusted friend. In 1856, Butler became a Republican, and his dinner was probably arranged in hopes that Van Buren would support the Republican ticket and possibly JCF. Van Buren (1782–1862), who had known Jessie since childhood, was, like her father and Francis Blair, a part of the old Jacksonian alliance. Blair had written enthusiastically about JCF to Van Buren in January, but Van Buren considered him too young and inexperienced for the post (Jan. 25, 1856, DLC—Van Buren Papers). Despite his opposition to the extension of slavery, Van Buren, like Benton, would remain in the Democratic party and endorse James Buchanan.

4. Dr. Frederick John May (1812–91), chair of surgery at Columbian College Medical School in Washington, D.C., was the Benton family physician and would care for Thomas Benton during his later struggle against cancer. In 1865 he would successfully remove a tumor from Lizzie Lee's right breast (KELLY, 2:155–56; CORNISH & LAAS, 153–54).

To Elizabeth Blair Lee

[Apr. 18 (1856)]

Dear Lizzie,

We dined yesterday at Mr. Butler's and Mr. Van Buren himself was my allotment for dinner—John[1] being opposite Mr. Frémont. Both were as gracious as good intentions could make them. John has not called upon me at all this winter. "He did not know Mr. Frémont" he said, so a friend of his told me. Between Mr. Frémont and Mr. Seward I presume he would not hesitate.[2] Last night he was profuse in apologies.

I want to know much more than a letter could tell even if it were safe to write but I do not think I can go to Washington. I have made one thing a fixed resolve—not to be hurt at heart any oftener than it is forced upon me—to go deliberately into agitation and pain is almost suicide.

I know both my people too well ever to look for concession from either side. And with Father this is only the expression of years distrust of Mr. Frémont's judgment. Since the revoked sale of the Mariposas, nearly five years ago, Father has put great constraints on his temper and now he has what he considers a fair occasion for an opposition.[3]

I think Mr. Frémont could not have done otherwise than revoke such a sale. I know more facts than Father did. Indeed Mr. Frémont would have had small respect for himself to allow of such administration of his estate during his life.

I can think as much as I like and give no offence, but if I were in a place where I must express an opinion or a feeling against either it would be very hard upon me & so I think it best not to go.

This is my own thinking out. Father shocked back & chilled all my feelings when I looked to him for sympathy the winter Mr. Frémont was in the mountains last. Your Father saw one little proof of it in the way he told me of Babbitt's news.[4] Tears may be sweet that are shed upon the bosom of a friend whose heart grieves with yours— but tears wrung from you in solitude and embittered by the want of a friend are such as I do not wish to feel burning my eyes again.

So I stand aloof. Success if it comes, gives a more graceful position to be friendly from and if it should be so I think Father cannot resist the influence of it. And if not, it would be a mortifying thing to add to the other annoyances of a defeat, that of having appeared to conciliate for a purpose.

I have written constantly to Father. I always tell him whatever I think may interest him—never saying politics—but for four months I have not had a line from him nor Liz except one stiff note about Cousin Anne.[5] So I am put into Coventry[6] and all I can do is not to show myself conscious of it which I could not succeed in doing if I were on the spot.

Just here & just now I am quite the fashion—5th Avenue asks itself, "Have we a Presidentess among us—" and as I wear fine lace and purple I am in their eyes capable of filling the place. So I go out nightly—sometimes to dinner & a party both the same night and three times a week to the opera where I hold a levee in my box. Nina is profiting by it all. She made her debut last Friday at a beautiful ball given by the bachelors to the crème de la crème. She looked very lovely & enjoyed her success very much.

I am chaperone now. We go next week into our new house 56 West 9th st.[7] Do come and see me there. I am getting as artificial as Mrs. Gales[8] for want of a heart warming such as you would give me. Mr. Frémont might as well go back to Washington for we only meet in company and when we get home silence is a luxury. May ends all gayeties however so that we will have a home life again after a while & perhaps more of it than we might like after the 17th of June.[9] Write as often as you can & thank you again for your promise about Mrs. Weaver. Yours affcty,

Jessie

Friday 18th April

ALS (NjP—Blair-Lee Papers).

1. Martin Van Buren's son, "Prince" John (1810–66), was a charming, witty man and a brilliant, popular orator who in 1848 had been a leader in the formation of the Barnburners, the free-soil wing of the New York Democratic party. However, drinking and womanizing had blighted his career, and by the time JBF saw him at the Butler dinner, he was prematurely aged. He died a broken man in 1866 (SCHLESINGER, 398–400; E. B. SMITH [1], 175).

2. John Van Buren would support neither JCF nor New York senator William H. Seward (1801–72) but James Buchanan. Initially Seward had been the leading free-soil candidate in 1856, but many party leaders, including his astute political manager, Thurlow Weed, became convinced that his outspoken antislavery views made him unelectable that year. JCF, whose stance on slavery was believed to be less radical, seemed the more acceptable candidate. Although Seward was again the leading Re-

publican candidate in 1860, he lost the nomination to compromise candidate Abraham Lincoln. Ironically, during the Civil War, Seward, as Lincoln's secretary of state, grew more conservative and JCF more radical on the slavery issue.

3. In 1851, when JCF had expressed interest in selling Las Mariposas, Benton had negotiated its sale to Thomas Denny Sargent for one million dollars, with an advance payment followed by a series of annual payments. But JCF, concluding that the mines were worth far more, exercised a clause in the contract that allowed him to revoke the sale. Benton disagreed; moreover, he believed John was "not adapted to such business and it interferes with his attention to other business to which he is adapted" (M. L. SPENCE [2], xlix–l; 331–32). From this point on, relations between the two men were strained.

During the campaign, a story circulated that when JCF cancelled the deal, he stalled in returning the advance payment. When Horace Greeley investigated, he found the accusation less serious than he feared, "but I still wish F[rémont] had sold Mariposa, or had ratified Benton's sale of it" (ISELY, 164–65).

4. In Apr. 1854, Mormon official Almon W. Babbitt had brought grim news about JCF's fifth expedition to Washington (see JBF to Francis Preston Blair, [Apr.] 13 [1854], above). Benton evidently felt that JCF had bungled his mission to find an all-weather railway route through the Rockies and was unsympathetic in giving Babbitt's news to his distraught daughter.

5. Cousin Anne was Thomas Benton's niece, Anne Benton Potts of St. Louis, the widow of the Rev. William Stephen Potts (1804–52), a prominent Presbyterian minister (J. B. FRÉMONT [1], 159; SCHARF [2], 2:1702–4).

6. JBF explained her family's use of the term "put into Coventry" in her "Memoirs": "From our early childhood it was a punishable offence to bring discord to the table. The child who so offended, by tale-bearing or sulks or anything unsuitable to general society, was not reproved then, but the next day, by having no place at table and was served at a side table. 'Put into Coventry,' in short" ("Memoirs," 38 [first draft]). The term may have originated in England during the seventeenth century when supporters of King Charles were seized and exiled to Coventry, a town whose citizens supported Parliament against the king (OED, 3:1071).

7. The Frémonts' newly rented house, one of a group of handsome row houses built in 1853, was located at 56 West 9th Street, just off Fifth Avenue (WRIGHT, 201–2).

8. Probably Sarah Juliana Maria (Lee) Gales, a cousin of Lizzie's husband and the wife of Joseph Gales (1786–1860), the Whig copublisher of the Washington *National Intelligencer*, longtime rival to Blair's *Globe*.

9. The date of the Republican nominating convention in Philadelphia.

To Elizabeth Blair Lee

Friday morning
April 25th [1856]

Dear Lizzie,

Mr. Frémont tells me to apply to you for advice. He wishes very much that I should go to Washington just now. I have not told him anything of what I wrote you—that would prevent his availing himself of whatever service I can render & although I do not count much on it myself, he seems to think you & I could act as peace makers. Will you please help me in this, and let me know at once what your Father thinks.[1] If he says so I will come on next week with some one of the children. Mr. Frémont will remain here—he says [he] cannot go into the house with Mr. Jones.

I write constantly to Father but have not had a line from him since I left there at Christmas. He always drops me that way when he is offended with Mr. Frémont.

I wrote about a month ago, saying I would go on to make him a visit when Mr. Frémont returned, but as he made no answer I feel like asking again before going even into what used to be my home.

One outlives many things. The burning of our old house was the funeral pile of home bonds and old ties.[2]

However nothing shall make me fail in my respect and duty to Father and if he will ever have it my affection too. I think if he had softer natures about him it would greatly add to his own comfort.

This is all a sore point to me. Mr. Frémont does not think how much I mind it and you must not tell him—but if I can help in anyway I will swallow my wounded pride and go.

Tell me at the same time if I can be of any shopping use to you— or perhaps you would rather see me first & Mr. Frémont is always on hand as courier & carrier. Yours affectionately,

J. B. Frémont

ALS (NjP—Blair-Lee Papers).

1. Upon receiving this plea, Francis Blair went to see Benton to smooth the way for JBF's visit. Blair found him "very amicable," in high spirits because he had just completed the second volume of his *Thirty Years' View* (Elizabeth Blair Lee to S. Phillips Lee, Apr. 28, 1856, NjP—Blair-Lee Papers). Blair accomplished his purpose: that same day Benton wrote JBF urging her to visit.
2. On Feb. 27, 1855, the Bentons' cherished C Street home in Washington had burned down when a fire originating in a defective chimney spread out of control (Washington *Union* and Benton interview in *Globe*, both Feb. 28, 1855).

Jessie Benton Frémont at twenty years of age. From a miniature by Dodge (courtesy of the Huntington Library, San Marino, Calif.).

John Charles Frémont. Photograph by Samuel Root (courtesy of the California State Library, Sacramento).

Thomas Hart Benton
(courtesy of the Southwest
Museum, Los Angeles).

Frémont's Rocky Mountain Flag (from John Charles Frémont, *Memoirs of My Life*).

Christopher (Kit) Carson (from
John Charles Frémont,
Memoirs of My Life).

Elizabeth Blair Lee at the age of
eighteen. Portrait by Thomas Sully
(courtesy of Mrs. P. Blair Lee, Philadelphia).

Samuel Phillips Lee, c. 1844. Portrait by Thomas Sully (courtesy of
Mrs. P. Blair Lee, Philadelphia).

Francis Preston Blair, Jr., Francis Preston Blair, Sr., and Montgomery Blair. Photograph by Gurney (courtesy of Blair House, The President's Guest House, Washington, D.C.).

VIEW OF THE LAST GREAT CONFLAGRATION IN SAN FRANCISCO ON THE 22ᵈ OF JUNE, 1851
TEN SQUARES BURNED, LOSS $3,000,000
VIEW TAKEN FROM THE HEAD OF CALIFORNIA STREET DURING THE PROGRESS OF THE FIRE
Pub. & Lith. by Justh Quirot & Co., California St., Corner Montgomery, S. F.

The San Francisco fire, June 22, 1851, burned Jessie Benton Frémont's home (courtesy of the California State Library, Sacramento).

John Charles Frémont in 1856. Portrait by T. Buchanan Read. The bullet hole in the lower right corner occurred in 1863 during the draft riots when the portrait hung in a New York City club (courtesy of the library of the Sons of the Revolution in the State of California, Glendale).

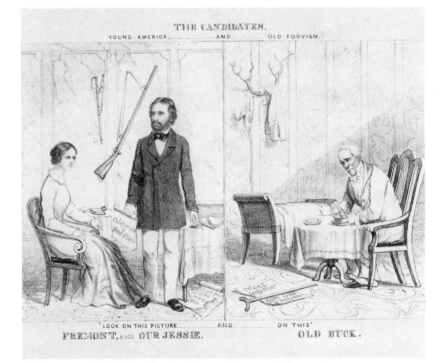

Republican cartoon, presidential campaign of 1856 (courtesy of the Huntington Library, San Marino, Calif.).

Bear Valley, Mariposa County. From *Hutchings' California Magazine*, Sept. 1859 (courtesy of the Huntington Library, San Marino, Calif.).

The Frémonts' home in Bear Valley. From a photograph by Carleton Watkins (courtesy of the California Historical Society, San Francisco).

Jessie Benton Frémont in 1861 at home on Black Point overlooking San Francisco Bay (courtesy of the Bancroft Library).

Thomas Starr King, c. 1861
(courtesy of the Bancroft Library).

Col. Franz Sigel, Gen. Frémont, and Capt. Constantine Blandowsky. John A.
Scholten's photograph of a painting by Carl Wimar, mentioned in Jessie Benton
Frémont to Thomas Starr King, Dec. 29–31, 1861 (courtesy of the Missouri
Historical Society, St. Louis).

Elizabeth Benton Frémont, early 1860s (courtesy of the Billings Mansion
Archives, Woodstock, Vt.).

Francis Preston Frémont in corporal's uniform, at the wedding of Frederick Billings, Mar. 31, 1862 (courtesy of the Billings Mansion Archives, Woodstock, Vt.).

Frederick Billings (from *New-England Historical and Genealogical Register*, 1891).

James T. Fields (courtesy of the Hougton Library, Harvard University).

THE STORY OF THE GUARD:

A CHRONICLE OF THE WAR.

By JESSIE BENTON FRÉMONT.

" Their good swords rust,
    And their steeds are dust,
    But their souls are with the saints, we trust."

BOSTON:

TICKNOR AND FIELDS.

1863.

Title page from Jessie Benton Frémont's first book.

Jessie Benton Frémont with Charles Zagonyi, John Raymond Howard, and John Charles Frémont. Another photograph (see letter to Thomas Starr King, [early 1863]), taken about the same time, included Rossiter W. Raymond (courtesy of the Bancroft Library).

John Greenleaf Whittier (from *Harper's Monthly Magazine*, Jan. 1884).

John Charles Frémont. Portrait by Guiseppe Fagnani in 1867 and the subject of Jessie Benton Frémont's letter to Emma Ballard, June 26, 1902 (courtesy of the Missouri Historical Society, St. Louis).

To Elizabeth Blair Lee

[Apr. 29 (1856)]

Dear Lizzie,

I had a very kind letter from Father who asks me to "come on and bring the whole" — Mr. Frémont & Nina will stay at home but all my blood I will take to him. It has been a sore thing to me to see Father and Mr. Frémont arraying themselves against each other & with Father's high sense of hospitality he would feel it a breach of honor to do anything against Mr. Frémont while I am under his roof — so I go to keep peace. It will be happier for himself in any event to be softer hearted. If we succeed Father will be cold & proud if he had worked against it — & if we failed his generosity would be very unacceptable to Mr. Frémont & I want to keep them on such terms that in any event neither will have to feel in a wrong position.

It will be only pleasure — no *arrière pensée* [ulterior motive] — with all your kind household. I shall not have the pleasure of seeing Mr. Lee or shewing him his manly little godson but you must make it up by admiring Frank as much as Charley.

I think I shall go on on Monday. Give our best love to your Mother who will appreciate my little Frank. Mr. F. has your Father's letter[1] in his hand. His lips are closed but his face is saying — to write — or not to write — that is a question that puzzles.[2] Yours affcty,

J. B. Frémont

Tuesday 29th April

ALS (NjP — Blair-Lee Papers).

1. Blair's letter was his "Voice from the Grave of Jackson!," a twenty-five-page statement condemning the South for splitting the Democratic party over slavery and claiming that if Andrew Jackson were alive, he would be a Republican. Blair's letter, copied out by Lizzie Lee, appeared on May 2 in the New York *Evening Post* and other newspapers. While the Democratic press branded it the senile ramblings of an old man, the letter exerted a powerful influence on moderate voters torn between the two parties.
2. JCF and his advisors were undecided about whether to use the public letter he was writing at the Republican mass meeting that night. Lizzie Lee reported the outcome to her husband: "F[rémont] did write to the New York Meeting & *so strong* that [Horace] Greel[e]y & a majority of the Committee would not allow it to be read — for fear of a spontaneous nomination — & then it would have [been] put forth that that was the object of the meeting — so the Ultras got more than they called for &

are now for keeping quiet" (June 9, 1856, NjP—Blair-Lee Papers). In his letter, JCF took his strongest stand yet against slavery: "I am opposed to slavery in the abstract and upon principle.... While I feel inflexible in the belief that it ought not to be interfered with where it exists ... I am as inflexibly opposed to its extension on this continent beyond the present limits." JCF's letter was finally published on June 17 (New York *Tribune*) during the Republican Convention and later in BIGELOW [1], 449.

To Charles Upham

[May 31, 1856]

Will Mr. Upham let my alterations stand? There was no "dash"[1] in our marriage—it was done in sober sadness on my part and as sober judgment on Mr. Frémont's. Two offers much more suited to my Father's ambition were favored by him, and we put between myself and any urging to the contrary the bar of the marriage ceremony. I returned to my Mother's house and was there until some six weeks after (Mr. Frémont going to Charleston for that time) when both gave their consent to our avowing the marriage.

I was not born at St. Louis but in Virginia at the family seat of my grandfather Col. McDowell where they had all been born for generations before me. I am through my mother a regular "F.F.V."[2] as the newspapers have them, and am not without my weakness in favor of good blood and gentle birth at least a century and a half—the time in which the family have occupied that place.

Both my brothers were born in St. Louis, where they both chanced to die—after many absences from that place—and there they are buried,[3] but I and my sisters are all Virginians.

As for the flattering termination[4] I can say as Portia did to Brutus

"Should I not be stronger than my sex
Being so Fathered and so Husbanded"—[5]

and that accounts I believe for any merit I may have.

I only got in last night from Washington[6] and am thoroughly tired & hurried also as Mr. Frémont is waiting to take this with him to the Post which must explain & excuse its scragginess.

It is quite fortunate I do not mind in the least having it known what my age is. This is my 32d birthday and Mr. Frémont was good enough to say I had not the traces of so many years.

Some of them have been heavy and bitter but few ever had so much to be grateful for as I. Very sincerely yours,

Jessie Benton Frémont

May 31' 1856.
56 W. 9th St.

ALS (MHi—Quincy, Wendell, Holmes, and Upham Family Papers in the Collection of Hugh Upham Clark. Microfilm). Harvard-educated Charles Wentworth Upham (1802-75) was a Unitarian clergyman and former Whig congressman who by 1856 had become a Republican. In the spring of 1856, at the urging of Charles James, Isaac Sherman, and others, and with the cooperation of the Frémonts, Upham had embarked on a campaign biography, *Life, Explorations and Public Services of John Charles Fremont,* to be published by the Boston firm of Ticknor and Fields (Upham to Isaac Sherman, June 27, 1856, editors' copy). In his preface, Upham would acknowledge receiving "details and dates, with some very interesting documents" from JCF. In reality, he, like Bigelow, was furnished with a version of JCF's background that covered up such aspects as his illegitimacy.

1. Upham evidently eliminated the "dash" to which JBF objected, writing of the marriage: "On the 19th of October, 1841, he [JCF] was married, in the city of Washington, to Jessie, daughter of the Hon. Thomas H. Benton. . . . It is not at all strange that objections were made to the match. A second lieutenant . . . surely had nothing to recommend him, in the way of worldly goods or prospects. He had not then commenced his great career,—no world-wide lustre had begun to emblazon his name. . . . But the instincts of a pure heart are often the truest wisdom; and he was preferred before all that fashion, wealth, and great station could offer" (UPHAM, 20-21).
2. "First Family of Virginia."
3. Both JBF's brothers died young: James McDowell, "a doomed consumptive," in 1831 at age four; and John Randolph, a probable alcoholic, of a sudden fever in 1852 at age twenty-two.
4. Upham's "flattering termination" was evidently, "All that it would be proper to say of her in this work, is all that could be said of any woman,—she is worthy of her origin, and of her lot" (UPHAM, 21).
5. JBF often paraphrased lines spoken by Portia, Brutus's wife, in Shakespeare's *Julius Caesar,* act 2, sc. 1, ll. 292-97.

> I grant I am a woman; but withal
> A woman that Lord Brutus took to wife.
> I grant I am a woman; but withal
> A woman well-reputed, Cato's daughter.
> Think you I am no stronger than my sex,
> Being so father'd and so husbanded?

Also see versions in JBF to A. K. McClure, June 25, 1877, and to [W. A. Croffut], [Nov. 30, 1885], below; and JBF, "Memoirs," 96.
6. JBF had postponed her Washington trip several times. When she finally arrived in late May, perhaps by a mutual wish to avoid a confrontation, Benton had already

set out for St. Louis, stopping en route at the Democratic Convention in Cincinnati on June 2. There he campaigned "hard and hot" for James Buchanan who was nominated on the seventeenth ballot (HALSTEAD, 22). Meanwhile, in Washington, JBF endured the antagonism of her sister Liz and her husband, William Carey Jones. Both JBF and Lizzie Lee blamed much of the breach with Benton on "the everlasting Jones's envious din" (Elizabeth Blair Lee to S. Phillips Lee, May 6, 1856, NjP—Blair-Lee Papers).

To Charles Upham

New York, June 4th 1856.
56 W. 9th St.

My Dear Mr. Upham,

Mr. Frémont was just leaving for an engagement down-town as your note arrived and he leaves it for me to answer. The Delaware is named "Saghundai."[1] Through Mr. James's perserverance we were able to get a very good daguerreotype of him & Mr. McNevin[2] is such an admirable artist that it will be the fault of the wood-engravers if that and Carson's[3] portraits (both of which will be ready to-morrow) are not perfectly faithful and characteristic. The likeness of Mr. Frémont is so excellent that it is not to be risked away from Mr. McNevin's superintendence. It will be engraved here. When I say that *I* am quite contented with it, there remains nothing more to say in its praise. It will be ready in the time you give.

This summer will go by like a dream in the pleasant work of preparing his work & overlooking the progress of the illustrations—which is Mr. Frémont's plan for the next six months. It is his vocation & mine too—a more refining one than experiences in political selfishness and treason—in either case however he is not wanting in the will as well as the capacity to "make his mark."

You were so necessarily behind the conventional curtains with which society forces one into covering from view their real feelings, that I make no fashion about speaking to you so sincerely of Mr. Frémont. It is such a luxury to speak without thinking. Yours very sincerely,

J. B. Frémont

ALS (MHi—Quincy, Wendell, Holmes, and Upham Family Papers in the Collection of Hugh Upham Clark. Microfilm).

1. Delaware Indian chief James Sagundai (variously spelled Saghundai, Secondi, Secondai), with approximately eight other Delawares, had accompanied JCF on his third expedition (1845–47) (SPENCE & JACKSON, 6, 10n, 113-19). Upham and later JCF in his *Memoirs* describe Sagundai's vengeful bravery when JCF's party was ambushed by Klamath Indians while camped near Upper Klamath Lake in southern Oregon.

2. John McNevin was an obscure historical painter and illustrator working in New York City in the 1850s, who later contributed to *Harper's Weekly* (GROCE & WALLACE, 418). A portrait, presumably of Sagundai but labeled only "One of the Delaware Body Guard," appears in UPHAM opposite p. 342. A different portrait of Sagundai appears in JCF's *Memoirs*.

3. JCF's guide during his first three expeditions, Christopher ("Kit") Carson (1809–68), was an experienced trapper and scout with a photographic memory for terrain. His loyalty, courage, and knowledge proved invaluable to JCF; in turn, the expedition reports did much to make Carson famous. It was most probably JBF who wrote the first newspaper account of Carson's exploits, an unsigned article published in the Washington *Union* (June 15, 1847; partially reprinted in BIGELOW [1], 139-41). See also her later accounts in New York *Ledger,* Feb. 20, 1875; *Wide Awake,* 30 (Feb. 1890): 193-98, reprinted in *The Will and the Way Stories;* and *Land of Sunshine,* 6 (Feb. 1897), reprinted in *Historical Society of Southern California Quarterly,* 42 (Dec. 1960): 331-34.

To Elizabeth Blair Lee

Monday June 9th [1856]
56 W. 9th st.

My dear Lizzie,

I had written to Susy that I would be with her Saturday evening[1] and was to have been also bearer of verbal despatches to your Father — but Friday morning (just one year from the last year's illness) I had a violent attack of neuralgia — beginning as the other did in cramping at the heart. This time my head shared the attack & I write now with one eye blackened & nearly closed by the stagnated blood which will have to be leeched off. Last year my recent accouchement made it more dangerous for the pain fell upon every vital part in the trunk. I doubt however if human endurance could stand worse pain than I had at intervals for two days and nights — and you know I cannot take chloroform.

I am worn out by it, although I am over it now. That was a very bad visit I had to Washington. The disappointment of missing Father, the want of hospitality in the house and the fatigue were altogether too much. I felt when at your house that I was a little from under my own control. I heard myself saying things I was not pleased with but had not the control of myself to restrain & I half thought I needed care—but up to a given point I am strong as Sampson, then I am just as good for nothing, and once at home I fell into the good for nothing state.

After this I will watch myself and not let such another accumulation of anxieties and fatigues overtake me.

Do come with your Father to Philadelphia[2]—and get there the 15th or 16th. I would go there to meet you if it was before the Convention. All the proprieties forbid it after the 16th.[3] After the Convention you are bound to come—to triumph with us I hope—and if not, to see how much we have to fall back upon at home in case of defeat. So in any event we shall see you. I hardly think it safe for me to leave home after such severe pain but I wish to go to Susan—and may do so. When I look at my strong frame & see how sound the covering is, I cannot realize that it is all so at the mercy of every agitation that touches too keenly that one little organ. But this last week I realized it entirely. I did not get to see Mrs. Weaver at all & may never now. I know you will care for her. How differently do we two fare in illness. It does not seem right that one should have so much & another nothing. "But they shall inherit the Kingdom of Heaven."[4]

[*Margin note:* Your enclosures (will?) be attended to. Mr. B.[5] was at Cincinnati & is not here yet. See the Tribune of the 6th.[6]]

AL (NjP—Blair-Lee Papers).

1. Susan Benton Boilleau was expecting her first baby.
2. Lizzie Lee did accompany her elderly father to the Republican convention in Philadelphia on June 17, ostensibly to watch over his health since he had been ill with diarrhea the previous week (Elizabeth Blair Lee to S. Phillips Lee, June 14, 1856, NjP—Blair-Lee Papers). Blair carried a letter authorizing him to represent JCF at the convention (JCF to Blair, [June] 17 [1856], NN—Bigelow Papers). A reporter in attendance found Blair "a little old gentleman, thin, slender, and feeble in appearance, yet moving about with considerable activity. . . . He is treated with distinguished consideration, and the mention of his name is invariably followed by uproarious applause. . . . The old fellow's big head glistens with intelligence" (HALSTEAD, 92, 101).
3. Mid-nineteenth-century political etiquette dictated that presidential hopefuls not appear at conventions. Even after the nomination was secured, the candidate remained at home, issuing occasional public letters and greeting visitors, while others stumped on his behalf. Both JCF and Buchanan would conform to this tradition.
4. See Matthew 5:3.
5. Here "Mr. B" seems to be John Bigelow, who was evidently covering the Democratic Convention in Cincinnati for the New York *Evening Post*. Blair's "enclosures"

were probably for publication in the *Post,* where his public statements first appeared during this period.

6. In an influential editorial on June 6, the astute, powerful, and eccentric New York *Tribune* editor Horace Greeley (1811–72) had endorsed JCF as the most electable of the Republican candidates. "Though young and born poor, he has done more service, braved more peril, and achieved more reputation, than any man of his years now living. That must be a very dark and squat log cabin into which the fame of Col. Fremont has not penetrated ere this." Privately, however, Greeley still had doubts about JCF: "All would be well if F[rémont] were not the merest baby in politics," he wrote Schylur Colfax. He was also concerned about "shabbiness" in JCF's Las Mariposas venture (ISELY, 164). Nonetheless, in editorials on June 11 and 12, Greeley strongly endorsed JCF: "There is no name which can find such favor with the masses." Even JCF's political naivete had become an asset: "We have had enough of third-rate lawyers and God knows what rate generals."

To Charles Upham

[June 12, 1856]

My Dear Mr. Upham,

I am entirely put out by the engraving of Mr. Frémont's likeness being taken away from Mr. McNevin. The likeness was perfectly natural and good, but they judge differently at the publishers and are I think going to make a fancy head according to the received flash idea of a "dashing adventurer."

Will you oblige me by preventing this. Messrs. Ticknor and Field[s][1] are on my black list already for the paragraph they had circulated about the book & of which both Mr. Frémont & I spoke to Mr. Andrews.[2] They look at it as a speculation but I hope you have it in your power to keep some check upon their ideas and at least let a true likeness of Mr. Frémont be inserted, or none at all, & please do not leave it to them to send on the proof sheets. Yours very truly,

J. B. Frémont

ALS (MHi—Quincy, Wendell, Holmes, and Upham Family Papers in the Collection of Hugh Upham Clark. Microfilm). Endorsed "J.B. Fremont, June 12 1856."

1. William Davis Ticknor (1810–64) had founded the prestigious Boston publishing firm of Ticknor and Fields in 1832. James T. Fields (1817–81) became his partner in 1854, and when the firm acquired the *Atlantic Monthly* five years later, Fields assumed its editorship. JBF would correspond extensively with the genial and highly capable Fields when the firm published her *Story of the Guard.*

The paragraph JBF found objectionable was probably Ticknor and Fields's advertisement for Upham's forthcoming biography of Frémont, in which they incorrectly stated that its illustrations would be based on "scenes taken in daguerreotype by himself while on his great expeditions" (New York *Times*, June 6, 1856). In reality, the only expedition daguerreotypes in existence were those taken by Solomon N. Carvalho during the fifth expedition; no illustrations based on these appeared in the Upham biography.

2. Israel De Wolf Andrews of Nova Scotia, a political associate of Nathaniel Banks, had acquired an unsavory reputation during his promotion of the Canadian-American trade reciprocity treaty of 1854, for which he openly purchased votes and editorial support. There is some evidence that during the 1856 campaign, he and Charles James schemed to steal Maine campaign funds (GIENAPP, 377). Andrews died of alcoholism in 1871.

To Charles Upham

June 25th. [1856]

My dear Sir,

Ticknor & Fields have by their unjustifiable hurry ruined the mouth in the likeness of Mr. Frémont. A half hour's work will make it correct, but I hardly expect of them to do the justice, by delaying it even that long.

A really good likeness under my superintendence will be put in a life now preparing here—and if the publishers there do not put the face as it should be, the daily papers here shall say the only authentic likeness of Mr. Frémont—the only one he does not feel to be a misrepresentation & caricature, is in the life to be published by Derby.[1]

I really think this is the only [way] to get them in Boston to give Mr. Frémont his true face. That under lip ought to prejudice thousands against him & will do it.

I write in the full vexation of the first look at the caricature & have to ask you to so understand my positiveness—but I mean to prevent that from being looked upon as an authenticated likeness unless they much alter that mouth. Yours truly,

J. B. F.

I think the closing chapter very very well written.

AL initialed (MHi—Quincy, Wendell, Holmes, and Upham Family Papers in the Collection of Hugh Upham Clark. Microfilm). Endorsed "J. B. Frémont, June 25, 1856."

1. John Bigelow's campaign biography, to be published by Derby & Jackson of New York City.

To Elizabeth Blair Lee

[June 29, 1856]

Dear Lizzie,

Mr. Frémont is entirely put out by the idea that you or your Father may feel unattended to by neither of us having gone down to the boat.[1]

It is in vain I tell him you will not feel so. His late ill turn & my own ailments for which you have experienced sympathy, are reason enough for not going through the form of sitting opposite you in silence — for none of us speak on Broadway.

Do give me a message of comfort to him for the wrinkle will not leave his forehead for my telling.

You know how fully I appreciated your Father's giving up his own sweet country home for our heated air & narrow space. Nothing but his political triumphs present & to come could have reconciled me to his being so uncomfortable and we have been so busy & I so weary with the heat that I have not attended to you at all as I wished — but you are both so full of sense and I hope so assured of my love and gratitude that I do not think of any misinterpreting on your part.

Thank Mrs. Blair for lending us Mr. Blair so long. Mr. Frémont says he is going to come in suddenly some day & make his thanks himself — and thank you for listening to your unselfishness in staying & Mr. Lee, (if he doesn't scold about it), for his in letting you. Yours affectionately,

J.B.F.

Sunday evening

AL initialed (NjP—Blair-Lee Papers). En route home from the Philadelphia convention, where JCF was nominated by cheering delegates on the first ballot, Lizzie Lee and Francis Blair spent a celebratory ten days with the Frémonts in New York. Blair reported afterward to his son Frank: "I have just returned from New York where I left a vast deal of enthusiasm [around?] Frémont which I think will continue to rise and to spread until it carries him to the Presidency. But you know my sanguine temperament, I never think a good cause can fail" (July 1, 1856, DLC—Blair Papers).

1. The boat was probably the Jersey City Ferry, which departed from the foot of Cortlandt Street and connected with the New Jersey Railroad, bound for Philadelphia, Baltimore, and Washington. On another occasion Francis Blair wrote his son Frank, "Jessie & Frémont could not be satisfied without crossing [on] the Jersey City ferry to see us all the way" (May 14, 1857, DLC—Blair Papers).

To Dr. John Roberton

New York, June 30th 1856.
56 West 9th street.

My dear Dr. Roberton

Your friendly letter has been here some days but it is quite impossible to control the tide of interruptions which sweep away all our private arrangements[1]

I can only find time now to say this much and to assure your enquiring friend that Mr. Frémont was born and educated in the Protestant Episcopal Church—for more exactness, at St. Phillips Church in Charleston, that he is now in the same church—that I am too an Episcopalian and our children were all baptized in that church.[2] Neither has either of us ever owned any slaves, which is the other bugbear.

I think with you that no question should be made of any one's religion and that all religions should be respected but since many people think differently this is an answer to them.

We shall see you on Sunday perhaps. Mr. Frémont is tired out and has just had to go down town but I add his kindest remembrances to you. Yours with the highest regard and respect,

Jessie Benton Frémont

ALS (MoSHi—Thomas Hart Benton Papers). Seventy-year-old Roberton was a classical scholar and teacher educated at the University of Edinburgh, with whom JCF had studied Greek and Latin as a youth in Charleston. In a long, laudatory passage in the preface to his 1850 translation of Xenophon's *Anabasis*, Roberton described JCF as a slender, graceful youth with a "keen, piercing eye" and a "noble forehead, seemingly the very seat of genius. . . . whatever he read, he retained. . . . It was easy to see that he would some day raise himself to eminence." During the campaign the complete passage was reprinted in the New York *Tribune* (June 24, 1856) and other newspapers and in BIGELOW [1], 24–27.

1. "This house has people pouring in from all quarters from 6 oclk in the mng until late at night," Lizzie Lee reported from the Frémonts' residence on June 27 (E. B. SMITH [1], 231).

2. Although the Frémont campaign had barely begun, JBF was already trying to deal with the false but persistent rumor that JCF was a secret Catholic. The rumor was based on the fact that his father was French and presumably Catholic, and that he and JBF had been married by a Catholic priest. However, JCF's mother was Episcopalian, and in June 1827, at age fourteen, JCF had been confirmed in St. Paul's (Episcopal) Church in Charleston by Bishop Nathaniel Bowen for St. Philip's congregation (JACKSON & SPENCE, xxiv).

Bigelow [1], 27, includes the following affidavit, which JBF secured from her parish rector:

Washington City, July 12, 1856.

The following children of J. Charles and Jessie Benton Fremont have been baptized in the church of the parish of the Epiphany, Washington, D.C.—their baptisms being recorded in the register of said parish:

1848, Aug. 15, Elizabeth McDowell Benton Fremont.
1848, Aug. 15, Benton Fremont.
1853, Dec. 28. John Charles Fremont.
1855, Aug. 1, Francis Preston Fremont.

As none were baptized in a house, *but all were brought to the church,* the order of the Protestant Episcopal Church for "the Ministration of Public Baptism of Infants," was that which was used.

J. W. French
Rector of the parish of the Epiphany, Washington, D.C.

To Charles Upham

June 30th. [1856].

My dear Sir,

The corrected engraving came this morning and I must ask you to thank Mssrs. Ticknor & Fields for the delay which I recognize as a loss to them.

The advertisement of Derby was without any authorization from Mr. Frémont & without the knowledge of either of us. That of Ticknor & Fields cannot be hurt by it, but I have sent a note to Mr. Bigelow to have the notice altered—if I can, so as to make the exception in favor of your work.[1]

Please do not misinterpret any vehemence I may have manifested about the picture. It is my weakness to wish all to share my admiration of Mr. Frémont's character as shewn in his face. Yours very truly,

Jessie Benton Frémont

I have not time to write two notes & beg you to say all this for me to Mr. Fields and Mr. Ticknor.

ALS (MHi—Quincy, Wendell, Holmes, and Upham Family Papers in the Collection of Hugh Upham Clark. Microfilm). Endorsed, "J. B. Frémont, June 30, 1856."

1. Upham had complained to Frémont aide Isaac Sherman that Derby & Jackson were advertising Bigelow's forthcoming biography as "the Only Authorized Edition," thereby discrediting his own work. "It ought not to be forgotten that I have incurred expense, and given my time to this labor, and my interests and rights are to be considered." Ticknor and Fields would also be upset if JCF sanctioned such an advertisement: "My publishers are men of influence. Mr. Fields stands high among our literary men—is a popular poet and his genius has been kindled to a high pitch by interest in the cause. I send you with this a Boston Transcript of to-day containing a song by him, entitled, 'Jessie Frémont.' He ought not to be estranged" (June 27, 1856, editors' copy).

On July 1, the Derby & Jackson advertisement in the *Tribune* (but not in the *Times* or the *Evening Post*) was altered to eliminate the word "only" from the phrase "authorized edition," but later the word reappeared. Finally by July 12 in the *Evening Post*, Bigelow's paper, the "only" permanently disappeared. Meanwhile Ticknor and Fields, advertising the Upham biography as "the authorized life of Frémont," profited from the fact that it was published on July 1, while Bigelow's was delayed, evidently due to JBF's additions on Frémont family background, until Aug. 6 (New York *Tribune* and New York *Times*, June 28–30, July 1–7, 1856; New York *Evening Post*, July 1–15, Aug. 7, 1856; CLAPP, 103–5).

To Elizabeth Blair Lee

July 2. 3 P.M. [1856]

Dear Lizzie,

Your note is just received—one from your Father (in wonderfully legible hand-writing) came this morning. I am as usual, tired, so I only answer to say your note ran the gauntlet of the Washington Post Office safely and Mr. Frémont has your Father's suggestions in time.[1]

I have most acceptable and good letters from Virginia. I go on Saturday to Old Point Comfort. Mr. Frémont says I must go by Washington & stay there a day. I don't know if I shall. I think no time is to be lost in seeing into all that can be collected in regard to Mr. Frémont's Mother.[2] I am invited by her great niece & her nephew Kennon Whiting to Hampton (near Richmond).[3] Mrs. Cocke (my cousin)[4] writes me from Old Point & says if I will come at once I shall be in the midst of Mr. Frémont's relations who all want to know us. (This horrible pen is *Mr.* Frémont's & blacks my finger without making any headway.)

Miss Whiting (who seems a very nice person) writes to ask me to come & see them at their own place. She is at Old Point. I am horribly tired & don't write sense I'm afraid.

Buchanan Read[5] is making a very sweet head that resembles me "as the dew resembles rain"—it is barely founded on fact & weighs thirty pounds more than the present remains of your affectionate friend & "fellow laborer"

Jessie B. Frémont

I send you a printed version of our parlor talk—the last sentence especially is something cruel.[6]

[*Margin note:* Mr. Frémont says "Thank Mr. Lee for his attention to the Beverley matter."[7]]

ALS (NjP—Blair-Lee Papers).

1. Blair's suggestions were probably intended for JCF's major postconvention pronouncement, contained in a July 8 letter in which he accepted the Republican presidential nomination (New York *Tribune,* July 9, 1856; reprinted in BIGELOW [1] 456–60). In it, JCF condemned the South for its attempt to impose slavery across the continent and advocated the admission of Kansas to the Union as a free state. Unlike his letter to the Apr. 29 New York Republican meeting, it expressed no moral opposition to slavery, but instead stressed the harm done free labor by competition with slaves. These themes, which reflected Blair's less radical position on slavery, would be emphasized by Republican campaign speakers eager to garner moderate northern votes.

2. Hoping to silence questions about JCF's legitimacy, JBF planned to gather material in Virginia on his family background for inclusion in Bigelow's campaign biography.

3. JBF had located several relatives of JCF's mother, the former Anne Beverley Whiting, including a sister, Susan (or Susanna), who in 1792 had married John Lowry; a nephew, Kennon Whiting (1796–1886), son of Anne's brother, Thomas Beverley Whiting, and his wife, Elizabeth (Kennon); and a grandniece, Elizabeth ("Lizzie") Tomasia Whiting (b. 1833), daughter of Kennon Whiting and his wife Anne (Mallory) (1803–76). For Whiting genealogy, see *Virginia Magazine of History and Biography,* 32 (1924): 130–31 and 33 (1925): 203; *William and Mary College Quarterly Historical Magazine,* ser. 1, 8 (1899–1900): 55; *Tyler's Quarterly Historical and Genealogical Magazine,* 12 (1930–31): 259–62; and BROCK, 689.

4. Elizabeth Randolph (Preston) Cocke (1808–89) was a daughter of Thomas Lewis Preston, brother of JBF's grandmother, Sarah Preston McDowell. Elizabeth was the widow of William Armistead Cocke (1798–1855) of "Oakland," Cumberland County, Va. (DORMAN, 303–6; *Virginia Magazine of History and Biography,* 4 [1897]: 447–48). She wrote JBF cordially on June 26, describing the Whiting family, enclosing a note from Lizzie Whiting, and inviting her to visit (NN—Bigelow Papers).

5. Fashionable poet and artist Thomas Buchanan Read (1822–72) painted campaign portraits of both JCF and JBF. Read's work was highly regarded in his day; as JBF suggests, he tended to prettify his female subjects.

6. JBF's enclosed clipping, reprinted from the Cleveland *Herald* by an unidentified newspaper, recounts an admiring editor's interview with the Frémonts during the Blairs'

postconvention visit. A final paragraph recalls Benton's opposition to his daughter's marriage, cites JBF's pride in her husband's rise "from obscurity to the confidence and hearts of his countrymen," and quotes her as saying, "I long to see dear father, and say to him that for once he was mistaken,—the Colonel [JCF] has not been used and thrown by!"

7. The Beverley matter presumably relates to JCF's mother, Anne Beverley Whiting.

To John Bigelow

Silver Spring
Monday 7th July [1856].

Dear Mr. Bigelow,

We made an overhauling of Sparks[1] & other authorities last night & I give you results by telegraph. Would it not be well to print what you have ready and put on another page or wrapper (it would in that way strike the attention more) such information as I may have to add. For some reasons, (good & of weight if I had time to go into telling them) I think it best to republish at once your life as given in the Post—& that without delay. What I gather can be added, as what it really is, information given by Mr. Frémont's relations, from having [read?] that.

[George] Washington was the grandson of John Washington & Catherine *Whiting* of *Gloster* or Gloucester Co. (it is written both ways).[2]

Mr. Frémont's grandfather was "Col. Thomas *Whiting* of *Gloster* Co— a member of the House of Burgesses & a man of great note & wealth." This was written me by his [great] granddaughter Miss Lizzie Whiting who has the will of Col. Thomas Whiting in which Mr. Frémont's Mother Anne Beverley Whiting is included with his other children.[3]

I have only to find the exact relationship between Washington's grandmother & Mr. Frémont's grandfather & then it is all clear statement.

The Blairs will not let me go alone to Old Point, where the Whitings now are & where they have invited me to meet them—so that Mr. Lee goes with me. He says his is a better name to travel south with than Frémont or Blair—but I am not much afraid of any rudeness on that score. Very truly yours,

Jessie B. Frémont

Sparks Life of Washington
Vol. 1, page 553. & the Chapter [preceding?]

ALS (NN—Bigelow Papers).

1. Jared Sparks's *Life of Washington* (1839), first published as volume one of his *Writings of George Washington* (1834–37), included what for JBF was a real coup, a memorandum by George Washington himself in which he sketched his ancestry, including his Whiting connection. JBF had appropriate portions reprinted in BIGELOW [1], 12–13.

2. George Washington's father, Capt. Augustine Washington (d. 1743) was the brother of John Washington (1692–1746), who in 1716 married Catherine Whiting (1694–1734), a sister of JCF's great grandfather, Maj. Henry Whiting (d. 1728). Therefore, George Washington (1732–99) was a nephew, not a grandson, of John Washington; and John's wife, Catherine (Whiting) Washington, was his aunt by marriage (*Virginia Magazine of History and Biography*, 32 [1924]: 130; SPARKS, 505–7).

3. Thomas Whiting (1712–81) was a member of the House of Burgesses from Gloucester County from 1755 to 1775 (*Virginia Magazine of History and Biography*, 32 [1924]: 130). JCF's mother, Anne Beverley Whiting, the last of his many children by three wives, was born shortly before his death. His will, dated Oct. 15, 1780, is printed in BIGELOW [1], 14–16.

Notes for John Bigelow on Frémont Family Background [July 1856]

Elizabeth Sewall [Seawell] married, had five children-1st Thomas Whiting & by him [number left blank][1] 2nd Sam'l Cary & by him had four children, dying left Sam'l Cary guardian to her children by both marriages.

Sam'l Cary was sued by the five children of the lst marriage for their father's estate.[2]

Anne Beverley Whiting, the youngest child of Thomas Whiting and Elizabeth Sewall [Seawell], was but six months old at the time of her Father's death. Consequently her share of property and slaves which should have increased greatly before her coming of age was the most defenceless in the hands of Sam'l Cary.

Mrs. Lowry (Catherine Whiting) was married when Mrs. E[lizabeth] Sewall [Seawell] Cary died,[3] & the stepfather's home being disagreeable from the vexations of law suits, Anne Whiting went to her sister Catherine to live.

Catherine (Mrs. Lowry) arranged a marriage between her sister & Major Pryor who was a very rich man. She was but seventeen & he 62 at the time of the marriage. Her sister Mrs. Lowry told me her sister was very unwilling to marry Major Pryor—and was a very melancoly woman.[4]

They had been married about 12 years when they separated by mutual agreement & being divorced, both married again, he a Miss Gray & she Mr. Frémont.[5] ...

Anne Beverley married,—very young & a lovely woman—through the arrangement of her sister Mrs. Lowry, to Major Pryor. [*Margin note*: Courted the mother Elizabeth Sewall (Seawell) who married a Cary & had several children all dead grand children living.] A man of wealth, but of not equally high social position & not at all of refinement of character. He was about sixty years of age and not in good health— gouty. Major Pryor engaged as French teacher for his wife Mr. Frémont who was then teaching French in an Academy there.[6]

Miss Kitty Cowne,[7] [*Margin note*: Catherine her aunt] was living with Mrs. Pryor in Richmond at this time. Mrs. Pryor had no children. Col. Pryor became suspicious of Mr. Frémont. Miss Kitty Cowne, then about twenty-four years of age (this is direct information from her sister Susan Lowry Cowne—now Mrs. Dr. [W. M.] Helme of Warrenton, Farquier Co. Virginia) was with her Aunt at the time of her separation from Mr. Pryor. [*Margin note*: Her Father Robert Cowne came for her & took her away afterwards.] A separation brought on by Mr. Pryor's suspicion & violence. He charged her in the presence of Mr. Frémont & Miss Cowne with ill conduct threatening at the same time to kill her. She told him "to spare himself the crime that she would leave his house the next morning." She did wait until the next day when she left him and went with Mr. Frémont to Norfolk. (how long)[8]

Then went to the South—the first child was born Jany. 21—1813(?).[9]

Mr. Pryor re-married a Miss Gray within ⟨*a very short time*⟩—as soon as a ⟨*month afterwards*⟩. Legislature in session granted divorce at once. woman housekeeper.

(The power to re-marry must be looked into. See Mr. Kennon Whiting & Dr. Helm.)[10]

The marriage of Mr. & Mrs. Frémont was immediate on Mr. Pryor's divorce.

AD (NN—Bigelow Papers). Endorsed, "Mrs. Frémont's memorial of the family of Col. Frémont. Recd July 15, 1856." During her visit to Frémont relatives in Virginia, JBF took a series of discursive and incomplete notes to be used in preparing the chapter on JCF's parentage and birth for Bigelow's campaign biography. Hidden in the notes is the dramatic and poignant tale of a young woman, Anne Whiting Pryor, caught in a loveless marriage, who ran off with a French emigré, Charles Fremon, in a desperate bid for happiness. The notes also reveal that JBF found no proof of her divorce or remarriage. In contrast, JBF's version as it appears in BIGELOW [1], 12–21, first plays on the "gilded wretchedness" of Anne Whiting's marriage to John C. Pryor, then neatly ends the story with a prompt divorce by the state legislature and remarriage for each, she to Fremon and he to his housekeeper. Printed here are those notes that relate to JCF's mother, her marriage to Pryor and her elopement with Charles Fremon; omitted are several irrelevant or repetitive pages on Whiting family ancestry.

1. Elizabeth Seawell was Thomas Whiting's third wife. Presumably their children were Henry, Horatio, Susanna, Jane, and "Ann" (Anne Beverley), listed as "my five youngest" in Thomas Whiting's will (ibid., 15).

2. JBF located a June 13, 1810, Superior Court of Chancery, Richmond, decree evidently relating to the litigation between the Whiting children and their stepfather, Samuel Cary. In it Anne Beverley Whiting and her then husband, Pryor, received from Thomas Whiting's estate "the negroes contained in lot No. 3, viz.: Phil $400, Black Peter $400, Peggy $300, Hannah and children Stirling and Salley $580, Billey $250" (ibid., 17–18).

3. According to John Pryor's Dec. 1, 1810, ms. divorce petition (Vi), Elizabeth (Seawell) Whiting Cary was still alive when Anne Beverley married.

4. Maj. John C. Pryor (d. 1823) was an elderly Revolutionary War officer who owned Richmond's largest livery stable as well as Haymarket Garden, a two-acre amusement park adjacent to the Pryor home (NEVINS [1], 4). He and Anne Beverley Whiting were married in 1796 (Pryor ms. divorce petition). While JBF's notes blame Catherine Lowry for pushing the marriage, Anne Whiting later explained to her sister's husband: "To exculpate myself from blame, I shall not pretend to do, only to relate simply the truth, I was married too young to be sensible of the importance of the state in which I was about to enter, and found when too late that I had acted with too much precipitancy, and could never feel that love for him to whom I was united, without which the marriage state of all others is the most wretched. . . . I could always have respected, and esteemed him as a father, but to love as a husband I could not" (Anne Beverley [Whiting] Pryor to John Lowry, Aug. 28, 1811, attachment to Pryor ms. divorce petition).

5. Pryor's divorce petition is endorsed "Dec. 11, 1811, rejected," and no record of a subsequent divorce has been found.

6. In his divorce petition, Pryor states that he and Anne met Charles Fremon when the Frenchman rented a small house on Pryor's property: "In a short time after this, the said Charles Fremon became very intimate in the house of your Petitioner, and as was customary, was treated with civility and hospitality, taking advantage of which, the said Fremon (as your Petitioner has since discovered) used every strategem in his power basely and perfidiously to seduce by intrigue your Petitioner's said wife Anna; in which, unfortunately, he was too successful so as to alienate her affections totally from your petitioner and persuade her to a criminal intercourse with him."

7. Kitty Cowne, a niece of Anne (Whiting) Pryor and Catherine (Whiting) Lowry, was the daughter of Capt. Robert Cowne (1754–1829) and his wife Sarah (Whiting) (WULFECK, 1:166).

8. Anne Pryor, in her letter to her brother-in-law, claimed, "I did not run away, but was turned out of doors at night and in an approaching storm . . . my treatment

becoming such I was compelled to leave." Both she and John Pryor stated that he had allowed her to take two female slaves, "Hannah and her little girl," from her inheritance from her father. In his divorce petition, Pryor denied any ill treatment.

9. According to John Pryor's petition account, Anne told him she was going to her sister's. Instead, she took the stage to Norfolk with Charles Fremon and then went on with him to Charleston, intending eventually to settle in Savannah. It was in Savannah that their first child, John Charles Fremon, was born (JCF later added the "t"). JBF's question mark after JCF's birthdate suggests she was unsure of even this point.

10. The notes here are confused, as was JBF, about whether John and Anne Pryor had divorced and whether Anne and Charles Fremon were able to marry. Nonetheless, it was JBF's task, through her Bigelow chapter, to transform the scandal in the Republican nominee's past into sentimental romance.

To Elizabeth Blair Lee

Staten Island[1] July 23d [1856].

Dear Lizzie,

The sea air has kept me from "melting" but not from illness, but I am up again and answer your letter directly to points.

Question 1st says

Whether application was made to any other minister than the Catholic one to perform the service? Mr. Frémont says yes. He went to see Mr. Seaton,[2] making an application to him in general terms, and received an unfavorable answer. This was after failing with the clergyman whose name Mr. Frémont tries vainly to recall. [*Margin note:* I don't know any of those details & so leave it to Mr. Frémont to answer.]

Q. 2d Civil contract or Sacrament.

Civil contract only, I should say. It was in a drawing room—no altar lights or any such thing—I was asked nothing but my age—& the whole was very short.[3]

Mother did wish the marriage to be made again by a Protestant clergyman—but Father said it would cause scandal—you can easily see why.[4]

Mr. Frémont was confirmed by the then Bishop of South Carolina in 1826 [1827], at Charleston in the Church of St. Philip. His brother and sister were also members of that church. [*Margin note:* They were both buried in its church yard by their Mother.][5]

Mr. Frémont's mother was very decided in her attachment to her own church—the Episcopalian & when Nina was but six years old, every morning of the time she was with us, Nina and herself read the morning lesson together, and she was very anxious I should keep Nina firm in that faith.

When Mr. Nicollet went to Baltimore a room was always kept for him in St. Mary's College at Baltimore & Mr. Frémont as his friend & companion was always invited about with him—to dine there & at the Bishop's. Bishop Chanc[h]e[6] especially, afterwards Bishop of Natchez wrote to him when we were married blaming him for the manner & regretting he had not consulted him—but as it was done, recommending his going to Kentucky to tell Father in person. I have that letter, but not here.

Mr. Hassler[7] also with whom Mr. Nicollet & Mr. Frémont kept house jointly, ⟨*was Catholic*⟩ mistake. Mr. Frémont says it was an education in itself to hear those two men discuss scientific & political matters.

Those were his Catholic associations but he never was at any time or in any way more closely connected with that Church.

If I except flirting with a very pretty Catholic girl in St. Louis[8] but that spoils my romance so we won't tell it generally. Yours affcty,

Jessie

Mr. Frémont says,
Three years spent with Mr. Nicollet brought him into acquaintance and friendship with many Catholic gentlemen—clergymen and laymen.

A room was always kept for Mr. Nicollet at St. Mary's College in Baltimore and Mr. Frémont as an associate in his labors & travels was included in the hospitality extended to him there, and the Bishop's residence (where once he dined with twelve Bishops, Mr. Nicollet & himself the only laymen) and at many private houses.

Bishop Chanche afterwards Bishop of Natchez had a real regard for Mr. Frémont and gave him some most friendly counsels just after our marriage. He regretted not having been consulted—said the open course was the only one but as it was done he offered all his skill as negotiator with Father.

Mr. Frémont wrote it all to me at the time & the letter is in the box I left in your care.

I give Mr. Frémont's own version—mine was from memory & not so accurate.

It is too late, I am afraid, to do anything in the Burlingame duel if it must end so. They are all back together. How little those northern men seemed to understand Mr. Brooks—nothing was so easy to prove as his unwillingness to fight but it has been badly managed for Mr. Burlingame.[9]

We are in great peace here at our really rustic retreat—the simplest & cleanest of old fashioned farm houses. Charley and Frank play about on the fine grass under old trees and take their meals al fresco until their cheeks are blooming again. Lily too looks very well. Nina is a little too fine-ladyish to profit as much as she might by the country life but our simple food & early hours tell favorably even on her.

Mr. Frémont comes over nearly every evening & returns in the six o'clock boat. It is always cool here at night & the air is very pure as we are on a hill & have all the ground to the water.

I have been a little ill—but I always get well again & this is only one of ill turns that I am accustomed to.

I trust the heat will not injure your Father—with love to you all and especial remembrances to Mr. Lee whom I was too excited & tired to thank enough for his kind care of us. I am always dear Lizzie yours sincerely,

Jessie Frémont.

ALS (NjP—Blair-Lee Papers).

1. In mid-July, after her return from Virginia, JBF and the family retreated to a rented farmhouse on Staten Island (New York *Tribune,* July 18, 1856).

2. William Winston Seaton (1785–1866) was the mayor of Washington, D.C., 1840–50, and coeditor of the *National Intelligencer.*

3. There are several stories about exactly *where* the Frémonts were married, ranging from a parlor in Gadsby's Hotel (NEVINS [1], 69) to the home of John J. Crittenden (PHILLIPS, 57). JBF's vague reference to "a drawing room" is her most revealing statement on the subject.

4. A Benton relative wrote more bluntly that Thomas Hart Benton was outraged to find JBF "privately married & would not let her remain in his house nor would he allow a second marriage by a protestant clergyman which her mother desired" (Sarah Simpson [Hart] Thompson to Nathaniel Hart, Jan. 19, 1842, KLoF—Edmund T. Halsey Collection).

5. JCF's brother, Horatio Francis, left home at fifteen to become an actor, but he was injured in a riot in Buffalo and died on Feb. 7, 1839, at age twenty-three in Charleston, leaving a wife, Jane, and infant daughter, Frances Anne Cornelia (Nina). Burial services were conducted at the home of his mother by the Rev. Paul Trapier, and he was buried in St. Philip's churchyard. Eleven days later Nina was baptized at the house of her grandmother by the Rev. Trapier (TRAPIER, 99, 255; BIGELOW [1], 28–29). See also JBF to John Roberton, June 30, 1856, note 2, above. JCF's sister reportedly died in the early 1830s at age seventeen (BIGELOW [1], 29).

6. The urbane and cultivated Dr. John Mary Joseph Chanche (1795–1852) became president of St. Mary's College in 1834 and the first Roman Catholic bishop of Natchez, Mississippi, in 1841.

7. Swiss-born Ferdinand Rudolph Hassler (1770–1843) was the first superintendent of the U.S. Coast Survey. While working on the upper Mississippi–Missouri rivers map, Nicollet and JCF shared Hassler's Capitol Hill house with him and used his roof for astronomical observations.

8. JCF's bachelor years were filled with flirtations. A colleague in St. Louis commented on JCF's flair for romance: "I never knew a more fortunate man in my life, he steers through life like a Portuguese man-of-war over the crests of the waves . . . & I should be mistaken very much if he is not in love already again" (Charles A. Geyer to Joseph N. Nicollet, Jan. 1, 1840, RPB—Lownes Collection). For other early romances, see HERR, 55–57.

9. The Brooks-Burlingame imbroglio had begun on May 22, 1856, when Congressman Preston Brooks (1819–57) of South Carolina, maddened by a vitriolic speech against the South by Senator Charles Sumner of Massachusetts, savagely attacked him with a cane in the Senate chamber and beat him senseless. A month later, when Massachusetts congressman Anson Burlingame (1820–70) publicly accused Brooks of cowardice, Brooks challenged him to a duel. Burlingame, in a note reportedly written by Nathaniel Banks, tried to avoid the duel by making a half-apology. But in a second note dated July 21 and reported in New York newspapers on July 23, Burlingame, stung by suggestions of cowardice for his partial retreat, accepted Brooks's challenge but cleverly proposed the Canadian side of Niagara Falls as the site (New York *Tribune,* July 23, 24, 1856). It was at this point that JBF commented on the situation to Lizzie. The next day, Brooks withdrew, stating that he would be assassinated if he tried to travel through the North to reach the proposed site. For a firsthand account by Frémont campaign aide Charles James, who was evidently Burlingame's principal advisor in the episode, see the Washington *Post,* Oct. 27, 1901.

To Lydia Maria Child

[late July/Aug. 1856]

You are quite right in supposing the report true that I refused to buy a slave. We were in San José,[1] and had no woman servant, and could procure no one to wash or iron. Mr. Frémont had an Indian, who took care of the horses, and a free mulato man, named Saunders,[2] who had married a slave. He left his family in Washington, and went with us to California. He was so faithful during the many trials and difficulties of our over-land route, that Mr. Frémont gave him his time to enable him to dig gold with his company on the Mariposa, and supplied him with everything necessary for his support while thus engaged. Saunders dug gold enough to buy his wife and his two children, and returned to Washington for that purpose. His absence reduced our establishment to the one Indian, who was very good to take care of the horses, but not exactly suitable for a lady's maid. There were but few women in San José, and they were all so rich, that twelve dollars a dozen would not tempt them to resume their old occupation of washing and ironing. Juan, the Indian,[3] offered to wash, and did get the clothes quite white; but I had some doubts how long they would stand his fashion of pounding them between flat stones at the river side. I managed to smooth the collars with my hands, and we all wore our garments un-ironed.

In this state of things, all San José was aroused by the announcement of an accomplished "cook, washer, and ironer for sale." As I was thought to be the most helpless woman in town, it was supposed that I would hasten to secure her. But both Mr. Frémont and myself declined the proposition. She was bought by some one in town for $4000; a price that would have gratified Gov. Wise.[4]

While we were living in this rough way, Mr. Frémont's workmen sent down two great bags of gold from the Mariposa. They arrived late, and were put under the foot of the mattress. In the night, one of them rolled out, and we heard the lumps and dust spilling on the floor. Fleas swarmed there, as they do wherever the Spanish language is spoken, and the fear of exposing our naked feet to their attacks prevented our getting up to replace the scattered treasure. We laughed at the contrast between present and former circumstances, and realized thoroughly that gold was not the greatest good of life.

When we returned to Monterey, an Englishwoman from Sidney offered her services as cook, and I engaged her instantly. She proved an excellent woman, and did all my housework so promptly, that I was left quite a fine lady. But if she had not presented herself, I would never have bought a servant.

Mr. Winthrop, in his letter, alludes to Gov. McDowell's Anti-Slavery speeches and bills.[5] He was my mother's brother, and if he had had her courage in the cause, he would have left a name like Wilberforce. But when the South grew stormy, he grew silent, and took refuge in fine sentences about his native State and Northern aggression. My mother was of a more enduring nature. She brought us up to think it good fortune to be free from owning slaves. She urged upon us many reasons why we ought never to own them. She dwelt especially on the evil influence of slavery on the temper of children, making them domineering, passionate, and arbitrary. I would as soon place my children in the midst of small pox, as rear them under the influences of slavery. When the State Convention was held at Monterey,[6] some of the members came to hear from myself that I would never buy a slave, and to inquire whether we would reside in California if slavery was introduced there. Finding we were sincere in our determination not to remain in that case some, who were themselves indifferent on the subject, were influenced to vote against the introduction of slavery.

Extract, JBF to Lydia Maria Child, copied by Child for Horace Greeley, Mar. 2 [1862] (NN—Horace Greeley Papers). In an attached note, Child wrote Greeley: "I enclose an extract from an old letter of Mrs. Frémont's, which you may perhaps think worth publishing. *I* was the person who inquired about her objection to buying a slave, but I had rather not have my name published." The extract was evidently never published in the *Tribune*. JBF repeated much of its contents in J. B. FRÉMONT [3], 91–96 and "Great Events," 121–22, 126.

Lydia Maria Child (1802–80), the noted New England writer and abolitionist, strongly supported JCF's candidacy in 1856 and was even more enthusiastic about JBF (L. M. CHILD, 291). She was the author of the influential early abolitionist work, *An Appeal in Favor of That Class of Americans Called Africans* (1833).

1. JBF had joined her husband in California in June 1849, at the height of the gold rush. They established their headquarters in Monterey but spent much of the summer traveling on the San Francisco peninsula, "putting into San Francisco for news or San José for soft weather" (J. B. FREMONT [3], 91). Journalist J. Ross Browne encountered JBF on Aug. 11 in San Jose, a town of hastily built shanties and tents, "busily engaged preparing some corn to cook, for here every lady has to do her own work" (BROWNE, 123).

2. Formerly a servant in the Benton household, Jackson Saunders was employed as JCF's personal cook and orderly on his disastrous fourth expedition to the southern Rockies and continued on with him to California in 1849 (M. L. SPENCE [2], 52, 55n).

3. According to JBF, Juan was a California mission Indian who, along with an Indian named Gregorio, had "been with [JCF] for years, coming and going between the United States and California." JBF found them "bright and observing" and "the most graceful horseman I have ever seen" (J. B. FRÉMONT [3], 78–79; "Great Events," 121; see also M. L. SPENCE [2], 56n).

4. Gov. Henry Alexander Wise (1806–76) of Virginia, a fiery and pugnacious speaker, was an outspoken defender of slavery and a supporter of James Buchanan. In a widely publicized speech, Wise condemned JCF as "a Frenchman's bastard" and warned that the election of the "Black Republican" candidate would bring civil war (quoted in NEVINS [1], 451).

5. JBF refers to a public letter on slavery by former Massachusetts senator Robert Winthrop (1809–94), published in the New York *Times*, July 24, 1856. In the letter, Winthrop mentioned a notable 1832 speech by JBF's uncle, James McDowell, Jr., to the Virginia legislature, in which he condemned slavery as a moral evil and urged a system of gradual emancipation. Unlike William Wilberforce (1759–1833), the British abolitionist, McDowell later changed his view. As Virginia governor and congressman,

he accepted slavery as an "indispensable institution" in the South and pleaded for northern understanding to avoid a "monstrous struggle of brother with brother" (S. MILLER, 182–85). For a discussion of the 1832 legislative debate, "the final and most brilliant of the Southern attempts to abolish slavery," see ROBERT.

6. When Congress, deeply divided over the issue of slavery in the new western territories, failed to provide recently conquered California with a civilian government, delegates met at Monterey in Sept. 1849 to create a state constitution and petition for immediate admission to the Union. Contrary to expectations, the delegates, including known southern sympathizers, voted unanimously to prohibit slavery in California.

To Elizabeth Blair Lee

Staten Island
August 12th [1856]

Dear Lizzie,

Marie was made very happy by yours and your Father's remembrance of her—the tears that gathered in her great bright eyes were the best thanks to your kind recognition of her feeble health.

I shall grieve to lose her as I fear I must before very long.[1] She will "die in harness" however—there is an insane energy about her that renders quiet painful to her. Mr. Frémont & all of us recognize her condition & I make it a constant charge to the servants to give her no vexation & they are all very good to her.

Marie has been with me long enough to be a sharer in many things & consequently to be quick in understanding my feelings & since the whole family have dropped me I value her the more for their loss. However there is nothing for that and greater griefs than submission— it is soon over with the rest of our lives and the little time we may have should not be given to useless & selfish regrets.

I am the more reminded of this as I am blazing with fever from the sudden anger I felt last night on reading Mr. Bigler's motion in the Senate.[2] Mr. Frémont says if Father takes no notice of that & continues to work with them he will never speak to him nor shall any of his children. I will let it make no outward difference but I have just written a long letter to Cousin Sarah[3] that she may tell it to Father—not what Mr. Frémont says—that I only tell you—you are my confessional— but telling him what I felt he ought to do. There will be no loss to him now from speaking the truth for Mr. Frémont, since the election is over. Whether for or against him yet we do not know. I am glad you have the pleasure of your brother's success.[4]

Mr. Frémont had intended to go for a week or ten days into some remote spot where he could have complete silence & solitude—but this act of Mr. Buchanan's—for all feel it such, has altered his ideas. He says now he would like to be at Bedford Springs & meet Mr. Buchanan who is to be there.[5] I would go with him.

But it would do him more good to go off into repose. I don't know what mischief might come of temptation and if our friends have the boldness to fix this attack upon Mr. Buchanan it will end in good— for the cause I mean. Mr. Frémont will keep silence until November. I suppose they wish to force him into some act of resentment. I wish they could understand how useless that is. He considers himself as belonging to the greatest cause ever at stake since the Revolution & his whole life shows that he "throws away his body" for his duty. In this case he "throws away his heart" & lets them slander & attack, in silence—knowing how injurious violence would be & how inadequate anything but death would be as punishment to such slanderers.

The best answer will be in the triumph of our party. You will see by one of the slips that Govr. Ford is at work in the right place.[6]

Urge every available man to go into Pennsylvania & speak. The Democratic party will fill that state with documents of their own but the human voice will exercise a magnetic power which will undo their work. Mr. Frémont works like a Cataline at Pennsylvania & but for the treacherous P.O. I would shew you with what certainty of good results.[7]

I have written a note to Mr. French. He ought to know Mr. Frémont would not go there to help in the children's baptisms if he were a Catholic but people are so weak & his congregation may not like what he has done.[8] I wrote to him to say I begged he would not feel constrained by his regard for me to do anything for Mr. Frémont.

The leader in the Evg. Post of the 11th (yesterday) ought to be the text of our friends' discourses. Bennett will yet tell the whole about "the abandoned woman to whom the passport was given."[9] It was an act which will insult every man whose name is worth keeping—being the giving to a woman of notorious ill fame a pass-port under the name of an American married lady then leaving London. Her name I cannot repeat without permission, but they are rich & his income flows like water into sustaining newspapers & attacks on Buchanan. He intends yet to use this fact if necessary but naturally shrinks from his wife's being printed about.

Little Frank has been very ill. His eye teeth gave him great pain & his head swelled & he drooped so that I feared inflammation of the brain. For nearly a week he was never out of mine or Mémé's arms—the only sleep or rest he took was when walked about but he is entirely well now & gay & bright as ever—walking about and eating with great appetite. Mémé is a good faithful nurse—we both look a little haggard but this fresh air is very health-giving & we shall soon sleep it off.

I am not afraid of the fever here where we are.[10] It is five miles from us that the only original cases on the island took place & that was from clearing away a wood from around a swamp. But we are on a high hill & in the healthiest locality here & are all well in spite of politics. Mr. Frémont comes over every night & refreshes his wearied head by an active romping with the girls who are real country lasses now. Did you notice in the Post the account of a portrait by Buchanan Reed [Read] of Mr. Frémont & one of myself?[11] The gentleman by whom they were ordered gave mine to Lily & Mr. Frémont's to me—in *such* frames. Mine is a lovely picture but looks like I did once not now. Lily will value it always.

Write to me as often as you find leisure. I wish you would think the heat debilitated Mr. Lee & then come here. Salt air ought to be his best medicine and you know how very very happy I should be to aid you in making him take care of himself. There is no yellow fever near us—none anywhere out of the Quarantine & it is so quiet & cool that we only know of the world by the guns of great steamers as they come to anchor in full view from our porch & by the crowds of sailing vessels going & coming all the time.

Don't you really think change of place could do good—"the ounce of prevention," is a great hobby of mine, and although I trust your fears are from affection more than reason I would not regret them if they brought you here. Tell Mr. Lee it would not be like him not to take care of you & the surest way to do it is to let you take care of him in your own way & not let you be uneasy. Men don't understand that it's a little selfish to refuse to attend to little illnesses—we must be uneasy whether they are or not.

I am glad Mammy [Ceely?] remembered me & did justice to our care of them. Yours most affectionately,

Jessie Frémont

[*Margin note:* The confirmation record had best be asked for by some one out of our family.[12]]

ALS (NjP—Blair-Lee Papers).

1. Actually, JBF's French servant, Marie, remained with her intermittently until about 1867, when she retired to France, "for no Frenchwoman can endure perpetual exile" ("Great Events," 170–71).

2. Senator William Bigler (1814–80) of Pennsylvania, a Buchanan ally, had demanded a Senate inquiry into JCF's financial transactions during his first California expedition. Bigler's motion called for the president to supply copies of JCF's expedition vouchers and asked whether any public money in JCF's hands was unaccounted for or if any papers on file charged him with malfeasance (New York *Tribune*, Aug. 11, 1856). The anti-Frémont Washington *Union* applauded the Bigler resolution, adding that there had been a "veil of romance" over all Frémont's expeditions. Referring to JCF's leadership of the California Battalion during the 1847 conquest, it questioned how, "in a service of five or six months, a small battalion of men, numbering, perhaps, three to four hundred, [could] incure liabilities . . . amounting to more than a million dollars" (Aug. 20, 1856). In contrast, the pro-Frémont New York *Tribune* dismissed Bigler's motion as "a political game" instigated by Buchanan and deliberately made at the end of the congressional session so that the charges could not be fairly investigated (Aug. 11, 1856). The Frémont forces cleverly parried the attack by publishing favorable testimony given by James Buchanan, secretary of state during the conquest, to a special claims commission established in 1852 to investigate JCF's California expenditures. Buchanan stated that JCF was "better entitled to be called the 'Conqueror of California' than any other man." Buchanan's testimony was republished in the Sept. 20, 1856, *Tribune*, with Horace Greeley editorializing, "We have caught the old rat at last! . . . In THE TRIBUNE of to-day our readers will find JAMES BUCHANAN squarely out in favor of JOHN C. FREMONT." For information on the claims commission investigation, see M. L. SPENCE [2], 375n, 490.

3. Sarah (Benton) Brant, a niece of Thomas Hart Benton, was the wife of Joshua B. Brant, a wealthy St. Louis businessman. Benton regularly stayed with the Brants when he was in St. Louis.

4. In June, Benton had been nominated for the governorship of Missouri by the antislavery faction of the Democratic party. In a forty-day campaign, he spoke to immense crowds throughout the state, condemning the extension of slavery into Kansas and other new territories, yet supporting Buchanan as the candidate best suited to preserve the Union. Ironically, the opposition charged that Benton was a secret Republican scheming to secure the election of his son-in-law. In voting on Aug. 4, Benton was defeated by Trusten Polk, a proslavery Democratic candidate. At the same time, Frank Blair, Jr., was elected to Congress from St. Louis (New York *Tribune*, Aug. 11, 1856). An ardent free-soiler, he had managed the delicate task of supporting, publicly, Thomas Hart Benton, his political mentor, for governor and, privately, JCF for president.

5. James Buchanan was scheduled to make his annual visit to Bedford Springs, a "watering place" in the Allegheny Mountains of Pennsylvania.

6. Lt. Gov. Thomas H. Ford (1814–68) of Ohio, a powerful and entertaining speaker, was campaigning for JCF in Pennsylvania. There is evidence that he was also distributing funds furnished by the national campaign to pro-Fillmore newspapers to induce them to support the Frémont candidacy; later some suspected he kept a portion of the money for himself (GIENAPP, 399; RAWLEY, 69). For the Democratic party's more blatant and better financed attempts to influence the Pennsylvania election, see JBF to Elizabeth Blair Lee, Oct. 9 [1856], note 10, below.

7. By late summer, populous Pennsylvania had become the campaign focus for both major parties. If, as expected, JCF carried New England and the upper Midwest, and Buchanan the South, the states of Pennsylvania, Indiana, and Illinois would be pivotal. Since both Pennsylvania and Indiana held state elections in early October, the results could serve as both bellweather and bandwagon for the winning candidate.

8. Rumors were circulating that the Frémonts' pastor, John William French (1810–71) of Washington's Episcopal Church of the Epiphany, claimed JCF was or had been a Catholic. See JBF to Dr. John Roberton, June 30, 1856, note 2, above; and to Elizabeth Blair Lee, Aug. 20 [1856], note 6, below.

9. The New York *Evening Post*'s Aug. 11 lead editorial condemned Senator William Bigler's motion to investigate JCF's California accounts as "maliciously unjust" and attacked Buchanan's record in several areas, including, without giving details, the "issue of free passes [passports] to abandoned women" during his tenure as American minister to Great Britain. The reference may be to Fanny White, a New York prostitute who was the mistress of Daniel Sickles, secretary to the American legation during Buchanan's tenure. Leaving his pregnant wife in the United States, Sickles had taken Fanny White to London, where it was rumored he presented her to the Queen as "Miss Bennett of New York," a slap at Sickles's enemy, James Gordon Bennett (1795–1872), editor of the sensationalist New York *Herald* (SWANBERG, 88–92; KLEIN, 226). The *Herald* had unexpectedly endorsed JCF, despite Bennett's reputed sympathy with the South.

10. Yellow fever cases had developed on ships arriving from southern and Central American ports, and by early August, 120 ships were lying in quarantine offshore. Arriving passengers and crew were required to pass through the Quarantine Marine Hospital on Staten Island, where they were washed and their baggage fumigated; actual cases were kept in the hospital. Since it was not then known that yellow fever is transmitted by mosquito and not through human contact, residents feared it would spread over the island. It wasn't until mid-November that the danger was pronounced over (New York *Tribune*, Aug. 9, 11, 18, 22, Nov. 18, 1856).

11. New York *Evening Post*, Aug. 8, 1856.

12. JBF probably refers to JCF's confirmation record at St. Philip's (Episcopal) Church, Charleston, which she feared might be difficult to obtain by the family because of southern antagonism toward JCF.

To Elizabeth Blair Lee

Staten Island
August 14th [1856]

Your note & one from Mr. French both reached me yesterday my dear Lizzie. Mr. French is quite right in doing nothing more. I am only afraid he has done too much already for the semi-barbarian latitude he is in. I would be very unwilling that regard for me should give him any trouble with his congregation—many of them are office holders who cannot afford themselves the luxury of thinking their own thoughts, and might be told to leave his church. In that case the loss would all be theirs but Mr. French's nature is not the kind to defy storms.

As to any one's speaking by authority for Mr. Frémont's religion, it is impossible for them to say he is or was a Catholic. He says himself that he never was one—not once has he ever gone into a Catholic Church for service—only to weddings & some shows in Paris where it was like an opera box & we were all talking as in a theatre.

But he was a great deal in Baltimore during Mr. Nicollet's time & through him much at St. Mary's College & liked some of the clergy, Bishop Chanc[h]e especially, very much.

Sarah [Benton Jacob] was (in her own estimation) a burning & shining light to the family enhancing our darkness by contrast & she was always pitching into me & Mr. Frémont about religion. In those days I always argued for the Catholic Church—more to enrage her than anything else and Mr. Frémont used to make fun of the St. Louis ideas.[1] But within a few years all that ended & there never was anything more to base it upon than what I tell you except always the Catholic girls he flirted with but if they had been Jews it would have been quite the same provided they were agreeable & pretty.

I send you what the Herald says about Bedford.[2] As Frank is variable, now well & then suffering again, I shall not leave him. Mr. Frémont will take a holiday and go off alone & incog.[3] I am the poste restante and hope to hear much from you.

We are preparing for Marie's fête to-morrow. She is going to bring over some friends & have a country fête. The 17th is Nina's birthday which we will celebrate on Monday.

I am very glad your Mother & Father are to have Frank with them. You ought to take holiday then. If you would only come here but although we are all well & I am assured there is no fever out of Quarantine limits yet I am afraid the newspaper fuss about it will keep Susan away & frighten you too. With love to all. Yours most affectionally,

JF.

AL initialed (NjP—Blair-Lee Papers).

1. The "St. Louis ideas" probably refer to the strict Presbyterianism in which JBF was raised. In St. Louis the Bentons's pastor and relative, the Rev. William S. Potts, a man known for his "exalted piety," condemned such amusements as theatre-going, card playing, and dancing (ROSIN, 41). Even as a child, JBF felt temperamentally at odds with this dour Calvinism, with its emphasis on sin and predestination.

2. The Aug. 14 New York *Herald* contained the following item: "We understand that some of Frémont's friends are anxious that he should take a trip to Bedford Springs in order to see the Senators who have voted for an inquiry into his accounts, and also to call upon his rival Mr. Buchanan. Some other friends of the Colonel think he had best write a long letter to the papers, giving a full account of his birth, marriage, and religion, and explaining the whole affair about his christening and Sunday practice."

3. On Aug. 13, JCF had written Nathaniel Banks: "I am going north west for a brief change of scene & ideas" (DLC—Banks Papers).

To Elizabeth Blair Lee

Staten Island
August 20th [1856].

Dear Lizzie it is easy to say "possess your soul in patience"[1] but not so easy to do it & far harder for me than for you for I have a bad rebellious nature that is always escaping even when I watch it.

It is of no use to say anything to Father who could by one line set right this Bigler movement. His old pride would have led him to do justice to an opponent—it was his boast that he so aided Genl. Jackson[2] & it would do him honor to speak the truth now for Mr. Frémont— but Mr. Frémont says I shall not write to him—that the breach is made now & he accepts it for himself & his blood. I am free to do as I choose for myself but nothing he says will atone to him for Father's causeless hostility, pushed far beyond the limits of political difference.

The manner in which the Buchanan party have slandered his Mother[3] (although but vaguely known to Mr. Frémont) and their sneers at his early poverty have given him the feeling that it was not honorable in Father to so completely identify himself with them. I think his silence on this last movement a reproach to him—he who has always been so quick to resent attacks on Mr. Frémont's California operations. But I suppose he is afraid it may injure his prospects for Senator.[4] A place he will not have even offered to him. Another generation will fill the seat; it is intended for younger men, & you will see, that he is ignored.

I should like to know if Susy has returned & how her baby is. She has not written for two weeks & I have something to send her & don't know how to address the box.

Little Frank is well now but has been very ill—we have no fever here, everything is healthy around us. I hope Mr. Lee is over the symptoms that disturbed you. Could you possess your soul in patience if your Father and brothers were openly aiding the Coast Survey to break down Mr. Lee—discrediting his capacity, impeaching his character and outraging his mother's memory? Could you. I don't think you would obtain or wish to obtain Mr. Lee's forgiveness for such acts—& silence on Father's part is complicity.

Old [William Carey] Jones writes a letter every week or so—the prospects of success have their usual affect on him & he offers assistance in refuting slanders "although national(!) considerations" "will make him vote for Buchanan."

Mr. Banks urges a visit to Penn. because of the rivalry between Penn. & N.Y. Says it would compliment—not Bedford but some where else. I am against it. I want to fight with stronger weapons than courtesies & I will do mischief if I am let loose among opponents. I am better on my island here where I can get over indignation by myself—& Mr. Banks insists on a family move.

Tell your father of it. Mr. Frémont hates the idea but will do whatever will aid in Penn.[5] I wish he could meet your Father somewhere except in Washington. I sent Mr. French a copy of a letter said to be written by him to a man in Troy & read at a Fillmore meeting.[6] I think it a forgery. If not, he is no longer among the people I respect or would speak to. "It's all a mad world my masters—a mad mad world."[7] Yours affcty,

Jessie

ALS (NjP—Blair-Lee Papers).

1. A paraphrase of Luke 21:19.
2. In 1813, Benton and Andrew Jackson had taken opposite sides in a quarrel that escalated into a violent brawl during which Jackson was shot and wounded by Benton's brother Jesse. Ten years later, Benton and Jackson reconciled, and Benton eventually became one of Jackson's most important political advisers (CHAMBERS, 50–52; 118).

JBF was bitterly reminded of her father's opposition to JCF as well as his old quarrel with Jackson when an outspoken letter from Benton was published in the press. In it he stated that JCF's candidacy had dangerously divided the Union. "There are cases in which public duty rises above personal consideration, though there are a great many people who cannot conceive it possible. Thus, when I supported Jackson (with whom I had been on ill terms), thirty years ago, the sordid motive of office was assigned for it; now, when I support Buchanan (with whom I am on ill terms), and support him against a member of my own family, the same class of persons can see nothing in it but falsehood and treachery. Incapable themselves of anything disinterested and patriotic, they believe others to be equally so" (Benton to Thomas L. Price, Aug. 10, 1856, printed in New York *Tribune*, Aug. 18, 1856).

3. Anti-Frémont newspapers, including the *Express* in New York, had vigorously contradicted the sanitized version of JCF's parentage provided by JBF in Bigelow's campaign biography. The Richmond *Dispatch*, for example, presented a cynical but essentially correct version of the love affair between Charles Fremon and Anne Pryor, and asserted that they had never married. The account concluded, "These incidents in the life of the progenitor of the free-soil candidate for the Presidency, show that he was at least a disciple of Free-love, if not of Free-soil" (undated clipping, NN—Bigelow Papers).

4. The indefatigable Benton now hoped to be elected senator when the Missouri legislature convened in Jan. 1857. His opposition to slavery extension, however, made it unlikely he would be chosen.

5. Banks's novel idea was not carried out.

6. The Rev. John William French purportedly wrote that he understood JCF had once been a Catholic. The letter was featured at rallies for Millard Fillmore, candidate of the northern wing of the antiforeign, anti-Catholic Know Nothing party, whose supporters felt threatened by Catholic immigrants pouring in from Ireland and Germany (New York *Tribune*, Sept. 3, 1856).

7. An old expression, it was used as the title of a dialogue by Nicholas Breton in 1603 and of a play by Thomas Middleton in 1608.

To Francis Preston Blair

Staten Island
August 25th [1856]

My dear Mr. Blair,

I should like to judge your health by the freshness & vigor of your letter which we have read with great interest and satisfaction. Mr. Bigelow told me on Wednesday that it would "make the fur fly." I like your grouping of Lafitte, Buchanan & Woodbury—since Charles Woodbury's speech I especially approve your fling at "oily-gammon." Mr. Frémont was amazed at the picture of young Jackson—such weakness, malice & ingratitude how undeserving of his great name.[1]

Mr. Bigelow brought me the Union of Monday with the editorial setting forth Mr. Frémont as "speculator & peculator."[2] It's of no more value than the Express here with its slanders on Mr. Frémont's Mother (which by the way I have still managed to keep him ignorant of)—but Father's silence when he has always been so prompt to do battle for the right hurts me literally to the heart. I hoped I might have served as hostage for at least his being just but I see he is with them altogether. This shuts off all future relations between Mr. Frémont & himself. Mr. Frémont says he would not willingly see his children go where he has been so injured — so you see why it hurts me for Mr. Frémont is right. A Father-in-law has not the right to the forbearance and duty of a child unless he gives the protection & love of a parent. I mean to the forbearance of a "law-child" — his own born child cannot but feel one way and Mr. Frémont is good enough to leave me to do as I feel for myself. But I have not written to Father since early in June. He answered me then that it was useless to do so as he would be travelling about until his return in August — that was the purpose of the letter — a setting aside of future remonstrance of which there was no danger from me. All this has made me ill. The pain in the heart lasted longer than usual & a general inflammation has followed making me tired & feverish & still after five days quiet and care, in pain if I do not keep perfectly hushed & quiet. Dr. Van Buren[3] says "no newspapers, no ideas, no excitement of any kind" & by way of forgetfulness I am to get well enough to go to town next week when the opera re-commences & lead a life steadily devoted to amusements disconnected with politics" [*Margin note:* which I shall not do] — but you know this is an old wound for the opening of which politics are only an excuse. Father has absolutely disliked Mr. Frémont since the refusal to sell the Mariposas.

All this I tell you dear Mr. Blair with an object. Mrs. Blair did us all a kindness we will never cease to be grateful for in doing for Susan at her marriage what my poor speechless Mother would have said had she been there.[4] I know you cannot talk to Father as you once did but Mr. Rives might, as they are together in politics.[5] Do not let him say things personally injurious to Mr. Frémont. Mr. Bigelow tells me such are repeated & even in print — he will send you them if he meets them. Such things would keep me too away from Father's house & I want you to keep it open to me as Mrs. Blair did for Susan by preventing an insult to her husband. I am going against orders in thinking over this matter but I cannot rest unless I do all I can think of to prevent this unnatural state of things which brings no advantage to Father & really hurts me. I hope you are as well as Mr. Frémont who is as gay as a boy. We let him read no papers (unless you write them) and he has the pleasure of doing daily good work in the cause. He hopes to see Frank [Blair, Jr.] today who will give you particulars. With love to all. Your affectionate,

Jessie Frémont

F. P. Blair, Esqre.

[Note on separate sheet:] I am afraid to address it on the outside.

ALS (DLC—Blair Papers). Envelope addressed: "Capt. S. P. Lee, U.S. Navy, Silver Spring near Washington, D.C."

1. JBF refers to Blair's lengthy Aug. 15 public letter, "Gen. Jackson and James Buchanan," which appeared Aug. 23 in the New York *Evening Post*. In it Blair detailed Buchanan's role in the notorious 1824 "corrupt bargain," in which Henry Clay supported John Quincy Adams for the presidency against Andrew Jackson, allegedly with the understanding that Adams would name him secretary of state. Adams won the presidency, Clay was named secretary of state, but both denied a deal. Before Clay threw his support to Adams, Buchanan, then a young Pennsylvania congressman, had suggested a similar bargain with Clay to Andrew Jackson, which Jackson had indignantly rejected. In a letter made public during the 1856 campaign, Jackson stated that Buchanan "showed a want of moral courage" in the situation and that his offer suggested "deep corruption." On Buchanan's role, also see JAMES, 421–23 and KLEIN, 49–53.

To combat this Jackson letter, the Buchanan forces had persuaded "young Jackson," Andrew Jackson's adopted son, Andrew Jackson, Jr. (actually a nephew by marriage), to state publicly that Jackson had always spoken highly of Buchanan and to hint that Blair had no authorization to quote from Andrew Jackson's letters in his earlier "Voice from the Grave of Jackson." In his Aug. 15 letter, Blair detailed his authorization and correctly described young Jackson as "a weak-minded, credulous, dreamy schemer," whom Jackson had loved even though his adopted son's flagrant mismanagement of Jackson's property had put Jackson so deeply in debt that Blair and his partner, John C. Rives, had several times loaned him money. Confirming Blair's account, see JAMES, 748–49, 760–61, 777–778, 783.

In explaining how Jackson could have named Buchanan minister to Russia if he distrusted him, Blair pointed out that Buchanan could thus be kept out of further political mischief and that Jackson had similarly employed both the French pirate Jean Lafitte (c. 1780–c. 1826) during his 1812 victory over the British at New Orleans and Levi Woodbury of New Hampshire as secretary of the treasury. Woodbury's son was lawyer Charles Levi Woodbury (1820–98), a brother-in-law of Montgomery Blair but a supporter of Buchanan for president.

2. The Washington *Union* editorial of Wednesday, Aug. 20 (no paper was published on Monday), entitled "Col. Frémont's Financial Operations," asserted that investigation of JCF's California finances showed "covered up speculations and peculations of large and small degree."

3. New York surgeon William Holme Van Buren (1819–83), chair of anatomy at the University of the City of New York, had recently become the Frémont family physician, probably on the recommendation of Dr. Hugh Hodge of Philadelphia with whom he had studied. During the Civil War, Van Buren became a founding member of the U.S. Sanitary Commission, and JBF solicited his aid on several projects; in 1867 Lily Frémont was a bridesmaid in his daughter's wedding (JBF to Sydney Gay, June 21 [1862], and JBF to Elizabeth Peabody, Mar. 20 [1864], both below; Elizabeth Benton Frémont to Nelly Haskell, Jan. 16, 1867, CU-B—Frémont Papers).

4. Benton had evidently only grudgingly consented to Susan's marriage to Gauldrée de Boilleau. Perhaps tellingly, the marriage reception was given by the Frémonts (CHAMBERS, 416).

5. John C. Rives (1795–1864) had been Francis Blair's business partner at the *Globe*, and after Blair's retirement, he continued to manage Blair's finances. Although Rives supported Buchanan in 1856, he remained on cordial terms with Blair (E. B. SMITH [1] 49, 170–72).

To Elizabeth Blair Lee

[late Aug./early Sept. 1856]
New York, 56 West 9th street

Dear Lizzie, Frank [Blair, Jr.] gave your note to Mr. Frémont who put it in his pocket & changed his coat for a thicker one to cross to the island & so my note lay perdu [lost] until the day Frank left. You had an enviable place that of keeper of the peace the day you were with Father.[1] The good effects of the seed you dropped that day are shewing in more ways than his letter to me. He only wrote of family matters but it was enclosed in a very kind note to Mr. Frémont (family altogether) which Mr. Frémont answered immediately.

He asks us all to come on. I must stay with little Frank and although he is doing much better since the eye teeth are through, yet the two lower ones still keep up his disorder. Mémé is a most faithful nurse but the little man loves me best and is much quieter with me than with Mémé. I have carried him so much that Mr. Frémont said this morning I looked like a "wilted plant" and took me off with him to a private conference room down town, where by way of relaxation I copied letters to California & Pennsylvania.

But a pen is less weight than Frank who is still large and heavy.

But to return to the main point. I see that Father resents the attacks on Mr. Frémont, and Mr. Colfax[2] writes that he expresses great indignation of Mr. Bigler's involvement. Perhaps in his position he cannot do more than speak. But there are many repeated things, personally injurious to Mr. Frémont, which are pretended to have been said by him. Mr. Bigelow told me they were circulated in print — one that "he said nothing of Frémont for that if he were forced to speak it must be in such a way as to ruin his prospects." I have not seen Mr. Bigelow for some days — their youngest child is ill & he of course has to nurse it.[3]

Such things as I have quoted, we know do not come from Father but he might be worried into some depreciatory remark which would be most eagerly caught up and Mr. Frémont has not my motives for indulgence. So that this timely visit of yours may serve as a warning & check any such impulse if it should rise in him. You know how much I thank you. Many words could not tell you better.

I will thank your Father for his kindness in writing me so long a letter but not just now for I have worked today. With love to all Yours affectionately,

Jessie.

We "drove a nail into Mr. Fillmore's coffin" yesterday. Look out for a letter not written or signed by Mr. Frémont however.[4]

ALS (NjP—Blair-Lee Papers).

1. Before JBF's Aug. 25 plea for help in preventing a permanent break with her father reached the Blairs, the tactful Lizzie Lee had paid a visit to Benton, ostensibly to get Susan Boilleau's address, which JBF had requested in her letter of Aug. 20. "Your Father talked lovingly of you in his way," Lizzie Lee wrote, "& when I said that your only annoyance was the Bigler attack . . . his face flushed & a few minutes afterward he said, 'You need not tell her Susan's direction. I'll do that' . . . & said he would send you a letter by the next mail" (draft letter, [late Aug. 1856], NjP—Blair-Lee Papers).
2. Young Republican congressman Schuyler Colfax of Indiana (1823–85) was an early JCF supporter. He would later be Speaker of the House and Ulysses S. Grant's first-term vice-president, but his involvement in the Crédit Mobilier scandal ruined his political career.
3. During 1856, Bigelow's young son Poultney (1855–1954) was seriously ill and only recovered when the Bigelows moved to the country (BIGELOW [2], 1:163).
4. Several letters subsequently appeared in the press to counteract Fillmore campaign charges that JCF was a Catholic: see, for example, the letters of John A. C. Gray and Robert F. Livingston, New York *Evening Post*, Sept. 5, 6, 1856.

To Elizabeth Blair Lee

Tuesday morning [Sept. 16, 1856]
C street.

Dear Lizzie,

We came in full force last night to stay a week with Father. Only Mr. Frémont & little Frank left behind. You know why I can't go out as I used to without any delay, but I hope to see much of you whilst here.[1] Father is much changed I think—very much thinner and so still—it seems as if sadness and silence were so fixed upon him that he could not shake them off. I will keep with him all the time I can and if possible will get him to come to see us this fall.

One of the good things in Mr. Frémont's success would be the enlivening of Father. He could not help taking interest too in public affairs & I think he is too much left to find resources within himself.

Give my morning greetings to all your home & with love to yourself believe me always yours,

Jessie

ALS (NjP—Blair-Lee Papers).

1. During JBF's visit, Francis Blair, though "in an exceedingly ill-humor" with Benton because of his opposition to JCF, had both father and daughter to dinner at Silver Spring (Blair to Martin Van Buren, Sept. 22, 1856, DLC—Van Buren Papers).

To Elizabeth Blair Lee

Thursday evening.
October 9th [1856].

Dear Lizzie,

It would do you good to see your Father and Mother going regularly into evening amusements. Last night at La Grange's opera[1]—tonight at Wallack's Theatre to see "London assurance."[2] Tomorrow evening your Father dines with *Bennett* (Herald)—Monday evg. with Mr. Cooley.[3] Tuesday evg. Burton—at my asking—is going to play "the Serious Family" and "the Toodles" especially for your Father's amusement.[4]

Your Mother reads, talks, listens, goes out to drive or walk as she chooses and is well and cheerful. I am on my p's & q's in housekeeping and Marie says she can't sleep at night (à la Wise)[5] for thinking how to vary the dinner. Your Mother has so good an appetite however that I am getting less nervous. You know I don't mind you at all & Mr. Lee still less. "A clean table cloth and a smiling welcome" are what the old saying declares make a good meal & I can always be sure of giving you both, but I am anxious to stand well in your Mother's eyes as a careful housekeeper.

It is rather decided that Betty goes to a school out of town—*not* Bolton Priory[6]—but not quite settled. We mean to keep your Father with us to rejoice over the 14th or to aid us in bearing defeat whichever it may be. If it were not for the false notes in Philadelphia I should consider the state safe. As it is, wiser people say it is safe but "je suis de l'école de St. Thomas" [I am of the school of St. Thomas].[7]

For a wonder I am absolutely alone with Mr. Frémont. He is reading Paul Ferroll[8] & we are as quiet as if the air was not rife with war and rumors of war. I had to see a lot of clergymen & their wives & so all the rest left me when they went to the theatre. Lily is in bed & the little ones also. Lil works away busily with a governess who is making also some light in Charley's vacant mind.

Let me know if I can do anything for you in the bonnet way as that seems to be my specialty. Weed[9] & some others have come in so good night—my quiet is ended.

                                                            J. B. F.

Mr. Weed has just left—he says we have *three* combinations which will overthrow the illegal votes in Philadelphia & all is safe there.[10] So after Tuesday I will order that signet ring Mr. Lee asked for.

AL initialed (NjP—Blair-Lee Papers). Francis Preston Blair and his wife Eliza had journeyed to New York to await results of the crucial Oct. 14 Pennsylvania election with the Frémonts.

1. The Oct. 8 program at the City Assembly Rooms on Broadway featured Anna de La Grange and other stars of Max Maretzek's Italian Opera Company singing selections from Giacomo Meyerbeer's *Star of the North* and Verdi's *Rigoletto* (New York *Tribune*, Oct. 8, 1856).

2. The comedy *London Assurance* was performed at Wallack's on Oct. 9 with the playwright, Dion Boucicault, among the cast (New York *Tribune*, Oct. 9, 1856).

3. Mr. Cooley may have been James E. Cooley (1802–82) of the book firm Cooley, Keese, and Hill, once associated with Benton's publisher, William Appleton. Cooley was a public-spirited reform Democrat who served as a New York state senator and on the commission to plan Central Park (ROPER, 127–28; STRONG, 2:371).

4. On Tuesday, Oct. 14, the popular English comic actor William Evans Burton (1804–60), who had just leased the Metropolitan Theatre on Broadway, featured "by desire and for the first time here" a double bill that included the comedy *The Serious Family* by English writer/actor Morris Barnett with Burton in the starring role. The second play was not *The Toodles*, however, but a drama entitled *The Wreckers* by the English playwright and actor John Baldwin Buckstone (New York *Tribune*, Sept. 8–9, Oct. 14, 1856). It was evidently on this evening, before JBF and Blair set off for the theater, that John Bigelow brought unfavorable preliminary results from Pennsylvania. JBF later described how she decided to spare the elderly Blair the bad news until the next day, although at the theater Blair could not understand why she was so uninterested in the performance ("Great Events," 206).

5. Possibly a reference to Methodist clergyman Daniel Wise (1813–98), who wrote several popular advice books for young women in the 1850s.

6. Betty did attend Bolton Priory, located in Tarrytown, N.Y. For a description of the school, see JBF to Elizabeth Blair Lee, Oct. 20 [1856], below.

7. I.e., a doubter (John 20:24–29).

8. The novel *Paul Ferroll*, a sensational crime story by English writer Caroline Wigley Clive, was published anonymously in London in 1855. An American reviewer praised its "stern fatality of plot" and "diction of bare and rugged strength," but concluded that "such an experiment in the deliniation of morbid psychology is neither of a pleasing nor healthful nature" (New York *Tribune*, June 23, 1856).

9. Thurlow Weed (1797–1882), the astute former Whig boss of New York State, had early joined the Frémont campaign, having concluded that his protégé, William Seward, would have a better chance at the presidency in 1860.

10. Blair, Weed, and other Republicans were convinced that well-financed Democrats were engaged in massive fraud in Pennsylvania, including the illegal naturalization of thousands of emigrants in exchange for votes. Democratic campaign manager John W. Forney implied as much in an Oct. 3, 1856, letter to James Buchanan: "We have naturalized a vast mass of men. The opposition are appalled. They cry fraud. Our most experienced men say *all is well*" (GIENAPP, 404–5).

To Elizabeth Blair Lee

New York, October 20th [1856]

Dear Lizzie,

I enclose you the receipt for Betty's first session. We found only Mrs. Bolton at home. She is a very gentle lady like woman and I liked her countenance and quiet manners very much. The house is good. I went into Betty's room & the various dining & school rooms—in short saw to everything your Mother and yourself would have done and I think Betty is very very well placed. Much better than in a town school. There is a beautiful country all around—every comfort of a great city at hand & none of its drawbacks. I think I would insist on Betty's exercising in the gymnasium they have there—mere dancing is not so good; for with her singing she should also develop her chest as much as possible. An hour in a bowling alley puts me at peace with all the world.

There are but eight boarders with Mrs. Bolton. The dining room is elegant and spacious with fine pictures. My fastidiousness rejoiced in the evidence of daily good breeding which shone throughout the house. Two very lady like girls, one daughter to the Governor of Rhode Island,[1] were introduced to Betty & I left her to their care.

I think Betty will not like the quiet & seclusion of the place at first but I am sure the good effects will tell on her soon, and children all imitate each other. She will soon learn to think the present the best and it is a happy faculty of youth that we elders will do well to imitate & make the most of the present phase.

I heartily regret the defeat we have met and do not look for things to change for the better.[2] The Democrats will follow up their advantage with the courage of success & our forces are unorganized and just now surprised and inactive. I wish the cause had triumphed. I do wish Mr. Frémont had been the one to administer the bitter dose of subjection to the South for he has the coolness & nerve to do it just as it needs to be done—without passion & without sympathy—as coldly as a surgeon over a hospital patient would he have cut off their right hand Kansas from the old unhealthy southern body. I think too that it would have called out great qualities in him and he would have so much enjoyed the greatness of the occupation. But he bears it nobly. I do admire his self-control. Tell your Father he must come to us for example & comfort in November for I don't think we will wear any but black feathers this year.

I hope Mr. Lee will not be punished for going with me to Old Point. That will be a great sin now. Give my love to your Mother & Father and with real love for your aid & sympathy, believe me always yours affectionately,

Jessie Frémont

Betty needs a fork spoon six napkins & 12 towels. Shall I get them?

ALS (NjP—Blair-Lee Papers).

1. William Warner Hoppin (1807–90) served as governor of Rhode Island, 1854–57, but no information on a daughter has been located.

2. In a crushing blow to the Frémont campaign, the Republican party lost the Oct. 14 Pennsylvania state election by less than 3,000 votes. The party was also narrowly defeated in Indiana, which voted the same day.

To Elizabeth Blair Lee

[late Oct. 1856]

Dear Lizzie,

Arnold[1] has put all my things with your Mother's into one bill & sent me a blank to fill up for your Mother's. I think I have everything on it but a bill is a mystery to me except what Mantalini[2] calls "the dem total."

Your dress, two of chally—eight yards each, a cravat & "habit" (silk shirt I presume) two cloaks—is that right? I put Madame Mas[3] on the same bill & the cap with it. I will send their separate receipts to you.

Mrs. Bolton said Betty only needed fork & spoon & some towels & napkins—half a dozen or a dozen of each. I did not get them, as she said there was no need to be hurried & I wait your orders.

I am distressed about little Frank. He was perfectly well, good appetite good digestion and gay as Charley, when suddenly Tuesday morning he was taken with a convulsion—slight but enough to bring before me all the sorrowful images I had shut down in my heart until I thought them forgotten.[4]

Since then he seems wavering between life and death. The weather changed to decided cold with heavy frost last night, so today he is much better, but he is so feeble looking yet it makes my heart ache, and Dr. Van Buren says I must "watch him closely"—in a way that makes me feel he is liable to a return of his illness.

I have not been out since Tuesday morning except to take Frank for a drive daily. Sleeping in the nursery & starting out of bed a dozen times in the night do not improve my courage. I don't care for the election. Let it go. I care more for your Father's disappointment than for Mr. Frémont's—although I dare say when Frank is well I shall be less careless about it.

Our people here don't give up the ship by any means—even Mr. Frémont who is almost as much of a cold comforter as Mr. Lee, and always looks failure in the face, thinks we shall win. An immense amount of work is going on & money comes in by 15. & 30.000 (thousands). I find I do take interest but I think I know myself when I say it is not on my own account.

Nina & Lizzie Whiting are on a visit to Mrs. Grey Staten Island.[5] Lil & I keep home. We hope to see some of you the 4th Nov.

Let me know anything you want done for Betty. She is as near as Silver Spring used to be to her—only an hour & I like the occasional shake-up of going out of town. With love to you all & good hopes to your Father. Yours affcty,

Jessie Frémont.

Susy writes me she had seen you & your Father. I hope with her, cheerfulness has returned to the house. She says Father was furious at the Penn. elections! I knew he would be.

ALS (NjP—Blair-Lee Papers). Enclosure: bill for Arnold, Constable & Company.

1. Aaron Arnold (1794–1876) had established a fashionable dry goods emporium in 1827; it became Arnold, Constable & Company in 1842 when his son-in-law, James M. Constable, joined the business (New York *Times* obit., Mar. 19, 1876).
2. A dissipated fop in Charles Dickens's *Nicholas Nickleby.*
3. Leonide Mas, a dressmaker (New York City *Directory,* 1857–58).
4. JBF refers to the deaths of two of her children, Benton on Oct. 6, 1848, at age ten weeks, and Anne Beverley on July 11, 1853, at five months (HERR, 177, 231). Eighteen-month-old Frank had the measles.
5. Possibly the wife of John A. C. Gray (b. 1815) of Staten Island, a wealthy merchant and strong Frémont backer (New York City *Directory,* 1857–58; New York *Evening Post,* Sept. 6, 1856).

To Elizabeth Blair Lee

Sunday morning
Nov 2d [1856].

Dear Lizzie,

We came home from the Acadamy of Music Friday night and found your Father sitting before the fire toasting himself.[1] Marie had fed him and he was resting and warming. We were very glad to see him— especially Mr. Frémont values just now your Father's intelligent confidence in the results for our side.

I don't dare say anything more than to tell you we may be successful. Telegraphs will do the rest. You will be in town Wednesday any way— either defeat or success is best met at once & we shall telegraph you at your brother's.[2] Your Father is very well—by way of neutralizing the effect of politics I took him to the German opera last night where the little opera of Martha was very well given.[3] "The last rose of summer" is sung again and again in it & your Father was really interested and pleased—found it very short.

There are no Sunday trains or your Father would have gone up to day to see Betty. I have everything ready for her and shall send you the receipted bills early in the week. I did not forget anything in the list I sent you but some boots for yourself & Betty came in afterwards which with her linen & fork & spoon made a little in addition which Mr. Blair can attend to without getting a draft for so small a sum.

I do trust for your Father's gratification that we may be the winners on Tuesday but he is best here if we are defeated. We will comfort him & cheer him up. Tell Mr. Lee from me that his "aggrieved face" must be laid by until Wednesday—I hope for four years.

I have so many things to tell you but the Post Office will read them first so I dare not. If we get in I shall ask that we do not have a Catholic for Post Master General[4]—absolution & the doctrine of doing evil that good may come, are tempting recollections to aid political inquisition.

Until Tuesday, in Hope & Faith—& without a grain of Charity for our "persecutors enemies and slanderers." [*Margin note:* Post Master please send as soon as read, to Mrs. Lee.] From your affectionate

Jessie Frémont

Little Frank is thoroughly well again—only he has grown so fond of me that I have to sl :ep with him the last half of each night in his own little bed. He lies with his eyes open—screams if Mémé comes to him, but smiles on me & murmurs "Mama Baby" & so goes to sleep again. After the 4th I am going to make him give me up for it gives me too little sleep but I like him to love me so.

ALS (NjP—Blair-Lee Papers).

1. On Friday, Oct. 31, the Academy of Music was "crowded from pit to dome" for a massive Republican rally of "the workingmen of this City" (New York *Tribune,* Nov. 1, 1856). Francis Blair had again come to New York to await election results with the Frémonts.

2. Montgomery Blair's house on Lafayette Square had been purchased by Francis Blair in 1836. Today "Blair House" serves as a U.S. government guest house.

3. Baron Friedric von Flotow's opera *Martha* was playing at Niblo's Garden (New York *Tribune,* Nov. 1, 1856).

4. Postmaster General James Campbell (1812–93) was a Catholic politician from Philadelphia who had been appointed to the Pierce cabinet with the support of James Buchanan (GIENAPP, 94).

To Elizabeth Blair Lee

Tuesday Nov. 18 [1856].

Dear Lizzie,

We are subsiding into former habits, not without some of the giddy feeling one has after having been a long while on ship board. Things hardly have their natural value and attraction after the engrossing excitement of the one idea we have had in our heads for so many months.

Mr. Frémont however has already mounted his old hobby and is in full chase after his butterfly[1] — this time with solid prospects of success. But as you know I am the most skeptical of mortals and until I see actual thousands I shall give small heed to the promised millions.

In the mean time can you bring down your ideas to the level of my small affairs — will you send me the box of papers I left with you and my feather rug? Send them by Adams express please.

I am gathering up my household belongings from California and elsewhere. Mr. Frémont says I may live where I like & I like here. Washington I fret against — yourselves Father & Susan comprise all my lovings there, & likings I have none. So look upon me as your hotel here for the future. Your Mother will I know come again. Betty will draw her here and your Father finds here a host of political allies and admirers. You must contrive some reason to come yourself. I am afraid Mr. Lee will receive some evidence of disfavor for having gone with me to Virginia. If he is sent to sea you will hate me.

We are all well. Frank fattens visibly as your Mother said he would. Charley has on cloth pantaloons (to the knee only) and is exceedingly proud. He learns well. We are all working at something, Lil & I at German. I am going to Germany when I have money enough & I want to speak it. We have a charming opera season. I am quite a dividing attraction there & it amused me last night to see Bel[l]e Cass[2] wedged in among ladies & watching with her cold venomous eyes, the succession of clever & fashionable men who came to my box. We have upset her throne. She & Aunt Catron[3] both have new white opera cloaks — they will wear them at the inauguration. See if they don't. I enclose Betty's last list — is anything else needed? Yours affcty,

Jessie

2 Spoons & a fork	9.00
Towels & napkins	4.75
Boots (2 pr) (Cork soles)	9.00
Bonnet (drawn black velvet)	12.00
	34.75

I can get very pretty chinchilla sets from 20 to 30—Cape & muff. I like it better than the dyed furs—they fade & grow rusty. The other, too, is much more used & lasts perfectly well. I have not gotten them yet—waiting your decision. The other kind are fifteen & seventeen to twenty dollars.

ALS (NjP—Blair-Lee Papers). On Nov. 4, 1856, JCF was defeated for the presidency.

1. JCF had resumed direction of Las Mariposas (The Butterflies) gold mines.
2. Isabella Cass was a daughter of widowed Michigan senator Lewis Cass (1782–1866), an old Jacksonian whose family JBF had known during her Washington childhood. Cass, defeated for reelection by the Republican candidate, would soon be named secretary of state, and his daughters would entertain lavishly during the Buchanan administration. Belle Cass married the Dutch ambassador, Baron von Limburg (WOODFORD, 296).
3. Longtime Buchanan favorite Matilda (Childress) Catron was the wife of another Jacksonian, Supreme Court Justice John Catron of Tennessee (c. 1786–1865). JBF may have disliked Catron in part because he was one of two dissenting justices in the 1855 Mariposas title decision otherwise favorable to JCF. The opera JBF and her rivals saw on November 17 was Meyerbeer's *Star of the North* with Anna de la Grange in the starring role (New York *Tribune,* Nov. 17, 1856).

To Elizabeth Blair Lee

December 6th [1856]
New York.

Dear Lizzie

The box and check came ten days ago nearly but Charley was so ill[1] and I so tired that I have not acknowledged them.

I begin to feel at ease now that Frank shews no symptoms of scarlet fever. Dr. Van Buren thinks one poison (measles) will drive the other away. He is certainly beautifully well notwithstanding his illness. Charley is entirely well. His voice is weak & low and the skin is peeling off his thin cheeks and hands but he plays all day & last night slept from ten 'till eight this morning without stirring. I keep him in Mr. Frémont's room which I have taken from him for the time. Frank disturbed him in the nursery & so I moved him here at once (here means in the bedroom where I read sew write & stay except for breakfast & dinner). I gave Mr. Frémont your pretty room & Lizzie Whiting & Nina have the one your Father had & Lil takes half of Frank's room. You see it has been a regular upsetting but we all get on quite as well as the other way. You owe no man anything but the little package of bills is rather bunchy & I will send them to you by Mr. James who goes next week. Mr. Frémont has had a very light form of scarlet fever—a little of each thing, sore-throat fever & nausea enough to make him headachy & very uncomfortable but nothing more.

I was very glad to know your Father was so well. Give our best love to your Mother & Father. Tell Mr. Lee I thought of him when Charley's life was trembling in the balance. He really loves him and I knew both of you would feel my pain, it reminded me of that other night I watched the same struggle in your room.[2] This time daylight brought quiet and sleep. Charley was delirious almost all the time for four days—Sunday night painfully so but at three in the night he began to calm down and in the morning the Dr. said "everything has changed—the dangerous symptoms are past"—the Dr. praises Charley so much—says he is so good and docile and obeys so well. He is as good as possible— this is the eleventh day he has been in this one room & he has not been fretful or disobedient at all. "Charley is my darling" & my weakness you will say. I believe he is but you have indulgence for me. Yours always affectionately,

Jessie Frémont

ALS (NjP—Blair-Lee Papers).

1. Five-year-old Charley Frémont had scarlet fever.
2. JBF refers again to the death of her baby, Anne, at Silver Spring on July 11, 1853.

To Elizabeth Blair Lee

New York
January 23d [1857].

Dear Lizzie

Since our labors as corresponding secretaries ended I think we have both rested on our pens—the one grand topic was so full of excitement that other things seem flat in comparison. We were reminded of you the other day by a young scamp calling himself Thomas Benton Blair and calling Mr. Blair "Father." Mr. Frémont amused himself by enclosing his letter to your Father and pretending to take it in earnest. He had none of the family talent for he made a most lame story & I gave him only enough to get him a night's lodging & supper for which he seemed entirely ungrateful.

I am looking for Father by the 27th. I was very sorry he was not returned to the Senate, it would have been agreeable to him every way. But I never expected it—states and republics are like any other business associations—they have neither memories nor sentiments only necessities and whoever serves those necessities best is the one preferred. The Democratic party has always shewn itself especially remorseless in that way. The Whigs kept on with Clay & Webster again & again but the Democrats follow Napoleon's example and divorce their oldest friend without flinching when they want a new heir.

With all this experience of others to go upon you will think us wise in turning our backs upon political life & putting our hands to other work—Mr. Frémont to money making & I to Lil & Nina. Lil has a thorough English governess who gives Nina drawing & music lessons & the girls both read aloud with her. She is my ideal of an orderly thorough well educated woman. Charley is quite strong & well again & at his lessons. He is not a rapid scholar except in fairy tales & Irish songs. Betty wrote me that she was well in spite of quantities of heavy cake & I look for her here her next vacation if you think the house safe.

We have the opera again the only amusement I indulge in. You will give me praise for my long walks—always two & sometimes four miles almost every day. I have a museum of shoes. Some for frozen & some for thawed ground, and one devoted dress short & cheap and a cloak that defies rain or snow & so disguised I walk out entrenched. Nina & Lil do the same & of course we are all well. Mr. Frémont is remarkably well—positively fattening & very contented with things as they are. Yours with love to all,

Jessie.

P.S.

Go see our french friend Matilda & engage her services[1]—for me— rather for yourself. I have not had a sight of bloody mse [menses?] since the fifteen of November. I am so old that there is a hope tis change of life—but a sick stomach & other familiar symptoms warns me that I may want my good friend Matilda's services. Still I don't tell this to any body—for I hate to be joked. So tell her from the middle of August to the 1st of October to hold herself disengaged & if necessary I do as they do [. . .] pay her in part before hand as a retainer. You have money of mine to arrange all that for me. I'll pay her for her time just as I would if she worked for it & that would not be disagreeable to me—for I dread the ordeal. Tell [her] she will be called to a house where she has often been & where she knows & likes every one & they her.

ALS (NjP—Blair-Lee Papers).

1. Thirty-two-year-old JBF, who had already borne five children, wanted Lizzie Lee to arrange for the services of a midwife. JBF was either mistaken or miscarried, for she does not mention a possible pregnancy again. This note follows her Jan. 23 [1857] letter in the chronological arrangement in the Blair-Lee Papers (NjP). Context suggests this to be the most likely date, or possibly the previous year.

To Francis Preston Blair

New York, January 31st [1857]

My dear Mr. Blair,

Mr. Frémont laughed out over your exculpatory letter—your name-sake had light hair, blue eyes & was a coarse stoutish likeness of Frank & Montgomery. He has been to Mr. Howard & Mr. Beecher.[1] Mr. Howard made him talk & so unmasked him. Mr. Beecher gave him some money without much investigation. You will see he knows who your friends are.

Your true namesake [Frank Frémont] has distinguished himself this morning by his "love of adventure." He walked off alone and in trying to walk down stairs rolled himself to the bottom of the dining room flight. Of course he made a sensation among us but he was only badly scared and very little hurt as he rolled side wise. I expect to grow grey rapidly now that there are two of them to make experiments on their bones.

Yesterday was a spring day and the softened snow is now being mixed with a fierce sleeting rain that makes man and beast go on their way with bowed heads. Mr. Frémont has gone down town and as it is Saturday the girls are off duty. They both study well with an admirable new governess I have for them. She comes every morning and returns to her own home at two o'clock. One of our German republican friends, himself a man of distinguished position as historian, told me of this Mrs. Seiler (an Englishwoman married to a German political refugee) and he had also the kindness to trace a plan of study and reading for Lily and said he would come from time to time to examine her progress.[2] Mrs. Seiler was a governess in England & has the highest letters from good families there. As her husband is employed on a newspaper here she is a fixture and I have her for years. In the summer when we go to Staten Island she says she will find board near us so Lil's & Nina's lessons will not be interrupted. She is a fine musician, sings & reads aloud well & is also a good artist. This is more for Lizzie than yourself. Lizzie knows my hobby & will be glad to find I have been able to gratify myself at last—and at a rate consistent with my finances—five hundred a year. Nina has for that her lessons in music drawing and reading aloud, Lil in everything & Charley in as much as his age can take. Mrs. Seiler speaks French as well as I do & Charley's books are in French.

You asked for a letter about myself and the children and you must not complain if I have given it to you. Mrs. Blair and Lizzie will fully appreciate the importance of my acquisition. I mean to adhere to my plan of keeping in one place until Lily is well grounded in her education and I see nothing to alter my plans for years to come. California has no attraction for me and I trust a stay of a few months may be all it requires of Mr. Frémont. We should only be in his way for any visit that was not to last for a year or two.

Mr. Brook's death brought up a crowd of political ideas and memories. A few centuries ago it would have been called a "jugement de Dieu" [judgment of God]. I see Mr. Buchanan attended his funeral. Considering his intention of "seizing the Treasury" the text of the funeral discourse was sarcastic.[3] Mr. Sumner should get well now. He is avenged now in a more complete and awful manner than could have been brought about by human agency.

Do any of you come on this spring? We have gay times here now in the artist world. Madame de Wilhorst,[4] a little lady about Lily's size, stepped at one step from her drawingroom and private life to the topmost round of the theatrical & musical ladder. A more charming voice one cannot hear and she acts like she was alone in her own house & walks without any stride. She couldn't if she tried—she is too short, but I wish you could see and hear her. A family quarrel about the amount of money her Father ought to give her brought her out.

Miss Heron[5] of whom you must have seen notices is the other great star. Mr. Frémont and I went to see her last night. She is large with hands and arms like pink wax moulded by a sculptor & such shoulders and figure as are enough in themselves to create enthusiasm. I will not tell you what we thought of her—only that I saw tears in Mr. Frémont's eyelashes & found it hard work to keep my own stormy eyes from overflowing. You would cry outright like an honest play goer as you are, and you must not fail to see her either here, or if she goes to you. She makes fifteen hundred a week—clear—& will not lessen in attraction.

All these new temptations with the old one of coming where every body has a warm welcome for you should bring you to us again. Father stayed a day & night with us—cheerful & quite himself again. We're all dead men in the political world so we have all our talents free for private life and the hatchet is buried and we are ourselves again.[6] Lizzie owes me two letters now for I shall expect her to answer this. With kindest love to all, yours affectionately,

                                                        Jessie Frémont

ALS (NJP—Blair-Lee Papers).

1. The man claiming to be Thomas Benton Blair, mentioned in Jan. 23 [1857] to Lizzie Lee, above, had also solicited money from John Tasker Howard and Henry Ward Beecher (1813–87). Howard, a business associate of JCF's whose New York office at 34 Broadway was used as a campaign headquarters, would work for JCF at Las Mariposas and remain a lifelong friend. Beecher, the renowned pastor of the Plymouth Congregational Church in Brooklyn Heights, had taken a two-month leave of absence to campaign for Frémont. JBF must have appreciated Beecher's gallant defense of her marriage by a Catholic priest: "Had we been in Col. Fremont's place, we would have been married if it had required us to walk through a row of priests and bishops as long as from Washington to Rome, winding up with the Pope himself" (New York *Tribune,* July 4, 1856).

2. JBF's German friend was most probably the noted scholar Francis Lieber (1800–1872), who had just resigned his South Carolina College professorship and moved to New York because his opposition to slavery had prevented his selection as college president. He would become a chaired professor at Columbia in Mar. 1857. In an undated early 1861 letter to Thomas Starr King (CSfCP), JBF mentions Lieber by name as having once volunteered to plan a study program for Lily. Mrs. Seiler has not been further identified.

3. The assailant of Massachusetts senator Charles Sumner (1811–74), Congressman Preston S. Brooks of South Carolina, had died unexpectedly on Jan. 27, 1857. During the funeral service in the House of Representatives, attended by President-elect Buchanan, a number of brief eulogies were given. In one, Congressman John H. Savage of Tennessee shocked the North by referring to the attack as an act "the world has approved and lauded." However, JBF probably refers to the eulogy of the House

chaplain, who used as his text Christ's words to the thief on the cross, "this day thou shalt be with me in Paradise," in order to show the necessity of repentance (New York *Herald*, Feb. 2, 1857; New York *Tribune*, Jan. 30, 1857). Sumner, who remained wounded psychologically if not physically, would not return to the Senate for nearly four years.

4. JBF had probably attended the opera debut of Cora de Wilhorst on Jan. 28 in Gaetano Donizetti's *Lucia di Lammermoor* at the Academy of Music. The *Herald* reported a huge and enthusiastic audience that included "the crème de la crème of the fashionable world" and predicted a "brilliant future" for the singer (Jan. 29, 1857).

5. Matilda Heron (c. 1833–77) was starring in *Camille* at Wallack's Theatre, a play the *Herald* condemned as "a deification of prostitution" that appealed to the "worst passions of the human heart" (Apr. 12, 1857; New York *Times* obit., Mar. 12, 1877).

6. In a letter to his son Frank, Blair reported Benton's visit less generously: "It seems he deigned to spend a night at Col. Frémonts! & Jessie . . . is happy that he is willing to forgive her for desiring her husband's election to the presidency & banishes the thought that he greatly contributed to prevent it" (Feb. 5, 1857, DLC—Blair Papers).

To Elizabeth Blair Lee

New York, March 1st, 1857

Dear Lizzie

I was very glad to get your letter and fully appreciate all your feeling about your good friends. You had the attachment to them that I have for your Father and Mother. We almost all find out during our lives that our best friends are not always those whose birth brings them nearest and there is no supplying their places when we lose them. I will not say any more about that—my experience of life has been a hardening one and I keep my mind from it as far as possible and I know you always regret to hear me say what I cannot help thinking, or rather, remembering.

I have had the real pleasure to have Father with me quite often this winter. At first he was formal and restrained, but he comes and goes now with a cheerful informality that brings a choking sensation in my throat. I have noticed, as no one could fail to do, the alteration in his person, and the complaint he contracted in Missouri continues to wear upon him.[1] But through myself I know Father and physical remedies alone will not reach him. He is wounded & irritated in his political associations. I wish with all my heart he had never returned to Missouri after his election to the House—then was the time to abandon them. Staying in Washington keeps alive all those worrying ideas. Here in the

North he is treated with the deference and respect due to his age &
past services—in Washington any successful man with a place & a
vote outranks him—Gwin, Broderick, Herbert, Keitt[2] anything in place.

Mr. Frémont has earned my positive gratitude—it is the right word—
by his deference to Father and his efforts to please him. One might
think Mr. Frémont had tried to defeat Father so much does he do to
make him feel everything on the old footing. Mr. Frémont is at work
on his book & Father was greatly interested in the plates &c—and
pleased with the deference to his judgment in various matters connected
with the publication.[3] Altogether he is as he ought to be in my house
a most honored and welcome and contented guest, and you know
what a relief it is to me.

Charley has taken a great affection for Father—following him about—
taking his hand & talking his nonsense to him & it pleases Father. He
likes too Charley's intelligence & good progress. Mrs. Seiler has him
for a daily lesson but I prepare it & he goes on famously. Father laughed
at Charley's geographical definitions of the States. I had told him things
in my fashion—rather depreciatory of slave states which he repeated
innocently to Father who was very much amused.

Lily, of course, is doing well—her handwriting is getting good &
she writes ten good sized sheets of dictation with only as many errors—
omissions of words counting. Nina is not well. She is quite dyspeptic
(I don't even know how to spell the word) and Dr. Van Buren says
nothing will really help her except some weeks of active country life,
walking, riding & simple hours & living. I have not taken her to more
than half a dozen balls for I found she danced herself ill & the only
way to prevent it was not to let her dance at all. She studies but without
interest, has no appetite & although we certainly live regularly & simply
I am not contented with the state of things for her. Nina has one of
those inert natures that yield to depression without one struggle. If
she had some motive to animate her I know she would get quite well.
I think our life too serious for her disposition. If the right person were
to appear I would be glad to see her get in love, it is the natural state
of mind for her age & would be a stimulant not disagreeable to take
but it all lies in whether the "right person" is right or not. As yet Nina
has no turn that way and it is as well with her delicate constitution
that it is so. We go to Staten Island in May but unless she is much
improved soon I will ask for an exchange & while I look after Betty
in the Easter holidays I will beg you to let Nina breathe the pine air

at Silver Spring. Susy is to be here soon and I look to that as an amusement for I think Nina is only half dyspeptic & the other half ennuyée. You know some children play alone & amuse themselves with any odds & ends & are happy & others must be walked about & given new toys constantly & even then they fret—& Nina needs new toys. Do write to me soon. Give my best love to all and tell your Father all the faithful stop here on their way to take their seats in the Senate. The Dixons, Doolittles (contrast between those two women) & our good friend Preston King[4] who is I believe truly friendly to Mr. Frémont. Yours afftcy,

J.B.F.

AL initialed (NjP—Blair-Lee Papers).

1. Benton had lost nearly fifty pounds and his face was "sharp & discolored by disease" (Francis Preston Blair to Frank Blair, Jr., Feb. 5, 1857, DLC—Blair Papers). Benton, but not JBF, would soon learn he had cancer (CHAMBERS, 434).

2. JBF had known proslavery senator William M. Gwin (1805-85) since they had both journeyed to San Francisco on the *Panama* in June 1849. Elected to the Senate in 1849 with JCF, Gwin had drawn the long term and served until 1856. Reelected to a second term, he would reportedly spend $75,000 a year to maintain his lavish Washington mansion during the Buchanan administration. In 1861, he would be arrested as a Confederate supporter and spend much of the war in exile. Gwin's bitter rival, David Broderick (1820-59), a rough, charismatic Tammany-style politician, had just been elected senator from California on a free-soil platform. In 1859 he would be killed in a duel with a Gwin ally, California Chief Justice David S. Terry. Alabama-born Philemon T. Herbert (1825-64) was a California congressman, 1855-57, who in May 1856 had murdered an Irish waiter at Willard's Hotel in Washington but was acquitted (POORE, 444). After Herbert was helpful to the Frémonts during their 1858 mining dispute, their opinion of him improved (see JBF to Francis Preston Blair, July 18 [1858], below). Congressman Lawrence M. Keitt (1824-64) of South Carolina was despised in the North because he had accompanied Preston Brooks to the Senate chamber and prevented others from intervening while Brooks brutally beat Senator Charles Sumner with a cane.

3. "I am engaged in writing up our expedition of 1845, '46, and '47," JCF wrote Kit Carson on Mar. 2 (CtY). He had begun the project in 1855 but put it aside during the election campaign. For the next several months he would work on the account, with JBF, as before, taking down his narrative. By now a book contract had been signed with publisher George W. Childs of Philadelphia. However, the lure of Las Mariposas business soon diverted JCF from the project, and the contract was eventually cancelled. During the Civil War, Childs sued for reimbursement of advances with only partial success. JBF, who enjoyed writing far more than did her husband, kept the accumulated illustrations and notes until the Frémonts finally made use of them in JCF's 1887 *Memoirs*. See JACKSON & SPENCE, xxxii-xxxvi, for a detailed history of the project; and JBF notes to [William A. Croffut], [Nov. 30, 1885], below, for additional information.

4. James Dixon (1814-73) of Connecticut, James R. Doolittle (1815-97) of Wis-

consin, and Preston King (1806–65) of New York were all newly elected Republican senators.

To Elizabeth Blair Lee

[late Apr. 1857]

My dear Lizzie I am so surprised by your last letter that I hardly know how to write to you.[1] I wish I could come immediately to see you but that is a gratification I must delay. You must not take so painful a view of the result. Mary [Schooff?] (Mrs. Stevenson) has a superb child and all her family anticipated the worst result from the lateness of the affair & she had not had your advantage of fifteen years married life. With chloroform (you can take that safely) you may go to sleep and wake up from a dreamless sleep to find my godson waiting your recognition.[2] Mr. Lee will be so happy in the possession of a child of his own that it ought to nerve you to think of it. Your godson will lose and mine gain by the event. Think of "fifteen years of accumulated parental enthusiasm" and Mr. Lee has parental instinct, a gift denied to Mr. Frémont and not tremendously developed in yourself.

I had made my wondering cry and told Mr. Frémont the great news before I read the postscript. It shall go no farther. He says the election did it, that it brought out all your dormant energies.

Frank [Blair, Jr.] is here & I have written for Betty to come down, as he asked, and see him. She will stay with me of course, but Frank promises himself to give her a little frolicking. He dined with us Saturday. I am happy to announce to your Father that Frank wears a moustache and beard as every genuine republican does. Some calling themselves so, but at heart preferring the name democrat, have not raised the emblem but the genuine ones are bearded.

I wrote to Nina to come home at once. Will you trouble yourself to find her an escort? Affcty,

J.B.F.

AL initialed (NjP—Blair-Lee Papers).

1. After fourteen years of marriage, thirty-eight-year-old Lizzie Lee was expecting her first child in August. For her earlier gynecological problems, see JBF to Elizabeth Blair Lee [Feb. 1856], note 3, above.
2. JBF's sister Liz wrote similar advice: "I wish you as few aches as one can have,

& in case they are many remember ether—it proved such a blessing to me" (Eliza Benton Jones to Elizabeth Blair Lee, Monday [summer 1857], NjP—Blair-Lee Papers).

To Elizabeth Blair Lee

New York, May 4th [1857]

Dear Lizzie,

Nina got home very well and I have written to your Mother to thank her for her care of her.[1] Let me thank you for your care of her mind. I see already where you have dropped good seed which are not fallen on stony ground. I will try to take care that they take root before the wind comes.

I have just had a letter from Susy—they stayed a day at Liverpool to recruit & Susan was sick every hour of the passage, Pensée well as a lark.[2] While I think of it let me tell you that Mr. Frémont says Mrs. Preuss can have nothing of importance to him, only books he would like to have but the results are worked out long ago for it is about eight years since Preuss was in his employment.[3] The $300 she claims was paid Preuss in California & $1500 gotten for him for surveying two ranches near San José—in '49.[4] I know you would not believe her nonsense but it is as well to give you Mr. Frémont's answer. I am only sorry you had the annoyance of coming in contact with such a coarse nature.

Do write to me as often as you feel like fatiguing yourself so much. As you cannot come to me I will come sometime in the early summer to see you before we go quite out of town. All the astronomical & tedious part of the work is now finished as far as Mr. Frémont goes into it. If Jacob[5] were here he could get rapidly through another part, but he seems dull about coming.

I hope Mr. Lee will soon be with you again. I believe in Landor's saying—"There is a vast deal of vital air in loving words"[6]—and one bad feature of childbearing is depression of spirits.

Something that I suffer from occasionally without however having your cause—but this continued pain at the heart wears out strength of mind as well as body. I have been in bed three days, quieting down a congestion that threatened badly and sad unto death but with returning strength I feel cheerful again. Don't say exercise, food or any thing of that kind, for I do not deserve reproach. I eat much and walk better than you do—rain or shine I make my four sometimes six miles daily. When the rain is too bad I get in an omnibus at the door & take twelve miles of shaking up and I do diligently my teaching of Charley & my helping of Mr. Frémont—but it is beyond my control and Dr. Van Buren says nothing can help me but entire undisturbed equanimity and such a placid brain & heart as I never have had & cannot well have unless I were an idiot.

You see dear Lizzie we both have our horizons bounded but we cannot say how far yet we may travel. You I trust will not realize your forebodings although I see all their justice but there is no limit to God's power and your life has been so self-sacrificing and good that you need not fear the result even if you should not live—but I trust you will recover to be more happy than ever in this new tie between yourself and Mr. Lee who will value his child and if he can, love you more than ever for the pain you endured in giving it to him. I would greatly like to go to you now but I am not well & have much to do at home, but I will bring my two beautiful boys to encourage you in giving me a godson like them. In our nursery talk we have let your Father be forgotten. Give him my love and tell him I will bring him a budget of *Albany* gossip—for & against. Yours most affectionately,

Jessie Frémont

ALS (NjP—Blair-Lee Papers).

1. JBF to Eliza (Gist) Blair, May 4, 1857 (NjP—Blair-Lee Papers).
2. Susan and Gauldrée de Boilleau, with their young daughter, Pensée, had just embarked for France and ultimately India, where Boilleau would be the French consul in Calcutta. Lizzie Lee reported that Susan was "dreadfully afflicted at leaving her friends and Country" (to S. Phillips Lee, Apr. 3, 1857, NjP—Blair-Lee Papers).
3. The Frémonts had asked Lizzie Lee to obtain the notebooks and sketches of JCF's skilled German cartographer, Charles Preuss, evidently for use in their projected book (see JBF to Elizabeth Blair Lee, Thursday night [Apr. 18, 1857], NjP—Blair-Lee Papers). Preuss, a morose man in poor health, had hung himself in 1854, and his widow clearly harbored deep resentments against JCF. When Lizzie Lee, accompanied by Nina, called to ask for the material, she found Mrs. Preuss "such a virago—she first said she had no books—then said she would burn them before giving them to Col F., her statements contradicting one another. I soon saw she was not a fit person for to enounter so came off & gave Jessie a full report of the woman's attack & my prompt retreat" (to S. Phillips Lee, Apr. 23, 1857, NjP—Blair-Lee Papers). The Frémonts never acquired the journals, which reveal Preuss's cynical feelings about JCF and the expeditions. For an account of their rediscovery in Germany, see PREUSS, ix-x.
4. Preuss had drawn and certified a map of Mariano Castro's Rancho de Refugio, dated San José, Dec. 26, 1849 (PREUSS, xxviii). William Carey Jones testified that Preuss had surveyed and drafted a map of Las Mariposas (now lost) for JCF in the summer

of 1849 (DNA-49, California Private Land Claims Dockets, Docket 1, p. 99). If JCF owed Preuss money, he would be one among many claimants through the years.

5. Presumably Jacob Dodson, the free black who had been on several of JCF's expeditions.

6. English author Walter Savage Landor (1775-1864). JBF also quotes these lines to Nelly Haskell, Nov. 1 [1864], below.

To Elizabeth Blair Lee

New York, June 2d [1857].
56 West 9th street.

Dear Lizzie,

We are in all our preparations for leaving which keep us busy enough.[1] I think we ought to be readier to die than other people for we are always setting our house in order & making up our minds to part with some one or other of the few we like. Now, it is Father. This railway accident has I fear jarred him more than he will confess and I want to know how he really looks.[2]

Father unbends to Mr. Lee for whom he has a real affection so that I can trust Mr. Lee's report of his looks & manner of moving. Ask Mr. Lee to do this for me—the next time he goes into town please to see Father & judge well if he is hurt. If he is I must see him again before I leave even if it is but for a night.

I wish I could add anything to his happiness—if I could I should have remained here this summer—but he will only see things his own way and I must not always give up, only think he wanted me to call on Mrs. Floyd[3] the other day. With him I should be meeting all the men who were so personally malignant last year & with whom nothing can make me associate.

Father goes for the summer to the Virginia Springs & I had enough of Virginia hospitality last year not to risk it again.

But all this does not take from me the regret that I can do nothing for him in his lonesome life.

Jacob [Dodson] came on with me & I have had my pen in hand as much as five hours & a half at a time. We finish with him today & that much work is done.

I can't tell you how grateful the rest of home was after that week's travel & fatigue. The house had been made brilliantly clean & of course

Marie had flowers everywhere—all in honor of my return & my birthday which is composed now of the crooked backed figures.

Tell me how you are yourself. I saw Mr Lee's name as witness on
one of the courts of Inquiry[4] so that I hope you sleep well. He is not
to scold because I kept you awake that night—for it is a long time
before I shall talk to you again. When I do I hope to find you very
well and very happy & to see your home completed by a child of your
own. Yours most affectionately,

Jessie Frémont

ALS (NjP—Blair-Lee Papers).

1. JBF had cancelled her plans to summer again on Staten Island and was preparing
to go to France with the children while JCF journeyed to California on Las Mariposas
business. She had recently returned from a visit to Washington, where she said goodbye to her father and the Blairs.

2. Benton had just been injured in a railway accident near Pittsburgh, suffering a
gash on his head and, more seriously, a painful bruise on his back. Despite his injuries
and a high fever, he had insisted on delivering a scheduled speech before returning to
convalesce in Washington. Although his back pained him severely, he was now writing
daily to meet a publisher's deadline (CHAMBERS, 431).

3. Both Sarah Buchanan (Preston) Floyd (1802–79) and her husband, former Virginia
governor John Buchanan Floyd (1806–1863), were first cousins of JBF's mother (DOR-
MAN, 289–90). John Floyd had been among a group of southern Democrats who had
discussed the Democratic presidential nomination with JCF in 1855, but Floyd explained, "I broke off all communication with [JCF] on political subjects because I saw
that the influences which governed him were abolition" (see New York *Evening Post*,
Sept. 4, 1856; New York *Tribune*, Sept. 13, 1856). Floyd campaigned against JCF,
giving a New York speech "spouted with great vehemence" according to STRONG,
2:298. Floyd was named secretary of war by Buchanan.

4. In a major reorganization of the navy stipulated by Congress, a special examining
board had met in June-July 1855 to evaluate the careers of naval officers and eliminate
dead wood. Later, in answer to charges that the board had acted unfairly in some
instances, Congress had authorized courts of inquiry to reassess individual cases. Lee
was now serving as a witness in one such case. (CORNISH & LAAS, 78–79; New York
Times, June 26, 1857).

To Samuel Phillips Lee

Tuesday evening
New York, June 9th [1857].

My dear Mr. Lee,

I did not look for so quick & so full an answer to my request so
that my pleasure was doubled by the surprise. I am going to ask that

you will go sometimes to see Father and have a friendly talk with him—to keep his heart as gentle as possible to his old friends and some young ones—who love him although he will not think so because of this political difference.

Father really likes you. When I was away before, Lizzie was my home authority. She has happier occupation now to keep her in her own home. She will write to me often I know and there is one letter I shall look with deep anxiety to receive from you.

I am glad you keep your love for your godson. He sends you his autograph with his portrait. Writing is not among his accomplishments yet and I will not hurry it, but he has learned through his history of the United States and a whole set of verses & such things. I am satisfied with my scholar.

Until you write to me claiming me as godmother (I trust you quite agree with Lizzie's choice?) I shall demand for Charley the first place with you. After that he shall descend a step but he is really a fine natured boy and one you will take pride in aiding to train.

We are looking for Mr. & Mrs. Blair every day.[1] The house is bare of everything but a welcome which is always to be found for all your household wherever they meet theirs and your sincere friend,

Jessie Frémont

ALS (NjP—Blair-Lee Papers).

1. Francis and Eliza Blair, who had just spent several weeks in St. Louis with their son Frank and his family, planned to stop in New York to see the Frémonts en route home. (E. B. SMITH [1], 244).

To Francis Preston Blair

Thursday night
Half way—[June 1857]

I have been thinking of you very often my dear Mr. Blair for we have two ladies on board who have your illness,[1] both of whom are reviving in the fine air we have had. This has been a rare day for the Atlantic—the sea has been like a lake & the sky blue and such a sunset as I never saw on this foggy sea before. There is so little motion that the table is set without guards and to judge by the well filled seats & well emptied dishes no one remains sick. This is a truly noble ship.[2]

I have chosen two staterooms for you—for Lizzie must come too—& Mr. Lee will be needed to take care of you on his element. No. 1 & No. 22—they face each other & are the largest & best rooms in the upper saloon. Don't wait for illness to drive you but come for the pleasure. I only wish I could cross with you instead of being wasted on people I don't care to know. The girls amuse themselves very well with some young people but I have had the blues desperately. I should like to hear from Lizzie every steamer if she finds leisure & when she cannot you will. I quite arrange in my own mind how you ought to do. All come away in October—it is a quiet month—and let Frank take care of Silver Spring for the winter. Mr. Frémont will be crossing about that time and I would meet you all at Havre & take you up home to Christian quiet & tea.

I hope this will not look too fanciful to you. It is not anything like the trouble or [fatigue?] of your journey to St. Louis this spring and the very novelty would amuse you—& in a great five thousand ton ship you would change your ideas about sea travel.

With kindest remembrances to all around you I am always yours affectionately,

Jessie Frémont

ALS (NjP—Blair-Lee Papers).

1. In May, sixty-six-year-old Blair had coughed up a trace of blood, but fears of tuberculosis proved groundless. (E. B. SMITH [1], 244).

2. JBF and children had departed June 20 on the steamship *Vanderbilt* (New York *Tribune*, June 22, 1857).

To Elizabeth Blair Lee

St. Germain en Laye
July 19th 1857.

My dear Lizzie

The first flight of my butterfly[1] (I hope you admire it as much as I do) is to Silver Spring where to use the words of an author we all admire "it finds among grass and flowers its natural and appropriate home."

I am wanting to hear from you very much—it seems a great deal longer than a month since we left home and in that time I have had no letters except from Mr. Frémont. Tell me exactly how you are—this will get to you very shortly before your confinement and you may be sure that from under your own roof there will not be another such anxious heart as mine. I think above all women I know, except Liz, you have the most right—under the promise to length of days, for you have truly honored your parents. With that you have loving care around you and Dr. May is eminently skillful.

I am full of concern for Susan who starts on her long journey tomorrow with the great disadvantage of being two months enceinte. I have asked in vain to have Pensée left with me, the little thing is teething and although sound and well now may not resist the heats of the Red Sea as well and by that time fatigue will be doubly disagreeable to Susan. She will not hear of it however. With the addition of a war in India the resources for coolness are cut off, for the summer retreat of the English was where the worst of the rebellion now is.[2] I should think our southern people might take a lesson from this Indian uprising. While one is filled with the deepest pity and horror for the cruel fates of the English there we can but remember how much the natives have had to provoke them. No well written dispatches tell us how many native women met revolting fates at the hands of the English. We know in other ways that when a native prince was "subdued" his household met "the fate of war." It seems they remember it among themselves. Calcutta is in safety and if there should be any doubt about it Boilleau's instructions have been altered this week to meet the case and he has the range of the Indian ocean and all it washes.

Susan is very well this time—no sickness. One whim only has seized her and that is an entire aversion & disgust to every thing french except french washing (I mean doing up clothes). It is funny to see how she has reversed her tone. She says Boilleau has nothing french in him and talks to Pensée in English. She protests roast mutton is better than any french cooking & what is more absolutely eats it. Boilleau and I laugh at it & say it will last to the frontier when she will change again.

We are charmingly placed here. This old castle is really old and is dilapidated enough to let the sunlight strike through its broken windows & doors and shine out the other side just as in pictures of ruins. We have a house on the terrace—a high table land some five hundred feet in a steep ascent from the beautiful valley of the Seine which lies at our feet. We are only ten miles from Paris and get to town with less thought & in less time than you do. We are three minutes walk from the station, which is a fine affair of iron pillars & glass roof as large as the President's house—the train has its 1st, 2d & 3 class carriages. The 2d are like ours only divided into seats for ten—the 1st are admirably built private carriages ten feet wide with seats for eight. You buy your ticket & it secures your seat, a privilege we do not have in our country. The station in town is ten minutes walk from the Tuileries & the best show places—no noise or confusion or crowding, all is regulated and orderly with policemen in every direction who answer questions or get you a carriage or do anything you need done. We have indulged ourselves with quiet and rest since getting here. One morning we went to see the pictures of this year's exhibition because there were several there of modern subjects & people. The Empress on foot & on horseback, with her child in the nursery & in the salon receiving Queen Victoria—who has been made by the artist (French-man of course) to look as hot and stout and ill dressed as he dared, while the Empress cool and elegant and in the most delicate of morning dress is making her a graceful salute.[3] The Emperor's favorites are there large as life—their portraits attracting knots of people. Isn't it an odd country where they care so little for that? How long would the English let a portrait of Prince Albert's mistress hang with that of the Queen. We are in a rustic atmosphere of simplicity and sobriety of every kind. There are many good French & English families here for the season which lasts to October. Our next neighbor is the son of the great Wilberforce.[4] We go to the same church & visit each other. Mrs. Wilberforce and himself have some of their grandchildren with them and Charley plays with them every morning. Our grounds are divided only by a little hedge. We have only a room for service here and about a hundred in the congregation. Charley behaves beautifully there, and is improving in every way. "Pauk" as he calls himself is growing visibly— he will be very tall and is a beauty. Nina & Lily walk every morning in the forest with the two little boys and Mémé. I did not tell you that in front of our house was the forest—a true forest of twenty one miles enclosed by a wall. Real trees & grass with lakes & deer—and rabbits innumerable. Their usual walk is to a lake two miles from the castle and with their divergings in the wood they make about five miles each day. They do that from seven to nine or ten—having first taken bread & milk—Nina her chocolate. At eleven we have our breakfast which is the best meal of the day to me, taken at the hour I like. One dish of meat, two of vegetables, curds & fruit. Then come lessons until two, then rest as it is warm weather. At six we dine and at half past seven we are on the fashionable promenade here which is a high walk on the edge of the steep hills—trees & the forest are on one side and the other slopes down to the Seine, vines covering it thickly all the way. In the distance lies Paris & we see the railway trains sending their white smoke in a dozen different directions over the wide view. There we sit on straw chairs, or walk, a military band playing, until nine when even the long twilight of this latitude begins to fall. I have a very good piano which with books gives us employment at odd times. At ten the girls go to bed. Charley & Frank at 8 & I later. I won't say how much. All our former servants are in their old places. They all gathered up & were ready for me—quitting other places without scruple. I have a man cook, a head man & an under one, Marie & Mémé—the gardener & the lodge keeper are included in the house rent. The house is three stories with eight fine rooms and several smaller ones on each floor—there are carriage house & stables with a pretty porter's lodge & servants' rooms, every place very prettily furnished—all clean as sunshine—in every room mirrors, fine clocks & vases, all the beds & windows very prettily curtained, china, glass, everything except house linen & silver, for three hundred dollars a month. That does not include the wages of my own servants but they cost me only half what my New York household did. The living here is less than in New York & no pen can do justice to the cooking.

I go into all these details because I know you will like to picture us to yourselves & I have given you our life for the last fortnight, which will be the same until Mr. Frémont comes in October. If you are not tired of me I will give some of the rest to your Father. Yours most affcty,

Jessie

ALS (NjP—Blair-Lee Papers).

1. JBF's new stationery featured a butterfly, symbol of Las Mariposas, perched above her entwined initials.

2. In May 1857, Indian soldiers had revolted against British rule and seized the capital. The British would retake Delhi on Sept. 20, but nearly a year passed before they regained complete control of India.

3. The Paris Exhibition was the annual display of paintings sponsored by the French Academy. Napoleon III (Louis Napoleon) (1808–73), nephew of Napoleon Bonaparte, had declared himself emperor in 1852. His wife was the Spanish beauty, Eugenie de Montijo (1826–1920).

4. William Wilberforce, Jr. (1798–1879), the least successful of Wilberforce's sons,

lived at St. Germain during this period (WILBERFORCE, 3:134). JBF found him polite but dull, with "nothing of his father but the name" (to Eliza [Gist] Blair, Sept. 16, 1857, DLC—Blair Papers).

To John Charles Frémont

Saturday 25th July [1857].
10 Avenue du Boulingrin
à St. Germain en Laye.

My sweetheart I spoil quantities of my pretty paper writing you things that begin well enough and then degenerate into the most selfish laments at not being with you. I cannot bring myself to be reconciled to your staying a month longer "and I far away on the billow."[1] Mrs. Blair was one of your many little strokes of good fortune. I am glad you like your physician and more than glad you have one who appreciates you. So many people think of you that way and except the Howards I don't think you have given your liking to any who really did see your highest qualities—the Blairs I except. But I get indignant when I see you wasted on people to whom you are simply a rich man or a society man. You laugh at my "infatuation" but you must see how many share it although you say truly only I know you well. What I liked in Mr. James was that he had a glimmering of your true character & our good friend Mr. Sherman[2] has not. He gets astonished at things in you that are as natural as the thunderbolts in Jove's hand. Mr. Selover[3] is stone blind to your best side but I won't take them to task for they all like you although they cannot comprehend you. I think Mr. Banks sees deeper than any except Mr. Howard who is your Melancthon.[4]

We had a scene with the leeches here. Twenty-eight were put on Boilleau—François who adds to his other merits that of being an excellent nurse—put them on. I would not let Susan go in where she could risk seeing them but going in myself I stepped upon one that had fallen. I leave you to imagine my horror. Susan saw me from the dressing room, with my eyes starting & my hand over my mouth & taking it into her head that Boilleau was in some frightful state rushed in & saw the hideous crushed thing in François' unflinching hand. Such a face as she had! Wasn't it a proof of regard she gave Boilleau not to scream? She jerked & wrung her hands and crammed them in her mouth but made no sound.

Are you sure you are quite well? I shall not be at rest for you until I hear you are well in California. I fear the isthmus heats. I was so entirely surprised to find you ill when I read your letter last night that I could not realize it at first. You were suffering nearly a week and really ill three days. How I should have loved to be with you and take care of you. You make yourself so present to me by your good letters. I could see the sunset sky & hear Annie Laurie.[5]

Wednesday. I know what interested you in the Initials.[6] Hamilton had your talent for letting the current carry him on, sure of turning when it grew dangerous. If Hildegarde had not been of a higher order of nature than his it would have ended badly. She knew she could make him happy as she did but it was an experiment to make with his disposition & as you remarked they lived a very retired country life. I don't think it is reasonable to lose sight of his propensity for adventure. Novels have that failing—they cannot or dare not tell how things end. It amuses me to see how certainly the author kills the married lovers in french novels. It being a received maxim with them that love must fade after marriage, they always give them a violent death in a period varying from the next day to three months—never exceeding a summer in the country, or a winter in Italy. I shall not rest until I have written out some of the criticisms that make themselves insensibly as I read french novels & I mean the best by the severest writers.

Boilleau has given me a list of books good for the girls—History, Biography & travels of a clever and entertaining kind. We will work together when it is a little cooler. It is really hot here this summer—the papers say "the hottest and dryest summer known in France since 1791." (By inference, the next year was one of revolution.) I send you the [band?] of [Saligman?] for a recuerdo [souvenir]. You must like this letter decousu [discursive] and gossiping as it is for I had written you several very bad ones but I persevered in destroying them & I gradually drew off all the troubled waters. Always though my darling I love you with all my heart and trust to you to give it health.

It would have been very bad if you had not told me of your illness. You must always let me feel you trust me and keep nothing from me that touches you. I am proud & happy to be your trusted friend and would rather be pained than not know what others [can't?] know of you.

I had written you a sorrowful letter when I read of your loneliness & illness but I thought it might come to you at a bad moment perhaps & I burnt it but I am so sorry for you there in pain my darling.

AL (CU-B—Frémont Papers).

1. The fifth verse of "The Burial of Sir John Moore after Corunna" by Charles Wolfe (1791–1823) ends with the line, "And we far away on the billow!"

2. New York businessman Isaac Sherman (c. 1817–81), a successful dealer in fancy woods until he retired in 1865, was a close associate of Nathaniel Banks. He advised the Frémonts both during the 1856 campaign and the early Civil War period. A self-educated political economist, he became an authority on taxation, international law, and railroad law (New York *Tribune* and New York *Times* obits., Jan. 23, 1881).

3. Abia A. Selover (1823–98) reached California in 1849, where he invested in San Francisco real estate and JCF's Las Mariposas mines. In 1861, he followed JCF to St. Louis, acquiring an unsavory reputation for profiteering during JCF's tenure there. When Las Mariposas was sold in 1863, he reputedly made a fortune. Retiring to New York City, he became a Wall Street financier (New York *Tribune,* Oct. 30, 1861; Statement of Abia A. Selover, Nov. 30, 1886, CU-B—Misc. Calif. Ms. Collection).

4. Philipp Schwarzert Melanchthon [or Melancthon] (1497–1560) was a German scholar and Protestant reformer known as a conciliator between diverse viewpoints. JBF seems to be using his name in this sense.

5. William Douglas's popular song, "Annie Laurie."

6. *The Initials* (London, 1850) was the first and most popular of the novels of Jemima (Montgomery) von Tautphoeus (1807–1893), an Irish woman married to a German baron. Its two main characters were Hildegarde and Hamilton.

To John Charles Frémont

Wednesday evening
July 29 [1857].

The money came very safely & I put it at once with the rest at Mr. Monroe's [Munroe].[1] This has been my most expensive month for I have had my "frais d'installation" [installation expenses] & Boilleau's illness has made their intended week with me stretch to three. Thanks to your generous provision for me darling I could well add them & their servants without embarrassing ourselves. I had enough even with such unforeseen expenses. It is just as well however that the horses have not been sent, for everything is very dear even in this village and I should be kept to my arithmetic to keep a carriage.

Still I think Mr. Lakeman[2] might have written to say why they did not come. Nothing at all has been heard from him & I would rather not write to him.

I had intended staying in this house until you came but they have built a caserne [barracks] that overlooks our garden and the windows of which face ours so that as it is to be moved into the lst of October I will not remain beyond the time for which we have the house—the 15th.

Please give me some kind thoughts the 19th.[3] I know we shall not be together. Do you know I was really happy the last year—the 19th. You made it a very good day to me and told me very kind things. You did not remember it until I told you in the morning and then all the rest of the day you were so very good to me. You scold my memory sometimes but there is so much that is sweet to remember that I would rather remember all than forget all. Love me in memory of the old times when I was so dear to you. I love you now much more than I did then.

Only see I have written the same foolish way in my money letter. "I didn't mean it Uncle Charley" and like that little culprit[4] I am sure to be found repeating the offence(?).

AL (CU-B—Frémont Papers).

1. John Munroe (d. 1871) and Company, established in Europe in 1836, served as the Frémonts' Paris bankers through the early 1870s (JCF to Frederick Billings, Mar. 12, 1861, Billings Mansion Archives; "Great Events," 410; New York *Times*, Dec. 2, 1904).
2. Stephen Charles Lakeman was an English investor who, with Palmer, Cook & Company, had promoted certain Las Mariposas mines under a JCF lease; in June 1853 JCF had borrowed 13,000 pounds from him. David Hoffman, a Las Mariposas agent in London, called Lakeman "a very notorious speculator, altogether in *bad odour here.*" For details, see M. L. SPENCE [2], xlvi–xlvii, liii, 246, 251n.
3. Oct. 19 was the Frémonts' sixteenth wedding anniversary.
4. Nina Frémont, JCF's niece.

To Francis Preston Blair

St. Germain en Laye
Sunday the 30th August [1857]

My dear Mr Blair,

Last night's mail brought not only your letter of good tidings but one from Cousin Sarah giving me a feminine version of the same and

equally welcome, almost, a letter from Father in which he shews me
there is no longer any feeling in his heart against Mr. Frémont. As you
say in yours "it was a shower of blessings from Heaven." I have been
more uneasy for Lizzie than I would even acknowledge to myself. I
was already in bed when the letters came—it was after ten (I keep
country hours) and seeing the great black seals on letters from Father
my sight grew too troubled to recognize the next letter. I took the
writing to be Mr. Frémont's and had a moment's wonder at hearing
so soon from Panama, when I recognized it was Mr. Lee's, which he
had rather altered in writing larger than his ordinary style. That re-
assured me completely and I read the first few lines and found my
sight gone again for I was crying so heartily that I could not read
beyond "my grandson & your godson Preston Blair Lee."[1] Lizzie is so
much a part of your life that that much would have gone with her
and for her Mother it would have been an entire loss of health. I could
not bear to think what would have followed. Thank God it is not so.
Everything is shining with new light around you. Frank is carrying out
your work in Missouri and you are winning old laurels over again in
his person. I dared not believe in our success in Missouri until Father's
letter.[2] I am so glad he is with you again—it was kindly done of Frank
to refer to him as the head of a party. Father does not find pleasure
in many things. You are very different but you understand him. Since
Mother's long illness shut off his affection and confidences in her, no
one took her place. I tried, but while I grieved at being unable to
succeed in giving Father that consolation, I could but honor his faithful
heart that rolled the stone over the mouth of her grave. We have
narrow channels for our love but terribly deep. If they cannot come
to the surface they wear inward. Father has thrown himself violently
into writing but work never yet filled the heart, it only uses up time.
When I saw how he was embittered last summer it went to my heart
that the injury, fancied as it was, should have come through me. I
wanted success that I might put it at his feet and let him make use of
it and feel his old power returned. Mr. Frémont was very good and
very forbearing—and you know how he was hurt by the St. Louis
speech in November.[3] It was a sort of Brutus stab. I am afraid I am
not of the right stuff for a political woman. I find myself thinking it
was the "world well lost"[4] since family harmony and peace for my
Father's old age has come out of defeat. Mr. Frémont has everything
else—health and youth and in his home there is no blank and a

moderate man might be contented with the vote he had last fall. I want the party to prevail. I am so very glad of its success in Missouri—only one thing makes me wish for Mr. Frémont's being the candidate—or rather a successful one—and that is to triumph over the enemies who made it a personal matter last year. I see that now, in India, when there is a fight the English troops as they load pass the word "remember the ladies—remember the babies." If I go into the fight again it will be with the same watchword "remember Mr. Frémont's mother." The sepoys in India have done nothing more brutal than did Mr. Wise and Mr. Toombs last year.[5] Their speeches were worse, when you remember the difference of country and education and religion; and they are not forgotten.

These are the first political souvenirs I have given way to since leaving New York. I came for rest and I have found it. "In these green solitudes" as my dear old favorite Héloïse calls them.[6]

I devote all my time and all my energies to growing strong. We have miles and miles of old forest around us and I often walk there from seven to ten. The girls go every day with Charley and a servant—Mémé's husband. All our old servants are back with us—there is nothing changed. God has even given me a child in place of the one born here. Frank is at this moment playing on the gravel walk before me, a great healthy boy with a crown of bright curls around his sun burnt face. I am writing in the garden with blue sky and trees around me. As it is Sunday we do not go to the forest today & our outdoor habits are so strong that seven o'clock finds us all spotted about. Lil near her rabbit & goat—she has a snow white goat fit to offer up to Jupiter—Nina with an india rubber ball taking exercise on the lawn & Charley building houses & stables in a remote corner given up to his litter. Frank has enough of the baby left in him to play near me in preference to ruder company. It is the most delicious weather possible, warm enough but cool & bracing. The country around is rejoicing in the great wine crop. This is one of the remarkably good years and following as it does so much agricultural distress it is doubly welcome.[7] I am going to take the girls the end of this month to Epernay—it is in the heart of the champagne wine district and only two hours & a half from Paris by railway. There, I am told, they have great rejoicings at the close of the vintage—real peasants dance real peasant dances and wear country clothes. You have no idea of the comfort of travelling here. Boilleau was very ill here in July, from engorgement of the liver.

Father will have told you of their departure for India so much sooner than we had counted upon. The delay granted him for his illness was given to trying the benefit of the waters at Vichy where the baths have great effect on diseases of the liver. It is over two hundred miles from here to the south. I kept Pensée until it was time for them to leave there & then with only a servant took her to Susan. It is eight hours ride in the most luxurious of private chariots for eight dollars. For a little less price you have carriages of eight seats built like a great private carriage — cushioned and carpeted so that neither noise nor motion interrupts the pleasure of the ride.

Susan is not strong. She insisted upon accompanying Boilleau although he left it to her to stay with me as I wished. On the other hand I am glad she is with him. Those long breaks in married life are dangerous — one must either be unhappy or indifferent & if one is bad the other is almost worse.

Susan will not be in an exposed place. Boilleau has every liberty given him and his tenderness and care for Susan are so great and so sincere that I have no fears of harm coming to her. She is very fortunate in her marriage.

It is near church time — we have a little English chapel here with so small a congregration that we would make a breach by not going. Charley behaves very well there. This will be the first Sunday in many that I shall not feel my heart grow heavy when they pray "for all women in the perils of childbirth." Thank you very much for your quick thought for me and with my warmest love to Mrs. Blair and Lizzie believe me my dear Mr. Blair yours most affectionately,

Jessie Benton Frémont

ALS (NjP — Blair-Lee Papers).

1. Francis Preston Blair Lee was born Aug. 9, 1857, at Silver Spring. The Lees considered calling him Frémont but ultimately decided to name him after Lizzie Lee's father (Francis Preston Blair to Martin Van Buren, Feb. 4, 1858, DLC — Van Buren Papers).

2. Benton had probably informed JBF that James S. Rollins, an independent candidate backed by the Benton Democrats, seemed to have won the Missouri governorship, causing the New York *Herald* to editorialize: "the election of Mr. Rollins . . . is tantamount to the declaration of . . . Missouri in favor of the gradual abolition of slavery in the State" (Aug. 13, 1857). Ultimately, however, Rollins lost by a few hundred votes to the proslavery candidate.

3. In a campaign speech on Nov. 3, Benton explained that while in the past he had stood by his son-in-law "as a father would stand by a child," he could not support

him as the candidate of a sectional party. "All advice, all my remonstrances, were useless. . . . I told him from the beginning that it was impossible that I could support any such nomination (Cheers). No matter what came, he must be national, he must have a vision that could look over the Union [or] I must take ground publicly against him" (New York *Times*, Nov. 10, 1856).

4. Evidently a reference to the subtitle of John Dryden's play, *All for Love: or, The World Well Lost* (1678).

5. The sepoys were the native troops of India. Both Virginia governor Henry Wise and Georgia senator Robert Toombs (1810–85) had attacked JCF viciously during the 1856 campaign and claimed his election would bring civil war.

6. JBF refers to Héloïse (c. 1101–64), mistress and wife of the French philosopher Pierre Abelard (1079–1142). Banished to a convent, where she eventually became an abbess, Héloïse exchanged several celebrated letters with Abelard from its solitudes. Alexander Pope's *Eloisa to Abelard* (1716) opens with a similar line, "In these deep solitudes and awful cells."

7. France had suffered a severe depression, 1846–51, precipitated by bad weather and ensuing crop failures, from which rural areas were only gradually recovering.

To John Charles Frémont

St. Germain
Wednesday the 23 Sep. [1857]

Your letter from Aspinwall came to me a day before the usual mail my darling and gave me the pleasure of knowing so far well on the way. I do hope the remainder has been equally good and agreeable and the return will be in keeping. You must not look for a good letter from me this time. I have seen nothing and done nothing this week but walk and take exercise and sew & read a little. Susy sails from Trieste the 25th. It keeps me thinking of her and until she is past hearing from, India dwells in my mind. But as somebody says Les malheurs prévues n'arrivent jamais [expected misfortune never comes]. If you like French books I know some you will read with pleasure and will send you a few by Captain Lines the 20th of October.[1] I wish I could think they would miss you but I feel you will not be in New York when he gets there early in November.

My darling I want to see you more than you can think. I am well but I am such a great fool I want to be still beside you with nothing to think or do but sit and wait for a little kind word from you — Sirius[2] by the dear master.

I am trying to make the sun go from west to east — that is trying to look young and pretty. Je deviens coquette dans mon vieux temps

pour te plaire [I am becoming coquettish in my old age to please you].
I walk like Queen Caroline[3] did and I eat when I don't want and I try
generally to follow all the rules for that sort of thing, but one affectionate look from you will give me more life than all the rules.

You see I have nothing to tell sweetheart. Much to wish and hope
and my darling so much to thank you for. Since Mr. Monroe keeps
an inquisition over my purse it is especially gratifying to have it well
filled. I should not like to get near the bottom even with the certainty
of each month's remittances, since I know what comments I am subject
to.

I think we share a dislike to being scrutinized. I send you a note
from Nina. Pitcher [Lily] was greatly obliged by your kindness to Mrs.
Seiler. You know I was pleased by it. We are all well and all look to
your coming for the only real happiness we know.

Most of all darling I love you and want you.

Your Jessie

ALS (CU-B—Frémont Papers).

1. D. Lines was captain of the U.S. mail steamship *Arago,* departing for New York
Oct. 20 (New York *Times,* Nov. 4, 1857). According to JBF, Lines spoke "the most
atrocious grammar but the kindest words & is a man designed by nature for the place
he fills" (to Elizabeth Blair Lee, Sept. 23, 1857, NjP—Blair-Lee Papers).
2. In Greek mythology, Sirius was the larger of the two dogs of Orion, the hunter.
3. Probably German-born Caroline of Anspach (1683–1737), wife of George II of
England, an intellectual woman known as the king's most influential advisor. She often
accompanied him on long walks, even when ill, and supposedly died of overexertion
(HALE, 241).

To Elizabeth Blair Lee

Paris, 3 Rue d'Angoulême
October 13th [1857]

Dear Lizzie,

Yours & Mr. Lee's letters came to me last Thursday and although
they assured me of Father's present safety they increased my wish to
go to him.[1] You know that nothing ever did or ever could estrange
me from Father and I know few sons who would have behaved as well
as Mr. Frémont did to Father last fall. I shall remember it to him.

No letters at all have come for me this or Saturday's mail. It has made me so restless that it decided me to do what has been my uppermost wish since I first heard of Father's illness. This only precedes me a few days. I go on Tuesday next—the 20th—in the Arago, taking only Charley with me. He will be a trouble at sea but in this evil thinking nation a woman cannot travel quite alone unless she be old & ugly & I am only halfway to that state. The Arago takes generally thirteen days so that I will be with Father the 4th. How things fade. I don't care two straws for the last fourth of November now—personally I mean—for I shall always regret the lost time for the party and most for your Father. But this year I only hope that day will give me the sight of Father, in health, & quite free from any bad thoughts about me. I would go farther to cure him of a heart ache than of a bodily pain. It [must be?] so weary to feel all your love given for nothing and I can go into parental feelings now. My dear good girls, Nina almost as much as Lil, help me now. They will be under the care of Lady Olliffe & our real friend Sir Joseph[2]—and have very near them, only a few doors off, Mdme de Potestad[3] & her sister both of whom we like very much. More than I have liked any one since Mrs. Key[4] whom she resembles in sweetness of nature & quick feeling. I will bring my love to all & will be so glad to see you all again & the new baby. Most affectionately,

Jessie Frémont

ALS (NjP—Blair-Lee Papers).

1. In early September, Benton had suffered an "appalling" intestinal attack, diagnosed as cancer of the rectum. Temporarily improved by early October, he kept the grave nature of his disease from JBF (CHAMBERS, 434; Francis Preston Blair to Martin Van Buren, Apr. 2, 1858, DLC—Van Buren Papers; physician's statement, New York *Evening Post*, Apr. 27, 1858).

2. Sir Joseph Francis Olliffe (1808–69), physician to the British embassy in Paris, also maintained a large private practice. He and his wife, the heiress Laura Cubitt, entertained lavishly.

3. JBF described Madame de Potestad, the former Gabriella Chapman of Philadelphia, as "beautiful and full of quick intelligence and feeling" but found her husband, the Marquis Louis de Potestad-Fornari (c. 1818-1917), "commonplace." A Spanish diplomat whose mother was a member of the Lee family of Virginia, he would later serve as ambassador to Washington (JBF to Eliza [Gist] Blair, Sept. 16, 1857, DLC—Blair Papers; New York *Times* obit., Feb. 19, 1917).

4. Ellen (Swan) Key was the deceased wife of Philip Barton Key, a son of Francis Scott Key and a longtime Benton family friend. It was Barton Key who had rescued Thomas Hart Benton's portrait from the Bentons' burning house in Feb. 1855 (JBF, "Memoirs," 91). See also JBF to Elizabeth Blair Lee, Apr. 2 [1859], below, regarding Barton Key's subsequent love affair and murder.

To Elizabeth Blair Lee

Astor House, Nov. 4, 1857

Dear Lizzie,

Your triple letter was handed to me by Mr. Howard on the deck of the Arago & I thank you all for your kind manner of reassuring me—but Mr. Frémont had been beforehand in telling me I was right. We got in by ten & they were ready to meet us as soon as we were worked in to the pier.[1] I assure you I never had a morning to be more thankful for in my life. The 4th of November hereafter represents health and prosperous voyages and all sorts of happy home images. Let the other keep what the last fourth brought him. We can afford to spare that much.

We had a very rough crossing—so much pitching that even I was laid low. I took my passage so late that the only state room I could get to myself was quite at the bow where I was upset at every plunge. So I slept in the little parlor in the centre but could only go to bed at midnight & had to be up at six. Not much sleep for my habits. I missed sleeping again last night. I was too excited even to lie still & I got up twice & sat before a coal fire in the parlor realizing the strange coincidence of the morning and my relief about Father[2] & by way of occupation brushing my hair, a family oddity I get from Grandmother Benton[3] who used always to brush her long white hair when she was wakeful. Mine is no longer long but it is getting hard on to white. Mr. Frémont too is silvered over, much, since the spring—but we are both very well except that he has a cold (& I am stifling in the hot room he keeps).

I am going to rest a little before going on but I will follow this soon. Kiss my godson for me and get everything ready for the christening except the dress—that has passed the custom house in spite of its box & blue ribbons & I intend to put it on him myself. But you must look out for my providing a wet nurse also, if you are still imaginative enough to suppose yourself one. I have been interrupted by something. I will tell you all. Thank Mr. Blair for his kind note & your Mother for all her unspoken thoughts & get my corner ready "for I'm coming, I am coming." Most affcty yours,

J.B. Frémont

ALS (NjP—Blair-Lee Papers).

1. "Mrs. Col. Frémont, child, and servant" reached New York Nov. 3 on the *Arago* after a "rough" passage (New York *Herald*, Nov. 4, 1857). JCF left San Francisco Oct. 11 on the *Golden Age*, reached Panama, and transferred to the *Star of the West* on Oct. 24, transfered to the *Quaker City* at Havana, and like JBF, reached New York on Nov. 3 (New York *Herald*, Nov. 3, 1857).

2. The newspapers reported that Benton was well enough to go horseback riding (JBF, "Memoirs," 95).

3. JBF refers to her paternal grandmother, Ann (Gooch) Benton (1758–1838), a forceful and intelligent woman who was left a widow with eight children at age thirty-two. She successfully homesteaded in Tennessee and later lived in St. Louis, where JBF knew her.

To Elizabeth Blair Lee

Boston, December 15th [1857]

Dear Lizzie,

You will think me dead and embalmed from my long silence and as I have not your excuse you can make no allowance for me. We have been "dreadfully well" treated here. I am tired down but Mr. Frémont thrives on campaign diet & all the kind speeches & complimentary things he hears said to him have restored his old good looks of the campaign times.[1] Just now he is playing chess and regularly mad at being checkmated. He was sure of his game & made a false move through over confidence. He won a very brilliant game Friday night from a crack chess player & chess is a serious thing to both of them. "Sarah Battle — rest her soul! — loved what she called 'a serious game of whist' — a clear light, a clean fire, and the rigor of the game."[2]

I have been writing a budget of letters to Paris arranging for the girls' return. Let me have the pleasure of telling your Father that as usual after a brief rebellion I am led in docile & already making the most of my coming position.

I refused so flatly to hear even of going to California that I suspected myself at the time & of course I am going. So is the whole caravan. We are only to stay six or eight months — to go immediately up to the Mariposas where Mr. Frémont will write as well as direct his work there.

I held out a little about taking Lil and Nina but gave up to day — feeling a little convinced by Mr. Frémont's arguments but much more influenced by the wish he expressed to have them all around him. I am too old to learn new ways, so I agreed to that too. They will be

home early in January & then we go but we will all see you first. I
hope your Father will be satisfied now. Mr. Frémont will begin on our
return to New York to prepare the manuscript for Mr. Childs[3] and I
am to do what he said I ought.

This is my last wail against my retreat to the mountains but since
my country, my spouse & thy sire demand that this victim expire
Strike—or rather take the passage and say no more about it.

This is for Silver Spring only. I don't write our plans home yet—
but I know it will gratify your Father to have done with France & go
into "serious realities"—serious enough—I quite hate some of them,
but I shall have the great pleasure of being of use & then some others
too. I'm glad you like all the things especially the baby's. I can't make
the list of our friends here who shew us attention. All the good names
& many less known but as sincere. It is very gratifying. Mr. Frémont
goes to a party every night, sometimes two & behaves charmingly.
Visits public schools & other institutions in the mg. & makes little
speeches, in fact does the whole duty of man in a public position.

We must see Frank when he comes on. Let me know the time. His
references will be ready.[4]

I can hardly find a cloak like mine but will do my best when I go
back. Thank you for the long letter.

Isn't it a sight to see. Mr. Walker & Mr. Douglas suffering for
conscience! sake.[5]

AL (NjP—Blair-Lee Papers).

1. JCF's main purpose in visiting Boston was to raise capital for Las Mariposas,
but the 1857 financial panic and ensuing depression made his task more difficult.

2. JBF loosely quotes from Charles Lamb's *Essays of Elia: Mrs. Battle's Opinions
on Whist.*

3. George W. Childs (1829–94) had recently founded the publishing firm Childs &
Peterson in Philadelphia. For information on the Frémonts' ultimately aborted book
project and their relations with Childs, see JBF to Elizabeth Blair Lee, Mar. 1, 1857,
note 3, above.

4. Frank Blair, Jr., had evidently asked JCF for technical information to support
the feasibility of a central route for the projected transcontinental railroad. On Christmas day, JCF (in JBF's hand) wrote Blair, Sr.: "I take it for granted that Mr. Blair
(Frank) holds steadily to his idea of the railroad. I have been preparing maps and
figures, these are ready and I have been endeavoring to finish the necessary chapter"
(NjP—Blair-Lee Papers). Frank Blair, Jr., would quote JCF extensively during a May
25, 1858, House speech advocating the central route (*Congressional Globe*, 35th Cong.,
1st sess., pt. 4 (Appendix), 421–25).

5. In late spring 1857, Buchanan had named Mississippian Robert J. Walker (1801–
69) territorial governor of Kansas. A proslavery southerner, Walker nonetheless insisted

on fair elections in Kansas on the issue of slavery, enraging fellow southerners who anticipated defeat because there were far more free-soil than proslavery settlers in the state. When southern forces engineered the Lecompton constitution, which protected slavery in Kansas and prevented a referendum on the issue, Walker branded it "a vile fraud"; in turn, southerners like Jefferson Davis denounced Walker's "treachery." At first supportive of Walker, Buchanan later succumbed to southern pressure and endorsed the Lecompton constitution. Illinois senator Stephen Douglas (1813–61) denounced Buchanan's position. It was at this point that the Democratic party split irrevocably into southern and northern wings, insuring a Republican victory in 1860 (MCPHERSON, 162–69). For JBF it was ironic that Walker and Douglas, who had condemned JCF for his stand on Kansas, would now be subject to the same abuse from the South that he had experienced in 1856.

To Francis Preston Blair

Christmas day [1857]

My dear Mr. Blair,

I can't avoid the usual style of Mr. Frémont's agents which is to do a little business for themselves by the side of his & so make my addition to his letter.[1] Tell Lizzie (I consider a letter to any one of you at Silver Spring as written to four persons—five, if Frank cares for it too) that her last letter was just the reasonable lady-like answer I had expected from her in reply to my caution. I row over Lizzie's gentleness sometimes as being hurtful to my vanity & not discriminating enough for me, but oftener I feel its softening influence. I should like however to talk out my side about California. I am going & so are the children but with all the conceit left me I can't take in Lizzie's idea of teaching Lily, moral training Nina & Charley (Frank has no morals yet), writing out all Mr. Frémont has to dictate for the book, keeping house (in Bear Valley that will not be as in Paris or 9th street)—all that I am to do—and with all entertain country visitors.

I think a stouter woman than myself might fall back dismayed from such an array of work. And as for Lizzie's grand argument of being with Mr. Frémont, we will see if that comes to more than being in the same state with him—at least a large half of the time. And as for the clever & intelligent young men, I think they are myths here or there. I look all the time for the coming man for Nina but I shall feel great distrust of even the best appearances. Lizzie has faith and I have knowledge. She has lived where there was no clashing of interests except political & all her people are on one side. I have seen that & the money test applied & it is a great searcher out of truths.

Last night I had put all Charley's things in Christmas order & came back from his bedside where he was so soundly asleep, to the toys & presents & I could but think how full of trust we begin our lives. He believes firmly that Santa Claus comes down the chimney & proportions gifts to good behavior. We don't keep that state of mind long in life. You & Lizzie are still well off in credulity but I am poor. "Naked came we into the world & naked we go out"[2] applies as much to the heart & its belongings as to our worldly goods—after my sermon comes the moral that having proved many things I hold fast to that which is good which is the friendship of Silver Spring for one thing. Affectionately yours,

Jessie Benton Frémont

ALS (NjP—Blair-Lee Papers).

1. On JCF's letter, see JBF to Elizabeth Blair Lee, Dec. 15 [1857], note 4, above.
2. Miguel de Cervantes, *Don Quixote*, pt. 1, bk. 3, chap. 11.

To George W. Blunt

[winter 1857–58?]

My dear Mr. Blunt,

My friend Mrs. Blunt of whom we were speaking this morning, is with me for a day or two and it would be very agreeable to me if you could give half an hour tomorrow morning to the business on which she is here. Mr. Blunt had an invention for lowering lifeboats with safety, which she has had patented here & in England. Last winter Mr. Dobbin[1] (Sec. of the Navy) recommended it should be bought by the govt. for the use of the navy. That would have given her eight or ten thousand dollars & lifted the mortgage (5000) on her California property. But other patents having been put into the same bill, all were set aside by a resolve of Congress not to buy any patents.

Ellen hopes & so do I, that as Mr. Maury[2] of the Navy & other authorities recommended this most highly, something (an indefinite hope but I trust not an unfounded one) may be done here in the merchant service.

You may remember I told you Mrs. Blunt had supported herself by writing for the Patent office. I obtained the place for her. This administration have stopped her employment for no reason—but we can but infer because of my having gotten it for her. When you remember she is the *daughter of Frank Key and the niece of Judge Taney,*[3] it is carrying their spite far.

I know you will give us the aid of your advice and we will be as brief & clear as two men and I will thank you very much for helping me to help Ellen. And if "something" does come of it, it will give you the additional satisfaction of having helped the widow and the fatherless.

At any early hour—from 7 on—that you say, we will be ready with the patent, the model & all to show you. With no excuses for asking this favor of you for I know your kind heart will be glad to aid us, I am yours very truly,

Jessie Benton Frémont

Sunday evening

ALS (CLjC). Envelope addressed to "Mr. Blunt, 139 12th Street." George W. Blunt (1802–78) and his brother Edmund were noted hydrographers and nautical publishers in New York City from whose firm JCF had purchased navigational instruments for his expeditions. In 1857 George Blunt was also a commissioner for New York harbor (New York City *Directory,* 1860; JACKSON & SPENCE, 70).

On JBF's earlier concern for Ellen Blunt, the young widow of naval officer Simon Fraser Blunt, see JBF to Elizabeth Blair Lee, Mar. 7 [1856], above. Ellen Blunt evidently failed to obtain much, if any, money for her husband's invention; in 1860–61 she was in London and in 1862 in Paris attempting to earn a living by giving dramatic readings. For comments on her European venture, see MORAN, 1:705, passim; and New York *Tribune,* Mar. 5, 1862.

1. James Cochran Dobbin (1814–57) was Franklin Pierce's secretary of the navy.

2. Matthew F. Maury (1806–73) was the author of *The Physical Geography of the Sea* (1855), regarded as the first textbook on modern oceanography. A friend of S. Phillips Lee, he became a special agent for the Confederacy in England during the Civil War.

3. Supreme Court Chief Justice Roger Brooke Taney (1777–1864) was married to Anne P. C. Key, a sister of Francis Scott Key.

To Francis Preston Blair

New York Astor House
January 8th. '58

My dear Mr. Blair,

Mr. Frémont asks me to write to you & get you to ask Frank to obtain for him, Carson's reports. He has made several & Mr. Blair can perhaps get them with more facility than any one else. They are most probably published among the yearly reports to Congress from the Indian Dept.[1]

Any reports of the officers engaged in the military expeditions in North Mexico, might be useful, as they were usually accompanied by topographical officers.[2] If these can be conveniently gotten at once Mr. Frémont says he would be much obliged.

Will you please also, he asks, keep your eye on Mr. Gwin's Arizona bill[3] as it would if passed destroy some arrangements otherwise successful.

- - - - - - - - - - - - - -

"Thats all"

Mr. E. D. Morgan and Mrs. Morgan[4] go to-day to Washington & stop at Willard's. Mr. & Mrs. Bigelow go also & will be at the same place.

If there were any fellow feeling for me among the "folks at home" I should write to ask for these friends (the Morgans) some attention but I have ceased looking for favors or even justice to our side there. I will write to Lizzie Whiting however, who as Mr. Frémont's cousin can shew some politeness to Mrs. Morgan.

I was at first hurt at Mr. Bigelow's defection[5] especially as so silly & untrue a ground is given for it—Frank said Mrs. Bigelow had given him many specifications, which I did not ask to hear—I know I never said any thing to justify a change so complete in Mrs. Bigelow—she dresses like a [. . .] wild fire & is very selfish I think but that, even if I told it to him point blank, is not a reason for turning the cold shoulder *immediately after the loss of the election*. There ought to be a grave motive for such an ungraceful act & so peculiarly timed. I know I never failed in my part towards them when it was in my power to give.

- - - - - - - - - - - - - -

Let him go too. You blame me for my little faith in people but I have enough left yet to give half a page to my surprise & regrets at Mr. Bigelow's fall from the high place I used to give him.

We are "putting money in our purse" — before I join the mining population in person, I will bring the children all with me to see Father & invade Silver Spring for a day. Your godson can speak French & German but says no English yet but he will soon get that & for all the rest he is an honor to his names. I shall be glad to have them all & it is not long now before I do see them. They will leave Paris Monday & it is only two weeks crossing.

I went to see Betty yesterday but she was out walking. I shall try to propitiate her duenna & amuse her occasionally.[6]

With love to Mrs. Blair but not a word to Lizzie who has deserted our alliance for the baby. I am always yours affectionately,

Jessie Frémont

ALS (DLC—Blair Papers).

1. In 1853, JCF's former guide, Kit Carson, had been appointed Indian agent for the tribes of northern New Mexico. JCF evidently wanted to consult his reports either in connection with the material on the projected central railroad route he was preparing for Frank Blair or for the account of his own expeditions on which he had been working sporadically.

2. One of the "military expeditions in North Mexico" may have been Stephen Watt Kearny's 1846–47 expedition to New Mexico and California, which resulted in a much-used survey of the Gila River route, William H. Emory's *Notes of a Military Reconnaissance from Fort Leavenworth ... to San Diego* (1848). However, JBF may be referring to other reports connected with the work of army topographical engineers during the Mexican War, the Mexican boundary survey, or the railroad surveys along the thirty-eighth parallel. Another possibility is J. H. Simpson's *Journal of a Military Reconnaissance from Santa Fe, New Mexico in the Navajo Country Made with the Troops under Command of Brevet Lieutenant-Colonel John M. Washington* (1850). Simpson, a topographical officer, was assisted by Richard and Edward Kern, who had been stranded in New Mexico as a result of JCF's fourth expedition.

3. On Dec. 17, 1857, Senator William M. Gwin of California had introduced a bill "to organize the Territory of [Arizona], and to create the office of surveyor general therein; to provide for the examination of private land claims; to grant donations to actual settlers; to survey the public and private lands" (*Congressional Globe*, 35th Cong., 1st. sess., pt. 1, 62).

4. Edwin Denison Morgan (1811–83), a farm boy from Connecticut who had become one of New York City's most successful businessmen, was chair of the Republican National Committee during the Frémont campaign. He would later serve as governor (1858–62) and senator (1863–69). He was married to Eliza Matilda (Waterman) of Hartford, Conn.

5. JBF was seemingly unaware of the reason behind John Bigelow's defection: shortly after the election, convinced that JCF had "debauched" a servant girl in the Frémont household, Bigelow had abruptly broken with the family. For speculation on this

rumored affair, see Preston King to Gideon Welles, Mar. 3, Apr. 9, 21, 1860, DLC—Welles Papers; and Welles to Francis Preston Blair, Apr. 9, 1860, DLC—Blair Papers. In a July 14, 1890, journal entry, Bigelow commented: "As a candidate for President in 1856, [Frémont] did everything pretty much that he could do to bring his party into contempt though it was not only partially [*sic*] discovered until after the election" (CLAPP, 107).

6. Betty Blair's "duenna" was Miss Henrietta B. Haines, whose private girls' school in New York City she was now attending.

To Elizabeth Blair Lee

Monday Jany. 11 '58.

Dear Lizzie

I have just had the pleasure of a letter from you in good company— as with it came letters from the girls who had just received their recall. Nina was fluttered out of all coherence. Lil says "you hold out *a hope* of our going to California with you" & is quite happy at the prospect of being back here with us. They leave Paris today & tomorrow we will remember them as "on the deep." In two weeks I hope to have them all safe under my care and it will not be my act if they are again from under it. The girls keep my letters from Susy but Liz sent me hers to read. I returned it yesterday. I was very glad to get it—things seem comfortable to her and as she does not seem to feel the heat painfully. I trust she will have a good accouchement & a boy as she wishes. Mr. Frémont says she will be disappointed if the law that the most vigorous parent gives sex, is true—but it is all a great mystery to my thinking & she may be pleased with a boy yet.

I am glad you nurse yours less. You ought to stop it altogether— all the theories about what nursing does for the mother & what it does for the child are fudge & nonsense & there is no rule for that any more than for the sex, so that you & the Queen & many other mistaken women drain your heart's blood to make bad milk & wake up to a second nurseling [*sic*] in spite of your pains.

The only certain thing is to discontinue what you find weakening & keep yourself as strong and healthy as possible. I was ill more or less all the time in Boston & have been steadily selfish in nursing myself back to the health I brought away from France. I do very well now & am energetic enough to make Charley learn a little every day. We have such beautiful weather generally that I am much out of doors. I went to see Betty last week but she was out. I will see after her & when the girls come she will find some amusement in talking over France. Nina will be a deposed monarch but we will manage that — my dear little Pitcher [Lily] will be glad to be with me and we shall find many things to like although it is not the thing I would have chosen. No man can know what a wear & tear the detail of family life in a new country without servants is to a woman. Especially if she is like myself unable to see things out of order. I shall have my time all filled but perhaps I may get shaken out of my unwillingness for noise & motion & do all the better for it. Mr. Frémont thinks of the climate & the sunrise over the fine mountain scenery, the spring flowers & horseback rides that send him with a vigorous appetite to breakfast & a clear healthy mind to write. I am to be ready to do that writing but I am to know & provide the component parts of that breakfast first — & I remember country life in California very accurately. We know the mysteries of washing & ironing too — think of Nina's skirts & mine & Lily's & two piggy boys to say nothing of Mr. Frémont's unbounded linen & we shall have "open house" & if I don't do something extraordinary in the way of feeding & entertaining generally I will be called disdainful & proud & indifferent to Mr. Frémont's interests. And when I have done ninety-nine polite things the missing hundredth will wipe them all out as with the Bigelows — my last awful warning of the uselessness of civilities.

Marie, Mémé & a man are all that it is reasonable to take with us. Fortune may favor us with some indigenous "help" but can't you picture Marie in her new position? & Nina! Remember we are to be eleven miles from Mariposas town & one mile from the nearest neighbor & there are mountain rocks & roads to be overcome for all our movings even to get letters from the Post Office. Keep Susy's letters from India & mine. I will write you from California & they will picture existences differing as far as the places — "from farthest Ind to new Cathay."

Now if I were to say any part of this to Mr. Frémont he would not let me go, but as I consider the one good attained worth the trouble it will entail on me, I look only at the good side with him & relieve my mind by this outpouring to you & remember you are four & no more. Your mother will understand my side — your father in his petted existence comprehends nothing of it, & will think all "these trifles unworthy of attention." Mr. Lee has learned something at sea, but your mother is my main reliance for sympathy.

I assure you it does a great deal of good to talk it out. I think one gets rid of a little grievance that way.

In the meanwhile I am as I said absolutely selfish. I have not made five visits or in any way taken trouble for any one. Sometimes I am of use to Mr. Frémont for writing, but the rest of the time I walk with Charley or go to picture galleries or morning operas or read just as the fancy of the moment dictates—& it is a very good way for a short while.

I don't wonder you shiver at the idea of parties. Send your friend to Minna [Blair] who likes them & who is invulnerable.

I shall always be thankful for a letter from you no matter how short. I expect to find the baby much grown & beautified—as intelligence marks their faces they improve daily. Tell Mr. Lee not to talk nonsense—there is no satisfactory shopping without limitation & I am very vain when I keep under for I don't think economy is a natural gift with me. With best love to you all Yours affectionately,

Jessie Frémont

I am entirely pleased that the cloak pleases you. I had the pockets added—mine are [issues?] of comfort & convenience.

Admire my new seal. A ring of Mariposas gold.

ALS (NjP—Blair-Lee Papers).

To Elizabeth Blair Lee

New York   February 1st '58.

Dear Lizzie,

I was very much obliged to you for your long letter—the fagged neuralgic state you are in makes such an exertion very much valued by me.

The girls go on tomorrow with Marie & Charley to escort them. I don't know whether I shall send Frank or not. He is a darling beauty and I am a little afraid of the chicken-pox which Liz has written me of. Mr. Lee is going to begin his godfatherly duties on Charley. Charley's second teeth are coming up inside of the first row & I would rather have Maynard put them in shape, than Parmlee [Parmly].[1] Parmlee is very well, but I have faith in Maynard. I don't go on until the end of the week & as they must be back here about this time next week I will ask of Mr. Lee to make an appointment with Maynard for Charley. Marie will be with him & he will not be a trouble, I hope, to Mr. Lee. It will be aiding me very essentially if Mr. Lee has the time to attend to this. From a landed estate to milk teeth, is the range I give his good will to exercise in.

Father insists on keeping the girls until our return. Mr. Frémont rarely makes a plan for the family. You know he leaves them to me but he wishes to take them with him & although it was no choice of mine I have looked at its desirable side until I found it all good & this little opposition settles the question. They could not stay in Washington even if they did not go. It is not the fit place for us since the abusive tone of last year in which the south & the democrats generally joined to such a degree that I make no distinctions among them but avoid the whole lot of them. And Lily and Nina feel as I do. They are eager to go to California.

So you are to stand by me when the fight comes on for Father is going to make one. I am very well & shall come away from there all upset again by having to displease him. It is not easy to serve two masters and I would like so much to obey both of mine, but if I must choose it will be for the one that I think needs & wishes me the most.

The girls are perfectly well & so are the little ones. Frank is splendid and as unruly as a young wild turkey—Charley is much tamer.

The girls have gone to see Betty. I hope Miss Hayne [Haines] will allow them to see her.

With love to your Mother & Father. Most affectionately yours,

J.B.F.

Nina has asked enough questions & made enough ejaculations about your baby to satisfy even Mrs. Burns.[2] Lil is not a baby fancier but says she is very glad you and it got on so well.

AL initialed (NjP—Blair-Lee Papers).

1. Dr. Edward Maynard (1813–91) was a Washington dental surgeon whose patients included members of both the Blair and Benton families (E. B. SMITH [1], 171). He was also an inventor who had developed a percussion primer (known as the Maynard tape primer) as well as improvements in the breech-loading rifle (DLC—Maynard Papers; STRONG, 3:90). Eleazar Parmly (1797–1874) was New York City's leading dentist. His daughter Julia would marry Frémont lawyer Frederick Billings in 1862.

2. The name of young Blair Lee's nurse, Martha Byrne, is variously spelled in the Blair-Lee Papers (NjP); sometimes she is simply referred to as "Birnie." By Mar. 25, 1859, she had married Joseph Cook, who lived in the Silver Spring neighborhood.

LAS MARIPOSAS AND
SAN FRANCISCO

When the Frémont entourage reached San Francisco in April 1858, they set out almost immediately for Las Mariposas, their gold-rich property in the foothills of the Sierra Nevada, some two hundred miles away. They traveled by steamboat up the San Joaquin River to Stockton and then changed to a stagecoach for the two-day, eighty-mile ride across the great Central Valley. They settled into a small white-washed cottage, approximately half a mile from the straggly little village of Bear Valley. Eight or nine miles away was Mariposa, the county seat, much of which was destroyed by a fire on June 4, allegedly originating "in a Chinese house of ill fame."[1]

Bear Valley was a company town and the hub of Frémont's operations. Its most substantial building, the Oso House, had been constructed a few years earlier by Frémont's direction. It was a two-story hotel with pillars, balcony, and rooms partitioned by cotton sheeting. The miners came to drink at its bar, and young John Howard, who stayed at the hotel, noted that the occasional pistol frays that followed drinking and gambling "made the town less agreeable to an effete visitor from 'the States' than it might be, and 'the hotel' a too frequent center of public attention."[2] Frémont had his office in the hotel. Not too far away was his store, which sold supplies to the miners. Two miles north were the valuable Pine Tree and Josephine mines, in contention between Frémont and the Merced Mining Company. Four miles south was the Mt. Ophir mine and mill, also in dispute, and still further south was the rich Princeton mine.

Although the seventy-square-mile property with its gold mines had figured prominently in the Frémonts' lives and fortunes since Thomas O. Larkin purchased it for John in 1847, this was Jessie's first residence on the estate, indeed her first visit. Shortly after her arrival, she was devastated by the news of her father's death. John postponed a trip to San Francisco to comfort her and "got her through the first & worst two weeks."[3] Nonetheless, she fell ill and later in June joined him in San Francisco, where they hoped the sea breezes would improve her health and spirit. No sooner had they returned to Las Mariposas in early July than they were confronted with violence.

The trouble had been brewing for some time. After John received confirmation of his title to Las Mariposas in 1855, he had succeeded in having the final survey made to include Bear Valley with the central vein of the mother lode running through it. These boundaries were quite different from those he had claimed in 1849 and 1852; and to the Merced Mining Company and individual miners who were working within the new boundaries, it was "an outrageous bare-faced piece of downright stealing." The angry miners, encouraged by the Merced Mining Company, organized the Hornitos League and vowed to defend their interests against Frémont's "aggressive, rapacious claims."[4] Tiring of the lengthy court battle and upset by Frémont's new operations to develop the property, the miners, on July 9, "jumped" Frémont's men who were working a rich section of the Pine Tree mine known as the Black Drift. Jessie gives the Frémont side of the conflict in her July 16, 1858, letter to Francis Preston Blair.

The heat and nervous strain of the siege so told against Jessie that John took the entire family to San Francisco again. In the late fall they returned once more to Bear Valley, where Jessie continued to pen much of John's correspondence and in the process became thoroughly acquainted with his ambitious plans for developing the mining properties.

Within a short time John had built a storage dam on the Merced River, and at the bottom of the river canyon installed improved ore crushing apparatus—the Benton mills—running seventy-two stamps. Chinese labor helped build a railroad to carry the quartz ore from the Pine Tree and Josephine mines down the steep mountainsides to the new crushing mills. Smelting works were erected in the village, new shafts were sunk, tunnels opened, and buildings constructed. While the developmental work stimulated the local economy, it was extremely expensive. John's monthly payroll was estimated to be at least $10,000.[5] In addition, he had large outlays for the advice of mining experts and engineers, and for taxes and endless litigation. His name appeared on the Mariposa County delinquent tax list for 1858, and shortly after he arrived in California, he wrote Montgomery Blair that "in addition to the cases in the U. S. Ct. I am engaged in four or five others in the Supreme Court of this State."[6] The stream of costly lawsuits that plagued the Frémonts' lives made Jessie "very suspicious of the legal fraternity." Young Howard reported that she remarked of John's fast-paced horse: "The Mexicans must have named him *Abogado* [lawyer] because he was a natural pacer as a lawyer is a natural liar."[7]

By late 1860, Frémont's average monthly income from all sources, including royalties paid by miners and revenues from the leasing of grazing land and town lots in Mariposa and Bear Valley, was estimated at $39,000. Thomas Starr King reported an even higher figure: "$16,000 a week in solid gold" from the mills alone.[8] The income might have been princely, but John had incurred "a magnificent indebtedness." Interest rates were exorbitant, and Las Mariposas was heavily mortgaged to many people. In May 1859, just as Jessie was about to start out on a camping trip to Yosemite Valley with Lily, Nina, and their guests, Hannah and Joseph Lawrence, a group of lawyers arrived to try a suit in the Mariposa court and John requested her services.[9] Later, when the temperature at the Bear Valley cottage grew oppressively hot, she, Lily, and the two boys did manage to camp for several weeks atop nearby Mount Bullion. "The spring at which they are encamped is the resort of Grizzlys," mused the editor of the local paper, "and a dispute regarding the water privilege is quite likely to arise between these beasts and the present squatters."[10] The family had no sooner settled back into home life, when an old political ally, Horace Greeley of the New York *Tribune*, arrived for a visit.

Jessie cheerfully made the best of frontier conditions, but she felt "as if the moutains of Bear Valley bounded" her world and she longed for a more congenial life.[11] Early in 1860, John purchased a home and thirteen acres for her on the tip of Black Point, a finger of land jutting into the Bay of San Francisco. Jessie wrote Elizabeth Blair Lee on June 2 that it was "more beautiful than any Sea Dream that Tennyson or any poet ever fancied." She was glad to escape the isolation of Bear Valley and to enjoy the comforts of city life with its opera, private parties, lectures, and newspapers. She met interesting people like Thomas Starr King, the new Unitarian minister, who became a devoted friend; Bret Harte, whose budding literary career she nourished; and Carleton

Watkins, a lively young commercial photographer. Her salon was frequented by literary figures and politicians. Thomas Starr King could write a friend, "I have just returned from Mrs. Frémont's where I have made a visit with Herman Melville," or "I am going to dine today at Mrs. Frémont's with Col. Baker the new republican senator from Oregon."[12]

Jessie, pronounced "unseaworthy," was left behind at Black Point when John set out for Europe in January 1861 to raise capital for Las Mariposas, now more than a million dollars in debt. He was accompanied by his lawyer, Frederick Billings, who also owned one-eighth of the estate.[13] John delayed his departure from New York, hoping to receive from the incoming Lincoln administration a promise of the French ministry, which he and Billings both thought would help them raise capital in Europe.[14] He finally sailed in late February.

Back in San Francisco, Jessie, living on $1,000 a month from funds of the estate,[15] followed the secession news and waged an unsuccessful crusade to save a former black servant from the gallows. In late April she was thrown from her carriage when the horses bolted. "My head received the force of the fall," she reported, "& it has brought on constant spasms of neuralgia in the back of the neck and in the left side—often the whole spine thrills like a harp cord."[16] In May, John wrote that he had been given a military command and asked her to meet him in New York. Announcing the news to their former accountant, Jessie wrote joyfully "I have not been so happy in years for him as now. . . . An army of cares has been boring into our lives these few years past, and I thank heaven for this noble chance in a great cause, which has come to Mr. Frémont now. . . . I am so glad I am going into an atmosphere where dollars and cents are not the first object."[17] And to the Reverend John A. Anderson, she wrote emphatically, "We go to join Mr. Frémont & I will be with him everywhere—I will."[18] Jessie, Lily, and the boys said a final good-bye to Black Point and left San Francisco on June 21. Several months later, Thomas Starr King asked the president of the U.S. Sanitary Commission if he had met Mrs. Frémont. "I hope so," he added. "Her husband I am very little acquainted with, but she is sublime, and carries guns enough to be formidable to a whole Cabinet—a she-Merrimack, thoroughly sheathed, and carrying fire in the genuine Benton furnaces."[19]

Notes

1. *San Joaquin Republican,* Apr. 24, June 6, 28, 1858.

2. HOWARD, 80.

3. JCF to Francis Preston Blair, June 4, 1858 (NjP—Blair-Lee Papers).

4. M. L. SPENCE [2], lxiii–lxix; CRAMPTON, 240–53.

5. Mariposa *Gazette,* Nov. 29, 1859; *San Joaquin Republican,* Dec. 22, 1859; SARGENT, 15.

6. July 4, 1858 (DLC—Blair Papers).

7. HOWARD, 84.

8. SARGENT, 15; King to Randolph Ryers, Oct. 19, 1860 (CU-B—Thomas Starr King Papers).

9. E. B. FREMONT, 101–4; Mariposa *Gazette,* May 20, 1859.

10. Mariposa *Gazette,* July 8, 1859.

11. To Elizabeth Blair Lee, Sept. 4 [1859] (NjP—Blair-Lee Papers).

12. To Randolph Ryers, Oct. 19, 29, 1860 (CU-B—Thomas Starr King Papers).

13. Summary of the condition of the Mariposas Estate as to title encumbrances & debt (CU-B—John T. Doyle Papers).

14. Billings to Trenor W. Park, Feb. 4, 6, 11, 19, 1861 (Park-McCullough House Archives).

15. Billings to Trenor W. Park, May 24, 1861 (Park-McCullough House Archives).

16. To John A. Anderson, May 28 [1861] (KHi).

17. Undated letter to John C. Hopper, printed in NEVINS [1], 472.

18. May [June] 11 [1861] (KHi).

19. To Henry Bellows, Mar, 18, 1862 (MHi, photocopy, CU-B—Thomas Starr King Papers).

To Elizabeth Blair Lee

Sunday 28th March [1858]

Dear Lizzie

Tomorrow we get in to Aspinwall and I send you back this news of our progress.[1] Mr. Frémont has been somewhat ill but is in such a general state of contentment at the good position of his affairs and the prospect of the quiet & yet usefully occupied life before us that he is contented & himself again for cheerfulness. I broke down the second day, had fever & heart ache & afterward sea sickness & after three days of this dismalness emerged to a weak satisfaction at being no longer in pain. We get off at Aspinwall tomorrow & will I hope find ourselves on the Pacific at Tuesday noon.[2]

The children get on famously, Frank [Charley] not down a moment & the baby as gay as a lark. Neither Mémé nor Rose luckily were sick so no one has suffered for want of care. One pleasantly familiar thing we have is the captain's voice. It is so identical with Mr. Lee's that Mr. Frémont & I both remarked it at once. He is a Captain Grey[3] of the Navy once I believe—but his voice, gestures & manner of speaking are curiously like Mr. Lee's. There is a friendly tenant of ours on board who tells me grapes & peaches abound within a mile of our house. He himself keeps the public house at Bear Valley & is a sensible tidy looking New England man. You don't know the beauty of cleanliness until you are on a little thousand ton ship with 772 passengers—such pigs the greater part of them.

I am in a half stupid state and can send you nothing worth reading except that we are all well. Keep dear Lizzie your promise to me and let me hear from some of you about Father. He will write only the favorable side & Liz too will soften things to me. Go to see her too somtimes.

Give my love to your Mother and Father and to yourself dear Lizzie the best love of your affectionate friend Jessie.

ALS (NjP—Blair-Lee Papers).

1. The Frémonts, including Nina, had sailed from New York on Mar. 20 in the steamship *Star of the West* (New York *Herald,* Mar. 20, 1858). They were accompanied by two maids and a retinue of lawyers, mining experts, and business associates. Young John Raymond Howard was along and would later chronicle, with some inaccuracies, the journey and stay in California in *Remembrance of Things Past.*

2. The party crossed the Isthmus by special train, in comfortable contrast to earlier mule-back, malaria-plagued trips, and boarded the steamship *Golden Age* at Panama for San Francisco, arriving there on Apr. 12 (HOWARD, 78).

3. Alfred Gilliat Gray (1818–76), brother of Andrew B. Gray, who in 1851 had been with the commission to survey the new boundary between the United States and Mexico.

To Elizabeth Blair Lee

Bear Valley
Mariposa County
April 24th [1858]

My dear Lizzie,

We have been here for over a week now and my letters to Father & Liz will have let you know how comfortably and safely the journey was made. I was the only one ill. I find going to sea is not the pleasure it used to be — rough motion disturbs the circulation so much that I get the most distressing pains — bleeding at the nose & entirely upset. But the smooth sea on this side made me quite well again and we had such luxury of space, baths & cleanly food that illness was impossible.

Your mother would be pleased with my energetic planting here. I sowed mignonette maderia vine & scarlet runner thick around the four sides of the house. A fine pine was blown down the week before we got in and the trunk stands thirty feet high, a black column on the lawn, for you must know we have a lovely natural lawn sloping off on each side, covered with wild geranium — a small variety in bloom and fragrance resembling rose geranium & wildflowers of a beauty and fragrance I never had met before.

Remembering your mother's description of the beauty she gave to what had been ugly objects such as stumps & cabins I vetoed the cutting down of the pine trunk & planted around its base (it is over three feet in diameter) scarlet runner & the chemise honeysuckle which grows like Jack's bean stalk. Will it not be a beautiful sight? My share of the little Brussels cabbages are planted out & today we set out a hundred tomato plants. There is a pretty good garden already underway & Lea, a colored man (grandson of Mr. Calvert of Riversdale[1]) who came overland with Mr. Frémont the last time, is a thorough gardener & works famously at it. We get quantities of milk, buttermilk & fresh butter & eggs & so you see my housekeeping goes on brilliantly. Mémé

& Rose are a host & a Spanish negrowoman from the West Indies comes by the day (three dollars a day) to wash & iron.

It looks incongruous with such slender working power to come into the house & find velvet carpets & a fine piano, bronze clocks, a marble-topped furniture—great stupidity or rather wastefulness as freight is so high over these mountains, but as it was an agent did it of course it was done regardless of expense.[2] We have a fine pair of carriage horses and Lil has a horse of her own. Lea is teaching Charley & Frank to ride bare back. They are already browned with red cheeks & the baby Frank thrives on the fine milk & pure air.

All of us are well and very contented & I tell you this whole sheet of details that you may form some idea of how much reason we have to be so.

Mr. Frémont is in San Francisco. He will be here again in a week. He does not mind the late decision of the Court for it must be reversed & in the meanwhile his agents here took squatters claims over 100 acres over all the richest veins, and so in point of actual possessions he is better off than before.[3] There is a great deal of kind feeling to us all & I am told that it gives great satisfaction that the family are here. They had a great bonfire on Mount Bullion[4] the night we got in & they fired off quicksilver flasks which sounded just like cannon echoing through the hills grandly.

We are so far from certain post offices that I sent my last letter for Susy to Mr. Lee's care with a vague sort of an idea that he in his capacity of sea king might know how to get it to her. Mention what you hear from her in your letters. Hers might chance to miss me and I am anxious to know the result of her confinement. Tell me exactly how everything is with all of you. I don't ask about Father for you all will keep your promises to me. Dear Lizzie remember how short the time is, only 25 days from here to Washington & do not fail to write and tell if Father wishes to see me. I can always come—there is no trouble about it now.

Mr. Frémont thinks a little that your Father & Mother may come out here this summer. If we only had a railroad it would be a certainty and they would enjoy so much the beauty of the scenery & the excitement of the mining, and your Father would have only to cross the orchard to find deer & fat hares & quail. Bears I am relieved to find have left the neighborhood. A few rattlesnakes come up in the heats but they are legendary & only known of at second hand. Already the days are hot—quite 90° today but a cool breeze & the nights almost cold. If they do come either Mr. Lee or the Judge ought to be with them to take charge of the sea sick part but for that I should beg them to come. It would be such a great pleasure to have them at our own home. We drank to your healths in the tea your Mother gave me, last Sunday evening. Mr. Beecher gave me a beautiful Sèvres cup for my tea here & it was a combination of friendly ideas.

This letter goes by private hand early tomorrow. I will take my chances with the democratic postmaster in town for another & hope you will get it. Write to me how the little man grows—if he gets his teeth easily & if his Mrs. Burns keeps him from forgetting his godmother. I want such letters as I will write you all "I do & I am & we are." You may put in a little politics but very little. I've cut the shop & taken to farming. Most affectionately yours,

Jessie Frémont

ALS (NjP—Blair-Lee Papers).

1. The grandfather would have been George Calvert, son of the Sixth Lord Baltimore. George Calvert had married the daughter of Henri Joseph, Baron de Stier, a wealthy financier who built a fine mansion in Riversdale, Md., at the turn of the century. As the young Calverts moved into the residence around 1803, it became known as the Calvert Mansion.

2. A former agent of Frémont, Rufus A. Lockwood, had built the Bear Valley house (SARGENT, 35n). For a biographical sketch of Lockwood, who was drowned at sea on Sept. 12, 1857, see HASTINGS.

3. At issue was the ownership of the minerals within JCF's land grant. The boundaries of Las Mariposas, finally patented in 1855, were quite different from those marked out by Frémont in 1849 and by the surveyor, Allexey W. Von Schmidt, in 1852 and included gold-bearing properties that had not been a part of the first two surveys. Many considered the final location of Las Mariposas "an outrageous barefaced piece of downright stealing." There would be a number of suits and appeals, with one of the more important cases being Biddle Boggs *vs.* Merced Mining Company. To test his ownership of the underground minerals, JCF, on Apr. 22, 1857, leased the mines at Mt. Ophir, then occupied and worked by the Merced Mining Company, to Biddle Boggs for a seven-year period at a monthly rental of $1,000. Biddle Boggs brought suit to oust the Merced Mining Company from the property. The Mariposa County Court upheld the Frémont-Boggs claim in July 1857, but the California Supreme Court reversed the lower court in Mar. 1858 and entered judgment for the defendant, Merced Mining Company. JCF, in turn, appealed this decision. The litigation tied up the Mt. Ophir property, but both sides kept up mining operations within other areas of the disputed territory of Las Mariposas. When the Merced Company took possession of a portion of the Pine Tree and Josephine mines, Frémont commenced an action

of forcible entry and detainer and won again in the Mariposa courts, only to be reversed and then sustained in the California Supreme Court. See JBF to Elizabeth Blair Lee, Nov. 15, 1859, below. He also began actions of ejectment against many occupants of the estate, and, as JBF notes in this letter, his agents took squatter claims as a further means of securing the property (M. L. SPENCE [2], lxii–lxix; Mariposa *Democrat,* Mar. 25, 1858; *San Joaquin Republican,* Feb. 12, 1858; CRAMPTON, 240–57).

4. Named after JBF's father, who was known as "Old Bullion" as he favored hard currency.

To Francis Preston Blair

Bear Valley, Mariposa Co.
May [1858]

My dear Mr. Blair,

I will not attempt this time to write you or Lizzie any part of what I feel for all your kindness in writing so fully to me.[1]

I knew my Father had a mortal disease but Dr. May let me think I should see him if I returned in September—and he forbid my staying. This miserable weakness about the heart condemns me to be selfish or to be myself an invalid & no aid. I am deeply thankful that the time of extremest suffering was so short and that no cloud dimmed his great mind. How different his last days from my poor dumb Mother's speechless suffering. I had a letter from Father the day I left New York. In it he tells me I ought to go—that it is not right for a family to be divided. It was a hard choice—one that left lasting regret for whichever was set aside but it is done and I am more than justified in being here when I see how much I do to keep Mr. Frémont where his interests require. The children too are so strong & well here & so entirely free from any influence but our own. Lil has her favorite exercise on horseback & I never taught her so well and so thoroughly as here. She has asked me to take up music again and we have time for that also.

Mr. Frémont has a great deal to do, for the present lawsuits carry him occasionally to San Francisco but a few more weeks will give order & then he enters regularly on his writing. It is quite impossible until he is through these interruptions. With all he finds time to take more care of me than ever in all the time we have been together and when I remember that my Father's last days were untroubled about me &

the children because he could rely on Mr. Frémont's care for us, it gives a new value to my home here & a new reason for making it every way pleasant for Mr. Frémont.

The scenery is so varied that each ride gives some beautiful new picture. We will try to have photographs of some to bring you for you and Silver Spring are the point to turn to now.

I go out often on horseback with Mr. Frémont & sometimes with Lily—the carriage could never go where the most beautiful views are to be seen from. We climbed a mountain a few evenings since from which we saw the San Joaquin plain—two lines of timber marked the course of the Mariposa Creek & the San Joaquin 100 miles off. Nearer around us were circling ranges of mountains to the San Joaquin side falling away into low hills like waves, or rather heavy surf—around us was fine timber and flowering shrubs, the wild oats & grasses giving a regularly farm-like look & at the foot of the hills the immense yellow plain without a tree except the two river lines of timber. We had to go on foot the last part of the ascent—slate & quartz & granite cropping out in such pointed jagged ends that even a mule could not get up. We came back to where the horses were tied & took another way down, making our own trail, & found ourselves hemmed in such a thicket of buckeye & chemisal bushes that Mr. Frémont got down & broke away an opening.

As he was leading my horse through the brush I heard a singular noise, half growl, half bark—very gruff & deep—the crashing bushes & the care of the horses kept it from Mr. Frémont's ears & he only said in answer to my saying it was a bear, it could not be a bear there were none here since long ago; but he ran for his mule & taking my horse by the head we came over the ends of the rocks down the hill at a pace we thought unsafe to go up. Lil was following on her horse— a very good mountain horse—her father called to her, as I thought rather sharply, to keep up, that that was the first rule in riding. When we were well down in the valley Mr. Frémont told us why he hurried so. Lily broke in as he began to say he had a good reason for hurrying us & that I had kept my seat well. I know why, Lil said—there was a bear in the ravine by the bushes you led Mother's horse through. That brave little girl heard the noise I did, an unmistakeable wild beast growl, both of us heard it from the same quarter. Lil thought it a dog until her horse snorted & hurried on so differently from its usual cautious pace on the hill sides that it flashed upon her what it was.

But she said nothing for fear of alarming me until she found I had heard it also. You may be sure we will not go into the bush again. We were about a mile above a farm near the foot of the hill where last week many hogs were destroyed one night by a bear. I told Mr. Frémont we had come up on the true Lord of the Manor but he thinks one visit to him enough from us. We have killed under the parlor window a young rattlesnake & by the spring one with ten rattles. The greater absorbs the lesser always. I used to fear caterpillars & spiders but I do not mind a housesnake or a chapparal snake now since I have seen the fresh trail of a rattlesnake crossing the patch to the kitchen. "You can tell 'em by the short crooks & they're fatter than other snakes" so old Isaac[2] directed Charley.

Frank last evening was stoning a long snake Lea had killed—he saw it move & called out "I miss killee him—senek turn he tail—he not dead—killee him Charlee" & away he stoned. But snakes & sounds of grizzly bears do not follow indoors where everything looks as secure and peaceful as at Silver Spring. We found stoves in the house. Mr. Frémont has had them carried off and a stone chimney put up. It is nearly done & when the cool evenings come now we shall sit around a fire of oak & pine & realize how Silver Spring is doing. Only we have cool nights & mornings always. Only the sun's presence gives heat—as it begins to go behind the high range facing us it grows very fresh & we need woolen clothing & all, even I sleep under blankets. This range back of us & nearest the Sierra was named years ago for Father & the tallest peak is Mount Bullion. On its summit a bonfire had been prepared by Mr. Frémont's friends (these are more friendly than unfriendly here) and it was lit the evening of our arrival. It was Friday the 16th at the time he was laid in the ground at St. Louis his mountain was a blazing beacon of welcome to us. You know how fond Father was of the classics & classical comparisons—it seems to me he would have liked to hear me—his favorite scholar—tell him what thought links itself with that day. How as the old Greeks sculptured a jet of flame on the tomb to typify the soul purified & ascending, so that great flame rising from the mountain of gold rock is to me an image of his great heart & mind freed from the clay and rising to the great master.

> "When through fiery trials thy pathway shall lie
> My grace, all sufficient, shall be thy supply;

> The flame shall not hurt thee, I only design
> Thy dross to consume, and thy gold to refine."[3]

How the fiery pains of that dreadful disease did that for my Father—how patiently he bore it all in silence working so hard for Liz & her children. We had a last talk together the Sunday of his birthday. When he saw my heart too full he changed the topic for he evidently dreaded excitement or emotion. But he knew he would not see me again and I did not know the end was so soon but I saw his changed face & evident pain & his voice was like a death knell while he was telling me of his will & his motives in making it. Mr. Frémont will be steady & faithful to his trust as Trustee & so must Montgomery & Mr. Lee—it was the safeguard devised by Father for Eliza's protection & if Mr. Jones makes it hard to be Trustee is it just to Father or manly to Liz to leave her to battle alone against him—how much harder will he make things to her.[4] We need not look for different or better conduct from him—he has not the elements that purify & restrain character & tendencies. And the labor of such a Father under such circumstances must be kept sacred for the purpose he willed. I did not intend to write you more than a little note of love and thanks for I have been less strong than usual lately & I nurse myself by avoiding thoughts that tell on me but this is too much in my heart to pass over. Write to me what came of Mr. Appleton's visit.[5] Did Father derive any encouragement or pleasure from it? Was it any advantage to him to have seen Mr. Appleton? Through Dr. Van Buren I sent Mr. Appleton on to tell Father the book would bring money and that at once. No one knew of it but Dr. Van Buren & Mr. Appleton. Did he do what he ought? I wanted to give Father peace about Liz & this feeling that his work was not in vain. I hope he felt so. I have so many things to say to you and Lizzie but this must end now. I did not get your article from the Eveg. Post but [. . .].[6] Why did the Tribune attack him so coarsely? I keep that editorial.[7] Not one man of them would have read it aloud to my Father. The dead Lion inspires them with no feeling but [detraction?] & security.

> Sage head in the cumber
> Red hand in the foray
> How sound is thy slumber![8]

J.B.F.

1. Thomas Hart Benton had died of cancer of the rectum on Apr. 10 (physician's statement, New York *Evening Post,* Apr. 27, 1858). Two days later, his little grandson, McDowell Jones, suddenly fell ill and died. After a double funeral at the Benton home, family and close friends accompanied the caskets to St. Louis. On Apr. 16, immense silent crowds lined the streets as a two-mile-long funeral cortege carried the bodies to Bellefontaine Cemetery for burial (CHAMBERS, 438–44).

2. JBF had known Isaac since 1849 when he had acted as her coachman in California. She described him as a "spare, wiry Tennessee Indian with enough colored blood to have been a slave," and she fancied that he had freed himself "sharply." In the nine intervening years, he had hunted and mined, maintaining a "thorough" allegiance to JCF (J. B. FRÉMONT [1], 196–98).

3. The fourth verse of the hymn that begins "How firm a foundation, ye saints of the Lord." It is often played and sung to the Lyons tune and was arranged in 1822 from J. Michael Haydn.

4. Benton willed the rebuilt house on C Street and all its contents, except his books, to his daughter Eliza (Liz) Jones. The library went to his son-in-law William Carey Jones. Out of the royalties received or expected from D. Appleton and Company for his various publications, including the two-volume *Thirty Years View,* ten thousand dollars was to go to Eliza, five thousand to his youngest daughter Susan Boilleau, and any remainder was to be divided equally among Eliza, Jessie, Sarah, and Susan. His executors were to be his sons-in-law Jones, Frémont, and Jacob, aided by Montgomery Blair and Samuel Phillips Lee, but Lee declined to serve (CHAMBERS, 434–35; CORNISH & LAAS, 83). Benton was plagued by financial stringencies to the end and shortly before his death borrowed $1,000 from Joshua B. Brant to meet expenses (CHAMBERS, 437).

5. A reference to William Henry Appleton (1814–99), who with his father, Daniel, had founded the book publishing firm of D. Appleton & Co. in 1838.

6. Since the *Evening Post* article was not published until May 25, 1858 (it also appeared in the New York *Tribune* of that date), it is possible that Blair had written JBF much earlier, mentioning that he was preparing one and would send her a copy. More likely, however, she is referring to a communique published in the New York *Tribune,* Apr. 8 (two days before the senator's death) in which the feeble Benton had reportedly whispered his disillusionment with the Buchanan administration, his satisfaction with the House vote to return the proslave Lecompton constitution to Kansas for another popular vote, and warmly praised the intrepid and the incorruptible Douglas Democrats who had resisted the powers and wiles of a corrupt and deluded administration. This conversation was enlarged upon in the Blair article of May 25. This, in turn, brought replies from two of Benton's sons-in-law, William Carey Jones and Richard Taylor Jacob, still proadministration Democrats, who charged the Blairs with political motives and insisted that Benton had remained friendly toward Buchanan and his administration. The controversy over the dying Benton's words went on for several months. In addition to the newspaper accounts, see William Carey Jones, *To the American Public* (Washington, 1858).

7. An editorial in the New York *Tribune,* Apr. 12, assessing Benton's character, had noted that his great adversaries, Clay, Calhoun, and Webster, had never been impressed by his "intellectual strength" and that "it was his intense individuality and animal force, acting upon an intellect of common scope and character that gave him all his triumphs." JBF may have also taken umbrage at the remarks upon his daughters' choice of mates. The newspaper concluded they had all had his final approbation, but believed "the most repugnant of the matches to the paternal care" had been "the marriage of his daughter [Jessie] Ann to the late Republican candidate for the Presidency."

8. JBF is quoting, somewhat incorrectly, from the coronach in Sir Walter Scott's *The Lady of the Lake.*

To Elizabeth Blair Lee

Bear Valley May 28th [1858]

Dear Lizzie,

I have written your Father a long letter but I will not leave you without my loving thanks for your visits to Father and your letters about him. Only by talking to you can I learn all I want to know. I have no details from Liz or Sarah—no messages. I do not wonder that Liz should have written briefly for she has been tried in every way. Her letter was very affectionate but did not tell me if Father spoke of me or did anything to be repeated to me. Sarah alluded to "messages" but did not give them.

I see from a newspaper slip that there is a mortgage of $10,000 upon the house & also that two members of the House were to ask Congress to take a number of copies of the book. Did Father know of this? Was he willing? Please write me all details about Father's affairs or perhaps Mr. Lee will do so that Mr. Frémont may know if he can in any way help. He says he certainly will hold to any power that secures to *Liz* what Father strove so hard to gain for her. Keep your brother & Mr. Lee in the same mind. If it is disagreeable to be a Trustee in connexion with Mr. Jones how much more so to be his child or wife without the aid of friends or protection from his habits. Depend upon it, if it is a harsh it is a clear opinion that he will make no upward move. I want the Congressional Globe with any debate that may rise upon the motion to buy Father's work. His memory and name are our care now. You will know dear Lizzie what things I would wish to know or ought to know and I can depend on you to let me know.

I hope your boy is as well as Charley & Frank. A month has altered both so that it looks as if they had mountain air for six months. Frank's curls are all cut off—they blew in his eyes & got tangled & dusty & he cried morning & night when I combed them so his birthday I cut his hair close & he looks so square faced & stout & healthy that it makes up for the vanished grace of the curls. Charley too grows finely & is busy & sometimes useful—drawing his wagon full of wood or water (he found the watering pot too heavy to carry)—riding on the hay wagon & helping rake it up—he thinks he helps to milk. He has many a good ride on horseback & many tag ends of other rides & can be said to be well on the way to horsemanship. Lea is very fond of him & bent on making a good rider of him. We have also some ropes & rings hung to a high oak limb where both the boys are trained at gymnastic work. They play hard about twelve hours & sleep nearly ten. They eat regularly at 7, 1, & 6 & sleep without turning.

Dear Lizzie I speak in preference of the living interests around us in which I know you take almost my interest. I do not like to think of the change & blank where our feelings have been so centered lately. Keep me informed of everything you judge I ought to know and with the greatest gratitude for all you have done and for your affection dear Lizzie Yours affectionately,

Jessie Frémont

I am so glad Susy had a son—it will help to fill her time & console her.

ALS (NjP—Blair-Lee Papers).

To Elizabeth Blair Lee

San Francisco
July 4th [1858]

Dear Lizzie,

I did not write the last mail because I wanted to keep my mind quite turned away from any thoughts that might agitate me. I have been ill and·came down here for sea air which is a great medicine to me—it was very hot in the mountains. We go back tomorrow and send you only this line now to thank you for your last letters—indeed for all of them and to tell you to thank your brother from me for his care to carry out Father's care for Liz. I will write to him myself when I am out of this torpor of convalesence.

Do keep me posted in all the details. Mr. Frémont says he will not give me my letters another time because I was so grieved to find all the Jones family desecrating the old home—it looks as if they had held back as long as they could & now had settled down. It hurt me—

such indecent haste to take possession it must have hurt Liz, too, deeply especially when she so needed quiet. I want to know especially about the mortgage on the house. Does Corcoran[1] hold it? What is the interest. It must not lapse to him by any chance.

I hope this war breeze[2] does not take Mr. Lee from you—if it should little baby must comfort you.

All ours are well. Lily very good & very happy—studying & riding on horseback. Frank is with me here at the Palmers[3] who are very hospitable and kind.

Do Lizzie give my best love to your mother and to Mr. Blair and affectionate remembrances to Mr. Lee & the Judge. I am very glad Frank made his speech when he did[4]—the English will make the first railway through. This new gold land will stimulate them to promptness & they will secure the overland trade while we are kept out by the dog in the manger southern politicians. I will be glad to see a little humility taught to our boasting people—"greatest nation for enterprize" &c. They have had India & China in their hand & let it slip to catch what?—a postponement of the slavery question. Now England makes fast the only link wanted to bind the globe with her flag.

I had rather have it so than see a railway that ran through Mexico & added more slave troubles. I find I am thinking—something I am not to do—I vegetate—I think of you always when I pass your brother's former home. It looks as it did with the addition of beautiful roses & geraniums about the entrance. All peace and happiness to you all dear Lizzie. Your affectionate friend,

Jessie Frémont

I make no excuse for sending you my letters for France & India. Both are rather important this time & they would be lost if sent in the usual way. I'm so used to all kinds of kindnesses from you that I go on asking.

ALS (NjP—Blair-Lee Papers).

1. Corcoran, sometimes known as Corcoran & Riggs, was a banking firm in Washington, D. C. The founder, W. W. Corcoran, had retired from active business in 1854.

2. In her zeal to stop the illicit slave trade, some Americans felt England had exceeded the right of search and committed outrages on the American flag in the Gulf of Mexico. This "war breeze" of the early summer of 1858 quickly blew over.

3. Originally from Nantucket, Joseph C. Palmer (1819–82) and his wife Mǎrtha (Field) Palmer were noted for their lavish hospitality. JCF had a long association with Palmer, who was one of the principals in the San Francisco banking firm of Palmer,

Cook & Co. JCF was a heavy borrower of the firm until its failure in 1856. Palmer supported JCF for the presidency, encouraged him to buy property at Point San Jose (Black Point), and received government contracts from him during the Civil War when JCF commanded the Western Department in St. Louis (BOSQUI, 112–19; San Francisco *Call* obit., May 2, 1882).

4. Frank Blair, Jr.'s May 25, 1858, speech advocating a central route for the railroad to the Pacific and quoting JCF extensively is printed in the *Congressional Globe*, 35th Cong., 1st sess., pt. 4 (Appendix), 421–25.

To Francis Preston Blair

Bear Valley
July 16th '58.

My dear Mr. Blair,

The papers will give you the news of our broken peace in this valley which was to have been our place of refuge against bad passions & bad climate. I have had to stay four weeks in San Francisco to recover from the exhaustion of the heat here & coming back was waked from my first sleep after the journey by the alarm of regular border ruffian warfare.[1] It is a week today that everything has been merged into the one thought—how to save life & keep off the impending fight. We made an armed truce with them on Wednesday. The governor's decision is to be the signal for the cessation or the renewal of hostilities. I think nothing paints our situation more vividly than the fact that Mr. Herbert (of Irish fame) has volunteered & gone on a peace mission to the governor & on his representation & on Mr. Weller's sense of right our future hangs.[2]

Mr. Howard left on Sunday last with a letter from Mr. Frémont to the governor—a copy of which I send, fearing you may fail to get the paper—we will hear tomorrow perhaps—perhaps not till Monday. Under Wednesday's truce we slept in peace that night & last night. All the men have dispersed & the lull will last until Monday. The Sheriff [Joshua D. Crippen] is of the most approved frontier type. The deputy sheriff [Thomas Howell] came promptly on Friday & read the riot act & then went for warrants to secure the rioters, as they refused to disperse. Then the Sheriff took it up & executed no warrants until Monday—then only on three persons, leaving the rest armed & angered—70 to our 19—(seven of our men were inside the drift). The arrested men soon returned & incited their camp by tipsy speeches.

Our men were kept from retaliating & firing with the greatest difficulty. The Sheriff, being applied to again, said he would have to arrest all if any & did so. He had warrants for nearly all our men beginning with Mr. Frémont & Mr. James. But he has not yet arrested Mr. Frémont, although Mr. Frémont was on the ground all Wednesday morning. Yesterday however the greater part of our men had to go 12 miles to Mariposas to be tried as rioters for taking up arms in self-defence & in defence of the property they were employed to work upon. Among the men on the other side are the most noted criminals of the country — one who has served two years in the penitentiary here. This one was to lead a party to set fire to our House & the mill & mill buildings, in case of a fight. Five nights we kept guard — Lea & Isaac — our trusty colored men, both mountain men & good shots, — a fierce dog named Rowdy, & Mr. Frémont made the home force. With pistols & double barrelled guns we had 32 shots. Only four men could be spared to keep guard at the mill. There were gold in amalgam & some coined & much machinery & so on.

The besieging men attempted to starve out our men & refused to let provision be passed in to them — but the boarding house for the men is kept by a Mrs. Ketton & her husband[3] who happened to be in the mine. The little woman took a revolver & a basket of provisions & presented herself at the mouth of the mine — they refused her entrance. She said she would go & pushed on & told them if they "offered to touch her she'd fire" & if she fired our men would have rushed in & fired also & at the same time they would all have been blown up for the men in the drift had laid a train & put their tools & old iron & blasting powder near the entrance & were ready to do their part by making a blast at the sound of firing. You see the carnage there would have been.

They let her in & after that she went in twice daily, carrying food in her hands & under her clothes pistols & powder & caps. I went yesterday & paid my respects to her.

The first day, Friday, was the most concentrated anguish I ever felt — the three hours in which I was without news from the mine seemed endless. When Mr. Frémont did come & I found no fighting had been done and that it was not imminent again I felt suddenly let down into a stupor from which I did not recover until the next day. Up to this time the only blood drawn has been from my mouth. But I grew somewhat used to it & whenever Mr. Frémont was in sight I was very brave.

I send you the printed part of the correspondence.[4] I send also a copy of the final letters & that to the governor.[5] Please notice how the leaders of the riot, consent to await the govrs. decision, which has to be made on Mr. Frémont's version of the case.

It is a compliment to his uprightness which we should be forced to decline imitating towards them. All this is the result of the decision of the State Supreme Court—& one of its Judges, Judge Terry,[6] says he will not decide for a free soiler. Like old Judge Thurston[7] deciding against the Catholics. I think if it were the property of a southern democrat it would have every legal protection.

I've had so much to copy & write that I cannot write to Lizzie. I got into such an excitement a few days ago that I wrote you 44 PAGES— but you are spared them by this truce. It was my last will & testament in case of loss of life here.

Now everything is our way the tide has turned & is rushing up— I trust it will fill our coffers as well as give peace. Mr. Frémont thinks this storm has finally cleared the air—provided always that the governor does right.

We never see any but the steamer papers that we buy—none are sent us. Please send me the comments of good papers on this—misrepresentations too, send.

AL (NjP—Blair-Lee Papers).

1. As noted above in the letter to Elizabeth Blair Lee, Apr. 24 [1858], the California Supreme Court's decisions earlier in the year had encouraged the Merced Mining Company to hold on to its operations on the Mariposas and even to extend them, since it was confidently expected that Frémont's title to the minerals beneath the land would soon be dissolved. The points of friction in the summer of 1858 were the Josephine and Pine Tree mines, very close to each other in Bear Valley and which both the Merced Mining Company and the Frémont miners were working, but in different tunnels. Furthermore, JCF had stepped up his operations by building a quartz mill nearby and by making a down payment on the purchase of the Merced and Mariposa ditch with which it was expected that a steady supply of water, so necessary to mining, could be introduced into Bear Valley from the South Fork of the Merced River.

The incidents recounted in this letter by JBF began when a rich section of the Pine Tree mine known as the Black Drift, and being worked by her husband's men, was "jumped" by the Merced Company's workers in the Josephine. Then at daybreak on July 9, about seventy men from the Hornitas League, a body of miners and settlers opposed to JCF's ownership of the mines, seized the mouth of the unguarded main entrance of the Pine Tree mine. Four or five of JCF's men were at work inside and prevented the "jumpers" from entering. The pro–Merced Company forces then took up positions above and below the tunnel, thus preventing ingress or egress, and awaited developments.

When compared with contemporary newspaper accounts, JBF's record of events and near warfare seems to be fairly accurate, although we might question her assertions of "tipsy speeches," "noted criminals" among the opponents, and the intention to fire the house, mill, and mill buildings. See *San Joaquin Republican,* and Mariposa *Gazette,* July 14, 18, 1858. Later, in "Beseiged," a chapter in her book *Far West Sketches,* JBF gives a dramatic and exaggerated account of the incidents.

2. As noted earlier, Gov. John B. Weller's third wife was a cousin of JBF. Weller had preceded JCF as chief of the Mexican Boundary Commission and succeeded JCF in the U.S. Senate. JBF was skeptical that former congressman Philemon Thomas Herbert, who had killed an Irish waiter at Willard's Hotel, Washington, in 1856, would be an adequate messenger.

3. In the U.S. Census Records for 1860, Mariposa County, the name is given as Ketten. Elizabeth and her husband, James, a head miner, were native Virginians, and the parents of five small children.

4. See Mariposa *Gazette,* July 14, 1858, which printed the miners' July 12 call for JCF to withdraw his forces and close up the Pine Tree vein until the California Supreme Court made its decision, and JCF's July 13 refusal to do so.

5. JBF enclosed handwritten copies of JCF's July 10, 1858, letter to Governor Weller, the "rioting" miners' July 14 agreement not to commit hostile acts at the Pine Tree vein until the decision of the governor was made known to the parties, and JCF's July 14 promise not to act aggressively.

6. David S. Terry was chief justice of the California Supreme Court from 1857 until shortly after he killed U.S. Senator David C. Broderick in a duel in Sept. 1859. His own checkered career concluded violently in 1889, in a Lathrop, Calif., restaurant when the bodyguard of U.S. Supreme Court Justice Stephen J. Field shot him after Terry supposedly struck Field in the face. For a biography of Terry, see BUCHANAN.

7. Judge Buckner Thurston (1763–1845) had served in the U.S. Senate as a Democrat from Kentucky before being appointed by President James Madison as judge of the U.S. Circuit Court of the District of Columbia.

To Francis Preston Blair

Sunday 2 pm.
18th July [1858]
Bear Valley

Dear Mr. Blair,

I keep the pen as I have been writing, but Mr. Frémont speaks. (You are willing for me to keep that share of telling you things?)

"Mr. Herbert has just passed here with a letter addressed by the governor [to] a committee of the rioters. As the letter may not get in time to the papers going East by this mail I send you a copy & beg you to see that some published notice of Mr. Herbert's good conduct on this occasion may reach here in time to be of service to him by September, when his election to the State Senate comes off.

The Governor sent me word by Mr. Herbert that he had telegraphed to the military companies at Columbia, Sonora, & Stockton, to hold themselves in readiness to start at a moment's notice to our protection.

Friends in San Francisco have sent me up 100 muskets with bayonets & abundance of ammunition & 50 good men have volunteered to come & use them.[1] (They are all stored up in my store room & my clothes & the groceries are stacked under the trees. J.B.F.)

This is a great triumph and ensures the peaceable protection of the property from this time on."

We have not another moment but take one to say that you must let our love for you somewhat compensate for the annoyance you have from Mr. Jones. The true sting to him is in Montgomery's faithful execution of Father's wish to secure Liz & her children from Mr. Jones's bad conduct. Beg him from me to hold to it. I am arranging a way to take up that mortgage & hold that house myself. Mr. Frémont says the first spare money shall go to that. Most affectionately Yours with love to all of you,

Jessie Benton Frémont

Mr. Fremont says consider his renunciation as sent—troubles here delayed the paper going but it will go to him next mail & so act accordingly.

ALS (NjP—Blair-Lee Papers).

1. On July 18, 1858, the *San Joaquin Republican* reported that it had been informed "that four cases of muskets were sent up to Col. Frémont by wagons, Friday, from Stockton, being forwarded by the United States Marshal."

To Elizabeth Blair Lee

San Francisco, August 17th '58.

My dear Lizzie your letter gave me great pain. Your Father and yourself have grown together & can no more live separate than the tree & the bark. I perfectly recognize & advocate a separate home. I see the greater content & the gratified pride & self esteem of a married man in his own home, but my dear Lizzie that is not to be begun after sixteen years spent otherwise. Part of the new nest will be made of the very fibres of yours and your Father's hearts.[1] I wish with all the love in mine for you that I could be near you both. Your Father loves me and I could be something to him—& to you too. I had this same thing too when we left for New York three years ago—but it is harder far for both of you than it was on my Father & myself for he was sufficient to himself in his work & there as in so many other things you are second nature to your Father. You both too see things—in general—in a softened light. Your Father feels a hard judgment & a stern manner of making it, even if he feels it deserved, as something unpleasant & uncongenial from which his taste winces as his lungs do from gusts of wind. Mr. Frémont is so like him in that & I am so gusty by nature that as it is my steady instinct to avoid making him wince I have learned to notice in others the same thing. You are a steady south breeze—hardly a wind—& your Father needs you for your healing properties. Indeed it is not nonsense to me the idea of six miles being a break up to yours & your Father's habits & ways together. But since it is done let it be well done. Mr. Lee was an oak in a flower pot narrow for his roots & I think he has given you the longest & most thorough possible proof of loving you better than himself in so long consulting your wishes at the expense of his own. For it is simply impossible that he should not have chafed at not having his own home—his silence about it makes the merit greater & I can but think you must like it best too. It is my insanity to have some spot where I can retire into myself. Foxes have holes why not people. I am even persuaded that we should introduce no foreign element of any kind into our holes—no governess or friend or ward. Indeed Lizzie "an enlightened selfishness" is needed to keep all peaceful around one. I think your Father will be the one to feel it most for one cannot change habits at his age as easily as at yours and he likes movement & animation around him & baby is just getting his pretty ways & making himself a resource against little times of weariness & crossness. Frank is that here. Mr. Frémont is as fond of him as Mr. Lee used to be & (I trust will remain) of Charley. When Mr. Frémont has had some repented folly of business disagreeably kept before him, I slide in Frank & the dogs for a romp & Frank is so sure he is wanted that you are obliged to want him & then the fog is dispersed. My dear blundering Charley doesn't answer the same purpose. He asks questions—above all he sees shades of displeasure & acts on them & Mr. Frémont's nature demands to be met two thirds of the way—and I think Mr. Lee is somewhat the same way. But I know no harvest so abundant as that from well sown seed of harmony & attention in a home.

You have given me so many useful lessons that I beg in turn to teach you a little in this. I have gone about like a stork with my young ones, building new nests summer & winter & rebuilding again & again as fast as they were abandoned or destroyed. All my energy—and I think I must have started with an unusual share for it to hold out yet—has gone to keeping a home & home feelings in our scattered little set. And of late I am getting a great reward. I am friend and adviser now— outwardly nothing is changed but to Mr. Palmer it is really very different—he finds an invisible obstacle & I am the confidante of his foiled plans. Children are so happy in their own homes. My little godson does not care yet but it will come and a happy childhood & youth gives its brightness all through life. At least they had it all fair and happy once & the mother who could dim or sacrifice that for a selfish reason is a criminal—she murders her children's faith in all sacred things. Let them find it out for themselves that there is no great happiness in living—they may & some by chance may not—give them as Father used to say "the benefit of the doubt."

I feel like saying pages more—I could talk to you until four in the morning & defy Mr. Lee's hints the next day—but Mr. Howard leaves tomorrow & that gives so much writing for the rest of the day & I have yet to write to Liz. She needs to feel there is such a thing as home affection. She is forever separated from her Father—from her only true friend and protector & with him she has lost all security of a home for her children.

Lil is learning well, music, singing, German & *parsing* & arthmetic— she goes about on horseback a great deal. We are out of town in an admirable house, with 8 acres of land—hills & valley & plenty of low oaks & willows.[2] Mr. Frémont has been ill—pleurisy—I am only too glad to keep him out of the mining country & can't be sorry for the cause. Write often & be sure I understand everything as it is I pity you a little & your Father very much & think the others quite right. I think it what they call "a painful necessity"—but all of you & you most must keep the good side uppermost. I wish you all happiness under the new roof & I know you will have it. We I think will be here some months longer—I'll tell you when I know. Au jour le jour [as the case may be]. Yours most truly & affctly,

Jessie Frémont

I never wrote & never shall write anything for print. Jack Howard wrote that letter & others in the Post & we were vexed at it. We want to keep silent. I never see the Post—that one Mr. Howard had sent from home to him.[3]

ALS (NjP—Blair-Lee Papers).

1. Jessie implies that Lizzie and her husband planned to build a home of their own and move from Silver Spring. Perhaps these plans spurred Francis Preston Blair to build them a three-story home in Washington, D.C., adjacent to the home of Montgomery Blair. He approved the specifications and signed the contract in Apr., 1859. The house shared a common wall with Montgomery's, although Phillips and Montgomery were not then on speaking terms (CORNISH & LAAS, 83).

2. The Fremonts had gone to San Francisco for the balance of the summer.

3. A heavy investor in the Mariposas, John Tasker Howard had published a general description of the estate in the New York *Evening Post*, July 15, 1858, under the pen name "Iota." Then on Aug. 12, 1858, the *Post* carried his account of the "riot," with copies of the correspondence that had passed between the opposing forces.

To Elizabeth Blair Lee

April 2 [1859]
Bear Valley.

Dear Lizzie,

I have written you long letters & put them in the fire as too much truth in the mail. My Father's affairs were unknown to me and your brother's letter made me so sick at heart that I have not had the courage to read it again. I must do it & answer it—but putting it off to the last moment the mail came in and brought me my poor Susy's last sorrow—dear little Pensée is to be sent to yours & Mr. Lee's care to be laid in the graveyard that was in sight from the windows of the cottage where she was born. Mr. Beecher will see to its passing the Custom house & put it in Adams Express—ah dear Lizzie how often that name has made me wince.

Susy is on the path of the cross fairly now—how her changed & humble resignation hurts me you can imagine. I know the process that breaks down a heart like hers & that child was the first thing in life to her. We will try to make some things happier for her. They are in France now & we will try to smooth money matters for them.

I never wanted money so much as now. Ah if I could have guessed what Father was enduring it breaks my heart to think of such a weight on his mind & no one to share it and love him and tell him it should be made right. I will write by the overland mail to your brother & a duplicate by the next steamer. I have sent a thousand dollars to Susy—I wanted to do more but you know something of Mr. Frémont's affairs—in a year half a year we shall have, we believe, many thousands to spare. Now it is difficult to spare tens. But he can do more little by little for Susy & I think Father himself would have put her first.

I should like to send something to Betsy[1] but I have nothing for any but Susy. Tell her I value her care of Father as it deserved. She knows it. I always gave her my thanks & large presents of money each time I saw her last winter. I should so much have liked to save Father's horse & send it to Lizzie Whiting to take care of—but my money will come too late. Dear Lizzie can you find who got Susy's & my photographs when Father's things were sold? I should like them back so much. There were many things of mine & Susan's there—the [piano?] Father sent over to the cottage to Susy—it was his gift to her. She will regret his only present. I am very much obliged to your brother for writing us so long a letter—please make him know that I understand it all but it gave me so much pain that I waited to feel used to it before answering it & I do not feel so yet.

Whatever Barton did at the last, his wife was loved & made happy to a degree very few women ever reach. I know them so well & I see plainly she was most happy & beloved. It seems to me that Mr. Sickles talked too much before acting & acted with a due regard for safety when he did act and the extracting a written confession before two women witnesses from a woman in her state of mind & in the family way was an accumulation of heartless cruelties that show a character to justify his wife's looking elsewhere for something to love.[2] Do write to me often. Mr. Jones has stopped Liz's writing to me & I hear nothing from any one. Will you let me know what you can of Liz & her children. I hope they will stay with Sarah—who never writes to me either. Kiss your dear boy for me—ours are so well and happy. I'll tell you all about us—not now though for I have no time as the mail goes

at ten. With love to your Father & Mother most affectionately dear
Lizzie Your friend,

Jessie Frémont

ALS (DLC—Blair Papers).

1. Benton's cook (JBF to Elizabeth Blair Lee, Mar. 7 [1856], above).
2. JBF is referring to Philip Barton Key's tragic love affair with Teresa Bagioli Sickles.
The handsome Key, who was U.S. attorney general for the District of Columbia and
the son of Francis Scott Key, was the widower of Jessie's friend, Ellen Swan Key.
Several years after her death, Congressman Daniel Sickles, a notorious womanizer even
after his marriage, and his beautiful young wife arrived in Washington. Teresa Sickles
and Key became enamored with each other. On learning the details and exacting a
written confession from his wife before two women witnesses, the aggrieved husband
shot and killed the unarmed Key in Lafayette Square on a Sunday morning, Feb. 27,
1859. In the trial that followed, Sickles was acquitted on the grounds that he was
rendered temporarily insane by rage and grief at the time of the slaying. Details of the
romance, trial, and later reconciliation of the Sickleses are given in SWANBERG, 1–76.
At the time there was a report that Mrs. Sickles was pregnant, but SWANBERG by his
silence implies there was no truth in the rumor.

To Francis Preston Blair

Camp Jessie on Mt. Bullion
4,000 feet above the sea &
facing the Sierra Nevada.
(Add to that the date the
2d of July '59 & I think
you never before saw so
long a heading.)

The slip I enclose you my dear Mr. Blair will sufficiently account to
you for our Excelsior movement. If we could have got, like the old
woman "Seventy times as high as the moon,"[1] we'd have been willing
while that moon lasted. When it grew to be 104° & 107° at sunset in
the most shaded & enclosed room of our Bear Valley cottage we grew
desperate & out of the heat came a lightning flash of remembrance;
how the year before when riding along the crest of this range we looked
down on our parched & hot valley on one side & just below on the
other a green & cool looking ledge of rocks & large-leaved oaks. Isaac
said there was a fine spring also but it was late & the stones very thick
so we only looked down upon it & across to the snow mountains

[Sierra Nevada] & returned to our heat, which was so sickening that we all left soon after for San Francisco & there I stayed until fall. But this year Mr. Frémont could not possibly leave and to go off & have sea breezes ice fruits & good health while he was bearing, literally in more senses than one "the heat & burden of the day" was what Lil & I couldn't do & so we bethought ourselves of this place. Before sunrise next morning Lil & I were climbing the mountain—the stones rolling at every touch of our horses hoofs—armed with a thermometer & a luncheon basket. We were to spend the day & come back at sunset to report.

We made our way, Isaac guiding, (Isaac is an oldish Tennessee Negro—a born hunter & for four years employed here to drive teams & do watch duty with his rifle & dog). The spring was in a cluster of fine oaks & the water so cold that we were shouting for joy over it. At mid-day under a June sun it was only 55° in its waters and so sweet & light. Remember we had no ice below & the water always tasted boiled & lukewarm—more than that when it had been drawn some time. We found it so cool & such a sweet breeze that we went home like conquerors. You know we never have moderation in our fortunes. They are either very good or very bad & this is a very bad year—the more felt as it should have been the reverse. Mr. Park[2] pretending to act for himself but really urged on by Mr. Palmer, of whose true character Mr. Frémont has no longer a doubt, has sued for part ownership & attachments & all sorts of law processes resorted to, to drive Mr. Frémont into terms. So we have had a storm to weather. It is not over yet but they find they will gain nothing & that Mr. Frémont will sink the whole property before yielding. So that left us no money for summer tours—every demand has to be promptly met or it is converted into a law demand—it is in fact like a run on a bank. Judge then of the great happiness it was to find health and quiet & delightful change for us all without money & without price. God's own free gift.

We had planks & common drilling at the mills—a man or two was turned from other work & two days after our reconnaissance we were installed in a great tent with a board floor, the sides held up to posts & over all the thick shade of an oak grove. The spring is about fifty yards off with its own settlement for cooking. Isaac & one of the women do everything and we are as happy & free as Robin Hood & Maid Marion.[3] You should see the boys. Charley is grave about watering horses, finding good pastures, *picking birds* (horrid work but he enjoys being useful). Frank skims into everything & sings "Don't you remember sweet Betsy from Pike" from dawn to dusk. Mr. Frémont gets up to us at five or earlier every evening. We have the most delightful open air dining room with a view that cannot be matched out of the Alps & not there I feel nearly sure. Every morning we get our garden & dairy supplies with meat, &c., from below & we make such good dinners with "appetite sauce."

We face an amphitheatre of mountains which rise from the river Merced—ourselves being on the steep descent to its banks. It is about thirty miles as the crow flies to the snow mountains but in this transparent, rarified air they look not ten. The cliffs & chasms of the Yosemite Valley are perfectly distinct. A few hundred feet behind us Mt. Bullion raises its stern head & we have this bench with its fine oaks & pasturage & spring to break the descent to the river bed. And it's only two miles from our door. Mr. Frémont goes back to his work below in the cool of the morning. The sun does not strike our side of the valley until six so he is almost there before the heat begins. Are we not fortunate in being able to keep well & keep together also? We have books & lots of papers & light reading & it is such a rest to Mr. Frémont to cut off business & put this high wall between himself & the money making.

We talk of you every time we hear Isaac's "wifle" as Frank calls it. Quail, doves, hares & squirrels are overflowing in camp. There are many deer around but the undergrowth is dense lower down the hill & though Isaac has seen some fawns & heard deer whistle he has not had a shot at them yet. Our horses scare them from this neighborhood. But the very talk of them rests Mr. Frémont's weary mind & he goes with new heart to his work. The sleeping is something fine. The roof of our tent is square & twelve feet high. As it doesn't rain in the summer I could go by fancy & not by rule. A board floor raised two feet from the ground keeps cleanliness about our beds which are made in Oriental fashion on the floor quite along one side. Oak leaves & a sort of soft heather which is abundant here make a delightful bed. Matting covers it next & then the usual pillows &c. for we are near enough to home to have clean things in abundance. The side of the tent that is at the bed's head is fastened down. The other sides are lifted to tall poles & make broad piazzas. Two great oaks are two of our tent poles & cast their boughs above and around the enclosure. The others are so near that the sun does not penetrate. It is as charming as an idyll. I have pasted a lot of engravings & colored views on the wall at the head. Some book shelves hang there also from the ridge pole. Little evidences of crinoline being around in the shape of work boxes, writing desks, flowers & so on make it the pearl of camps. Mr. Davenport,[4] one of Mr. Frémont's party from '45 to '48 took great part in making all right for us up here. He gave it my name. It is not on the post office book yet so all letters must come as usual to Bear Valley. Indeed before an answer to this could reach me it will be cold here. In August frosts begin up here. But I am sure you more than anyone can appreciate the rare good fortune we have had in finding such a place so near to us where we can all share the good together.

I will write to Lizzie about Miss Lawrence[5] who has made us a long visit & who leaves on this steamer. But this camp letter is for Lizzie too. Indeed Mr. Blair, yourself & Lizzie are so necessary to one another to my mind that I feel you one & indivisible. Nina goes on a visit to today with Miss Lawrence & may meet Betty or some of you & can tell you of the past year—not much however for it has not been in her style exactly. With best love to you all, dear Mr. Blair Yours affectionately,

Jessie Frémont

ALS (NjP—Blair-Lee Papers).

1. From the Mother Goose nursery rhyme that begins, "There was an old woman tossed in a blanket,/Seventeen times as high as the moon."
2. Trenor W. Park (1823–82) was a Vermont lawyer who had come to California in 1851 and for a time became affiliated with San Francisco's most prestigious law firm, Halleck, Peachy and Billings. Park was a heavy investor in real estate in and around San Francisco and in 1857 obtained an interest in Las Mariposas by taking a $65,000 mortgage on the property. Over the next few years, he purchased other mortgages and judgments against the estate. In 1860, he worked out an arrangement with JCF whereby he was to take over the management of the estate. In exchange for the 5 percent commission to which he was entitled as estate manager, he was to receive one-sixteenth ownership of the property. By July 1863, Park claimed he held 180 bonds against the estate with a value, including coupons and interest, of $334,021.66. For an article on Park, see BELL; the Park-McCullough House Archives indicate the intricacies of the business and legal arrangements. See, especially, JCF's mortgage to T. W. Park, Dec. 1857; JCF's statement of agreement with Park, June 14, 1860; and Park's Statement of Bonds, July 1863.
3. The Ballad of Robin Hood and Maid Marian may be found in F. J. CHILD, 3:218–19.
4. "Mr. Davenport" was Alfred Davenport from Ohio, whom the U.S. 1860 Census for Mariposa County listed as a mine manager. He seems not to have been a member of any of JCF's exploring expeditions, but in 1846, he was in Company A of JCF's California Battalion (PIONEER REGISTER, 775).

5. The daughter of Judge Effingham Lawrence and Ann Townsend, Hannah Townsend Lawrence, born in Bayside, Queens, in 1833, was the sister of Effingham Lawrence,
who had a plantation on the Mississippi River near New Orleans, and of Joseph E.
Lawrence, a San Francisco newspaperman. JBF's friendship with Hannah Lawrence
would continue until Hannah's death in 1898.

To Elizabeth Blair Lee

Camp Jessie, Mt. Bullion.
July 2d '59.

Dear Lizzie

I was to have written you a long letter but I walked to the top of
the mountain & took me over a day to right myself after it. I am so
well that I forget the old leaven is still there & that I cannot accelerate
my heart's work without suffering. I have had such good health almost
all the time this year, that I never think of it & should not speak of
it but that a day's pain cut off my intended letters. I have written today
to your Father but it is for you also.

Nina goes home with Miss Lawrence — a sister of Mrs. Cornelius
Lawrence[1] of New York who has made us a good long visit up here.
She says she would like very much to know you all. Don't fail if you
go to New York to send your cards to her. She is the most upright
truly honorable nature imaginable. Fine health, fine spirits & an impossibility to see one going wrong without trying to turn them right.
She has been a happiness to us all. Even my poor fastidious husband
gradually forgave her for not being in the true American standard of
beauty a sulky dyspeptic skeleton whose few smiles are kept for the
outside & whose ill feeling pour out over all within doors. Miss
Lawrence is larger than I like but I would not change an ounce of her.
Nina has been fretting at the seclusion here & Miss Lawrence invited
her to go with her which she did with an eagerness that surprised her
uncle (but no one else) & quite hurt him for this is not one of our
sunny times. But it is her nature & she is not to be blamed for an
irresistible tendency to glare any more than a moth.

I intend she shall go in October to Cousin Sarah [Sarah Benton Brant]
& from there to make a visit to her Mother,[2] who plies us with abuse
for keeping her only child from a mother's love.

Do write to me much & often & about everything. I can't imagine you in a house in town. Kiss my dear boy for me, teach him my name & let him learn about the boys. They are so happy here. So is Lil. She studies as usual & sings & rides & is happy in her own silent fashion. Frank is perfectly charming. The sweetest manner & the sweetest voice & so beautiful. Charley is a little cubbish, but a fine boy.

Give our best love and remembrances to Mr. Lee. Will the increase of the Navy move him away from you?

Do write much. In many ways this has been a hard sad year of loss and trouble. In some other things great gain. I have good health again & we are all at peace & very contented within doors. Most sincerely & affectionately Your friend,

Jessie Frémont

ALS (NjP—Blair-Lee Papers).

1. Hannah Lawrence's sister, Lydia, had married her cousin, Cornelius Van Wyck Lawrence, financier, merchant, and one time mayor of New York.

2. Nina's mother, Jane, seems to have remarried. JBF's July 13, 1864, letter to Biddle Boggs (copy, Mariposa County Historical Society) implies that she was a Mrs. Drew.

To Nathaniel Banks

Bear Valley, Aug. 20, '59

My dear Mr. Banks,

I am not sorry that continued headaches put me out of the way for answering your letter which reached me in our mountain camp. A little delay has cleared away many clouds and we have now what "ce respectable Ritchie" would have called "Skies bright." The last agreeable thing we have to thank you for—the letter telling that you have seen to, and can assure Mr. Frémont of safety in your quarter. That is a great relief to him as it bars any malice from bond holders in other quarters. Mr. Frémont has as you will have learned from Mr. Howard bought back all but one eighth of the estate & large as the obligations seem he felt sure of his own power to pay them if he were only free to work—and if his work-men were to come back to himself. For that he has taken upon himself the entire overlooking of each department—going at sunrise to the mines—praise my housekeeping a little—he has a good breakfast & is in the saddle at six, often at half past five,—examines rock & directs the source of supply—visits the mills & sees each branch there managed with its utmost economy as well as skill & so on through it all. He tells me to say he is preparing a little budget for you—sketches, accounts, estimates, &c.—in the mean time he wishes you to share his pleasure in the first weeks results of "the master's eye"—from the river & stream mill for the week the yield was five thousand eight hundred dollars. He intends to double it with some new amalgamators which will be in place within a week.

Few will feel so understandingly as yourself what a satisfaction this is to Mr. Frémont—not only for the money, but for the evidence of his power & capacity to manage this business profitably. I have always been the Didymus[1] of this estate—not as to its capabilities but as to our profiting from them. Now I believe.

My other pleasure is in having my sister Mrs. Boilleau back in America. She leaves France about this time for New York. Boilleau is sent to Quebec & they come through that way. It is quite fit Boilleau should represent France there for his grandfather was first cousin to Genl. Montcalm. As climate it is all they wish and I don't care a fig for the dignity part being beneath his deserts for I rather think about the time we are getting solid in princely revenues here there will be only fragments of the French throne. I don't understand the peace— it is a promise broken. The Emperor is very clever but I think he has made a mistake this time. But let him go his way for my sister is my object. I want you to ask Mr. Andrews[2] who knows Canadians to let any friends he has in Quebec know of their coming and bespeak a little cordiality for her. Poor Susy has had a very sorrowful two years since she left us. Her little boy born in Calcutta was but a few weeks old when she read on a paper around a package the mention of the ceremonies at my Father's funeral. Boilleau had known it some time & kept it from her. The shock hurt her & hurt the baby also. From her own illness she was [roused?] to Boilleau's. He was four months hanging on the edge of the grave from the illness so fatal to Europeans in India. Suddenly her little girl, the loveliest and most precocious child of nearly three years, died. All these things would have told upon any one but Susan has the power to suffer that goes with great capacity to feel and know what we lose. I am so glad to have her back. I fell asleep thinking Quebec & waked to speak of it the first thing. If I could get letters to her in time I would tell her to stop a day or two in Boston & see my friend Miss Richardson & Mrs. Banks & yourself. It warms one's heart to come back to home thoughts and appreciating sympathy after years among strangers. I think your boy is a little older than my youngest.[3] We will trot them out together when I see you. Frank rides bare-backed—horse or mule—climbs trees & sings Villikins & his Dinah[4] with proper expression. Is little Frémont so far advanced? Frank also tells immense snake & hunting stories. If his imagination remains as vivid & prolific he will surpass Sinbad or Dumas. Make my best regards to Mrs. Banks. Nina returned to New York with Miss Lawrence & may meet you somewhere. Very sincerely yours,

Jessie Benton Frémont

ALS (DLC—Nathaniel Banks Papers).

1. A surname of the Apostle Thomas, called the Twin, who doubted at first the disciples' report of the resurrection of Christ. See John 11:26, 20:24, 21:2.
2. Israel De Wolf Andrews had served as American consul in New Brunswick and had been the chief promoter of the Canadian-American trade reciprocity treaty of 1854.
3. Joseph Frémont Banks.
4. For a list of variant forms and modern sources of this comic parody of a street ballad, see BRUNNINGS, 327.

To Elizabeth Blair Lee

Bear Valley, Nov. 15th, '59.

My dear Lizzie it is so long since I have had a good old time letter from you that it made me very glad to see the two sheets come out of the envelope—pray don't drop it again. If you are busy with country housekeeping, and one small child, what have I not to do? All that only much more of it like Judge Gaston's creed.[1] Some day your father will write to me again. I get little pistol shots of notes from your brother once in a while but I like a whole doublebarrelled concern crammed full of little friendly shots against all people but our own. Mr. Jones is so unreliable from his bad habits & his alliance with the Administration that I have not ventured to write to Liz since his prohibition & I know nothing whatever of any of the family. When he dies it will all be right again.

You will have seen Susy by this time—write to me of her looks &

her talk & all about her. You know all I wish to hear. I was grieved to hear of Alice Key's broken health for she is the stay of the whole family for common sense.[2] I have thought so much of her in their distresses. Last Spring I wrote to her but feared to send my letters least she should feel it an intrusion. I think I knew Barton in his true and best nature—he was a truly loving & good husband and Father and his cruel death came to me with a shock that few could have caused. Now his Mother & Ellen's unsettled ways.[3] I saw Ellen's conversion noticed. She is one of the people who don't know when they are well off. Her children were originally very fine little creatures, but I wouldn't introduce Mason to Charley again. Marie & I were on guard to keep them separate all the latter days he was at my house. Ellen used to keep saying, "But you see the thing is there's no money. How can I do anything for my children without money." There are several ways. I find it possible to do a great deal for Lily with less than Ellen paid for railway tickets and you will see if the boys are not as much little gentlemen as they are healthy manly little men. They know the habits of horses, cows, calves, dogs, fowls, and birds. They know what woods are best for firing and what for props in the mines. They know the sound & flourish of ox-talk. We have been so lucky as to have a man & his sons as lumber men who did the cutting & hauling for the mill and were most steady men who never swore & many a delightful tramp Charley has had with them. Then I let him go hunting with safe men & when he came in yesterday with a great hare dropping blood on a clean new suit (only corduroy but whole & clean) & his face bright & red-cheeked as the fresh blood I hadn't the heart to say clothes. He was so pleased that he had seen the hare first & he had brought it out of the brush after it was shot & his dog was as good a pointer as its mother (ten puppies were her May day present to us). All these made him so happy & he had walked near six miles & was so hungry & laid in such a stock of bread & cold beef as he talked as well nigh choked him.

For Mr. Lee's gratification I tell that Charley's deepest love is the sea and the ships that go down upon its waters. A great colored picture of the Great Eastern hangs in his little bed-room—a dog guarding a dead soldier is the only land idea in his collection. Russian frigates in dock, big ships firing salutes, all the large illustrations he can get are pinned up to his papering & he sits on the bed with all seriousness copying parts of them. He whittles out schooners, takes all my linen

& cambric out of my work basket for sails & my biggest needles to sew them on their masts so as to slip up & down & then gets permission to sail them in the reservoir. He climbs already—very well. The oaks here are pretty-even-barked and don't help him up much, so he has tough practice. In all these Frank imitates him as nigh as he can. He is a most beautiful boy and has developed the right paternal foolish fondness in Mr. Frémont at last & the door once opened, the rest have gone in also.

I have written you a quantity about the children but you will forget them if I don't. I don't let them forget you and yours. They always eat from their cups when they are at table but their evening's feed is a tin cup of fresh warm milk & a great hunch of dry baker's bread at least one day baked. By six they are scoured & nightgowned and have said their last jokes to Mr. Frémont & each in his own room is singing himself to sleep. For them this long stay here has been all good.

Lil feels beat as much as I do & it has very much hurt her health to have stayed through these two long hot summers. But she will not leave me. I try to make it up to her and all I can do in talking, reading, seeing after her barnyard & stable pets, every talk of hers I follow up & share. She has learned a great deal. Luckily she loves real reading & you know how she systematizes and saves time. We have finished a French history by one of the learned & at the same time elegant French authors, in thirteen volumes, the size of the Spectator. In this everything was verified by references to maps, by lighter works on the same points, some committing to memory, & much writings out of abstracts. The work began in the dark ages & came down to the consulate. It took just eleven months to do this but now Lily knows France, French history & the biographical & anecdotical part of French history as we know our own family story. On this foundation I have put her to work now on a work from the end of Louis 14th's reign to our days, a compact law argument for the advance of liberty in religion & social life & equality in law. With that, Madame deGenlis' Memoirs in 10 volumes giving the social life (in its respectable side) of the time from the marriage of Marie Antoinette to the Restoration.[4]

Nov. 29

I was interrupted and hurried so for the last mail, that I let slip my letter for you—and ever since I have been both ill & busy.

The decision in Mr. Frémont's favor (I do not send it as you will

see it noticed & it will be in pamphlet form soon, then I'll send it)
has brought lawyers & consultations & quartz claimants & talks &
leases & more for me to do than I have quite time for.[5] This decision
is a great point gained and makes the labor here easy by comparison
but it will take months on months yet to shape things so as to leave
them. I wish Mr. Lee had not built that stupid house & then you
would be foot-loose to travel and you could so easily come & see us.
Else, I don't see how we shall meet again. Please think of it—anyway
write to me. Tell me what my godson can do & if his eyes are as
beautiful as when I saw him. Frank's are not what they were in his
baby days but they are beautiful still. He has a true gift in singing &
whistling. Think of the little man—(in corduroys & a red flannel shirt
over the white one)—hands in pockets & thick-soled leather shoes,
whistling perfectly well tune after tune—all the turns, bends & graces—
& he only 4 1/2—is your boy half-way to that?

Mr. Frémont has gone to start his new mill today and a nine day's
rain, snow & wind storm has stopped just in time to favor the ceremony.
We shall get the reward of our long stay here and I know no one who
will be more glad to be assured of it than you. Mr. Frémont is very
well and so busy that it keeps him out all day & early to rest as he
is early up also.

We should have some grand talks if we ever did meet. Doors might
be slid and coughs might be coughed with the greatest significance,
but we'd snub both of them.

I don't believe you are greyish even. My hair is a queer tawny color,
neither grey nor brown—a kind of feuille morte [dead leaf]. I'm decidedly the worse for my two years stay in bad climate with wearing
anxieties & a total want of the rest and physical luxuries I need. But
it was a reward for all and a foretaste of the great "well done, good
and faithful servant" when Mr. Frémont told me after the court gave
him the support of the law, that without my care for him & sharing
the long hard waiting, he could never have endured it.

It has brought out all his old best qualities. They were rusting a
little & his friends had not been good for him, but these keen winds
of adversity have swept away all that were not hearts of oak.

We have many things to be very thankful for & chief among them
for the happy family life we lead.

This will get to you about Christmas. Our best love and best wishes to you all and show me by a letter that I have some part in your lives yet. Always affectionately yours,

Jessie Frémont.

Dec. 1. The new mill began working yesterday; the "remittitur" came up yesterday—a law suit of importance was gained also yesterday.[6] December ushers in splendid weather and every prospect of a secure and prosperous future—a "near future" at that. The mills are almost entirely paid for & there is the best feeling toward Mr. Frémont. It is a good ending to many cares.

ALS (NjP—Blair-Lee Papers).

1. The reputation as a statesman and jurist of the North Carolinian and Federalist William Gaston (1778-1844) was national. His "creed" is probably a reference to his Catholic faith, which he said had been instilled into his mind by maternal piety.

2. Philip Barton Key's sister Alice, christened Mary Alicia, had married Ohio politician George H. Pendleton in 1846 (LANE, 63).

3. JBF seems not to have heard of Mrs. Francis Scott Key's death on May 18, 1859 (ibid., 58). The reference to "Ellen" is to her daughter, the widow of Simon Fraser Blunt, and not to Ellen Swan, the deceased wife of the murdered Philip Barton Key (ibid., 62, 63). On JBF's efforts to help Ellen Blunt, see JBF to George W. Blunt, [winter 1857-58?], above.

4. Comtesse de Genlis (1746-1830), whose first husband was guillotined in 1793, was born Stéphanie Félicité du Crest de Saint-Aubin. She was a governess to the children of the duchesse de Chartes for a time. Revolutionary events forced her to leave France, but she returned in 1802, found favor with Napoleon and, after the Restoration, with her former pupil, the duc d'Orleans. Her writings fill some eighty or ninety volumes. There are several editions of her *Memoires,* most of which are in eight volumes. See DOBSON for an account of her life.

5. The California Supreme Court held that the minerals underneath the soil belonged to JCF and thus reversed the lower court's decision, which had held for the Merced Mining Company. See 14 *California,* 279-380; Mariposa *Gazette,* Nov. 22, 1859; and JBF to Elizabeth Blair Lee, Apr. 24 [1858], note 3, above.

6. This case has not been identified. JCF was involved in many, many lawsuits, both as plaintiff and defendant.

To Horace Greeley

Bear Valley, November [1859]

My dear Sir, You were very kind to my Mrs. Johnson and her little brood, & it was a mark of attention which we fully appreciate, that you should write me so fully of it when you have so many claims on your time. I must make you my thanks—my astonished thanks—for the number of facts you have put together in the account of the mines here & Mr. Frémont's affairs relating to them. To all future questions as to what we are about & what we intend to do & especially "when are you coming back" I shall refer them all to the Tribune of October 5th.[1] That tells the whole story—if you will allow me the slang phrase. We are in the contentment following a great rain storm which restores the mills to full running time, has laid the dust until next May & makes the air light and, to me, health-giving. Mr. Frémont intends sending you some statistics, for yourself, (we don't belong to the public—your heading was in the most beautiful good taste) of the amalgamators recently put up. We hope too that some law points about being decided will lessen expense & give Mr. Frémont less to think of. Then, he goes back to the book.

We were quite sure you would not be taken in by the letter pretending to be from Mr. Frémont if only from its cruel style—one good writer can feel for another under such an imputation.[2]

A letter of introduction to Mr. Beecher for Mr. Bell,[3] a clergyman of this State, saying about what you did (& at the same time) of the absorbing nature of the duties & engagements here, is the sum of his letter-sinning. The stuff about regretting the part in '56 was nonsense— it was one of the most honorable episodes in Mr. Frémont's life & remembered as such—a good fight well fought. Very truly yours,

Jessie Benton Frémont

ALS (DLC—Greeley Papers). On his far western journey in the summer of 1859, Horace Greeley had visited Yosemite and the Frémonts at Bear Valley on both Aug. 11 and 14 and was very admiring of JBF's household and executive ability. He sounded them both out on another presidential contest, but JCF was not interested.

1. Greeley's article about California mining in general appeared in the New York *Tribune* on Sept. 9; about his trip to Bear Valley and Yosemite, Sept. 24; and about JCF's mines, Sept. 26. This last article, which praised JCF's management, may have been included in the Oct. 5, 1859, issue of the *Tribune* for California, Oregon, and the Sandwich Islands, since special issues of the *Tribune* were published on the departure of each mail steamer for Aspinwall. See the notice in New York *Tribune*, Oct. 5, 1859. Greeley's articles were republished the next year as *An Overland Journey from New York to San Francisco in the Summer of 1859.*

2. In the letter that falsely bore his name, the alleged Frémont had declared that he was not and would not be a candidate for the presidency in 1860. To the query of the New York *Daily News*, Oct. 7, 1859, as to the validity of the letter and statements, Greeley answered: "Col. F. is giving his whole time and energies to his own private affairs and is writing no letters at all about the Presidency." Montgomery

Blair also saw the letter and sent JCF a copy (JCF to M. Blair, Nov. 17, 1859, DLC—
Blair Papers).

3. The Rev. Samuel B. Bell (d. 1897) from New York, builder of the First Presbyterian
Church in Oakland and one of the organizers of the Republican party in California,
had served Santa Clara and Alameda counties in the state senate.

To Elizabeth Blair Lee

Black Point   June 2d 1860.

My dear Lizzie I hardly know how long it is since I wrote to you. You
have been kind enough to keep on writing to me & Mr. Frémont
always claims the hearing of the letter—it is a little family fête that
all share. I had gotten so out of health with the many anxieties of the
last two years that it gave fullest play to the heat & the effects of high
mountain climate. The want of pressure in the atmosphere kept the
blood thrown to my head & I have really suffered from that—headaches giddiness & actual fainting of late until I began to feel very
insecure. Now, I look for health again. The sea is my life. I have always
gotten solid health in sea air & Mr. Frémont has found me here a
"house by the sea" that is more beautiful than any Sea Dream that
Tennyson or any poet ever fancied.[1] If Mr. Lee should go to sea &
you carry out your good idea of making me a visit I will make you
love it as I do. For your sake I want Mr. Lee to be kept with you.
For mine I shouldn't grieve at his going. It would bring us together
again, for if you don't come to see me I don't know when I shall see
you. We had to stay here to put things in order & now we must stay
to keep order. Mr. Frémont can I hope give himself a summer of
comparative rest & be here most of the time. Then he will try to write
his book. Until now it has been impossible for one head to think more
than his has done. These years have had some points harder to bear
than any we have known—although they have not been sybaritic—
but withal in looking back there is nothing to regret for it has been
work faithfully & well done & hard duties stood to. In one way they
have [been] better than all the days of my life. When I knew I should
never see Father again I turned my whole heart into this house and
sometimes I think I magnetized Mr. Frémont into home life. He takes
part in & likes all the details of our household—the children's plays
& witticisms & lessons—he looks after our comforts, & is in fact

head of the house. No "wild-turkey" left. It's so easy to take care of children when two help. I feel now as if we were a complete & compact family & really Mr. Frémont used to be only a guest — dearly loved & honored but not counted on for worse as well as better.

> To him the palms
> To us the shade —

Now we share & share and he is far happier for it. As for me you need no telling how satisfied my craving heart is.

You should take new life in here. The soft warm air joined to sea breeze makes it so different from the usual sea side weather. I have the prettiest little house you ever saw — furnished like a picture. I put my own experience into it & this is like Paris for beautiful things at most reasonable prices. The scenery is a combination of every beauty in nature. I am going to send you a photograph of the Point as soon as I can get it copied.

If Mr. Lee should be sent to the Pacific, I am going to claim his old offer of taking Charley [on] a cruise. Charley is working up to it.

I have a very thorough & experienced teacher for them who keeps them working four hours a day. Charley has great intelligence but is like his Mother in fitfulness. Lil is a steady worker & Frank will be in the same style. The little man can spell cat already & is on the way to know[ing] how to read. I have to let him for he worked at it all alone. A little time at disciplined routine life would be marrow to Charley's lazy bones. Lil works at her German & keeps up her course of English reading, but I am making her go out a little. She has known & shared & helped endure all the business cares & has been so often anxious about my health that her [letter incomplete][2]

AL (NjP — Blair-Lee Papers).

1. *Macmillan's Magazine,* Jan. 1860, had published Alfred Lord Tennyson's poem "Sea Dreams," with the subtitle "An Idyll."

The formal purchase of the property that JBF is describing seems not to have occurred until Sept. 28, 1860, but the Frémonts may have occupied it even earlier than June. There would be many, many appeals and even a suit with respect to the title to the property, which was never recognized by the U.S. Government, but none of the appeals mentions the exact date of occupancy.

The property, a thirteen-acre tract on Point San Jose, often called Black Point and later Fort Mason, overlooked tiny Alcatraz Island to which Frémont also laid claim — unsuccessfully, it might be noted. The house was one of several homes on the Point and seems to have been built originally by New Englander Leonidas Haskell in 1854 and occupied by one of his business associates, George Eggleton (RATHER, 28–29). JCF formally purchased it for his wife from the San Francisco banker Mark Brumagim for $41,000 in gold, so Jessie claimed in 1892 (Senate Report 898, 52nd Cong., 1st sess., serial 2915). The day previous to the purchase, she had mortgaged the property to Haskell and his wife for $16,000 and to William Dana and Haskell for $5,000 (House Report 527, 43rd Cong., 1st sess., serial 1625). After taking occupancy, JBF spent $20,000 on improvements, enlarging the parlor, adding a glass veranda on three sides, building a stable and summer house, and planting roses and fuchsias. In 1863, JCF described it as "a wilderness of flowers & flowering shrubs" (RATHER, 31; JCF to Albert Tracy, Sept. 23, 1863, NN). Old business associates, the Cooks and Palmers, also lived on the Point as did Haskell and his daughter, Nelly (later Browne), who became a dear friend of the Frémonts and a steady correspondent of JBF and Lily.

To this day, the U.S. government has successfully contended that the land had been reserved for public purposes, especially military purposes by presidential orders of Nov. 6, 1850, and Oct. 28, 1851, and that the developers were squatters without legal rights. During the Civil War, it took over the property for defense purposes, leveled JBF's house, and erected fortifications. In 1866, JBF offered to settle her claim for $250,000, and by 1892 House or Senate committees had investigated and reported at least twelve times on proposals for relief. Many documents relating to the claim may be found in DNA-77, Land Papers, Point San Jose. See also JBF to Charles Sumner, Jan. 28, 1868, below.

2. The reason for this incomplete letter and the one that follows is given in JBF to Elizabeth Blair Lee, Aug. 10 [1860], below.

To Elizabeth Blair Lee

Black Point, June 14 [1860].

Dear Lizzie,

Is it your Capt. Lee who is so much with the Japanese?[1] I take hope from it that we will surely have a visit from you all for if he goes to sea at all it will I trust be to this coast & then you will be sure to come & make me the promised visit. How very glad I should be to have you, you do not need telling. My little house by the sea is a fairyland picture. I have tried many kinds of houses in top places as Landon Carter[2] would say, but this has more perfections combined than any. I am getting so strong & well again too. In place of Charley's picture I am going to ask that Mr. Lee take Charley's self. He is at this moment working away with Miss [Pfiffe?], Japan being his promised reward.

I heard him talking with Isaac (our black coachman who has lived with us all the time here). "Isaac do you know I'm going to have a chance to go on a man of war?" "You'll break her down," Isaac says,

"You'll get so full of yourself you'll be too heavy to carry." And that's about his condition of mind. He looks like a baby apple each morning after his dip in the surf.

I talk Charley to you because Mr. Lee & yourself have something of my weakness for him & your own boy will make you understand how large such a topic may seem. And then outside of ourselves there are no local things here of interest to you.

Starr King the new Unitarian clergyman has been our event.[3] I have none but a parlor acquaintance with him but he is new life in a literary way. He is so clever & charming in conversation. There are several people of that kind here & they make me visits as people you liked used to go to Silver Spring—to walk about & admire until they are hungry & then have a delightful chatty luncheon from one to three hours at table. You know the sea is my life and my love. I love the light—& the sound and the smell of its water & here on this point of land we have it on three sides while the slope down to the very water's edge is covered with wild holly & laurel & other native trees & good taste & money have been for seven years adding all sorts of planted flowers & vines & shrubs. The flapping of the sails as the schooners round this point & the noise of their paddles as the steamers pass are household sounds really that come to us through closed doors. It is like being at the bow of a ship—the place of honor among Japanese. We have cows, horses & dogs—in fact thorough country comfort with a city at our door & San Francisco is a true city in its resources.

Can you realize Lily nearly eighteen & myself preparing her dresses for all the trotting out that 18 year olds have to do? Mr. Frémont makes great fun of her very long dresses & other insignia of young ladyism. There is a very good opera here & lots of private parties, visiting & yatching is Lil's last enjoyment. Mr. Haskell, who owns this neighborhood & has lived here with his colony (rather than family for there are aunts, wives, daughters, sisters-in-law & partners) has great wealth & his habits & tastes are English—fine horses, dogs & boating are family themes. So Lil is in several congenial elements. Mr. Frémont gave Lil last Christmas a perfect little Spanish mare—young & sound and of thorough beauty. She rides well & it is a pretty picture to see her on Chiquita. Miss Lawrence's brother[4] rides a great deal & several others make this a point in their rides so that we have added to the life & gayety of this place. I feel drawn on to tell you of its attractions that you may come to see it—although your true attraction would be the keeping nearer to Mr. Lee's ship. It quite animates me to think of the immense talks we should have—& you don't know how it would renew & refresh you to come to a new place although some sad memories are [letter incomplete]

AL (NjP—Blair-Lee Papers). JBF encloses a sketch of the bay, including a view of Alcatraz Island with its lighthouse, and labels it "an unprofessional topographical view from my house."

1. This seems not to have been Lizzie Lee's husband, but Sydney Smith Lee, also a naval officer, and a brother of Robert E. Lee.
2. Landon Carter (1710–78), a distant, but oft-quoted Lee relative, had been a member of the landed gentry of Virginia. Possibly there was a younger Landon Carter, but the editors have been unable to identify one.
3. Thomas Starr King (1824–64), his wife, Julia, and their daughter Edith (1852–1909) had recently arrived in California. King, an avid reader and a master of six languages, had been the popular minister of Boston's Hollis Street Unitarian Church. To JBF, King became a loving friend to whom she could not only speak her mind and heart but unleash her wit and intelligence.
4. Newspaperman Joseph E. Lawrence (1825–78) had been in California since 1849. In 1860, he became editor of San Francisco's *Golden Era* and published the writings of Bret Harte, Mark Twain, and Joaquin Miller.

To Elizabeth Blair Lee

San Francisco, August 10th [1860].

My dear Lizzie,

The best way when one has a doubt is to ask & find out is it not? so I am going to ask you why such a dead silence follows all my letters to you all. Except one letter from you I have heard nothing from any of you since your Father's long kind New Year's letter which I answered when I was down in February & mailed from here, & one from your brother enclosing the Pescadero papers.[1] Did he get any from us since then? Mr. Frémont wrote in acknowledgement & so did I. One letter I wrote in regard to my Father's affairs which I wish very much to have an answer to—I enclose you about the substance of what I wrote before & it may in that way reach your brother, as I shall take the precaution to send this through a business house.

For all our doings I send you extracts from today's papers & I am sure you will be glad of our success.[2]

I've been huffed enough not to send you letters that I could not help writing—I send you parts of them to shew how much you have been in my mind.

We have passed the morning on the beach of our little cove. The willows & laurels made delightful shade and the water is as blue & the sky as golden as the bay of Naples. Charley had a boat as a reward for learning his multiplication table & of course I had to see its first working.

Put the rather shaky handwriting to having been boating—isn't it a happy change in health to get back so much of my old strength. Write to me soon & *enclose* your answer to "Mark Brumagim Esqre.,³ Montgomery Street, San Francisco["]—then I shall get it. If they care to have it give my love to your Mother & Father & tell Mr. Lee I hold Charley subject to his wishes. Kiss my little boy for me and believe me as always Your affectionate friend,

Jessie Frémont

ALS (NjP—Blair-Lee Papers).

1. El Pescadero was a ranch in San Joaquin County in which JCF had purchased a half interest from the claimant in 1852. Montgomery Blair handled some of the complicated legal work in obtaining the patent for this property (M. L. SPENCE [2], 324–25; DNA-49, California Private Land Claims, El Pescadero, Case 272; JCF to M. Blair, May 4, 1860, and M. Blair to Leonidas Haskell, Aug. 11, 1863, DLC—Blair Papers).

2. The San Francisco *Alta California*, Aug. 10, 1860, described the gala train ride, banquet, and ball that heralded the opening of the four-mile railroad that would carry quartz ore from the Pine Tree and Josephine mines down the steep mountainside to JCF's new crushing mill on the Merced River. Lily had represented the Frémonts at the various celebrations in which one of the speakers, D. Arnot, the builder of the railroad, had asked, "Who ... but a Frémont, would have the nerve to expend the vast sums of money necessary to erect such works in such a locality?"

3. A pioneer forty-niner from Montgomery County, New York, Mark Brumagim (d. 1914) had opened one of the first banks in Marysville, Calif. Eight years later, he and his brothers established the banking firm of Mark Brumagim & Company in San Francisco. Brumagim became a heavy creditor of JCF, obtained a lien on the Mariposas estate, and eventually participated in the reorganization of the Mariposa Company. For his change of name to Mark Birmingham and his twenty-five year legal battle to gain control of the rich Candelaria silver mine in the state of Durango, Mexico, see PAULSEN.

To Thomas Starr King

[early 1861]

My dear Mr. King,

I have hunted myself stupid for the key of my book case until I remembered yours was its twin & so send Isaac for your key. While

I am trying it Mrs. King can decide which day she will be bored for my benefit. Shut up with myself I take fancies that become positive wants if they are thwarted.[1]

I want that key to open the case & put over the Palmetto sword,[2] a little flag (every star in its place however) that Mr. Frémont gave me eighteen years ago—the flag he raised on what has since been named Fremont's Peak.[3] It was made to carry among savages & for that an eagle is placed among the stars, & in its extended claw it holds the long red pipe of peace—the other is keeping the arrows dry against his breast. We gave Mr. Frémont a parting salute with this cherished old flag &, I can't get at it for want of a key. I hope this explains & justifies my sending for yours.

"Friend" is not the next thing to "angel"—it is "minister of grace." That you were in the days when we were lodged on Ararat before any good thing had come to us out of the boiling waters, but I shall hold to the "friend" & ask as a proof that when you. can make the time "any reasonable length," that you will bring my mind some fresh air. I hope soon to be able to go about & be left less to my own thoughts. The fear of what may be in store for us all if this cloud of civil war takes shape, makes me restless & I am unfortunate in not being able to live more away from myself just now.

J. B. Frémont

Tuesday mg.

ALS (CSfCP, Alice Phelan Sullivan Library—King Papers).

1. JCF, his lawyer Frederick K. Billings, his old business associate George W. Wright, and if we are to believe Billings, JCF's mistress, Margaret Corbett and child, had gone east (Billings to Trenor W. Park, Jan. 14, Feb. 22, 1861). For a strong denial of Billings's story, see Geroge W. Wright to Montgomery Blair, Mar. 12 [1861], DLC—Blair Papers. JCF (with Corbett) and Billings would continue on to Europe in an attempt to raise money for development and discharge of Las Mariposas debts.

2. In 1847, the citizens of Charleston, S.C., had presented JCF with a sword in appreciation of his role in exploration and the conquest of California. BIGELOW [1], 222, notes that "the head of the hilt, around which is coiled a rattlesnake belonging to the old arms of the State, is formed to represent the summit of the Palmetto tree."

3. The flag was probably raised on the peak now known as Woodrow Wilson Peak.

To Thomas Starr King

[(Jan.) 16th (1861)]

My dear Mr. King,

I return your Emmerson's [Emerson's][1]—they're not in my style— above or beyond me in some way & the words are like Kanaka[2] to the ear. Lily (Frank too) gets from Mr. Frémont a slight stammer—I proposed to her reading Emmerson aloud when the tide was going out, as a modern pebble system. How much the tide is in the South Carolina style—roaring as it recedes & coming back with a stealthy swift silence to the old mark. As my hands are empty I have taken a young author[3] to pet & you are to read something of his the next time you suffer capture & transportation by the black van.

I have cut out your letter about Bear Valley & sent it to Mr. Frémont as nothing is so hard to get as "last week's paper."[4] Haven't you always seen how little children get hurt & have taken their cry out, it all breaks out afresh when some new person is told of it & pities & pets them? So that it's a nursery maxim not to revive a grief or it will be all to go over again. Although the large grief of those two years is given in outline & no more yet I was brought low as a little child by your vivid summing up. "J'eus pitié de moi-meme" [I took pity on myself]. You can't think however how much comfort there is in being understandingly pitied. I have to thank you that we did not die unsung.

My great reward has come to me every time Mr. Frémont has told me that but for me he could not endure through it—but what can atone to him for so many years of such a life given to do such uses.

Hortense tells her son in one of her last letters—"Believe firmly there is another life. Mine here has been such as to render this hope a necessary belief without which I could not endure it."[5] Poor Hortense was not a model woman in many things but she is as right as possible in that faith.

I have not been in town for a month & considering my name is on a pew in your church you are a negligent pastor not to have been out to know the reason why. Mrs. King is better—she even wore her last new bonnet into the country—a refinement of attention that only women could feel in all its force.

J.B. Frémont.

Wednesday 16th

ALS (CSfCP—King Papers). Commenting on this letter, King wrote an eastern friend on Jan. 20, "Mrs. Frémont sent me a gem of a note the other day, thanking me for my letter in the Transcript about their gold-estate" (to Randolph Ryers, CU-B—King Papers).

1. Ralph Waldo Emerson (1803–82), American essayist and poet.

2. "Kanaka" was the word used for Hawaiian and South Sea Island sailors as well as for their language.

3. A reference to the young writer [Francis] Bret[t] Harte (1836–1902), whose serious literary career began in 1868 when he became editor of the *Overland Monthly.* Today he is best known for his stories of the California gold rush. For JBF's sponsorship of him, see her letters to Edward F. Beale, May 21 [1861]; and James T. Fields, Oct. 26 [1862], Jan. 5, 26, Feb. 20 [1863], below.

4. King's letters on California topics, including Bear Valley and the Yosemite region, were appearing regularly in the Boston *Evening Transcript* (WENDTE, 120).

5. Hortense was the daughter of Josephine, stepdaughter of Napoleon I, queen consort of King Louis of Holland, and mother of Napoleon III. A translated version of the letter that she wrote to her exiled son shortly before her death in 1837 may be found in ABBOTT, 362–63.

To the Editors of the *Alta California*

San Francisco, Tuesday Feb. 26, 1861.

Eds. *Alta:*—There is two sides to every case, and since one has been given in to-day's *Alta,* justice to [Albert] Lea requires that equal publicity be given to the other. It would fare ill with men if some one act of their lives, and that the very worst, should be the only one by which they are to be judged. It is true that Lea did murder his wife; but Lord Bacon says, "a wise man will not judge the whole play by one act;" and in this life, of which but three days now are left, there were other acts that deserve to be known also.

Lea's mother was for years employed in the family of Colonel Benton; liked and respected during her life, and regretted at her death. When her son was just grown, he applied for a place under Col. Frémont, on the winter journey overland of 1853–4. Lea and his mother were born free, but with that feeling which is one of the mitigating features of Southern domestic life, he felt the bond between employer and employed an inheritance to be respected and claimed, where good conduct and faithful services had made it as much a pleasure as a duty to both. During the long illness which interrupted the commencement of that journey, Lea was Col. Frémont's faithful nurse—it was to Lea that parting charges of care and watchfulness were given, when, in the Delaware Indian country, the party finally made their start at the beginning of winter. A winter journey over the bleak prairies, with their sharp snow storms and icy winds—the harder struggle for life, when their scant and diminishing supply of food added starvation to all other trials—one last wearing fast which would have ended in death to all, but for the kindness of some Indians who gave up their own slender stores, enough to enable them to get through to the Mormon settlements of Cedar City—all these Lea shared, with cheerful courage and timely words of home, that kept the heart from fainting. When educated white men refused to leave the safety and comfort of that place Lea had the nerve and loyalty to stand by his leader, and start once more into the snows and an unknown bed of mountains from which no traveler had ever yet returned.

When the Supreme Court of this State made a decision that left no rights in the owners of mining land, and converted a country cottage residence into a Fort Sumter, Lea and one other brave faithful man of the same race, were for weeks the sleepless guardians of the women and children in that house.

It was not in Col. Frémont's early circumstances, and, certainly, not fostered by the habits of his later life, to require the attendance of a "*valet*." Lea had been a tried and brave companion in danger, and when times of quiet came, a place was made for him by giving him charge of the horses. It is due to Lea to deny the charge that he drank; and because he did not smoke, Col. Frémont chose him to share his tent.

In the spring of '59 so great a change took place in Lea, that the servants and family watched him with concern. From an active healthy manner and walk he became silent and pre-occupied, staying apart, eating, and, at last, even cooking for himself, at a distance from the house. Finally he left Bear Valley, and when the news of the murder reached there, there was an instant expression that "Lea *was* mad."

This is eminently a case in which to ask "Who was she?" *She* was the mother-in-law. Like many women in higher life, she found, what she thought a "good match" for her daughter, and then, being disappointed, tried to make moves with two human beings full of passions, as though they were figures on a chess-board.

Through the truly Christian care of the Rev. Mr. [Francis Marion] McAllister, and a young clerical associate, whose name it is a regret not to know, Lea has been brought to feel more than willing—he is glad and thoughtful—to give his life in atonement for his sin. He shrank from the manner of his death; and friends who knew the facts of the case, and regarded the recommendation of the Jury to mercy, applied for a change of sentence to perpetual imprisonment.[1] This

Governor [John Gately] Downey did not see fit to grant.[2] Lea, now, neither wishes a reprieve, nor could any one who wishes him well, ask it. Those who have had charge of him for a year and a half, the clergymen whose kind care has been given him for nearly as long a time, and those who have seen him but a few times, all receive the same impression. His sincere manly penitence is unmistakable. The mere privilege of retaining the breath of life, when all that makes life useful or desirable, is lost, is never so great a boon that it should be begged for or clung to. It would be a poor exchange, indeed, for such hopes as Lea now has. He goes now before a Judge who saw the influencing causes as well as the crime. His final sentence is to come from one to whom no true penitent ever appealed in vain for mercy. J.B.F.[3]

Printed in *Alta California*, Feb. 27, 1861. For additional information on the Lea controversy, see *Alta*, Feb. 26, Mar. 1–3, 1861.

1. The Frémonts had led the appeal to have Lea's sentence of death by hanging commuted to life imprisonment.

2. To JBF's letter, the editors added the information: "Whilst giving place to the above it may be well to add, that Lea sent his wife to her long home without a moment's warning, and that he had a fair trial by jury and was convicted. There are several other persons now awaiting trial for the crime of wife murder, and if Governor Downey should interpose his hand in the behalf of Lea, he might be called upon to follow the example thus set with the rest; they might be able to make as good a showing as does the present pleader for Lea. Mercy, in this instance, with several almost parallel cases occurring subsequently, would be but a poor terror to the vicious, or check to stay the hand of the wife murderer."

3. To write a public letter was a daring act for a woman of the nineteeth century. When the *Alta* published a rebuttal from Lea's mother-in-law, a San Francisco man wrote the manager of the Mariposas, "You probably saw the controversy between Mrs. Frémont and Mr. Lea's wife's mother in the papers. It may lead to something serious,—as they are both fighting cusses" (Calvin Park to Trenor W. Park, Mar. 2, 1861, Park-McCullough House Archives).

JBF made arrangements for Lea's funeral and burial, which were conducted by a lodge of black Masons since Lea was a Mason.

To Elizabeth Blair Lee

Black Point, March 10th [1861]

My dear Lizzie,

The enclosed letter & newspaper slips will shew you what I promised to do for Lea. Better than writing would be a personal visit to his grandmother & sister & in these disturbed times I fancy a parcel would go more safely to you than to an obscure name.

I went to see Lea a few days before the end & it is not in mere words to give you the impression he made on me. No knightly cavalier going to the block for his king & his cause ever had a more truly noble aspect with it the gentleness & quiet of faith, like that of a little child. I shall never forget how it made one feel to see that true repentance and simple faith in the forgiveness of sin had transfigured this uneducated colored man & made him the equal of heroes.

His execution could not have taken place where the executive was unprejudiced. But Irish & extreme southern principles (?) were the determining powers & nothing could avail.

Will you tell his sister & grandmother that over a thousand of the best citizens attended the funeral services which were held in town at the undertakers—from which place most strangers are buried. I will put a cross at his head. You know I will not give up that emblem to the Catholics—and on it "Christ died to save sinners," with his name at the foot.

We saw Col. Brant's death[1] in the Pony news. Lily & I wear mourning for him. We were often at his house and as friends go he was a friend.

My best dates from Mr. Frémont are only to the 8th. By Tuesday we shall hear to the 4th inclusive. I trust all is peace around you. My thoughts & hopes for good were with you all that day.

You will know as well as I do when we are to leave here & in the meantime our movements are so uncertain that it is unsatisfactory to write of ourselves. Mr. Frémont writes that he had a letter from your Father which he will send me. Did you get mine through the Bakers?[2] With love to your Mother & Father & remembrances to the others. Affectionately yours,

J. B. Frémont

ALS (NjP—Blair-Lee Papers). JBF enclosed the newspaper print of her Feb. 26, 1861, letter to the editors of the *Alta California* and a clipping describing Albert Lea's execution.

1. Col. Joshua B. Brant of St. Louis, who had married Sarah Benton, the first cousin of JBF. He had settled in St. Louis in 1823, and after he resigned his army commission in 1839, he entered the construction business. By the time of his death, he had built many of the city's tallest (five- and six-story) buildings and was among its wealthiest citizens (ROWAN & PRIMM, 274).

2. Edward D. Baker (1811–61) and his son Alfred W. Baker. Oregon had elected

Baker to the Senate in the fall of 1860, and on his way east he had settled his wife and some of his children in San Francisco, where he had also made an effective speech for Abraham Lincoln and the Union and been entertained by JBF (T. S. King to Randolph Ryers, Oct. 29, 1860, CU-B—King Papers). He took his seat in the Senate on Dec. 5, 1860. Alfred became a lieutenant in the Civil War and was acting as his father's aide when the senator was killed at Balls Bluff, Va., on Oct. 21, 1861 (BLAIR & TARSHIS, 108, 112, 114, 168).

To Edward F. Beale

[May 21 (1861)]

My dear Mr. Beale,

This will introduce to you my young friend Mr. Frank Harte who wishes to make his thanks in person.[1] Very sincerely yours,

Jessie Benton Frémont

Black Point 21st May

ALS (DLC—Beale Papers).

1. JBF had arranged with Beale, just appointed surveyor-general of California by Abraham Lincoln, to give Bret Harte a position in the surveyor-general's office in San Francisco. In 1863, when Beale resigned his office, a job was found for Harte at the U.S. Mint.

To William Armstrong

[June 10, 1861]

My poor William,

We have all been so grieved by the fearful accident to you. You were so faithful in your services to us & gave proof of so much interest and sympathy in Mr. Frémont's many and hard troubles during your stay with us in Bear Valley, that it is a real regret to us that you are not where we can give you some personal care. But all that can be done, is I am assured, being done for you, and Dr. Anderson[1] will be your best physician in caring for what we all must surely meet—and which first? You, crushed and wounded, may outlive those who to day are so full of sympathy for your sufferings. My letters, by the Pony this morning, from Mr. Frémont, tell me to meet him in New York, where he intended to be by the end of May & where he hoped to arrive as he says "not too late to strike a blow for the Union." You know Mr. Frémont is not given to much talking so you can judge how much he is feeling when he breaks out "God bless the dear old flag." We will go to join him on the 21st. and I will keep with him when I get there. It is not more danger than we went through together in Bear Valley & that was only for property. But this is a worthy cause to labor for. And if we feel this about our country's flag how should we feel for the great banner of the Cross. In that noble army there are no unrewarded soldiers. There is no promotion by purchase there. The humblest soldier is more the care of their great Leader than if he went on his way with all the help of rank and friends and favoring fortunes. What is the highest promise held out to us all? That one day we may be told "Well done good and faithful servant." Sometimes, the best acts and most trying sacrifices of our lives have to go unrewarded and unsupported by human sympathy or else they might fail to accomplish good. But in that crowd none are so low or so far but that the loving eye of our Father is on him and be sure every suffering, mental or bodily, cheerfully borne for his sake, meets with the love and reward promised us. People are always saying, "it is such a world of uncertainties and change" & you see them fret at losses and illness and death as though the good gifts of life, and life itself was their patented and vested property and death an infringement of rights. There is no uncertainty in God's world, and the only quiet and real good we can have in this world is from being very sure of that and acting up to it. I am telling you what I try to feel and live up to myself, although I do often break down and get ill with grief for partings that have had to be. But if my turn comes to be tried, and what is more—so much more than my life to me that I can't compare it—if I am called to part with that I must try to say with my heart and in my conduct & not only with my lips We have received good from the Lord—shall I not receive evil also? The Lord gave and the Lord taketh away. Blessed be the name of the Lord. Even so Father—not my will, but thy will be done.

All over our country now we are being called to lay aside self. You, in this breaking up of all your hopes and health can feel what a solemn time it is, for you are at the point of view when worldly aims, when the things we work for that end with life, seem so trifling as we look into eternity. I believe that our cause is the cause of truth and that

God is with us. You, are sure he is with you. Mr. Anderson will tell you all these things better than I can but it is the root and the life of all that can or ought to be said to anyone in great trials. And the trials are never too great to bear when we go for strength to our Father in Heaven.

Into His care I try to leave the future — and into His care you can trust yourself. You were good and faithful in serving us and you may hear the sentence first. I pray we may all deserve it.

Jessie Benton Frémont.

Black Point, June 10th

ALS (KHi). William Armstrong, a former coachman of the Frémonts at Las Mariposas, had suffered an irreparable spinal injury when his horse fell upon him in a rodeo.

1. John A. Anderson (1834–92), son of William C. Anderson, the pastor of the First Presbyterian Church in San Francisco, began his ministry in Stockton in 1857. After JBF heard that William had been brought to Stockton for medical care, she wrote the young Anderson requesting that he find him and help him meet his sufferings "in the right spirit." Later, to give the injured man "pleasant thoughts," she sent duplicate pictures of the Frémont family with the plea that Anderson "see that they go to no one but William or yourself as they contain mine & my daughter's likenesses." She thanked him for his comfort to the injured man and, remarking that she was leaving San Francisco to join JCF in the East, expressed a desire to know when William "goes" (to John Anderson, May 22, 28, June 11 [1861], KHi). During the Civil War, John Anderson served as a chaplain in the California volunteer infantry. Later he was president of the Kansas State Agricultural College, a U.S. congressman, and, finally, consul general in Cairo, Egypt.

THE CIVIL WAR YEARS

When Jessie Benton Frémont left San Francisco in June 1861, she was determined to play an active role in the war. She saw herself as part of a great cause, one that would permit her, as well as other women, to step beyond the boundaries of their separate sphere. "The restraints of ordinary times do not apply now," she explained.[1]

For Jessie, the Civil War years would be both the most invigorating and, ultimately, the most disappointing of her life. Passionately dedicated to the abolition of slavery, and as passionately devoted to her husband, she would see slavery ended but the credit go to Abraham Lincoln, a man she came to view as having a "sly, slimy nature."[2] Although John Frémont would be the hero of the emancipationists in the first years of the war, by its end most would see him as both a military and political failure.

Jessie, with her three children and maid in tow, reached New York on July 13, after an anxious voyage from Panama, chased by Confederate privateers. Ten days later, as newspapers reported the disastrous Union defeat at Bull Run, the Frémont family journeyed by train to St. Louis. They found the city tense and the Western Department in near chaos. In urgent letters to Lizzie Blair Lee and her brother Montgomery, Lincoln's postmaster general and their personal conduit to the president, Jessie outlined the problems they faced: a desperate lack of troops, supplies, and arms, and an enemy "thick and unrelenting as mosquitoes."[3]

Although Congressman Frank Blair and Brig. Gen. Nathaniel Lyon, aided by the large German immigrant population and other loyal Unionists, had managed to keep Missouri from seceding, it was still a slave state overrun with rebel sympathizers. St. Louis was so tenuously controlled that recruiting for the Confederate army went on openly, and Union soldiers were harassed in the streets. Moreover, Confederate troops threatened both the strategically vital Union garrison downriver at Cairo, Illinois, and General Lyon's small army at Springfield in southwestern Missouri. Acting swiftly, John assembled nearly four thousand troops and a flotilla of eight steamboats to relieve Cairo. "The sound of the shouts with which we were welcomed at Cairo stays in my memory," Jessie reported afterward to Montgomery Blair. "Undisciplined & untrained they are, but the volunteers are knights and crusaders of the best kind."[4]

Although John moved quickly to save Cairo, he felt he did not have the troops to reinforce Lyon as well. He instructed the general, ominously outnumbered by rebel forces, to fight or withdraw as he saw fit. Lyon chose to fight, and when he was killed at Wilson's Creek on Aug. 10 and southwest Missouri fell to the rebels, the first murmurs against John's generalship were heard.

Lyon's defeat brought hundreds of wounded to St. Louis for care. Together with William G. Eliot, a Unitarian minister and founder of Washington University, Jessie organized a relief organization, the Western Sanitary Commission, and brought long-time friend Dorothea Dix, director of the new army nursing corps, to St. Louis to advise on the establishment of hospitals and the training of nurses.[5] Sensitive to public concerns about woman's proper role, Jessie, with Eliot's help, prepared a newspaper article to explain the Dix visit and the still controversial idea of professional female nurses.[6]

The Frémonts had established their St. Louis headquarters, as well as their personal residence, in the opulent Brant mansion, where Jessie plunged into work as her husband's aide and confidant. She would be only partially successful in concealing her active role, however, and enemies soon branded her "General Jessie." The Frémont staff was an unconventional mixture of regular army officers, longtime abolitionists, former European revolutionaries, and California cronies looking for quick profits in war contracts. To many ordinary citizens, the foreign officers seemed flamboyant and impractical, the abolitionists subversive, and the California contingent unscrupulous outsiders using their friendship with Frémont to gain lucrative contracts that should rightly have gone to St. Louis merchants. The situation was made more difficult by the fact the Frémont's chief quartermaster, career army officer Justin McKinstry, would prove to be personally corrupt.

Despite such potential problems, much was accomplished during the first weeks of command. Fortifications to protect St. Louis were begun; innovative iron-sheathed gun boats ordered, and new army barracks erected. Attracted by Frémont's name, men flocked to enlist. John took a special interest in establishing an elite bodyguard of three hundred cavalry troops, who patroled the Brant mansion and accompanied him, in a showy spectacle of galloping horses and flashing sabres, on his journeys about the city. "Frémont has stirred up things in St. Louis & given new life there," Lizzie Lee wrote her husband. "If he & Frank can't take care of Missouri I am mistaken in the men."[7]

But when Frank Blair himself returned to Missouri from Washington in mid-August, he was barraged with complaints about inefficiency and favoritism at Frémont headquarters, as well as about John's own aloofness and ostentation. At the same time, Blair found his place as leader of the pro-Union forces usurped by the new Union general. Although the ambitious young congressman found John unfailingly courteous, he seemed remote and apparently unwilling to discuss the desperate military situation in Missouri. While St. Louis was now firmly under Union control, forty thousand Confederate troops held the southern half of the state, and marauding rebel guerrilla bands plundered the Union-held areas of the countryside.

In late August, alarmed at the disintegrating situation, Frank Blair wrote a long, critical letter about John to his brother Montgomery. Three days later he wrote again, more strongly.[8] Montgomery passed the letters on to the president.

While Frank Blair wrote his damning letters, John made a fateful decision. On August 31, after consulting only Jessie and Quaker abolitionist Edward M. Davis, he declared martial law and issued a stunning decree—a limited emancipation proclamation freeing the slaves of Missouri rebels. While he was no doubt influenced by his abolitionist sympathies, his specific purpose was to force Missourians in the rebel army to return to their homes or face the loss of their slave property.

In the North, this first emancipation decree created a sensation. "The hour has come, and the man," proclaimed Harriet Beecher Stowe, speaking for many Northerners eager to make the abolition of slavery the clear purpose of the war.[9] But Lincoln, whose moderate stance on slavery was calculated to keep border states like Kentucky loyal, asked

John to revoke it. At this point, convinced of the moral rightness and military necessity of the proclamation, Jessie, carrying letters from her husband, journeyed to Washington to see the president.

In many Civil War accounts, the resulting confrontation merits an entertaining paragraph, in which Jessie Frémont is dismissed as an overwrought and foolish woman trying the patience of the busy president and damaging her husband's career in the process. The correspondence between Jessie and the president, as well as her several accounts of the incident, provide an alternative version to what has generally been a one-sided story. Certainly, Jessie was a forceful speaker who was fully informed on the situation in Missouri. Moreover, the arguments for such a decree were strong and worth discussing. But Lincoln, who normally listened attentively to opposing views and tolerated vigorous debate, received her cooly, called her "quite a female politician" when she attempted to explain her position, and dismissed her quickly. "The General should never have dragged the Negro into the war," she recalled his words. "It is a war for a great national object and the Negro has nothing to do with it."[10] In addition, although Lincoln had seen Frank Blair's critical letters, discussed them with his cabinet, and already instructed Montgomery Blair to go to St. Louis to investigate, he withheld this information from Jessie.

She learned of Frank Blair's letters the next day when his father, Francis Preston Blair, came to see her. The two old friends argued long and bitterly. When Lizzie Lee was told of the angry meeting, she dreaded the consequences. "A formal quarrel fills me with a terror I can't articulate." But as the situation unraveled over the next weeks, she sided with her brothers and father. "The more I think of that couple, the more bitterly I feel my disappointment in them — it is so humiliating to have bolstered up such unworthy people so long."[11]

The resulting feud made John Frémont's position in Missouri increasingly precarious. The Blair family marshaled their considerable influence in a concerted press attack on John, and, more privately, on Jessie. In the Blairs' version of events, John was a brave but inept commander while Jessie was a clever and vengeful woman who had stepped beyond her proper sphere. "Did you ever hear of such a superb jackass as 'John C. & Jessie Benton Frémont Major General Commanding," jeered one Blair ally.[12] Long experienced in press manipulation herself, Jessie countered in kind, while John, prodded by Jessie if the Blair view is to be believed, even briefly jailed Frank Blair twice for insubordination.[13]

Amid the vituperation, the military situation in Missouri reached a crisis point when Union troops were decisively defeated at Lexington, near Kansas City, on September 21. Rumors circulated that John would be replaced. Surrounded by enemies, both military and political, and desperate to prove himself, John wired the president that he would lead the Union forces himself. Departing for the field a week later, he left Jessie in virtual control of his St. Louis headquarters.[14] Over the next month, as John attempted to assemble and move an army in pursuit of the Confederate forces of Gen. Sterling Price, she worked tirelessly both to get him the troops and supplies he needed and to counter the continued attacks on his generalship.

A long string of observers, both hostile and friendly, made their way to St. Louis to investigate the situation. In mid-October, Secretary of War Simon Cameron arrived with a dismissal order for Frémont, signed by the president, to be used at Cameron's discretion. Although Cameron decided to withhold the order, since John was in active pursuit of the enemy, he froze funding for all contracts until they could be reviewed in Washington and, in a decree aimed at John's controversial personal staff, suspended pay for officers whose commissions had not been approved by the president. Adj. Gen. Lorenzo Thomas leaked his own damaging report to the press, including statements by two of Frémont's generals questioning his competence. Meanwhile, a hostile congressional committee had begun hearings in St. Louis. "Such robbery, fraud, extravagance, speculation as have been developed in Frémont's department can hardly be conceived of," wrote one member of the Special House Committee on Government Contracts. "There has been an organized system of pillage right under the eye of Fremont."[15]

As such reports emerged, the president grew increasingly distrustful of Frémont. Even the daring recapture of Springfield on Oct. 25 by Frémont's elite bodyguard disturbed the Lincoln administration, which feared that the guard's battle cry, "Frémont and Union," had ominous political implications.

Fremont was a careless administrator, and his neglect of the conservative establishment in St. Louis was politically unwise. Yet the task of creating a vast army from scratch in a few months time would have been daunting for anyone. Nonetheless, he had secured St. Louis, inspired intense enthusiasm among his troops, and, by the time of his dismissal, virtually driven the rebel forces from the state. Over the next years, the corruption and inefficiency uncovered in Missouri would seem minor compared to later wartime scandals, while Lincoln himself would prove far more tolerant of a long string of blundering generals. Many shrewd observers suspected that the hamstringing of Frémont was, at least in part, the act of a consummate politician not unwilling to watch the downfall of a formidable political rival.

Jessie's correspondence during the last weeks of her husband's Missouri comand reflects the disintegrating situation they faced. In letters to lawyer Frederick Billings and political advisor Isaac Sherman, to Lincoln's friend Ward Hill Lamon, who in a visit had shown some sympathy for Frémont's dilemma, and to her own friend Dorothea Dix, she expressed her frustration, anger, and growing desperation. Eventually she came to feel that the president's policy—neither removing John nor supporting him adequately with troops, arms, and funds—was the most dangerous course of all. She was almost relieved when, on Nov. 2, as Frémont's army chased retreating Confederate troops to the southern Missouri border, he was removed from his command by the president.

John was now the martyred leader of a growing portion of the North passionately opposed to the continued existence of slavery. A chorus of support greeted the Frémonts as they returned, weary and embittered, to New York City. Although as a woman Jessie's actions were limited, she was determined to justify her husband's record to the public. Hitting on an ingenious plan, within weeks she had sketched out what became *The Story of the Guard,* an account of the heroic victory of the Frémont bodyguard at Springfield and less directly, a subtle and persuasive defense of her husband's command. "Don't be frightened," she would assure her publisher, James T. Fields, "it's as soft as carded wool."[16]

While Jessie would be circumspect in print, she was less careful in private letters and conversation. Writing to friends like Thomas Starr King, who shared her abolitionist sympathies, she condemned the "Washington Dictators"; in conversation with friends, she bluntly called Lincoln "an ass."[17]

In January 1862, the Frémonts took their case to Washington. "She has scarcely slept or rested," reported an acquaintance. "To see her Husband vindicated, is the restless burning of her soul, and she is mistress of every statistic, every item, that can weigh for or against him.''[18] Jessie helped John prepare a elaborately documented statement for the powerful Committee on the Conduct of the War, dominated by sympathetic radical Republicans. Predictably, committee chair Benjamin Wade pronounced it a total vindication while Frank Blair branded it "an apology for disaster and defeat."[19] By the time the Frémonts attended Mary Lincoln's controversial White House gala in early February, the Republican party was deeply split over Frémont and slavery. Anxious to heal party differences, Lincoln bowed to radical pressure and, on March 11, named Frémont commander of the Mountain Division with headquarters at Wheeling, West Virginia.

Jessie's letters from Wheeling, and afterward from her temporary home at Little Neck, Long Island, swing between hope and cynicism. With the cooperation of congressional supporters like George Julian and Schuyler Colfax, and journalists like Sydney Gay of the New York *Tribune,* she saw to it that pro-Frémont reports continued to appear in the press. Her only diversion was a visit from Rebecca Harding (later Davis), a shy young *Atlantic* writer whom she met in Wheeling. But for the most part, Jessie was forced to watch, helplessly and from afar, as John, along with Generals Nathaniel Banks and Irvin McDowell, were brilliantly outmaneuvered by Stonewall Jackson. In late May the Confederate general briefly threatened Washington itself. After an unsuccessful attempt to coordinate his three generals in trapping Jackson, Lincoln decided to merge their commands under a single man. Convinced by now of Frémont's incompetence, he chose Gen. John Pope, a blustering West Pointer who had been publicly hostile to Frémont while serving under him in Missouri. Angry and humiliated, John resigned his command.

Although he retained a small staff in the expectation of a new assignment, John Frémont would never receive another command. His own mistakes and the Blair smear campaign had done their work. Settling in New York City, he turned to the mounting problems of Las Mariposas, which had suffered under the self-serving management of Trenor Park. When he finally sold the debt-ridden estate in June 1863, Jessie was relieved.

She herself kept busy with the publication of *The Story of the Guard* and a frenzy of charitable and social activities. But as the war dragged on in seemingly endless slaughter, and one inept general replaced another, her mood was often bitter. She joked mordantly that the administration changed generals "nearly as often as a bad housekeeper changes servants."[20] Summering at the Massachuesetts coastal village of Nahant, in a cottage next to the poet Henry Wadsworth Longfellow, she was heartened by a visit to John Greenleaf Whittier at nearby Amesbury. "Remember me to the General," he wrote her afterwards. "Would that he were in Washington, commander-in-chief."[21]

In early 1864, Jessie and countless other New York City women became involved in an ambitious Metropolitan Fair, an astonishing outpouring of energy that alarmed traditionalists and raised more than a million dollars for the U.S. Sanitary Commission. Jessie superintended the publication of a series of small books—memoirs and letters relating to the war—to be sold at the Fair and also raised several thousand dollars by staging a lavish children's production of "Cinderella."

By 1864, as the daily casualty list reached three columns in the newspapers, Lincoln was in political trouble. Conservatives favored Gen. George McClellan and a more conciliatory policy toward the South, while radicals remained discontented with Lincoln's moderate stand on slavery. Although the president had finally issued his Emancipation Proclamation in September 1862, to many it seemed a tardy concession to party pressure. Moreover, the president's proposals for reconstruction suggested that once the war was over, he would allow former slaveholders to dominate the South at the expense of black rights.

Although Frémont was frequently mentioned as an alternative candidate in the upcoming presidential election, many of his former supporters were uneasy. Charges of incompetency, corruption, and persistent rumors of personal scandal lingered on. Frémont is "mildewed and rotten," one dedicated abolitionist warned Wendell Phillips.[22] Nonetheless, in early 1864, John begun to spend liberally to promote his candidacy. Some committed abolitionists, including Phillips and Elizabeth Cady Stanton, remained loyal. After a conversation with Jessie, Stanton sent her a memorandum of suggestions to be used in writing a call for a dissident convention.[23] When the convention, an odd mixture of idealists and dubious hangers-on, met in Cleveland on May 31, 1864, Fremont was nominated for the presidency.

Although Lincoln was nominated by the regular Republican convention in June, over the summer, as seventy thousand Union troops died in a grim struggle toward Richmond, party leaders began to of calling a new convention to choose a more electable candidate Frémonts' hopes must have temporarily soared, although Jessie her husband would withdraw in favor of the right third candidate.[24] Then Gen. William Tecumseh Sherman's stunning victory at Atlanta on Sept. 2 electrified the North and suddenly Lincoln seemed electable. Nonetheless, the beleaguered president still feared that John's independent candidacy would divide Republican voters and throw the election to McClellan, the Democratic nominee. In September, through intermediaries, Lincoln offered a deal. Although the Frémonts always maintained that John's subsequent withdrawal was made solely for the good of the party, Lincoln's dismissal of Montgomery Blair from the cabinet the next day no doubt sweetened an otherwise bitter occasion.[25]

The Frémonts' political hopes ended with John's withdrawal. "Jessie rages at all sorts of people, especially Greeley, Beecher, and Garrison," reported Congressman George Julian. "According to her the General was shamefully betrayed by pretended radical and anti-Lincoln men who deserted him in time of greatest need, after encouraging him to stand in the breach."[26]

In April 1865, as the terrible war drew to a close, the Frémonts purchased a hundred-acre estate overlooking the Hudson near Tarrytown, New York. Over the next decade, Jessie would retreat to Pocaho, as they called their luxurious country seat. Bruised and disillusioned, she wanted no more public life.

Notes

1. J. B. FRÉMONT [2], 223.
2. To Thomas Starr King, Oct. 16 [1863], below.
3. To Elizabeth Blair Lee, July 27 [1861], below.
4. Aug. 5 [1861], below. JBF evidently joined the flotilla without her husband's prior knowledge. When Benjamin Grierson, a soldier who met her at Cairo, talked with her years later about the episode, she told him she had concealed herself in a stateroom until the steamboat started downriver, "when much to the General's surprise and apparent annoyance she made her appearance in the cabin, but her persuasive faculties proved sufficiently powerful to carry the point in sharing the danger" (Grierson ms. autobiography, "The Lights and Shadows of Life," 91, IHi).
5. Eliot later praised JBF's work, noting "I have now in my possession the original order establishing the Commission in *her own handwriting*, and signed by the General" (St. Louis *Globe-Democrat*, Oct. 22, 1877, clipping in MoSW—Eliot Papers).
6. See JBF to William G. Eliot, [Aug. 27, 1861], note 2, below. Probably

at JBF's instigation, the New York *Tribune* also praised the Dix visit (Sept. 6, 1861).

7. Aug. 20, 1861 (NjP—Blair-Lee Papers).

8. Aug. 29, Sept. 1, 1861 (DLC—Blair Papers).

9. *The Independent*, Sept. 21, 1861.

10. Lincoln Interview, Excerpt from "Great Events," below.

11. To Francis Preston Blair, Sr., Sept. 15 and 27, 1861 (DLC—Blair Papers).

12. Barton Bates to Edward Bates, Oct. 10, 1861 (MoSHi—Bates Papers).

13. Frank Blair's arrest, Montgomery Blair stated, "was as the phrase is 'Genl.' Jessie's doing altogether" (to W. O. Bartlett, Sept. 26, 1861, DLC—Blair Papers).

14. JBF justified her position as resulting not only from "Mr. Frémont's long habit of referring all manner of work and duties to me as acting principal in his absence, but because nearly all the General's reliable officers were with him. Of those remaining, his quartermaster became ill of fever, and was in a critically dangerous state from the time of the army's leaving. The adjutant, Captain McKeever, who was very active and thorough in his attention to his duties, had his right arm disabled by a relapse of injuries received at Bull Run, causing several times so much fever and suffering as to leave actually no other head than myself" (J. B. FRÉMONT [2], 88–89).

15. BARTLETT, 79.

16. [Oct. 8, 1862], below.

17. Dec. 29, 1861, below; JBF quoted in Lucretia Mott to Martha Wright et al., Aug. 1, 1862 (NSyU—Osborne Family Papers).

18. KASSON, 65.

19. E. B. SMITH [1], 306.

20. To John T. Fiala, July 10 [1863], below.

21. WHITTIER [2], 3:48–50.

22. Theodore Tilton to Phillips, May 31, 1864 (MH—Phillips Papers).

23. [May 4? 1864], (NjR, Douglas College—Stanton Papers). Transcript courtesy of Ann D. Gordon, coeditor, Papers of Elizabeth Cady Stanton and Susan B. Anthony.

24. To John Greenleaf Whittier, Aug. 22 [1864], below.

25. For JBF's accounts of the arrangement, see JBF to Rutherford B. Hayes, July 7 [1881], and to Samuel T. Pickard, May 28, 1893, both below.

26. JULIAN, 330.

To Thomas Starr King

My dear Mr. King,

I wrote you a long letter two days ago & tore it up today—there was a great deal too much in it to run the risks of Missouri RR riots[1] or even the gulf pirates.[2] I send you my chief, however.[3] Do you notice the sword? And that he is keeping the rattles under his hand. I want to send a copy with my regards to the city of Charleston where Mr. Frémont says he wants to make his headquarters. We shall not be able to indulge ourselves in burning Richmond. St. Louis is getting hot enough to be tempting and we will be on our way in another twenty four hours. Lily and the boys, and the silent bewildered Ellen,[4] who has heretofore lived decently & in order & by decorous rules—her breath leaves her at my pace and contempt for bonnet boxes & extra wraps & such like. Everybody thinks we are going by Buffalo &c.— but we take the only six foot track in that line of travel (through Pennva.) and so will have a quiet travel all to ourselves. A rest we all need. Mr. Frémont has stacks and stacks not only of bayonetted muskets to examine but of work of all sorts. We have really had no chance to have a talk—[. . .] to have speech of each other but I remind myself of what I was told once when I thought that I had made the discovery that the insects took the color of the bush they lived on (I had seen a blue fly on some blue phlox) & got for my announcement the answer that certain insects belonged to certain plants & could not live away from them.[5] I haunt around taking my chances of a word— sometimes it is only a look—but after the hungry yearning of that far off blank life at Black Point it is enough.

I could write you so many things of interest but the chances of the mails are not good to run. I am looking for letters from you all and you must not disappoint me. Did Mrs. King take any comfort in making "steamer things"?[6] Mrs. Dewey[7] needn't wish to go any farther. It's bad style here to dress or have entertainments and you hear of nothing but the war. Eugene[8] would be off for a soldier—sure. Mr. Dewey too. All that energy he displayed in defending the climate of San Francisco would find a better cause & where would Mrs. Dewey be then? Less sunshine than in the big parlor. I am going along so I can't feel as left out as the others do but there is a side to all the excitement

that is sober enough. With love to Edith and best love and remembrances from Lily and myself always. Sincerely and affectionately Your
friend,

J B Frémont

N.Y. July 20th

ALS (CSfCP—King Papers).

1. JBF feared her letter might be seized by Confederate guerrilla bands who were
sabotaging railroad operations in northeastern Missouri (New York *Times,* July 13,
17, 18, 1861).

2. JBF refers to Confederate privateers who preyed on merchant ships along the
southern coast in the first months of the war. During her recent voyage from Panama
on the *North Star,* which carried $1.2 million in California gold, the steamer had been
chased by the notorious sailing privateer *Jeff Davis* just after passing Cape Hatteras.
"It was a sparkling cold and windy day, and we had the out-of-date sensations described
in pirate stories as the wind now helped, now hindered our pursuer; but the wind of
the North was our ally, and we outran her before night" ("Great Events," 218; see
also E. B. FRÉMONT, 122–25 and New York *Times,* July 13–15, 1861).

3. JBF enclosed a recent carte de visite photograph of JCF in military uniform,
clasping a gold and silver-mounted sword with a rattlesnake curled around its hilt, an
1847 gift from the citizens of Charleston, S.C. Copies of the photograph survive in
the Billings Mansion Archives and the New-York Historical Society, among others.
JBF also refers to the sword in JBF to King [early 1861], above.

4. Ellen, a "staid, painstaking" English maid and "trained nurse," had accompanied
the family east in part to aid JBF, whose foot and arm were in "splints" as a result
of her San Francisco carriage accident (JBF to Anne C. Lynch Botta, Jan. 22 [1863?],
courtesy of Paul J. Scheips, Arlington, Va.; "Great Events," 218, 269).

5. The first expedition report contains a similar observation: "All these plants have
their insect inhabitants, variously colored; taking generally the hue of the flower on
which they live. The *artemesia* has its small fly accompanying it through every change
of elevation and latitude; and whenever I have seen the *asclepias tuberosa,* I have
always remarked, too, on the flower, a large butterfly, so nearly resembling it in color,
as to be distinguishable at a little distance only by the motion of its wings" (JACKSON
& SPENCE, 178).

6. JBF alludes to the fact that Julia King was outspokenly critical of California and
homesick for her native Boston (HERR, 312).

7. Orville Dewey (1794–1882) was a noted Unitarian minister and author, recently
retired from his Boston pastorate. He and his wife, Louisa (Farnham), were visiting
the Kings in San Francisco.

8. Eugene was probably a Frémont family employee, possibly the coachman, in a
note to JBF written during the Black Point period, King had requested a return message
via "Prince Eugene" (King note quoted in JBF, "Distinguished Persons I Have Known:
Starr King," New York *Ledger,* Mar. 6, 1875).

To Elizabeth Blair Lee

St. Louis July 27th [1861]

My dear Lizzie,

Your letter reached me last night and but for the genuine interest you have in the cause I should have taken it for a sarcasm. You say all we need is "Generals." That is simply and literally the whole provision made for this Dept. An arsenal without arms or ammunition — troops on paper and a thoroughly prepared and united enemy thick and unremitting as mosquitoes. The telegraph in the enemy's hand & the worse for us as not being avowed enemies. In Ohio & all the way we met western troops on their way to the Potomac — the western waters left to defend themselves as best they might. I promise you that "if Trelawney die,

> Then twenty thousand Cornish men
> Shall know the reason why."[1]

It is not safe to say on paper all that should be said at Washington. The President is a western man and not grown in red tape. If he knew the true defenceless condition of the west it would not remain so. I have begged Mr. Frémont to let me go on & tell him how things are here. But he says I'm tired with the sea voyage — that I shan't expose my health any more & that he can't do without me. It's making bricks without straw out here & mere human power can't draw order out of chaos by force of will alone. Don't be surprised if you see me some day at Silver Spring. I will obey a higher law than my dear chief's and open out the view to the M[ississi]ppi. It seems to stop now at the Potomac.

Dear Lizzie I can't go backward & I'm too old to begin on new faiths. I believe in the United States. I am not ready to cramp down to United States Army. Although we won't think the worse of a good man for being in it. But this is a day for men, not rules, to govern affairs.

Precedent & courtesy are two fatal words just now. And it takes one's heart away to see how little private war hatchets are dug up, when only the one sword should be in every hand.

Mr. Frémont says your boy is a fine fellow. We read of Mr. Lee's independent change of orders and felt proud for you — no *precedent* work there.[2] Is your brother Frank coming out here? Ask him if he brings his arms or is he like the rest here to wait on chance for them. If I write of nothing else it is because nothing else is of moment compared with this. With love to your Mother & Father, always affcty. yours,

J.B. Frémont

ALS (DLC—Blair Papers).

1. JBF is paraphrasing lines from "The Song of the Western Man" by Robert Stephen Hawker. This popular nineteenth-century ballad commemorates the 1688 imprisonment in the Tower of London of seven Anglican bishops, including Sir Jonathan Trelawny of Cornwall, for refusing to recognize the Declaration of Indulgence issued by King James II, a Catholic.

2. S. Phillips Lee, commanding the sloop of war *Vandalia,* had been at the southern tip of Africa en route to China when he learned of South Carolina's secession. Disobeying his official instructions, he brought his ship back to New York (CORNISH & LAAS, 85–89).

To Montgomery Blair

[July 28, 1861]

My dear Mr. Blair,

Mr. Frémont asks you to take this from him, I write it from his telling—not absolutely from dictation.

The enemy have already occupied, & in force, points which Mr. Frémont intended holding against them. For want of arms to arm new regiments & because not a cent of their pay has been given to the others which disheartens & indisposes them to re-enlist, it is almost impossible to make head against them. He is doing the best he can without money without arms without moral aid. This city needs a force to repress it. All the arms & well equipped troops of Ohio & Indiana we met moving *to the East.*

Mr. Frémont says send anything in the shape of arms—but arms we must have. Send money, & both arms & money by the most rapid conveyance. His English arms he says were bought for himself & begs that you will not allow them to be intercepted.[1] His battery rifles & pistols might save the State—but it looks now as if it was intended to let it slide (that's my own).

It is also my own to say that I don't like this neglect & I look to you & to the President to see that it has not a fatal effect. Just now the Potomac is so interesting that I do not blame every care for it but don't expect miracles on the M[ississi]ppi.

This is very abrupt. Mr. Blow[2] is waiting. It is odd to feel in an enemy's country here in St. Louis but it is unmistakably so. With best love to all, Yours,

J. B. Frémont.

[*Margin note:* "Money & arms without delay & by the *quickest conveyance.*"]

ALS (DLC—Blair Papers). Dated July 28, 1861, in another hand.

1. While still in Europe in late May, JCF had pledged $50–60,000 in government funds to purchase 2,000 French rifles, 500 revolvers, eight rifled cannon with shot and shell, and 2,000,000 percussion caps (Frederick Billings to New York *Tribune,* Oct. 30, 1861; "Great Events," 220). When JCF returned to the United States, Secretary of State William Seward approved this transaction and authorized funds for additional European arms. JCF then directed Frederick Billings, who was still in London as his agent, to purchase 5,000 cavalry sabres; 1,000 cavalry saddles, bridles, and halters; 5–10,000 rifled small arms; and "one or two batteries of six pounders." This second order was evidently never completed, because the government preferred to use its own agent. See JCF to Billings, July 1, 13, 17, 1861, Billings Mansion Archives; JCF to Montgomery Blair, Aug. 19, 1861, DLC—Blair Papers.

2. Virginia-born Henry Taylor Blow (1817–75) was a successful St. Louis businessman and antislavery politician who from 1863 to 1867 served as a congressman from Missouri (SCHARF [2], 1:607–11).

To Montgomery Blair

Head Quarters   Western Dept.
St. Louis   July 31st [1861]

My dear Mr. Blair,

Mr. Frémont finds his hands too full in these last hours before starting[1] to write to you himself but he wishes you to know the condition in which he found this Department, and the causes of delay in his appointed work. I put down his own words as he talked & give them to you in unshaped sentences.

JBF.

"Everything here I found in the most disorderly condition and the State, this city included, insurrectionary. The want of money & arms made my hands weak, until I got angry—& if any more sub treasurers[2] stand in the way of necessary work for safety you may look to see secession newspaper columns dressed in mourning for my blood thirsty acts.

I judge from all information, that the enemy is forming himself into bodies along the southern frontier. Appearances indicate that he designs a simultaneous movement from M[issou]ri. to Washington, and I think he wants to get the same position in M[issou]ri. that he has in Virginia. You may be sure he is vigorously organizing south of Memphis.

Within a circle of fifty miles are in & about him (so Genl. Prentiss reports)[3] twelve thousand men,—increasing daily. On Current river the enemy have 5000 infantry & 2000 cavalry well armed—they are Tennesseeans & Arkansas men led by Col. Hardee.[4]

Genl. Lyon[5] reports large force gathered in his front. Morton[6] of Indiana reports him preparing to attack Cairo from New Madrid with 20,000 men.

I begin to move to day but I am distressed by singular inadequacy and scarcity of equipments and great want of arms. At this moment I learn from the Adjt.[7] that two regiments are refusing to move— refusing pay unless they get the whole. My boats have fires up, and my movements are checked by this most inopportune want of money. I do not write to complain but to let you know the facts.

One regiment had to be compelled to go on to Ironton yesterday by arresting officers—it had been in a state of mutiny all day. I should have had to go farther had they not obeyed at once. The money needed to prevent this is in the sub treasury here.

I don't care for my commission—I am determined not to risk my character here for want of means within my reach, and what is needed I will take.

On my return to this place I shall undertake the re-organization of the Home Guards.[8] Wyman is at Rolla.[9] I hold the R.R. from that place to St. Louis by Col. Almsteadt's [Almstedt] command.[10] I have placed Gratz Brown[11] at Ironton with 600 of his regiment. He has Bland's regiment[12] under his command re-inforced last night by Hecker,[13] and I hold the roads from Ironton to St. Louis by a good man, Col. Kahlmann [Kallman][14] & 250 men.

This is no complaint. I am doing all I can but I wish you to see the ground on which I am working.["]

Yours truly J. C. Frémont
(by J. B. F.)

AL initialed by JBF, and signed for JCF by JBF (DLC—Blair Papers).

1. JCF, accompanied by nearly four thousand troops and a flotilla of eight steamboats, was about to embark for Cairo, a day's journey by water, to relieve its beleaguered Union garrison. Strategically located at the juncture of the Ohio and Mississippi rivers, Cairo was threatened by an estimated twelve thousand Confederate troops, who would quickly retreat when the flotilla arrived. For accounts of the enterprise, see MOORE, 2:467–68; "Great Events," 235–36; New York *Tribune* and *Times,* Aug. 3, 1861.

2. Desperate for money to pay troops and buy equipment and supplies, JCF had seized subtreasury funds in St. Louis without waiting for federal authorization. He explained his action to Lincoln on July 30: "Our troops have not been paid, and some regiments are in a state of mutiny. . . . The Treasurer of the United States has here $300,000 entirely unappropriated, I applied to him yesterday . . . but was refused. We have not an hour for delay. . . . This morning I . . . will send a force to the treasury to take the money, and will direct such payments as the exigency requires. I will hazard everything for the defense of the department you have confided to me, and I trust to you for support" (OFFICIAL RECORDS, ser. 1, vol. 3:416–17).

3. Brig. Gen. Benjamin Mayberry Prentiss (1819–1901), a Mexican War veteran turned Illinois lawyer-politician, commanded the Union troops at Cairo. JBF quotes from his July 28, 1861, report (see ibid., 411).

4. Recently promoted to brigadier general in the Confederate Army, William Joseph Hardee (1815–73) of Georgia was the author of the widely used military textbook, *Rifle and Light Infantry Tactics.* Hardee's forces were moving from Arkansas toward Ironton, a vital rail terminus in southeastern Missouri (JCF to Lincoln, July 30, 1861, in ibid., 416).

5. A West Point graduate who served with distinction in the Mexican War, Brig. Gen. Nathaniel Lyon (1818–61) had been instrumental in keeping Missouri in the Union during the first months of the Civil War. With a force of 5,400 men, he was now at Springfield in southwestern Missouri and, like Prentiss, demanding reinforcements to meet an anticipated Confederate attack. But JCF, deciding he could not reinforce both Springfield and the strategically more important Cairo, would leave Lyon to retreat or fight as he saw fit; choosing to fight, Lyon, his forces outnumbered, died heroically at the battle of Wilson's Creek on Aug. 10. With this defeat, southwest Missouri fell to the Confederates (see ibid., 53–130, for documents of the battle, and SCHOFIELD, 39–45, for a convincing defense of JCF's role by Lyon's second in command).

6. Indiana governor Oliver P. Morton (1823–77).

7. The reference is probably to Capt. John C. Kelton (1828–93), a West Point graduate who had been serving as assistant adjutant general since at least July 28, although he was not formally appointed until Aug. 3 (OFFICIAL RECORDS, ser. 1, vol. 53:498; BOATNER, 451–52).

8. Originally organized by Frank Blair and Nathaniel Lyon largely from among St. Louis's intensely pro-Union German citizens, the more than four thousand Home Guards (more formally the U.S. Reserve Corps) had been vital in holding St. Louis for the Union at the outset of the war. The state's moderate Unionists, led by Gov. Hamilton R. Gamble, wanted to disband the guards or integrate them into the regular army since many citizens resented their radical antislavery views; JCF, however, would retain them as a separate unit (see OFFICIAL RECORDS, ser. 3, vol. 1:794–96; PARRISH, 15, 17, 19, 55–56; ROSIN, 214–15).

9. Col. John B. Wyman commanded an Illinois volunteer regiment. He would be killed at Chickasaw Bayou, Dec. 28, 1862 (OFFICIAL RECORDS, ser. 1, vol. 17, pt. 1:653–54).

10. German-born Col. Henry Almstedt (d. 1884) commanded the First Missouri Reserve Corps, a regiment in the Home Guards (HEITMAN, 1:161; OFFICIAL RECORDS, ser. 3, vol. 1:794).

11. Yale-educated Benjamin Gratz Brown (1826–85) briefly headed the Fourth Missouri Reserve Corps of the Home Guards. Related to both the Blairs and Bentons, he was a radical antislavery lawyer/politician who would endorse JCF's quest for the presidency in 1864. Elected senator in 1863 and governor in 1870, he advocated woman's suffrage and civil service reform.

12. Col. Peter E. Bland (1824–70), a lawyer, commanded the Sixth Missouri Volunteer Regiment (SCHARF [2] 2:1509; HEITMAN, 2:81).

13. Friedrich Karl Franz Hecker (1811–81) was a celebrated German idealist and revolutionary leader who had emigrated to Illinois with the failure of the 1848 revolution. A successful fifty-year-old farmer, he nonetheless joined the Union army, leading Illinois regiments throughout the war.

14. Col. Herman Kallman [sometimes Kallmann] commanded the Second Missouri Reserve Corps of Home Guards (HEITMAN, 2:117; OFFICIAL RECORDS, ser. 3, vol. 1:794).

To Montgomery Blair

St. Louis Aug. 5 [1861].

My dear Mr. Blair,

The General cannot make time to put his pen to paper except for necessary signatures. But he wishes you to know things in which your aid may be of vital importance & you understand I am a faithful reporter when he has not time to dictate.

Whilst we were at Cairo a despatch came from General Scott[1] himself granting two companies of artillery which were idle at Cincinnati. Mr. Frémont answered at once with thanks for the well timed relief. In the morning came another despatch also from Genl. Scott, saying one Company was sent to western Virginia (after being asked for by & promised to us here) & that the other had no guns. By letter, Mr. Frémont is today informed that the company without guns is still idle there. Mr. Frémont asks for it again. Experienced artillerists decide the day. Seigel [Sigel] had some & thence success.[2] The new men who come in are absolutely raw in all war matters. This is a great scandal—this dept. By dint of begging and bullying some guns & money are being gotten in, but every useful thing is being concentrated around Washington. The town is ready for a rising in aid of the rebels who are marching in on the southern part of the State in force. Well armed and having good cavalry. If they would hold off ten or fifteen days we should carry the day, but they don't seem to intend holding off. Quite a force is reported as only fifteen miles below Cape Girardeau. Everything is being pushed to the uttermost to get them reinforcements which I hope will reach them in time—and—be of use when they get there. The sound of the shouts with which we were welcomed at Cairo stays in my memory. Only a weak & threatened garrison seeing aid coming could make such sounds. Gen'l Prentiss's voice as he said "I shall sleep tonight" said volumes. Should Ohio & other western troops be sent East when such a point as Cairo was being left almost abandoned for the three months men were leaving.[3] It is a hard life at best that of private & such moral aid as can be given by entering into their local feelings should be added to the physical comforts needed by them. War on paper & war on the ground are two sides of the medal. Undisciplined & untrained they are, but the volunteers are knights and crusaders of the best kind and a little loving care such as the first Napoleon gave would make an invincible army of them. Five regiments chiefly Ohio river men are now ordered East. They must come here & the President will feel that it is necessary they should.

J.B.F.

AL initialed (DLC—Blair Papers).

1. The old Mexican War hero, General-in-Chief Winfield Scott (1786–1866), was suffering from dizziness and dropsy; he would retire on Nov. 1 (MCPHERSON, 313). Scott's two mentioned dispatches (both dated Aug. 2) and a third (dated Aug 6) ordering "Hoffman's battery of artillery, from Cincinnati" to St. Louis can be found in OFFICIAL RECORDS, ser. 1, vol. 3:419, 428.

2. JBF refers to the July 5 success of then Col. Franz Sigel (1824–1902) at the battle of Carthage, Mo., where his well-drilled artillerists carried the day (OFFICIAL RECORDS, ser. 1, vol. 3:14–37; and newspaper reports in MOORE, 2:246–50). Sigel, the youthful commander of the revolutionary forces in the duchy of Baden during the unsuccessful German revolution, had emigrated to the United States, where he campaigned for JCF in 1856. When the Civil War began, he organized a Missouri regiment of German-American volunteers and was active in securing the state for the Union.

3. Six of the eight regiments at Cairo consisted of men who had enlisted for a three-month term that ended in late July. Since they had not been paid and their families were without support, they were leaving despite the desperate situation. Many, moreover, were sick with fever and dysentery. By the time JCF reached Cairo, the garrison had been reduced to 1,200 men (NEVINS [1] 483; "Great Events," 236).

To Abraham Lincoln

[Aug. 5, 1861]

Genl. Frémont has read Col. Palmer's letter with the President's endorsement. The plan suggested by Col. Palmer is about what Genl. Fremont has been doing since arriving in Missouri.[1]

The State is in a disorganized condition but much worse in the South where it is mixed up with Arkansas people, than in the North where it connects with a loyal population. The battle is in the South upon which fifty thousand men are now advancing and closing in with our posts.

A large part of the Illinois force has been already transferred to Birds Point opposite Cairo. The State is being occupied militarily by the Home Guards & the occupation would have been complete but for the absolute want of arms.

Knowing how many affairs press upon the President's attention, General Frémont returns the letter in order to recall the subject to his mind.

Head Quarters Western Department
St. Louis, Mri. August 5th, 1861

AL (DLC—Lincoln Papers). JBF evidently composed this letter from JCF's cursory instructions; her use of the third person allowed her to avoid signing her own name, which might have been looked on askance. She responds to a July 24 letter from Col. John M. Palmer (1817–1900) to Lyman Trumbell, which the Illinois senator had passed on to Lincoln. The president sent it to Frémont on July 31, with the endorsement: "The writer of the within I personally know to be a most reliable man, both for integrity and judgement; [now?] as the matters he speaks of are in Gen. Fremont's field, I submit them to him, asking his special attention to the item." In his letter, Palmer, an Illinois politician who commanded the Fourteenth Illinois Volunteer Regiment stationed in northern Missouri, suggested that local citizens, organized into Home Guard and other military units, could more effectively counter possible Confederate guerrilla attacks than the federal forces then on duty. "If this course is adopted, our [federal] forces could be employed in a better business than watching bridges and disturbing women and children in searching for arms."

1. On Aug. 2, JCF had reorganized the Home Guard ("Great Events," 237, 240); on Aug. 6 he ordered Palmer's and three additional Illinois regiments to St. Louis for other duty (OFFICIAL RECORDS, ser. 1, vol. 3:428).

To William G. Eliot

[Aug. 27, 1861]

My dear Mr. Eliot,

Miss Dix[1] answers that she will be here this week.

I have been so conquered by headache yesterday & this morning that I have not done all I wished but I shall be like Punch's caricatures of [long blank space] until "Reform" is carried. Read the Democrat in the morning.[2] Your letter & plan will find every assistance in this house & I have written to ask Mr. De Camp[3] to come see me & I can have him on our side. His signature is needed I think. His services we [he?] will let me delegate to younger men. Did you telegraph for the physician you spoke of? Very truly yours,

J. B. Frémont

Tuesday evening

ALS (MoSW—Eliot Papers, Notebook 6.) William Greenleaf Eliot (1811–87), a Unitarian minister and founder of Washington University, St. Louis, worked with JBF to establish the Western Sanitary Commission. A distinguished and energetic civic leader, he was a longtime abolitionist and, incidentally, the grandfather of T. S. Eliot. On Aug. 31, 1861, Eliot recorded in his notebook: "For a week past or more I have been investigating Military Hospital business: have proposed a plan to Genl. Frémont, had several long talks with Mrs. F., who has sent for Miss Dix, whom we expect tomorrow." Within weeks the Western Sanitary Commission had set up four hospitals with more than two thousand beds. For additional details, see MAXWELL, 97–100.

1. The noted reformer Dorothea Dix (1802–87) had recently been named superintendent of nurses for the U.S. army. JBF had known her since 1848, when Dix had begun her campaign to provide federal funds for the care of the insane, blind, deaf, and dumb. For Thomas Hart Benton and JCF's support of Dix's early work, see D. WILSON, 171; 187–91.

2. The Aug. 27 St. Louis *Democrat* contained an article on the forthcoming visit of Dix, "our American Florence Nightingale," written by JBF and revised by Eliot. Its purpose was to prepare the way for the still controversial idea of professional female nurses: "Amateur or indiscriminate nursing is not enough for the stern realities which war has already brought amongst us. The modern system of female nurses has been found too acceptable to the suffering to be dispensed with; but to bring this element into efficient use requires the practical discrimination of some one—like Miss Dix, we were going to say, but no other like her can be found" (*Democrat* clipping in Eliot Notebook 6, Aug. 31, 1861).

3. Although JBF, as well as members of the U.S. Sanitary Commission, considered the aging army surgeon Samuel G. De Camp (d. 1871) too old for active work, he nonetheless was named the first medical director of the Western Department. He retired

in Aug. 1862 (MAXWELL, 101, 103, 105; New York *Times*, Aug. 3, 1861, Sept. 15, 1871 obit.; HEITMAN, 1:364).

To Abraham Lincoln

[Sept. 10, 1861]

Mrs. Frémont brings to the President, from Genl. Frémont, a letter and some verbal communications, which she would be very glad to deliver with as little delay as possible.[1]

If it suits the President's convenience will he name a time this evening to receive them — or at some early hour tomorrow.

Tuesday night, 8 o'clock[2]

Willard's Hotel.

AL (DLC—Lincoln Papers). JBF's visit to Lincoln and its repercussions are discussed in the section introduction.

1. JBF carried a copy of her husband's negative reply to Lincoln's Sept. 2 request that he rescind his emancipation decree. JCF wrote: "If upon reflection your better judgment still decides that I am wrong . . . I have to ask that you will openly direct me to make the correction. . . . I acted with full deliberation, and upon the certain conviction that it was a measure right and necessary, and I still think so." According to "Great Events," 264–65, JBF also carried a second JCF letter for the president, dated Sept. 8, which proposed a complex military strategy designed to secure Kentucky and then take Nashville and Memphis. For the texts of JCF's proclamation, Lincoln's Sept. 2 response, and JCF's two Sept. 8 letters, see OFFICIAL RECORDS ser. 1, vol. 3:466–67, 469–70, 477–79.

2. The time of JBF's note, "8 o'clock," confirms that she did not seek "an audience" with Lincoln "at midnight," as Lincoln's secretary, John Hay, quoted the president as recalling two years later (HAY, 133, and repeated in NICOLAY & HAY, 4:415).

The Lincoln Interview: Excerpt from "Great Events"

I left by the night train with only my English maid who was needed, for my hurt arm still kept me helpless. We had only common cars and I had to sit up the two nights in the overcrowded train; there was so much travel, the cars were crowded like street cars and it was the hot early September weather. At the end of the third day we got into Washington and I went to Willard's Hotel where some New York friends had been telegraphed to meet me and go with me to the President. Mr. Isaac Sherman who had great influence with the President and had proved his value, was ill and unable to come; Judge Edward Co[w]les[1] and Mr. Frederick Billings[2] however had both arrived. I sent my card at once to the President with a line to say, I had a letter from the General to deliver and asking when I could do so.

After a little delay the messenger brought back a card on which was written,

"A. Lincoln.
Now."

As I rose to go Judge Co[w]les insisted on my waiting until morning — that I was too tired, and looking at his watch, said it was nearly nine o'clock. I thought it best to make no delay and though my baggage had not been delivered and I was still in the dusty dress in which I had been two days and nights, I walked across to the White House, taking the short way at the side nearest Willard's.

All my life I had been at home in the President's House — as well received there as in the family circle, and with the old confidence of the past I went forward now.

We were shown into the red parlor and told, the President would be there presently. It was some time before he came in, though it was an appointment of his own making and the "now" had indicated I was to hasten. When he did enter it was from the far door of the dining room which he pushed to, but it was gently set open again from the other side. The President did not speak, only bowed slightly, and I introduced Judge Co[w]les as a member of the New York bar, and as the President still said nothing, I gave him the letter, telling him General Frémont felt the subject to be of so much importance, that he had sent me to answer any points on which the President might want more information. At this he smiled with an expression that was not agreeable, then moving nearer the chandelier to see better, read the letter standing. Judge Co[w]les had withdrawn to the door way of the blue parlor where he walked up and down like a sentinel. I had not been offered a seat though I was looking as tired as I felt. The President's unusual manner was a reversal of the old order of things. As he remained standing reading the letter, I drew out one of the row of chairs and sat down for I was trembling from fatigue and recent illness and instinct told me the President intended to discourage me, and I did not intend to appear nervous.

At length the President drew up a chair and sat down near me with the letter, saying, "I have written to the General and he knows what I want done."[3] I answered the General thought it would be an advantage for him if I came to explain more fully what he wished him to know, for, I said "the General feels he is at the great disadvantage of being perhaps opposed by people in whom you have every confidence."

"Who do you mean?" he said, "Persons of differing views?" I answered; "the General's conviction is that it will be long and dreadful work to conquer by arms alone, that there must be other consideration to get us the support of foreign countries—that he *knew* the English feeling for gradual emancipation and the strong wish to meet it on the part of important men in the South* [*note:* *General Wm. Preston, John Breckenridge and others][4]: that as the President knew we were on the eve of England, France and Spain recognizing the South: they were anxious for a pretext to do so; England on account of her cotton interests, and France because the Emperor dislikes us."[5] The President said "You are quite a female politician."

I felt the sneering tone and saw there was a foregone decision against all listening. Then the President spoke more rapidly and unrestrainedly: "The General ought not to have done it; he never would have done it if he had consulted Frank Blair;[6] I sent Frank there to advise him and to keep me advised about the work, the true condition of things then, and how they were going." The President went on almost angrily—"Frank never would have let him do it—the General should never have dragged the negro into the war. It is a war for a great national object and the negro has nothing to do with it."

"Then," I answered, "there is no use to say more, except that we were not aware that Frank Blair represented you—he did not do so openly."

I asked when I could have the answer? "Maybe by to-morrow," said the President, "I have a great deal to do—to-morrow if possible, or the next day." To my saying I would come for it—"No, I will send it to you, to-morrow or the day after." He asked where I was staying, and was answered at Willard's—and we came away.

As we walked through the grounds Judge Co[w]les said, in his calm way, "Mrs. Frémont, the General has no further part in this war. He will be deprived of all his part in the war; it is not the President alone, but there is a faction which plans the affairs of the North and they will triumph, and they are against the General. It will be like General Gates,[7] it will be thirty years before he is known and has justice. They will give reasons for keeping him down. But they hold the power and will keep him down."

I had to let the General know the result of the interview; I knew that to telegraph directly was impracticable; but the cipher and address I had arranged for, told him exactly what I found was the policy decided on.[8]

The elder Mr. Blair came to see me early the next day. He had always been fond of me, I had been like a child in their family; but Mr. Blair was now very angry: "Well;" he said, "who would have expected you to do such a thing as this, to come here and find fault with the President;" I laughed at first—laughed at him; but he was too angry; "Look what Frémont has done; made the President his enemy!"

Mr. Blair stayed over two hours and got heated up with his own words and from old habit of intimacy told far more than he should as he said finally, "If you had stayed here in Washington and done what I wanted you to do—it is not fit for a woman to go with an army. If you had stayed here in Washington you could have had anything you wanted as I wrote you, but there you went straight out to the West without even coming to Washington."[9]

All that painful day of broken friendship passed and there was nothing from the President. Mr. Blair had said the President would send Montgomery Blair to talk with General Frémont "and bring him to his senses."[10] Now I doubted my being given the answer the next day and wrote to ask the President if Mr. Blair's statements were exact and if he could let me have the answer for the General in time for me to leave by the evening train.

Typescript, "Great Events," 269–72. JBF wrote three essentially similar accounts of the Lincoln meeting, of which the most detailed, written in 1891 as part of "Great Events," appears here. A first skimpy report, written in June 1888, and a fuller statement, dated Apr. 10, 1890 (both also in CU-B—Frémont Papers) were provoked by publication of a distorted version of the meeting in John G. Nicolay and John Hay's *Abraham Lincoln: A History,* which JBF first read serialized in *Century* magazine (36 [June 1888]: 297–98). JBF prepared her accounts as rebuttals but then withheld them to avoid controversy (see JBF to Robert Underwood Johnson, Apr. 7, 1890, Apr. 24 [1890], CLjC).

1. New York lawyer Edward Pitkin Cowles (not Coles, as JBF writes) (1815–74) had campaigned for JCF in 1856 and served a term on the New York State Supreme Court. In 1861, he was reportedly looking for a civil service appointment. Unsubstantiated testimony before a congressional committee would link him with JCF's corrupt quartermaster Justus McKinstry (STRONG, 2:296, 3:151; Special House Committee on Government Contracts, 37th Cong. 2d sess., *Report* 2, serial 1142, pp. 941–42; New York *Times,* Jan. 5, 1875).

2. Vermont-born Frederick Billings (1823–90) journeyed to California in 1849, where he cofounded Halleck, Peachy, and Billings, soon the state's leading law firm. In May 1860, he purchased a one-sixteenth share in Las Mariposas; later that year, in exchange for an additional one-sixteenth interest, he agreed to provide JCF with legal services for one year and to accompany him to Europe to raise additional capital for Las Mariposas (JCF to Billings, May 2, 1860; agreement between JCF and Billings, Nov. 26, 1860, Billings Mansion Archives). He remained in Europe after JCF's departure to purchase arms and equipment at JCF's request (for details, see JBF to Montgomery Blair, [July 28, 1861], note 1, above). Just after returning to the United States, Billings received a telegram from JCF, dated Sept. 9, asking him to meet "a friend [JBF] on Tuesday night [Sept. 10] or Wednesday Morning at Willards in Washington. It is important" (Billings Mansion Archives).

3. Lincoln was evidently referring to his Sept. 2 letter, in which he asked JCF to rescind his emancipation order "as of your own motion" because there was "great danger" that it would "alarm our Southern Union friends, and turn them against us — perhaps ruin our rather fair prospect for Kentucky. . . . This letter is written in a spirit of caution and not of censure" (LINCOLN, 4:506).

4. William Preston (1816–87), a former Kentucky congressman and minister to Spain, was an aide to Confederate general Albert Sidney Johnston. John Cabell Breckinridge (1821–75), U.S. vice-president under Buchanan and a presidential candidate in 1860, had become a Confederate brigadier general. JBF was related to Preston and Breckinridge as well as Johnston through her mother.

5. JBF's point, one commonly made by emancipationists during this period, was that if emancipation was made an explicit goal of the war, the North would gain a powerful moral edge that would deter European nations from recognizing the South. See the New York *Times,* Sept. 14, 1861, for a similar argument by the newspaper's London correspondent.

6. In reality, Frank Blair disagreed only on the timing, not the content, of JCF's proclamation: "His recent proclamation is the best thing of the kind that has been issued but should have been issued when he first came when he had the power to enforce it & the enemy no power to retaliate (to Montgomery Blair, Sept. 1, 1861, DLC — Blair Papers). Lizzie Lee commented that Frank was "so radical" he would not have opposed JCF's emancipation proclamation (to Francis Preston Blair, Sr., Sept. 15, 1861, ibid.).

7. Gen. Horatio Gates (c. 1728/29–1806) had been suspected of plotting to supersede George Washington as commander-in-chief of the Revolutionary army in 1777–78; after the defeat of American forces under Gates at Camden, S.C., on Aug. 16, 1780, his reputation was further tarnished. Congress demanded an investigation, and Gates was relieved of his command. Despite Gate's pleas for a court-martial to clear his name, no formal inquiry was ever held.

8. JBF seems to be referring to a third telegram, since the two known telegrams ([Sept. 11?, 1861] and [Sept. 12?, 1861], both below) appear to be written later and are addressed directly to JCF.

9. Blair's version of the meeting was quoted by Lizzie Lee in a letter to her husband:

"In a word [the Frémonts] hate & fear Frank & are also hostile to everybody in the administration who is supposed to stand between them & imperial power which is they think to be clutched as easily as martial law by proclamation. I talked 3 hours & sounded her to the bottom, her natural secretiveness [and] Benton cunning giving way under the passion I provoked. . . . I then stated what Frank had done to give him his command—what I & Montgomery had done to elevate him in the public eye—what we had done to advance his private fortune. . . . She bridled up at this & put on a very *high* look—I told [her] she saw she was to play the part of Empress Catherine. 'Not Catherine but Josephine,' she said. I said you are too imperious for her & too ungrateful for me. You have never made any return for services & you never shall—so I quit her" (Sept. 17–18, 1861, NjP—Blair-Lee Papers).

10. Spurred by Frank Blair's criticism, JCF's "alleged general mismanagement and incapacity formed the subject of a long session" of the Cabinet on Sept. 9 (John G. Nicolay to Therena Bates, Sept 17, 1861, DLC—Nicolay Papers). As a result, Lincoln sent Q. M. Gen. Montgomery C. Meigs and Montgomery Blair to St. Louis to assess the situation, a fact Lincoln chose not to mention to JBF. After a brief investigation, Meigs would conclude that JCF was unfit for his position: "he is prodigal of money; unscrupulous, surrounded by villains, inacceptable to the people and ambitious; should he see the opportunity he would not hesitate to play Aaron Burr" (Meigs Journal, Sept. 10–18, 1861, quoted in WEIGLEY, 193). Meanwhile, Montgomery Blair telegraphed Lincoln that the situation was "deplorable," and Meigs should immediately be appointed in JCF's place "to save the state" (Sept. 14, 1861, DLC—Lincoln Papers).

To John Charles Frémont

[Sept. 11?, 1861]

Genl. Meigs and Postmaster Genl. Blair leave this morning for St. Louis to investigate that Department. See New York Times of Tuesday.[1] It is true and sent by the Cabinet. Things evidently prejudged. Collateral issues and compromises will be attempted but the true contest is on the proclamation. It is your Lerida.[2] Listen but remember our Salem witch. Remember and by note about General Washington. Guard originals and have copies ready. Some true active friends here and the heart of the country with you everywhere. I will wait for Billings. Will repeat this dispatch until you answer. That I may rely on the answer sign the name you gave one of Bronte's puppies.

I am really well and Dr. Van Buren[3] has just sent up his card.

Major General Frémont
Head Quarters
St. Louis
Mri.
Ans. to care J. B. Swain 503 12th St.[4]

AD (telegram) (ICHi). JBF signature in another hand.

1. The Tuesday, Sept. 10, New York *Times* stated that Blair and Meigs would leave "in the morning" for St. Louis "to personally examine the condition of the Western Division."

2. JBF's prearranged code has been only partially deciphered by the editors. "Lerida," a city in northeastern Spain, is celebrated as the site where Julius Caesar decisively defeated the forces of his rival, Pompey, in 49 B.C. In Frémont family parlance, "remember our Salem witch" meant "be silent," as Lily Frémont noted years later when JBF used the same term in a telegram on mining business (Elizabeth Benton Frémont ms. journal, Dec. 17 [1879], NNC—Nevins Papers). Bronte and her puppies were Frémont family dogs at Bear Valley (E. B. FRÉMONT, 110).

3. JBF's New York physician, William Van Buren, was in Washington for meetings of the U.S. Sanitary Commission, of which he was a founding member (STRONG, 3:178–80).

4. James Barrett Swain (1820–95) was a New York *Times* correspondent in Washington in 1860–61, who had edited pro-Frémont publications during the 1856 campaign. Lincoln appointed him a second lieutenant in the First Cavalry on Nov. 1 (LINCOLN, 4:501n). Swain's name and address appear to be in another hand.

To Abraham Lincoln

[Sept. 12 (1861)]

To the President of the United States:

I was told yesterday by Mr. F. P. Blair Sr. that five days since a letter was received from his son Colonel F. P. Blair, containing certain statements respecting Genl. Frémont and his military command in the Western Department: which letter was submitted to you as President.

I was further told by Mr. Blair that, on that letter you sent Postmaster Genl. Blair to St. Louis to examine into that Department, and report.

On behalf of, and as representing General Frémont, I have to request that I be furnished with copies of that letter, and any other communications, if any, which in your judgment have made that investigation necessary.

I have the honor to be, Very Respectfully,

Jessie Benton Frémont.

Willards Hotel, Washington City. September 12th.[1]

ALS (DLC—Lincoln Papers).

1. For Lincoln's reply to this and JBF's second note to him, see Sept. 12 [1861], note 2, below.

To Abraham Lincoln

[Sept. 12 (1861)]

Mrs. Frémont begs to know from the President if his answer to Genl. Frémont's letter can be given to her without much farther delay.[1]

Mrs. Frémont is anxious to return to her family and takes the liberty of asking a reply by the messenger.[2]

Willards Hotel
Sep. 12th.

AL (DLC—Lincoln Papers).

1. In answer to JCF's Sept. 8 letter, Lincoln wrote that he "very cheerfully" complied with JCF's request to make "an open order" to modify the proclamation in regard to the "liberation of slaves." Through some misunderstanding, Lincoln sent his reply to JCF by mail rather than giving it to JBF. Lincoln dated his answer Sept. 11, but in a copy of the letter given to the press, the president wrote across the top of the first page, "The following letter from the President to Gen. Fremont was transmitted to the latter by mail, on the 12th Inst." On Sept. 16, when JCF still had not received the letter, he telegraphed the president: "I have seen in the papers your published telegram to me. The original has never reached me. Shall I act on that?" (LINCOLN, 4:517–18).

2. Lincoln replied to JBF the same day (Sept. 12): "Your two notes of to-day are before me. I answered the letter you bore me from Gen. Fremont, on yesterday; and not hearing from you during the day, I sent the answer to him by mail.

"It is not exactly correct, as you say you were told by the elder Mr. Blair, to say that I sent Post-Master-General Blair to St. Louis to examine into that Department, and report. Post-Master-General Blair did go, with my approbation, to see and converse with Gen. Frémont as a friend.

"I do not feel authorized to furnish you with copies of letters in my possession without the consent of the writers.

"No impression has been made on my mind against the honor or integrity of Gen. Fremont; and I now enter my protest against being understood as acting in any hostility towards him. Your Obt. Servt A. Lincoln" (LINCOLN, 4:519).

To John Charles Frémont

[Sept. 12?, 1861]

The countersign is still *Lerida*. All made satisfactory here to-day. Attend only to the country's enemies. Have not received your letters, but got the good telegraphs from home. I leave to morrow morning. Telegraph Billings fully about cavalry equipments, and write also. I am really well.

J.B.F.

To Maj. Genl. Frémont
Head Qrs. St. Louis Mri.

AD (telegram) initialed (CLjC).

To Isaac Sherman

Saturday night. [Sept. 28, 1861]

My dear Mr. Sherman,

Your nephew[1] left last night for Jefferson City with Lieutenant's straps on his shoulders, he may bring back a higher grade. The General will see to him when he is there. Charley went with his Father—he said, when he was told that the cannon balls would whistle around him—he "didn't think there would be any of his size." If Price[2] stays still he can be cut to pieces, if not it is the repetition of the French army in Spain.[3] There is immense work to do here. To day some money is to arrive—a million, it is said. Too late to give saddles & bridles to our cavalry who have taken the field—for the greater part—with rope halters, & on bare backed horses, and armed with spears like Indians. The contractors in Cincinnati decline to send on the things made by them, cavalry equipment & clothing, for fear their contracts will not hold good as it is possible the Genl. may be removed.

I hope you will never find fault with my giving a copy of your letter before it went to you.[4] Some things here made it immediately necessary & as the Genl. has left I had to [line illegible].

The Genl. gave an unconditional release to Frank Blair at the request of his brother "for public reasons" but it was generosity thrown away as we knew it would be. He was ordered to resume his sword & join his regiment for duty. He refused on the ground his character had been attacked & he must defend it.[5]

Good night. I am interrupted & tired but will keep you posted. Mr. Billings will be at Astor House when you get this. He can tell you everything.

AL (editors' copy). After the disastrous Union defeat at Lexington, Mo., on Sept. 21, Frémont resolved to take the field and drive the rebel forces from Missouri. On Sept. 26, he set out for Jefferson City, 120 miles west of St. Louis, where he would mass nearly forty thousand troops to pursue the enemy southward. Meanwhile, JBF remained in virtual command at their St. Louis headquarters.

1. The nephew was Freeman De Witt Clarke (1838–89), a son of Sherman's half-brother, banker Freeman Clarke of Rochester, N.Y. (New York *Tribune,* Dec. 2, 1861; WARD, 327).

2. Gen. Sterling Price (1809–67), a Mexican War veteran and former Missouri governor, had joined the Confederate cause in June 1861. Leading Missouri volunteer troops, he had helped defeat the Union forces at Wilson's Creek and Lexington.

3. During Napoleon's disastrous Peninsular Campaign, 1807–13, Spanish guerrilla forces hobbled several hundred thousand invading French troops in a long, bleeding war. In Missouri, marauding pro-Confederate bands had been successful in similar hit-and-run raids. Since JCF was now pursuing Price deep into southwestern Missouri, JBF seems to be suggesting that if Price refused to stand and fight, the Union army could be worn down by guerrilla tactics.

4. JBF refers to a Sept. 26, 1861, letter from JCF to Sherman, the original in JBF's handwriting, published in the Sept. 28 New York *Tribune*. In it JCF lamented having to face not only the enemy in the field but "the enemy at home." In phrases that could be JBF's, he stated: "It is a shame to the country that an officer going to the field, his life in his hands, solely actuated by the desire to serve his country and win for himself its good opinions . . . should be destroyed by a system of concentrated attacks utterly without foundation. Charges are spoken of when there are none to be made. . . . Already our credit, which was good, is shaken in consequence of the newspaper intimations of my being removed. . . . To defend myself would require the time that is necessary to and belongs to my duty against the enemy. If permitted by the country, this state of things will not fail to bring on disorder." The New York *Tribune* later cited this letter as JCF's only lapse from an otherwise "manly" silence, despite his ill treatment by the Lincoln administration, and conjectured that it had been written "by a secretary, and published by some injudicious friend" (Oct. 30, 1861).

5. Just after JBF's return from Washington, JCF had arrested Frank Blair for "insidious and dishonorable efforts to bring my authority into contempt with the government," an action Montgomery Blair believed was " 'Genl' Jessie's doings altogether." In response to a plea from Montgomery, JCF released Frank but rearrested him after Frank sent a long list of countercharges against JCF to Lincoln through Adj. Gen. Lorenzo Thomas. On Oct. 1, Gen. Winfield Scott ordered his unconditional release. For details, see "Great Events," 278; Montgomery Blair to W. O. Bartlett, Sept. 26, 1861, telegram to JCF, Sept. 19, 1861, and draft letter to JCF, Sept. 20, 1861, all in DLC—Blair Papers; Frank Preston Blair, Jr., to Lorenzo Thomas, Sept. 26, 1861, DLC—Lincoln Papers; E. B. SMITH [1], 301–3; New York *Tribune*, Sept. 28, Oct. 1, 7, 10, 1861; New York *Times*, Sept. 17, 28, 29, 1861; New York *Herald*, Oct. 9, 1861.

To Frederick Billings

[Oct. 12 (1861)]

My dear Mr. Billings,

I sent you a dispatch last night in answer to your letter of the 1st which, with Mr. Sherman's, had followed the Genl. to Tipton[1] & from there was sent by him to me. Mr. Cameron is here[2] & will leave for the camp at one o'clock to day if not prevented by dispatches hourly expected from Genl. Frémont. Not many people are willing to travel through an enemy's country even in the rear of an army. But I trust he will go on & see Mr. Frémont. If he has not already made his decision in Washington (and I think he has too much cleverness for that) he will have his eyes wonderfully opened, & have some facts to carry back which will turn the tide. As it is he must recognize many mis-statements have been made although here all that meet him are of the Blair clique—the good men have gone to the war & the slanderers only are left.

I hope you received the muster rolls. They were sent to you at the Astor House enclosed to Mr. Stetson.[3] So many letters fail to reach us that we employ only the Express & don't trust the Post office.

What a way to help one's country—rebels to front of him, slanderers & spies all around him & a malignant stealthy cabinet using every engine at its disposal to destroy him.

The latest is to restore De Ahna to his rank as Col. after being dismissed for cause. The cause given was enough but there were many other reasons also. He was degraded in the same way by Garibaldi for making money by his place—as he did here, & making debts on debts for personal luxuries & refusing payment—swindling in fact.[4] At the same time Mr. Frémont's commissions are declared valueless. Take one example. Capt. Totten[5]—24 years an officer in regular service—never a brevet even for Mexico or for Springfield where his battery did such heroic work. Mr. Frémont makes him head of the artillery with a Col.'s commission. That is refused & a swindler, dismissed by a regular court martial Genl. Pope presiding, restored to rank & pay. Now Totten & all the others have their feelings chilled as they go into battle. If success comes the Times, speaking for its owners says only the grossest incompetency could fail with such an army so appointed & officered.[6] If it fails will they ever tell the truth?

I have thought of these things and pictured my brave husband battling with these moral snow storms until I have given way under it. It is too much for the body to bear if the mind must. One of the low fevers of the country has fastened on me & yesterday I was too ill to answer your letter except by the dispatch Lily took down for me.

This morning I will get up & see Mr. Cameron who has promised to come. He may or may not do so. I don't know anyone who will speak the truth without fear or favor but myself & though my Dr. says I shall not yet I shall get up for an hour. It may do real good. At all events he cannot after that say he did not know the truth.

I send you several newspaper slips & remarks—it's an economy of strength to let print talk. Dr. Lieber, Mrs. Shaw[7] of Staten Island & some others whose names I shall enclose ought to see you. If you see

Mrs. Shaw you will want to marry one of her beautiful daughters & be son in law to her beautiful self. She is sister to Sturgis of the Barings.

J.B.F.

October 12th.

AL initialed (Billings Mansion Archives).

1. JCF's troops were encamped near Tipton, 160 miles west of St. Louis.

2. Lincoln had dispatched Secretary of War Simon Cameron (1799–1889) and Adj. Gen. Lorenzo Thomas (1804–75) to investigate the tangled Missouri situation. Cameron carried a general order for JCF's dismissal, to deliver at his discretion. Lizzie Lee, reading of Cameron's journey, remarked: "I see Jessie who moves by 'Special trains' is back in St. Louis [from a visit to JCF at Jefferson City] to meet Cameron. I hope the wily Scot will be her match at least in cunning if nothing else" (to Francis Preston Blair, Oct. 12 [1861], DLC—Blair Papers).

3. Charles Augustus Stetson (1810–88) was the well-known proprietor of the fashionable Astor House hotel in New York City.

4. In an early Sept. 1861 court-martial presided over by Brig. Gen. John Pope (1822–92), German-born Col. Henry Charles De Ahna had been sentenced to dismissal from the army for "conduct unbecoming an officer and a gentleman" (New York *Times,* Sept. 6, 1861). According to the St. Louis *Democrat,* De Ahna had been "broken" by JCF (who had approved the sentence) because he had used "violent and insulting language" while passing sentries at JCF's headquarters, saying "D——d Body Guard. Hungarian humbug" (quoted in New York *Times,* Sept. 29, 1861). While De Ahna may have been temporarily restored to his rank, possibly at Frank Blair's behest, his promotion to brigadier general would be rejected by the Senate on Apr. 25, 1862, after Gen. Henry Halleck accused him of accepting bribes (De Ahna to Lincoln, May 30, 1862, DLC—Lincoln Papers). Meanwhile, Frank Blair, Jr., had requested Lincoln to assign De Ahna to McClellan's staff, but this appointment seems never to have been made (Blair to Lincoln, May 13, 1862, ibid.). In early 1864, Treasury Secretary Salmon P. Chase came to suspect that De Ahna was involved in a rebel plot that again involved bribery. Despite De Ahna's claims of innocence, he was evidently never able to clear his name (see De Ahna to Lincoln, Jan. 31, Feb. 10, 1864, ibid.)

5. As JCF fell into disfavor, the Lincoln administration refused to recognize his commissions (New York *Tribune,* Oct. 8, 1861). One of those affected was James Totten (c. 1818–71), a West Point graduate from Pennsylvania, whom JCF had promoted to major on Aug. 19 and chief of artillery with the rank of lieutenant-colonel on Sept. 1. Totten would eventually be breveted for gallant and meritorious services in action at Boonville, Mo., and at Wilson's Creek (near Springfield), perhaps in part because the New York *Tribune* publicized the oversight (Oct. 12, 1861). Totten was promoted to major on Nov. 12 by JCF's successor, but he would not reach lieutenant-colonel until 1867. Breveted brigadier general in 1865, he was dismissed from service in 1870 for "disobedience of orders," "neglect of duty," and "conduct to the prejudice of good order and military discipline" (CULLUM, 2:89–90).

6. The New York *Times* favored the Blairs in the feud while the *Tribune* (although not all its correspondents) supported JCF. By early October the *Times* had become outspokenly critical, and JBF's paraphrase echoes several recent editorials: "It will be a sorry result indeed if so perfect an army, under such splendid officers, shall fail to

win back some of the prestige lost in Missouri" (Oct. 3, 1861). And, "There is little doubt that Gen. Fremont is now fully prepared for an encounter with Price, and that whenever he does start in pursuit of him, it will be with an army confident of success, and with appointments which only bad generalship can render insufficient" (Oct. 8, 1861).

7. Sarah Blake (Sturgis) Shaw (1815–1902) of New Brighton, Staten Island, was a dedicated abolitionist who numbered among her friends Lydia Maria Child and, before their deaths, Margaret Fuller and Elizabeth Barrett Browning. She was the daughter (not the sister, as JBF writes) of Nathaniel Russell Sturgis, a wealthy Boston merchant associated with the influential London banking firm of Baring Brothers. Sarah Shaw, as well as her husband, philanthropist Francis George Shaw, strongly supported JCF in 1856. The Shaws had four daughters and a son (L. M. CHILD, passim; New York *Times* obit., Dec. 31, 1902; STRONG, 2:290).

To Isaac Sherman

[Oct. 15?, 1861]

My dear Mr. Sherman,

A letter from you of the 9th October came this morning and after reading—(and approving it) I send it on by a safe hand tomorrow to Mr. Frémont.

The copy of Mr. Frémont's last letter to me will shew you how much foundation there is for looking to Washington for help or aid of any kind.[1] Genl. Cameron may mean well or he may mean to color previous intentions by a flying visit here. He came with a well considered plan, sprang it at the Genl. and as far as I know gave him no assurances that he should have anything but a "chance." Mr. Frémont, unfortunately for himself & his work, is not a man to make terms. The command should not have been left to him by the Secty. unless he supported it in a way to render it effective.

On his return,—he was only a very few hours in camp,—he ordered the fortifications to be suspended & at the [text missing] payment of officers commissioned by the Genl. refused to them by the Quarter Master.[2]

The fortifications are some of them finished, not stored or guns mounted. Those ordered by Mr. Frémont were finished in 25 days. Those begun by the govt. a month previous are not finished. This also stops the employment of several thousand men in various ways & renews the discontent & want among the Irish & our own laboring people. The sewing for the troops which gave employment to over a thousand women, also is cut up & the future work is to be done through Washington.[3]

This town is only held by the German strength for the American Union force is less than that of the American secession. The Germans are tired of fruitless patriotism. They are rewarded for their early services by being called Dutch & finding the papers chorus against foreigners being employed. (Let a foreigner be a Prince & it's all right) but Seigel [Sigel] is all wrong.[4] The last insult to Hecker will turn all Germans more from the administration for he is known to have had efficiency rendered impossible by the jealousies & quarrels of his officers & their various bad qualities.[5] Restoring them, restoring De Ahna, different such acts making a certain reversal of sentence in Washington against any discipline attempted here, demoralizes an army. This, the general order, whispered around by the drunken Wilkinson [Wilkeson],[6] proclaimed by the Blair set, & virtually sustained by the stopping of Mr. Fremont's plans here & the non payment of officers necessary to him—these things defeat an army before it takes the field. For one thing, for a purely selfish view I wish Mr. Frémont had had the drums rolled & the force called together & then bid Mr. Cameron read his secret order aloud.

Three wagon loads of broken muskets were brought for mending to the arsenal after the news that Wool was to come here in Mr. Frémont's place.[7] They were broken by the troops at Benton Barracks in their rage at the news. The officers there came to town to avoid being called on to take notice of what they could not have stopped. That night the Germans who were organizing their Home Guard, stoned a Mr. How[8] friend of Mr. Blair who came to address them, & made a committee of fifty to take Frank Blair & hang him as the source of the trouble. That was fortunately stopped by the longer headed among them who suggested they should wait until the truth was known from Head Qrs. Their committee came here & the telegraph from Mr. Seward—so true to himself, true as to words, false in spirit & intention—quieted them. But they resolved, & have, stopped all further organization until they are assured that Mr. Frémont remains in command here.

Yesterday, on the part of five thousand Germans, I had a letter & visit from one representing them.[9] They know that whatever is done outwardly the real animus of the Govt. is to break down the Genl. & make success impossible to him. So they say that with the fortifications stopped & the Genl. taken from them their hope of protection is ended & better peace with Jefferson Davis than the rule of Frank Blair. This fire only waits a signal to be ten thousand here & wherever Germans are in this West and North West. The universal feeling is they have been patriotic in vain & are used & flung aside for politicians.

I do not know Mr. Cameron in a way that enables me to think him a man who seeing & knowing the truth dares single handed to sustain it. I am told by those who know him well that he is true to a promise & makes no offer that he does not sustain. He may have some queer understanding as to how he is sustaining the Genl. but it seems to simple minds like pulling away props.

It is a very very difficult position & Mr. Cameron was in the highest degree unfair & unjust in giving no time for thought on such a matter, & I am very sure, no promises that it should be justly & fairly an honest opportunity for success.

Look at it

The President nullifies his means of punishing rebels.

The Secretary at War nullifies his protection of St. Louis & removes all danger from enemies within & without the town & many of Price's army are here & gathering in daily.

The Germans are cast off by the want of respect to their wishes & the ignoring of their military & political services — the Irish who were nearly all secession had become five thousand the other way but now will relapse.

With this Mr. Frémont is sent on against an enemy whose government I was yesterday informed through a private secession source (& as an act of personal feeling from an old acquaintance) is sending Genl. Johnston of Kentucky to finish the work in M[issou]ri.[10]

I have gotten that information vouched for & sent on to Mr. Frémont this morning. Also that the city is defenceless from the German feeling & the want of fortifications. It must modify all his plans. I will try to go to him myself tomorrow but the best will cannot govern one's body always & I am for the last week very tired with fever which keeps me without appetite or enough sleep & makes me nervous.

But I must see him & talk to him. He must feel how deadly & treacherous is the enemy in the rear & know how strong is the united force against him.

With all this if you wish a surface view it is easy enough to say I look only at the worst aspect. Did I in Washington? Was I wrong about that raging wicked old man [Blair] who boasted he could & would "unmake" Mr Frémont & have not he & all his [house?] done everything that nature & education in wicked political warfare can suggest?

The general tells me he will wring some success out of things yet, but even his firm will cannot do miracles. I hope but I do not believe & you must take this as a Cassandra view, as the other was.

This is for Mr. Billings as well as yourself. My head aches so much it is hard to write at all but Mr. Eliot will leave at 3 & I want you to know him.[11] He represents all that is honorable & of good repute in St. Louis for 27 years & knows facts.

Mr. Howard[12] has returned from camp—they have moved on all in high spirits & intending success, replying on truth & ultimate justice & bringing it about by their own right hands.

I must close this—share it with such friends as are friends indeed. Why is it that an editor of the Tribune drinks so much that he is confidential with railway acquaintances. Of the four who went with the Secty. only one did not drink—the others did all the time & Mr. Wilkinson [Wilkeson] most of all & yet tens of thousands of people will rely on his statements.

J. B. Frémont

My fear is growing so high that I see I can't rely on myself for work.

ALS (editors' copy).

1. In his letter to JBF, JCF described his Oct. 13 meeting with Secretary of War Cameron, who agreed to withhold, at least temporarily, the order he carried relieving JCF of his command so that JCF could continue his pursuit of Price. "But I much doubt whether the Administration will permit me to make any progress. . . . Do not be the least uneasy or discouraged, it is really now a matter of indifference whether I retire from this business or not. It has become almost too disgusting to endure" (Oct. [14?] 1861), editors' copy). After seeing JCF, Cameron reported to Lincoln: "I had an interview with General Fremont, and . . . showed him an order for his removal. He was very much mortified, pained, and, I thought, humiliated. He made an earnest appeal to me . . . that he was in pursuit of the enemy, who he believed were within his reach; and that to recall him at this moment would not only destroy him, but render his whole expedition useless" (NICOLAY & HAY, 4:430).

2. On Oct. 14, Cameron had suspended payment to all officers whose commissions had not been approved by the president and on all contracts until they had been investigated in Washington. He also stopped the construction of fortifications around St. Louis, one of JCF's most controversial projects (OFFICIAL RECORDS, ser. 1, vol. 3:532–33).

3. Critics had charged that the California firm of Beard and Palmer was making exorbitant profits in constructing the St. Louis fortifications. They also suspected favoritism in awarding the contract, since E. L. Beard had reputedly worked a quartz

mill on the Mariposas estate while Joseph Palmer was a longtime business associate of JCF. For charges against Beard and Palmer, see the Thomas Report in OFFICIAL RECORDS, ser. 1, vol. 3:542, 550; and Special House Committee on Government Contracts, 37th Cong., 2d sess., *Report* 2, serial 1142, pp. 73–83, 916–20, and serial 1143, pp. xlvi–xlvii, 696, 1485–89. JCF later defended both the firm and contract, arguing that in the emergency he had faced, quick results were more important than economy (JCF statement on his administration of the Western Department, New York *Tribune*, Mar. 4, 1862; see also Beard's defense of his project in Joint Committee on the Conduct of the War, 37th Cong., 3rd sess., *Report*, 3:270–79).

4. Along with JCF, Franz Sigel had received much of the blame for the Union defeat at Wilson's Creek: it was reportedly Sigel's battle plan that Lyon had followed, and during the fight, Sigel's brigade had retreated in disarray after confusing Louisiana with Union troops because their uniforms were at that time a similar gray (see OFFICIAL RECORDS, ser. 1, vol. 3:60–71, 86–88; SCOFIELD, 43–44; ROWAN & PRIMM, 280n).

5. Former German revolutionary leader Frederick Hecker had quarreled with some of the officers in the regiment he commanded and persuaded JCF to dismiss them. Since they had been commissioned by the governor of Illinois and could not be discharged without a court-martial, Secretary of War Cameron reinstated them, pending an investigation. Hecker eventually resigned over such problems but later effectively commanded another Illinois regiment (KOERNER, 2:150–51, 193–94; New York *Times*, Oct. 15, 1861).

6. The New York *Tribune*'s Washington correspondent, earthy, hard-drinking Samuel Wilkeson (1817–89) had studied law under Judge Daniel Cady and married a sister of Elizabeth Cady Stanton. A close associate of Secretary of War Cameron, Wilkeson had accompanied him and Adjutant General Thomas to St. Louis on their investigative mission for Lincoln. JBF's charge of drunkenness was also suggested by a Columbus, Ohio, reporter, who noted the "unmilitary" condition of both Thomas and Wilkeson during their railroad journey to Tipton to see JCF, which "entirely unfitted them . . . for doing justice to anyone" (ANDREWS, 43–44, 131n). Through Wilkeson, the *Tribune* would confirm that Cameron had carried a secret order for JCF's removal (Oct. 20, 1861); it would also be the first to publish Thomas's highly critical report of JCF on Oct. 30.

7. The news that Lincoln had summoned Brig. Gen. John E. Wool (1789–1869) to Washington for consultations had led to rumors that Wool would either replace JCF or preside over his court-martial (New York *Times*, Oct. 4, 1861; New York *Tribune*, Oct. 5, 1861). At 8 P.M. on Oct. 3, JCF aide B. Rush Plumly had telegraphed the War Department: "From the reports of General Fremont's removal we are in a state of incipient revolution. Committees besiege the headquarters; mass meetings are being prepared all over town; all is excitement and rage among Union people. If he is removed, don't be surprised at anything the people do" (OFFICIAL RECORDS, ser. 1, vol. 3:517). Secretary of State Seward immediately telegraphed: "Gen. Fremont is not ordered to Washington, nor from the field, nor is any court-martial ordered concerning this" (quoted in New York *Times*, Oct. 6, 1861). Plumly replied: "Your dispatch has revolutionized the town with joy. We send it to all the hotels and to the public meetings now in session and to Camp Benton. There is great rejoicing. All thank you" (OFFICIAL RECORDS, ser. 1, vol. 3:517).

8. Former St. Louis mayor and merchant John How (1813–85) had sided with Frank Blair in his feud with JCF (HOLLI & JONES, 171). In fact, JCF later testified that the quarrel actually began when he and his chief quartermaster, Justus McKinstry, refused to grant a large clothing and equipment contract to How and another Blair associate. For details, see JBF to Colfax, Dec. 30 [1861], note 3, below.

9. JBF enclosed a printed copy of the letter. Presented to Secretary of War Cameron upon his arrival in St. Louis, it asked that the government give Frémont its "most zealous, active, and efficient support" and asserted that his dismissal would cause "utter confusion, demoralization of the army in the field, great damage to the recruiting service, and wide-spread dissatisfaction of the people of the West."

10. JBF's fear of an attack on St. Louis had some basis in fact. As the new commander of the western region of the Confederacy, Gen. Albert Sidney Johnston (1803–62) had recently reinforced Columbus, Ky., just fifteen miles south of the Union stronghold at Cairo, adding to speculation that he was preparing to attack Cairo and St. Louis. Moreover, on Oct. 16, Gen. Sterling Price would write him that St. Louis was "almost defenseless, and may have an important bearing on your operations." Price wrote again on Nov. 7 to suggest that Johnston threaten St. Louis to force Frémont north to protect it, leaving him open to entrapment between the two Confederate forces (OF-FICIAL RECORDS, ser. 1, vol. 3:720, 729, 731–32; SHALHOPE, 184–87). Despite Price's urging, Johnston, convinced that he lacked adequate troops and arms, made no plans either to aid Price or to attack Union forces in Missouri himself. However, Johnston was also attempting to create an illusion of strength to prevent a Union attack, and the information JBF received about a Confederate offensive under Johnston may have been a deliberately planted falsehood, designed to conceal Johnston's own weakness. For details of Johnston's plans during this period, see ROLAND, 260–72, and JOHNSTON, 318, 325. Ironically, Johnston was a Kentucky relative of JBF, and his first wife, Henrietta Preston, had been a favorite cousin of JBF's mother (JOHNSTON, 23).

11. William G. Eliot was going east on Sanitary Commission business, but he would also meet with Lincoln to plead that JCF not be replaced. For Eliot's defense of JCF, see Eliot to Salmon P. Chase, Wednesday, 4:30 A.M. [Oct. 1861] and Eliot's Aug. 18, 1886, account of his interview with Lincoln, copies in "Great Events," 316–20.

12. "Mr. Howard" was most probably John Tasker Howard, JCF's longtime political and business associate, rather than his son, John Raymond Howard, who had become a private secretary on JCF's staff with the rank of captain. Howard, Sr., made several trips to St. Louis during this period as an arms purchasing agent. According to testimony before a congressional investigating committee, he was acting as J. P. Morgan's lawyer in a complex deal in which Simon Stevens, later a JCF aide, using money borrowed from Morgan, had purchased five thousand "useless" government surplus Hall's carbines for $12.50 each, refurbished them, and resold them to Frémont at $22 each. Others involved included George Opdyke and Morris Ketchum, who would be among the purchasers of Las Mariposas in 1863. The notorious Hall carbine deal is summarized in Special House Committee on Government Contracts, 37th Cong., 2d sess., *Report* 2, serial 1142, pp. 40–52, and serial 1143, pp. lxiv–lxxii; see also WASSON, a later account financed by Morgan funds.

To Frederick Billings

St. Louis
October 18th [1861].

My dear Mr. Billings,

Before this can reach you the telegraph will have told you of Mr. Frémont's movements.[1] "Boy's play" is an easy phrase to men who read their morning paper in a comfortable room & know no greater hardship than waiting for an omnibus to carry them through the rain down town. The steady forward march made by Mr. Frémont through not only rains & cold winds but with the far more chilling influences of a hostile administration and a doubting, if not blaming country, is not "boy's play."

That something true and loving, some reminder of all he leaves to serve his country, goes with him is not a fault. If he wins a victory it will be called a beautiful thought. It is neither that nor a whim. I have had more of the fair side of life than usually comes to one person. The result of what I have felt & seen is to make me more than willing that my children should die young. Charley begged to go—he said "I am as old as Casabianca"[2]—and in my heart if he should end his little life in his sincere belief that he is helping defend the flag, I should be glad for him that he had not lived to become changed into what men usually become. The loss to me will not be for long. I am wearing out with suspense & weariness of heart. Such simple true patriotism as we both brought to the work—honestly we thought it was the country to be served. But I am unworthy of my chief who writes to me that I must keep well & full of faith for he will wring success from all this yet.

Mr. Plumly[3] & the Revd. Mr. Eliot of this place will see you & the Genl's. other friends. But Mr. Frémont himself will best see to all false charges with the sword first & then the pen.

You will see Mr. Hopper, so long bookkeeper on the Mariposas[4]— he is to arrive with the Deweys & will give you the last information from there.

J. B. Frémont

Frank has gone to sleep. He shall have, & answer your message.

ALS (Billings Mansion Archives).

1. In pursuit of Price's army, which was rumored to be only thirty to fifty miles ahead, JCF's forces had moved forty miles southwest from Tipton to Warsaw, on the Osage River, in three days (JCF to JBF, Oct. 17, 1861, printed in J. B. FRÉMONT [2], 94).

2. In 1798, ten-year-old Giacomo Jocante de Casabianca died trying to save his wounded father, French naval officer Louis de Casabianca, when the latter refused to abandon his burning ship during the Battle of the Nile in Napoleon's Egyptian campaign. Charley probably learned the story from a popular ballad celebrating the boy's heroism written by the sentimental English poet, Mrs. [Felicia Dorothea] Hemans. Impressed

with Charley's bravery, staff officer Gustave Koerner admonished his wife: "Little Fremont, only ten years old, wants to go with the body-guard into the fight. Victor [the Koerners' son] should take an example, and not be afraid" (KOERNER, 2:179).

3. The author of a volume of Quaker poetry, Maj. Benjamin Rush Plumly (1816–87) of Philadelphia was an aide-de-camp on JCF's staff with special duties as postal director (SCHARF [2], 1:404). In 1864, conservative Attorney General Edward Bates would pronounce him "a scatter-brained zealot that teaches negro[e]s in Lou[isian]a" (BATES, 392).

4. John C. Hopper, formerly of New York, had edited the Mariposa *Chronicle*, 1854–55, and served as secretary of the Republican party in Mariposa County. In 1862, he would join JCF's staff in West Virginia as chief of scouts and spies. JBF later wrote that Hopper's "silence was as proverbial as his cool courage and high honor" (SARGENT, 48, 64–65; HEITMAN, 1:542; TRACY, 185).

To Ward Hill Lamon

[Oct. 26 (1861)]

General Lamon will find the copies he asked for enclosed.[1] The originals I had rather not risk in the mails & they would have to be returned to me as necessary parts of the evidence which may or may not be required — certainly will be, if Genl. Frémont's enemies succeed in carrying out their intention to remove him from this Dept.

On the transportation point, if the divisions under Genls. Hunter,[2] Pope & McKinstry[3] had had transportation enough — they do not march light as Genl. Frémont does — there would have been a complete victory over Price & his whole force about the 20–22d. But it is another chance gone.

There remains another which depends on the will of the Administration. It can take its choice between a victory that, followed up, will end the war & give peace by spring, or more delays — time & fine weather gone, snows & rains on land & ice in the rivers & dispirited soldiers. If any one had the power to put this truth clearly before Mr. Lincoln so that he would recognize it as the simple truth it would be a benefit rendered to the country. He is too prejudiced against me, I can't do it. I wish he could read the whole of Mr. Frémont's letters to me. He can be calm & just even in the midst of these injustices & wrongs. But when I think of this great rich country giving generously its men & money to end the war, & see our army in the field feeding only on meat & coffee, not a pound of flour, I speak of those at Warsaw & in advance under Sigel, of the poor muskets, of the delayed transportation, of the work stopped here on the gun boats for want of payment to the workmen, of the stopped fortifications, & then to crown all, daily despatches over wires governed by Washington that the leader whose whole past life has been one steady act of unselfish devotion to his country is to be taken from them to gratify private malice, I despair.

[Two lines blotted out.] I beg pardon for the blot but I have not the right to talk to you so except that I am getting to be like the ancient mariner & must tell my tale when I see the right man.

No better service can be rendered to the country just now than to settle promptly this vexed Dept. question.

To remove Mr. Frémont will be a great wrong as the necessary investigation following it will prove. It will make immense confusion & require all his control over his friends & the army to get them to do as he will—accept it as an act of authority not of justice—but in time of war it is treason to question authority.

To leave him here without money, without the moral aid of the govt. is treason to the people. I cannot find smoother phrases for it is the death struggle of our nationality and no time for fair words.

J.B. Frémont

St. Louis
26th October

ALS (DLC—Lincoln Papers). Ward Hill Lamon (1828–93), a former law partner and close friend of Abraham Lincoln, often served as the president's personal agent, as here in investigating the problems in the Western Department. JBF's Oct. 26 letter indicates Lamon had asked her for more information on the Missouri situation. On the same day, Lamon telegraphed the president: "Just returned from Warsaw. Saw Gen. Frémont. Doubt the policy of his removal. Will be Home in a few days" (DLC—Lincoln Papers). Unfortunately for the Frémonts, Lincoln had signed JCF's final dismissal order on Oct. 24.

1. JBF enclosed extracts from three JCF letters to her, dated Oct. 18, 19, and 20, 1861. In them, JCF expressed his eagerness to catch Price and make him fight, and his frustration and anger over the Lincoln administration's thwarting of his plans by cutting off funds, canceling contracts, and refusing to pay the officers he had appointed. Most immediately, he lacked wagons and mules to move his army: "Send me transportation and I will go ahead like a prairie on fire" (Oct. 20). JBF also included portions of these letters in J. B. FRÉMONT [2], 91–94, 108–10.

2. Maj. Gen. David Hunter (1802–86), a West Point graduate who was wounded at Bull Run, had accepted assignment as JCF's second in command at the president's personal request. Lincoln wrote Hunter on Sept 9: "Gen. Frémont needs assistance

which it is difficult to give him. He is losing the confidence of men near him. . . . His cardinal mistake is that he isolates himself. . . . He needs to have, by his side, a man of large experience. Will you not, for me, take that place? Your rank is one grade too high to be ordered to it; but will you not serve the country, and oblige me, by taking it voluntarily?" (LINCOLN, 4:513). Despite Lincoln's hopes, JCF did not confide in Hunter, who soon pronounced his commander "utterly incompetent" (OFFICIAL REC-ORDS, ser. 1, vol. 3:544–45).

3. It was unfortunate that when JCF arrived in St. Louis, the devious and corrupt Justus McKinstry (1814–97), a swashbuckling West Point graduate, was serving as chief quartermaster with responsiblity for purchasing war supplies. In the emergency, normal procedures such as competitive bidding could be ignored, allowing McKinstry to grant lucrative contracts to cronies in return for a share in the profits. While Frank and Montgomery Blair had been instrumental in getting McKinstry the position, his rep-utation in the army was already dark. Lizzie Lee had tried to warn her father about him: "I told you months ago he was a rogue. . . . Mary [Jesup Blair] says Genl. [Thomas Sidney] Jesup thought him 'dishonest' & he gave him endless trouble & that she heard him say that he never staid a year anywhere without giving disgust to citizens as well as Army people" (Sept. 15, 1861, DLC—Blair Papers). JCF, both naive and careless, ignored McKinstry's dubious activities and in September promoted him to brigadier general commanding one of the five divisions JCF was leading in pursuit of Price's army. After JCF's dismissal, McKinstry was court-martialed. Although JCF testified on his behalf, the evidence was overwhelming, and McKinstry was dismissed from the army for defrauding the government. Despite the conviction, he served as a political operative for JCF during the 1864 presidential campaign and developed a successful postwar career as a New York City stockbroker and Missouri land agent. For further details, see LONGACRE; WEIGLEY, 187–97; Special House Committee on Government Contracts, 37th Cong., 2d sess., *Report* 2, serials 1142–43, passim, and particularly 1142, pp. 83–136, for the committee summary.

To Dorothea Dix

[late Oct. 1861]

My dear Miss Dix,

The General sends a letter on public business which should reach the President.[1] The ordinary means being unreliable we send a bearer of dispatches who will do what he is told & convey it to the President in person. I have given him a note to Mr. Hay, Secty. to the President,[2] but as you are the only leader of a forlorn hope that I can count on in that subjugated province & he may fail with Mr. Hay, I have to ask that you will aid him to place it in the President's hand.

I can but think that if the President had had one interview with Mr. Frémont there never would have grown up this state of injury to the public service[3]—two honest men can quickly understand each other but the same good brain & bad heart that made the President so unjust and deaf to me has influenced not only the President but the newspapers of the kind that don't offend Govt. patronage. The truth has to come out victorious finally. Mr. Frémont can well afford to wait, but this lost time can never be regained for the country. Soon the river will be filling with ice & land work will be harder than the Valley Forge records. While it is yet day the work should be done. All we knew in the early summer, of the intrigues with France is becoming more & more sorrowfully apparent. If the south can bring themselves to play that last card—& you know as I do that Mr. Slidell[4] is a gambler every way—politically as well as with money—their recognition by both England and France is very near. The worst would be that with all their enormities they would have the moral triumph too. You know from long experience abroad that America was neither loved nor hated, but very much feared & very much resented. Their chance has come to push us back and they will not lose it. The double bait of free trade & gradual emancipation (*very gradual* it will be) but enough to make a pretext for England, will not be repulsed by them & Slidell has the backing of the Rosthchilds [Rothschilds]. Their feelings have been sufficiently shewn in the [London] Times. This is our last chance—it's a very hard pull but a strong pull, above all a *pull together* will bring us through. My dear chief is doing his duty—he will do it for the country whatever he meets, but it's a shame & a crime to hamper & as far as they can disable him when so much depends on his success. There is nobody however to tell the President the truth & he is being ringed in by the evil minded of the Cabinet. Well—we will hope for our country & its Cause care proportionate to that which "marks the sparrow's fall."[5] We must do our best but we cannot influence that Power only strive to deserve the final "well done" which He never fails to give to the true & faithful servants.

Your hospital friends have done noble work here. I tell you nothing of them for you have had Mr. Eliot with you. He ought to be back soon. I have missed his faith & goodness in these late days of trial. I have not Mr. Frémont's patience & I get ill & heart sore. But we two shall rest some day. Do pardon my crowded letter. I meant to write one page only, but have gone on talking to you it's such a relief to speak out.

J.B. Frémont.

ALS (CU-B—Frémont Papers).

1. JBF refers to JCF's Oct. 26 letter to Lincoln reporting that on Oct. 25, "Maj. [Charles] Zagonyi, of my Guards, as the head of only one hundred fifty men, charged and routed two thousand of the enemy . . . at Springfield" (DLC—Lincoln Papers). JBF would make this dashing attack the centerpiece of her book, *The Story of the Guard.*

2. JBF had met Lincoln's young private secretary, John Hay (1838–1905), in late August when he briefly visited St. Louis. Hay noted that JCF was "quiet, earnest, industrious, imperious" and JBF "very much like him though talking more and louder" (HAY, 26). Hay would become a prominent journalist and author, and, under Presidents William McKinley and Theodore Roosevelt, secretary of state. With John G. Nicolay, Lincoln's other private secretary, he wrote the monumental *Abraham Lincoln: A History* (10 vols., 1890), in which both JBF's meeting with Lincoln and JCF's Missouri administration are described critically and, in part, inaccurately.

3. Lincoln had also considered a personal meeting at one point. A copy of a Sept. 19 note from the War Department to JCF in the Lincoln Papers (DLC) requests JCF to come to Washington to talk with the president, while leaving Gen. David Hunter temporarily in command of the Western Department. The note was evidently never sent.

4. Former Louisiana senator John Slidell (1793–1871) had recently been named agent for the Confederate government in France. The "last card" JBF feared Slidell might play was a proposal to incorporate slaves into the Confederate army in exchange for their freedom, a plan for gradual emancipation that might persuade England and France to recognize the South and even intervene on its behalf. Slidell and other Confederate negotiators actually broached this plan to England and France in 1865, in a desperate attempt to prevent a final Confederate defeat. For a discussion of the plan, see OSWLEY, 530–41.

5. A common sentiment, probably from Matthew 10:29. A variation occurs in Shakespeare's *Hamlet,* act 5, sc. 2, l. 230–31.

To Ward Hill Lamon

[Oct. 30–31 (1861)]

I am very glad to avail myself of your asking for more facts & enclose you some which require very instant attention. The administration have the power to do as they like about removing officers but neither the power nor the excuse for perilling this State & the army now on the march in it.

That you may judge for yourself how deadly a virus is infused into the whole business I have only to refer you to the acts of Genl. Hunter.[1] It would be an unjustifiable act to put him in Mr. Frémont's place on the gossip collected by Genl. Thomas, but the administration can meet that issue better than the array of facts in regard to this command at present. From all I hear the President is only told one side & on the money part he is no doubt told what is true, that over a million has been sent here. But who tells him that it is not paid out, & that his Govt. officer Mr. Farrar,[2] announces it will not be paid out so long as Genl. Frémont remains in command here.

As for the letter of which you ask an extract I have not the right to copy that for it is to Mr. Frémont. It may be stretching a point not to copy what I gave you to read but I think I see a difference. I have been going over today other letters to the Genl. from Mr. Blair & others of equal position & I wonder at his magnaminity. But the time must come when they succeed in removing him. Better far to remove him if it is only then they will defend the State from secession. As it is now they are preparing all the horrors of war—unpaid workpeople have to meet cold as well as hunger—the soldiers on the march are suffering everything because requisitions here are not filled & now part of the army lags sixty miles in the rear carrying pilot bread[3] in the wagons they refused for the transport of ammunition. If this does not result in a massacre of the advance, it will be because some brave man influences the President to act promptly on the truth, or because God is always on the side of the oppressed.

J. B. Frémont

St. Louis
30th October

The incessant telegraphic & other uncontradicted statements from Washington that Genl. Frémont was to be removed, have produced results in this military command fatal to an army if not immediately altered. I will not ask of the officers in charge of the bureaus any official statement of facts—they have their obligations of position which do not allow them to furnish these until officially asked, but, I have my obligations equally great knowing the facts, to lay them before the only authority that can act summarily. Since Genl. Hunter was informed by Adj. Genl. Thomas that he was to take command of the Army, & the steady reports from Washington confirming him in that belief, he remains in the rear until within two days, at the railway terminus. Want of transportation is the excuse.

Genl. Frémont's express sent through after he started into Springfield, which he was to reach that night, had orders to Genl. Hunter, Genl. Pope & Genl. McKinstry to hurry up & especially to bring forward the ammunition at Tipton.[4] Wagons, mules & harness are in plenty at that point, but teamsters are yet wanting. They will require ready money

& although the Sub Treasury has a great deal yet we must believe the Sub Treasurer Mr. Farrar who says, "not a dollar will be paid out until Frémont is removed," since none is to the order of the QuarterMaster & none can be paid out. Genl. Pope had teamsters & many wagons complete. He utterly refused to spare any & loaded ten of them with pilot bread, leaving all the ammunition at Tipton. There is enough with the advance for an ordinary battle but not for contingencies. Genl. Hunter & himself are moving by slow marches, at a rate which will bring them to Springfield by the 7th of November. They say openly that Hunter will order the army back so that they do not trouble themselves to go forward.

With the aid of private enterprize we are arranging to day a supply train of ammunition to be pushed through to Genl. Frémont & reach him by Saturday. Maj. Allen[5] although personally hostile to Genl. Frémont does not let that interfere with his duty. I am glad to record this exception. But every engine that moneyed & political power, assuming & as yet without contradiction the authority of government sanction, can bring, has been brought to bear, to dishearten, demoralize & defeat the army. With what success, I leave Fredericktown, Lexington & Springfield to answer.[6] As the army goes on the mails are re-opened. The first since July left yesterday for Springfield; other towns along its route are already receiving theirs. If not prevented from Washington Genl. Frémont is certain of having this State quieted for the winter— which will be terribly hard at best on the devastated families every where the enemy has passed.

From the same disturbing cause, removal of Genl. Frémont, his plans & orders for the protection of the lines of travel are much & dangerously interfered with. Genl. Prentiss & Genl. Harding[7] are doing their utmost to enforce the instructions given them but Genl. Curtis does some fresh mischief daily[8]—partly from not understanding the true limits of his authority, partly because he listens to & pleases the heirs-apparent.

This state of things, bad in time of peace, is simply treason in time of war. No man however loved and believed in by his army & those who know him, can take the place of the law. In view of the united front & bold policy of the enemy, our distracted state here, encouraged by the silence of Washington, if not more decidedly by official communications—Genl. Thomas's for example—will lead simply to the destruction & massacre of the advance of the army. If the President could see the facts as they are he would be appalled at the result of this indecision. Genl. Frémont relies on his divisions under Hunter & Pope, on his supply train of ammunition & on the gun boats to co-operate with him in following up his land movements—certain of victories which would so greatly [aid in] terminating the war by the spring, relieving Missouri & Kentucky at once & preventing the immediate recognition of the Southern confederacy by France & Spain—perhaps England, but it is some time since he had reliable information from there.

But Hunter is waiting his authority to order the army back & Genl. Pope is of that inferior nature of man which runs to the rising sun. The ammunition we will get to him as fast as we can by private means—ten teamsters were sent up today but it's uphill work going to war on private resources. The gun boats have been so illy supplied with money that they will not be ready until ice has made the river travel impossible & all this time, the newspapers & the Govt. officers give positive names & dates of removal. Genl. Curtis sends a flag of truce to Price by an open secessionist to negotiate exchange of prisoners. Of course Genl. Frémont sends it back but in the meantime the man has studied our resources & informs Price.[9] In face Price is in good heart—knowing how effectually Mr. Frémont is being weakened—by finding an ally he had no right to look to for help—the govt. of the United States. For so long as this state of things continues they must be held as a [unit?]. That part which wishes & works for the removal of Genl. Frémont is less blood guilty than those who retain him but deprive him of the necessaries for his army.

Oct. 31.

I had written & copied a great deal to you. But the usual leakage at Washington makes public Genl. Thomas's & Genl. Hunter's plans. This explains to all why Hunter does not advance & why orders from Genl. Frémont are left unattended to. In addition to the distress & ill feeling among the poorer creditors of the govt—those who had worked on the fortifications, the boats, & the soldiers' clothing &c. is now added the danger of disloyalty from them. An officer came down last night to give information that at Tipton where great stores of ammunition & other supplies are banked up waiting transportation—no money in the QuarterMaster's power to move them—the rebels are gathering in tens & twenties.[10] Their plans are all made to take advantage of this state of things produced by the want of protection from Washington & unless there is an instant authority given to some one to be the military head, in fact & not in sham, there will be scenes which cannot be atoned for. The Govt. have no right to send Genl. Frémont out without the fullest security for his plans being sustained. They have no right to give him "a chance." It is not theirs to give or his to take. The people have a right to demand *certainties*. So far as lies in one man's power Genl. Frémont is making this, but it is impossible for him to protect any but the force immediately around him, when [many?] chief govt. officer[s?] as if in obedience to secret orders, delays disobeys & thwarts all his orders & plans. I refer you to Capt. Foote's[11] letter to the Navy Dept. To Major Allen's to the Q.M.'s Dept. (both of these are doing their duty honorably) for the proofs of criminal want of attention to the needs of this Dept. I cannot send to the chances of the Wash. P. O. Genl. Frémont's plans. If he had not been thwarted by these reports from Washington which leave him no real power things would have been done which would have gone far to procure peace. [on separate page] I send something more, of proof, by to-night's mail.

I find that I cannot write less strongly [than] the facts make me feel. If an instant determination is not made at Washington the blood be upon their heads.

J.B.F.

ALS (CSmH).

1. JBF refers to Hunter's reluctance, either from want of transportation (as Hunter asserted) or deliberate disobedience (as the Frémonts believed) to move his division to Springfield, where JCF's forces were massing in anticipation of a confrontation with the enemy. JBF may also have already seen Hunter's highly critical comments about JCF quoted in the New York *Tribune* on Oct. 30 when Adj. Gen. Lorenzo Thomas's report was made public.

2. Bernard Gaines Farrar, Jr. (1831–1916), had been an aide-de-camp to Gen. Nathaniel Lyon. Now hostile to the Frémonts, Farrar claimed that when he had tried to deliver an urgent message from Lyon just before the Wilson's Creek disaster, he had been forced to wait three days to see JCF (NEVINS [1], 493). After JCF's removal, Farrar became provost-marshal of the Western Department (OFFICIAL RECORDS ser. 1, vol. 8:405). Ironically, Farrar's father had been a close friend and political ally of Thomas Hart Benton, even serving as his physician during the notorious 1817 dual when Benton killed his opponent (CHAMBERS, 72–75).

3. Hardtack.

4. JCF's Oct. 30–31 orders to his generals can be found in OFFICIAL RECORDS, ser. 1, vol. 3:557–59.

5. Maj. Robert Allen (1812–86), a career army officer who had served since 1849

mainly in California, was the new army quartermaster at St. Louis. Allen had tried unsuccessfully to have his assignment changed because "General Frémont is aware I am not his friend, and he is surrounded by some half dozen of unscrupulous speculators from California, some of whom, *I know*, are with him by his own special invitation" (to Q. M. Gen. M. C. Meigs, Sept. 24, 1861, DNA-92, consolidated correspondence file: Allen, Col. Robert.) Soon after his arrival in St. Louis, the Thomas report quoted Allen as finding "great irregularities" in his department (OFFICIAL RECORDS, ser. 1, vol. 3:542).

6. On Oct. 21, Union forces under Col. J. B. Plummer had routed rebel troops near Fredericktown, Mo. (OFFICIAL RECORDS, ser. 1, vol. 3:206-9). While the Sept. 20 battle at Lexington had been a major disaster for the Union, JBF refers to a daring and successful Oct. 16 raid on the town in which Confederate arms and supplies were seized and Union prisoners released (ibid., 246-47). Springfield was seized by Zagonyi's Guards on Oct. 25.

7. Col. Chester Harding, Jr. (1826-75), had been assistant adjutant general on Gen. Nathaniel Lyon's staff, and briefly on JCF's, before assuming command of a regiment. The Harvard-educated son of a noted portrait painter, he would practice law in St. Louis after the war (SCHARF [2], 2:1493; HEITMAN, 1:500; Joint Committee on the Conduct of the War, 37th Cong., 2d sess., *Report*, 3:254, 258).

8. Brig. Gen. Samuel Ryan Curtis (1805-66) commanded Benton Barracks, the large Union army training camp outside St. Louis. A West Point graduate and three-term Republican congressman, he had resigned his office to serve in the war. Lincoln, wanting "an intelligent unprejudiced, and judicious opinion from some professional Military man on the spot," had written Curtis on Oct. 7 to ask whether JCF should be replaced; Curtis had replied in the affirmative (LINCOLN, 4:549). Curtis's newest "mischief" was probably his statement, recently made public in the Thomas report, that JCF was "unequal to the command of an army" (OFFICIAL RECORDS, ser. 1, vol. 3:541).

9. Asst. Adj. Gen. Chauncey McKeever also cited this as insubordination in testimony regarding JCF's Missouri command (Joint Committee on the Conduct of the War, *Report*, 3:251-52).

10. A messenger from Col. George Washington Deitzler at Tipton had reported that rebel forces were gathering on the Missouri above Booneville, threatening Tipton and Sedalia. "Very much alarmed," Deitzler asked for reinforcements. McKeever, JCF's assistant adjutant general in St. Louis, ordered Curtis to send six companies of the First Iowa Cavalry to reinforce Tipton but admitted he was not certain that Curtis would obey the order (McKeever to JCF, Oct. 31 [1861], copy by Elizabeth Benton Frémont in editors' possession).

11. Andrew Hull Foote (1806-63), commander of naval operations on the upper Mississippi, was the son of a Connecticut senator and thus known to JBF from Washington years. JBF had probably already seen his Oct. 31 letter to JCF, written from St. Louis, in which Foote detailed his problems in obtaining funds to complete, equip, and man his gun and mortar boat flotilla (CSmH). On Foote's eventual success with the flotilla, see JBF to Foote, Feb. 15 [1862], below.

To Isaac Sherman

[Printed letterhead]
Head Quarters. Western Department
[Oct. 31 or Nov. 1, 1861]

My dear Mr. Sherman,

Lily will make the copy of the asst. adgt's report for the day to Genl. Frémont. It is the result of interference from Wash. with his authority & the upsetting of his plans.[1]

A larger force is needed at Jeff. City on account of no fortifications allowed. Genl. Harding has come down to attend to it and a special train goes up with all that can be done to guard Tipton, but all Mr. Frémont's plans for protecting the line of march & rear of the army are altered by quarrelling officers Curtis, Pope &c. & by the doing away of the fortifications & especially by the want of money. This last order not to pay the reserve corps deprives St. Louis of its only reliable defence. They are chiefly Germans & used to war. But they speak their mind in their papers.[2]

Each general is on his own hook out here now & the State will quickly be gone to the rebels if this is not undone immediately.

The Govt. must not lose a moment in announcing what it has done for McClellan, that it will sustain him fully.[3] With that certainty the general uprising may be met no matter who is in command, for the army is fine & the supplies good but without it, the massacres that will follow rest on the President. I have sent full copies of this report & the causes for this state of things to him, & he will get them, as they go by sure hand.[4] He cannot plead ignorance. I will write you more fully tonight. Isn't it fine that Mr. Weed's letter was published before Springfield?[5] Look out [text missing] appointing. Match them if you can in the army of the East.

Mr. Frémont sent a letter to the President, written immediately after Springfield asking a confirmation of Zagonyi's commd. & "such promotion as he might judge fit to add." I had yesterday a despatch to say the letter was delivered into the President's hand. This at the cost of private messenger & a bribe to the porter that a communication of a victory from a Genl. in the field can reach Mr. Lincoln—if that Genl. is Genl. Frémont. It is nearly two months since Mr. Frémont has had any official recognition from Wash. His letters, dispatches & plan of campaign unanswered. Match me the Genl. who lifting this dead weight raises, equips & marches his force successfully. He is a perfect Dr. Windship[6] compared to the rest. When the time comes to have a Genl here who will be favored like McClellan with Govt. aid for the war, you will see what might have been if they had had love as well as money to inspire them. What will the country say to this appropriation to private vengeance of the blood & treasure it has given so gladly to restore peace. Is it for peace making it is used? Who misuses it? & then

why?

They cannot shirk the question. It is coming upon them & they will break down under it.

It is from Genl. Hunter again that this Weed letter has been furnished. Date & all shew that—& it is his regular talk.

Ask Mr. Billings if he is dead or gone away or why is he silent? My sister Mrs. Boilleau is in town. Will you see her, ask at attn. Mickle's, 36 Broadway.[7] Will you see & share my letters with my friends true & dear & good friends the Deweys. Just from California. Ask their address at the Metropolitan Hotel. I've so little time to write for myself. My chief is well and in good heart. He is a brave heart. Charley, he writes me gets on very well, learning as he goes. I am proud my boys wear the Guard uniform. Very sincerely yours,

J. B. Frémont

[*Margin note:* Won't you see Dr. Lieber & Mrs. Shaw of Staten Island & give them facts from me.]

ALS (editors' copy).

1. Asst. Adj. Gen. Chauncey McKeever (1829–1901) reported a litany of problems resulting from the government's virtual freezing of all federal funds in St. Louis and its general undermining of JCF's authority (McKeever to JCF, Oct. 31 [1861], copy by Elizabeth Benton Frémont in editors' possession).

2. The German press, principally represented by the radical antislavery *Anzeiger des Westens* and *Westliche Post,* was strongly pro-Frémont. For a useful study of the German press in St. Louis during this period, see ROMAN & PRIMM.

3. George B. McClellan (1826–85), commander of the Army of the Potomac, had not yet launched his long anticipated offensive, and critics had begun to question his courage and competence. Nonetheless, Lincoln remained fully supportive, and on Nov. 1, McClellan succeeded Winfield Scott as general-in-chief.

4. JBF refers both to McKeever's Oct. 31 report and her own Oct. 26 and 30–31 letters to Ward Hill Lamon. Neither the report or JBF's Oct. 30–31 letter is among Lincoln's presidential papers, but JBF's Oct. 26 letter is, indicating that the president received it.

5. In a report first published in his Albany *Evening Journal,* Thurlow Weed had "reluctantly" concluded that the Union army under JCF would never catch up with the Confederates. He also reported corruption in contracts and pronounced JCF to be as difficult to see as "a monarch in the darkest days of despotism" (New York *Herald,* Oct. 30, 1861).

6. Dr. George Barker Windship (1834–76) was a Harvard-educated physician celebrated as a weight lifter and lecturer on physical fitness. When he died at age forty-two of "paralysis," his premature death was attributed to carrying "lifting too far" (New York *Times* obit., Sept. 18, 1876; see also Windship's "Autobiographical Sketch of a Strength Seeker," *Atlantic Monthly,* 9 (Jan. 1862): 102–15).

7. The headquarters of Andrew H. Mickle (1805–63), a wealthy tobacco merchant and former New York City mayor, was located at 36 Broadway (HOLLI & JONES, 252–53; New York City *Directory,* 1860).

To Frederick Billings

[Printed letterhead]
St. Louis
Head Quarters. Western Department
Nov. 4th 1861.

My dear Mr. Billings,

Your letter of the 31st has just reached me & I will answer at length through the same channel. Meantime I acknowledge it & only save the mail by hurrying. Price was near, at Neosho.[1] But jealousy was nearer & it is quite believed here that on Friday Hunter reluctantly took the price of his treachery & falsehoods. He will march the army immediately back, so his fuglemen say & go into winter quarters— not these. I have made a chance & broken the lease for this house.

Under the 5th article of war Genl. Thomas must answer for his publication.[2] What a long pull & a strong pull & a pull altogether it has taken for them to dislodge Mr. Frémont & evidences pour in daily from the neighboring states, that it's nothing but a dislodging from place—not from power. [*Margin note:* Mr. Sherman always has the caissons full—apply to him.]

I have just been told that the QuarterMaster has directions, written, to hold over a payment until the arrival of "the new commander." So we shall see you soon & talk over the subjects of your letter & the subject I scared you from mentioning. But the General & Lily take great interest in the place. Frank is uncommonly good & handsome—

getting a little priggish with too much admiration but I am not the
one to put him on half rations. Yours very sincerely always,

J. B. Frémont

I knew on first seeing the gun article in the Tribune that it was yours.
Only you or Mr. Sherman had the facts & the style at once peremptory
& polite was not Mr. Sherman's—& the "all sorts of speculators"
meant A.A.S.[3] I had sent it two days since to the Genl.

ALS (Billings Mansion Archives).

1. JBF's remark on Price's whereabouts relates to a controversy about whether or
not JCF had been on the brink of battle when he was replaced. Lincoln had instructed
that JCF not be given his dismissal order if he was "in the immediate presence of the
enemy in expectation of a battle" (OFFICIAL RECORDS, ser. 1, vol. 3:553). Although JCF
asserted he was about to engage the enemy, the order was nonetheless delivered on
Nov. 2. Rebel commander Price's correspondence confirms that he intended to make
a stand, but since he was at least fifty miles away on Nov. 2, moving south from
Neosho to Pineville, the battle would probably have occurred several days later (see
Price to Albert Sidney Johnston, Oct. 16, 27, Nov. 7, 1861, and to Ben. McCulloch,
Oct. 26, 1861, OFFICIAL RECORDS, ser. 1, vol 3:719-20, 727-29, 731-32). When Hunter
replaced JCF, he immediately ordered Union troops to St. Louis, a retreat suggested
by Lincoln, who believed JCF had moved dangerously far from his supply lines in a
futile pursuit of Price (Lincoln to Hunter, Oct. 24, 1861, in OFFICIAL RECORDS, ser. 1,
vol. 3:553-54). For evidence that JCF was close to battle, see CASTEL, 59-60 and NEVINS
[1], 656-57.
2. JBF refers to Adjutant General Thomas's damning report on JCF published Oct.
30 in the New York *Tribune,* but the fifth of the Articles of War in effect during this
period only loosely fits the case: "Any officer or soldier who shall use contemptuous
or disrespectful words against the President of the United States, against the Vice-
President thereof, against the Congress of the United States, or against the Chief
Magistrate or Legislature of any of the United States, in which he may be quartered,
if a commissioned officer, shall be cashiered, or otherwise punished, as a Court-martial
shall direct." Conceivably JCF could be called a "chief magistrate" and Thomas "quartered" in his region during his brief investigation. For a complete list of the Articles
of War, which were read every Sunday to the troops, see the New York *Times,* Sept.
29, 1861.
3. In an Oct. 30 letter to the New York *Tribune* signed "One Who Knows," Billings
had defended JCF's arms purchases, asserting that government agents were now paying
far more for European weapons than had JCF, and that JCF's later, more expensive
St. Louis arms purchases were justified by the emergency. "A.A.S." was JCF's California
business associate Abia A. Selover, who the Thomas report claimed had written to a
San Francisco friend "that his share of the profit of the purchase of these [European]
arms was $30,000" (OFFICIAL RECORDS, ser. 1, vol. 3:544).

To Frederick Billings

[Nov. 23, 1861]

My dear Mr. Billings,

This will be posted at Cincinnati by Judge Corwine[1] late judge advocate of the late staff & is to tell you that we leave here on Tuesday. The General asks that you will, through some business person, get us in a small furnished house at a rate suited to our lamentably low finances. We should like if possible to avoid going to a Hotel at all & you must not be misled by the beauty of this house to judge of my requirements. It's my cousin's—not mine—she has $25.000 a year & I have less than nothing.[2] But sunshine, a good neighborhood—*accessible I mean,* will be the chief things; for Ellen & I will make things around us right very quickly. The Genl. begs you will be there to meet him. Genl. Halleck[3] told him you were to leave in a fortnight (from a week since). But you will wait I trust for public as well as private reasons of interest. Genl. Halleck has behaved like a gentleman—a method out of use in the army. There are so many things of great interest to tell you but our well founded distrust of the mail will not allow of writing. But one thing is sure that Mr. Frémont can more than prove he has the right on his side in all that is charged against him—there will be enough evidence to break down his accusers & leave them no escape.

Your boy Frank came nigh his death from a chance shot last week— a mark on the forehead is all that will remain but I will put them at school as soon as I get to civilization.[4] We are all well and "eager for the fray." You see Price is proving Hunter in the wrong for bringing back the army. Everything is put under Washington rule here & no letters or dispatches allowed on army matters but there's a tale of woe from the South West & the citizens here last night held a meeting to censure Hunter or *whoever ordered the retreat.*[5]

Nov. 23 1861.

I had five minutes only to write in.

J. B. F.

I have sent a sort of duplicate request to Coles Morris[6] en-cas you are in Vermont.

AL initialed (Billings Mansion Archives).

1. Richard M. Corwine of Cincinnati, an "easy, clever fellow" according to former law partner Rutherford B. Hayes, would continue as judge advocate on JCF's staff in West Virginia (BARNARD, 184).

2. The Frémonts had been criticized for renting the St. Louis mansion of JBF's cousin, the widow Sarah (Benton) Brant, for $6,000 a year. However, supporters pointed out that it served as general headquarters and residence for JCF's entire staff.

3. On Nov. 9, Maj. Gen. Henry Wager Halleck (1815–72) replaced Hunter as commander of the newly organized Department of the Missouri. A West Point graduate, Halleck had served as secretary of state during the military occupation of California, but resigned from the army in 1854 to establish a lucrative San Francisco law practice in partnership with Frederick Billings and Archibald Peachy. Halleck's Civil War record would be mixed: a poor military commander, he nonetheless proved an able administrator as Lincoln's chief of staff.

4. While building a play fort with his brother, six-year-old Frank Frémont received a superficial wound when the two boys "put both ball & powder in a model of a cannon & it burst & sent a mimic bullet jagging across Frank's forehead, tearing the skin only. His perfect coolness charmed his father." Two days later Charley was also injured when he "touched off a 'mine' in the same fort (all forbidden) & it exploded sooner than he counted on & he is less eyebrows, lashes & part of his hair, most mercifully the eyes are saved and he has no powder under the skin, but suffers enough to keep his memory awake for a few days" (JBF to Billings, Nov. 18 [1861], Billings Mansion Archives).

5. Union troops under Hunter had retreated from Springfield in southwest Missouri, harassed as they moved north by detachments of Price's dwindling rebel force. As the troops withdrew, rebel bands plundered pro-Union farms in the region. JBF's "tale of woe" doubtless included the many destitute pro-Union families who fled north with the troops; the New York *Tribune* correspondent reported more than a thousand refugee families gathered at the Union stronghold of Rolla (SHALHOPE, 188–91; New York *Tribune*, Nov. 27, 29, Dec. 5, 1861).

6. Coles Morris was JCF's New York lawyer. A reclusive bachelor with a large art collection, in late 1876, he would misappropriate $500,000 in family trust funds. His doctor attributed his concurrent "mental derangement" to his sedentary habits (New York *Times*, Dec. 29, 1876, Jan. 7, 1877; Washington *Evening Star*, Jan. 1, 1877).

To James T. Fields

[Dec. 14 (1861)]

My dear Sir

Because I know what it is I want to do I am afraid I made the mistake of talking to you this morning as though you too knew all about it. Mr. Ticknor and yourself both talked "book" when I am incapable of writing a book—sunshine puts out little fires, & I have known too much of those who lived as well as wrote books to pale my ineffectual fires by comparison. But I can tell what I know and Mrs. Fields[1] quoted the exact idea today—"drunk with a belief" I am. I believe that those truly soldierly young men, worthy of a place in chronicles of knightly deeds, were misrepresented, slighted & finally insulted out of the service because of the name they bore.[2] It has not altered the feeling with which they took that name and we feel to them as towards the foremost in sharing a long siege. It seems to me as much an obligation of feeling and honor to do them justice and heal the hurts to their natural pride, as it would be to visit them in the Hospital had they been wounded bodily in the discharge of their duty near the General in the field.

They were all young, many with younger members of their families looking to them for protection and assistance, some few married— some were sons of widows, and it was an additional sorrow to find that those killed at Springfield comprised the greater number of the married men & some of the most needed sons. I cannot let those mothers & wives feel our name only the synonym of sorrow and loss to them. In the first nights after hearing of Springfield—the days were too busy for dwelling on thoughts—this thought troubled me. The idea of making the whole conduct of the Guard there the means of providing for their families, came to me very gratefully. It leaves no sense of obligation, & their protection from such of the ills of life as money affects, will be due to the same true hearts and strong hands that defended the country at Springfield.

Mr. Raymond[3] was at the piano while I was thinking this over & chanced upon one of his German student songs which so fitted to & embodied the charge that we adopted it at once as the war song of the Guard, & then & there in the midnight hours we made each our contribution to this Story of the Guard. I had the General's letters telling me very fully of the charge and many incidents connected with it. Major Corwine, who was Judge Advocate, had the deepest interest in the "Kentucky Company" which he had mainly recruited himself, & the song is from the memories of Capt. Howard & Mr. Raymond who arranged it for the piano & made an English translation. The song is perfectly charming from its appropriateness as well as its beauty. Written by Herwegh[4] in '48 it is dear to German patriots. Bold, & full of eager life in a full open key, each verse ends with a minor chord that collects the fibres of the verse into one quivering word—"Dying."

Here, where the war is only one among the large questions of the day, it is hard to make real the feeling with which union people hold to each other in a rebel state actually at war. In St. Louis, the rebel city of a rebel state where, until September, the uniform of a Federal officer made him at once a target, those who shared the chances of that earlier day of insecurity were as one family. The house used as Head Quarters was strongly built and fire proof and while the disturbances in the city were of almost nightly recurrence part of the basement was a regular armory—arms & ammunition were issued more than once "in the small hours" to the Guard for some dangerous duty in the City & its suburbs. We—literally, & the City, figuratively, slept over a magazine. Those were wearing days and anxious nights but the City learned to rest in peace trusting to the watchfulness of Provost Marshall McKinstry & Col. McNeill [McNeil].[5] Few knew of the constant activity and perpetual vigilance of Zagonyi[6] & the Guard. Many of these young men were citizens of St. Louis & knew the sources of danger. As the work of the Department became more centralized & telegraphic & other government records were to be taken care of, the Guard was put on duty inside of the house & so little by little they came to be a feature in our daily lives.

It is smooth sailing in St. Louis now but the first company of the Guards are among those who remember a different order of things. This is diverging, to you, but I mean to shew you why, apart from their unusual claims of character & education, we had for the Guard a more personal feeling than could grow up in ordinary war or in the formal life of barracks. (Will you by "we" please understand that I mean the General & the Staff & myself & all of us who were working— each according to their scope—for the success of our cause.)

You will see it is not anything to make a "book" of—it is really nothing more than the fire-side story of an incident of the war— interesting from the facts—interesting because in ten thousand homes some vacant place will lend its own interest to the tale—then I hope something from the kindly interest of old friends of my Father's.

These young men gave their blood to save the State he loved so well and served so long. Some rest there, as he does, until the last trumpet call.

For any personal object I should never use my name which is to me a double charge to keep, but I think my Father also would more than approve when it is to do justice and to aid the widow & the orphan.

In Catholic countries no lady thinks it wrong to go around the church in person, or stand at its door & receive gifts for a charitable purpose. I like that infinitely better than being manager of a ball for that same purpose.

Such as it is, my offering goes to make a fund for the Guard and their families and I turn over the manuscript & pictures to you relying on your experience & good sympathy to manage the rest. My part is to give you the story of the Guard and yours is to make it profitable to them. If Mr. Ticknor & yourself will be their bankers, the Revd. Mr. Eliot in St. Louis & Judge Corwine in Cincinnati will see a just use made of the fund. But all this part I leave to you—my share shall be to collect & arrange some facts & incidents & give them, with my best wishes for success in their object, to a tribunal in which I was educated to trust—our American people.

Jessie Benton Frémont

Astor House   New York   14th December.

In reading this over I see I have left unsaid things which needed telling & I've told lots of things intelligible enough to me but in their present shape without force to you. But there is no time to write it over—the thirty-times-over style doesn't answer when the world is all alive & steam & lightning give us no thinking time. To get a quiet time I have stayed up to write this until I hear now the clocks tolling two. We always come here on our return to New York—always for many many years to this side of the house overlooking the churchyard with its old grave stones.[7] From France from California from Missouri & its Civil War each episode comes back to the minor chord "Dying."

"Dear banished T.S.K." [Thomas Starr King] used to join me in pitying the people who had not the privilege of temporary insanity. German music is one of my crotchets—and when you hear "The Trooper's Death" I shall look for an intelligent sharing of my madness of the hour or give you my great pity. Is Mrs. Fields "privileged" musically?

J. B. F.

Mr. & Mrs. Fields

ALS (CSmH—Fields Papers). The proposal JBF mentions would result in her first book, *The Story of the Guard* (Ticknor and Fields, 1863), an account of the capture of Springfield, Mo., on Oct. 25, 1861, by the Frémont Bodyguard. JBF planned to use the book's royalties to create a fund for the families of the sixteen men who had died during the battle. A lightly edited version of this letter, redated Dec. 5, 1861, and without the postscript, appears as the preface to *The Story of the Guard.*

1. Annie Adams Fields (1834–1915) was a poet, essayist, and celebrated Boston literary hostess. JBF would later conclude that Annie Fields never really liked her (JBF to Elizabeth Peabody, Mar. 20 [1864], below).

2. JBF refers not only to the group's name, the "Frémont Bodyguard," but also to the fact that during the charge at Springfield, they had shouted "Frémont and the Union," disturbing the Lincoln administration so much that when JCF was dismissed, the Guard were mustered out of service for expressing, in Gen. George B. McClellan's words, "sentiments rendering their continuance in the service of doubtful expediency." Given the option of forming a regiment unattached to JCF, the unit refused. For documents of the controversy, see Charles Zagonyi's testimony in Joint Committee on the Conduct of the War, 37th Cong., 3rd sess., *Report,* 3:186–94; his letter of explanation, New York *Tribune,* Mar. 1, 1862; and J. B. FRÉMONT [2], 206–14.

3. Rossiter ("Ros") Worthington Raymond (1840–1918) would become an aide-de-camp on JCF's West Virginia staff with the rank of captain. A brilliant engineering student who had studied in Germany for three years, he would later have a distinguished career as a mining engineer.

4. Georg Herwegh (1817–75), a popular German poet of the 1848 revolution, led an unsuccessful uprising in Baden.

5. Col. John McNeil (1813–91), a St. Louis businessman/politician, was military commandant of St. Louis under JCF (OFFICIAL RECORDS, ser. 1, vol. 3:410; HEITMAN, 1:679).

6. Maj. Charles Zagonyi (b. 1826), a Hungarian emigré who fought in the revolution of 1848, was the organizer of the Frémont Bodyguard. A flamboyant cavalry officer, he commanded its successful recapture of Springfield and was thus the overt hero of JBF's *Story of the Guard.* He would serve as chief of cavalry during JCF's brief West Virginia command, but his loyalty to JCF kept him from further war service. For further information on Zagonyi's life, see R. MILLER.

7. The Astor House was built in 1836 by John Jacob Astor at what is now 225 Broadway, between Vesey and Barclay streets. JBF probably refers to the churchyard of St. Paul's Chapel, built in 1766 and still standing today (WRIGHT, 106–9).

To Thomas Starr King

Astor House, New York
Dec. 29, 1861.

My dear Mr. King,

Your letter of November 1st has at length reached me and I was heartily glad to get it. Lukewarm or forgetful I never judged either of you. You would not think so of me if years went by without hearing. None of us (the strawberry marked)[1] are over confident of friendships, but such a real loving friendship as our little circle had for each other is not dependent on the chances of mails & travel. Especially was I sure you were truer than ever when "stone him" was the cry of the slavery party. You have heard enough of that in your time & it is an honored few among whom Mr. Frémont has been received. For himself he thinks he did right and is willing for the personal results. He is not willing or reconciled to see the cause muddled away and betrayed by those elected to uphold & promote it. Mr. Lincoln would be in Springfield to day & Mr. Seward in Albany if the voters of last November could have seen the record this November was to shew. Now that we are in the dust before England & the rebels feel they have Europe with them, it will become more than ever evident that we were strong from ideas as well as by strength of numbers. The Germans are chilled & nearly alienated by the treatment to the Missouri Germans, Sigel and Mr. Frémont,[2] & the repudiations of Liberty and Free Labor. The Irish are almost in mutiny on the Potomac at the yielding to England. How Northern men feel you can imagine. Of course you saw Wendell Phillips's speech[3]—he is to repeat it in Philadelphia & Washington. The officers of the Potomac army are generally subservient & silent—the men loudly for emancipation. Burnside's expedition intended to attack Fredericksburg (Va.) while McClellan attacks at Centreville, has hung fire for weeks. It is promised now for early January.[4] If they win a great victory the administration can stand. If they keep still or are beaten then all the malcontents give tongue. I should delight beyond telling in having you here during all this time but I am shy of planning. Our lives move in such an eccentric orbit that it would seem we jerk out of place all nearly connected with us. Yet I suggested to Mr. Fields (blue & gold Fields)[5] that you ought to have a summer's furlough to bring Mrs. King home for her health. Let that congregation know by your absence what you are. They will call for you fiercely. I did not know your gifts as a lecturer until I measured you by Mr. Phillips. I do not like a lecture with the chill on. It may be high Boston. But your voice & gestures are greatly beyond his & you have the magnetic power much greater—the Rarey element.[6] Mrs. King knows that. I was surprised by you into emotions and enthusiasm & it takes an uncommon kind of fuse to touch off this grim siege piece in my left side. Mr. Dewey entered into it favorably too—can't it be done? It does such a world of good to change houses once in a while & by the time you get here who can tell what will be happening?

I have so many things to talk of to you that I fairly halted as I took a fresh sheet—but I hope to have a proof sheet[7] to send you which will tell you something of the coming judgment against the Washington Dictators. The President, the Cabinet, Genl. McClellan & their families and jobmen constitute an irresponsible body who appoint & remove, praise & censure, enrich or impoverish, imprison or release at their own pleasure without consulting or listening to the popular voice. The New York press belongs to them in part. The Tribune was nearly ruined for not giving in to them & is scary—the Post is kept well flattered & its patriotism appealed to not to excite or add to criticism. The Herald belongs to Mrs. Lincoln because she visits, invites to the White House, Mrs. Bennett.[8] This is a formidable body to combat having as they do 500.000.000$ & 5.000 000 of men at their irresponsible bidding. But it's as exhilarating as a sea breeze to make head against. They are like all houses built on sand & we are on the rock. Our eyes may not see the perfect day but it is good to feel sure it is coming & bear a part in bringing it quickly.

Indeed it is nobler, & one can but feel it so, even after having had the charm of power, to work without visible reward. And good work we are doing. Perhaps serving to point the evils of this tenderness toward slavery. I think there is a little more bold speaking wished for, than is given to the people. As in all great & lasting reformations the movement is from the roots upward. A brave true eloquent speaker who should devote himself to this crisis & cry aloud & spare not, would be hailed as a Luther by the people. Mr. Seward would wish to send him to Fort Warren but he can be twitted about his jailorship too much now for him to be feared. The Herald would cry out for his imprisonment perhaps his execution but it's more than likely the Herald office will be level with the ground before long. Even the polite Evening Post tells it so.

It will not do to trust on paper the combinations which will soon test the power of the Washington Directory to stop the will of the people.

Only an overwhelming victory on the Potomac can delay their fate. Wellington used to say a battle was always uncertain until ended & the rebels have numbers, skill, & fanatical enthusiasm on their side. We have only principle on ours. The prestige of success is with them & they are about sure of recognition from Europe—certain if they hold their own many weeks longer. All this could have been averted by two words—Be free—but they are not allowed to be spoken.

I send you a card picture just sent me from St. Louis.[9] Sigel is on the eve of resigning, only kept from it by the hope of Mr. Frémont's having another command. His best regiments are taken from him &

he is kept inactive. The whole work of the summer is given to Pope & other West Point inefficiencies to make capital of. The Germans everywhere are in deep rage & this picture is one result. They couple Sigel & Mr. Frémont & behind is the Guard—now disbanded by Genl. McClellan's order "for expressions used at Springfield." The expressions means "Frémont & Union." This picture is the Mulbery leaf of the [grounding?]. I wish I had more copies I should so like to send some to Mr. Beale & Mr. Harte & my artist friend Mr. Watkins[10]—but unless he copies it I shall have to ask waiting until I can get some more.

Dec. 31.

The proofs are all corrected but the impressions will be too late for this mail. I shall send them. The Sergeant at arms of the Senate has just been in to give the subpoena of the Joint Committee for the Genl. to attend on Monday 6th.[11] This is the end of our silence & now will come justice & retribution. Be glad for us dear friends for the cup has been full & every drop bitter. If it was drunk in silence & without spilling a drop, it only proves a firm hand & the habit of endurance. Now Fortune turn thy wheel.

Mr. Frémont has gone off with Zagonyi to ride over on Hoboken heights—the same horse as in the picture, a grey which he rode all the time in M[issou]ri. He is a little too contented for in doors. I keep in to share my joy with you & ask your halving of this good as you so often halved less good news to me.

Mrs. Dewey was here yesterday. Mr. Dewey has a bad cold & otherwise ill from feverishness. She looks well & calm—a shade less of the old smiling serenity. New York is a large city. There is but one Oriental & Serena was its prophet.[12] Mr. Dewey's cold opens a vista of Nice or Naples. They are both bored. We all miss you but their lives are monotonous & you gave such zest to it there that Mr. Dewey lends your & Mrs. King's attractions to San Francisco. Just think how fitly spoken you would be here & wouldn't the breezes be invigorating if we could all go skating stones & bowling ten pins together again with this stage & decorations (See dress skirt). I wish I could stay & take tea & not go home 'till ten. How many more Japanese things has Mrs. King? Is the faithful & diplomatic Sarah still there with that good tea & that inimitable English-cut bread & butter? My love to Edith whose hair must be just right about this time—a curve from the pure

Teutonic. Most love to Mrs. King (to whom I am writing) & to Mr. King every kind & affectionate remembrance & may the opening year bring you health & keep you happy.

Jessie Frémont

ALS (CSfCP—King Papers).

1. JBF and King evidently both had small red birthmarks.

2. The Missouri Germans had been the backbone of Union support in St. Louis, but their continued enthusiasm for JCF disturbed the Lincoln administration. In December, when Brig. Gen. Franz Sigel was superseded as commander of Union troops in the newly organized Southwest Missouri Army, German-Americans protested what was in effect a demotion, and Sigel tried to resign. In early Feb. 1862, the administration would receive intelligence from St. Louis alleging that German-speaking officers and newspapers were plotting to restore Frémont and Sigel to command (OFFICIAL RECORDS, ser. 1, vol. 8:828–29). Meanwhile, the Germans charged that the administration was deliberately bypassing German officers like Sigel and forcing German regiments to join American brigades (ROWAN & PRIMM, 297–300). Responding to these protests as well as Sigel's courageous leadership of German-American troops at the battle of Pea Ridge, Ark., on Mar. 7–8, 1862, Lincoln promoted Sigel to major general. Nonetheless, midwestern German-Americans would remain among JCF's strongest supporters. KOERNER, 2:194–203, provides a useful first-hand account of the Sigel controversy.

3. On Dec. 19, the noted abolitionist orator Wendell Phillips (1811–84) had spoken before a huge crowd at the Cooper Institute in New York City. The Frémonts slipped in at the last moment to avoid notice; and when Phillips alluded to JCF, the crowd cheered wildly (HERR, 350–51; New York *Tribune*, Dec. 20, 1861).

4. In reality, the Army of the Potomac was stalled. In mid-December, the already reluctant McClellan had contracted typhoid fever, leaving the army virtually without a commander for almost a month. However, Brig. Gen. Ambrose E. Burnside (1824–81) was readying a massive amphibious expedition that in February would seize Roanoke Island and other key points on the North Carolina coast. (MCPHERSON, 367, 372–73).

5. Many Ticknor and Fields volumes had blue covers with gold lettering.

6. JBF evidently refers to John Solomon Rarey (1827–66), a well-known Ohio horse trainer celebrated for his compelling power over animals. In 1857–60, Rarey had demonstrated his skills in an immensely successful European tour and even given lessons to Queen Victoria and Prince Albert.

7. JCF had collected official correspondence and other documents for the Joint Congressional Committee on the Conduct of the War, which was investigating his Missouri administration. For the documents, plus JCF's supporting statement, see New York *Tribune*, Mar. 4, 1862.

8. The president and James Gordon Bennett, editor of the previously anti-Lincoln New York *Herald*, had indeed reached a rapprochement. The courtship had begun when Lincoln sent Thurlow Weed to persuade Bennett to support the administration (CARMAN & LUTHAN, 122–25). By the fall of 1861, the *Herald* was defending not only Lincoln's policies (including his dismissal of JCF) but also Mary Lincoln against her critics, resulting in several invitations from her to the White House (FERMER, 214–15). While the *Herald* recounted Mary Lincoln's social rounds in lavish detail, its archrival, Greeley's *Tribune*, hinted that she was ostentatious and vulgar. In a Nov. 11, 1861, editorial, the *Herald* condemned the personal attacks on Mary Lincoln "by the ab-

olitionist press" and added, in a subtle jab at JBF: "Even when a lady sometimes stepped into the *melee*, as did 'our Jessie' [in the 1856 campaign], there was no hand bold enough to strike at her, no matter how strongly it might fall upon the cause her husband represented."

9. The card picture was a photographic reproduction of a black and white oil painting by German-born St. Louis artist Carl Wimar (1828–62), which had been commissioned for the purpose by St. Louis photographer John A. Scholten (see SPIESS, 16–29; GROCE & WALLACE, 695).

10. The Frémonts had given the talented young photographer Carleton E. Watkins (1829–1916) his first important outdoor commission when they asked him to take a series of photographs of Las Mariposas to show potential investors. Watkins's subsequent views of nearby Yosemite, which JBF saw displayed in New York City, were important in persuading Congress to pass legislation in 1864 making Yosemite the first public park. For a study of Watkins's art and life, see PALMQUIST.

11. The Joint Committee on the Conduct of the War was established by Congress in Dec. 1861 as a result of public outcry over Union defeats and Lincoln's seemingly ineffectual war strategy. It was dominated by radical emancipationists, who could be expected to give JCF a sympathetic hearing. After testimony from JCF and thirteen others, including Frank Blair, a majority of the committee would conclude that JCF's Missouri administration "was eminently characterized by earnestness, ability, and the most unquestionable loyalty" (Joint Committee on the Conduct of the War, 37th Cong., 3rd sess., *Report*, 3:6).

12. Evidently a reference to the Oriental, a fashionable San Francisco hotel where the Kings stayed when they first arrived in the city. King described it as "a forlorn looking wooden building in a wretched part of the city, but the best kept house in the place" (WENDTE, 84).

To Schuyler Colfax

[Dec. 30 (1861)]

My dear Mr. Colfax,

I have had but one letter at all from you since I saw you in St. Louis.[1] It is dated Dec. 21.

I answered that about three days since, directing to you at Washington & sealing with my butterfly seal. I have been waiting for a safe hand to send you some information which is being printed, but we are only at the proof sheets & it will go on later.

Mr. Fields of Boston told me he had written two letters to me & mailed them in Washington. One only has come to me & that ten days after it was mailed.

Major Zagonyi's letter from St. Louis with much information troublesome to gather & mailed there by himself, has never reached me although I wrote to the Post Master to ask for it opened or unopened. The same with important letters from Col. Fiala[2] & others to the Genl.

We never write by mail to St. Louis or Washington (except this one experiment I've made three days since to you) except in disguised hands or under cover to names not dangerous to the Blairs.

Now that the proof of Frank Blair's sharing in contracts are so clear & so known the end is at hand.[3] If there is any public virtue it will resent the use of public trusts & government means to screen dishonorable men by the sacrifice of honorable men who would not be their accomplices. But until that day has come Montgomery Blair uses the Post Office for his ends & Frank the military power of St. Louis, & the Investigating Committee[4] have kept back their proofs of his ill conduct & put insinuations & charges upon honest men. It's about time for honesty to assert itself & send the shams to their original level.

I had put your paper away & forgot it in answering your letter.

J.B. Frémont

Hon. Schuyler Colfax   Dec. 30th

ALS (CLjC).

1. A loyal supporter of JCF, Colfax had visited the Frémonts in St. Louis in mid-September and afterward issued a report favorable to JCF (New York *Times,* Oct. 3, 1861). He presented a major defense of JCF in the House on Mar. 7, 1862, in response to a scathing attack by Congressman Frank Blair (New York *Tribune,* Mar. 13–14, 1862).

2. Col. John T. Fiala (1822–1911), a former Hungarian revolutionary, was a skilled topographer known for his 1860 map of Missouri. He was JCF's chief topographical engineer in St. Louis and West Virginia (VASVARY, 52; HEITMAN, 1:418).

3. There is no evidence that Frank Blair, Jr. (or JCF for that matter) profited personally from any contract made during JCF's Missouri administration. JBF probably refers to Blair's attempt to obtain a $750,000 contract for two friends, John How and W. S. Gurnee, to furnish equipment and clothing for 40,000 troops. In Jan. 1862, JCF would testify that after intense pressure from the three, he had reluctantly recommended a contract to furnish supplies for one-third the original number of troops, but his chief quartermaster, Justus McKinstry, with JCF's tacit approval, rejected the entire proposal. JCF claimed that it was this rejection that provoked the feud with Blair. For testimony on the contract, see Special House Committee on Government Contracts, 37th Cong., 2d sess., *Report* 2, serial 1142, pp. 703, 967–68, 977–79; and Joint Committee on the Conduct of the War, 37th Cong., 3rd sess., *Report,* 3:75–77, 178–79, 184–85, 202).

4. JBF refers here to the Special House Committe on Government Contracts, which during October hearings in St. Louis had collected damaging testimony about alleged corruption in JCF's administration. In his March defense of JCF, however, Colfax

would point out that the committee had held hearings while JCF was in the field, giving him no chance to respond to accusations, and had leaked negative testimony to the press (New York *Tribune*, Mar. 13, 1862). For the complete hearings, see Special House Committee on Government Contracts, 37th Cong., 2d sess., *Report* 2, serials 1142–43; and leaked excerpts in the New York *Tribune*, Nov. 29, 1861.

To Frederick Billings

Washington Jany. 21st 1862.

My dear Mr. Billings,

I have been waiting for something fixed to tell you & so waiting have not written since we reached here just a fortnight ago. I hope the New Year's letter reached you with Frank's souvenir. I enclose the Sigel picture which has reached me since. His ill treatment by the govt. has made the Germans embody all their resentments in this collection of rejected corner stones. The background as you will see is made by the Guard. My Guard story is partly in type. The plates are being finished & the charge is near. Here, in the absence of the staff I am sole pen in waiting & have rather more writing than I can get on with but there's nothing like good hating for carrying on a war & being born on the rebel side of the line I think I have some advantages in the way of vindictiveness. The General made an abstract of the printed evidence (all the papers you saw & others of the same kind—we had them put in print, but not published) giving points & proving them— commencing by giving the condition in which Missouri was when he went there, the carte blanche given him for operations & all their details of management, fortified by special permits to points, (witnesses & papers given to each position), the Lyon matter, the reasons thereafter for fortifying St. Louis, the Lexington time, for which the papers are conclusive, and an exposé of the Investigating Committee's [on Government Contracts] report ending with a summary of the State as it was, "when, without reason assigned" he was removed. The whole will occupy, quoted proofs & all, about four columns of a newspaper. It is really admirable as a condensation.[1] The Committee [on the Conduct of the War] were, a part of them, for deciding the case then & there on its reading. The Chairman, Mr. Wade,[2] said no witnesses were needed, that it was all proved up & every charge against Mr. Frémont exploded. Some technicalities prevailed, but the thing is fixed & now we are trying to give it immediate publicity. After that the administration has only two courses open. One, to give Mr. Frémont such a command as his position entitles him to & as the public will demand for him, or formally to recognize that he is so much identified with the principle of emancipation that they dare not endorse him & for that rule him out of the war. Either course will hurt them — the last will bring about the immediate action of Congress. The Confiscation Bill is under preparation which will test the govt. & Congress on the slavery question.[3] They have tacked a point to the South in the putting Mr. Stanton in the War Dept.[4] It is becoming fast a question of money. The North is wanting its money's worth & only the promise of an immediate, concerted, simultaneous forward movement from here to Missouri has kept the people at bay. But "time's up" and nothing has been done. The notes are offered for renewal but find no takers. Isn't that the banking slang? Meantime, the General's position strengthens—hourly,— is not too much to say. We are a centre of revolution against this hideous return to all our troubles. It's wonderful how few men *are* leaders. But without going into speculations & theories we can sum up just now on the points gained, which are Mr. Frémont's presence here, his satisfactory answer to the Committee, & his recognition as the indispensable popular war cry. The signs thicken daily & we have many episodes both amusing, as well as some very gratifying which will not do to risk on paper but which will keep for telling. It is already a question as to which command he will *accept*.

Your friend Frank is the only one of the family with us. Charley is contented and progressing nicely in his New England school.[5] My sister insists on keeping Lily until April. I believe Boilleau is then to go to China as minister. Lil is quite happy in the atmosphere of calm & elegance which our very broken up life has deprived her of for so many years. In Quebec there is always a good foundation of French as well as English society & just now it is largely added to from England. She is, like Charley, studying, skating, & having generally the right life for a young lady. This is the General's birthday. I have just made him a bouquet. We send you all our best wishes overseas & hopes for success. It is coming here — the next letter will give the form. Very sincerely,

J. B. Frémont

ALS (Billings Mansion Archives). Addressed to "Frederick Billings, Esqre. Frankfort on the Maine, Germany. To the care of W. W. Murphy, Esqre., U.S. Consul Genl." Billings was again in Europe to raise capital for Las Mariposas.

1. When JCF appeared before the Committee on the Conduct of the War on Jan. 10, they had requested a written defense of his Missouri administration to accompany the documents he provided. He and JBF completed the statement by Jan. 17 (Joint Committee on the Conduct of the War, 37th Cong., 3rd sess., *Report*, 3:32–33).

2. Ohio senator Benjamin Wade (1800–1878) was a leading radical Republican who advocated immediate emancipation and deplored Lincoln's cautious policy. As chairman of the Committee on the Conduct of the War he was a powerful Frémont ally.

3. Seven bills relating to emancipation or confiscation were reported out of congressional committees in Jan. 1862. JBF probably refers to the most important, a new article of war forbidding army officers from returning fugitive slaves to their masters, passed by Congress on Mar. 13 (MCPHERSON, 496–98).

4. Amid charges of corruption in the War Department, Lincoln had sent Secretary of War Simon Cameron to Russia as ambassador and appointed Edwin M. Stanton (1814–69) in his place. Stanton, who had served briefly as attorney general in Buchanan's cabinet and voted for Breckinridge in 1860, was blunt, efficient, and incorruptible.

5. Charley was attending a boarding school near Litchfield, Conn., while Lily was staying with JBF's sister Susan in Quebec City, where her husband was the French consul (JBF to Thomas Starr King, Mar. 10 [1862], CSfCP—King Papers).

To Frederick Billings

February 7th 1862.

My dear Mr. Billings,

After waiting for points until I feared my letter would cross you on your return I can at last give them. The War Committee [Joint Committee on the Conduct of the War] waited on the Secretary at War last week & told him that everything was more than explained & justified in regard to Mr. Frémont's Dept. and that they came to ask for him a command. The Secretary said he had only waited for their decision to give him one of which his friends should have nothing to complain—that it would give him ample scope for his military talent & satisfy their pride as well as the Genl.'s. Tonight, by appointment, Mr. Frémont is to submit a plan & his preferences for a command to Mr. Stanton at his own house where they can be "uninterrupted & have the evening."[1]

(Vide Stanton.) Mr. Frémont has just returned from a visit to the President who told him he wished to talk with him & but for the illness of their youngest child would do so now.[2] Neither of us had called at the President's—or in fact made any first visit—but to the ball given by Mrs. Lincoln—(which has been a regular apple of discord here)[3] we received invitations & the President made our reception marked. You would have been amused to see people taking their cue from that & from Mr. Stanton's stopping to speak to us. We had friends enough there already but these things added the cyphers so that the sum total was a complete success. From that trunk which was the object of your sarcasms I had extracted a white & violet dress of tulle & blonde & fragile beauty & fearful cost & in my secession cousin's finery, emancipation shook hands with modification & Kentucky. Sixtus wore his crutches until he was well in the seat you understand.[4] It will be about ten days before I throw mine away but they will hit hard when they are thrown. At my instance—I am responsible for all impertinences—the General wore with his regulation military dress his cross of merit. A gentle hint that a prophet is not without honor save in his own country. Baron Gerolt[5] was very much pleased with him for wearing it—so were many of our ultra republican home friends. Your beautiful friend Mrs. John Sherwood[6] was there & said some very nice things of you. Miss Shaw[7] too and the Morgans (Peabody Morgans) of London.[8] It was a really beautiful ball for dressing & flowers & music. No dancing & we came away early, staying only an hour—stopped by the President in person, in the hall made to take off my cloak & be introduced to Genl. McClellan. I behaved myself perfectly well but I didn't like it. I had my compensation in seeing the eyes that followed us across the hall & East Room, the President & Mr. Frémont, Mr. Sumner & myself, while the introductions were gone through.

February 8th

I am so constantly interrupted that I will not attempt to write you a regular letter but only add that a third freshet in Cal. has carried away every mill & bridge (inclusive) from Chapin's to Stockton, on every river. Murray's, the Stanislaus everywhere, & those on the Mariposas only, are uninjured.[9] We accept the good omen, and look to hear good results from you although up to this hour there is not one word of you or line from you since we wished you bon voyage at the Astor. I trust our letters were more fortunate—for I think you must have written. We leave here in about a week now victorious & vindicated. Always sincerely yours,

J.B.F.

Frank has made his sensation here & is quainter & more winning every day. He is out or there would be a message to Mr. "Billins."

AL initialed (Billings Mansion Archives). Addressed to "Frederick Billings, Esqre. Frankfort on the Maine, Germany."

1. Three days after this meeting with Stanton, JCF submitted a proposal to establish a military department comprising California, New Mexico, Texas, and Louisiana, with the immediate goal of seizing Texas, New Orleans, and the Tallahassee Railroad (JCF to Stanton, Feb. 10, 1862, DLC—Stanton Papers). On Feb. 6, the day before the meeting, JCF aide Albert Tracy noted in his journal that he and another officer had been assigned to investigate and report on a plan for a Frémont expedition of twenty thousand men to take Texas. To Tracy's surprise, on Mar. 11, just after they submitted their report, the administration assigned JCF to command the newly created Mountain Department in West Virginia (TRACY, 168).

2. Twelve-year-old William ("Willie") Wallace Lincoln died of typhoid fever on Feb. 20, 1862.

3. Many radical Republicans had refused to go to the Lincoln gala because they thought it inappropriate to attend a lavish party while soldiers were dying. The Frémonts went only after Lincoln sent a special messenger to urge them to come. Years later JBF remembered the president as preoccupied about his son's illness and the evening as "a ghastly failure." For a fuller description, see HERR, 356–58.

4. According to legend, Pope Sixtus V (1521–90) used crutches to feign old age while awaiting his election as pope but tossed them aside once he was chosen. JBF evidently planned to imitate Sixtus by deference to the administration until John was given a new command, expected in about ten days. At that point, they could publish JCF's defense of his Missouri administration, prepared for the Committee on the Conduct of the War, as well as JBF's own *Story of the Guard*. The defense finally appeared in the New York *Tribune* on Mar. 4. JBF again used the Sixtus allusion in her Oct. 28, 1890, letter to William Carey Jones, Jr., below.

5. In 1860, the Prussian government had awarded JCF a prestigious cross of merit in the sciences, which was announced in a letter from the Prussian ambassador, Baron Friedrich von Gerolt (c. 1798–1879), a longtime family friend. Ten years earlier, Gerolt had transmitted to JCF a letter from the distinguished explorer Alexander von Humboldt awarding JCF a large gold medallion from Prussia for his contributions to "scientific progress" ("Great Events," 136–37, and following 215; M. L. SPENCE [2]:205–6).

6. Mary Elizabeth (Wilson) Sherwood (1826–1903) was a writer and literary hostess whose work appeared in the *Atlantic* and other magazines. When her husband, a New York lawyer, suffered financial difficulties in the 1870s, she, like JBF, began to write for a living. Her most successful work was a popular etiquette book published in 1884.

7. One of Sarah and Francis Shaw's three unmarried daughters, Susana, Josephine, or Nellie (Ellen).

8. JBF most probably refers to Juliet (1816–84) and Junius Spencer Morgan (1813–90). Junius S. Morgan was a partner in George Peabody's London-based international banking firm. The Morgans' son, John Pierpont Morgan, recently married and beginning his financial career, was in Europe on this date.

9. The damage at Las Mariposas was actually serious. The *Alta California* reported that "the Benton Mills and dam have been ruined. The loss not less than $70,000"

(Jan. 17, 1862). Estate manager Trenor Park estimated losses at $100,000 (BELL, 166–67). The *Alta* also reported that "all the bridges on the Stanislaus, Tuolumne, and Merced are gone," including the bridge at Murrays on the Merced, the location of a comfortable inn where the Frémonts had often stayed en route to Stockton and San Franciso (J. B. FRÉMONT [1], 195–96). Chapin's, a costly mill at Johnson's Flat, near Bear Valley, owned by Flint, Peabody & Company of San Francisco, was also largely destroyed (*Alta*, Jan. 22, 29, 1862).

To [George W. Childs?]

[Feb. 8 (1862)]

My dear Sir,

I have your second note in regard to publishing Mr. Frémont's works & find by it that you did not get my answer. I trust this will reach you. Mr. Fields writes me on the 4th from Boston that he has received only two days before a letter from me dated 19th January. As he says, "Heaven & the Post Office only know where it was all that time."

Starr King is the only person I know who could do justice to the work. We had talked over many points with a view to this very arrangement. He has been on some of the ground, he is full of local coloring & is everyway more qualified for the task than Major Dorsheimer[1] whose style & habits of ideas are so radically different to those of Mr. Frémont that I think only failure would result from the attempt you propose. Major Dorsheimer's style is excellent in its way but it is in no manner related to the subject to be treated. Starr King has the habits of affectionate personal intercourse with us, the full sympathy in political faith & above all the nervous susceptibility to feel & reproduce vividly the intangible impressions of scenery & sentiments.

If the General is given a command in which I cannot follow him I should be glad to have such work & would help Mr. King ten hours a day. We are trying now to get him a leave of absence that he may have six or eight months on this side. If you could add this inducement he would, I am nearly sure, accept it. It's all quickly & easily managed by telegraph.

My Story of the Guard waits only for the signal, to appear. I would not let it have the look of sentimentalizing public opinion & it will follow public justice to the General. When it comes out read it & then read our friend's account of the same in the Atlantic, & you will see what I mean by his style. My Zagonyi is pre Raphaelite in simplicity & fidelity. But the Major has served him up with sensation sauce until Zagonyi grew red with vexation at the unmilitary & improbable ideas which make it nearly absurd. I shall look to hear from you again & hope this will reach you. We shall not be here more than a week now, I think. Very truly yours,

J. B. Frémont

Washington City
8th Feby.

ALS (MHi—C. E. French Collection). The recipient of this letter was probably George W. Childs, with whom JCF had a long-standing contract for a book on his explorations. The Frémonts had worked sporadically on the book since the mid-1850s, but the election campaign, Las Mariposas business, and the Civil War all intervened. In early December, Childs called on the Frémonts at their New York hotel (New York *Times*, Dec. 8, 1861), and JBF's letter may be a result of that visit. In 1864 Childs would try to get JCF to reimburse him for expenses for the unfinished book (JACKSON & SPENCE, xxxiv). Years later JBF would charge that Childs had refused to publish her own *Story of the Guard* because he had a lucrative printing contract with the Treasury Department and found it "unprofitable to criticize the administration" (to Henry Preston Child, Oct. 18, 1897, KyLoF).

1. William Edward Dorsheimer (1832–88) was a young Buffalo, N.Y., lawyer who had served as a private secretary to JCF in St. Louis (New York *Tribune*, Sept. 30, 1861). His highly sympathetic account of JCF's aborted pursuit of the Confederate army, "Fremont's Hundred Days in Missouri," was currently appearing in the *Atlantic Monthly* (Jan.-Mar., 1862). Later, as a New York congressman, he would try to help JCF secure a government pension (JBF to John Sherman, Apr. 14 [1884], below).

To Andrew Hull Foote

Washington Feby. 15th [1862].

Among the many congratulations that reach you does there come up a remembrance of the weary times in October? When no money, no powder, no small arms, no attention in short to any wants of the fleet could be had? The time when "*Capt.* Foote" was "forgotten to be telegraphed for" when the gun boats could have saved so many lives. Now that you have the gunpowder & the men & the rank to make them available in spite of envy—or "forgetfulness"—no one can send you more hearty & sincere congratulations on the use you are making of them than I who tried in vain to help you into an earlier use of them.

Both mine & the General's satisfaction in the Fort Henry victory was without alloy, for the honor and credit, for once, lodged where it deserved.

Feb. 17th

We are watching hopefully but anxiously for the result of your return to Fort Donelson with the Benton.[1] You will understand how it deepens my interest to have the dear brave name connected with the victory you have, doubtless by this time, won.

My dear Commodore I am very sure you share the regret that another name for which I feel the same is not having part in these results of the hard work of preparation in which we all shared last year. It makes patriotism the purer to have no selfish joy in our returning national strength but this late justice now being accorded to Mr. Frémont cannot atone for the wrongs to him in letting others reap what he sowed.

I have written you a halting letter for I have been quite ill & am yet unable to leave my room or sit up long, but we have such great satisfaction in your safety as well as your victory that I must express it to you. Very sincerely yours,

Jessie Benton Frémont

ALS (MeHi—John S. H. Fogg Autograph Collection). As commander of naval operations on the upper Mississipi, Foote, with JCF's active support, had supervised the construction and equipping of ironclad gunboats, which in early 1862 brought important results. On Feb. 6, Foote's flotilla seized Fort Henry on the Tennessee River. On Feb. 14–16, as JBF wrote, troops under the still obscure Ulysses S. Grant, aided by Foote's gunboats, were taking Fort Donelson on the Cumberland, destroying the Confederate line of defense in northern Tennessee.

1. The *Benton,* a converted Mississippi salvage boat that had been sheathed in iron for military use, was the largest of Foote's gunboats.

To Frederick Billings

Wheeling, Virginia,
April 8th 1862.

My dear Mr. Billings,

The General answered your letter by a telegram agreeing with your views & giving his more than consent to your going on the 11th. I am very glad for Mrs. Billings's[1] comfort that it is such a good connection of steamers. I hope everything connected with California will shew its fairest side to her. Her marriage is a coup d'état—all my letters come to me wide-eyed. Col. Savage,[2] on the staff, made his most emphatic "In-deed" and mourns the loss to the artists' reunions of one of the most beautiful faces to be seen there. It was through a mutual friend who has married in Boston (Creswell or some such name) that he knew more of "Miss Julia Parmly's" inner claims & he hopes her fastidious delicate taste is fully justified. He spoke for the lady (who has spoken for herself) & I could answer for the other side. But you are the wonder & envy of many for from Miss Lawrence & others who know New York I learn that Miss Parmly had been such an idol of the highest inner circle of art, that for her to condescend to a mortal is as if the Statue had chosen Pygmalion. But you know your wonderful good fortune better than it could be told you.

In this state of things how am I, work-a-day mortal that I am, to look for attention to my prosaic requests? I put them on another sheet—they are not worthy to touch the initials of her name, & employ my infallible method to attract your attention.

I will direct to Madame Julia as Starr King calls his wife (all the nicest women are named names beginning with J) and held in her hand it will become sublimated & so pass into the notice of Frederick the Happy.

The General has been trying to accomplish a letter to you & has one page finished but Col. Cluseret[3] is there also with a plan for mountain transportation & being French he talks & I left him reaching Cheat Mountain by way of Algeria, so on a despairing look from my patient Chief I came off to repeat the substance of what he had been talking over. He is very glad you go. From you he will hope for full & immediate information in regard to all moneyed matters. Telegraph (I hate this word) if necessary & certainly letters each steamer. Slowly but surely as fate the northern sentiment is ruling the war. It is not blood but brains that will decide it and at last a firm organization has taken place on the subject. It is not possible to write you any more than the fact that all in regard to Mr. Frémont's Dept. is clearly known to the guiding heads & he has their constant & warm support. On his side patience & watchfulness—on theirs watchfulness and activity. Mr. Frémont is so well again. The governor—Pierpont[4]—is a good and honest man who works with the Genl. & has faith in him. Already the vitality of an idea with a man behind it warms into new energy this country side. I don't know what the Govt. meant by sending Mr. Frémont here, but the result will be to kill the *conditional* union sentiment & bring out the healthy feeling, which we find with pleasure does exist but has had no nourishment. You must care about these things. It is all important to success and you know that much as I wish & hope for smooth money success yet this is the noble part. This is something which remains when we leave the Astor House & take our places among its "neighbors gone before to the unknown & silent shore."[5]

My little requests to you are to make any use of my dear little marine villa[6] that Madam Julia dictates. When you leave—if it seems safe to you to do so—you can let go into execution the accompanying lease. The place is Lily's and as a matter of choice & feelings I would rather not have Mr. Brumagim there. I am afraid he will cut some of my wild looking laurels. There are both quail & rabbits there in the brush & it was so pretty to see them & hear the quail calling its little ones. His taste would lead to flower beds and open squares planted with those ghastly statues & urns that now brave the sand drifts & the breeze high up Pacific street. But he has always wanted the place & if it pacifies him & is a useful move you may let him have it. I like Mrs. Brumagim, she is genuine & good and has insight & capacity but he is managed by Mr. Park.

The rent for the place I want made payable to some reliable person for my sister Mrs. Jones—better in the name of little Betty her daughter. Mr. Childs (of Childs & Peterson) publisher, told me that the sales of my Father's Thirty Years View had been immense since the war, but Montgomery Blair is executor & he has never rendered an account to any one.[7] I will give it to Coles Morris to look into & as soon as Mr. Frémont gains a victory then I will have position to work from. In the meantime, my poor sister is at the mercy of a husband who drinks. When I was there I could see she did not suffer in one way from it & I rented the house to Mr. Beale to provide a little income for her chiefly for Betty's education.

Betty is my godchild & it gives me the right. But Mrs. Beale prefers the mission road to Black Point & so that was broken up.

I have troubled you with my reasons for letting Mr. Brumagim have the place because it is a matter of feeling & on my theory you are going to be a better man than ever, and except the one abiding charge to see that Mr. Frémont is not worried, I think is the only money-tainted idea I shall ever have to present to you. I should be very thankful to have his mind quite quiet about his private affairs. This will be done I know if intelligence and friendship can compass it. If there is any insuperable difficulty we shall meet it as we have done other evils, but I will not look for evil with you on the ground.

J. B. F.

AL initialed (Billings Mansion Archives). The Frémonts had reached Wheeling, W. Va., where JCF assumed command of the Mountain Department on Mar. 29.

1. On Mar. 31, 1862, after a month-long acquaintance, Billings had married Julia Parmly (1835–1914), daughter of the noted New York dentist Eleazar Parmly. On Apr. 11, the couple sailed for California, where Billings would continue as JCF's agent and legal advisor for the increasingly debt ridden Mariposas mines.
2. Col. James Woodruff Savage (1826–90), a New York City lawyer, was an aide-de-camp to JCF in St. Louis and West Virginia. After the war, he moved to Omaha, where he was elected a district judge. The Frémonts visited him en route to Prescott in 1878 (*Transactions and Reports of the Nebraska Historical Society*, 4 [1892]: 61–71, 218–32; JBF to John Gutzon Borglum, May 30, June 18 [1890], DLC—Borglum Papers).
3. Gustave Paul Cluseret (1823–1900), a French military adventurer, had commanded the French Legion with Garibaldi's forces in Italy. Recruited for Civil War service by the American envoy to Sardinia, he was assigned to JCF's staff after McClellan rejected him. For his gallantry at the battle of Cross Keys on June 8, he was promoted to brigadier-general. In 1864 he edited a New York weekly promoting JCF's presidential candidacy. Returning to France in 1867, he was in his later years four times elected to the Chamber of Deputies (WARNER, 85–86; MCCLELLAN, 176).
4. Francis H. Pierpont (1814–99) had supported Lincoln for president in 1860. When Virginia seceded, he lead West Virginians to form a new state, admitted to the Union in 1863. After the fall of Richmond, he would serve as governor of Virginia.
5. The quotation is from Charles Lamb's short poem, "Hester."
6. Black Point.
7. See JBF to Philip Fendall, July 6, 1866, below, on the same issue.

To George Julian

[Printed letterhead]
Head-Quarters, Mountain Department
Wheeling, May 1st, 1862.

My dear Mr. Julian,

I think you know how much pleased I was to find that no committee restrictions could keep you silent when Mr. Dawes made his suggestio falsi [suggestion of falsehood] for the second time.[1] I enclose you a copy of the General's letter to Col. Shanks[2] for him to use on a question of privilege in answer to Mr. Odell,[3] who is more true to his pro-slavery demands than to the truth.

Won't you, with all the force of one knowing the truth refuse to assist these slanderers? and insist on the justice of giving publicity to what you know of the Western Dept.? It is not one man they are striking at but a representative of a clear policy against slavery. It is all work for the summer elections that they are doing. Col. Blair has arranged to be the conservative candidate in Missouri.[4] The Germans know him & have cast him out but the semi-secessionists (their paper the Missouri Republican) are to support him. This is to prevent the emancipation candidate from success. Of course every government aid in mails & patronage is bent to this aim, & so it is in other states. I can take care of Mr. Odell & will attend to his defeat next week[5] but I think a man or two might be found to attend to the West & prevent the next House from being crammed with men whose speeches are like editorials in the N.Y. Herald[6] or like the arguments used in Cincinnati against Wendell Phillips.[7] I have no more time. This goes by private hand. Will you make my thanks to Mr. R. Conkling. I've just read his little speech. He knows about the "co-partnership."[8]

I am perfectly thankful none of the intriguing Genls. got New Orleans.[9] Why is Com. Foote never rewarded? Because he is puritan anti slavery & successful? Now he is ill—& if he dies without reward we shall have imitated England's conduct to Havelock. Com. Foote is our Havelock. He ought to be immediately attended to.[10]

This is a very scrappy letter. *Don't let troops be withdrawn from this Dept.* They are trying to take away the Blenker Division & that leaves nothing.[11] It's bad enough to be shut up here *under restrictions* but too bad to have what little is promised withdrawn. Still we are patient for this is no war of blows. And it must have moral force to settle it. Either now or later—we can't see but we will wait in faith.

The people here are unconditional union—the rich secession & its twin Holt-unionists.[12] The working & middle class all for emancipation & we are doing a good political work here (which was not intended). The Governor is good enough but not a fierce man & wants re-election. Once in power he might be clearer but he is muddy about slavery just now.

It is such a privilege to write a letter that is not to go through the

Washington Post Office that I give you a full tide of my own thinking. Will you share it with our true hearted friend Col. Shanks. The Genl. is about going to hunt for the Blenker Dv. which has been a month on its way & is not yet in this Dept. Very truly yours,

J. B. Frémont

[*Margin note:* Col. Shanks has two letters to share with you.]

ALS (DLC—Giddings-Julian Papers). Congressman George Washington Julian (1817-99) of Indiana, another sympathetic member of the Committee on the Conduct of the War, was a deeply sincere reformer of Quaker background who advocated immediate emancipation.

1. In an Apr. 25 House speech, Massachusetts congressman Henry Laurens Dawes (1816-1903), a member of the predominantly anti-Fremont Committee on Government Contracts, had vigorously defended the committee's methods and findings. JBF's "suggestio falsi" seems to relate to Dawes's own reference to an earlier speech by JCF supporter Thaddeus Stevens, in which Stevens pointed out an error in the committee report and concluded "falsus in uno, falsus in omnibus" [false in one thing, false in all] (Washington *Globe*, Apr. 26, 1862).

2. Col. John P. C. Shanks (1826-1901), a Republican congressman from Indiana, served on JCF's staff in both St. Louis and West Virginia. In 1865, Shanks would be promoted to major general for "faithful and meritorious service" during the war (POORE, 618; MORRIS & MORRIS, 518; HEITMAN, 1:876). No JCF letters to Shanks have been found.

3. Moses Fowler Odell (1818-66), a Democratic congressman from New York, was an opposition member of the Committee on the Conduct of the War. When the majority issued its final report favorable to JCF, Odell did not sign it (FAUST, 541).

4. Amid charges of voter fraud, Frank Blair, who now advocated a policy of gradual rather than immediate emancipation, would be narrowly reelected to Congress in 1862 (E. B. SMITH [1], 334).

5. Despite JBF's threat, Odell was reelected to Congress.

6. The *Herald* was strongly antiemancipation.

7. During a recent speech in Cincinnati by Wendell Phillips, an antiabolitionist mob had thrown rotten eggs and charged the stage of the lecture hall. Afterward, a bottle of explosives was found in the lobby (STEWART, 237).

8. In a House speech on Apr. 29, New York congressman Roscoe Conkling (1829-88) had chastised the Committee on Government Contracts for its "semi-judicial, one-sided trial and condemnation" of JCF's Missouri activities (*Congressional Globe*, 37th Cong., 2d sess., pt. 2, vol. 129, pp. 1862-65). In her reference to the "copartnership," JBF seems to suggest that the committee's unfair treatment of JCF put it in virtual league with the proslavery forces.

9. New Orleans had been taken at the end of April by naval forces under Flag-Officer David Glasgow Farragut. The "intriguing generals" were most likely John Pope, who had publicly expressed contempt for JCF while serving under him in Missouri, and Henry W. Halleck, who had replaced JCF as commander of the Department of the Missouri. Pope was now commander of the newly formed Army of the Mississipi, while Halleck, having taken credit as department commander for the Grant/Foote victory at Forts Henry and Donelson, had been promoted to commander of all Union

forces west of the Appalachians (MCPHERSON, 406). The newspapers had been full of speculation on who deserved credit for these victories and well as for the more problematic one at Shiloh on Apr. 6–7, 1862. MCFEELY, 104–10, 116–21, provides a detailed account of Halleck's rivalry with Grant during this period. See also GRANT, 5:78–83, on the newspaper controversy over Grant's role at Shiloh.

10. On Apr. 7, Pope's army, with vital support from Foote's gunboats, had seized Island No. 10, an important southern stronghold on the Mississippi. JBF doubtless thought Pope, who was lionized in the press, had received credit at the expense of Foote (MCPHERSON, 415). Broken in health, in part as a result of battle injuries, Foote died on June 26, 1863.

Sir Henry Havelock (1795–1857), like Foote an earnest, deeply religious man, spent most of his career in subordinate positions with the British army in India. During the Indian revolt of 1857, his military ability was finally recognized, but just as he became a hero in England, he died of diarrhea in India.

11. Louis Blenker (1812–63), an emigré who had led troops in the failed 1848 German revolution, had organized German-American regiments into a ten thousand-man division. On Mar. 31, Lincoln reluctantly assigned the division to JCF, explaining to McClellan: "This morning I felt constrained to order Blenker's Division to Fremont; and I write this to assure you that I did so with great pain, understanding that you would wish it otherwise. If you could know the full pressure of the case, I am confident you would justify it." Unfortunately, Blenker's Division, lost en route in snow and rain without tents and sufficient food, did not reach JCF until May 11. By then the men were so exhausted that JCF aide Albert Tracy believed the division "should rest and recuperate on full supplies, for not less than ten or twenty days, and yet it is to move with us tomorrow!" (FAUST, 67; MCCLELLAN, 219–20; TRACY, 171).

12. Joseph Holt (1807–94), a Kentucky lawyer who served briefly as Buchanan's secretary of war, had been instrumental in persuading his native state to support the Union cause, although he opposed the abolition of slavery. Holt-Unionists were thus pro-Union but antiemancipation. When JCF issued his Missouri emancipation decree, Holt wrote Lincoln opposing it (LINCOLN, 4:520).

To Frederick Billings

Astor House, 7 May [1862].

My dear Mr. Billings,

We got in too late for the Long Island boat last night but go over at one. Will you remember "Little Neck Long Island," is the address. I trust the whole journey was in keeping with the first move and that Mrs. Billings (are you used to the name yet?) has only happy associations with California & the oceans we have to cross to reach it.

The Pacific R.R. bill has passed the House & will the Senate.[1] That will make a great difference to us all & render Mariposas no longer a bug bear. The Genl. had a letter that pleased him from Mr. Park dated 12th March. I hope you will send him only good news. You will be glad to know how well & how contented the General is. I left him at a camp in the mountains deep down in Virginia, with the advance guard of the Blenker Division fine soldiers & filling the air first with shouts of welcome & then with full throated songs. Blenker is a horror but the Division is soldierly—genuine—& its officers admirable. There will be a compact body of 25.000—Ohio, Indiana & Virginia troops with the Germans, and nearly a hundred pieces of artillery. This was Bonaparte's favorite moveable column & a happier (or handsomer) man never headed a column than the one I left at New Creek. Each day he makes about 20 miles & you will hear of results. The Govt. forbid his going to Knoxville.[2] Of course the Herald (the only organ left to the Blairs) attacks him for neglecting it. But the record is fully kept & the second volume will be as compact and conclusive as the first which was issued on the 4th March.

Genl. McClellan has another victory by default and one side cry shame and the other side shout glory.[3] You can take your choice. The war is not ended. Nor will mere blows settle it.

My friends the Kings are happy over a little Viking who has come into port lately, but Mrs. King will before this reaches you have been able to give a welcome to Mrs. Billings.

Ellen tells me you were the most agitated bridegroom she ever saw. You are a very happy man to be able to have your whole heart stirred & Mrs. Billings must feel like a real enchantress to have been able so to glorify your life.

With our best and warmest remembrances to her. Always sincerely yours,

J. B. Frémont.

The Corporal[4] is not in—he is more military than ever having had his hair cut to the skin, camp fashion. Evidently he feels himself as essential a bolt in your matrimonial structure as the ring or the certificate.

ALS (Billings Mansion Archives). While JCF remained at his field headquarters at New Creek, W.Va., JBF returned to New York, where she rented a house at Little Neck, Long Island.

1. The Pacific Railroad Act of 1862, signed into law by Lincoln on July 1, authorized the construction of a transcontinental railroad along a central route, subsidized by land grants and generous loans for each mile of track laid. After selling Las Mariposas in 1863, JCF invested in western railroads.

2. JCF had discussed his plan to seize Knoxville, Tenn., and its strategic rail line with the Lincoln administration before he assumed command of the Mountain De-

partment. On Apr. 21, Lincoln asked, through Secretary of War Stanton, "when you intend to move toward Knoxville, and with what force and by what route." JCF responded the same day with a detailed plan for moving up the Valley of Virginia, seizing the Baltimore and Ohio Railroad, and continuing on to Knoxville; but on April 24, Lincoln, through Stanton, "modified" the plan "so far as to direct you after striking the railroad, as you propose, not to advance toward Knoxville without further instructions" (OFFICIAL RECORDS, ser. 1, vol. 12, pt. 1:5–7, pt. 3:96, 104).

3. JBF refers to the Confederate evacuation of Yorktown on May 3–4 after a month-long siege by McClellan's forces. Many, including the president, believed that McClellan's strategy was overly cautious and that Yorktown would have yielded far more quickly to a vigorous Union assault (MCPHERSON, 426–27).

4. Six-year-old Frank Frémont had been an attendant at the Billings wedding on Mar. 31, evidently accompanied by JBF's maid Ellen since the Frémonts were in Wheeling.

To James T. Fields

[May 22 (1862)]
Little Neck
Long Island

My dear Mr. Fields,

Miss Harding[1] writes me that she is going to Boston & having promised herself for the earliest day there can only give me half a day here. She is so conscientious that I shall not be able to keep her without a formal release from you. Won't you write one & send it to me here? You shall not lose by her staying with me a little. She has never seen the sea & I want to shew it to her—& she is proud & shy & I want to help her to a coat of armor against she gets into your formidable sharpshooters' circle. Remember too she is in my department & these war times I claim mine as a first right.

The winter was such a weary time of forced silence and patience that I had no heart for my work. Since then I have put my little quête [quest] into order but we thought it best to hold it back so long as there was any chance to recall the Guard into service. Every effort for that has failed. Perhaps the new call for fifty thousand more may bring them in, but now they are dispersed & most of the officers on duty in other branches—all the General could, he has gotten commissions for, but only by *not* telling who they were. I see no reason to keep it back any longer & shall send it on to you as soon as it is fairly copied out. I find nearly all the illustrations were left here. I shall have to sandwich them into place & I think it will attain the object I propose. With best remembrances to Mrs. Fields. Very sincerely yours,

Jessie Benton Frémont

May 22d.

ALS (CSmH—Fields Papers).

1. JBF had met the young writer Rebecca Harding (later Davis) (1831–1910) in Wheeling. Harding's startlingly realistic story, "Life in the Iron-Mills," had appeared in the Apr. 1861 *Atlantic,* launching her literary career. See OLSEN for insight into Harding's career.

To Annie Adams Fields

Little Neck
Long Island
May 29th [1862].

My dear Mrs. Fields,

Thank you for your very kind invitation to Lily & myself. At another time I should be glad to go with Miss Harding & see her great pleasure in realizing the Revolution (which I never did until I was in Boston). But I am not quiet enough at heart just now to live out of myself— it is so hard to have one's body in one place when all one's heart & soul & strength are in another. Here I can wear it down but until I am delivered from my apprehensions of Washington (I never had any for it) I can know no rest.

Mr. Copeland[1] was fearfully unmilitary in telling his knowledge as adgt. to Genl. Banks but I should like to tell him how much indebted I feel for his being so much of a man in spite of being an officer. I've long suffered from a regular congestion of facts in regard to the negligence and niggardliness & ignorance of the war managers: Mr. Lincoln & Mrs. Lincoln, Mr. Holt, N.Y. Herald, Mr. Stanton & a camarilla of aged & spiteful old army officers & some who are not old, but alertly spiteful—especially against "Abolitionist generals."

These receive constant re-enforcements from the Border states & from such of their allies in the North as would be found after death to have "cotton" stamped on their hearts.

Patience & silence are all the weapons I have. I should risk losing them if I met with you all. For through Mr. Banks you are feeling in your own innermost lives the results of this sort of war management, & sympathy is a great weakener of the nerves.

When I do go to Boston I shall consider myself privileged to come at once to see you, & receive privately & before publication all yours & Mr. Fields's criticisms, erasures & modifications. Although I write with a curb bit as I want to make friends for the object & property *is* timid. Very sincerely yours,

Jessie Benton Frémont

ALS (CSmH—Fields Papers).

1. Maj. Robert Morris Copeland (1830–74), a committed abolitionist, was assistant adjutant general to JCF's longtime political ally, Nathaniel Banks, now a major general heading the Department of the Shenandoah. Copeland had been on leave in Boston when Banks's forces were routed by Gen. Thomas J. ("Stonewall") Jackson at Front Royal and Wincester. On May 26, Copeland issued an imprudent public statement blaming the administration for Banks's defeat; as a result, Copeland was dismissed from the army (BURCHARD, 56; New York *Tribune*, May 28, 1862).

To Biddle Boggs

[June 17 (1862)]

My Dear Mr. Boggs,

You have behaved just as I knew you would and I am proud of you. I have to thank you for many personal kind acts which helped lessen the trouble of frontier life but you are caring for my chief now in a way that gives you honor as well as satisfaction. Capt. Howard wrote me about your getting between the General and the angry horse at Franklin & I asked the General to tell you I knew you did it half for him and half for me & we both thanked you for the feeling which prompted it.

The General wrote me of your cool courage at Cross Keyes.[1] Buena Vista & California had not left much to surprise you but it was a great pleasure to me that you had the chance to shew what our Mariposas Californians were. To Mr. Haskell[2] also the Genl. owes a great debt for his cool intelligence & daring.

Some day you will tell me all about it. The telegraph just tells us that on the 16th a much greater force was coming upon you & no re-enforcements on their way.[3]

I hope that God will do much for you. It would be hard to say in which Capitol, Richmond or Washington, it would give most joy to have Mr. Frémont cut off. But God is with you. I am glad you fought on Sunday for all that morning I was at church & many hundred thousand women everywhere were joining in prayer for our armies. Not on Sundays alone do those prayers ascend and be sure they are listened to.

J. B. Frémont

New York 17th June

ALS (C). A copy, made by Biddle Boggs in the 1880s, is in the possession of Mrs. Barbara Brock, Fresno, Calif. Boggs (1822–86), the Frémonts' faithful general handyman at Las Mariposas, had joined JCF's Mountain Department command as a lieutenant. According to one San Francisco source, JBF had written Boggs "requesting him to serve his country by enlisting. She has also written to Gen. Sumner requesting him to give Boggs a place" (Calvin Park to Trenor Park, Sept. 4, 1861, Park-McCullough House Archives). An acquaintance described Boggs as "one of the most thoroughly *Dickensy* characters I ever knew. . . . He was a Pennsylvanian ('Me mother was a Biddle, and me father was a Boggs: so there you have it') but looked a typical dried-up Connecticut Yankee, with sparse yellow hair . . . skin of face, neck and hands corrugated and hardened by years of exposure . . . tireless on foot or horseback, lazy as to all regular employment, good-natured and kindly, shrewd of judgment, deliberate in speech, with a perfectly delightful conceit of his own wisdom and importance—in which he was not so far out" (HOWARD, 81; Shirley Sargent ms., "Biddle Boggs and the Frémonts," copy courtesy of author).

1. At the battle of Cross Keys on June 8, Boggs had shown exceptional bravery. JCF recorded that he "got dismounted twice by shells & had his horse killed under him" (to Frederick Billings, June 13, 1862, Billings Mansion Archives; see also TRACY, 333, 338).

2. Leonidas Haskell (d. 1873) and his family had been neighbors of the Frémonts at Black Point. Haskell joined JCF's staff in St. Louis as police director, but substantial testimony before congressional committees linked him with other Californians in profiteering from war contracts. Specifically, Haskell was involved in a system of corrupt inspectors that allowed him to purchase mules from local citizens and sell them to the government for a profit (see Special House Committee on Government Contracts, 37th Cong., 2d sess., *Report* 2, serial 1142, pp. 95–97, 531–32, 544–45, 707–11, 794, 1045; serial 1143, pp. lxi–lxii, 536–37, 1489; and Blair's repetition of these charges in Joint Committee on the Conduct of the War, 37th Cong., 3rd sess., *Report*, 3:182). Following JCF to West Virginia, Haskell served as an assistant chief of cavalry under Charles Zagonyi. A fellow officer called Haskell "a bird of evil omen. . . . a most thorough disorganizer, and disliked by us all" (TRACY, 177). To the Frémonts, however, Haskell seemed a loyal aide, executing his duties, according to JCF, with "boldness and celerity" (OFFICIAL RECORDS, ser. 1, vol. 12, pt. 1:16, 23, 35).

3. From Mount Jackson, W.Va., on the same date, JCF informed Secretary of War

Stanton: "Harrisonburg is reported occupied by a large body of enemy's cavalry, and Jackson's main body reported crossing Shenandoah [River] to this side at Port Republic yesterday morning" (OFFICIAL RECORDS, ser. 1, vol. 12, pt. 1:662; for additional correspondence on the alleged threat, see ibid., 401–2, 406–11). In reality, Jackson was retreating south to join the main Confederate army.

To Sydney Howard Gay

June 21 [1862].

My dear Sir,

Your note of yesterday had some good in it although you like myself evidently feel the Govt. indifferent to the fate of that branch of the army. Sigel, Schurz,[1] Banks & Frémont nicely tucked in a corner to be taken like Jack Horner's plum by Jackson's thumb.[2] It would be hard to say in which Capitol, Richmond or Washington, most *real* sympathy would be given to the rebel general who should rid them of this quartette—including those Germans who never will vote for slavery & are therefore of "not the least consequence."

I enclose you copies of the two last dispatches from the General. It is absolutely all I know, but I infer there is to be some active service for which the fragments of separate corps are being united—this time I trust under one head.

As I get my dispatches by favor I dare not make the information known except to a few useful friends who will give all the help possible without telling why.

When I have a safe chance (you see the General cannot even get my letters—I wish they would read them in cabinet meetings) I will give the General the compliment wrung from our Colbert(!).[3]

In the meantime do stir Massachusetts feeling for Genl. Banks. It was not my chief's own feeling of which you have heard—but the atmosphere of impatience among some of the best foreign officers around him telling on tired nerves with no one who understood him to say he should hold his own ideas even against men who had been doing vital good service. We know that [these are?] not at war to make brilliant reputations & gain sudden honors—faith & patience & almost hope will be worn out before the objects we have are obtained. We may wear out in the work but there is nothing [that] can bring self above duty in this war of the purification. Even now it is to me the crowning good fortune of the Genl's life that he has the opportunity to take a share in it. Knowing what he did in the West & what he had prepared to do even with this meagre command at Stanton & Lynchburg it tries me to the heart to see him cramped & thwarted & misrepresented but it can never dishearten either of us. Hawthorne in comparing open fires & stoves says (what a mess of nonsense he has put in the last Atlantic)[4] "what man would not die for his hearth? Who would die for his air tight stove?"[5] The Govt. is the air tight stove but the dear old hearthstone of country is not to be abandoned. Zagonyi feels this in all his knightly nature. Col. Albert[6] does not. My daughter says, "How can Col. Albert have patience when he has no faith?" (He says he is without belief in any future.) Naturally to him present immediate rewards & opportunities to bring those rewards are paramount, & those come from an ephemeral source. (I wish it was literally ephemeral but, patience.) [*Margin note*: Cluseret too is selfish but they are both invaluable. Col. Albert especially so.]

I have written with all my heart about this to the Genl. I embodied, in a few enigmatical words to others, something which I telegraphed to him—it is that he means by "your good telegraph." If I could only see him—he has no one with him to whom he can rest his mind, & laying off that burthen start again. But I am growing personal. You will know how to rouse German feeling about the condition their troops are in. Can't Germany & Massachusetts make a rescue? Do you know the editor of the American Baptist? There have been brave editorials in that paper & it's bad interfering with religious papers—they have all a woman's privileges of tongue. If I were not Mr. Frémont's wife I could speak out but as it is for his benefit, as well as that of others that I am working, I must do it through friends who will not misunderstand & who know the beauty as well as the utility of silent activity.

J B Frémont

Copy

Woodstock 19th.

Arrived here with my command. Made connection & received your good dispatch on the road. All right in camp.

J. C. Frémont

Strasburg 20.

Dispatch of today received. All quite right in camp. Have had no letters from you for some time. Can you have some hospital comforts sent to me for our men, and soon.

J. C. Frémont

———

I have written to Dr. Van Buren (not time to get answer) about the hospital wants. He will do his part thoroughly. Do you think it is for past or coming wants?

I am steadily in all day until 6. I go out then for two or three hours for air.

ALS (NNC—Gay Papers). A dedicated abolitionist, Gay (1814-88) edited the *Anti-Slavery Standard*, 1844-57. He then joined the staff of Greeley's New York *Tribune,* becoming managing editor in 1862. Enthusiastic about JCF, he told Rebecca Harding Davis: "My creed is short. I believe in Almighty God, His Son, and John C. Frémont" (DAVIS, 175-76). During this period, JBF regularly furnished Gay, who also lived on Staten Island, with reports from and about JCF, thus insuring that her husband's version of events appeared in the influential *Tribune.*

1. Carl Schurz (1829-1906), a renowned student leader during the failed German revolution of 1848, emigrated to the United States in 1852. A gifted speaker in English and German, he campaigned actively for JCF in 1856 and Lincoln in 1860. Lincoln appointed him a brigadier general of volunteers, and on June 10, 1862, he assumed command of a division under JCF. Asked by Lincoln to report personally to him about JCF, Schurz generally justified JCF's actions but noted that his "whole personality appeared rather attractive—and yet, one did not feel quite sure" (SCHURZ, 2:344). Schurz, along with Sigel, Banks, and Frémont, were all "political generals" and thus viewed with disdain by many professional soldiers (MCPHERSON, 328). After the war Schurz would have a distinguished career as a journalist, senator, and secretary of the interior.

2. Confederate general Thomas J. ("Stonewall") Jackson (1824-63), using fast-moving, hard-hitting tactics, had initiated a brilliant campaign in the Shenandoah Valley to divert Union forces and so disrupt McClellan's imminent attack on Richmond. On May 8, Jackson had defeated JCF's outnumbered forces at McDowell; and on May 21-25, he had routed Banks's troops at Front Royal and Winchester, sending them fleeing across the Potomac. Alarmed that Jackson might invade Washington, the administration panicked. It called off the long-planned transfer of Gen. Irvin McDowell's forces at Fredericksburg to McClellan's army, then attempted by telegraph to direct a strategy to trap Jackson in the Shenandoah between McDowell and JCF. But neither Union general was able to move as quickly as Jackson, who slipped through the trap, fighting effective rearguard actions against JCF at Cross Keys on June 8 and against McDowell at Port Republic the next day. For accounts of Jackson's campaign, see NEVINS [3], 2:123-28; MCPHERSON, 454-60; and JCF's report in OFFICIAL RECORDS, ser. 1, vol. 12, pt. 1:3-26).

3. As Louis XIV's finance minister, Jean Baptiste Colbert (1619-83) inaugurated

sweeping reforms in France's tax and tariff systems. Thus "our Colbert" was probably Secretary of the Treasury Salmon P. Chase (1808–73), who was overseeing vast changes in the nation's fiscal system to finance the war. A compliment about JCF may well have been "wrung" from Chase, since he, like JCF, favored immediate emancipation and was also hostile to the Blairs.

4. An essay by Nathaniel Hawthorne (1804–64), "Chiefly about War-Matters by a Peaceable Man," had just appeared in the July 1862 *Atlantic* (available in June). Hawthorne's ironic, detached tone and his concluding hint that a compromise with the South might be possible must have annoyed many readers besides JBF. In fact, the *Atlantic* had felt it necessary to add a series of editoral notes to the text to contradict Hawthorne's views. For a discussion of Hawthorne's attitude, see FREDRICKSON, 1–3.

5. JBF paraphrases a remark in the last paragraph of Hawthorne's "Fire-Worship," an essay published in 1843 and reprinted in his *Mosses from an Old Manse* (1846).

6. Col. Anzelm Albert (1819–93) was JCF's chief of staff. A professional soldier who had participated in the failed Hungarian revolution, he emigrated to the United States in 1851. Settling in St. Louis, he joined the Union army at the start of the Civil War and was severely wounded at the battle of Wilson's Creek (New York *Tribune,* Apr. 25, 1862; VASVARY, 43–44).

To Frederick Billings

1st July [1862].

The General is back—attending to the Mariposas this day.[1] He says he looks for you immediately. Everything of the Philadelphia arrangement is fully arranged. Mr. J. of Phil. taking 450.000 & the other part in two portions in this City.[2] If we are defeated at Richmond all money matters fall—but the whole chapter is open—foreign intervention—splits at home, everything bad.

My head is (as usual) aching. The General is off with some business people & the steamer is going. The President went to West Point to get Genl. Scott's backing in removing Mr. Frémont[3]—said on his return he had not been there to make or unmake Genls! & today exults in the success of his work there. Throw up your hat for *Honest* Abe.

On a clean page I put the name of Mrs. Billings to whom we all send our warmest regards & wishes to see her again.

Frank has gone to Mass[achusetts] for his 4th of July—uniform included, with Mr. Haskell. Very sincerely & warmly always your friend,

J. B. & (for) J. C. Frémont

ALS (Billings Mansion Archives).

1. On June 26, 1862, the Lincoln administration had combined JCF's Mountain

Department with those of Banks and McDowell into a single unit under Maj. Gen. John Pope, an outspoken critic of JCF in St. Louis. Deeply humiliated, JCF resigned his command rather than serve under a man whom he viewed as both an enemy and a subordinate. See JBF to George Julian, Jan. 16 [1864], below, for JBF's explanation of his motives.

2. The "Philadelphia arrangement" proved to be yet another unsuccessful attempt to raise capital for Las Mariposas, which had become increasingly indebted under Trenor Park's dubious management, despite the fact that the mines produced $53,000 a month in 1861 and $42,000 per month in 1862 (Billings to Park, Oct. 31, 1862, Park-McCullough House Archives). CRAMPTON, 269, estimates the Mariposas debt at $2 million by early 1862, with interest payments draining profits drastically. According to a nine-page "Summary of the condition of the Mariposas Estate as to title encumbrances & debts," indebtedness as of Jan. 1863 was $1.1 million with the interest on some loans as high as 2 percent *per month* (CU-B—John T. Doyle Papers). JCF had gradually sold pieces of the estate to creditors, including one-eighth each to A. A. Selover and Frederick Billings, and, in a series of complicated arrangements, a greater proportion to Park. For information on Park's business arrangements with JCF, see JBF to Francis Preston Blair, July 2, 1859, note 2, above. On the "Philadelphia arrangement," see Billings to Park, Mar. 20, 29, 1862, Park-McCullough House Papers; JCF to Billings, Mar. 4, Apr. 8, June 13, 1862, Billings Mansion Archives; and "Great Events," 381–82).

3. Most of the rumors provoked by Lincoln's visit to Scott on June 25 did not concern JCF but McClellan, whose removal was anticipated after the failure of his Peninsula campaign (STRONG, 3:233; LONG, 230; NEVINS [3], 2:143).

To Frederick Billings

[August 1 (1862)]

The General is putting himself in walking trim and dictates to me as he moves about—that, he has done nothing yet in the Mariposas matters owing to the pre-occupation in every one's mind caused by the continued reverses large & small to our arms. "Everything is in abeyance—looking either for the capture of McClellan's force or the taking of Baltimore & Washington"—both of which are among the near probabilities.[1]

The General has had nothing from you by the last two steamers. He says if there is anything he can do to aid affairs let him know. The Texas command is under discussion[2]—if it includes California, as we will try to have it, then he says he "can reach malefactors with a strong arm."

Meantime I rely on you not to let your friend & Frank be entirely robbed by Mr. Park.[3]

We are all well, although we have not fresh San Francisco air to keep us so. Mrs. Billings should be in highest health as she seems to be in happiness. Her kind pleasant letter has been unanswered because young Raymond's brother was killed,[4] Jack Howard & Col. Savage have had army fever (a mixture of ague & typhus). Col. Savage nearly lost his life & so I've had all the letters & in door work & no time for gentler things.

You can't think how the sensation of coming disasters has passed into the very air—making us all feel aimless & nervous & watchful— a sort of sultry silence in the moral world.

This is a focus of consultation & intelligence. The General is in the field although not in the saddle, but it is a question now to be settled out of Washington. Kindest remembrances to Mrs. Billings & from us all to you both. Frank & Lily got home two days since from a month at the sea side.

J. B. F.

Aug. 1.

AL initialed (Billings Mansion Archives).

1. On July 11, 1862, Lincoln had appointed Henry Halleck general-in-chief of the Union army. Shortly thereafter McClellan's Army of the Potomac was withdrawn from its position on the James River to protect Washington. As JBF reflects, northern morale was at a low point after the collapse of McClellan's Peninsula campaign.

2. JCF remained interested in commanding an expedition to Texas (see JBF to Billings, Feb. 7, 1862, note 1, above, on JCF's earlier Texas proposal), and his supporters continued to lobby Lincoln on his behalf (PEARSON, 2:124–26). However, abetted by the Blairs, Lincoln now seriously questioned JCF's competence, and the Texas post eventually went to Nathaniel Banks.

3. By now the Frémonts viewed Park's management as corrupt, believing, for example, that during the 1861–62 winter flood, Park had deliberately neglected to open the sluice gates of the expensive Las Mariposas dam and so destroyed it ("Great Events," 382). By late fall, Billings would also be suspicious (see Billings to John T. Doyle, Nov. 29, 1862, quoted in BELL, 167; and to Park, Nov. 8, 1862, Park-McCullough House Archives). Frederick Law Olmsted, as Las Mariposas superintendent, concluded in 1864 that Park had managed the property to "take the cream" of the gold, postpone its debts, and artificially inflate profits at the time of the sale (OLMSTED, 5:196–200). For further evidence of Park's misconduct or mismanagement, see Billings to Park, Oct. 31, Nov. 12, 1862, Park-McCullough House Archives; A. A. Selover to JCF, Aug. 10, 1862, Billings Mansion Archives; and ROPER, 233–79, passim. Later, Park was a principal promotor of the notorious Emma silver mine (for details of this scandal and Park's role, see C. SPENCE, 139–82).

4. "Ros" Raymond was the eldest of seven children; his brother has not been identified.

To James T. Fields

[Oct. 8, 1862]

My dear Mr. Fields,

I can't get along without seeing you & I can't leave home. I'm pinned down like Gulliver by little people.[1] Charley is at home for his vacation & my daughter is quite seriously unwell, and yet I wanted you to read over the manuscript, &, if it answered announce it in this month's Atlantic—(on one of those slips attached with book notices). The 25th October is the anniversary of the charge[2] & I like to keep anniversaries. I can't possibly send you the manuscript because you will have to talk it over with me. I may consent to leave out some things but I'll make a death struggle for each lost projectile & I will not alter facts. As it is although I have put down the truth & nothing but the truth it's by no means the whole truth. Don't be frightened—it's as soft as carded wool—the goring apparatus is sous entendu [understood].

Are you coming to New York soon? If you will let me know, I will have you met & brought over here—it needs a guide, & you can brace yourself to an exciting & protracted sitting in which I shall want you to be satisfied but I must tell the truth. Very truly yours,

J. B. Frémont.

The Genl. is in town every day & my letters come quickest simply addressed to me at New York.

ALS (CSmH—Fields Papers). JBF's letter follows on the same sheet an Oct. 8, 1862, letter to Fields from John Raymond Howard regarding minor changes in the music for the song "The Trooper's Death," which JBF planned to use in *The Story of the Guard.*

1. Gulliver was tied down by six-inch Lilliputian people in Jonathan Swift's *Gulliver's Travels.*
2. A reference to the Guard's capture of Springfield on Oct. 25, 1861, the focus of JBF's *Story of the Guard.*

To James T. Fields

[Oct. 26 (1862)]

My dear Mr. Fields,

Will you send me a line that I may let Mr. Harte know officially that you approve of him? and how many talents his talent represents.[1]

This assumes that he pleases you as he does Mr. King and myself. But of that there can be no doubt for his is a fresh mind filled with unworn pictures, & having the great advantage only shared in that field by "John Brent"[2] of cultivated perceptions. I should like, if it suits you, to be the one to announce any pleasant fact to him. I covet the post of bearer of good tidings, and it will be such to him to have your approval & to be admitted to a place of honor in the Atlantic.

Please let no one see what I have written. Now that I am rid of the [. . .] I see it as a whole & by erasures & substitutions & a very little addition in linking I can make it very much more coherent and forcible. I enclose the verses which make its termination—they were accidentally left behind on Monday.

I had the most characteristic talk from Zagonyi yesterday. He came from Brooklyn early & breakfasted with us. What a crying shame that such a man should be left to parlor duty. No wonder Stuart rides where he lists.[3]

When the proof sheets come down Col. Zagonyi will go over them with me. So must the General although they are slow in St. Louis but he will make his impatience felt.[4] With best regards to Mrs. Fields, always very truly yours,

J. B. Frémont

Sunday night   26th October

I don't *prefer* misquotations. That from Schiller, "I shall outlast this stroke I know. What does not man live down" &c.[5] is not thoroughly well quoted in the intermediate lines. The applicable parts—the first & last lines came correctly to mind.

ALS (CSmH—Fields Papers).

1. With the backing of JBF as well as Thomas Starr King, Bret Harte would make his eastern debut in Oct. 1863 when "The Legend of Monte del Diablo," a tale of Mexican California, appeared in the *Atlantic*. Despite pressure from JBF, no other material from the still obscure Harte appeared in the prestigious *Atlantic* until after Harte achieved sudden fame in 1868–69 for California gold camp stories like "The Luck of Roaring Camp" and "The Outcasts of Poker Flat." In 1871, the *Atlantic* would offer Harte $10,000 for exclusive rights to his work for a year, the largest amount ever paid a writer up to that time (HARTE, 1:382–97; GAER, 124–27).

2. *John Brent* (1862), a romantic adventure novel set on the western plains, was published by Ticknor & Fields after the death of its young author, Theodore Winthrop, killed in action on June 10, 1861, at the battle of Great Bethel. According to one reviewer, his style was "fresh, natural, strong, and direct" with "a dashing, daring, and jubilant vigor" (*Atlantic Monthly*, 9 [Apr. 1862]: 520–21).

3. In mid-June, the dashing Confederate cavalry officer J. E. B. Stuart (1833–64) had led 1,200 cavalry in a daring four-day reconnaissance around McClellan's forces massed near Richmond. JBF suggests that Stuart's exploit was successful because superb cavalrymen like Zagonyi were not being used against him by the Union.

4. JCF had gone to St. Louis to work unsuccessfully against Frank Blair's reelection to Congress (W. E. SMITH, 2:218), as well as to testify at the court-martial of Justus McKinstry, his former chief quartermaster. Although JCF believed McKinstry was a "true soldier and true and loyal citizen" (New York *Times,* Oct. 28, 1862), he would be dismissed from the army for defrauding the government. For further information on McKinstry, see JBF to Lamon, Oct. 26 [1861], note 3, above.

5. *The Death of Wallenstein,* act 5, sc. 3, by German poet and dramatist Friedrich von Schiller (1759–1805).

To James T. Fields

[Jan. 5 (1863)]

Dear Mr. Fields,

You're too good to be true. Is it possible that I have actually gotten tangible help for my people already?[1] or is it your contribution to a good object? It's all the same to them, but my satisfaction would be greater to believe it's really of my own earning. I like that word—it's a new sensation. I have now a dim perception of the protecting pride of a man who earns & gives of his own labor to those he loves. The Earl of Locksley hall didn't feel more gratified pride in giving Ellen his castle than I in my first "five hundred."[2] And I'm sure it will not kill any one for joy.

Mr. Eliot stayed over a train to take particulars from Zagonyi & we were all really happy over this unexpected assistance. If it is all right in a business view, I shall persist in thinking it very nice and kind of you to do it in the way it was done & so thank you. Mrs. Chamberlain[3] got the first $50, by telegraph. To her it was very necessary. Her son had been educated at the Washington University & known to Mr. Eliot who had high hopes for him. All fell for them at Springfield. Think how comforting to her it is to feel her son still guards her.

We have an idea—quite silently of course—that an edition on less expensive paper & with paper backs should be gotten out. After a little time. Several different kinds of minds have suggested this. They think it will be well to call it "the Army edition" and send it among the soldiers as an encouragement. Mr. Eliot says he will answer for the western armies.

You cannot realize what a fountain of sweet waters this little work has opened up for me. Our way is over the hot dusty highroad and neither grass nor shade belong to it—it's all bustle & keeping your own in the crowd & seeing the [hind?] wheels come to no grief while the horses' heads must be watched too & there be many rough words spoken there & kindly feelings cannot spring up in that toil & trouble. But this "aside" has brought to me from so many quarters the most charming evidences of sympathy and gentle feelings. Every way I am thoroughly gratified about it.

As soon as possible I want the full list of those in the charge added. It was due to them, for their feelings were wounded if not their bodies.

The misplacing of a period makes the mistake which has brought me a dozen written communications of the kind with this I enclose you. I have written to Judge Corwine to make it right—it should read "With the exception of that at Fredericktown all were small actions" (or something like that idea).[4] Would it be too much to ask a word of correction in the next Atlantic? It really is "influential" and our soldiers ought to get justice for they receive nothing else that is their due.

That reminds me of some new lines by my friend not Haste but Harte. I enclose them. As they are on Genl. Banks they may help him to notice (In the same proportion that the little girl helps Genl. Banks).[5] Let me know when he makes his debut in the Atlantic. Honestly, I foresee a calm well founded admiration for the Mt. Diablo legend. It's not Prescotty[6]—so much the better I think & lots of people like contemplative writing.

As I write as much for Mrs. Fields as yourself I send no separate message but best New Year's wishes to both.

J. B. Frémont

Monday evg. 5th Jany.

ALS (CSmH—Fields Papers).

1. JBF refers to a Jan. 3, 1863, note from Fields in which he announced that the just published *Story of the Guard* promised to be "so successful in point of numbers ordered" that $500 in profits had already been turned over to the Rev. William G. Eliot for the support of the families of the slain guardsmen. Fields's note would appear in the Jan. 12, 1863, New York *Tribune,* presumably at JBF's instigation.

2. JBF may be confused. In Alfred Lord Tennyson's poem, "Locksley Hall," the speaker revisits his childhood home and meditates on the girl who rejected him for a richer suitor. But the girl's name is Amy, not Ellen, the speaker is not an earl, and he gives her no castle. Perhaps JBF has in mind Tennyson's "Launcelot and Elaine," in

which Lancelot refuses Elaine's love but promises to endow her with broad land and territory, if her "good knight" be poor. A castle is not specifically mentioned, however.

3. Cpl. D. F. Chamberlain of St. Louis, a member of Company A of the Frémont Bodyguard, was killed during the assault on Springfield, Oct. 25, 1861 (J. B. FRÉMONT [2], 173).

4. JBF refers to an error in the Jan. 1863 *Atlantic* review of *Story of the Guard*, which resulted in the incorrect implication that the battle of Fredericktown, Mo., was a Union defeat.

5. Harte's poem, "Banks and the Slave Girl," describes the freeing of a slave child by Maj. Gen. Nathaniel Banks, commanding at the battle of Cedar Mountain, Aug. 9, 1862. The poem appeared in the Oct. 26, 1862, *Golden Era* (HARTE, 20:348–49).

6. William Hickling Prescott (1796–1859), author of *History of the Conquest of Mexico* and other works on Spain and its colonies, was known for his sweeping narrative style, with an emphasis on grand scenes and stirring events. Harte's story was more in the restrained manner of Washington Irving.

To Thomas Starr King

[early 1863]

Dear Mr. King,

I have had good long letters from both Mr. Harte and yourself and you know how glad I am to get them, and they should have had their answers long since, but every day for us has begun with an "if" for so long now that I lose my time because the horizon is so misty. Now I want to write first in regard to the California subscription.[1] Mr. Eliot tells me they have had not quite fifty thousand of it, the Revd. Bellows giving his own construction of the word "West." I enclose you a copy of the order which makes it a separate Department & frees them from interference.

The members of the Western Commn. take no salary & give their whole time. Mr. Eliot as clergyman & Samaritan both is very over-worked. Here in New York the Secretary Mr. Olmsted[2] receives $5000 a year. I do not know the salaries of the others but judge from what I have seen & known of the Revd. Bellows, self-denial is not his strong point. Did you read his speech about the physical superiority of the South? As a Virginian I have the privilege of dissenting—& this is no moment to flatter the South. Altogether I know of Mr. Bellows un-favorably and I am sure it was not your intention to leave that fund at the mercy of his prejudices. If you will say it was intended for the Western Sanitary Commn. for use in the West, that clears it. And take notice there is the most sanitary work needed there. Have I said enough?

I want you to let one third of the money go to western men to use for western men, & not leave them to the scant & unsympathizing mercies of the Revd. Bellows & his allies here. It is enough to say of them, that they speak of the north as lost *because* McClellan is not head of the armies. That gauges their capacities to me.

Then while we're on charitable topics, make use of Mr. Ticknor's note[3] to shew my venture is already meeting its object in getting money for the families of the Guard. As it is always to those who have that more is given, this will promote the sale of the bookling in California & I look to your friendly help in this. I get lots of compliments on it but don't care for any but the General's & yours (m. & f.) & Mr. Harte's and Mr. Beale's. The General likes it & you will all find something for each one in it. Mr. Beale would be friends with Zagonyi who has very much his own nature except more grim & less joke. Every day Lily has a grand ride with Zagonyi & often the General also. Isn't it a shame that such men have no higher use of their time than to train a girl to ride? The three horses have been together since July of '61 (the same groom for them) & they are all part of our lives. One the General rode at Cross Keyes & the one Lily rides is Zagonyi's own favorite horse which has shed its blood (pure blood it is too) from a bayonet stab given by a rebel in battle.

It's about the pleasantest thing they find to do. The General has had his hands over full with the misdeeds of Mr. Park who is without precedent in his shameless robberies. Rather than allow him a chance you must yourself come to the Senate.[4] But this would be an extreme measure for I know you do not want to break your plans, and besides that will be decided before this reaches you. If it should not be, don't let either Mr. Park or Mr. Billings get in.[5]

I send this by Mr. Howard who will be able to answer questions on many points to you. But it's all au jour le jour [depending on the circumstances] & we are not sure of much else than good health & good heart. Two good things. Add to them letters from you all. Don't judge from my infrequent writing. I am very often busy. I do a good deal of desultory work & in one way & another the General & the children fill the time. Charley was down for his Christmas & has returned—growing tall & behaving very well & learning very satis-factorily. Frank goes from ten to one daily to a French kinder-garten school, & has also drawing lessons as he has positive talent that way. Lily is deep in serious study of German & polishing off in French. That with skating & riding keeps her "alive." In among it all we see many pleasant people & get snatches at some really good music & I can get a bunch of violets (for ten cents) & lots of new reading matter. That makes up decentish happiness don't it?

I had intended to have some new cartes de visite for you by Mr. Howard but the sky has been dark every day since they were taken and so they are not ready. One is for a "frontispiece" for *giving* only— I am sitting with the General, Zagonyi & Ros & Jack around me.[6] The frame is the best part of the picture—for they surround me like a frame. I have not written a word to the Deweys. I can't. It's so shabby to go abroad for amusement just now. I am interrupted for the third time & give in—Affectionately to all, Yours,

JBF.

AL initialed (CSfCP—King Papers).

1. Under King's vigorous leadership, California had raised over $500,000 for the U.S. Sanitary Commission by the end of 1862 (and $1.2 million, a quarter of the national total, by the end of the war). Although King, in forwarding the first installment, stipulated that the Western Sanitary Commission in St. Louis receive "a fair bite" (MAXWELL, 185), Henry Whitney Bellows (1814–82), the authoritarian but public-spirited Unitarian minister who headed the national commission, was determined to control all fund distribution. JBF hoped to circumvent Bellows by persuading King to earmark one-third of the California money for the Western Sanitary Commission, which was resisting control by the national organization. JBF's pleas no doubt made King's dilemma more difficult, but he eventually decided to send all California's funds to the national organization for distribution. See FREDRICKSON, 100–112, on the conservative authoritarianism of Bellows and the Sanitary Commission; MAXWELL, 97–106, 131–32, 185–88, on the conflict between St. Louis and the national organization; and POSNER on King's fund-raising efforts.

2. Frederick Law Olmsted (1822–1903) had left his position as chief architect and administrator of Central Park to become executive secretary of the U.S. Sanitary Commission. In Sept. 1863, he would be hired by the new Mariposa Company, which purchased the estate from JCF and his creditors, as superintendent with an annual salary of $10,000 plus stock. His futile attempt to make the mines pay is fully described in ROPER, 233–79, and OLMSTED, 5:passim.

3. While Ticknor's note has not been found, it was presumably similar to copublisher James T. Fields's note in the Jan. 12 New York *Tribune*, which announced the distribution of the first profits of JBF's book to the needy Guard families.

4. JBF had long felt King would make a superb senator. In early 1862, King admitted there was "some talk of making me Senator," but he remained uninterested, explaining to Henry Bellows on Oct. 31, "I should consider an election to the Senate as the greatest calamity which could befall me in life" (WENDTE, 166; POSNER, 293).

5. In 1862–63 Trenor Park unsuccessfully sought election as senator from California. Las Mariposas investor A. A. Selover had already warned JCF that Park was neglecting his managerial duties to campaign (Aug. 10, 1862, Billings Mansion Archives), while Olmsted would later conclude that Park tried "to make the estate pay for his Senator's

seat" (OLMSTED, 5:61). Billings evidently had political aspirations as well, for JCF wrote him on June 13, 1862, "As to the Senate you should come there yourself & if you make at once this arrangement about the Mariposas I see no difficulty in it" (Billings Mansion Archives). JBF evidently believed that Billings had sided with Park and was no longer a friend, but in reality Billings would himself break with Park (OLMSTED, 5:93).

6. The photograph was probably intended as a frontispiece for gift copies of *The Story of the Guard,* which featured JCF and Zagonyi, and included excerpts from letters by JCF aides Rossiter ("Ros") Worthington Raymond and John ("Jack") Raymond Howard.

To James T. Fields

New York 26th January [1863]

Dear Mr. Fields,

I send you the corrected copy. Thank you for the assurance that the book is fulfilling its little destiny. I had intended to get the notices but somehow other ideas displaced that & it so chances I have not seen half a dozen. But your test of $'s is the one we are best pleased with.

If your publishing instinct says yes to a cheap edition—an "army edition"—I can promise it immediate wide & friendly circulation through the Potomac army under its new auspices. It is sure of all that in the West already where the Sanitary Commission will make itself colporteur [peddler] to it.

I shall distrust your readers, if not your own taste, if that Pear Tree & that lamentable ghost story are preferable to Mr. Harte's legend.[1] He thought he was writing for polished minds. I wrote to him to write as if for the mines—a tale full of everything startling—something to make Beacon Street say Fie! & rush up stairs to read uninterrupted. Is that what will do? He can do either. You may have the showman's motto—

> "You pays your money
> & you takes your choice."

I am in treasonable correspondence with Miss Harding. I quite disapprove of her Christmas Story & have asked her to modify her Fantinish proclamation.[2] She writes me she has finished a long story which she doesn't like but hopes you will. You know we are to have her in the north again soon? With kindest regards to Mrs. Fields. Very sincerely yours,

J. B. Frémont

ALS (CSmH—Fields Papers).

1. Part one of Mrs. Thomas Hopkinson's "Under the Pear Tree," the story of a New England woman who chose to marry a farmer rather than a more adventurous rival, and the unsigned "Ghost of Little Jacques," an improbable tale of multiple murder and revenge, had both appeared in the most recent (Feb. 1863) *Atlantic.*
2. Rebecca Harding's Christmas story, "The Promise of Dawn," appeared in the Jan. 1863 *Atlantic.* It told of an old man who refused to aid a starving prostitute, only to learn after her death that she was his own sister's child. Harding's "Fantinish proclamation" was her sympathetic portrayal of the prostitute as capable of redemption, a view Victor Hugo had espoused in his characterization of the prostitute Fantine in *Les Misérables,* published the previous year. Harding's "long story" was most probably "Paul Blecker," a "mawkish" tale according to one modern critic, serialized in the May, June, and July 1863 *Atlantic* (OLSEN, 114).

To James T. Fields

New York 20th Feby. [1863]

Dear Mr. Fields,

I had occasion to buy a copy of the Story of the Guard yesterday & the bookseller (who did not know me) said he had but the one copy—as I objected to the Irish binding—that the sale was about over because of its high price. "We could sell some every day if it was not so high." I ventured to suggest that it was rather expensively done up to which he agreed fully but said "paper backs sold better than boards." Won't you let this weigh with you? & make it fashionable as paper currency?

Just now I can dispose of the good will of the Potomac Army. I want to "stick a principle" into the soldiers as well as make more money for my Guards' people. It's a case for the "diffusion of useful knowledge on a war footing," and although I don't feel that I can move you, yet I shall growl very much if you don't begin to see I'm right. I know you have experience but grant something to instinct also.

I am so pleased to see Blind Tom[1] quoted in Littell from All the Year round. And Mr. Harte's Reveille.[2] He has something flaming in preparation for you.

Miss Harding will soon be near us as "Mrs. Davis of Philadelphia."[3] I am very glad she is to be transplanted. Philadelphia will do for a first stage.

The General has been in Washington a week—the newspapers say he is to go to Texas. I have not my final information yet & I don't know what to wish. Meantime isn't the Alabama burning enough ships to dignify her in Mr. Whipple's eyes? I long for the letters of marque.[4] Then the war will grow brisk for we shall "make mistakes" that will set the smouldering fires of English & French enmity ablaze.

I have been interrupted in a most welcome manner by a visit from Mr. Beecher. It's a case of "Watchman tell us of the night"[5] among us all round. The signs of promise are scanty just now but it's seed time as yet. I don't know that you care about the war in this way but it underlies everything else in my mind & I make no apology for speaking so—for in writing to Mrs. Fields & yourself I'm not on guard.

J. B. Frémont

ALS (CSmH—Fields Papers).

1. "Blind Tom" by Rebecca Harding, a short story about a slave child exploited for his musical ability, had appeared in the Nov. 1862 *Atlantic*. *Littell's Living Age*, a popular American magazine, mainly reprinted material from British publications. *All the Year Round* was an English review edited by Charles Dickens.

2. Bret Harte's "Reveille" was a Civil War poem (HARTE, 12:10–11).

3. On Mar. 5, 1863, Rebecca Harding married Lemuel Clarke Davis, a young law clerk who would later become an influential newspaper editor. The couple had three children, including Richard Harding Davis, one of the most celebrated writers of his day. While Harding herself continued to write, her earlier work is considered her finest.

4. At a Christmas dinner attended by the Frémonts, Edwin Percy Whipple (1819–86), a noted lecturer and frequent *Atlantic* contributor, had minimized the damage the Confederate raider *Alabama* was doing to U.S. commerce. However, before it was finally sunk in June 1864, the *Alabama* would seize or destroy sixty-four U.S. merchant ships (MCPHERSON, 547). On Mar. 3, 1863, Congress authorized the president to issue letters of marque, allowing privately owned and armed ships to plunder southern merchant vessels (LINCOLN, 6:126). See JBF to King, Feb. 27 [1863], below, for a more extensive description of the *Alabama* discussion.

5. JBF quotes from an 1825 hymn by John Bowring: "Watchman, tell us of the night/ What its signs of promise are." The phrase is derived from Isaiah 21:11.

To Thomas Starr King

New York 27th February [1863].

My dear Mr. King,

This will be taken out to you by Mr. James Hoy[1] of this place who tells me he was at your farewell dinner at the 5th Ave. Hotel.[2] He is therefore in a manner acquainted and I want you to treat him very nicely on our account. Capt. Hopper was directed to report to you & let you know he was the avant courier of the Mariposas Co. of which Mr. Hoy is President. Mr. Opdyke,[3] Mr. Morris Ketchum[4] & the General (I forget the other two) are directors. These are all men of millions (the present company excepted) & the whole business is on an honorable as well as a safe and profitable footing. More of the financial part you can have from those who do not realize Burns's[5] feeling about business so keenly as I do — "as for me I loathe detest & swoon at the very word *business*." But as Mr. Billings has complicated himself with Mr. Park and as there is much money with Parrott & Luning[6] I want Mr. Hoy to see that "all the decency" is not necessarily unprincipled. He said to me what a set they must be in San Francisco — to which I opposed you & some others & asked if he would like New Yorkers to be judged by the Aldermen & common council, by the wealthy & really influential Bennett or by their members of Congress, the Woods[7] or — he stopped me & said the case was gained.

I offered him letters to Mr. Beale as well as yourself. Mr. Beale is most likely to have some good horses and I would so much like if you all drove to San Mateo.[8] Didn't we have the sweetest days there — those trees after the bushes of San Francisco & that pretty brook & the lovely drive over to the place whose name I forget but I don't forget the trees & the crazy bowling alley and the wonderful French dinner Mr. Beale & I got there afterwards. Won't you shew him all that? & ask Mrs. King to pour him some tea into one of her newest Japanese cups (how many sets of china has she now?) In short shew him that though we be virtuous yet we have cakes & ale.[9]

In his grim way the Sachem Rand will marshal him about[10] & Mr. Beale must give him the freedom of the Land Office. If Mr. Harte is not, as is usual, utterly demoralized by being married I shall count on him also for adding to the "feast & flow" as Dick [Irisheller?] would put it. Mr. Hoy goes with power to enforce his position — legal, moneyed, & equitable power. The appointment of Judge Field[11] in place of that secession dormouse Judge McAllister[12] will gratify every one except Sister McAllister & the lawyer sons — & such clients as were in their hands already as a means of reaching the Father. I am happy to say this silliness Mr. Park was guilty of. D. Dudley Field (brother to the Judge & to Cyrus the cable & Henry the pastor) is lawyer to the General & to the Co.[13] It is a very good point in the case. Altogether we are quite calm about business & the General has plunged again into the war. He has been in Washington for the last few weeks with several different fingers in as many pies (it's not dignified but it would run that way off the pen) and doing them all brown. (If that is not slangy enough to make the Deweys shudder even in the remote splendor of their gilded halls!) The General's new command is to be announced just after Congress rises. This Mr. Stanton says he has sufficient reasons for & Mr. Sumner & others agree with him. But the telegraph will anticipate me in this.

We dined with your friends the Whipples on Christmas day, or rather dined where we met them. We were mutually disappointed. Mr. Whipple will tell you I am narrow, hard & fierce. I would tell you Mr. Whipple was shockingly narrow & without the instinct of the war. (It's only about the conduct of the war we differ.) Mrs. Whipple rather agreed with me—her eyes did. Mrs. Fields's role is to be sweetly gentle and lambent eyed & she's clever enough never to disagree with anybody. Mr. Fields & I & Mrs. Whipple were of one mind only I was most so. The Alabama was the matter.[14] Having had seven days of terror on the high sea from the Sumter I was not so cool as they that do not go down on the great deep & run the risks of rebel pirates. Mr. Whipple absolutely said the row about the Alabama was disproportioned to the damage she did for she had not yet destroyed as much in value as it cost to keep the army for a day (that was Christmas but she's "doing the sum to prove it" since).

I asked—without thinking—what was the money damage done to the flag at Sumter? Are you not glad we are to let loose privateers on our side? It has not quite passed into a law but it will & then for the row. I see Mr. Beale bristle at the prospect. Charley's aim is to live in just such a moment "own his own ship, sail her & fight her" is his idea.

Meantime tell Edith he is becoming quite a charming boy. We were all really sorry when his vacation ended & when mothers & sisters can say that of a boy it's something rare.

Frank goes to a French kinter-garten school where he "leads the band." He is making really good progress in drawing & in fencing. Just now that limits his list of studies. I shall look for details of the princess & heir apparent who is just cutting his teeth & wearing short dresses if my memory of the infant programme is clear. Why does Mrs. King never write to me? And why does Mr. King write so seldom?

We've heard from Mr. Howard but nothing from you all who I trust nevertheless received my package by him.

Didn't you like "Blind Tom" thoroughly? Miss Harding (who wrote it) is to be married on Thursday of next week & to live in Philadelphia. So we shall save her out of Virginia. She remains the one agreeable result of my stay in Wheeling & she is an acquisition. Have you taken part of the "burning egg" from the verbose Bellows? Did you ever in nightmare read such dispatches? We met him at a dinner & the General behaved like a shower bath to him. The Revd. Bellows couldn't make it out & I was divided between laughing "up my sleeve" as Zagonyi says, & horror at the opinion the General was making against himself— to snub a clergyman in the house of one of his devotees! & surrounded by his admiring believers (f.) You know the consequences to the man.

Sunday 1st March.

I only add a line to say that anything you can do to make Mr. Hoy's visit agreeable will be a great service rendered to us. As far as security in property matters is concerned, that is all right already, but time my dear Mr. King is a great point too. And I want Mr. Hoy to be kept there as long as his presence is needed & helped in such a way that he won't feel it irksome & not have to fall in with the enemy for company's sake. And the more thoroughly & quicker he consolidates matters the sooner we shall be assured of the "glorious privilege of being independent."[15] [*Margin note:* Mr. Brumagim is behaving well— encourage him please.][16]

Whenever I begin writing to you I rage at the inadequacy of such means of talking. There's so little ever put into a letter of all you meant to say or have to say. Lily sends her affectionate regards (or whatever represents that dignified young lady's warmest out-of-home feeling) to Mrs. King & yourself. She has been happy since October with a dear horse—a grey mare that follows her voice & they spend two or three hours daily together (Sundays excepted) but Chiquita[17] still has a golden halo that no other horse can attain. I like the riders better than their horses. Cavalry & infantry send you their heartiest love & good wishes.

J. B. Frémont

ALS (CSfCP—King Papers).

1. James Hoy (1810–71), a wealthy New York financier, was traveling to California

to evaluate Las Mariposas for a group of investors considering its purchase. Hoy's report would be favorable, although stories later circulated that Trenor Park had "salted" the mines for his visit (OLMSTED, 5:196). The Mariposa Company was organized on June 25, 1863, with shares valued at $100 each. Billings, A. A. Selover, and Park received 12,500 shares; Morris Ketchum, George Opdyke, and Hoy, 25,000. After giving David Dudley Field 2,000 shares for legal services and transferring 25,000 shares to Ketchum (for which he eventually received only one-fourth their value), JCF ended up with only 8,500 shares. In total, JCF realized about two million from the sale of the ten-million-dollar property. See CRAMPTON, 269; NEVINS [1], 583–86; and "Great Events," 381–82, for details of the sale. For scathing indictments of the Mariposa Company's subsequent stock manipulations as a deliberate fraud on the public, see New York *Tribune,* Nov. 30, 1875, and *Nation,* 8 (June 24, 1869): 488–90. The John T. Doyle Papers (CU—B) contain a series of letters and telegrams, Nov. 1862–May 1863, some in code, to Doyle, Billings's New York attorney, concerning the sale of the estate.

2. With William Cullen Bryant presiding, three hundred people had attended King's farewell dinner on Apr. 4, 1860, the day before he sailed for San Francisco (WENDTE, 71).

3. George Opdyke (1805–80), a millionaire merchant and early Republican, had been elected mayor of New York in 1862. In 1864, Thurlow Weed charged that Opdyke had profited unfairly from secret clothing and arms contracts with the government and that he had cheated JCF out of his fair share of Las Mariposas. In the sensational libel trial that followed, the verdict was indecisive, but during testimony by JCF, Weed's lawyers argued that Opdyke, Ketchum, and David Dudley Field had swindled $2.6 million from JCF in purchasing the mines (VAN DEUSEN [1], 313–15; NEVINS [1], 583–86). Observing the trial, future *Nation* editor Edwin Godkin pronounced Opdyke "a consumate rascal" (ROPER, 274–75).

4. Morris Ketchum (1796–1880) was a wealthy New York investment banker who had just purchased JCF's share of Las Mariposas. When the Mariposa Company was founded in June, he would serve as treasurer and principal stockholder until mid-1864. In August 1865 his personal banking firm, Ketchum, Son & Company, failed when his son and partner was arrested for forging $2.5 million in gold certificates of deposit. In 1867 Ketchum retreated to Savannah, Ga., where he successfully founded a bank (New York Times obit., Jan. 3, 1880; STRONG, 4:27; OLMSTED, 5:57–60).

5. Scottish poet Robert Burns (1759–96).

6. John Parrott (1811–84), former U.S. consul in Mazatlan 1838–50, and Nicholas Luning (1820–90) were wealthy San Francisco bankers (San Francisco *Directory,* 1863; ALAMEDA, 222).

7. The Wood brothers, Fernando (1812–81) and Benjamin (1820–1900) had recently been elected to Congress. Fernando, a former New York City mayor, was the leader of the powerful Mozart Hall machine. Politically, he was a peace Democrat who in 1861 had suggested that New York City become a "free city" to maintain commercial relations with the South.

8. San Mateo was a parklike region of rolling pastures dotted with live oak trees about nineteen miles south of San Francisco. JBF would describe the San Mateo expedition in "Distinguished Persons I Have Known: Starr King," New York *Ledger,* Mar. 6, 1875.

9. JBF alludes to Shakespeare's line from *Twelfth Night,* act 2, sc. 3: "Dost thou think, because thou art virtuous, there shall be no more cakes and ale?"

10. JBF puns on the occupation of Charles W. Rand, U.S. marshall of the Northern District of California. A former customs collector on Nantucket Island, Rand reached

California in 1847. JBF later credited Rand with helping Bret Harte retain his government job after Edward Beale left the California surveyor generalship in 1864 (BAN-
CROFT, 7:239, 278; J. B FRÉMONT [1], 205; LARKIN, 6:93).

11. Stephen J. Field (1816–99) trained as a lawyer in the office of his older brother,
David Dudley. In 1849 he joined the gold rush and soon built a flourishing law practice
in California. He was elected to the state supreme court in 1857 and became chief
justice in 1859. Field decided in favor of JCF in his case against the Merced Mining
Company (see JBF to Elizabeth Blair Lee, Nov. 15, 1859, note 5, above). He would
be named an associate justice of the U.S. Supreme Court on Mar. 10, 1863.

12. Matthew Hall McAllister (1800–1865) of Georgia had settled in California in
1850, where he practiced law with his two sons, Hall and Ward. In 1855, President
Pierce appointed him California's first U.S. circuit judge, a position he resigned in 1862.
"Sister" McAllister was probably Matthew Hall McAllister's wife, Louisa Charlotte
Cutler (1804–69), an aunt of Julia Ward Howe.

13. David Dudley Field (1805–94), the oldest of the Field brothers, was a longtime Republican who supported JCF in 1856. Distinguished as a codifier of civil,
criminal, and international law, his reputation would be tarnished by the $200,000
legal fee he charged JCF in the Mariposas settlement and by his work as counsel for
Jay Gould and Jim Fiske in the 1869 Erie Railroad litigation. Besides Stephen and
David Dudley, the Field brothers included Cyrus (1819–92), developer of the trans-
atlantic telegraph, and Henry (1822–1907), a noted clergyman and author.

14. Mrs. Whipple was the former Charlotte B. Hastings, a close friend of Oliver
Wendell Holmes and his circle. See also JBF to King, July 20 [1861], on JBF's experience
with southern privateers and JBF to James T. Fields, Feb. 20 [1863], both above, on
the *Alabama* discussion.

15. Robert Burns, "Epistle to a Young Friend," stanza 7.

16. Mark Brumagim, from whom the Frémonts had bought Black Point, held actual
title to Las Mariposas. He had purchased it from Francisco Ocampo, a Los Angeles
rancher, who had acquired it at a sheriff's sale in Nov. 1858 in lieu of the approximately
$8,000 JCF owed him. JCF had the right to repurchase the title from Brumagim by
repaying the debt plus 2 percent interest per month. However, JCF never repaid the
debt, which by late 1863 would reach more than $300,000 in gold. It was evidently
in not pressing for its repayment that JBF saw Brumagim as "behaving well." Later
the Brumugim debt would be assumed by the new Mariposa Company, which in
settling it would expend capital badly needed for development of the mines (OLMSTED,
5:12–13).

17. Lily's horse at Black Point.

To George Julian

[March 3 (1863)

My dear Mr. Julian,

A copy of your speech reached me since the General left & I had
read it before receiving your note.[1] I had written you a note telling
you my opinion of it, but tore it up thinking you had too much to
do to read what a lady had to say about the conduct of the war. But

I feel authorized now to tell you how glad I am to see plain words used at last. Never could the rebels have had such successes had not our own political chiefs helped them & you make the right date at which northern treason lifted its frightened head, looked, doubted its own senses, took heart & profited by the crime of the Blairs. When we reach the cooling stage of this lava flood, they will stand (it takes the three to make a man) as the Judas of the day. Had they not accepted the posts of sappers & miners the Democratic invaders could not have found such a breach waiting their arrival & now to crown their treachery the Senate is asked, and Republicans will vote to confirm as Major General the man who cannot be elected to the House in his own State because of his slavery-bargain, & whose habits of drinking caused his being defeated for the nomination of Speaker to your body.[2] And to this man your party will give over true brave men's lives & the honor of upright & thorough republicans. And then when a defeat follows, it's a pontoon missing, or it's muddy, or no coal for the gun boats — or anything except the voice of conscience crying against the unfaithful watchmen of Washington. Cry aloud and spare no man for you say truly we must have no pretences or soft words now. I shall not believe a command is intended for the General until it is announced. Then, he will make it a success in spite of them & jusify your noble praises for which I give you my heartfelt thanks. To the widest circulation of your speech I will use every means, & I think you will see it where you wish. Pray excuse my writing on the edges. If I take another sheet I will talk you tired, but when you stir truth as you have done in your speech other truth answers to it. We are at 236 4th ave. Blancards — and I shall hope to see you. Very sincerely yours,

Jessie Benton Frémont

New York
March 3d.

ALS (DLC—Giddings-Julian Papers).

1. In a Feb. 18, 1863, speech, Julian charged that the Lincoln administration had allowed Democrats sympathetic to slavery (such as McClellan) to dominate the war effort to the detriment of the Union cause. "This is a war of freedom and free-labor against a mighty aristocracy based upon the ownership of men. Our aim is the overthrow of that power, and the reorganization of Southern society on a republican basis; and it should require no argument to prove that men who believe in this aristocracy are not the most fit commanders in such a contest." Julian pointed out that JCF's emancipation decree in Missouri was at last government policy through Lincoln's recent

Emancipation Proclamation, and he urged that JCF, "the victim of the most cruel injustice and the most unmerited and mortifying humiliation," be restored to active service (*Congressional Globe*, 37th Cong., 3rd sess., pt. 2, 1064–68).

2. JBF refers to Frank Blair, Jr., who had been defeated for Speaker of the House by Galusha Grow of Pennsylvania in July 1861, a period during which there were reports that Blair was drinking (W. E. SMITH, 2:115–16, 118). In June 1862, Blair had accepted an appointment as brigadier general and joined Gen. William T. Sherman's forces in Arkansas. In December, he led an unsuccessful attack at Chickasaw Bluffs, near Vicksburg, where he distinguished himself for personal bravery. In Apr. 1863, he was promoted to major general. See E. B. SMITH [1], 306–9, and W. E. SMITH, 2:145–62, on Blair's military career.

To Horace Greeley

[March 3 (1863)]

Dear Mr. Greeley,

Mr. Julian of Indiana writes me that many think it will do good to have his late speech reprinted in the Tribune which will he says "secure it a half million of readers." And he asks me to use my influence to that end. I don't think I have any influence with you, but after reading the speech I certainly join in the wish to have it read & felt by the largest number. Mr. Julian's writing is as hard to read as your own so that I enclosed both speech and letter to one of your staff with whom I had the pleasure to renew acquaintance yesterday, & who will do the details for you. The speech is not long & I trust you will give it an honorable place—for the good it will do, and because I should be flattered to find I had influence. It ought to be a tremendously mighty reason that outweighs a lady's first petition, so that I shall hope to see "Speech of the Hon. Mr. Julian, &c. &c" in my morning paper very soon.[1]

Jessie B. Frémont

Tuesday evg. 3d March
Hon. Mr. Greeley

ALS (DLC—Greeley Papers).

1. Julian's speech did not appear in the *Tribune* until Mar. 27, and only after JBF had sent Greeley a reminder (see JBF to Julian, Mar. 23 [1863], DLC—Giddings-Julian Papers). In reply, Greeley explained that he had had trouble finding space for it (to JBF, Mar. 24, 1863, NN—Greeley Papers). In a brief editorial accompanying its publication, Greeley noted Julian's radicalism and added: "we do not concur in all it contains but there is much to approve."

To Elizabeth Cady Stanton

[May 4 (1863)]

My dear Madam,

I learned from Miss Dickinson[1] that you had not received my answer to your letter asking me to preside at your meeting of the 21st of May. It was sent as all our letters are and I cannot understand its failing to reach you.

Although it will not be in my power to do as you asked I hope it will not lose me the pleasure of seeing you. We are just changing to our own house which will be in order, I trust, by the end of the week. It is no. 21 West 19th Street & I rarely go out until after two o'clock.

Wishing you every success in your loyal undertaking, I am Very sincerely yours,

Jessie Benton Frémont

Monday 4th May
Blancards' (236 4th Avenue)
Mrs. E. C. Stanton.

ALS (NPV—Elizabeth Cady Stanton Papers, Scrapbook 1). Elizabeth Cady Stanton (1815–1902), the distinguished woman's rights leader and abolitionist, was a strong critic of Lincoln's moderate policy toward slavery. Stanton had been a supporter of JCF since the 1856 campaign and would remain so through his abortive 1864 bid for the presidency.

During a series of meetings in May 1863, Stanton, Susan B. Anthony, and like-minded women established the Women's National Loyal League, the only woman's organization created during the Civil War for the purpose of influencing political events. During the next year the league would gather more than 300,000 signatures on a petition urging immediate emancipation by constitutional amendment. The generally sympathetic *Tribune* (May 21, 1863) noted, however, that some women were reluctant "to unite in this movement from prejudice against those who have taken the lead." Such hesitation may have arisen not only because Stanton and Anthony advocated woman's rights but also because they were known to support JCF. While JBF did not preside at the meeting, she sent the league a contribution of $50. The league's activities are described in STANTON ET AL., 2:50–89; HARPER, 1:226–37; New York *Tribune*, May 16, 20–21, 23, 1863; and New York *Times*, May 16, 1863.

1. Probably Anna Elizabeth Dickinson (1842–1932), a young abolitionist of Quaker descent whose impassioned proemancipation speeches on behalf of Republican candidates were attracting large audiences in New York and other northern cities during the spring of 1863.

To Christopher Carson

[May 1863]

My dear old friend

As the General has the chance of sending directly and safely to you I cannot lose the opportunity of writing for myself and saying how often I have been watchful of your movements since the war began, and how glad I am that you are not only always successful but that you are spared for renewed service.[1] For although we will most probably never meet again, yet you are part of our early life and my Father, as well as my husband valued you and relied on you, and when the end comes be sure, if you go first, there will be two friends here to feel something has been taken from them not to be replaced.

I had lately a letter from my friend and yours, "Ned Beale" & in it you had large mention. He longed for a part in the war but he is too loyal and too useful to be in demand here.[2]

We should be so glad to hear from you. If you find the time let us know about yourself and your wife and all that makes your greatest happiness — the newspapers give us accounts of your military life, although it must be necessarily but in very small part.

My daughter, whose picture you have with mine, is a famous horsewoman and worthy to ride with you. My boys are little yet — the oldest only just twelve, but little men and in training for soldiers. The youngest who is not eight has been for six months, daily under drill. They are fine healthy boys — very intelligent and handsome and will do good service I trust. You were the first to warn me that my oldest boy could not live.[3] I always think of you in connection with that poor suffering baby. Grief was new to me then and I could not bear to give him up. But that, and many another sorrow has come since you were with me at my Father's house — it makes what is left more valued. I hope you will go on in good service & see peaceful days again in your home where your wife cared so kindly for the General when he came all starving and worn out to your care.[4] And let us hear from you or if anything brings you to the East, come to us, without fail. Always your friend,

Jessie Benton Frémont

New York
21 West 19th Street.
Col. Carson
Taos, New Mexico.

ALS (ICN—Graff Collection). Envelope addressed to "Col. C. Carson in the field, Taos, or Santa Fé, New Mexico." See LECOMPTE for a discussion of this letter.

1. Soon after the Civil War began, Carson joined the First New Mexico Volunteer Infantry and participated in the battle of Valverde in Feb. 1862. In 1863 he led the government campaign against the Navajo, culminating in their forced "Long Walk" to the Bosque Redondo Reservation in eastern New Mexico. For Carson's army career and the Navajo campaign, see GUILD & CARTER, 218-49.
2. In July 1861, Beale had written Lincoln requesting a military command, but before any action was taken, he accepted the surveyor generalship of California. Far from serving the war effort, Beale used his position to acquire a fortune in land, and in 1864 he was dismissed from office for irregularities and neglect of duty (G. THOMPSON, 128-55).
3. Carson had been godfather to the Frémonts' son, Benton, who died Oct. 6, 1848, at age ten weeks.
4. After his disastrous fourth expedition to the Rockies in the winter of 1848-49, JCF had taken refuge with Carson and his wife, Josefa Jaramillo (1828-68), in their Taos home.

To John T. Fiala

[July 10 (1863)]

Colonel,

The General received your letter this morning with its interesting & useful newspaper enclosures. As he had the day full of engagements he asked me to acknowledge it for him & tell you, what I am happy to be the one to repeat to you, that in the matter of the railway duty, you have only anticipated his own wish to secure your services.[1] It is among the agreeable features of the work before the General that, his power in it is such as to enable him to secure permanent positions for such of his faithful friends as have the capacity & desire to engage in the work.

A recent order has just dispersed the staff who wait now answers to their letters reporting, as directed, for duty.[2]

The General will write to you of this. It is very hard to bear but the Govt. is simply irresponsible. Thank Heaven & the Constitution that limits them to four years, & more than two are over now.

We learn from direct personal information that on Tuesday evening the military conclusion of the administration was that Lee would carry his whole army safely back into Virginia. It was no defeat & rout at Gettysburg, only a severe check. Lee did not lose a gun & carried off all his wounded except those who fell among ours on the actual field. The President already has found a flaw in No. 7 (as we call Genl. Meade).[3] The President approved of a certain line in pursuit of Lee, & Genl. Meade took another. To be sure the admin[istration]. changes Generals nearly as often as a bad housekeeper changes servants, but not quite in the first week. So Genl. Meade will be allowed to "stay his month" & if he defeats & utterly routs Lee he may be President & if he fails or gets roughly handled himself we will have a new Napoleon for the dog-days.

Will you remember me to Dr. Pre[e]torious[4] & tell him I have sent the Genl's likeness, two copies, & hope he has them safely. I wish we could have a talk with him here. Very truly yours,

J. B. Frémont

New York
21 West 19th.
July 10th.

ALS (MoSHi—Fiala Papers).

1. Fiala, JCF's staff topographical engineer, had extensive map-making and railroad survey experience that would doubtless be useful in JCF's new railroad ventures. A loyal friend, he promoted JCF's political interests in St. Louis during the Civil War.

2. On July 3, 1863, the War Department had directed all staff officers attached to generals without commands to join their regiments or report by letter to the adjutant general for assignment to duty (New York *Times,* July 3, 1863). That same day JCF asked Secretary of War Edwin M. Stanton to exempt his personal staff from the order, since he still anticipated a new command, "agreeable to your promise and that of the President that I should have it in time" (DLC—Stanton Papers). JCF's staff finally resigned in June 1864 in the wake of his own resignation to accept the Cleveland convention's presidential nomination.

3. George Gordon Meade (1815–72) had replaced McClellan as commander of the Army of the Potomac just before the battle of Gettysburg, July 1–3. Although he was the victor on the field, many, including the president, were disturbed that he failed to pursue and destroy Lee's retreating army, which might have resulted in an early end to the war (MCPHERSON, 663, 666–67).

4. Dr. Emil Preetorious (1827–1905) had received a doctorate in law from the University of Heidelberg. Forced to flee Germany after the failed revolution of 1848,

he settled in St. Louis and in 1862 was elected to the state legislature as a radical emancipationist. In 1864, he became editor of the *Westliche Post,* one of the most influential German newspapers in America (SCHARF [2], 1:941–42; New York *Times* obit., Nov. 20, 1905). Like John T. Fiala, he was active in JCF's 1864 presidential campaign.

To Thomas Starr King

Nahant   October 16th [1863]

Dear Mr. King

I go down tomorrow.[1] Down means to New York. All the time I've been here you have been a constant presence. Yours and Mrs. King's faces (she is wonderfully like Prince Napoleon) look down on us from the dining room wall and your old intimates all speak of you. But none of them know you as I do. I ventured to declaim on your behalf the other day. Mrs. Revd. Dewey, Mrs. Fields (T[icknor] & F[ields]) and others were talking of your great success in fortune as well as fame.[2] (I wish your fortune *was* as large as they make it—I always say it is.) And I informed those feminines—gazettes each one—that for a man who was actually in command spiritual & temporal (& when he pleased a touch at finance) of the whole Pacific Dept. that for habits of mind proportioned to such an enlarged growth as that, the Hollis Street Church would prove too small a flower [just?] now. When you want a trumpeter allow me to recommend myself.

I only send this to shew you that I *will* not go away from here without writing from here to you. My eyes have been off duty all summer and [I] waited for them to get quite well.

Everything goes so well for us now. Do write to me. We are going to make a good Christmas this year. I want to give the children a Christmas story from each of our best friends. I will write them one. Won't you & do ask Mr. Harte for one—short as you please but your carte de visite & something from you must be on the tree. It's only for ourselves & you too when we get together. Lots of nice people approve my idea & are going to help in it. I am going even to ask Whittier[3] to whom I made a ⟨nice⟩ visit—nice is a mean word for it was delightful & satisfactory to us both. What steadfast eyes that man has.

Don't fail me now. Frank has—unknown to him—a Shetland pony

under training & it is to be haltered to the tree. Also a big New-foundland dog for Charley who covets that for his sailing & boating. The children are good & handsome & a real pleasure. Edith must be all that & more now & the baby must be a great pleasure to you all. I can't realize Mr. Harte's baby. Tell him I can see him eyeing it critically & taking it to task mentally poor little mannikin—he is not of the species pater.

If I wrote a week I couldn't say what I have to say. Be sure no length of time between the letters or the biggest type in them when they do come, mean that I am different from the one who wrote oftener & in ordinary "joining hand."[4] I am hoping great things for the country from the growing knowledge of the President as he really is—a sly slimy nature. If we have more threats of a French war[5] you have your work under your hand. I will keep you informed on that point which promises to be serious. I must stop. Affectionately to both of you & good night.

J. B. F.

AL initialed (CSfCP—King Papers).

1. The Frémont family had spent much of the summer at Nahant, a small coastal village north of Boston, where they had purchased a cottage from Wendell Phillips. Neighbors included such Boston/Cambridge names as Longfellow, Agassiz, Lawrence, Prescott, and Motley (New York *Times*, Aug. 13, 1865).
2. On the advice of San Francisco businessmen, King had made a lucrative investment in a Comstock silver mine (WENDTE, 211–12).
3. See JBF to John Greenleaf Whittier, Oct. 17 [1863], below.
4. A now obsolete term for cursive writing.
5. When France seized Mexico in June 1863, overthrew the republican government of Benito Juarez, and installed Hapsburg archduke Ferdinand Maximilian as emperor, the Lincoln administration refused to recognize this European venture into the Americas. The Confederacy, however, offered to recognize Maximilian in exchange for French recognition of the South, temporarily causing talk of a northern invasion of Mexico and war with France (MCPHERSON, 683).

To John Greenleaf Whittier

the Anchorage, Nahant
Saturday the 17th October [1863].

Dear Mr. Whittier,

I have often said, (and only a little in jest) that the only thing of which I make sure is, that whatever I plan and am nearly accomplishing will be violently upset, & generally, exactly reversed. Thursday I had a dispatch from the General to say he could not come & that I was to come to New York today. So I go in a few hours now, & as you may imagine have had my time filled with closing up our summer home & all the packing & last letters and visits & the dozens of little things to always turn up at the last.

The storm assures me you will not venture out so that I am freed from the fear that you might take the trouble to come & find an empty house before my letter could reach you to tell of our change of plans.

In the new thoughts that came from seeing you I quite forgot what the General had asked me to say to you. You cannot think how much new strength & courage your noble lines gave him & he wished you to know it from me.[1] He was smarting under some fresh proof of the determination of the powers at Washington to make him fail & I had been enduring for him while all the harassing details of the interference of the Quarter Master at St. Louis were being gone over by the officer sent to examine where the leak was—when one of the staff officers came up to me with an Evening Post containing your lines. It was just sunset, we were in the open air & the hills around were white with tents & beyond them the autumn coloring of the trees was in sunset colors. I read the words to the General and it was like David's harp of old. His face lit up with such a different kind of look from the angry baffled resentful kind of face he had just had. His natural serenity came back & the whole tone of his mind was altered. Thanks to your true brave words. For it was brave at that time to believe well of the General. Such a skillfull use of the power of a great government against an individual naturally swept away many men. But seeing your steadfast eyes I recognize you do not look through the eyes of others, but that you can & do see for yourself & hold fast to that which is good & true. All the firmer for persecution. And both the General and myself feel these lines, and those you wrote in '56,[2] to be among the most highly valued honors of his life. [*Margin note:* Col. Zagonyi left early with the horses or I should have his reports to add.]

We have had so much to make us thankful & happy this summer and this little sea-side place is so unmarked with any care or grief, that I wish we could have had you with us this year. I'm afraid of "to-morrow." The rule of our life—our lives even—has been struggle & unrest. This summer has been so peaceful, so full of every good home blessing, that I am nervous about what must follow this lull in our stormy lives.

But if—the "if" always must come in—if we are here next year you and your sister³ will surely come to us and we will have some fire side as well as sea-side talks. You will both regret for me that my dear old anniversary⁴ has to lose such surroundings as these. The General has been enlarging & beautifying our town house so that it will be ungracious in me not to be pleased there but I nearly let "the tears downfall" for this little cottage.

It made a regular hurting in the little camp. When "Mother has a headache" it means Mother has been sorry. So when I emerged from a twenty four hours' sick headache it was a general "what's the matter." I told them it was nearly the worst thing they could think of. Zagonyi cried "the General is ordered on duty" & the children, "Father's not coming & we're to go to New York." My daughter is my dear friend as well as child & knew.

So, we tell you goodbye for awhile. I trust, to see you early next year and in the meantime now that the way is open you will let me recall myself to your sister & yourself occasionally. My eyes have been rather over tasked lately so that this summer—this good rare, ended, summer—I have scarcely used them & I save them now for great occasions. My daughter asks to be remembered to your niece⁵ as well as to yourselves & with kindest & sincerest regards from myself, I am yours most truly,

Jessie B. Frémont

ALS (MH). While at Nahant, JBF, Lily, and Zagonyi had visited the Quaker poet John Greenleaf Whittier (1807–92) at nearby Amesbury. A committed abolitionist and supporter of JCF since the 1856 campaign, Whitter wrote JBF afterward: "We have in some sort known and loved thee and thine for a long time, and seeing thee has confirmed our impressions. . . . The villagers have complained sadly because I did not let them know that Jessie Frémont was in the place. Our young men and women wanted to see Colonel Zagonyi, the hero of the Body Guard. When thee comes again we will have the bells rung and satisfy them" (WHITTIER [2], 3:48–50).

1. JBF refers to Whittier's poem in praise of JCF's Missouri emancipation decree, "To John C. Frémont," which she had read to her beleaguered husband in late Sept. 1861, during a visit to his field headquarters near Jefferson City, Mo. The poem begins, "Thy error, Fremont, simply was to act/ A brave man's part, without the statesman's tact. . . . Still take thou courage! God has spoken through thee,/ Irrevocable, the mighty words, Be free!" (WHITTIER [1], 334–35).

2. Whittier wrote a number of Republican campaign poems in 1856, but JBF refers to "The Pass of the Sierra," which celebrates JCF's dramatic Sierra crossing in the winter of 1843–44 and ends: "Rise up, Frémont, and go before;/ The Hour must have its Man;/ Put on the hunting-shirt once more,/ And lead in Freedom's van!" (ibid., 321–22). JBF mentions the poem again in her Feb. 14, 1864, below, and Mar. 5, 1868 (NHi) letters to Whittier.

3. Whittier shared a house with his sister, Elizabeth Hussey Whittier (1815–64), who was also a poet (WHITTIER [2], 1:38).

4. The Frémonts' twenty-second wedding anniversary on Oct. 19.

5. Whittier's young niece, Elizabeth ("Lizzie") Whittier (1845–1902), stayed with him often after her parents separated in the late 1850s. In 1876 she married Samuel T. Pickard, who became Whittier's official biographer (ibid., 2:407).

To Henry Wadsworth Longfellow

[Nov./Dec. 1863?]

Dear Mr. Longfellow,

Your kind remembrance gave me additional pleasure as it shewed you did not forget your neighbors of the sea side. We hope to go up early next year & the children promise themselves great swimmings & boatings, & wonderful drives & rides with their Shetland ponies, & "Annie & Edie"[1] come in for part of all the plans.

I saw you had been at Gettysburg[2] — the next time you go through New York won't you remember we are in our own home here & will be very glad to have you remember that we are "pays" [country] and should not give the go by as city neighbors do. Very sincerely yours,

Jessie Benton Frémont

21 West 19th street

ALS (MH). The poet Henry Wadsworth Longfellow (1807–82) had been an eager reader of JCF's expedition reports and made use of their descriptions of the western prairie in writing his long poem *Evangeline*. Longfellow, whose wife had died in 1861 from a tragic, accidental burning, summered annually at Nahant with his children. On Aug. 12, 1863, he wrote his (and JBF's) publisher, James T. Fields: "Mrs. Fremont is next door to us, which is very pleasant." But the following summer, when JCF was a presidential candidate, he would comment wryly to Charles Sumner: "what merry times I shall have with my neighbors the Fremonts, during the campaign for the Presidency, not meaning to vote for him" (LONGFELLOW, 4:351, 416).

1. "Annie & Edie" were Longfellow's youngest daughters, Anne Allegra (1855–

1934) and Edith (1853–1915), who later married Joseph Gilbert Thorp, Jr., and Richard Henry Dana II, respectively (ibid., 3:14; 6:216n, 225).

2. JBF probably refers to the dedication of the national cemetery at Gettysburg on Nov. 19, 1863, attended by numerous dignitaries, though not Longfellow (ibid., 4:367–68). The newspapers of the day featured Edward Everett's lengthy oration, but it is, of course, Lincoln's brief address that is remembered today.

To Thomas Starr King

[Jan.? 1864]

Dear Mr. King,

My head gave out & began hurting just as your turn came so I leave explanations to Capt. Hopper.

If good motives don't tell enough on your people let them see "that it will pay" to be kind to the Sanitary Comn. now. *Mrs. Belmont*[1] has accepted a place on the committee for the Fair & Mrs. McClellan & Mrs. Fremont work together on a committee for "Arms & Trophies."[2] After that let your lambs & lions go to work together too.

J.B.F.

AL initialed (CSfCP—King Papers).

1. Carolyn Slidell (Perry) Belmont (1829–92) was a member of the women's executive committee for the Metropolitan Fair to be held in Apr. 1864 for the benefit of the U.S. Sanitary Commission. The daughter of Commodore Matthew Perry and the wife of banker and Rothschild agent August Belmont, she was "among the loveliest of our New York duchesses" and her house "probably the most splendid and showy in the city" (STRONG, 3:36, 424). August Belmont was a strong supporter of McClellan for president.

2. Although JBF and Mary Ellen (Marcy) McClellan (c. 1836–1915), wife of the deposed general who would become the Democratic presidential nominee in 1864, represented opposite political viewpoints, they shared a mutual antipathy toward Abraham Lincoln. As members of the Arms and Trophies Committee for the fair, they helped collect an impressive array of weaponry, flags, and military accoutrements for display during the event, ranging from the original Bowie knife to George Washington's army uniform, cane, and sword (New York *Times*, Apr. 4, 1864). The committee published a 109-page exhibition *Catalogue of the Museum of Flags, Trophies and Relics Relating to the Revolution, the War of 1812, the Mexican War, and the Present Rebellion.*

To George Julian

New York January 16th [1864]
21 West 19th street

My dear Mr. Julian,

The General has been up to the eyes in his railroad work[1] & took today to write to you & some other friends in Congress on a matter which touches him very nearly. But it has rained interruptions & he did not get his letters written & went to bed in despair of getting a quiet half hour in any other place. But I can give you some points, briefly, which will go in with his letter but which he may not have time for.

The thing is this—that as it stands on the report of the Secty of War the General & six of his staff officers have been for sixteen months now doing no duty and drawing pay. On this showing the General is unwilling to stand before the country. It is not of his choice that he is not on duty and the officers would have long since resigned but that he was constantly promised a command, as you know, and they had each done good service and were unwilling to lose the hope of doing more. I ought to say to you that each of these has his merits and it is better to put them down briefly.

Col. Albert has been twelve years in America & gave up his farm in Wisconsin to take part in the war. He was in the first troops called out, was wounded & made prisoner at Springfield under Genl. Lyon & is partly crippled by a rebel ball still lodged in his hip. He has steadily done good duty until shelved with the General. He speaks as good English as we do & is thorough in French & German—is a Hungarian & a trained officer.

Col. Fiala is also a trained officer & a Hungarian—he, Col. Albert & Zagonyi all served in the Hungarian War. Col. Fiala is an engineer & has surveyed every foot of land from the Missouri river to near Little Rock. He too began at the beginning of the war & served faithfully until his health broke down completely from over-work. He too speaks & writes excellent English & German.

Of Zagonyi I will only say that he too has been in America nearly twelve years—like the others his own industry made him an honorable & comfortable living. They all knew what the work was that lay before the country & they gave up their hard-earned homes to aid in defending others. The beggarly pay given to officers off duty is no substitute for an intelligent man's independent earning so that the question of "pay & no service" does not fit them. The wrong of it does not lodge with them but with those who deprive the country of services to which it is entitled. Isn't that a species of defalcation—or breach of trust? [*Margin note:* Col. Pilsen[2]—less time in the country. Served in army of Potomac, transferred to Mountain Dept. Writes English perfectly & speaks it well & is a first-class artillery officer.]

Of the General's pay not one farthing goes to private use since he became satisfied that he was not to be given a part in the war. It comes from the people & he takes care that it all returns to them. It goes to a fund we set aside for our part in relieving the suffering caused by the war & that is a better way to do than to leave it in the public Treasury where it could help no one. As it is more than one family is comfortable from it.[3]

If it is said the General left active service of his own accord in Virginia, I wish you would turn to Vol. 3d of the report of your committee on the Conduct of the War & read Genl. Pope's letters put in as evidence by Genl. Hunter.[4]

It was only a question of time, the resigning. It would have been so contrived that the General would have been forced to do so, but if he had stayed they would have prepared defeats & destroyed his reputation. He knew the men & would not trust them. I think it was good of him to give only a technical military reason for resigning & not say as he was warranted in doing—this man you have put over me is my enemy & will endeavor to make good his assertions against me. I cannot trust him with my honor or the lives of my command so I retire knowing it to be useless to ask justice where he is a court favorite & I am denied the ordinary rights of military usage.

I'm tired of the bad behavior of those people down there. Can't you have a resolution to ask *why* these Generals are out of service.

Why is Genl. Harney out of service? Why was he "excused from active service during the war." I know. So do many others. Let every body know.[5]

I see you are on a committee which may bring you to New York. If you do come don't forget we are at home now—under our own roof & not a taint of government worries suffered to abide under it. You must come & see us & renew some of the ideas you took pleasure in discussing when you were here last year.

You will get a regular letter from the General but this is what I would say to you if you were here—and I write it for fear you should have no answer if unjust things are said of good men. Mr. Wade is a fearless man & will speak for them if needed in his places. So will Mr. Lane of Indiana[6] & Mr. Conness[7] & others whose names I need not recall for you know them. I see Major General F. P. Blair Jr. slipped into his fraudulent seat. It was no long tenable for him in the West.[8] Very sincerely yours,

J. B. F.

AL initialed (DLC—Giddings-Julian Papers).

1. In 1863, using proceeds from the Mariposas sale, JCF had purchased the franchises and property of the unbuilt Kansas Pacific Railroad ("Great Events," 382-83). Over the next decade he became involved in a series of railroad ventures that ultimately tarnished his reputation and left him poor.

2. Lt. Col. John Pilsen, a native of Czechoslovakia, was JCF's chief of artillery in West Virginia. In 1863 he wrote a fourteen-page pamphlet, "Reply of Lieutenant-Colonel Pilsen to Emil Schalk's Criticisms of the Campaign in the Mountain Department, under Major-General J. C. Fremont." He resigned from the army June 8, 1864 (OFFICIAL RECORDS, ser. 1, vol. 51, pt. 1:577, and vol. 12, pt. 1:15; HEITMAN, 1:792).

3. In an article on the Western Sanitary Commission, the Rev. William Eliot noted that "almost the whole" of JCF's salary was regularly sent to him "to be used at discretion for 'those that need' " (ELIOT, 527).

4. While serving under JCF in Missouri, Pope had written Hunter that he thought Frémont was "crazy or worse" and asked rhetorically whether JCF and his coterie should "be permitted to drag to destruction, or ... unnecessary suffering, the 30,000 men of this army, for no other purpose than to save, if possible, their official lives?" (Joint Committee on the Conduct of the War, 37th Cong., 3rd sess., *Report*, 3:246-48).

5. General William Selby Harney (1800-1889), a career army officer from Tennessee, had commanded the Department of the West at St. Louis when the South seceded from the Union. Convinced that he was too sympathetic to Missouri's proslavery element to be a reliable commander, Frank Blair, Jr., had persuaded Lincoln to replace him with Nathaniel Lyon. Because of her antipathy to Blair, JBF doubtless found it easier to agree with those who believed Harney would ultimately have been loyal. KOERNER (2:152), a close observer of the situation, also felt the suspicions about Harney were "unjust, as I knew personally; but he was very old and of course not as ardent and enthusiastic as Lyon or Blair." For details, see W. E. SMITH, 2:35-51.

6. Senator Henry Smith Lane (1811-81) had been president of the 1856 Republican convention that nominated JCF for president.

7. John Conness (1821-1909) was the newly elected Republican senator from California.

8. After serving under Sherman through the fall of 1863, Frank Blair, Jr., had taken a leave of absence and resumed his congressional seat. Some, evidently including JBF, believed he had left the military because he was not given the command he wanted. In Apr. 1864, when he was named commander of the Seventeenth Army Corps, Blair returned to the war (W. E. SMITH, 2:170-75).

To Elizabeth Palmer Peabody

New York, January 27 1864.
21 West 19th street.

My dear Miss Peabody,

The little book with its scarlet & blue & gold letter A came safely to us although after Christmas, and filled us with admiration for your niece's talent[1] and pleasure for your own goodness in writing not only so dear a little story with a proper moral for my boys, but for the time & eyesight you gave to putting it into such a legible form for Frank.

A short time before Christmas, only a few days indeed, Lily was thrown from the carriage & very much hurt. Her face was almost completely skinned and she not only suffered from it, but we had the fear that ugly traces might be left. But she is quite well again & not a blemish remains except one cut on the forehead which our physician says will also fade down with time & only shew when she is flushed or chilled. Charley too was hurt & a big boy with his knee in splints in skating time is a weariness to his Mother. Add to this that I have had diphtheria & was still in my room & you will see it poured when it rained. How was I to read to Charley with a throat just out of such an illness? We are just now in an interval of weather to make the lame dance. It's sweet beyond telling. I have violets, hyacinths & mignonette in bloom in the open windows, the sun & soft air drawing out a fragrance that seems more like April than January.

I am part of the Sanitary Fair work and because I know what you can do, & get done, I want you on my special staff. I think the beautiful fidelity of those who have carried out the work of the Sanitary Commission deserves a true & lasting record. Not to give them mere fame, for that would not be congenial to people who work for love and duty, but to give us an invaluable example of love of country and humanity, and to serve as that dear old Froissart says, "to the end that others taking example by them may be encouraged in their well doing."[2] Such memoirs are best made up from private letters written in the singleness of feeling which can't be had when a public is thought of — in personal recollections of those who knew the good women and men who have given, some their lives and many their health, in this work.

And with these I think it not inappropriate to put brief memoirs or collections from the notices already public of some young lives whose home training and social influences found their fittest expression in their beautiful heroism in battle. Some of these were so young & so surrounded with all the appliances for a life of happiness and ease that everyone feels for them the same sort of tender regret that one does for a woman's life ended by violence. Young Dwight — Young Putnam — Young Lowell and most touching of all because he died for a despised race, young Shaw.[3]

Won't you help me in this? — talk it over & systematize & condense it & let me know what can be sent me from your resources — "your" means all you can command. This was my suggestion & the committee for its execution was given to me with a promise of aid, if possible, from Mrs. Woolsey[4] & Mrs. Shaw. They are to be bound, uniform in size & binding, in thin little books like "Hospital Transports"[5] & to contain very much the same kind of matter only more personal. And we have a little book rack for the series designed by Darley & Rogers,[6] & with all this copyrighted for the Sanitary Comn. I hope to add to its funds. For once started the idea will be taken up by more practised people & form a collection of Memoirs pour Servir which will have value for History & the deepest interest for such of us as have been deprived of a belief in regular Histories by our own experience of how ours is made.

Such books would sell well at Christmas & I think it's a good idea to make a growing fund.

It would be very kind and very valuable to our Fair if Mr. Hawthorne would write some little thing especially for it and send it with a design illustrative by his own little daughter. I am not authorized to ask for that as it comes more under the autograph collector's work & there's a committee for every thing. I will ask today if he has been written to, or if I may stretch my commission to include such a request. Always my dear Miss Peabody Yours sincerely and affectionately,

J. B. Frémont

ALS (MH). Elizabeth Palmer Peabody (1804–94) was an author, publisher, and educational reformer long associated with the New England transcendentalists. Influenced by the ideas of the German educator Friedrich Froebel, she started the first formally organized kindergarten in America in 1859. When JBF settled in New York in 1862, she sent her youngest son, Frank, to a progressive kindergarten based on the ideas of Froebel and Peabody.

1. JBF had asked a number of friends to write brief Christmas stories for her children. Elizabeth Peabody had several nieces, but JBF probably refers to Rose Hawthorne (1851–1926), the thirteen-year-old daughter of Elizabeth Peabody's sister Sophia and her husband Nathaniel Hawthorne. Rose, who already showed a talent for drawing, later attended art school in London. She eventually became Mother Mary Alphonsa Lathrop, the founder of a Roman Catholic order that aided indigent cancer patients (BASSAN, 39–40).

2. JBF quotes from the opening of the *Chronicles* of Jean Froissart (c. 1337–c. 1410), which recounts the chivalric exploits of the French and English nobility during the Hundred Years' War.

3. JBF refers to several Harvard-educated Bostonians who died heroically in combat. Lt. Col. Wilder Dwight (b. 1833) of the Second Regiment Massachusetts Volunteers was mortally wounded on Sept. 17, 1862, at Antietam "while displaying his usual coolness and courage under the fire of the enemy" (OFFICIAL RECORDS, ser. 1, vol. 19, pt. 1:500–501). Second Lt. William Lowell Putnam (b. 1840) of the Twentieth Regiment Massachusetts Volunteers, was "shot in the bowels" during the disastrous battle of Ball's Bluff and died Oct. 23, 1861. Putnam's cousin, Lt. James Jackson Lowell (b. 1837), also of the Twentieth Massachusetts, was injured at Ball's Bluff and died of wounds received on June 30, 1862, during the Seven Days' battles (OFFICIAL RECORDS, ser. 1, vol. 5:317, and vol. 11, pt. 2:987). He was the younger brother of Charles Russell Lowell, who was married to Josephine Shaw, sister of Robert Gould Shaw and daughter of JBF's friend Sarah Shaw (BURCHARD, 48–49). Charles Russell Lowell himself would be mortally wounded at the battle of Cedar Creek, Va., and die on Oct. 20, 1864 (HEITMAN, 1:645).

Col. Robert Gould Shaw (b. 1837), commander of the celebrated Massachusets Fifty-fourth Regiment of black volunteers, died July 18, 1863, while leading his men in the tragic assault on Fort Wagner, S.C. (OFFICIAL RECORDS, ser. 1, vol. 28, pt. 1:362–65; the story of the regiment is told in BURCHARD and the 1990 movie *Glory*). Shaw admired JCF and, inspired by his explorations, had once dreamed of settling in the West. Earlier in the war, he had considered transfering to JCF's command. Coincidentally, as a child Shaw had attended the primary school of Elizabeth Peabody's sister Mary in West Roxbury, Mass., adjacent to Brook Farm.

Instead of William Lowell Putnam, JBF may be referring to Haldimand Sumner Putman, twenty-six, a West Point graduate from New Hampshire, who also died July 18, 1863, during the tragic assault on Fort Wagner (CULLUM, 2:680).

4. Jane Eliza (Newton) Woolsey (1801–74) and her daughters were active in Civil War relief work. On Mar. 9, Jane Woolsey urged daughters Jane Stuart and Georgeanna to contribute accounts of their activities for the fair: "Send whatever you have to *me*, that I may have the pleasure of handing it to the committee on *literature* (BACON & HOWLAND, 2:568–69). Georgeanna Woolsey's *Three Weeks at Gettysburg* (1863), an account of her own and her mother's experiences as relief workers at Gettysburg, was also sold at the fair.

5. Frederick Law Olmsted's *Hospital Transports: A Memoir of the Embarkation of the Sick and Wounded from the Peninsula of Virginia in the Summer of 1862* was published by Ticknor and Fields in 1863 for the Sanitary Commission.

6. Felix O. C. Darley (1822–88) was a popular artist who had illustrated the works of Irving, Dickens, and Cooper. The Rogers to whom JBF refers may be either her acquaintance, John Rogers (1829–1904), who was known mainly for his small sculptural groups, or a second John Rogers (c. 1808–c. 1888), an English engraver working in New York City for various book publishers (GROCE & WILLIAMS, 544). For mention

of a print probably engraved by the English Rogers after a drawing by Darley, see
Archives of American Art, Detroit, Roll No. N85, filmed from NN—Print Division.

To Sarah (Hildreth) Butler

[Feb. 8, (1864)]

My dear Mrs. Butler,

My bronchitis has come back so severely that I must get back at
once to the quiet of my own home and the care of my own physician.
Nothing but actual illness could have made me disappoint myself in
failing to be at your house tomorrow evening. The General will go,
and tell you how ill I was again last night and in bronchitits there is
no delay. You *must* mind it. You listened with so much interest to the
account of Col. Critcher's release[1] that you may like to judge the man
by the note I enclose. He had not been here for seven years but came
seeing our names here. His court met on Monday & he could not stay
over but we went together to see Genl. Butler and make him our
thanks again. That is a home into which you would be welcomed in
a way to warm your heart. I was very sorry Genl. Butler could not see
& feel all the good he had done. I asked Mr. Critcher what had decided
him to the Southern side finally—knowing how he held out for the
Union. And I think he had good reason to stay for he said he could
not give up his old home—for two hundred and forty years now in
direct succession from Father to son—never even mortgaged. It is but
forty miles from Richmond, on the Rappahannock & the boats stop
within three miles of them.

I don't think very pleasant things are so common that I need apologize
for this long* note, and it was a great pleasure to feel I had had part
in such a good act as Genl. Butler's release of my cousin.

Will you be kind enough to return Mr. Critcher's note to the General
at this Hotel (the Metropolitan). It may be needed. But first shew it
to Genl. Butler & give him my sincere regrets that I shall not be at
your house tomorrow evy. By nine tomorrow I shall have reached home
& be in bed with wet towels on my throat. Very sincerely yours,

Jessie Benton Frémont

Monday Feby. 8th

* (that reads as though the note was the pleasant thing—but I mean
the subject of the note)

ALS (DLC—Benjamin F. Butler Papers). [1862?] is marked on this letter in another hand, and it is filed in a folder marked 2/1–10/62, but context as well as the fact that Feb. 8 was a Monday in 1864, not 1862, indicates it should be dated 1864.

Sarah (Hildreth) Butler (1816–76), the daughter of a Massachusetts physician, had been a professional actress noted for her Shakespearean roles before her marriage to Benjamin Franklin Butler (1818–93), a wealthy Massachusetts lawyer/ politician and controversial Civil War major general. In her high spirits, intelligence, and attentiveness to the military and presidential ambitions of her husband, Sarah Butler resembled JBF. See BRADFORD, 201–34, for an assessment of her character.

Butler, commander of the Department of Virginia and North Carolina, was stationed at Fortress Monroe, Va., while his wife stayed in Washington. JBF evidently writes from Washington just before her return to New York City.

1. Lt. Col. John Critcher (b. 1820) of Westmoreland County, Va., was commander of the Fifteenth Virginia Cavalry when he was captured by Union forces in late May 1863 near Oak Grove, Va., while leading bushwhacking parties and reporting on Union movements to Gen. Robert E. Lee (OFFICIAL RECORDS, ser. 1, vol. 25, pt. 1:1114; pt. 2:826; ser. 2, vol. 5:706). Critcher, a lawyer who had studied at the University of Virginia and for three years in France, had served in the Virginia state legislature and participated in the state secession convention of 1861. He was married to Elizabeth ("Lizzie") Tomasia Kennon Whiting, a Virginia cousin of JCF's whom JBF had discovered and befriended during the 1856 campaign. When Lizzie Whiting married in 1857, JBF liked her husband but remarked that Lizzie was "no more in love . . . than I am with Mr. Critcher but he is with her" (JBF to Elizabeth Blair Lee, Nov. 22 [1857], NjP—Blair-Lee Papers). Critcher attributed his release from prison to JBF, who personally requested it of Butler (Critcher to John Alexander Meredith, Feb. 8, 1869, CSmH). After his release, Critcher returned to command the Fifteenth Cavalry (OFFICIAL RECORDS, ser. 1, vol. 51, pt. 2:985). Following the war, he served as a judge and congressman (POORE, 351, and *Virginia Magazine of History and Biography,* 5 (1897–98): 220–21; 35 (1927): 77.

To Elizabeth Palmer Peabody

Sunday 14th February [1864]

Dear Miss Peabody,

I am out of bed for the first day since last Sunday. I've just finished a note to Mr. Hawthorne but I fear my illness has put too much delay in my request.

Thank you very very much for your assistance. I have not made provision yet for the exact data of publishing. I am told by two publishers that they will do it at the lowest figure of actual expenses, & the money is to come from subscription or my own pocket. If it keeps within my means I shall make my contribution in that shape. As for the size &c — let that be regulated by that golden rule of saying in compact clear shape all there is [to] tell & not one word more. Let it make two pages or two hundred. This is my standard of true good writing.

A gentleman is to send me a large edition of a memoir of his son — dead at 22 after nearly three years of battles & wounds — made up from the young man's own letters & illustrated with his own drawings.[1] This had been partly prepared for private circulation, but learning of my wish, he has it prepared for me, all expenses paid by himself, & the whole edition given me for the benefit of the Fair. It is not everyone who can afford to carry out a feeling so thoroughly but this is a specimen.

I am at work this morning condensing a little notice to be printed & to serve as my circular.[2] I will send it to you. The fair opens the 28th of March[3] & will be fine.

Thanking you again very much & making no apology for adding to your work for none is sufficient, I am as always most sincerely yours,

J. B. Frémont

I must tell you that my forced quiet enabled me to read Theodore Parker's memoirs.[4] I knew him through Starr King & now through himself. Leaving out his ideas on the Bible and our Savior which seem to me harder to arrive at than the whole string of Catholic dogmas, I had almost entire assent to give. What a beautiful expression he makes about Govr. Andrew,[5] "his sense of justice amounts to the heroic" — how [Parker] recognizes that Lincoln "dodges" & "this is no way to fight the battles of freedom."

What's the matter with Mr. Garrison[6] that he can take "that thing" into his faith. What twaddle to talk of "magnanimity" toward the Pontius Pilate of the Slaves. Seward is the Judas of Freedom & Mr. Lincoln its Pilate. So far from magnanimity toward him, truth and duty compel his abolition & I'm thankful to know that even I have been of large service in that good work. Yours for unbargaining truth,

J. B. F.

ALS (MHi).

1. JBF most probably refers to the memoir of Walter Symonds Newhall (1841–63) of the Third Pennsylvania Cavalry, who died from wounds received July 3, 1863, during the Gettysburg campaign (OFFICIAL RECORDS, ser. 1, vol. 27, pt. 1:1051). The Newhall

volume was published in Philadelphia for the benefit of the Sanitary Commission in 1864. JBF specifically mentions the Newhall memoir to Elizabeth Peabody, Mar. 20 [1864], below.

2. The circular announced the formation of the Committee on Special Literary Contributions to collect and publish material relating to the war, including the private letters of soldiers in the field and of men and women engaged in Sanitary Commission work. "The materials so collected are intended to form a series of small volumes, bound in uniform style, copyrighted, with the object of forming a growing fund for the benefit of the Sanitary Commission." The circular was signed by JBF, Sarah Shaw, Mrs. Egbert Viele, Mrs. Robert B. Minturn (Mrs. Shaw's daughter Susanna), Mrs. George T. Strong, and Mrs. Alexander Clayton.

3. Although scheduled to open Mar. 28, the fair actually opened on Apr. 4 and continued through Apr. 23 (STRONG, 3:406, 432).

4. JBF refers to the newly published *Life and Correspondence of Theodore Parker* by John Weiss. Parker (1810–60), a distinguished Unitarian theologian and abolitionist, rejected the divine origin of the Bible and the deity of Jesus, whom he viewed as inspired by God but nonetheless human (WEISS, 1:355; 2:226). Parker's remarks about John A. Andrew and Lincoln, the latter in an 1858 letter written during the Lincoln-Douglas Senate campaign, also appear in WEISS (2:241, 360).

5. Massachusetts governor John Andrew (1818–67) was a vigorous antislavery leader who had organized two all-black regiments.

6. By early 1864, abolitionist William Lloyd Garrison (1805–79) had decided to support Lincoln for a second presidential term. At a meeting of the Massachusetts Anti-Slavery Society on Jan. 28, he responded to Wendell Phillips's praise of JCF by asking why JCF had not publicly supported Lincoln's Emancipation Proclamation. Garrison argued that JCF should have been "magnanimous. . . . What a glorious opportunity he has lost to show himself superior to all personal feelings towards the Government!" (GARRISON, 5:185–86).

To John Greenleaf Whittier

Sunday 14th February '64
New York, 21 West 19th street.

Dear friends

If you had received all the letters from me which have passed through my mind to you, you would have had a little box full. Few days have left so complete and charming a picture on my memory as that lovely October day when we found you & made you a visit in spite of your efforts to escape visitors. We have had a succession of illnesses and bad accidents in the family—the General is the only one who has gone through the winter in his usual health. I am just out of my room after a second illness and I've not time to get really well in the preparations we are making for the Sanitary Fair.

I have undertaken to collect and make public some of the evidences that deep down and governing every other feeling is the love of country. I will not write much more for my head is still easily tired, but I will send you a little printed slip which condenses what I want to say—it is only just ready for the printer now. This is my special work for my share in the Fair, but I want to add to it something written expressly for the occasion by yourself. I don't want to give you trouble— remember that. But I want something from you written at my request if you have time & health to indulge me in my wish.

I had intended sending you a large sheet of vellum with an illustration in the old missal fashion and asking you to write around it, in your own writing, the ballad of Barbara Frietchie.[1] I wanted the illustration to be where her grey head comes out of the high window & her hand is clutching the torn flag—the grey head could come out against a blue sky & the flag would add its coloring—below the serried crowd of troopers, dingy grey, & their sincere conscience struck leader commanding respect to her with his raised sword. But I can't make the picture and, as yet, I can't find the artist who feels it. If I can get it done will you add the verses? We have yet to the 28th of March and if you were willing I could have it photographed. You see what beggars we become when hundreds of women are pitted against each other to do their best. I have a little committee on which Mrs. Frank Shaw (including her lovely and clever daughters) & some names unknown to you are working to secure memoirs which will be of the deepest interest. Miss Whittier will let me add my collection to her own books and when I come to remind you of your promise to visit me at Nahant I shall look to see if they bear marks of reading.

How beautifully you have collected the noble ideas regarding California in the dedication hymn for our friend Mr. King's new church.[2] Distance is absolutely necessary to give poetry to that country. It's like Heber's description of Ceylon

"Every prospect pleases"

but when both the 7th & 8th commandments are "repealed" as Thackeray says the 7th is in Paris, inevitably "Man is vile."[3]

I trust we shall have Mr. King with us next winter. He says he only stays to carry that State through the Presidential crisis.

My daughter and the General join me in warm regards to your household & most for yourself. Did I tell you how in our home in California your verses on '56 & its needs, beginning "All night above their rocky bed," were fastened up by me in my room where none could go in or out without seeing them so that they grew to be part of the household words.[4] Now, the little volume you sent me[5] stands with Uncle Tom's Cabin, Wendell Phillips's speeches, Olmsted's Slave States, Fanny Kemble's diary & Theodore Parker's memoirs,[6] on a corner étagère while on a projection above the books I put a group of Rogers called the Slave Auction.[7] Have you ever seen it? And to finish the idea I have added a piece of a rebel gun taken at Fort Wagner—one of the guns which mowed down the 54th Mass. Young Hallowell,[8] a quaker of the war kind & now the head of the regiment, sends me the piece of the gun. Is it not well placed? Most sincerely yours,

Jessie B. Frémont

ALS (MH).

1. Whittier's famous 1863 poem, loosely based on a true incident, told the story of an old woman in Frederick, Md., who defiantly flew the Union flag while Confederate troops passed through town (WHITTIER [1], 342–43). The poem was probably included in a collection of poetry and prose by American authors in their own handwriting, "multiplied by the lithographic art," which was sold at the fair for six dollars a set (*Spirit of the Fair*, No. 7 [Apr. 12, 1864]: 75).

2. Whittier had written a hymn for the dedicatory services on Jan. 10, 1864, of San Francisco's new $90,000 gothic-style Unitarian church (WENDTE, 208–10).

3. JBF quotes from the "Missionary Hymn" by Reginald Heber (1783–1826), an Anglican bishop of Calcutta: "Though every prospect pleases/ And only man is vile." The commandments reputedly not followed in California were "Thou shalt not commit adultery" and "Thou shalt not steal."

4. JBF quotes the opening line of Whittier's "The Pass of the Sierra," written for the 1856 Frémont campaign (WHITTIER [1], 321–22).

5. Most probably *In War Time and Other Poems* (1863), Whittier's most recent volume.

6. JBF refers to a number of antislavery books: Harriet Beecher Stowe's *Uncle Tom's Cabin* (1852); Wendell Phillips's *Speeches, Lectures, and Letters* (1863); Frederick Law Olmsted's *Journey in the Seaboard Slave States, with Remarks on Their Economy* (1856); English actress Fanny Kemble's *Journal of a Residence on a Georgia Plantation* (1863); and *Life and Correspondence of Theodore Parker* by John Weiss (1864).

7. Many antislavery homes contained a copy of *The Slave Auction*, a sculptural group by John Rogers first exhibited in 1859. Rogers noted in a Feb. 28, 1864, letter that during an exhibition of his new work, JBF had especially admired *The Wounded Scout*, a depiction of a slave aiding an injured Union scout, and asked if she could bring "the General" to see it (D. H. WALLACE, 100–101).

8. Edward Needles Hallowell (1836–71), from a distinguished Philadelphia Quaker family, was wounded while leading the left wing of the Fifty-fourth Massachusetts during the attack on Fort Wagner. Hallowell's own terse report on the assault is in OFFICIAL RECORDS, ser. 1, vol. 28, pt. 1:362–63.

To John Greenleaf Whittier

[March 10 (1864)]

Dear Mr. Whittier

Your two letters reached me together on Monday. If the illustration proves worthy of the subject I will send you the paper by express — and thank you all the more since the copying will be disagreeable. I wish I had nothing more disagreeable than that to meet in my work for the Fair. If we have that visit I hope for from you next summer we will amuse your sister and yourself by the "inner view" of a fair.

I send you the only copy of the General's remarks which I happen to have.[1] This is from the Liberator, which was in the morning's mail. And I see it is accurate. It is not broken anywhere by the "applause." I mark with lines, according to the force of assent expressed, some places which I remember.

Does your sister use chloroform as an external application? I was thrown from the carriage (about three years since) on my head, and the jar to the spine gave me most terrible pains not only in the spine (I could almost *hear* it vibrate like a harp string stretched too tight) but caused neuralgia of the stomach. I had no respite for nearly five weeks except from rubbing with chloroform — aided by long lying daily in a warm bath.

Perhaps your sister knows all this but I should be glad to think I could suggest any rest from suffering.

It was at that time that my dear true friend Starr King came still nearer into our affections by his interest and sympathy & his efforts to help me through the time of convalescence. His brave pure soul has gone through those golden gates and to him it is well earned rest.[2] But to us it is a loss and loneliness that cannot be repaired. Most sincerely yours,

Jessie Frémont

March 10th
21 W. 19.

ALS (MH).

1. JCF's introductory address at a Cooper Institute reception honoring the British abolitionist George Thompson, appeared in the Mar. 3, 1864, *Liberator*.
2. Thomas Starr King, thiry-nine, died suddenly of diphtheria and pneumonia in

San Francisco on Mar. 4, 1864. In California, businesses and government offices closed, and his funeral was attended by twenty thousand people. At JBF's telegraphed request, violets were placed in his casket in her name (WENDTE, 217).

To Elizabeth Palmer Peabody

New York, March 20th [1864]
21 W. 19th.

(I saw your nephew¹ for a few moments.)
My dear Miss Peabody

Miss Smith gave me your notes and I am, as you know, more & more obliged by each package. It will not be possible to print them before the 28th. Will you add to your other kindnesses by letting me know (for publication) what memoirs I can promise "by authority."

The name of the person preparing need not be given, unless they choose. I send you a page of the first proof of the book which is ready. I will send you the book itself as soon as I get copies. It reads like the memoir of Hodson of Hodson's horse²—that & Tom Brown at Rugby³ should be in every boy's library. Our books must be of that kind & go to shaping the generous young hearts that will have grown chilled & careworn before they see the end of this strife.

Nobody has been disagreeable about the memoirs except Mrs. Fields.⁴ She could not "mistake" and ask in my name for the letters of living officers—that's against the ABC of military rule. I beg of you not to let Mrs. Holmes judge me by such a perverted view as that. Is it Dr. Holmes's wife?⁵ I don't want clever people to think me so stupid. I have an inerring instinct that tells me when I'm not in favor with people & Mrs. Fields never had a liking for me. But that's no matter if she will only not put me in a mistaken light of "intruding." Fortunately nobody else has taken my application as an "indelicate demand." (I say I don't care but I think I don't get used to that affront.)

The Gallery of arms & trophies is to hold the flags borne in battle, & those captured—the War Dept—Albany & West Point send each all they have. Mine is the only table in the Gallery. It is simply a library table with the volumes that are ready, & a large album for subscriptions. I want to have the list of what we are to have ready for Christmas, or earlier, ready printed, for distribution among those subscribing. The Arms & Trophy Committee is headed by Mrs. McClellan & I come next—we get on very civilly—even amicably. That gallery will be the military show room and on the opening night we shall all be in full bloom with generals attached, so you can see that it will be a neighborhood where something can be done if we have something positive to promise. I have five most attractive books under way but only two ready. Dr. Van Buren is writing me a preface to a new work of Miss Nightingale's.[6] The Appletons republish her book & give it as their contribution. Dr. Van Buren makes a preface adapting it to our American war & its wants & necessities &c—linking it "by request" to the Sanitary Commission, & giving it in to my table. This is a work of real value.

A memorial volume of our dear dear friend who held California in the Union & whose efforts obtained the half million for the wounded— this will be prepared by those who knew him* in that scene of his labors. *(mainly from Mr. King's correspondence & speeches &c.)[7]

I have a volume made up of letters from a mother to her children— she in New Orleans, they in the North. She, by birth & inheritance, a slave owner & by conviction an abolitionist, married to a northern man who was a secessionist. You can imagine the struggle in a loving heart. Of course it killed her. The names will not be given but the material is almost wholly from family letters. Only linked by explanations. They cover from the winter of 60, to within a year. Young Newhall's memoir & Mr. Curtis's memorial volume[8] make the five which are distinct to my mind.

Can you embody anything more for me—with or without names. I do so like young Bowditch's face.[9] He is the kind of boy who never outgrows sitting on his mother's knee & kissing her good night—or seeing her troubled turns instantly to his reserve of manliness & defies all man & womankind for troubling her. Oh what precious lives have been given—and how many more must go. But the word "lost" does not fit these deaths. And we will see that their examples are not lost. Mrs. Revere's letter[10] is so motherly & simple & sorrowful that I would like to keep it. If I might be allowed, I would like to give one or two sentences (without the name or any indication as to who wrote) to shew how a true mother feels.

My throat, today, is better. You know I was built to last a hundred years & I may yet get to half of that. But I think a little more of the present work would wreck me. Lily & Frank go early to Nahant. Lil is unnerved by her accident & longs for deep silence & the rest of the country as only nervous invalids can. My dear little Frank is not strong. He has never righted since his second attack of measles last year. He is too good & sweet & gentle for a healthy boy. His ponies & the boat & the soothing silence may make him like himself again, but now it lies like a shadow cast before, that we must all watch not to fatigue or worry him, and he is all eagerness to please every one.

I hope Mr. Hawthorne will find the health he seeks. Let me know if he comes to town & where I shall find him & I will go to see him. I don't think I would jar him. I believe in the Scarlet Letter, & I believe in some good traits in Mr. Pierce. Few men in power ever did a more unselfish & chivalrous act than I know of Mr. Pierce's doing—and for pure good feeling where he could have no benefit from it.[11] Good night & thank you very very much. I wait your answer. [Paper torn; sentence illegible.] I thank you very much and will be most indebted by your aid as offered. I will write fully and very soon but I am driving a four in hand team—society work, political work, sanitary comn. work and the looking after my two big boys & home which is a recurring work that takes its own hours every day. Throw in diphtheric sore throat for myself, runaway horses & wounded children & my sister's society & family duties which are being put into working order & you can see I have no "spare time." But Nahant will patch us all & make "auld *folks* amaist as gude as new." As an incidental bit of work I'm planning & directing roads & an enlargement of the cottage there. But this preface I can ready notes for quickly. Thank you again for undertaking so much labor.

J. B. F.

AL initialed (MHi).

1. Elizabeth Peabody had several nephews, the two oldest being Horace Mann, Jr. (1844–68), a son of Elizabeth's sister Mary and the educator Horace Mann; and Julian Hawthorne (1846–1934), son of Sophia Peabody and Nathaniel Hawthorne. Both young men were attending Harvard at least intermittently during this period (THARP, 291; BASSAN, 31).

2. British officer W. S. R. Hodson (1821–58), commander of a cavalry regiment known as "Hodson's Horse," was killed in Lucknow, India, during the unsuccessful 1857–58 Indian rebellion against British rule. In his letters, posthumously published under the title *Hodson of Hodson's Horse* (1858), he depicted himself as a Christian gentleman fighting for civilization against barbarism. FREDRICKSON, 155, sees aristocratic Civil War martyrs like Harvard-educated Robert Gould Shaw as reflecting a similar noblesse oblige.

3. *Tom Brown's Schooldays* (1857) by Thomas Hughes, based on the author's

experiences at the English public school Rugby, celebrates a similar ethic, a "muscular Christianity" combining physical prowess with loyalty to school and country.

4. When JBF wrote Annie and James T. Fields requesting their help with her book publishing plan, Annie Fields objected that it would be an invasion of privacy to publish personal memoirs and letters. JBF suspected other motives: dislike of herself and perhaps a reluctance to endorse a nonprofit venture that might compete with the publications of Ticknor and Fields (see JBF to James T. Fields, Sunday evening, [Feb. 14? 1864]; to Annie Fields, Feb. 24, 1864, Mar. 4 [1864], all CSmH—Fields Papers; and to Elizabeth Palmer Peabody, Monday mg., [Mar. 7? 1864], MHi).

5. Physician and author Oliver Wendell Holmes (1809–94) was married to Amelia Lee Jackson (1818–88), daughter of a Massachusetts supreme court justice. In Oct. 1861, their oldest son, Lt. Oliver Wendell Holmes, Jr., the future U.S. Supreme Court justice, had survived a "shot through the chest from side to side" at Ball's Bluff (OFFICIAL RECORDS, ser. 1, vol. 5:317).

6. JBF possibly refers to Florence Nightingale's *Notes on Nursing* (1859), with subsequent editions in 1860, 1861, and 1878 but not 1864. Van Buren seems not to have written a preface for a new edition, but he did contribute several of his own essays, including "Rules for Preserving the Health of the Soldier," to *Military Medical and Surgical Essays*, published in 1864 for the Sanitary Commission by J. B. Lippincott, Philadelphia.

7. *In Memoriam—Thomas Starr King*, a twenty-two-page booklet dated Mar. 28, 1864, includes poems by Whittier, Fitz-Hugh Ludlow, and Bret Harte, as well as excerpts from King's California letters. At the fair, JBF sold copies at her book table in the Arms and Trophies Department (New York *Tribune*, Apr. 21, 1864).

8. JBF may refer to author and journalist George William Curtis (1824–92), whose mother-in-law, Sarah Shaw, was on JBF's committee. Curtis's stepbrother, Lt. Col. Joseph Bridgham Curtis, had been killed at Fredericksburg, Dec. 13, 1862; a tribute to him by George Curtis would appear in John Russell Bartlett's *Memoirs of Rhode Island Officers* (1865). Curtis may also have helped prepare the memorial volume for his brother-in-law, Robert Gould Shaw. *Memorial. R. G. S.* (Cambridge, Mass.: University Press, 1864) includes a poem by Curtis and an Aug. 9, 1863, condolence letter from JBF addressed to Shaw's sister Nellie (Ellen) (pp. 141–42).

9. Lt. Nathaniel Bowditch (b. 1839) of the First Massachusetts Cavalry, was mortally wounded at Kelly's Ford, Va., Mar. 17, 1863 (OFFICIAL RECORDS, ser. 1, vol. 25, pt. 1:53). A *Memorial* by his father, the distinguished surgeon and Harvard Medical School professor Henry Ingersoll Bowditch, would be privately printed in Boston in 1865. Dr. Bowditch, who had long urged reform of the army medical service, also issued the poignantly titled *Brief Plea for an Ambulance System for the Army of the United States, as Drawn from the Extra Sufferings of the Late Lieut. Bowditch and a Wounded Comrade* (Boston: Ticknor and Fields, 1863).

10. Mrs. Revere was most probably the mother of Dr. Edward H. Revere (b. 1827), a surgeon with the Twentieth Massachusetts who was killed at Antietam, and of Col. Paul Joseph Revere (b. 1832), regimental commander of the Twentieth Massachusetts, who died at Gettysburg, July 2, 1863 (OFFICIAL RECORDS, ser. 1, vol. 19, pt. 1:116; vol. 27, pt. 1:375, 435–40, 445). A long *Memorial* to the two brothers was privately printed in Boston in 1874.

11. Nathaniel Hawthorne, who was seriously ill, was traveling to New York, Philadelphia, and Washington with his publisher, George Ticknor, to care for him. Ironically, Ticknor would die unexpectedly of pneumonia during the journey. Hawthorne himself died on May 19 while traveling with his former Bowdoin College classmate, Franklin Pierce (1804–69). Hawthorne had written a campaign biography of Pierce, who re-

warded him with the Salem Customs House job that provided such rich material for the celebrated autobiographical introduction to *The Scarlet Letter*. Although JBF disagreed with Pierce's willingness to compromise with slavery during his presidency, she was grateful for his "unselfish & chivalrous act" in inviting her father to stay at the White House when Benton's house burned in 1855 (JBF, "Memoirs," 91–92).

To Horace Greeley

[Mar./Apr. 1864?]

Dear Mr. Greeley

So few people have seen the grand scenery of the Yo Semite that it needs a little explaining. You who have been there and know how much endurance it takes to overcome those weary miles will be among the few who can fully appreciate not only this picture but all that went to its making.[1]

I wish you would come to the private view—it's, in a manner, my reception, and I shall look for you. I shall look too to find such a notice in the Tribune as will bring in money to the object for which it is exhibited & for which I know you are kindly interested.

To give some points, I enclose a rough memoranda which may be of service to some one who does not know the subject as yet so well as I do. Very sincerely,

J. B. Frémont

Wednesday mg. 21 West 19th

ALS (DLC—Greeley Papers).

1. JBF probably refers to a painting by artist Albert Bierstadt (1830–1902), who had visited Yosemite in August 1863. Bierstadt donated a painting of Yosemite to the Sanitary Commission to be exhibited and auctioned at the Metropolitan Fair. The first color view of Yosemite shown in the East, it sold for $1,600, the highest price paid for any painting at the fair (New York *Times*, Apr. 4, 1864).

To Maria Daly

[late May/June 1864]

Dear Mrs. Daly

Thank you for the book & your note about which I should like to talk to you, but as we go on Monday to Nahant I may not have the chance unless you come to see me there on your White Mountain tour. My name was put to the Washington "covenant" without my knowledge.[1] There is much for & much against it. To me it seems, en bref, that if we are to have Mr. Lincoln for another four years, the little our gowns & gloves would amount to wouldn't be the traditional drop in the bucket toward the embarrassments of finance which would inevitably follow. But you are not in need of having this proved to you & can understand why I have no interest in that particular mode.

From the World I cut a sensible idea.[2] The whole letter is too long & attempts too much for a start & is a little hysterical in its arguments, but founded on facts that justify regular hysterics so we can overlook the style.

The passage I marked is an excellent idea & if you New York people of good hearts & good heads will adopt something like this I will do my part as your (always invisible) aid de camp. I refer respectfully to Cinderella[3] & the Mrs. Frémont of eight years ago for my credentials as designer & decorator in dress. Seriously, this is something we *can* do. If the profits are made into a fund for the relief of sewing girls it will be a sacred object. I was here the winter of '57 when so many failures threw—*sixteen thousand* young women literally out of doors. One came to me then who had been with the French dress maker who made my clothes—in her necessity she did me what I felt to be the honor of coming to me not only for temporary employment but for such an introduction to steady work as should save her from the consequences of her position—she looked most (I mean she thought most) at starvation & it was the first person I had ever seen suffering hunger. After taking charge of her, only the same experience can make one know all I learned of the difficulties in the way of getting work for an intelligent, experienced, absolutely respectable woman. To be sure it was a time of great moneyed depression—but is it any thing else now for the class whose incomes are stationary while prices double. That one woman was saved, & after four years' absence from New York I find her healthy, well-married & independent but—she was one of sixteen thousand.

From that time it has been my hobby—& I have talked of it with different people who could advise—to see founded a place where sewing girls & women could come to receive orders for such work as is now given out by searching up seamstresses—where they could find a comfortable light lunch & tea & in the evenings a comparison of profits & resources—a workwoman's exchange in fact where they could meet not to complain but to learn from friendly people what could be done either to start them or to tide them over a season of illness or want of work. Where they should find some wholesome simple food for their bodies & wholesome refining food for their minds—good papers, periodicals, engravings, & works of the kind that would raise their standard of taste. A place where the lady managers would find it a pleasure as well as a duty to meet them not only as employers & employed but on the common ground of women caring diligently & jealously for the honor & protection of women.

I don't think this is too much to accomplish. Practical minds must be brought to the details but a little heart is always needed in what's to be done for women. Man doesn't live by bread alone & women must have kind words with theirs or it becomes the prohibited stone which we are ordered not to give in its place.

You can manage all this. You live among your own people & Judge Daly is not a candidate for the Presidency. No one can put their own constructions on your motives. If you do give it favorable consideration count me among your thorough workers—on condition my name is not put except among the privates.

Meantime I want enough American made stuffs to dress a doll for a Fair in Portland & I am told you have treasures. I shall come about five o'clock & ask for what I need.

You are in earnest in your work & I am too so I make no apology for this long letter. I'm new to the subject but if you will compact it & make it into a working fact with the other ideas that belong with it—& this in the World seems to me admirable—I shall be only too glad to obey orders in such a cause.

It's odd, but just at this moment arrives a sewing machine given me at the Fair.[4] Why shouldn't we accept omens & make of it an altar to this good work? Always yours very sincerely,

J. B. Frémont

Saturday mg.

ALS (NN—Charles P. Daly Papers). Maria (Lydig) Daly (1824–94) was the wife of Judge Charles Patrick Daly of the Court of Common Pleas in New York City. She had met the Frémonts in early 1864 through Baron Friedrich von Gerolt, the Prussian ambassador. Although Maria Daly was a Union Democrat opposed to abolitionism and therefore, she admitted, prejudiced against the Frémonts before she met them, she gradually warmed to both. She found JCF "very gentlemanly, talks little but well, has a soft, tender blue eye, and is, I am sure, rather a shy man. He seems to have a chivalric devotion for his wife and is, I feel certain, a brave soldier.... I liked him very much." JBF she pronounced "brilliant and original, has somewhat the manner of one accustomed to rule and direct others, fond of gentlemen's society, as most clever women are, has . . . no affectations of manner and no hypocrisy" (DALY, 276, 321).

1. A group of prominent Washington, D.C., women, organized as the Ladies' National Covenant, had pledged not to buy imported clothing for the duration of the war; the group listed JBF as a principal member of its New York state committee (New York *Times*, May 5, 1864). Responding to the Washington group, the women's executive committee of the Metropolitan Fair sponsored a meeting on the issue in New York City, attended by two thousand women. Angered to find it conducted and dominated by men, the women induced the men to leave before agreeing on a pledge against imported luxuries (New York *Times*, May 17, 1864). Maria Daly, president of the Women's Patriotic Association for Diminishing the Use of Imported Luxuries, commented sarcastically on the patronizing male speechifying: "They patted us on the back and said they were sure we would be good little dears and give up our laces, French bonnets, and sugar plums, if we knew how well the gentlemen would think of us.... they would think us just as pretty in homespun" (DALY, 290, 297, 299–300).

2. A May 25 New York *World* article billed as a "lady's opinion" argued that the "covenant" against foreign fabrics would increase the demand for domestic clothing, force up prices, and thus cause hardship to the working class and poor. In a vivid section, the writer depicted the plight of even the better paid "sewing girls," who earned $5 a week yet had to spend $3–3.50 on "a small miserable room . . . shared by other persons, and [a] poor lunch of a thin slice of dry bread and meat, or bread and butter, grudgingly bestowed. The whole distance from her wretched home to the shop and back the girl is obliged to walk, toiling laboriously between times, and oppressed with a sick faintness the result of scant and unwholesome food." For such young women, clothing was already almost unaffordable. The writer concluded that instead of buying domestic fabrics, wealthy women should wear their old clothes and devote the saved money to "some good enterprise, such as providing homes for working women."

3. JBF had financed and staged a lavish children's production of *Cinderella* at Niblo's Theatre. Complete with real Shetland ponies to pull Cinderella's coach, it netted $2,842 for the Sanitary Commission. Maria Daly, attending on Apr. 16, found it "admirably well done.... The court ball was beautiful. I think there must have been some 200 children on the stage in fancy dress and they danced the cotillion as well as any *corps de ballet*. Young [Charley] Fremont was the prince. The house was crowded so that there were not even places to stand" (DALY, 289; see also New York *Tribune*, Apr. 14, 17, 1864).

4. Three sewing machines, donated by Singer and two other manufacturers, were purchased during the fair by group subscription. The money raised went to the Sanitary Commission and the machines to the wives of Generals Frémont, Grant, and McClellan (*Spirit of the Fair*, No. 17 [Apr. 23, 1864]: 205).

To John Greenleaf Whittier

[August 22 (1864)]

Dear Mr. Whittier,

The General will be here on Wednesday and will be glad to talk with you. Thank you for your faith in him—it is fully deserved.[1] I hope your sister's health will permit you to stay the night of Wednesday and take the morning train to Boston, for we should so love to have you even for that short time share our peaceful home life here.

I am grieved to learn your sister still suffers so much. If it were not for the steady watching my own sister needs I would go to Amesbury in the hope of giving Miss Whittier even a little lifting of the weariness of confinement. Sometimes a new face and a different class of ideas coming with it leave refreshment to an invalid and it is such a pleasure to be able to bring them any rest. I would like to shew you my little Bible where two lines of yours stand with a date that marked both a cradle & a grave to me and made you part of that memory always.[2]

It would have been a great loss to me if you had not recognized that Mr. Frémont could not turn away from the truth. It has never been his allotted part to go with the current but the weariness of the strife against might & wrong is more than compensated by the companionship & reliance on his firm faith which he does get from such as you dear Mr. Whittier. He is clear as to the duty. We have very unusual means of knowing the real feeling of the South and of Europe. Mr. Lincoln's re-election will be the signal for the recognition of the South by France first then England, Austria, & so on. The West will separate from New England & have its treaties with the South. This is all ready and the [return of?] Mr. Lincoln's administration is hoped for by the Richmond administration as their most speedy & easy means of independence. Some one else must be put in his place.[3] It must be some one firm against slavery. Everything hinges on that. And the General will thankfully retire & give his most active support to such a man. He has said so before & will say it again very soon. Most sincerely yours,

Jessie Frémont.

Nahant August 22d

ALS (MiMtpT). For a discussion of JCF's 1864 candidacy and withdrawal, see the section introduction.

1. JBF describes Whittier's subsequent visit, during which he urged JCF's withdrawal for the sake of party unity, in a letter to Samuel T. Pickard, May 28, 1893, below. On Aug. 29, Whittier wrote William Lloyd Garrison to condemn attacks on Frémont published in the *Liberator:* "If Lincoln cannot be voted for without disparaging and sacrificing Fremont, his election is entirely hopeless. . . . I know that thou wilt agree with me, that the course of the Administration in regard to him constitutes one of those passages which the best friends of the President find most difficult to explain or justify" (WHITTIER [2], 3:75–76).

2. JBF refers to the death of her baby, Benton Frémont, on Oct. 6, 1848. The two lines she copied are from Whittier's 1847 poem, "Angel of Patience": "The throbs of wounded pride to still,/ And make our own our Father's will" (WHITTIER [2], 3:49, and [1], 425).

3. Republican politicians were talking of naming a new candidate who could unite the North as Lincoln seemed unable to do at this low point in his presidential career. Among the names mentioned were Chase, Sumner, and Butler. See, for example, Edgar Conkling to JCF, July 18, 1864, urging him to throw his support to Butler (BUTLER, 5:512).

To Nelly Haskell

Nahant
Tuesday Nov. 1. [1864]

Dear Nell

I won't pretend to answer your letter in size—although you did not write a word too much, but I do not write much as you know.

Sometimes in my life I have felt I could be of more use to some one than their usual regular people. Mr. Harte was one—Mr. Beale was another, each of these feel me—I really think—to be a friend. A friend to like them, & a friend to tell them themselves what others would only say of them rather than risk getting their ill will. For it's a very risky thing to tell the whole truth. Especially if people are displeased with themselves. But both of those men have had more useful lives & been more patient under trials & had more wish to do for others & put themselves aside, because of our talks together— and because they think I have tried to do as I talked. Each of them has chanced to know me under fire. Mr. Beale especially for he knew me when I was young and more gay and happy than you can imagine me. "Fair was she and young when in hope the long journey began." You see how the end looks, but looking back I do not regret that I did not contend for myself. It was not natural to me or easy for me to bend my pride and I was a great deal older than you are before it was sorely tried. I am sure if it was all written out in a book it would grieve any one to see how I got broken in. But out of that came a grieving whenever I saw a hot generous nature blindly striking out and trying to hold to some vanishing joy—unable to understand, much less to say, Thy will, not mine, be done. We have received good at his hand. Shall we not receive evil also? Even so Father—Thy will not mine be done.

Dear Nell even when that has become a fixed and governing thought—when it is so driven in that it comes of itself in the first stunned moment of trial—even then it needs fresh strength to act up to it cheerfully. And since I see that I can do you good I will tell you too to remember that God loves a cheerful giver.

You know how a favor loses all grace when the trouble it gives is set forth to you. So one's submission is to be made not with a parade of sacrifice but so thoroughly that only God knows it. Then, then I believe he *will* reward us. Under Miss [Henrietta B.] Haines's care I am sure you will do your utmost to be good which is of far more importance than being accomplished. She is so truly a lady that it is good to live in her atmosphere. If I had been in New York I should certainly have spoken to your Father about the schools and if there had been no serious reason for the other I should have urged Miss Haines. For I saw evils on evils for you in the change, and only good if [in] it you remained. The General thought as I did and I am very glad your Father was able to decide the way we all wanted. You had a pleasant week at the last—and you are sure your singing gave pleasure and your pretty hair was thought pretty & told so too.

One of the good English authors has died lately[1]—he was nearly or quite ninety but remarkably young in all ways. I remember a sentence of his which is so true, "I am growing old for want of some one to tell me I am as young as ever. *There is a vast deal of vital air in loving words.*" Age is not the number of years one has but the number of people who love one & to whom one's death would be a horrible blank. And if one lived just to be happy and do as one pleased regardless of duties or hindrances then it would be too bitter to endure to feel that one could be dispensed with.

But everyone can do something for others. And if it proves that our efforts bear [letter incomplete].

AL (CU-B—Frémont Papers). Born in 1849, Ella ("Nelly") Haskell (later Browne), the pretty teenaged daughter of JCF supporter and aide Leonidas Haskell, first met JBF in San Francisco in 1859–60, when the Frémonts were neighbors at Black Point. When JCF assumed his Missouri command, her father joined his staff; subsequently he continued to serve as an aide in various railroad ventures and during his 1864 presidential campaign. The Haskell family lived on Ninth Street during these years, and Nelly saw the Frémonts often in New York City and vacationed with them at Nahant. She would remain a loyal friend for the rest of their lives. Her own death came in San Francisco in 1941 (Tacoma *News Tribune* obit., Mar. 10, 1941). On the Haskell family and their association with the Frémonts, see Benjamin H. Brooks, "A Transcript of Certain Imprints upon the Tablet of Memory," typescript, c. 1925, CU-B. The letters Nelly Haskell saved and later, through the auspices of Catherine Coffin Phillips, deposited at the Bancroft Library, form an invaluable collection on the Frémont family.

1. English author Walter Savage Landor.

THE LOSS OF FORTUNE
1 8 6 5 – 7 8

After the Civil War, although the Frémonts kept their brownstone mansion in New York City, Jessie and the children spent more and more time at Pocaho, their newly purchased estate near Tarrytown. The place had formerly belonged to James Watson Webb, the owner of the New York *Courier and Enquirer*, and John had first seen it when he spent the Fourth of July holidays there in 1856, planning campaign strategy with Webb and other Republicans.[1] The house was surrounded by more than a hundred acres of orchards, woods, and fields and in Jessie's mind combined the best of all her former homes, including the beloved Black Point. She would spend the next few years decorating its large, airy rooms elegantly and simply, entertaining friends, and worrying about her children's futures and, all too soon, John's finances. In 1874, when the Frémonts were on the point of losing Pocaho, she estimated its value at $300,000.

The four sides of its fine library, a twenty-by-thirty-foot room, were lined with books from floor to ceiling, including Audubon's *Birds* (Jessie's favorite as a child), volumes on science, geography, and the art of war, and a portion of the library of Alexander von Humboldt, purchased after the death of the great German naturalist. Atop an oak stand holding Henry Schoolcraft's volumes on the American Indian was a bronze of the *Freedman* by John Quincy Adams Ward, which Jessie had commissioned. Above the library mantel was Albert Bierstadt's painting of the Golden Gate at sunset, purchased from Bierstadt, a neighbor, for $4,000. Nearby hung Giuseppe Fagnani's portrait of John, wearing his general's uniform and holding a sword given him by the Germans of the West, which had been painted for Jessie's forty-third birthday. Fagnani had also done a companion portrait of Jessie, framed in the same red velvet and heavy wood.[2]

A retinue of well-trained servants—maids, grooms, coachmen, gardeners, even a French chef—kept the estate running smoothly. There were horses and dogs, carriages and boats, croquet on the lawn in summer and ice skating on the pond in winter. The boys were sent to a private academy, and teenaged Charley had his own yacht, Frank a Steinway grand piano. But even the comforts of Pocaho were not sufficient, and in 1870, after their return from a European journey, the Frémonts acquired a small "splendidly wooded" Maine island where they planned to build a summer cottage. "We are going to have no plaster in the house—all hard wood & the furniture covered with bright plaid worsted stuffs, & Scotch carpets & everything as homespun and comfortable as possible," Jessie informed a nephew. Already, too, they had plans for a donkey and "a red morocco side saddle which shall come from England."[3]

In late May 1868, the Frémonts journeyed to St. Louis, where Jessie had been asked to unveil a large monument of her father. The bronze statue of the "Old Roman" was the work of Harriet Hosmer and showed Benton with an unrolled map in his hand, facing westward, with the words carved below: "There is the East, There Lies the Road to India." The event awakened in Jessie the deepest of emotions. A crowd of forty thousand filled Lafayette Park; a salute of thirty guns, one for each year Benton had served in the Senate, was fired at the beginning of the ceremony; and as she drew back the drapery, thousands of schoolchildren pelted the base of the Quincy granite pedestal with roses. Ironically, Frank P. Blair, Jr., her bitter enemy, delivered the dedicatory address and dwelt at some length on Benton's favorite idea—a Pacific railroad.[4]

Except for occasional trips such as this, Jessie retreated into domesticity, while John plunged into numerous speculative enterprises. He was often away from Pocaho, staying in New York City, Washington, and even St. Louis. During the summer of 1866, he wrote that he had "not had three days rest."[5] Railroading was absorbing all of his attention and money.

John had served briefly—in 1863—as vice-president of the Eastern Division of the Union Pacific Railroad Company, was a stockholder for a time in the Kansas Pacific, and a purchaser of the Southwest

Pacific. He tied the last into his Atlantic and Pacific Road, which received a congressional land grant and authority to build from Springfield, Missouri, to the Pacific. The reason for the purchase of the Southwest Pacific, he informed Missourians, was to assure St. Louis a connection with his Atlantic and Pacific in the race to the ocean. The San Francisco *Bulletin* expressed skepticism that he could be trusted to press the road to San Francisco; more accurately, it editorialized, he bought the Southwest Pacific purely as a land and townsite speculation, noting that land grants and bonds often filled private pockets rather than completed great enterprises.[6] He also had visions of building a Costa Rican railroad running from Puerto Limon on the Atlantic Coast to the Pacific Coast and of a line in northern Mexico that would connect Guaymas on the Pacific with El Paso.[7] But it was his actions in connection with the Memphis, El Paso, and Pacific Railway Company that brought financial ruin upon the Frémonts, a ruin from which they were never able to recover and that further blighted the general's reputation.

The Memphis, El Paso, and Pacific already had a charter and a conditional land grant (the certificates for land depended upon the mileage of track laid) from the state of Texas, when John entered into an agreement with the company in 1866 to furnish money to build the road, which he envisioned as stretching from Norfolk, Virginia, to San Diego, California. The lands yet to be received provided the security for the bonds that John proposed to sell in Europe to raise money for construction. For this purpose he enlisted the help of his brother-in-law, Baron Gauldrée Boilleau, who had been the French consul in Quebec and New York for the past ten years, but was now in France. Boilleau introduced him to Henry Probst, who after associating himself with a prominent French railway engineer, Antoine Lissignol, arranged with the great brokerage house of Paradis et Cie. to take up to $8,400,000 of the bonds provided they could be put on the Bourse. Getting the bonds quoted on the Bourse, however, was tricky, since French law prohibited the offering of securities for sale there unless they were regularly sold on the exchange of the country of their origin. But the bonds could not be quoted in New York until the railroad was built and the trains were running. Consequently, as the next best thing, a scheme was devised whereby they were advertised in the New York *Tribune* on October 1, 1868, and a few days later, the company's agent took to France forged certificates with signatures and gold seals as conclusive proof that the bonds were being sold on the New York Stock Exchange. The French promoters, spurred by high commissions, further misrepresented the company's situation, falsely claiming that it owned 8,000,000 acres of land all along the transcontinental route and that the principal and interest on the construction bonds were guaranteed by the U.S. government. Inquiries at the American embassy caused the U.S. minister, Elihu B. Washburne, to urge the American government to investigate. It was at this juncture, in June 1869, that the Frémont family, along with the railroad's chief engineer, James M. Daniel, arrived in Paris.[8]

John could not have been unaware of the false representations, but it was not until late summer that he publicly corrected them. Meanwhile, Daniel, who was genuinely interested in the construction of the road, became suspicious of Frémont. He wrote Benjamin H. Epperson, then president of the company, that although at least $4,600,000 had been realized from the sale, Frémont seemed reluctant to forward any of it to the states for construction. "If F continues in power with Probst & Lissignol and their complement of parasites, it would be much easier for a camel to go through the eye of a needle than for us to succeed."[9] Several weeks later, he wrote, "The same mystery exists here about all transactions that existed with you and him in N.Y. I am not allowed to investigate the company books or contracts."[10]

While in Paris, the Frémonts (except Charley, who was at the Naval Academy) settled for a few days into the Hotel Windsor on the Rue de Rivoli. The two women shopped, Frank rowed on the lake in the Bois de Bologne, and soon the three set off for Denmark where they attended various festivities in honor of the newly married crown prince and his bride, a princess of Sweden. Later, Jessie also recalled a beautiful day at the castle at Elsinore, "where Hamlet saw his father's ghost on the ramparts," and a visit with Hans Christian Andersen, who read them his "Tale of a Thistle." John joined them sporadically as they made a "long way round" return to Paris by Dresden, Prague, Munich, the Austrian-Tyrol, and Vienna, stopping at "leisurely characteristic old-world hotels," away from the rush of railroads and tourist ideas of food and lodging.[11]

Once back in Paris, they were met by Frémont, who took them to an opulent apartment in the Hotel de Jardins de Tuileries, which gave them a beautiful view of the old palace. Within a short time, they visited the studio of a young American sculptor, Vinnie Ream, who had come to Europe to sculpt her statue of Abraham Lincoln in marble. She had been making a medallion of John and now made a bust of Jessie and casts of Lily's and Frank's hands. If Jessie realized that the fifty-six-year-old John had been flirting with the talented coquette, she never gave any indication.[12] Outwardly her devotion remained unshaken, as it had in an earlier year when she may have heard rumors of a mistress named Margaret Corbett.

John and Jessie went to London for ten days and then on November 13, 1869, took passage from Liverpool on the *Java.* Lily, Frank, and a maid wintered in Dresden where Frank would be tutored in German, Latin, arithmetic, fencing, and music, while Lily improved her German and learned to paint flowers on china.

After a brief stay at Pocaho, John and Jessie headed for Washington. Already the congressional investigation into the Paris bond scandal had begun. A shrewd manipulator, John A. C. Gray, moved in to gain control of the company through bankruptcy proceedings, then slowly began to force Frémont out. So devious and arrogant was Gray that even the Frémonts's old enemy, Thomas Scott, declared that "nothing would please him better than to witness Gray's destruction."[13]

The letters printed in this section reveal a complex woman—one who enjoyed luxury and show but who was also remarkably resilient. Although Jessie was depressed and even made physically ill by her family's continuing adversities, she was also in some way exhilarated by the opportunity to be of use again. Writing to the shrewd Pennsylvania lawyer Jeremiah Black for help, she attempted to salvage what she could of their dwindling fortune. In early 1875, she began to write for a living. She produced a series of reminiscences of her eventful life for the New York *Ledger,* a high paying weekly, and then wrote a charming and polished account of her gold-rush experiences for *Harper's,* which later published it as a book, *A Year of American Travel* (1878).

Despite her efforts, the Frémonts were forced to sell Pocaho. Over the next years, they moved to progressively cheaper rental houses; in 1877, their household treasures—paintings, furniture, and books— were sold at auction.[14] That much of Jessie's idealism was gone is indicated by a comment she wrote to a friend: "But I am only a ghost of the past and my place now is not to work or help in great things, but to ask for my own and confine myself to 'putting money in my purse.' "[15]

Notes

1. CROUTHAMEL, 134–35.

2. F. P. Fremont, Memorandum for Allan Nevins, n.d. (CU-B—Frémont Papers); JCF to A. Bierstadt, Apr. 8 [1865] (DeWint); JBF to Emma Hill (Hadley) Ballard, Feb. 10, 1902 (MoSHi), June 20, 1902, below.

3. JBF to William Carey Jones, Jr., Aug. 22, 1870 (CSmH).

4. JBF to Wayman Crow, May 1, 4, 1868 (MCR—Harriet Hosmer Papers); *Harper's Weekly,* June 20, 1868, p. 398.

5. For JCF's various ventures, see JCF to Trenor W. Park, July 20, Dec. 23, 1865; July 16, Aug. 27, 1866 (Park-McCullough House Archives).

6. MINER, 40–59, discusses JCF's involvement in both the Southwest Pacific and the Atlantic and Pacific, as well as public reaction.

7. For JCF's unsuccessful attempt to obtain a railroad concession, vast mining and land grants, and six million dollars in bonds from the Mexican government in exchange for the use of his influence to market a sixty-million-dollar loan to Mexico and a U.S. guarantee of that loan, see FRAZER. Although his contract with Gaspar Sanchez Ochoa had not been ratified by the Mexican minister in the United States, JCF wrote Park as though all was settled: "In connection with the Mexican Bond business I can obtain the right to export silver from Mexico free of duty & to coin Mexican dollars. You are aware that these are at a premium of ten percent in Cala. for the Chinese market" (Sept. 1, 1866, Park-McCullough House Archives).

8. V. TAYLOR, 3–141, gives an excellent description of JCF's role in the tangled affairs of the railroad. In a Mar. 1870 letter to Jacob M. Howard, chairman of the Senate Committee on the Pacific Railroad, JCF wrote that "a sale to the amount of $8,400,000" was made to the house of M. Paradis (Senate Misc. Doc. 96, 41st Cong., 2d sess., serial 1408).

9. Daniel to Epperson, July 4, 1969, quoted in V. TAYLOR, 28.

10. Daniel to Epperson, July 24, 1869 (TxU—Benjamin H. Epperson Papers in the Barker Center).

11. Elizabeth Benton Fremont to Nelly Haskell Browne, Dec. 12, 1869 (CU-B—Frémont Papers); JBF to Whittier, Dec. 22, 1869 (MiMtpT); J. B. FRÉMONT [1], chs. 22–25.

12. See four undated letters (c. 1869–70) of JCF to Vinnie Ream and Vinnie Ream's Journal Abroad (DLC—Vinnie Ream Hoxie Family Papers).

13. V. TAYLOR, 95.

14. For notice of the auction, see New York *Times,* Oct. 10, 1877.

15. JBF to Nathaniel Banks, Jan. 30 [1877?] (IHi—Nathaniel Banks Papers).

To Samuel Phillips Lee

[Oct. 25, 1865]

Dear Mr Lee

When Lil came back from town she brought me your name & the date under it which you had left at the house[1]—thank you for remembering my home days as well as ourselves. We were all very sorry to have missed you. I never go to town, Lil rarely & the General about once or twice a week. But Marie is in command there, with a fag under her who chanced to open for you—a stupid thing who is only underground in her duties & could tell you nothing of us.

If you come to town again before December, when we shall be down for the winter, won't you come here and see us? It is only an hour from town & this is our true home. Often in going over the grounds & planning walks & opening mews & bringing all the brooks into one, my old walks at Silver Spring come to me & are talked over. A gulf like death lies between that time & now but all that went before that time died is very green in my memory. My own rooms I chose on the side of the house where the pine & hemlock groves come up close to my windows. It was but a short time since that I watched the rising sun bringing them into clear light—in the dark hour just before they are like a black wall, and it made living to me again the summer night I was in Lizzie's room—she sharing my unavailing cares—and how from the blackness the pine by her window grew into brightness with the sunrise just as Heaven opened for my suffering baby.[2]

All of you were always so good to me. I never have—I never tried to alter any part of the feeling of that time. But so much goes from us as life goes on that I gave up all that—keeping only the good memories of the past. When I was in Washington I realized that all my former life was only a memory. That hateful stuffy rented house on E Street—a street I never even walked through—strange people of every kind—of all the old faces only a few servants who came to see me—all were to me like so many proofs that the places which knew me once knew me no more.

One gets used to nearly everything. We have a lovely home here among people who are glad to have us. My visiting list for the summer is just twenty-five miles long for the Hudson is a great street & people dine & visit by rail when they are past driving limits. Charley is at a school for engineers, military & civil, only a dozen miles north of us.[3]

He keeps his passion for the sea. He is a very big boy—very strong & active and healthy and when he is over his cub days—he is only fourteen now—he will be splendidly handsome in a manly way. Frank is more delicate in health—more delicate in tastes & mind too but equally manly, but he is & always was & will be a beauty & with it a most rare refinement of nature. They have had a tutor at home until this summer when my long illness took me from the helm & gradually Charley was taken from me & put into men's care. Frank I keep.

The rest of us are about as we were except that quiet has told pleasantly on every one. Lily was very nearly killed by her horses running away & throwing her from the driving box—her forehead was cut & she had many serious hurts but now there is not a scar—only it has left her nervous, but two years more may take her beyond that as it has removed all outward marks. The General retains his firm health & youthful looks except that his hair is all grey. I am the most changed for I am much fuller in figure than I like & my hair is almost entirely white—it turned so suddenly that I had serious reproofs addressed me for "giving in to the frivolity of powdering my hair."

When the color was taken out of my life in that hard first year of the war, it was natural enough the color should leave my hair too. But when one has to give up a dear hope the very struggle leaves a calm. I am really peaceful and happy again for in these stone walls I centre the only remaining interests of my life.

Mary Martin[4] was in New York last winter & shewed me a picture of your boy. I had not seen even a likeness of Lizzie since the day I parted from you both when I was leaving Father.

When I was so ill this year I was much troubled for Charley who will do just right if he is in the right hands. But I know the sources of the Nile or some other such work would beckon the General away from an empty home & who to ask to keep a constant & friendly watch over my big healthy boy?

I thought of you but that was over. The new constitution they are giving Hungary will lose us that true gentleman our friend Zagonyi.[5] Dr. Van Buren's health is broken. I used to get so tired thinking & never coming to a resting place. But I am well again & may do my own work & now you have made the first move I feel I have regained a friend for Charley as well as ourselves & in the thousand recollections your name brought up I've taken a regular old time gossip over home & children, which I am sure will not tire you. I only date from '56 up here—there's nothing previous in the minds of these people. Very very pleasant people but my Father's & my friends & intimates of old early days belong to the lost time that went before.

J. B. Frémont

Oct. 25th/65
Pocaho near Tarrytown NY

ALS (NjP—Blair Lee Papers)

1. That is, the Frémont townhouse in New York City.
2. A reference to the death of her little daughter Anne Beverley on July 11, 1853, at Silver Spring.
3. Charley was at the Peekskill Academy, a military school twelve miles north of Pocaho.
4. The daughter of Enos Thompson Throop Martin, Mary Martin (d. 1884) lived at "Willowbrook" near Auburn, N.Y. (NHi—Willowbrook scrapbook). After her family's sudden impoverishment in the early 1870s, she began a jam and preserves business, running it as a women's cooperative with profit sharing among the employees. Making Mary the subject of her "Play and Work" article in the *Will and the Way Stories,* published in *Wide Awake,* 30 (Apr. 1890), JBF admiringly noted that her work "remains as a proof of what a woman's mind and will can do to make a way out of hard business care."
5. The new constitution for the Austro-Hungarian Empire was not adopted until 1867, but since it did give the Hungarians control over their internal affairs, Zagonyi, the rebel against Austrian authority in 1847–48, would be able to go home. Exactly when he returned is unknown, but in 1871 he was the owner of a tobacco shop in Pest, Hungary.

To Susan B. Anthony

Monday, April 22 [1866]

Dear Miss Anthony:

What I enclose is not much for the work you have to do, but it is all I can proportion out for it just now. You are quite right in relying on my regard for you, although I can not see the subject as you do, and I was pleased to get your note saying so.[1] I am sure you take great interest in following Mr. Gladstone's bill for the extension of suffrage in England.[2] His speech upon it is in great contrast to the shallow nonsense talked by many Americans against our democratic form of government.[3] Very sincerely yours,

Jessie Benton Frémont

Printed in STANTON ET AL., 2:911. Susan B. Anthony (1820–1906) was the renowned woman suffrage leader.

1. Some three months earlier, Elizabeth Cady Stanton had reported to a friend that when she had called on JBF to head a suffrage petition, she had refused, saying, "Oh, no. I do not believe in suffrage for women. I think women in their present position manage men better" (STANTON, 2:112).

2. In the spring of 1866, William Gladstone (1809–98), chancellor of the exchequer in Lord Russell's government and majority leader of the Liberals in the British House of Commons, introduced a reform bill that reduced the amount of property men must have to qualify as voters. The bill was defeated, as was John Stuart Mill's attempt to extend the suffrage to tax-paying women. For details of the reform bills and parliamentary battles, see F. B. SMITH.

3. Presumably a reference to Gladstone's speech of Mar. 12, but this is uncertain inasmuch as he intervened in the debate on numerous occasions. On Mar. 23, in a discussion upon electoral statistics, he let fall a phrase that reverberated through the discussion inside Parliament and out. He noted that the opponents of the bill acted as though they were ascertaining the numbers of an invading army. "But the persons to whom their remarks apply are our fellow-subjects, our fellow-Christians, *our own flesh and blood,* who have been lauded to the skies for their good conduct" (quoted in F. B. SMITH, 86–87).

To Philip Fendall

Private.
Pocaho, near Tarrytown
July 6th '66

Dear Mr. Fendall,

As you made my Father's will, you will know on what it was based. I wish I could see you for I have so much to know that by writing only I am afraid I cannot manage but I will make points for you, & I think I may rely on your regard for my Father and your former friendship for myself to assist me?

In brief, I believe and I know that my Father's arrangement with the Appleton's was for 30 or 33 per cent gross profits. This I know is always the contract with the best authors. There must have been a written contract for the "Thirty Years View"—Genl. Dix[1] made the preliminary arrangements & he is a cautious man.

Mr. Montgomery Blair's personal hostility to the General made it awkward to enter into investigations. However I did so through a lawyer whom I chose for his even calm dispassionate ways as much as for his position & skill—Mr. L. M. Fancher.[2] After repeated letters he has only one equivocal note of four lines from Mr. Blair which commits him to nothing.

I am assured by persons in the book trade that quite two hundred thousand dollars have been realized by the Appletons from the sale of my Father's works. Neither Mr. Blair nor the Appletons will admit anything but debts—no assets—(I think that's the word). I wish every thing entirely cleared up & out of Mr. Blair's hands. This I do for my Father's name as well as for the benefit of my sister Mrs. Jones. As you know to go to law with an executor, a rich man, a very pious man, a man having government officers in his control & newspapers in his service was a formidable undertaking & I had to wait until the General's own property had been put in a clear condition, & then Mr. Curtis Noyes[3]—(who had the case first, & who was my Father's admirer and friend & entered heartily into the work for me—) Mr. Noyes died. One never finds two lawyers with the same combination I had in him—personal & professional—heart & head—his services were given. But Mr. Fancher is able & clear. Can you help me with your memory or facts?

Was there not a written contract for the "30 Years View"

Who has it—or had it—and had not Mr. M. Blair knowledge of it?

I shall hope to hear from you very soon in answer to this. Tarrytown (N. York) is our post office. If you come northward will you not come & see me? We are but one hour from town & this is classic ground since [Washington] Irving made it known & is buried here. We are exactly in the Sleepy Hollow—but not exactly Rip Van Winkles. Very sincerely yours,

Jessie B. Frémont

Philip Fendall, Esqre

ALS (CLjC). Philip Ricard Fendall (1794–1868) was a highly respected Washington lawyer who had been U.S. attorney for the District of Columbia in 1853 and whom Benton had often consulted, as for example, when, acting under a power of attorney from JCF, he sold Las Mariposas to Thomas Denny Sargent in 1852. JCF repudiated the sale.

1. Before becoming a major general in the Civil War, John A. Dix (1798–1879) had been an attorney in New York and a U.S. senator. Shortly after JBF's note to Fendall, he was appointed minister to France and in 1873 was elected Republican governor of New York.

2. The Frémonts' lawyer was Enoch L. Fancher (1817–1900).

3. William Curtis Noyes (1805–64) was noted for his lucrative practice in commercial cases in New York City. In 1857, he was one of three commissioners appointed by the New York state legislature to codify the laws of New York, but the drafted code was never adopted.

To Benjamin F. Butler

[Mar. 11, 1867][1]

General,

The bill, or rather joint resolution of the Senate giving a million for the relief of those threatened by famine in the South will I hope pass the House with as few—and perhaps fewer dissenting voices than in the Senate.[2] It is a state of things which cannot be left unrelieved when it is once known, and as it is now generally known every reason requires immediate action. Only a government could act largely & promptly enough, although as you have seen Boston as well as this city has done something.[3] But if the Bill requires help I beg you to aid it.[4] Your generous conduct towards my rebel cousin Col. Critcher went deep into his heart & has influenced his whole course from that time. I think I told you that he resigned & would not take arms against us again. And this timely aid from Congress will I know go far towards the necessary relaxing of bitter feeling. I find those who suffered most by the war, & still, from the northern friends of the South, are the best aids in the work. Very little money comes from "sympathizers" while that noble family of the Shaws act with these ladies many of whom are quite rebels. Counting on your aid General I am very truly yours,

J. B. Frémont.

Sunday evg.
21 W. 19th [New York City]

ALS (DLC—Benjamin F. Butler Papers). JBF enclosed a copy of an appeal for aid issued by the New York Ladies' Southern Relief Association, which had its office at No. 14 Bond Street and an executive committee of prominent persons, including JBF, Mrs. James J. Roosevelt, president, and Mrs. S. L. M. Barlow, vice-president. The society had been organized by women of southern birth or family ties.

1. The letter was dated either by Butler or by Butler's secretary.

2. *Congressional Globe,* 40th Cong., 1st sess., pp. 39–48.

3. The New York Ladies' Association raised $71,000 for relief through donations, balls, benefits, lectures, fairs, and teas. Post office clerks contributed one day's pay, and the Russian Baths gave the proceeds of a day's business (BREMNER, 122–23).

4. Butler did not aid the bill. Rather, he proposed to amend the bill to have the million dollars relieve "the widows and children of Union soldiers starved to death in the rebel prisons of Andersonville, Salisbury, Libby, Millen and Belle Isle." When that amendment failed to garner much support, he suggested that the necessary money be raised by empowering military commanders of the various southern districts to assess persons owning over 160 acres or making more than $600 per annum. For the House debate on the propriety of federal relief for former rebels, see *Congressional Globe,* 40 Cong., 1st sess., pp. 83–91, 208–13, 233–37, 259–66, 281–82. Ultimately, Congress failed to appropriate new money, but did authorize the Freedmen's Bureau to employ unexpended funds from its existing appropriation to relieve extreme want (*U.S. Statutes at Large,* 15 [1867–69]:28).

To Charles Sumner

Pocaho, near Tarrytown, N. Y.
January 28th. '68

Dear Mr. Sumner

I have a petition before the Senate to which I want your attention and that given, I think your aid must follow. It is for the restoration of my San Francisco property called Black Point — rechristened Point San José by the military authorities who took it in '63 and still hold it under their claim as military reservation.[1]

I know you have any quantity of work always but finding myself among the petitioners I want the strongest aid I can get. Mr. Reverdy Johnson[2] has legal charge of the case which comes up soon before the Supreme Court in the case of "Grisar & Co." — a French claimant whose dwelling house & woollen mills were taken at the same time & whose claim rests on the same title.[3] But I do not want to have the expense & delay of a lawsuit against the Government. A Government is very hard to fight, & the right being on one's side only adds to the difficulty. The whole principle is in the old question which has been decided again & again — the old Mexican title as opposed to our laws. We fought that battle in the Mariposas case which had to be decided

400 *January 1868*

finally in favor of a title guaranteed by treaty. This is as clear but we had ten years delay and losses and expenses with all our clear right. Judge Field's local reputation was made as the defender of Mexican titles.

In a late "Harpers Weekly" with the (horrid) illustration affixed of likenesses of the Supreme Court & biographies also—I see this fact set out as Judge Field's merit in chief.[4] But as Mr. Justice Field he differed. I appeal from Field on the Supreme Bench to Field of the elective judiciary. Genl. McDowell[5] in a private letter to the War Dept.— sent to the Senate under a call for information on this point—says it is a "squatters title—that Frémont Haskell & Co. squatted on it knowing it was government land &c." This may be believed by Genl. McDowell but it is entirely out of the truth. We bought this place from Mr. Brumagim—banker in San Francisco & more recently an additional part from another banker, a German, Mr. Steinbach.[6] Neither the General nor myself had even seen the place or met Major Haskell until after the property had been rented from Mr. Brumagim with the right to buy. It is twelve acres, waterfront, in the City. I held it as a great solid fortune for my children. That, & this place here near New York were my own ideas as safe investments for them.

The death of Mr. Jones[7] gives me the care of my sister's boys who are fine lads and for whose education and future I need to add to & not diminish my income. The return of this property at this time will be very timely, and I am sure your old pleasant relations with my Father will give you an interest in assisting my sister & her family through me. I shall ask the General, who is in Washington on this business, to send you a pamphlet which gives the previous arguments in this case & the references to decisions affecting it. Very sincerely yours,

Jessie Benton Frémont

ALS (MH—Houghton Library). Charles Sumner, one of the first prominent statesmen to urge emancipation, was chairman of the Senate Committee on Foreign Affairs.

1. For a brief history of JBF's Black Point property, see her letter to Elizabeth Blair Lee, June 2, 1860, note 1, above.
2. Deemed one of the greatest lawyers of his day, Reverdy Johnson (1796-1876) had represented the defense in *Dred Scott vs. Sanford* and was currently representing Maryland in the U.S. Senate.
3. Grisar lost the appeal; the court upheld the earlier judgment that the lands remained the property of the United States (73 *United States Reports*, 363-82).

4. See *Harper's Weekly*, Feb. 1, 1868, p. 73. As a justice of the California Supreme Court, Stephen J. Field had favored Frémont's interests on the two occasions that *Biddle Boggs vs. Merced Mining Company* were argued before the court and indeed had the reputation for favoring large claim owners, holding under Mexican title, over the settler or squatter element. As U.S. Supreme Court justice, he wrote the opinion in the Grisar case that augered ill for JBF should she bring suit.

5. After his exoneration by a court of inquiry for his conduct during the Second Battle of Bull Run (he had lost the First Battle of Bull Run in 1861), General Irvin McDowell (1818–85) was assigned to the Pacific Coast. Frank Frémont noted that he was a distant cousin and one of the family's "most irritating enemies" (Memorandum for Allan Nevins, n.d. CU-B—Frémont Papers).

6. Rudolph Steinbach, a San Francisco banker (San Francisco *Directory*, 1872–89).

7. William Carey Jones had died in San Francisco on Nov. 5, 1867 (San Francisco *Bulletin*, Nov. 5, 1867).

To Horace Greeley

Private.
Copenhagen
August 14 [1869]

Dear Mr. Greeley,

I have offered this note of introduction to our minister Mr. Yeaman[1] who looks upon you as the old Danes looked upon their god Thor when his mighty hammer was lifted.

But I know you always make sure your hammer *ought* to fall before you let it go down. And this is to beg you to keep the hammer off until a fair hearing is given to both sides of the St. Thomas treaty. Against it is the abuse of power by Mr. Seward to whom no one has a right to feel more ill will than myself.

But if in addition to his other sins he leads us into doing a shabby thing to a weak power that will be a crowning sin. No cabinet ought to end the treaty now. Our character for good faith is at stake and it ought to come before Congress, and if it is obligatory, we must ratify it. And if it is not, let it go. But the public has the right to understand it & to act on it. It ought to have had these rights at the start, but that is past. And a full discussion will settle all precedent against such future disposal of the country's honor in future. You always intend to be just and fair—even to your own disadvantage—& I think you do me the honor to believe I intend the same & to think I know what I am talking about; and you may be sure I feel this seriously or I would not ask your personal attention to it so strongly.

We shall be back in the winter. The Genl. has just joined us from Paris where he has left everything in solid good shape. He adds a line himself. Very sincerely yours,

Jessie Frémont

The Genl. is carried off by visitors & asks me to say he will write by mail.

ALS (NN—Horace Greeley Papers).

1. Under the direction of Secretary of State William Seward, former congressman George Helm Yeaman (1829–1908) had negotiated a treaty with Denmark (signed Oct. 24, 1867) for the purchase of the islands of St. Thomas and St. John for $7,500,000 in gold, which failed of ratification in the Senate. Many in Europe expressed the opinion that Denmark had not been justly treated; at home it was seen as a disinclination on the part of the American public to follow Seward in his schemes for colonial dominion. Diplomatic negotiations and a copy of the unratified treaty may be found in TANSILL. To James Parton, who published a protreaty pamplet, JBF indicated that it was her affection for the Danish minister's wife and daughter that made her anxious that the treaty should be ratified (Dec. 12, 1869, MH). Greeley seems not to have taken a position either way.

To William T. Sherman

Pocaho
August 10th [1871].

Dear General Sherman,

You may not have seen a poem by a Mr. Joaquin Miller, which he names Kit Carson's Ride.[1] It came out first in London in the "Dark Blue" then in Harpers Weekly in New York with an indecent woodcut as illustration & now it is in Littell's Living Age.[2]

We cannot let our friend's memory stand so shamefully misrepresented as this puts it. Mr. Beale has written something which he will send you but for general circulation and especially for England something more brief but perfectly distinct in contradiction, will do better.[3]

Mr. Frémont and myself loved and valued Carson. When he was on his way home to die I went to see him in New York and he told me then of his friendship for you and yours for him.[4] All we can do to prove our love for our friend is to keep his name as he kept it clean and honored. You have the position to speak so as to command the widest attention, and my thought was that we should publish a short note signed by all of us (for in this case I am willing to go against all my prejudices & habit & go into print) to be published by the papers which first noticed this poem, and in England where I have friends who will attend thoroughly to giving it the fullest circulation.

It needs but to raise the voice & everywhere in our own country it will be taken up and those who knew Carson will join us in over-throwing this shameful false likeness of our modest brave unselfish old friend.[5] Sincerely yours,

Jessie Benton Frémont

My address is here at my country place Pocaho, near Tarrytown on the Hudson, New York.

ALS (DLC—William T. Sherman Papers). Endorsed, "Ansd." William T. Sherman (1820–91), commanding general of the army, was a long-time acquaintance of the Frémonts and of Kit Carson, having met them in California in the 1840s.

1. Dubbed "Joaquin" by his cronies after the colorful Mexican bandit Joaquin Murietta, Cincinnatus Hiner Miller (1837–1913) used it as his pen name. Miller had a varied career in the West as a miner, horse thief, and attorney before he started writing poetry. Londoners received his works enthusiastically, and he did everything possible to live up to the English image of the rough, democratic American frontiersman. He appeared in upper-class literary salons attired in sombrero, cowboy boots, buckskins, and with either cigar or chewing tobacco stuck in his mouth. For a biographical sketch, see FROST.

2. *The Dark Blue,* 1 (July 1871): 578–81; *Harper's Weekly,* Aug. 5, 1871, p. 713 (with an ethereal depiction of a naked man and woman riding on plunging steeds in burning long prairie grass surrounded by buffalo); *Littell's Living Age,* Aug. 12, 1871, p. 447. In his poem Miller had described a fictional ride in which Carson stole a beautiful Comanche girl from her people and then abandoned her when her weaker horse gave out as a raging prairie fire threatened to overtake them. The implication was that Carson's instinct for self-preservation overcame his sense of love and duty.

3. Beale, using the pseudonym "El Mariposo," wrote a lengthy letter to the editor of the Chester, Pa., *Republican,* attacking Miller and eulogizing Carson. He concluded that the poem was moral poison and regretted that Carson had not counted among his coups the "scalp of Joaquin" (G. THOMPSON, 188–89). Beale sent Bayard Taylor a copy of his defense, and on Aug. 27, the latter replied: "Thank you heartily for writing, as well as sending me your defense of Kit Carson, and sacrification of that vulgar fraud, Joaquin Miller. . . . The fellow really knows nothing about the life he undertakes to describe, and this is the 'great American poet' of the English literary journals. . . . We authors have really fallen on evil days when such stuff passes for poetry. However, patience is my watchword; we have but to wait and see these fictitious reputations go down as fast as they go up" (FROST, 113).

4. Carson had come east in the spring of 1868, and JBF, hearing that he was very ill, had hurried to New York City to see him and to urge him to come to Pocaho to recuperate, but he refused. Carson died on May 23, 1868, one month after the death of his wife, Josefa, who had given birth ten days earlier to a little girl.

5. The editors were unable to locate a protest by Sherman, but the outcry of Beale and others brought a response from Miller. "No sincere, impartial man can read my allusions to Carson and say I have represented him as anything but a true man," he wrote. "The Indian Girl is permitted to perish because it is the order of things. She represents a race that is passing away. It would have been contrary to the order of things to have allowed her to escape" (New York *Tribune,* Sept. 23, 1871).

To Oliver Otis Howard

Pocaho
Near Tarrytown N. Y.
September 7th [1871]

Dear General Howard

I enclose you this request from a former maid of mine who deserves that I shall say, in brief, that it will be a personal obligation to me if you can give her the chance she wishes. She belongs to one of the good old families of colored people in the District. Father was a grand-looking old preacher — blind in his later years — a really venerable man every way. Harriet came to me when she was but eighteen — then she could not establish herself as a dressmaker being colored but she is so capable that she made all mine & my sisters dresses for years. And in New York she has continued to work for me, and now she can give you not only my thorough recommendation as "respectable and in-dustrious," but she is also most capable.

Alice is the child of her first husband, and the child has been well brought up & educated in Rhode Island. If she has her mother's sweet voice and temper she is a most desirable teacher. The Father, Parks, had some of the touchiness that goes with the irritable white blood of which he had a great deal.

We all were very fond of "little Harriet" — there was an "Aunt Harriet" who was head nurse over me & then over my children, a free woman (as was little Harriet) and I have always kept sight of her and sometimes have been of service to her.

If she were not clogged by her little children she could make a great deal by dressmaking. Mrs. Morgan (E. D. Morgan, New York) and many other well known names can answer for Harriet's skill.

You have done a very kind & much needed thing in building these houses, but it does not surprise me. It is a good thing that good habits as well as bad increase their force by indulgence and it evidently became an incurable habit with you to do good. Sincerely yours,

Jessie B. Frémont

[Enclosure]

No. 934 H. Street
Washington Sept. 6/71

My Friend Mrs. Fremont

I write to you today to aske a grate faver of you that is will you please give me a letter of Introduction to Gen Howard to tell him that I am a respecteble and an Industrious Woman. The Object is this he is puting up a number of small houses out by the Uneversity and leting respecteble Familyes have them on very Easey termes leting what would be the rent go as monthely payments. I should like so much to get a house in that way as I cannot sell my house in Brooklyn untill Alice is 21 years of age.

I thinke a letter from you Mrs. Fremont will be a very grate service to me of which I will feal so very much obliged to you. My little children prevent me from doing much at my trade but I am so glad to tell you that Alice passed a very crediteble Escamination and has a School of which she get $50 per month that is a grate help.

My husband has some hopes of a Situation in the Patent Office this month if successfull. Alice [wanted again?] to write to you for the letter you promised to give her to Gen. Howard but she was told that all the Situation[s] ware filled by Graduates from the Uneversity but we both thank you just the same for you kinde offer.

I was going out to see about a place but I was Informed that Gen. Howard was very particular whome he sold the houses to and I being a stranger is why I aske you this faver [k]nowing a letter from you will be suficient.

Hopeing Dear Madame this will finde you with Miss Lilie and the rest of the familey is good health with much respect I remaine yours Obedientely,

Harriet

"Endorsed on Harriet's letter in JBF's hand: "Application of Harriet

Bell, thoroughly & warmly recommended by Jessie Benton Frémont, Pocaho, new Tarrytown NY. Sep. 7. '71."

ALS (MeB). Howard (1830–1909), a Union general and director of the Freedmen's Bureau, was known for his humanitarianism and church work. He helped to found Howard University in Washington, D.C., and became its president in 1869. He also promoted Barry Farm, a complicated project designed to help individual blacks in the District of Columbia buy an acre-plot of land each and build a house thereon. The farm of approximately 375 acres was located on the south side of the Anacostia River in the District, and no doubt it is one of these properties that Harriet desired to purchase (J. A. CARPENTER, 169, 185–87).

To Jeremiah S. Black

Pocaho April 5th [1873]

You must remember this,
my Father's seal   [SEAL]
given him by John Randolph
(after the Clay duel).[1]

Dear Judge Black

We have not yet received the conclusion of the French trial,[2] but in the midst of our translating the previous reports it has occurred to us that you might prefer the original french papers—the print also is less wearing to the eyes than mss.

If you would like the French papers will you let us know at once.

I am glad you are resting—even so little. Bronchitis tires the head. I know from several winters experience. You are very good and I am more grateful than I can put in words for the friendly spirit in which you have taken up this cruel wrong against our name. I am not yet at the point of looking at it as an outrage on Law—as yet it is too personal. With your aid the truth shall come uppermost and I told the General to say to you that I grieved I was not in your neighborhood for my long practice as amanuensis, & secretary should be at your service and would be a labor of love to me to do the heavy detail of work.

We should be so happy, my daughter and myself to have you come to us. It is not very out of the way if you had any time and we would like to do our little part in shewing you how much we appreciate what your manly right feeling as well as your sense of law has made you do to uphold the General in what has been — and to all of us — the hardest thing we have had to bear. Sincerely yours,

Jessie Benton Frémont

ALS (DLC—Jeremiah S. Black Papers). The legal connection between JCF and Black dated back to 1860, when much of the explorer's business concerned California. Black had then been retained *"permanently"* to assist *"whenever* and *wherever* it may be necessary in the future to maintain the legal rights of Frémont" (BRIGANCE, 131). Black (1810–83) was a Pennsylvanian, a former attorney general of the United States, and a great controversialist, often championing unpopular causes and participating in magazine article wars.

1. The seal was a *Lion Rampant,* which John Randolph had given to Benton for his services as a peacemaker in Randolph's duel with Henry Clay in 1826 (CHAMBERS, 140). JBF refers to the motto in a letter to William J. Morton, Oct. 17 [1873], below.
2. On Mar. 27, 1873, JCF, who was being tried in absentia in a Paris court, along with several Frenchmen, including his brother-in-law Boilleau, was convicted of swindling Frenchmen who had purchased the bonds of his Memphis, El Paso, and Pacific Railroad Company. He had prudently remained in the United States during the trial, for he received a sentence of five years; Boilleau, who was in France, spent two of his three-year sentence in jail during which time his wife, Susy, died. For a brief sketch of JCF's interest in railroads and railroad promotion, see the introduction to this section. For details of the participants and the enormously complicated manipulations, consult V. TAYLOR, 1–141.

To Jeremiah S. Black

Pocaho, Good Friday. [Apr. 11, 1873]

Dear Judge Black

You were very kind to me to write so long a letter when you were needing all the rest possible. I hope — as a fellow sufferer from bronchitis — that you know the merits of sunshine, beef essence, cream, and sleep. That four in hand pulls one up again.

The newspaper report in the Legal Gazette is now over ninety columns. This would make about eight hundred foolscap pages of manuscript. To have it well translated and copied so as not to try the eyes would take precious time now.

If you will let it be so, the General and myself will meet you wherever you prefer, and either of us can translate as we read along & you can specify while listening what points you need translated. There is no end of repetition. If a short-hand writer were present everything could go much faster.

From this on, until this case is understood and our names stands as it ought, I have no other occupation or wish for any other than putting it right, and so clear that any mis-apprehension must be intentional.

For that I will go to Philadelphia or York or wherever it bests suits you to appoint to meet us. If change of air did not hurt you it might do you good. We have a peaceful empty country house here—only an hour out of New York, and the four in hand I spoke of has been on duty for me and is in full train for you if you could come. This is one of the most healthy of places—an old pine and hemlock forest growth, on sandy soil, facing north towards the Catskills and having the salt water of the Hudson, (here three miles wide), just in front. We have our morning paper by 8 a.m. and the evening papers by 6 p.m. and yet we can shut off all they represent as easily as we can get at it.

But it will be entirely as best suits you, and I know I can be of use, and any place will suit me provided I am being of service. Very sincerely yours,

Jessie Benton Frémont

ALS (DLC—Jeremiah S. Black Papers).

To William J. Morton

Pocaho. October 17th [1873]

Dear Dr. Morton

This paper is stamped with my father's seal & family motto "Factis non verbis" [with deeds not words]. I never use it except to people I like for it is so much a part of himself that it's too good for commonplace or insincere people. I often use it to Anna[1] but I wouldn't to Mrs. Jay[2] and Mrs. Bancroft.[3] A maxim for you to remember and act upon is that the women past their youth rule society—and it is they who make or mar young careers. So I reach the heads of the legations through *their* heads. And remember one can't have too much good will and don't chill off an offered attention. A little going into the world is not going to hurt your studying and the greater part of the world value veneer & varnish more than unpolished oak—*that* is the connoisseurs's wood. Moral—you must not offer that remarkable sincerity of yours to all your patients and acquaintances. Get a coating of polite attention and keep those naif acts and speeches of yours for us and such as we who enjoy and prefer them. But don't change to us—come back just as young and fresh-hearted and simple in taste as you were during the "play-days." And don't be afraid of "that grey old nurse of Heroes." You are a true hero now and while you are in your first lonesomeness, just cast adrift among strange sounds and faces it may be some strength to you to know how I honor you for your thoroughness of moral courage in your battle of life. The staying at the Bay View while any of your patients had to remain was fine and the coolness with which you managed the white-eared lady[4] was fine but this is one of the unexciting solitary uncheered and maybe uncheerful acts of sacrifice to the sense of right which sometimes leave one doubting whether they were right or not in making it. So when you are a little heavy-hearted let me reassure you and I know you value my opinion. I tell my boys that I am "very old & very wise" and I have been alive all the days of my life and I have seen and heard much so I am entitled to speak with authority.

And among the things worthy of all respect and admiration is that of a young man turning all his faculties to a noble and self denying aim and going about it simply as though it were a matter of course. When in fact it's a matter of wonder to see it. I am full of humble and surprised thankfulness that my big boy who was fairly launched a year ago has gone on much in that way. There are so many chances against the home training—the powers for evil are so much more agreeable and so much more at hand always than the influences for good. But this comfort you have. Every self-denial practised secures not only ease and unconscious power to repeat it, but it puts a keen edge on all the simpler pleasures such as the self indulgent never know in any of their pleasures.

This sounds to you, maybe very like truisms, but some day when you realize it in your own case you will feel then it no worn phrase but a discovery.

If Mr. Pfeiffer[5] should have been absent & so unable to introduce you, introduce yourself to the Doctor of the ship. I was stupid not to think of that at first. You can say as the french lady did when a person of less rank offered to take her to some great house, "I do not need you, my name introduces me. I was born introduced everywhere" ("je suis née presentée"). Tell him you want to read & speak German & you want to know the Lutheran clergymen and it will all be done.

Lil and I thought this morning what a charming spot that aqueduct would make for a parting of lovers—the whole picture was so exquisitely beautiful and poetical. But if it was hard to say goodbye between friends I don't see how Rome[o] & Juliet ever could reach a parting.

"Good-luck to you." When you think of friends at home, count us all in and most your really sincere friend,

J. B. Frémont

[Admonitions were added to the letter with some appearing on the back of the envelope.]

Prevents cold feet: Be sure to take a warm rug or heavy shawl—Very useful at sea and needed in the railway carriages which are not heated as with us.

Education: Books.
> Thacker[a]y's novels   *Tauchnitz edition*
> Pendennis
> Newcomes
> &
> Phillip's adventures
> Lucille[6]
> pocket edition

B[a]edeker
> Christians foreign bookstore
> University place between 12th & 13th

ALS (CU-B—Morton Papers). William Jeremiah Morton (1845–1920), a graduate of Harvard Medical School in the class of 1872, was the son of the dentist William Thomas Green Morton (1819–68), who had pioneered the use of ether as an anesthesia. Young Morton had been Frank's physician and would become a close friend of the Frémonts. After 1878 he was a neurologist in New York City and editor of the *Journal of Nervous and Mental Disease* (1882–85).

1. "Anna" is Anna Raasloff, daughter of Waldemar Raasloff (1815–83), the Danish ambassador to the United States.
2. The former Eleanor Kingsland Field was the wife of John Jay, the U.S. minister to Austria-Hungary.
3. JBF had given Morton a letter of introduction to Elizabeth Davis Bliss (d. 1886), who had married George Bancroft, the U.S. minister to Germany. In the letter to Mrs.

Bancroft, also dated Oct. 17, 1873 (CU-B), she noted that Morton was going to Europe for "hard study" and wished "to be more personally known at some of our legations than by a mere passport."

4. Morton had treated a woman wearing white earrings at Bay View, a convalescent hotel in Bar Harbor, Maine. JBF had taken Frank there after a spot in his lung was discovered by Dr. Van Buren.

5. A friend of JBF, Carl Pfeiffer (1834–88) was a German-American architect who, after 1864, established himself in New York City where he attained a high reputation. Among his works are the Church of the Messiah, Roosevelt and New York City hospitals, and the Fifth Avenue Presbyterian Church.

6. *Pendennis, The Newcomes,* and *The Adventures of Philip on His Way Through the World* were by Thackeray; *Lucile* was by E. R. B. Lytton.

To James Parton

Pocaho Friday night
January 9th '74.

Dear Mr. Parton

I had not given up the project, but I have been very un-nerved & ill and now I must go away for a month or more. We go the 15th to Nassau.[1]

But after March I shall still hope to have your aid.[2] Other steps will have been taken which will render the writing I hope for from you rather Memoirs pour Servir than an exhaustive article. Judge Fancher is now off the bench and can resume this case.[3] He has been for twelve years our friend as well as our lawyer. He knows it in every step. We have had to wait for him. It is so long to study thoroughly an affair that the wrong once done we took patience and waited for the aid of those who knew the truth. Judge Black of Pennsylvania—a man of old fashioned force of language and also of old fashioned force of conviction & courage to maintain it—has charge of the international law part as Judge Fancher has of the financial and personally business part.

I do not mind the delay. It is better so. There will be more time for you to take in the truths if no time is fixed for the publication.

I wish it made for me as a lawyer would make a brief, I to pay the retaining fee. Publishers will not be wanting when we choose to offer it to them. They may add their payment also, but this is my affair with you if on consideration you undertake it.

The Saxon love of "fair play" belongs to us too. Our people are dreadfully in a hurry & they hate to have a second serving up of any idea. But there is a certainty of an honest verdict from the reading public when the truth is put compactly and clearly before them. And the truth is with us. Your special talent is to resume a subject clearly & calmly and yet with conviction. Because I am Mr. Frémont's wife I cannot speak for him. In addition to the more limited audiences Judge Black & Judge Fancher influence I want the more general public reached by you. So far from reconsidering or giving up this is the business of my life and the lives of my two sons.

We have lost much money through all this work against us but my children as well as myself have properties given us more than twenty years ago by the General. We are putting it into shape to use and there can be no use so sweet to us as to make others know as we do that no shadow can rest on the name we have seen so carefully kept clean and high.

I shall leave you a memorandum of points and references and between now and March you will perhaps consider them. Meantime I thank you very much for your personal kind impulses. I can promise you they would not lessen with knowing the whole case. Sincerely yours,

J. B. Frémont

ALS (MH). James Parton (1822–91) was one of the most popular and well-paid writers in the United States, his great achievements being the lives of Aaron Burr, Andrew Jackson, Benjamin Franklin, Thomas Jefferson, and Voltaire. His wife had been Sara Payson Willis, known to the reading public as the writer Fanny Fern.

1. The reason for the journey to Nassau is given in the next letter.
2. JBF wants Parton to write a popular article that would explain the Memphis, El Paso, and Pacific Railroad bond fraud case to the public.
3. Appointed to fill the unexpired term of an impeached justice, Enoch L. Fancher was defeated in his bid for election to the New York Supreme Court.

To Jeremiah S. Black

Clarendon Hotel
New York
Jany 14. 74.

Dear Judge Black

I go tomorrow to Nassau where Frank (my son who has been so ill) has been all winter.[1] He has had a return of illness and I go to him.

This will leave the General quite alone and free to move about. He wants me to say to you that if he were sure of finding you he would go to see you in relation to the case submitted by him to Mr. MacVeagh[2] in December. Now the holidays are over and the chief justice-ship bids fair to become a chronic excitement so that it can be taken leisurely[3] — perhaps Mr. MacVeagh has found time to see you in relation to it. Has he?

It is a good and solid title, one my Father always wished pressed, and you who know California titles so well will understand the value of this. Will you let the General hear from you in answer to this, to this address.[4]

Our country house will be shut until my return which is a little indefinite. Meantime I hope the General will have the advantage of your aid in this case.

I take a fresh Galaxy with me. You thrust a lance for me when you impaled Mr. Seward.[5] I always called him the Mephistopheles of our war. There is in Dante a passage where he finds a man below, whom he had met but just before in Pisa (I think). Are *you* a shade says Dante — did I not see you but yesterday in Pisa. To which the shade answers that he was long dead but that for his sins of hypocrisy a devil had been put into his former body and was doing openly the things which he had done covertly during his life. And his torture was to know & not prevent this unmasking defaming process. This is exactly Mr. Seward's case. Once broached my theory grew. I insisted the former Seward died somewhere from 56 to 60. You knew the grinning devil who had his own fun at your expense in the winter of 60 to 61 while covering his impishness with occasional maskings of patriotism &c— &c.[6] For this the knife of the assassin did him no harm — on the contrary it is known it pierced an abscess and did him good.[7]

For this he went roaming to & fro to the uttermost parts of the earth. In the opera of Faust Mephistopheles is attacked by the returned soldiers for the murder of Marguerite's brother — they close around him, when he draws about him a circle of fire with his rapier & they fall back recognizing his fatal character. The first time I saw this I told the General at once — that's Mr. Seward paralyzing our troops — (it was in '62) — I am sure, croaking as his voice was, if he had been given a guitar he could have sung "Dio del oro del mundo signor" perfectly well.[8] And his Aspasia is worthy of him.[9] I heartily enjoyed that article.

You have an old fashioned force of expression but you have the old lost old fashion force of conviction and courage in expressing it.

I've just had the pleasure to read that Mr. Cushing has had to retreat from his intended seat as Chief Justice. Genl. Butler will do anything but I kept Mr. Cushing in mind for their work against the General last spring. How my Father did despise the man.[10]

We had planned, the General and myself, seeing you together. But Frank's renewed illness takes me away. There is no telegraph to Nassau & mails only once a fortnight. It's a case to remember your dutch-woman and be resigned because I can't help myself. This is a stiff hotel pen, and my eyes are tired from want of sleep—and I'm so sorry to leave the General and yet I am sorry for my Frank.

But once writing to you the ideas grow.

Goodbye my dear Judge. What a kind heart and a clear brain can do I know you will do for us both and especially for yours, Very Sincerely,

J. B. Frémont

Wednesday night

ALS (DLC—Jeremiah S. Black Papers).

1. Frank, a cadet at West Point since July 1872, became ill with pneumonia after marching in his summer uniform in freezing weather at Ulysses S. Grant's second inauguration in Mar. 1873. This was followed by hemorrhages from the lungs, and JBF feared he had tuberculosis. He was granted leave from West Point to recover his health, but when illness persisted after his return from Nassau, he resigned in Sept., 1874.

2. Isaac Wayne MacVeagh (1833–1917), an attorney in Harrisburg, Pa. In the Grant administration, he had served a brief term as minister to Turkey.

3. President Grant was having a difficult time finding a chief justice for the Supreme Court. He had offered the position first to Roscoe Conkling and then to George H. Williams. Caleb Cushing (1800–1879) also requested that his name be withdrawn, since old slanders reputing sympathy for the South had been renewed against him.

4. It is uncertain what California property JBF had in mind. It could not have been her Black Point property, since her father was dead before she acquired it; it could have been JCF's old claim to Alcatraz Island, which he reasserted periodically; or possibly it related to Rancho El Pescadero in which members of the family still had interests, although the uncertainty with respect to the title had been removed in 1865.

5. Black had written a long reply to Charles Francis Adams, who in a memorial address had compared the late William H. Seward to Pericles, the illustrious Athenian statesman. Not only was there not the slightest resemblance, Black maintained, but also that Seward "knew less of law and cared less about it than any other man" who had held high office in the United States (BLACK).

6. A reference to Black's brief tenure as secretary of state in the closing days of

the Buchanan administration and his attempts to handle the crisis created by the secession of states and the movement of Maj. Robert Anderson from Fort Moultrie to Fort Sumter. To South Carolina's demand that Anderson be ordered back to Fort Moultrie, Black replied, "I cannot and I will not" (quoted in W. E. SMITH, 2:4). Seward, who not only became Lincoln's secretary of state but who also wished to formulate the policy of the administration, had more "appeasing" suggestions. One was to unite the North and South by provoking a war with foreign nations; another was to evacuate Fort Sumter and hold the Gulf ports.

7. At the time President Lincoln was assassinated by John Wilkes Booth, Seward was stabbed in his sickbed at home by Lewis Powell, a half-mad ex-Confederate soldier whose two brothers had been killed in the war.

8. The first American performance of Charles Gounod's *Faust* was in New York in 1863. JBF refers to Méphistophélès's sarcastic "Calf of Gold" aria.

9. This is a veiled reference to the young Olive Risley with whom Seward was infatuated. Although Olive was a friend, JBF implies that she stood in the same influential relationship to Seward as the Greek courtesan Aspasia had to Pericles. For a discussion of Seward and Olive Risley, see JBF to Black, Feb. 21 [1875], note 5, below.

10. Benjamin Butler and Caleb Cushing had been counsel to a group of French bondholders who wished JCF extradited to France to face criminal prosecution for his role in the Memphis and El Paso bond scandal (V. TAYLOR, 102). This, however, may not have been the sole reason for JBF's opposition to Cushing. As attorney general of the United States, he had appealed the California Land Commission's decision in 1851 confirming JCF's Las Mariposas title. On the other hand, he and Reverdy Johnson had been JBF's lawyers before the Supreme Court with respect to her Black Point property (JBF statement, May 7, 1872, CLjC).

To Nelly Haskell Browne

Steamer Merida
Monday noon [Jan.] 19th [1874]
at 2 we reach Nassau.

My Nelly it comforted me to know you and the General were left to each other as we slid away.[1] I thought of him in the carriage with you & your dear daughterly ways of comforting him. He is so solitary so lonely my poor dear darling—you know how tender hearted he is & he has no one now. So I loved you and blessed you for every gentle care you were giving him, and be sure it does help him.

Your dear GB. was so thoughtful for us.[2] Tell him we all went sadly to bed that first night—not sea sick but heart sick and little sleep came to any of us for it was very rough. Lil & Emeline[3] were both upset next day & I gave each some of your wine in crushed ice & Lil has been well ever since. Emeline returned to her performance during

a two days storm we had. Such a fury of wind rain lightning waves &
row generally that we lay to for eight hours. But today it is a new
heaven & a new sea—*such* soft air! Such blue above—and below! I
have thinner under clothes but above, the same old blue vigogne [vicuna
wool] & am not too warm (out of the sun). I can send this by the
purser to Havana. I will also send by him a cable message for the
General to let him know Frank and ourselves are well—I hope Frank
is entirely so. I know my coming must help him.

Some nice people are on board—Mr. Meert, Addie Van Buren's
husband—you saw him, the blond giant.[4] He is very agreeable & I
should judge good at home. He has been a real resource.

The Chief Justice of the Bahamas, Sir Wm. Doyle is also on board
& has introduced himself and will make us like Nassau he says. I'm
sure we will do very well every way and the Captain & purser and
cook are good—the ship is rolling again.

The grapes were globules of health & delight and I ate an orange
in my berth each morning & I said good thoughts to my Brownies
when I ate them.

I love you my dear dear child—I'm glad to get a little chance to
speak to you. This leaves Havana Thursday 22. The 27th or 8th you
will get it. Ask May to tell you about the sandwich man. Yours and
G.B.'s affectionate friend and loving,

                                                        J. B. F.

Mr. Meert sketches well. He says you have a delightful oval face—
and you are so "interesting"—pronounced by him (Iintheresthing). If
Mary[5] is with you say a good word from us to her.

AL initialed (CU-B—Frémont Papers).

1. JBF and Lily sailed for Nassau on Jan. 15, 1874, to be with Frank.
2. George Browne (1840–1912) had married Nelly Haskell in Gloucester, Mass.,
in 1873. He made enough money in the financial circles of Wall Street to spend the
five years following 1882 traveling with his family. In 1887–88 the Brownes moved to
Tacoma, Wash. (HUNT, 2:20–24).
3. Evidently, the Frémonts had rehired Emeline after she left their service earlier
(Elizabeth Benton Frémont to Nelly Haskell Browne, June 12 [1872?], CU-B—Frémont
Papers).
4. Charles Frederick Meert and Adelaide Mott Van Buren had been married in St.
Stephen's Church on Feb. 20, 1867 (*New York Tribune,* Feb. 25, 1867).
5. One of the Frémonts' servants who may have been in the temporary employment
of the Brownes.

William J. Morton (from I. A. Watson, *Physicians and Surgeons of America*).

Ella (Nelly) Haskell Browne (courtesy of Evelyn Browne, Durham, N.H.).

William King Rogers (courtesy of the Rutherford B. Hayes Presidential Center, Fremont, Ohio).

Prescott, Arizona, c. 1880 (courtesy of the Sharlot Hall Historical Society, Prescott, Ariz.).

The Frémont residence in Prescott, c. 1980, restored and moved from its original location (courtesy of the Sharlot Hall Historical Society, Prescott, Ariz.).

A portion of Jessie Benton Frémont's letter to Elizabeth Blair Lee, July 29, 1883 (Blair-Lee Papers; courtesy of Princeton University Library).

Jessie Benton Frémont, 1895. Photograph by Charles F. Lummis (courtesy of the Southwest Museum, Los Angeles).

John Charles Frémont, before his death in 1890. Engraved from a photograph by Doremus (from *Harper's Weekly*, July 26, 1890).

The Los Angeles home of Jessie Benton Frémont, given to her by the women of California (courtesy of the Huntington Library, San Marino, Calif.).

Jessie Benton Frémont in her Los Angeles home (courtesy of the Bancroft Library).

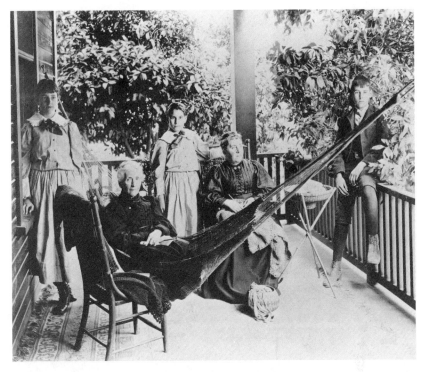

Jessie Benton Frémont with her daughter, Elizabeth Benton Frémont, and her grandchildren, Jessie, Juliet, and John Charles III. The fourth grandchild, the son of Francis Preston, is not present (courtesy of the Huntington Library, San Marino, Calif.).

Lt. John Charles Frémont II of the U.S. Navy, c. 1897 (courtesy of the U.S. Naval Institute Photo Collection).

Maj. Frank Preston Frémont, c. 1909 (courtesy of the Library of Congress).

Caroline M. Severance, c. 1900 (courtesy of the Huntington Library, San Marino, Calif.).

Jessie Benton Frémont, at age seventy. Bust by John Gutzon Borglum (courtesy of the Huntington Library, San Marino, Calif.).

To Jeremiah S. Black

private.

Pocaho
June 18th '74

My dear Judge

As you "take your information through the eye," will you read the enclosed slips. One will shew you an outside opinion of that "Empire" for which I have not more respect than for that of France, now exploded.

The other will shew you a first move made just to test our opposing power in Congress. The bill, to allow the mortgage of Texas Pacific bonds,[1] would have passed without opposition but for the objection raised by Genl. Shanks[2] a true and faithful friend of ours. Now it has gone back to the committee and will require a two thirds vote to pass it.[3]

We have also made alliance with two of the strongest forces in politics and the rest of the work we do now depends upon Mr. Scott's adhering to his last phase. You know my opinion of him. Therefore you will understand I was not surprised by his open repudiation of his word.[4] I was surprised he should so uncover himself to you however. What you can do now my dear Judge is to save for me the evidence you possess regarding Mr. Scott's pledged word. You can put it with Mr. Fancher only to be used in case of necessity. But your sense of justice as well as your kind feelings to me will not let you delay to grant this very earnest request of mine. It was my money from my portion of the Mariposas estate which went into the different expenses which have always been held and acknowledged as a just debt of this road.

I am putting order into all my affairs and my eldest son and my daughter I put in full knowledge of each thing, I have been too often ill in the last year and the evidences of hurt vitality are too fixed upon me for me to risk delays. Any excitement brings back the pains in the head, the loss of sleep and appetite—the waking with sharp screams when I do sleep—all the train of ills that follow over taxed nerves in women.

My sister and myself were very much alike. We were built to live a hundred years but she has been murdered and I am very hurt.[5] But I do not mean if I can help it—and you can aid me by placing the truth in the guardianship of Judge Fancher—that my children's fortune shall go without resistance to Mr. Scott.

First I must make my ground secure.

I shall wait your answer to this and on receiving it will explain to Judge Fancher, who has been my friend as well as my lawyer for many years, why I prepare this evidence.[6]

The General is in Washington. Possibly you may meet him there. But this is my own unaided idea which I am carrying out myself. And I hope you will answer it to me for I know you do not think me either incapable or indiscreet. Sincerely yours my dear Judge,

Jessie Benton Frémont

ALS (DLC—Jeremiah S. Black Papers).

1. The Texas Pacific Railway was incorporated by Congress on Mar. 3, 1871, with JCF as one of the 124 incorporators. On May 2, 1872, Congress changed its name to the Texas and Pacific Railway Company, and on June 12, 1873, it received the property rights and franchises of the Memphis, El Paso, and Pacific Railroad Company (V. TAYLOR, 141).

2. V. TAYLOR, 46–47, implies that Representative J. P. C. Shanks of Indiana, who had served on JCF's staff during the Civil War, was "paid" early in 1870 to be friendly to the interests of the Memphis, El Paso, and Pacific Railroad Company.

3. In the Senate, the bill had been introduced by John Scott of Pennsylvania, who later became general counsel for the Pennsylvania Railroad after Thomas A. Scott became its president. The House committee seems not to have reported the bill back to the floor (*Congressional Record*, 43rd Cong., 1st sess., pp. 3298, 4216, 4243).

4. The powerful railroad magnate Thomas A. Scott (1823–81) was the master mind of the Texas Pacific and, after the resignation of Marshall O. Roberts in Feb. 1872, became president of it and of its successor company, the Texas and Pacific Railway Company. Scott had agreed that the Texas Pacific would give Frémont $300,000 in paid up stock for his interest in the Memphis, El Paso, and Pacific and $300,000 in bonds for the actual cash expended in preliminary construction (V. TAYLOR, 75). In her notes to the Sept. 29–Oct. 3, 1874, letter, below, to Judge Black, JBF speaks of a pledged indebtedness of $142,000 as of Mar. 16, 1872. This may or may not be part of the $300,000 in bonds that Scott had promised JCF.

5. Susan Benton Boilleau had died earlier in the year in France "from accumulated grief." The implication here is that financial ruin and her husband's imprisonment had "murdered" her. Later JBF implied that another women had been part of the tragedy that ended her life as Boilleau remarried within a few months of her death (JBF to Mr. Farrington, Dec. 16, 1885, CLjC).

6. V. TAYLOR, 89, maintains that when Fancher was JBF's counsel, he was really working for John A. C. Gray, who was undercutting Frémont in every railroad transaction.

Mem. for Mr. Barlow

[July 17, 1874]

In 1869 the Manhattan Engraving Co. of New York obtained a judgment against the Memphis El Paso Co. for engraving and printing its Bonds. The Texas people had no money and all payments had been coming from the General. At his request I paid this judgment which was assigned to me and has since remained, as it was executed that day, in the hands of the attorney of the Manhattan Co., Chas. H. Jackson, Esqre., who still holds it for me.

Recently the General applied to Mr. Gray and Mr. Fancher for payment, but Mr. Gray[1] replied that no payment could be made until Mr. Scott had closed with him, and the Estate was settled, when there would be a pro-rata payment.

But I think I have the right to ask all circumstances considered — that this should be a preferred debt, and settled now.

This transaction was before the sale of the Bonds in Paris.

I wish also to say that my money was quite my own coming from the sale of the Mariposas in '63.

When the Texas Pacific franchises were transferred to Mr. Scott the road was indebted to the General about $142,000. This was cash expended in Texas as well as Washington for suits, lawyers, agencies journeys — in many sorts of necessary intermediate steps in getting those franchises.

This again was chiefly my money. These Railroad properties were placed by the General in control of Mr. M. O. Roberts[2] who transferred them to Mr. Scott.

At that time, now more than two years ago Mr. Scott assumed this indebtedness of $142,000 and promised the General and Judge Black that "it should be paid in thirty days" from the date of that interview May 16, '72.

Tied up as we are by the French suits this money became imperatively needed but it was only last fall that a part was paid — 42 Bonds — and the panic made these nearly valueless.[3]

Early in June Judge Black and the General had an interview with Mr. Scott in order to get the remaining one hundred bonds.

Col. Scott said it was impossible to give them — the exigencies of the Company were too great, but if the General could raise money upon the obligation he would aid him.

And so the matter stands. The security is too intangible and the prospect for re-payment as distant as two years ago.

I have sacrificed and exhausted my ready money property in California in these delays. The children have given up theirs and I am now waiting the action of the Court at San Francisco to sell a portion of their landed property involving minors rights.[4]

I am obliged to tell you this much to explain why it has become so urgent to get that judgment paid. To prevent reclamation from any french source I must keep within my own clear resources.

I had hoped if it was referred to you, you would have seen it was safe and right to have it paid.

I do not know if it is law, but I do know it is just and honest and equitable to give me what I claim.

Five or six thousand dollars, and the putting of the Bond indebtedness in a more tangible shape so that it could be used would carry me over safely until January when I shall have other resources.

With Judge Black and Judge Fancher perfectly satisfied, as to the equities, and fortified as I am by inside knowledge, documents, letters and witnesses, I have no doubt but that I should eventually be successful in a suit at law—only one sided or underhand action can pervert the facts.

But both my necessity and inclination lead me to try for a quieter settlement.

You will do me a greater kindness than you can realize now, if you can succeed in getting me this timely aid which will save everything to my children and myself.

And thank you from my heart for your kind attention when you are so occupied.

Jessie Benton Frémont
New York—July 17th '74

ALS (CSmH). Samuel Latham Mitchell Barlow (1826–89) and his wife, Mary Townsend Barlow, were long-time friends of JBF. As an attorney, Barlow specialized in corporate law and management, particularly in railroads, mining, land, and utilities, and was part-owner of the New York *World*.

1. John A. C. Gray, a retired merchant of New York, had been prominent in railroad enterprises before becoming interested in the Memphis, El Paso, and Pacific. He took advantage of every opportunity to discredit JCF and to get rid of him. He even succeeded

in having JCF sign the petition for Gray's appointment as receiver of the Memphis, El Paso, and Pacific (V. TAYLOR, 62, 69, 74–75).

2. The resignation of Marshall O. Roberts as president of the Texas Pacific was detrimental to JCF's interests. Thomas A. Scott's power increased as it did also when Marshall sold him the Southern Pacific.

3. Reckless speculation in railroads and the wholesale watering of stock in many industries were important factors in causing the Panic of 1873, as was an unfavorable balance of trade and a surplus of agricultural products. The crash came on Sept. 17, with the failure of the great banking house of Jay Cooke and Company. One substantial business after another toppled, and the New York Stock Exchange closed its doors for ten days. Over half of the railroads defaulted on their bonds.

4. Records in the courthouse at Stockton indicate that JBF, "in her own right and as Trustee for Francis Preston Fremont," who was nineteen at the time, sold 2,216 acres of El Pescadero for $8,400 in gold coin (Deed to H. W. Carpentier, May 13, 1874).

To Jeremiah S. Black

230 S. 21st street
Philadelphia
[Sept. 29–Oct. 3, 1874]

My dear Judge,

Mr. [Edward M.] Davis came about a half hour after you left. He had waited an hour in Quaker patience, then sent in a brief and not too Quaker message.

The result is that the great man's great man gave for answer that tomorrow at eight o'clock Mr. Scott would stop here to see me.

I shall write you what he says. And if he does anything then I will write what he does.

Meantime if you will be so good as to make a brief statement of the points as you know them it will be of immediate and valuable use to me.

Pocaho, Friday mg.

I finish this at home. I was quite ill Tuesday night but came home Wednesday after seeing Mr. Scott. I am a little at a loss whether his memory is intentionally at fault, or whether it is confused by the great pressure of conflicting affairs. He did not seem insincere. But his position is entirely at variance with your memory, that of the General, with the notes made at the time by the General in his notebook and with letters written me by the General and his talking with me at the time. I was as thoroughly polite and free from anger or even [just?] emphasis as you could wish. A night of pain and some danger, put me above all but the hope that I might get Mr. Scott to see it was a fixed position we took, and thanks to your letter, that we were supported in it. And that he might, seeing how established the facts were, act quickly to meet them. I copy his letter.[1]

Dudley Field is back. I wish your opinion as well as Mr. Field's upon the letter. I think it was something to get this much from Mr. Scott, but only as an admission in writing that in some form an obligation existed. It can do no good, as it stands, and gives up—if used—our strong position. Very sincerely yours,

J. B. Frémont

Notes

You will see Mr. Scott resolutely ignores—or he may forget—or rely on our not using—the fact that you and the General and the General's note book and letters and talks to me all fix the fact that in March of '72, he promised these bonds in thirty days—the time to have them printed. Mr. Scott quite grew loud in denying this. I only said then—we will not argue it—I was not present, and it is not my memory that you doubt, so that we will go to another point. Then he absolutely insisted on having given the 42 Bonds in *June* "June before leaving for California"—I asked "which year?" but he really seemed confused and only repeated "June, before leaving for California." And when I said, "Mr. Scott there was no illness before June of '73 in my family, so you see you could not have given them—as you say—because the General told you of illness in the family.["] My son's illness was not known to us or to himself until the 1st of July. We thought it a cold & his thin condition the result of hard study when Dr. Van Buren to whom he went for a prescription for his cough, examined his lungs and found fixed disease. All our dates are precise because he was at West Point and did not leave there until the 28th of June.

The date of the 42 Bonds is also fixed by the date of the personal obligation required from the General. By his sale of them Judge Black also was cognizant of this transaction. It was late September of '73.

And yet by implication Mr. Scott makes that date his first knowledge of the subject. Page 2 *fourth line Mr. Scott by his own showing not only hears this case for the first time but instantly and generously meets it out of his own pocket. "And I loaned him 42 Land Grant Bonds of my own." Where had the 142 of the General's gone? Those promised within 30 days, in March of '72.

Is not that great infirmity of memory?

I will not point out more evidences of Mr. Scott's intention to avoid this debt. I intend it to stand truthfully in order to avoid his counter charge for 42 Bonds—which he—or his family—will enforce, Mr. Scott's eyeballs give the sure indications of a fevered brain. He has great pluck—and has had luck also. It interested me to watch him and I was quite as quiet and cool and polite and guarded as even you would wish. And such an opposite and unsympathetic nature shut mine in and left my head only on duty. And I felt [thus?] armed by the justice of my quarrel. Your letter has gone deep into Mr. Scott. "Judge Black's letter surprised me."[2] (He said that twice.) I think *surprise* is the right word for his state of mind.

"Can Fulvia die?"[3] "Can Scott prove vulnerable to the law? Can that law so long defied, manipulated and perverted into a shield prove now the spear of truth penetrating all my defenses?" For Mr. Scott's plans now lie at my mercy. I was thinking this as he talked of the *"ruin"* that would come to him without this aid from Congress.

I have no mercy to shew at the cost of full justice to my own family—especially at the cost of a question of veracity between the General and Mr. Scott. But I thought also which is the wiser? to expose or to use him.

I cannot accept this letter for it gives up our clear case and allows him to assume the part of generous and timely friend, and with more generosity to follow contingent on the skies falling and sending us the breakfast of roasted larks. There is reason in his saying that if the South combine to demand that road as a measure of prosperity and wealth he will get what he asks. But there again is another "if." I suggested they would be sure to do that, but it might be good policy on the Democratic side to go on voting down expenditures &c now, and then revive this road as their own act for the South.

I dare say Erie will help Mr. Scott in Congress this winter. But it is all an if. And this comes [. . .].

On page 5 of the letter, Mr. Scott admits a half truth and includes your name.

This is enough at this time. I shall hope soon to get your brief points of the truth. Mr. Field's office is 4 Pine Street.

Mr. Green brought me the letter from Mr. Scott (who by the way had begun by saying he would write it "tomorrow" but sent it me in time for me to get to New York before dark) and said I was to read it and see if it would do. I read it. But only asked him to thank Mr. Scott for attending to it in time for me to get my train. And when he wanted more, but was too much of a gentleman to urge it, I only talked generalities and said I must pack my bag to get off. I hope you are satisfied with me. Sincerely yours,

J. B. Frémont

ALS (DLC—Jeremiah S. Black Papers)

1. In essence, in his letter Scott denied any indebtedness to JCF, maintaining that the forty-two bonds were a loan—not a partial payment of indebtedness (copy of Scott to JBF, Sept. 30, 1874, DLC—Black Papers).

2. To Scott, Black had written: "You have always admitted the justice of this debt and you have not forgotten that you once solemnly promised to pay it soon after you became president several years ago." Black asserted that there was no ground on which the claim could have be repudiated and urged him as a "courteous" gentleman to pay it before the Frémonts were ruined (copy, Sept. 29, 1874, DLC—Black Papers).

3. Heretofore, Scott had seemed to be invulnerable as had the Roman matron, Fulvia, wife successively of Clodius, Curio, and Mark Anthony. The question quoted by JBF comes from Shakespeare's *Antony and Cleopatra*, act 1, sc. 3.

To Jeremiah S. Black

Pocaho
Christmas night [1874].

My dear Judge,

It may interest Mr. Scott to know that I have received notice that the mortgage on my home will be foreclosed on the 1st of January. This place is worth three hundred thousand but for want of six thousand I shall lose it.

It cannot be a secret or even a quiet thing and I shall not feel bound to protect Mr. Scott's credit. Already those most concerned know of his indebtedness to us and the long delay which has brought this loss. It will help him in Washington. My friend E. M. Davis (the Quaker) will see it does not help him in Philadelphia. You know I do not say this for "a threat" but it is the simple truth. Do you think it worthwhile to bring this to Mr. Scott's notice? He may be hard pressed for money but the President of the Penna. Central should be able to pay six thousand on a debt of a hundred thousand to avert the loss of three hundred thousand.

If you will telegraph me, here, I will act on your advice. It will be a financial error for him to make me an active enemy. Sincerely yours,

J. B. Frémont

ALS (DLC—Jeremiah S. Black Papers)

To George W. Childs

The Arlington, January 24, '75

Dear Mr. Childs

Before leaving Philadelphia, I telegraphed my daughter to send you a Humboldt catalogue with our numbers marked.[1] I also wrote Mr. George Moore[2] to ask him to give you, briefly, a summary of the books & their value.

With time, and among people who feel their unique value they would certainly bring what they cost. This Mr. Moore said on examining them lately. But I cannot wait. Less money now will give quiet of mind for larger things than the books and I would feel it a deep kindness to get the half of their cost. This was £1000 gold when gold was 168 in '63–64 and even that I do not fix as a sum to be required for I should be only too glad and thankful for even a less sum if you can succeed in your kind effort to have them taken.

The General has been so tired and hurt by the undeserved grief of these two hard years that, to spare him, I have to do many things I hardly understand. But I am sure I understand the voice and manner in which you said you would do what you could to obtain us the money for these books. We used to do so many things of this kind that I know it is a luxury to give rest of mind. I shall go on writing but that is slow in its returns.[3] And I am needed for other work just now. March and April are the best time for real estate sales in New York (country property) and in March Clarkson Potter[4] will be free to go on with aid to me in selling some of mine advantageously. Meantime if you can do this for us — and I beg you to excuse the trouble I give in asking you to give so much attention to it — you will confer a greater favor than you can think and have our thanks and gratitude. Sincerely yours,

J. B. Frémont

ALS (PHi—Dreer Collection).

1. The Frémonts had acquired a portion of the old library of Alexander von Humboldt from an American book dealer in London, Henry Stevens. Among the volumes were three that included the 181 diplomas of honorary memberships in learned societies, called "Humboldtiana." A letterpress copy of JCF's account with Stevens, listing the purchases by the catalogue number and the title, may be found in MiU-C. The Frémont purchases have also been marked in the University of Illinois Library's *Catalogue of the First Portion of the Humboldt Library*, which was once in the New York office of Simon Stevens, Henry's brother and a JCF attorney. All of the Frémonts' Humboldt items later appear in the *Catalogue of the Library of E. G. Squier* (New York, 1876), thereby indicating that Squier, an American archeologist, ethnologist, and diplomat, purchased from the Frémonts directly or through an intermediary.

2. Probably George Henry Moore (1823–92), librarian of the New-York Historical Society and of the Lenox Library.

3. JBF had been writing a series of reminiscences, "Distinguished Persons I Have Known," which appeared periodically in the popular weekly newspaper, New York *Ledger*, Jan.–Apr. 1875.

4. Son of Episcopal bishop Alonzo Potter, Clarkson Nott Potter (1825–82), an attorney with an engineering background, was one of New York's Democratic representatives in Congress.

To [George Browne]

Monday afternoon [1874–75]

The Tax collector is here—says he can levy on anything moveable, no matter who it belongs to, even if to one of the servants; will you see Mr. Bryant about it as you come out—the collector is at the stable now looking at horses, carriages etc. with a view to moving them into the village, advertising them for six days &, if not redeemed, selling them. Mr. Weeks[1] will try to have him wait [thro.?] tomorrow afternoon; the man's name is Sylvester Van Tassel: Jennings will be able to tell you if he has taken them off or not, if I don't know in time. Disagreeable to have to write you but I can't help it.

Ask Mr. Bryant if it is possible the man has the right to do this? He was so positive yesterday that nothing of the kind could happen.

Mr. Weeks just tells me the collector consents to wait until Wednesday *morning* on condition a promise was given nothing should be spirited away out of the stable—of the contents of which he took a list—in the meantime, the promise was given & there is a thirty six hours' respite.

AL fragment (CU-B—Frémont Papers).

1. Mr. Weeks was the Pocaho manager.

To Jeremiah S. Black

Washington City, 2109 Penn. Ave.
February 21 [1875].

Dear Judge Black

You said we should know everything we needed to know but as no sound comes from you must I infer that there is nothing that concerns us? Meantime—as usual our name is put out to bear the brunt of a mingling of true & false which is not fair and which we only submit to because there is so much else demanding our attention and work. And because the truth would not be published even if it were given to those papers.

One good has come of it. We have burnt our ships and begun a new life. These attacks simply ruined the chance of getting my Black Point Bill attended to. That loses me my home on the Hudson. Even if Mr. Scott gets anything on his bill—which is possible—I am told his feeling against us is bad and so nothing will come of his promise to pay. We had a family council and the General accepted two offers made him from California and he has been there now since Saturday a week ago.[1] Both the boys can be with him in the work he will have and Charley will resign & follow him as soon as I have tied up some matters here.[2] The Harpers have very amiably accepted my offer to write a book and when I go back this week the arrangements will be perfected.[3] This will be my contribution to the family work.

After a little we shall be able to get together again and have our family life but now it is all work and sacrifice without the strength of being together.

It is only you who can give us a strength which would give us courage for all the separation and labor. You know how unjust it is to allow "Frémont fraud" to be a fixed heading to articles. But it is getting accepted for want of contradiction. And it brings its evil on all we engage in. Even to making men afraid to vote for my poor innocent Bill to go to the Court of Claims for my own property. I was so very sorry and surprised to find you had left here (I called an hour after you had gone to the train) that I felt hopeless and it made me ill. I have been at home and returning here last week have again been laid up by influenza. But I go back Wednesday and will hope to get an answer from you to Tarrytown to let me know if you do not think it possible to put out enough of the much truth you hold in regard to the french case, to stay this habit of defamation and prevent the evils it brings.

If you could find it right to say to the public what you have said to us, that you know the case—that it was an outrage on the Law as well as on the General, that the record of the trial is recorded evidence in the General's favor, and shew the utter difference between the french way of giving that sentence and any way possible to our law. If you could say that no financial establishment could have stood against the combination made to take that road from him & destroy his name, that he was defamed on [contract?], and that all this was clearly to be proved by documents you knew and had examined—in short if you can speak even a part of the much truth you hold, it would be new life to us each and all.

Everybody knows you only speak the truth. Your simple utterance, brief, in the words I had taken so much courage from hearing you use, would be worth the finding of a jury and we could go on waiting for full justice. Can you not do this? And now I think you would do it for justice's sake. And somewhat too for my sake for I am wearing out under this endurance of injustice. If I go, the last strength and restraint goes. It is hard to keep down the natural passion of resentment this continued and perverted persecution rouses in my son—and in the General too.

You alone have the knowedge, the position and the courage to speak the truth which would completely turn public opinion. My dear Judge it seems simple and right to me that I should ask this. You may have other ideas. If I thought it would do good I would go to York to see you about it but I am so hurt and insulted by this incessant coarse talk that I will go nowhere unless I am sure my dear name I love and honor so is to be met as I know it should. The people who wish us harm would be contented if they could see how well they have succeeded. Here in this town I cannot keep down the feeling how different it would have been if my dear brave Father were living. "Solitary and alone" was no reason with him for not attacking an evil.[4] And how the timid fall in like the sand in a wheel track when an iron will passes over their loose surface. You are of his ideas and his school and you have been so kind to me that I look to you for the justice of a timely word of truth.

I am ill and lonesome and discouraged. It would help me to know that you have received this and do not take it amiss. Maybe I may not be well enough to get off Wednesday, and a telegram could reach me — just a signal in answer. I am with my true hearted friend Miss Seward — 2109 Penna. Ave.[5] Sincerely yours,

J. B. Frémont

ALS (DLC—Jeremiah S. Black Papers).

1. On this trip to California, JCF wrote his poignant and despairing poem entitled "Recrossing the Rocky Mountains" and sent it to Jessie, who submitted it to *Littell's Living Age*, where it appeared anonymously in the May 29, 1875, issue (JBF to Whittier, [Jan. 21-22, 1880], MH). The manuscript is in the Southwest Museum.

2. Shortly after his resignation from West Point in Sept. 1874, Frank had gone to California and was there until July 1875.

3. JBF is referring to her "Year of American Travel," which would appear first as three articles in *Harper's New Monthly Magazine* (Nov. and Dec. 1877, Jan. 1878) and later as a separately bound book.

4. JBF refers to Benton's "Expunging Resolution" to remove Senator Henry Clay's censure of Andrew Jackson for withdrawing government deposits from the Bank of the United States. The "frontier" president viewed the national bank as an enemy of democracy, and the withdrawal of funds was one of the measures he used in his war against it (CHAMBERS, 218-19).

5. Around 1868, Olive Risley (c. 1844-1908), the daughter of Hanson A. Risley, began to receive marked attention from the sixty-seven-year-old widower, William H. Seward. She and her sister went around the world with him and in order to quiet tongues, he adopted her as his daughter in 1870 and left her part of his estate. *William H. Seward's Travels Around the World* (1873) was edited by her (VAN DEUSEN [2], 553-64; New York *Times* obit., Nov. 29, 1908). Exactly when the friendship between Olive and JBF was established is uncertain, but "Miss Risley" was an occasional visitor at Pocaho, and while she was on her world travels with Seward, JBF wrote John Hay that she knew "her differently and better than any one can who has only a surface or society acquaintance with her." As her intermediary and friend JBF sought information from Hay as to where Risley's own travel letters might be published and posed the possibility of submitting them to the editor of *Every Saturday* (June 24 [1871?], RPB).

To William J. Morton

Arlington House
Thursday evening [Feb. 1877]

Dear Dr. Morton

I want a jibber with you and I dare not — does jibber look like little stones? (Pebbles) I am going home Saturday. I am homesick now. So much so that I won't go down alone to dinner but I have rested on an afternoon tea at five which I had with some old friends to whom I always go. It is as warm as April. I was quite warm on coming in and made myself some orange juice which reminded me of you and the satisfied thirst at our midnight gossips.

Then I thought you too might miss the pleasant talks and regular irregularity of our good winter of ideas and castle building.

I have been divided into five minute rushes also — so to speak. My aid de camp met me at the station with the uncle's carriage.[1] My room was fragrant with flowers and a cold chicken and oranges were in place also. So I was welcomed. My work is not congenial but is made as little disagreeble as possible by friends in every position and I have effectually strangled the wrong Bill which was nearly through because it had borrowed our feathers.[2] That much is done or undone. What is not so easy is to put through the one we want. Mr. Conkling,[3] Genl. Banks, everybody of our friends are as helping as possible but all say there is no attention to any thing until this Presidential question is settled.[4] So I think I will go home and if it is needed I can come back. But I want to go home.

I have been asked to various places for the evening but I only came for work and have no gowns with me. I shall go tomorrow evening to see Mrs. Winchester.[5] Theatre parties to see her are the rage here. Mrs. Fish sent for her to see her "but did not ask me to stay to her reception." But as a family they are standing by her very thoroughly. And I have asked her to take breakfast with me tomorrow. That, in the Arlington dining room is equal to an editorial in the Times. I am just by Charles O'Connor[6] [O'Conor] and Mr. Conkling and others of that kind. And this morning I introduced her to General Banks who was *very* nice to her.

(Is italicizing bad?)

(I feel any way like a culprit up for sentence)

I was fortunate today in securing for Mr. Aguerro (my phonographic secretary) an excellent place with a Senator. And my old friends have promised to get him good and economical lodging with a lady. Genl. Banks took me in to see the Committee.

A knock — enter servant bringing a basket of glorious flowers from Babcock's uncle this time. Such roses! and orchids and lillies of the valley and hyacinths. The sweetness of it makes me want somebody I like to talk to. I chanced upon my own old room here and it makes a foolish of me to be in it alone and silent. I will put in a flower leaf for you as I am too far off to put in the boutonnière. What interpretation do you suppose would be put on this letter if it went to the Dead Letter office? How far from the reality they [letter incomplete].

AL (CU-B—Morton Papers). The Frémonts were living in New York City at 924 Madison Avenue, and JBF had gone to Washington to promote her Black Point claim.

1. The aide-de-camp was probably William C. Babcock (1853–96), a young naval friend of the Frémonts, who had recently been assigned to the Signal Service in Washington (DNA-24, William C. Babcock, vol. 6: 457–59). Babcock is mentioned several times in Lily's Pocaho and Arizona ms. journal (NNC—Nevins Papers).

2. The bill with respect to Black Point property was so worded that the Frémonts were fearful it would be construed as consent to relinquish title (JBF to Nathaniel Banks, Jan. 30 [1877?], IHi).

3. Roscoe Conkling, who was then representing New York in the U.S. Senate.

4. JBF implies here that JCF cannot hope for a federal office until the disputed election between Rutherford B. Hayes and Samuel J. Tilden is settled.

5. Mrs. Winchester, not otherwise identified, had a starring role in *Forbidden Fruit,* an immensely popular three-act farce by Dion Boucicault, which opened Jan. 29 for a week at the National Theater. JBF reported that Boucicault was surprised — "astonished" — by Mrs. Winchester's stage instinct (Washington *Evening Star,* Feb. 1; JBF to William J. Morton, Feb. 17, 1877, CU-B—Morton Papers). The Hamilton Fishs' connection with Mrs. Winchester has not been ascertained, but Lily noted to Morton that her mother "will have the amusement of seeing Mrs. Winchester act before the Fish set which as a side show won't be bad" (Feb. 1877, CU-B—Morton papers).

6. Charles O'Conor (1804–84), a lawyer with a national reputation. He had signed Jefferson Davis's bail bond and had prosecuted without compensation William Tweed and his associates, eventually destroying the ring in New York.

To Alexander K. McClure

924 Madison Avenue
June 25th 77.

Dear Colonel McClure

If there is something I can say better than another could say it, and if it is wanted that it should be said that makes a reason for writing. Another reason is that which drives the wolf down from the mountain.

Some few years ago I wrote for this last reason a brief series of sketches for the Ledger — Mr. Bonner's Ledger.[1] We had houses and lands and stocks and no money for unpremeditated uses. My youngest boy had been among the cadets (on the 4th of March '73) whose health was so hurt by the weather that day of the inauguration — summer uniforms and the thermometer below zero combine badly on young lungs. When it came to a second winter of change of climate for him he refused to reduce the home purse and vowed he would live through the winter at home. So I remembered Mr. Bonner had wanted me to write and although I had refused then, because I did not wish to do anything to be talked of — yet now I had more than enough motive to brave all criticising.

Without telling my home people I arranged everything through a friend, and think the sweetest pride I ever felt was in handing the check to my boy and sending him into a good climate. It was absurdly large for three weeks work so I could not cavil at the pruning and dismembering my writing received to "fit it into place." The subjects and the treatment were chosen and limited and Mr. Abbott's(!) style preferred so that I do not feel those articles are fair to me.[2]

In August, in their monthly, the Harpers publish something from me which comes under my first reason. They think well of it since they asked for it and put me with Castelar[3] and Mr. Bigelow, they tell me. It has a simple enough title. But it involves much that is distinctively peculiar to our country and countrymen and if you do me the pleasure to read it you will find it leads to much. I should like it to be noticed especially among old friends of my Father's and of the General. It would be a shame "being so Fathered and so husband'ed," were I not able to see and feel, and tell clearly and compactly, and although I have written so little for the public yet writing has been second nature to me. And I should be glad to save for our people such personal and more agreeable aspects of political and material life as might otherwise be left in letters or only in memories.

If you have the leisure when in New York to come this high uptown it would give me pleasure to talk with you and shew you my caissons of ammunition — the pigeon-holed collection which would make mem-oires pour servir to more than one large phase of our times.

The General will have his paper ready quite soon now.[4]

Only it would never do to say all we could say. Or probe. My early political training as well as all usage of good breeding make limits that lessen the interest but which are none the less imperative.

I have just had brought me the letter of Robert Dale Owen to Mr. Lincoln on emancipation—and the editorial upon it—in the Evening Telegram of today.[5]

On that subject I have a tale to tell, but the manner of Mr. Lincoln's death bars the truth at present.

This is a diffuse way of saying that I accept your idea of writing, if you think of something special to my capacity—the chapter on Gwendoline's interview with the music professor (in Daniel Deronda) should be pasted in full view of the writing table of all untried amateurs.[6] What friends say and what the public say make the swing to be or not to be a writer. Sincerely yours,

J. B. Frémont

ALS (PHi—Gratz Collection). Alexander K. McClure (1828–1909) had taken a special interest in the organization of the Republican party and, in 1875, in conjunction with Frank McLaughlin, had established the *Times* in Philadelphia.

1. Robert Bonner (1824–99) was a famous turfman as well as publisher of the New York *Ledger*. Early in 1875, he had paid $100 per column for JBF's sketches of such distinguished persons as Andrew Jackson, Hans Christian Andersen, Kit Carson, Martin Van Buren, and Thomas Starr King.

2. Probably Jacob Abbott (1803–79), who had a wide reputation for his writings and especially biographies for young people, many of which Harper's published.

3. A Spanish statesman and writer, Emilio Castelar y Ripoll (1832–99) had a reputation for writing with imagery and harmony. A translation of his *Life of Byron* had been published by Harper's in 1876.

4. Four months later JCF's "sketch" was still unwritten (JCF to A. C. McClure, Oct. 20, 1877, PHi).

5. The long Sept. 17, 1862, letter was published the day after the death, at age seventy-six, of the noted philanthropist. Owen had called upon Lincoln to "crush forever" treasonable cabals against him and at the same time destroy the underpinnings of the South's agricultural economy and fulfill his responsibility to God and man by emancipating the slaves. The editorial remarked that Lincoln had the letter before him when he penned the Emancipation Proclamation. Lincoln had already been greatly disturbed by George B. McClellan's "political" letter of July 7, 1862, from Harrison's Landing, in which the general gave advice on matters within the functions of president and Congress and warned against "forcible abolition of slavery." The dread of military dictation was "one of the main motives" for the president's issuing the emancipation, asserted the newspaper, and "McClellan unconsciously was an agent of Divine Providence in the liberation of the slaves."

6. In George Eliot's novel *Daniel Deronda*, the music professor had objectively analyzed Gwendolen Harleth's potential for a singing career. When he left, she exclaimed, "I had a mistaken idea about something I could do. Herr Klesmer has undeceived me."

To Henry M. Alden

New Brighton, Staten Island
March 4th. '78.

Dear Mr. Alden,

I return today the proofs, as you directed, to the Messrs. Harper. Will you say to them in answer to the message you conveyed in your letter that I accept their offer and will take the hundred dollars in full of my copyright in the Year of American Travel.[1]

I have made very few corrections but I would be much obliged if they should be left as corrected. Especially at the end where "to" had been substituted for the "in" as written by me. My idea was of travel ended and rest attained. The best grammarian and linguist I know sustains me. I only write by ear so to speak, but in my father's house and in my own, and greatly overbalancing chance hearings, my habitual education of the ear has been safe to follow.

I regret to have forgotten the note of which you send me a copy. From nothing being said at the time, and no intimation having been given me at any time that I was free to make corrections or additions at my own cost, I thought no more of it and later events put most things aside in my mind.

Certainly if I had known my offer was accepted I should have insisted on some things which were omitted. But they will remain for future use now. I get so many letters telling me to write fully & write more from leading men whose opinions have governed events and shaped thoughts, that I have made my programme for large writing. It will be much what I spoke of with you, but enlarged by the interest and co-operation of some who had governing parts in our history—especially my own southern friends.

I think this about ends all the trouble I have to give you about my initial little book—my year of odd rough experience. I am afraid my inexperience has made me ask more than my share of attention, but it was the fault of a recruit. Sincerely yours,

J. B. Frémont

ALS (NNPM). Henry Mills Alden (1836–1919) was editor of *Harper's Magazine* from 1869 until his death. He made it a "family magazine" and the most widely circulated periodical in the country.

1. JBF seems to have been paid $500 for "A Year of American Travel," which

appeared in three parts in *Harper's New Monthly Magazine,* beginning in Nov. 1877 (Henry Alden to John D. Townsend, Feb. 2, 7 [1877] DLC—*Harper's Magazine* Papers). Then on Sept. 29, 1877, "for value received," she assigned her copyright to that work as well as "the proceeds of a contract for writing for the Philadelphia *Times*" to William J. Morton (CU-B—Morton Papers). In the four-month interval between the assignment and this March letter to Alden, she must have repurchased the copyright. In the summer of 1878 Harper's issued *A Year of American Travel* in book form.

THE ARIZONA ADVENTURE

The inauguration of President Rutherford B. Hayes in 1877 provided an opportunity for John C. Frémont to seek federal office in an attempt to reverse the downward financial cycle in which he and Jessie had found themselves since 1873. Hayes had long been a warm admirer of the explorer. Not only had he served briefly under his command during the Civil War, but also, as early as 1849, when merchants in Sandusky, Ohio, had decided to rename the little town, they had accepted the suggestion of Hayes, then a young attorney, to call it Fremont. Moreover, Lucy Hayes had been enthusiastic about Jessie during the 1856 election; after the defeat, Hayes reported that "Lucy takes it to heart a good deal that Jessie is not to be mistress of the White House after all."[1]

In the 1860s, John had exhibited interest in the reports of mineral wealth in Arizona, but the Civil War and the attractions of railroading had precluded serious investigation. His old latent interests may have been revived, however, by a number of factors, not the least of which was Arizona's display of gold and silver ore samples at the Centennial Exposition at Philadelphia in 1876. The press was giving the territory more notice; Indian disturbances were passing away; and the Southern Pacific, building its railroad east from the Pacific Coast, had reached the west bank of the Colorado by May 1877. Moreover, the decline of rich workings on the Comstock Lode in Nevada had freed labor and speculative capital for Arizona enterprises, and the Bland-Allison Act (1878), remonetizing silver, appeared to guarantee a profitable market for the product of such mines. Stockraising and railroading also beckoned as rewarding enterprises. Arizona seemed right for the still hopeful entrepreneur. John declined an offer of the vacant Idaho governorship and sought political support, especially from Zachariah Chandler and James G. Blaine, in obtaining the governorship of Arizona, thus foreclosing on a debt owed him by the Republican party since 1864, when he supposedly had insured the reelection of Abraham Lincoln by withdrawing his own candidacy.

President Hayes nominated him on June 8, 1878, although as Jessie indicates in her letters, there was some opposition in the Senate. Nonetheless, John was confirmed, and the Frémonts made no attempt to hide from friends the fact that they intended to use the office to make money. In fact, Hayes's private secretary, William King Rogers, became a business associate in various enterprises, as did one of the territorial supreme court judges, Charles Silent. The Frémonts wrote bluntly to Rogers of their needs, and he no doubt intervened on their behalf, especially to protect John from charges of absenteeism.

Jessie, who was fifty-four, found much that was difficult in the new life on the Arizona frontier, but she was heartened by the public acclaim that came their way on both the trip out and in the territorial capital of Prescott, tucked high in the pines. In spite of its twenty saloons, the U.S. postal inspector, Benjamin C. Truman, pronounced it the "model frontier settlement of the United States." He even claimed that it reminded him, "with some few exceptions," of a quiet New England village, with little of the violent "man-before-breakfast style" so characteristic of settlements in Wyoming or Montana.[2] Jessie was impressed with the simple strength and endurance of the women she met. "Some of the quiet-faced women here tell me of things you would feel impossible for women to live through," she wrote Theodore Stanton, son of the feminist.[3]

Refusing to be "rolled in cotton wool" and treated like a fragile flower, Jessie quickly entered into the life of the community. Each Friday afternoon she went to the public school, called the Prescott Free Academy, to give a history lesson. She devoted long hours to writing, participated in the social activities of nearby Fort Whipple, collected Mohave pottery for friends in the East, and exalted in sunsets "above description." In March 1879 she wrote Anna Fitch: "I used to think no one (meaning myself) could be unhappy who can command the sea, plenty of music and flowers, and an open carriage. Behold me destitute of all these props of the mind, and not even lonesome."[4]

Almost a year to the day after her arrival, without ever having been out of town, Jessie left Prescott for good. The governor, under fire for a six-month absence from the territory, needed her "on the spot" in New York as his agent in the placing of mining properties and as his personal lobbyist in Washington while he was forced to remain in Prescott. She stayed with Charley and his wife, Sally, or friends, or in a hotel, working hard, optimistic that the Frémont fortune would be restored. Her letters to William King Rogers during this period reveal the totality of her involvement in efforts to regain some financial security for the family.

John managed to join her in March 1880, while Lily stayed in Prescott, "watching for telegrams on which the fate of mines & to some extent of ourselves hang."[5] The governor reluctantly returned to Arizona in October for the winter legislative session, but as soon as it adjourned, he quickly moved Lily and himself into the Carrillo House in Tucson, alleging that the lower altitude would relieve his "mountain fever." The Prescott *Arizona Miner* editorialized that the move was made so that "he could be 'check by jowl' with Judge Silent in manipulating mining claims."[6] Almost immediately, John traveled east again, ostensibly on territorial business, but really to promote his own ventures, especially a railroad and ranching operation. Political opponents kept up criticism of the absentee governor until President Chester A. Arthur, less sympathetic to the Frémonts' aspirations than had been Presidents Hayes and James Garfield, asked for his resignation in October 1881.

As soon as Lily recovered from a bout of typhoid fever, she joined her parents in the East. John continued to peddle his business schemes while Jessie tried to maintain an outward cheer. Writing twice to George and Nelly Haskell Browne on March 19, 1883, she noticed that Judge Silent, "who has been *very* successful," was with them and that "our Railroad is beginning to move. We are near enough again to fortune to feel its strength and warmth."[7]

Fortune came to Judge Silent and to their Arizona schoolteacher-friend, Moses H. Sherman, but it eluded the Frémonts. John's poor business reputation doubtless deterred investors. With hopes waning, Jessie quietly turned to writing again as a source of income. On August 16, 1882, she confidentially informed Nelly Browne that "as soon as the illustrations are ready something I have written will be published in Wide Awake."

Wide Awake, a popular children's magazine whose name was derived from a prewar Republican antislavery group, had serialized Margaret Sidney's *Five Little Peppers and How They Grew* and made its readers familiar with the writings of Sarah Orne Jewett, Harriet Beecher Stowe, Helen Hunt Jackson, Edward Everett Hale, and Jessie's beloved John Greenleaf Whittier.[8] John Frémont contributed "My First Buffalo Hunt," although the article was no doubt written by his wife, who also asked General William T. Sherman to write a "brief paper for boys, which would give some incidents of your march to the sea."[9]

In the seven years between 1883 and 1890, Jessie wrote more than fifty articles for *Wide Awake*. She called her sketches "fireside history"—personal reminiscences about presidents and congressmen, diplomats and socialites "without hurtful ingredients of complete facts." Drawing a parallel between her stories and nursery puddings, she asked Anna Fitch to "please remember that nursery puddings cannot have any flavor but nutmeg or cinnamon, so they are harmless (my papers and the puddings)."[10] Some of the *Wide Awake* sketches were eventually collected into a book, *Souvenirs of My Time* (1887), published in Boston by D. Lothrop Company.

In 1885, Jessie, with the assistance of John and Lily, embarked on a more ambitious project than "fireside history." It was a project designed not only to give the facts of history, at least from the Frémont point of view, but also to give credit to her husband and father for their roles in shaping and carrying forward the development of the West.[11]

Perhaps it was the probing of Josiah Royce about Frémont's role in the conquest of California or the monumental financial success of Ulysses S. Grant's *Memoirs* that spurred Jessie to pull out of storage the papers that she had been preserving for more than thirty years. In the 1850s, John had contracted with George W. Childs to bring out an illustrated book of his travels, but the volume had never been finished. The new work was to be his *Memoirs,* but in Jessie's mind it was "our book"—"ours because I am custodian guardian amanuensis & secretary with a memory," she wrote Charles Wood Irish.[12]

She sought advice from journalist William A. Croffut on how to proceed; Belford, Clarke & Company, a publishing house with offices in both Chicago and New York, offered a liberal contract. The advance was sizable enough to allow the Frémonts to rent a charming house in Washington, D.C., where they could be near the official records. Lily ran the house "as usual," and frequently went up to the two libraries in the Capitol, "where all the librarians know me now & help me hunt up references." Until she learned to type, she did in "plain hand" the last fair copy for the printers. Her father dictated, her mother did all the writing. She described a typical day: "We are all up early, teas & coffees over by 8-1/2 at the latest; then Father & Mother go at their work & no interruption is allowed till our noon breakfast comes, after which they rest till half past one when they go at it again till five—but very often till Mary goes up & forces them into coming down to the cooling soup. In the evenings they take a short walk & do no writing work though they sometimes talk over the programme for the next day's work." She noted that each was "somewhat fagged by the long continued mental pull of steady brain work indoors," yet they were both well.[13]

When the *Memoirs* appeared early in 1887, it also contained Jessie's biographical sketch of Benton, in which she papered over the differences between her husband and father and linked them in the acquisition of Mexican California. "Two men were in a position to use deciding influence, and both understood the crisis and each other, my father in Washington, with his established power in the Senate; Mr. Frémont on the ground where the decisive blow must be given."[14] Unfortunately, the large volume did not carry John's story beyond the conquest of California, although a sequel volume was promised but never published. Reviewers and readers were disappointed that there were no revelations about the campaign of 1856, the Civil War, or the controversies that surrounded his later career. Commercially, the work was a failure, and when the lease expired in June 1887 on their Washington house, the Frémonts moved to a more modest dwelling at Point Pleasant on the New Jersey coast.

Jessie wrote bravely to friends of the pine and sea air—her "vital air"—of the rehabilitation of her health after the long grind in Washington; of songbirds; of honeysuckle, roses, and wild pink laurel; and of the fresh eggs, strawberries, and peas she found in the local market.[15] She resumed her writing for *Wide Awake*, John traveled to New York "on business," Lily puttered in the cottage, called "The Anchorage" after their Nahant residence, but all the while the spirits and finances of the three worsened. By late fall, Lily had developed a steady hacking cough, and John's bronchitis was on the verge of pneumonia. When their physician advised a warmer climate, Jessie pocketed her pride and sought the financial assistance of the railroad magnate Collis P. Huntington in getting them and Mary, their long-time maid, to California, where they might recover health in the sunshine and possibly profit from a real estate venture floated by their old Arizona friend, Charles Silent.[16]

Notes

1. HAYES, 1:501.
2. San Francisco *Bulletin,* printed in *Weekly Arizona Miner,* Dec. 17, 1878.
3. Aug. 13, 1879 (NjR).
4. Letter fragment to Anna Fitch, printed in MOODY, 144–45.
5. Elizabeth Benton Frémont to Nelly Haskell Browne, Mar. 11, 1880 (CU-B—Frémont Papers).
6. Prescott *Daily Arizona Miner,* Mar. 17, 1881.
7. JBF to Nelly Haskell Browne and JBF to George Browne, Mar. 19, 1883 (CU-B—Frémont Papers).
8. HERR, 413.
9. July 17, 1885 (DLC—Sherman Papers).
10. Letter fragment to Anna Fitch, Jan. 30, 1887, printed in MOODY, 145. See also JBF to Charles Nordhoff [1887?] (CU-B).
11. Notes [for William A. Croffut], Nov. 30 [1885] (DLC—JBF Misc. Ms. Collection).
12. May 31, 1886 (IaU).
13. To Nelly Haskell Browne, Oct. 7, 1886 (CU-B—Frémont Papers).
14. MEMOIRS, 17.
15. JBF to Nelly Haskell Browne [June?] 1887 (CU-B—Frémont Papers); to Ella Pratt, June 21, 1887 (NjHi); to George Bancroft, Oct. 28, 1887 (MHi).
16. JBF, "Memoirs," n.p.

To Nathaniel Banks

Monday morning [June] 17th [1878]
the Arlington

Dear Genl. Banks

The General or Governor General[1] went to New York this morning and asked me to write this to you.

The N. Y. Sun, 12th June, says "nine or ten Democratic Senators voted against Frémont's confirmation because of his connection with the sale of the Memphis and El Paso Bonds in France which made him an unworthy person for Federal appointment."[2]

I have sent my only printed slip with this notice, to a Democratic leader who told me there would not be one Democratic vote against the General, but the above is copied.

Can't you get the truth of this? The General wants it very much. He has turned over a new leaf—is accepting all invitations to receptions of honor &c. and will give up his old proud silence which has been so misunderstood and taken advantage of. Pray see into this and let me know. Sincerely yours,

Jessie Benton Frémont

ALS (IHi).

1. A reference to JCF whose appointment as territorial governor of Arizona by President Hayes had just been confirmed by the Senate.

2. Initially, thirteen senators voted not to confirm the appointment, of whom eleven were Democrats, but by unanimous consent and before JBF's letter to Banks, the approval was forwarded to the president (*Journal of the Executive Proceedings of the Senate of the United States,* 21 [Mar. 5, 1877–Mar. 3, 1879]: 350).

To William J. Morton

the Arlington, Washington, D. C.
June 26th '78.

Dear Dr. Morton

It is not often I put off friends to the last but I am back at my old post of Secretary and I get cruelly tired and then can't amuse myself.

Lil will have told you enough to shew what a long contested fight it was—against invisible opposition too. The old Scott enmity—no one would avow it and as the President was not only firm but combative presently it was all unanimity and so the end was harmony. And since then, though I have been very tired, there are no end of letters to answer which must be answered because they are full of feeling.

I am coming to you for a little advice before I go. I have never had just the same disordered action of the heart that I have now. For three days, (after the end was reached) I coughed all the time from the throbbing in the throat and the jerking and fluttering at the heart. I have not had it so long at a time since but I am hardly at full rest from it a day—it feels so quiet when the engine does stop "wobbling" and goes on evenly. What I am to do in rarefied air 4000 feet up— you must think I cannot.

Great fortune is already opening there to us and each one will be the better for the mountain air. Maybe I will too—but it will be the first time and you will help me understand what to do if it hurts me. For I shall be very far from my Benjamin[1] or anyone who knows what a fagged out machine my heart has gotten to be.

That's enough of that. I was so pleased you had Dr. Hammond's[2] summer lectures—that is your Arizona exile. But there are compensations.

I am selfish enough to be glad we shall see you again. There is not much I regret leaving. Charley I am glad is happy in his own new home. Sally has all sorts of womanly and home tastes and gifts.[3] They will grow into real happiness together—it takes the sting out of leaving him. For the rest it is new life and we shall be a very thankful as well as happy family—on our journey and in our new home. Fancy—*fancy* our doing your African stage travel![4] What letters we can write back to you. I have been under such swing of writing answers for the General that in writing to him today I put yours very truly and it looked so odd that it stopped me but it was written before I knew it.

We think, Mephisto & I that on our return we may be asked by Judge Daly[5] to "read a paper." You know there are marked remains there of Aztec & Toltec settlements.[6] Also the Navajoes make blankets so fine they turn rain—and beautiful in colors and design—looking Egyptian in designs. I shall have them for portières.

My chief, Mr. Schurz,[7] is a charming man and we are allied &c. and the General will do something good with that Territory and there will be some interesting writing about it.

I am very pleased with the President. And indeed I have had a look into the better side of humanity. Govr. Noyes,[8] the minister to France is here at the Arlington—where I have been this week since Miss Seward left for Colorado. I will keep to tell you all the crowning good that has come from his being here at this moment. It is all un-really good. This time last year was so sad—it was all breaking up then. Now it is all new life and solid ground. Another year will certainly see us with funded properties.

I had a visit from an insane officer one evening lately. He had just been released under surveillance from the asylum. He came in full uniform—it was hanging very loose on his thin frame—his poor eyes were fixed and sad and his hands twitched at each other and plucked his own fingers all the time and his voice kept at one tone—a shot hurt the spine & the voluntary muscles are paralyzed—his leg flies out and his servant helps him about with a patient "Now then Mass George." He knew all my people, he is from here. But I was meaning to tell you that for two hours he talked on & on. And it was a look into a soul, naked, and not knowing it was uncovered. And it was a clean patient sad religious nature. Never, never have I been so sure of the abiding good of early religious training. I mean religious—not clerical. Again and again I thought of you and how you would see so much in such a man. He knew his state too. He asked me Do you think I am only like a child, to be kept under restraint? Ought I to be put in a House of Restraint?

He recited my own hymn I think of so often—"Abide with Me." His voice going into mere breathing—to him it was a prayer—he repeated often & over and over some lines in it.

> Hold thou thy Cross above my dying eyes
> Shine through the gloom

Shine through the gloom he kept on murmuring and then with such a low patient groan—Oh Lord grant me patience to endure to the end.

You have seen such things. I have not before seen a man of such family and such social belonging, every way a noble looking man too though only a shadow, so helpless. And it brought me one more source of gratitude—that the torture of these years of wrong and suffering had clouded no mind among us. Sometimes I feared it for one and at times for another but we are all saved. The poor gentleman was taken back to the "House of Restraint" the next day.

This is more like our old midnight talks than the work I have been in lately. We are going to do one or two bits of public speaking (we means my Govenor-General and the recording secretary & Francis the A.D.C.).[9] Then about the 15th or 20th we start.

We must take Thor.[10] Think how happy he will be out there. And Mary[11] the wonderful. She shall have a section of land and shares in mines and be astonished in turn, for her fidelity astonishes me.

I think I have met with an unusual number of good people in my time.

My General will be here Saturday and Monday we calculate—this is literally exact for we are calculating our time and our money all the time now and fitting each into the work—so "calculous" Monday, New York, Wednesday, Woodstock, Connecticut to "hold a reception" and Thursday the 4th a speech! by the General to ten thousand people perhaps—who will have out (so they write us) the old '56 flags and they require *me* also.[12]

It is all good for the General. He needs a little extra warming to thaw him back. Omaha claims the same privilege of welcome & god-speed and the Pioneer Society in New York and San Francisco ditto. So this tired hand of mine has been doing the polite all round.

I have never seen you at your house. I must before I go. Charley is to have a house too. Has Lil told you my good friends here arranged it for my wedding present to him—three years on Staten Island, house, fuel & lights free. *Secret as yet.*

Good night dear Sandy. If you are that & Benjamin too we must call you B & S. Your affectionate,

J B Frémont

ALS (CU-B—Morton Papers).

1. JBF is evidently calling Morton "Benjamin" after the biblical Benjamin, last son of Jacob and Rachel (Genesis 35:17–19 and Judges 21:1). In the last paragraph of the letter she also addresses him as "Sandy."

2. Dr. William Alexander Hammond (1828–1900), American nerve specialist and former surgeon general, had been court-martialed in Jan. 1864 on charges of making irregular purchases and lying. He was dismissed from the army in 1864, but President Hayes in 1878, after a review of the case, restored him to service and placed him on the retired list.

3. Two dates have been given for Charley's marriage in New York. The Washington *Post,* July 11, 1878, reported that he had secretly wed Sally Anderson of Washington in Oct. 1877 (as printed in New York *Times,* July 13, 1878). Juliet C. Anderson's sworn statement, May 13, 1911, in his pension file, indicates that she was present at their

marriage on May 17, 1878, by a Presbyterian clergyman at the Everett House (DNA-15, John C. Fremont, XC-2 683 652).

4. Morton had included Africa in his "grand tour," although in reporting the Associated Pioneers' reception for the Frémonts at the Sturtevant House, the New York *Times*, Aug. 2, 1878, noted that Morton had just returned from a trip "through the Australian diamond fields." At the gala event JBF had been hailed as "one of the best wives God ever made."

5. Judge Charles Patrick Daly (1816–99), husband of JBF's friend Maria Daly, was not only an outstanding jurist, but he was also president of the American Geographical Society and contributed valuable papers to its proceedings.

6. This was a common misconception in the nineteenth century.

7. Territorial governors reported to the secretary of the interior, who at this time was Carl Schurz.

8. Former governor of Ohio, Edward F. Noyes (1832–1890), who had served in the army under JCF, had placed Hayes's name in nomination for the presidency and, in turn, had been appointed minister to France. He had been called back from France to give testimony before Congress respecting his role in the canvass of votes following the Hayes-Tilden disputed election.

9. JBF was of course the "recording secretary," and Francis, that is, their son Frank, would serve as a sort of aide-de-camp to his father.

10. The Frémonts' staghound.

11. Mary McGrath, the Frémonts' long-time and faithful maid (see JBF to Nelly Browne, May 26, 1893, CU-B—Frémont Papers, wherein she notes the approaching departure of "Miss McGrath" to her native Ireland).

12. Ever since Henry J. Raymond of the New York *Times* made his great "Frémont and Jessie" oration in Woodstock, Conn., in 1856, it had assumed a national importance with some speaker or celebrity invited annually. In 1878, Hugh McCullough, a former U.S. secretary of the treasury (1865–69), was the speaker, and the Frémonts were invited guests.

To Nelly Haskell Browne

Monday [Sept. 23?, 1878]

Dear Nell,

I have been in bed three days—fatigue &c.—we go tomorrow and I want to be as rested as possible for the rest of the journey which is solid. To Yuma is by rail but there is to be a day and night at the Angeles and it is very wearing to be on duty and packed up and travelling all at the same time. Then comes a day of company and 100° of heat at Yuma and then the river travel and after that *five days* of ambulance. It will be charming I am sure but I shall be glad to go to sleep where we are not to "moof" on from. We get excellent accounts of Prescott. We have engaged a Chinese cook—Mary says the poor haythuns [heathens] are peaceful & industrious—they are more than that. Betty's cook is equal to Delmonico.

Georgie has been a triumph—Judge [Stephen J.] Field doubted his being a real child—I keep the photographs to prove him. The Cooks[1] (who are married) shiny-clean uninteresting little dots of women who echo each other—rave over him. So do all people. My Jack is, as usual not noticed enough. He never will be a picture like Georgie.[2] Thor also gets a great admiration and has been photographed—"by request"—I send you the first shadowy proofs and when I get them will send the other, finished things.

We are in full blast of going out—praises, invitations, flowers, fruits, books &c. &c. driving in four in hands & in landaus & coupeés & etc. The wheel has turned you see.

Once at Prescott, & unpacked, I can write you comfortably. You were my dear good loving child when friends were few and you know I have a long memory. Yours and G.B's loving,

JBF

AL initialed (CU-B—Frémont Papers). The Frémonts reached San Francisco on Sept. 12 and were reunited with JBF's sister Eliza and her daughter, Betty.

1. The Cooks—Mattie and Anna—were undoubtedly related to Charles W. Cook, a partner in the old defunct San Francisco banking firm of Palmer, Cook & Company (Elizabeth Benton Fremont to Nelly Browne, San Francisco, Thursday n.d., CU-B—Frémont Papers).
2. Georgie and Jack were sons of Nelly.

To William J. Morton

Prescott, Arizona, October 7th. '78.

This is my first letter from here dear friend. You were waiting here to greet me with good news about Sally and kind good words about my Charley.

I do not need the digestative—someway I do not feel myself. If one can actually live without caring for the body or being encumbered by it, I am doing so. All this new phase is so like another life that I do not feel myself but it is like a long dream with a purpose however, and I see my opportunities all the time to make the General's life softer and more suitable to his tastes. If you were here and I could have a talk as we have talked in the dead hours—dead that is to matter but alive to soul I think I would cry just a little—only because I would feel softened and comprehended.

All the time I tell myself to look back and feel the contrast, I mean, for good now. And you know I can have sense but you know too I don't want to have sense. I want just to be natural and have peace. We will get at peace through this time however for there are certainties of money making and we are all well and in hearty cooperation to make all things work to the same end of comfortable family life while we work and watch for the fortune.

Your letter is responsible for making me give this backward look. I have been only seeing the days and hours as they came and had to be met. And what was required of me was to be pleased and astonished and receptive, and sometimes, it was easy and sometimes it was not but I was taught my trade of society well, in the early days, so it is second nature to look it all.

The General would find it exile but for me. With me he feels it a term of voluntary labor from involuntary causes and together we make the labor light but oh so much of it is uncongenial—never mind we will succeed. And I keep telling over my rosary of blessed points—the justification—the public recognition of a wrong done—the gathering stream of friendly and indignant sympathy—it has been a regular widening gulf-stream of a current since we struck Chicago—all the evidences of the strength and warmth of feeling for the General throughout all our western country. It deserves its name of the Great West—great-hearted we have found it. All these I remember and dwell on and when I see the General flagging a little under new discomforts or old memories, I get my chance and warm his heart again. So he is now very well and sees his way clear. We shall have a peaceful and successful life up here. But all the same my Benjamin, your Marraine [godmother] yearns for some parts of the old life. I know you will be good friend and counsel to Charley but I could be so much to him, and I love him. He is more simply affection-needing and affection-giving than the others who have more power of mind, so I can be more to him. And I miss you more even than I thought. Every root cut off sends back that sap to the trunk maybe, but it only hardens and toughens and that I don't like to have to be.

It is ungrateful in me to make my moan for anything for greater kindnesses could not be shewn than we have had. My niece, Mrs.

Hughes, would not let me have a strange servant to add to Mary, but made me take her own cook who had been with her five years and for two years before had travelled here in Arizona with Major Hughes.[1] He is a Chinese of the better class—a gentleman's servant. A really first class cook and laundress! He asked Betty, "Are you tired of me? Do you want me to go away?" But she said it was because she knew he was a good man as well as a good cook, that she wanted me to have him and that he would take care of me and see I had no trouble. So in twenty-four hours Ah Chung was mine, a friend of his, warranted, was in his place at Mrs. Hughes, and we were on our way here. A contract signed in duplicate by Chung to stay with me one year as "cook and general servant" and they keep their contracts. So with Mary, who has been super excellent in conduct every way, we are, for this country, in aristocratic ease.

At San Francisco, in fact early in the day we reached there, we were met by a despatch from the Palace Hotel asking the General "and his party" to be their guests. Also a chief clerk was sent out to meet us and take charge of details. So we were franked through twelve days of wonderful comfort and elegance and thanked for accepting it. And the old Pioneers made much of the General and the Mayor and the Senators & the chief men—and women—all came to see us. Lots of old hatchets were buried and pipes of peace and indignant sympathy and good will offered in their place. We had a really swell reception from Mrs. Shillaber[2] who was most attentive every way and fortunately the General took a liking to her and behaved like himself—so he went about driving and sightseeing with her (her landau is lined with black satin, and corded, &c. with *gold* if you please) while I received visits by the bushel, and went to amateur theatricals & musicals and Luncheon parties, &c. &c. and had one charming drive in a french char-à-banc with a true four in hand team, through the park to the ocean (the young owner, Wm. Boothe[3] having just made a fortune in Arizona mines (Silver King). Genl. McDowell came in full fig to make the General a visit and invite us to the fort (my place)[4] the French & English admirals &c. the officers of our navy & army all in full uniform as was Genl. McDowell to receive us. One young officer, Fletcher[5] (I helped him out of a scrape at Annapolis once) told me they had been directed to come in full dress to meet Genl. Frémont. It was a lovely kettledrum govt. band and dancing; such fruits and flowers and such tea! The word W E L C O M E was made in roses over the hall fireplace, each letter over eighteen inches high and in a different rose for each letter—the O in yellow marshal neils [*sic*] and the C in Jacques minots.[6] It was charming.

At the Angeles we met your sister who had come down to meet us.[7] She was with a Mrs. Severance[8] who has a beauty of a place there. I have lots to tell you of that place and of Mrs. Otis, but this is only headings. There too, were receptions &c. and each day long drives. Then at Yuma we found Major Lord[9] had arranged everything for our comfort. No money could have bought such comfort—it was the best the government had and it saved us such lots and lots of money. I must not forget that the General and myself were given each a whole section and all our party others sections in the Palace Car and franked through to Yuma from San Francisco. Genl. Sherman met us near the Angeles and stopped the train while he greeted us most warmly and told the General (he came on our train and stayed half an hour) of all the arrangements he had made up here with the commndg. genl. for any travel Mr. Frémont was to make on tours of inspection &c.

We left Yuma in state—three ambulances, six fine mules to each—the third having tent & camp equipage and the invaluable Ah Chung. This is only headings remember. *So* often we remembered you. When you told us of the African travel how little did we foresee this. We looked back from one bank of the wide Gila river and saw our following ambulances plunge into the ford—the staggering wagon top—the lines of wagging mule-ears, the perilous plunge of the whole thing [*JBF draws picture*] in that river of fatal accidents and quicksand—and we felt better when it was over. How ever to tell the days of sun and sand and cactus—no rest for the eye anywhere—the glare of light on hot shifting blowing sharp sand—the dusty grey-green prickly bushes sparsely set in baked ground or sand or miles on miles of black volcanic rocks glistening like anthracite coal.

I took up a volume of Mrs. Browning last night and this is so strangely descriptive I quote it to you. She never saw a desert—and I could not have appreciated this but that for six days I had travelled over one. The last two days we met water and trees & farms and then mountains and the dear pines. Mrs. Browning, speaking of the numbing withering effects of the greatest griefs, says:

Thank God, bless God all ye who suffer not
More grief than ye can weep for. That is well—That is light
grieving!
(then) x x x x
I tell you hopeless grief is passionless.
[That] only men incredulous of despair,
Half-taught in anguish, through the midnight air
Beat upward to God's throne in loud access
Of shrieking and reproach.

(Now comes this wonderful photograph of what I have just seen &
she never saw, but with the eye of genius)—

Full desertness
In souls as countries, lieth silent—bare
Under the blanching, vertical eye-glare
Of the absolute Heavens.[10]

When we camped at Date Creek a long narrow valley with a wide
creek bottom & big green cottonwoods, we rejoiced. There the governor and the secretary of the state met us.[11] They travelled on with
us the two following days, and we made this entrée.

Near the town was a barouche waiting to lead with the chief men
to go in it. Genl. Wil[l]cox[12] was there with his ambulance and four
sleek big mules. Two carriages with ladies &c.

Barouche Two governors & Genl. Wil[l]cox

My ambulance Six mules, Lil & myself & Mrs. Hoyt (my predecessor)[13]

Genl. Wilcox's ambulance His son, a Lt. & two little sons

Next ambulance & six mules Frank on the driving seat by the
driver—black bearded, boots outside of blue jeans overhauls blue
flannel shirt. Inside Mary and baggage—also two New York men—
good but not known to you.

Then our third ambulance with Chung & the impedimenta.

Barouche and pair
Ambulance & 6
Ambulance & 4
Two ″ s & 6 each
Two carriages 2 horses each

——————

28 horses and mules

All the piazzas were crowded, cheers & flags and such met us, and we were driven through the village to a charming cottage which had been turned over to us by its owners for our use until we settled on a house. Pale blue drawing room with a harp among other christianities.

This has been written brokenly because the General has been really ill. He just slipped off into a fever and Dr. McKee[14] the post surgeon has now at the end of three days got him cool & at ease again. Nervous exhaustion he called it together with heat, changes of water and fatigue of mind. He is getting on all smoothly now but will not leave his bed before Friday. This is Wednesday.

We have a house for two months, maybe longer if the lady remains in San Francisco. Anyway we have breathing time. And two cows have been given to me. And there are lots & lots more of kind and good things done to us. And people like me for coming (as if I could keep away when the General had this hard pull—I *never* was so needed and of so many uses).

Thursday

I am going to send this off with all its imperfections for I am too cut to bits for any satisfactory writing—my dream is a writing table and a room of my own. But how to get that room in a five or at most seven roomed cottage? This morning we learn that the best house in town promises to be vacant from the illness of the owner's wife who has been gradually sinking to insanity from a local effect of the altitude which kills young mothers very easily and is generally relaxing. If we get that house we shall all rejoice.

Meantime the General is quite well again. Dr. McKee is a man of European as well as home study—an old army surgeon, and has had a theoretical attachment to the General which became actual and active on finding him his patient. Today the General is sitting up in bed (reading a novel) after a breakfast of one wonderfully broiled chop of mountain mutton, two soft eggs (eggs $1.00 a dozen), a glass of rich milk and such bread! baked thin and brown on purpose by that inestimable Chung. Orientals for me forever for service. Silence is as delightful as their skill.

Tomorrow night is the Ball. The newspapers & Lily will give you details—these are only my pheelinks as Thacker[a]y puts it.

I wish the wishing carpet did exist. How good it would be to join you at times. One admirable thing here is the total absence of any false standard—no sham of any kind whatever. It is cooling to the mind.

Goodbye my dear Benjamin. You are my youngest but you are nearest head for you are above me in some things and we have each a need of safe expansion which finds safe expression with each other. Your loving Marraine.

It may interest you to know how the General was ill. He took a chill one night on the way up—the 3d night. Feverish thirst the next day. No chill again but aching limbs. Here, he gave out the second day. The whole functions but one had struck work and only the kidneys acted. They seemed like a siene. Hot fever and b[l]inding headache. Dr. McKee gave first a nitre drink. The Genl.'s pulse was 97. A day and night brought a good change. Then next morning quinine, followed by a purgative (in a pill or rather three pills and some "Bitterwater"). This made a breakup of the torpid condition, and today the General has only taken his quinine, and feels all comfortable. He is in a pretty blue bedroom—one window lets in the morning sunshine & soft milky air and also the organ sound of a great pine tree just by. I have been reading to him and since I have been writing he has slid down and fallen asleep. Dr. McKee is entirely content with his condition. I am governor and see everyone & settle things if needed, for he is to be kept absolutely secluded from thinking or talking even until Friday evg. I am still well though a little "scant of breath" but that will wear off.

ALS (CU-B—Morton Papers).

1. William Burton Hughes (d. 1896) had married Betty Jones in 1870 or 1871. Before her marriage, Betty had been doing knitting and embroidery for San Francisco stores to earn money. Her mother was grieved and shocked by this, but cousin Lily Frémont thought it "noble."

2. The San Francisco *Evening Bulletin,* Sept. 17, 1878, described the reception given by Mr. and Mrs. Theodore Shillaber at the Occidental Hotel. Seven rooms were thrown open, and there was a "perfect stream of guests" entering the hotel to greet the Frémonts. Cynthia H. Shillaber and her husband would later become involved in the Frémonts' Silver Prince Mine.

3. William Booth was not the discoverer of the Silver King, north of present day Superior, Ariz., but had been one of the four trustees when the Silver King Mining Company was incorporated under the laws of California on May 5, 1877, with a capital stock of ten million dollars (*Arizona Weekly Enterprise* [Florence], Dec. 3, 1881). Eventually, the total recorded production reached an estimated $6,500,000, with the bulk of the yield coming before 1893 (DUNNING, 118).

4. A reference to her Black Point property upon which Fort Mason had been

constructed, but which she still claimed. Since his frontier duties had taken him to Arizona, Gen. Irvin McDowell was able to tell the Frémonts something about Prescott.

5. Probably Ensign Frank Friday Fletcher, who had graduated from the Naval Academy in 1875.

6. JBF is referring to marechal niels, a fragrant noisette rose, hardy on the West Coast and in the South, and to General Jacqueminots, a famous scarlet-crimson hybrid tea type from which have come many fine seedlings.

7. Morton's sister was Bessie Otis, who had come from Santa Barbara. Earlier Lily had written to Morton about the expected visit (Sept. 19, 1879, CU-B—Morton Papers).

8. Caroline Severance (1820-1914), a national leader in the woman's rights movement and in the movement to make kindergartens a regular part of the school system. She and her husband had moved to Los Angeles in 1875 because of his incipient tuberculosis.

9. Maj. James Henry Lord (d. 1896), the quartermaster at Yuma.

10. JBF has combined lines from Elizabeth Barrett Browning's sonnets on "Tears" and "Grief."

11. The governor was John Philo Hoyt (1841-1926); the secretary of state was John J. Gosper.

12. Orlando Bolivar Willcox (1823-1907) had relieved Gen. A. V. Kautz as commander of the Department of Arizona the previous March.

13. Lettie Lewis Hoyt (1849-1916).

14. James Cooper McKee (1830-97) had many years of service in the West before he became medical director of the army's Arizona Department in 1877. His *Narrative of the Surrender of a Command of U.S. Forces at Fort Fillmore, New Mexico in July, A. D. 1861,* was first printed at Prescott in 1878 and circulated among friends. McKee had also been assistant director in the Army of Virginia and, after the Battle of Antietam, took charge of a 3,000-bed hospital in Washington (A. WALLACE, 134-35).

To Carl Schurz

Prescott, Arizona, October 25th 78.

Dear Mr. Schurz,

It relieved me of some embarrassment to come upon a point here as regard to Governor Hoyt and I send it to you. Will you also tell it to the President. Especially as the Secretary of State for this Territory, Mr. Gosper, will be in Washington soon. And with the franchise of the frontier he told me he was very much opposed to the General's coming here, because "it had been aranged between Gov. Hoyt and himself, that he (Gosper) should succeed him as Governor," that Govt. Hoyt had resolved to give up the governorship because he could make more money by his profession—the law—than in his post, and as his request to be allowed to practice law had been discouraged from Washington he would resign.[1]

But this he thought only his friends knew, and he had not thought
it was known and would be acted upon at Washington—and Mr.
Gosper blamed the governor for telling it too widely, and thereby
making it known to the Executive. This is a demi-mot pour le sage
[half-word to the wise].

Mr. Gosper was good enough to add that he was reconciled since
meeting and knowing us, so the Administration may consider itself
both absolved and approved. Othello says "what's not known is not
there."[2] So at this incredibly aloof place Washington is a myth and not
recognized where it may be an obstacle. As you see in this instance
when calculations were based on the culminating point in place of the
foundations.

There is a great deal to be done here of large and enduring interest.
The General is greatly interested in the subject on which he is making
you a brief report. It cannot be in time for the 1st of November but
it will be of immediate service to Arizona and of great service to the
General officially here, to have it used as you proposed. So that although
it is a little delayed I hope we will find it in the documents you send
in to Congress.

The Indian question is one that comes, literally, home to us.[3] Genl.
Wil[l]cox postponed the outbreak by feeding the Indians but they are
too numerous to depend on one garrison command's supply and all
those supplies carried hundreds of miles over hot plains with infrequent
water stations—ten miles a day and ten cents a pound. It is an ele-
mentary phase of living. But it so seldom chances that minds capable
of seeing what should be done are united in positions to carry out
good ideas that the opportunity should not be lost. Neither yourself
nor the General care one straw for personal-political results of your
Indian policy—the officers here, and the highest in rank and experience
they are, have said to us that they trusted you would remain where
you were to carry out your views about Indians. They, meeting them
under all aspects, and meeting the consequences of bad faith and traders
&c &c &c understand, and their hope is in you. You, the General,
and General Wil[l]cox, could carry out in this Territory the ideal experiment of justice and fairness. When my Father had the General for
his active coadjutor in exploring and opening roads to the Pacific they
had the Washington inertia, ignorance and routine to contend with.
(The Colonel of the Topographical Bureau, Col. Abert, was honored
by the gift of the geographical medal of Prussia at the same time that

they sent it to Mr. Frémont—then still a Lt. and Bvt. Captain in that Corps). Col. Abert not only never drew up an order for these explorations—my Father and Mr. Frémont did that, and it was copied at the War Dept.—(my Father being too valuable on appropriations to be denied—) but actually Col. Abert countermanded and would have entirely broken up the second journey which resulted in the taking of California,[4] but for my keeping back his orders until it was too late to overtake Mr. Frémont. But the large results remain even if the wrong man was praised. And so it would be if order and security could be put into the Indian matters here.

All the moneyed interests, which are going to be immense here, would combine to keep a good system if it were once in process. Smaller interests would be powerless to regain control—and our government might keep its treaty obligations. English capital and English public opinion too would be a [power?] here to hold order.

I send you this enclosed through Miss Seward as this is a compound sort of P.O. service here. The Post-master being very busy at his "store" and his aid or aids may not be without curiosity. I act on information drawn from the experience of business men here!

Au reste [moreover] we are all well and so far from regrets are very glad to be here—at work—and seeing a clear way to private fortune as well as public usefulness—with help from your side.

Jessie Benton Frémont

ALS (DLC—Carl Schurz Papers).

1. The biographer of Hoyt maintains that President Hayes compelled the governor to yield his post to JCF. Hoyt was offered the governorship of Idaho Territory, but shortly after he declined that post he was appointed to the Supreme Court of the territory of Washington and ultimately became a professor of law at the University of Washington (GOFF, 62-71). Gosper became an ardent foe of the Frémonts.

2. The passage from act 3, sc. 3, l. 343, of Shakespeare's play Othello reads: "Let him not know 't and he's not robb'd at all."

3. By the mid-1870s most Arizona Indians had submitted to reservation life, but a few restless holdouts still watched for the opportunity to escape its confines. From 1874 to 1880, the Mimbreño Apache, Victorio, kept more than 2,000 troops in the field by leading destructive raids against scattered settlements and ranches. In 1878, Geronimo, who had been released from a guardhouse, slipped away with some Chiricahuas to pillage and murder for the next year and a half. Indian hostilities were exacerbated by feuds between agents and the military, graft of government officials, and greed of contractors. In addition, miners invaded reservations to develop mineral lands belonging to the Indians and in some cases succeeded in securing a reduction of the reservations through political channels. Mormon immigrants entered the south-

eastern part of the Apache reservation in the late 1870s and diverted so much water from the Gila River for their agriculture that downstream Apache farmers suffered partial crop failures. In general, throughout the territory, the Indians were sullen, restive, and hungry.

4. It was on the third expedition that California was taken.

To William J. Morton

[Printed letterhead]
Territory of Arizona,
Executive Department
Prescott, Nov. 23, 1878.

Dear Benjamin

I know you think a great many talks with me—sometimes they may take such shape as will bring them before me.

I send you this for *the* scrapbook [no enclosure]. Mine is an uncommonly good school here—the principal[1] a quiet enthusiast who is a born teacher and trained also. But his health failing he came here and from three scholars in his bedroom he has in four years built up this really admirable school—got from the Legislature twenty thousand for the building & fitting, and now the roll call has two hundred pupils. And six years ago the Indians scalped people in sight of these schoolroom windows. Mr. Sherman's health is perfect now—that detail of climate will interest you. Also his sister[2] who has been here but two years is cured of "teachers' bronchitis." I am just splendidly well and ready to take hold of Fortune's wheel and pull it to the place I would have it "stick." We shall get there.

Meantime we are all really well. Frank positively grows fat. Buttons come off his new waistcoats. Lil still has some headache but not the kind that oppressed her at first, while the General has a clean pink-tinged smooth skin, filled out so that fifteen years are off his looks.

You see even with all my work as secretary (and I *do* work!) I found energy to spare for volunteering a "history talk" at the Friday's review of history. I have had three "talks" and my class and myself are each learning and each growing in friendship towards each other. Some of the young men (it is the upper class of about thirty to forty) fairly *toil* that they may earn enough to live in town and go on with study. Some are old enough to vote, and did vote this Fall, but they had no chance before Mr. Sherman came. There is something pathetic to me in this intense striving for what is elevating where so much holds one down. You know how glad I am to join in the lifting process, and to make the dry bones of history take on flesh and color and life—and shew them how after all, the conditions of humanity are all made from the same elements and that pain and sorrow and certainly death come to all. In fact, though I wrap up my moral very thick & sweet, the comforting drop of a certain balance and equal compensation is to be found in the lesson. This is all I am going to write now for this is Saturday and ends a busy week. The last things [we had to write were] large official "safe-guards" to friendly Indian chiefs on which we put the big seal of the horse. The General gave one to an old Chief about ten days ago. Two others came in today "to get the same." Their retinue is sixty souls—some of them women and children. Ah-sa-keet is the name of one chief. Is it not a flowing sound? The General *likes* it all. Goodnight from your affectionate,

JBF.

AL initialed (CU-B—Morton Papers).

1. Vermont-born Moses H. Sherman (1853–1932) had been educated at Oswego (New York) State Normal School, which was a relatively new and then rather revolutionary teacher-training institution advocating the Pestalozzian methods of Object Teaching, something of a forerunner of Progressive Education. He instituted the first graded school in Arizona, drew up the territorial school laws, and selected the lands that were to help provide for the future of the University of Arizona. Sherman had a knack for finance as well as teaching and acquired various pieces of town property in Prescott and also built a hostelry. In the early 1880s he transferred his operations to the Phoenix area, investing heavily in banks, the Phoenix Water Company, and the city rail lines. Eventually, he became convinced that the future lay with Los Angeles, moved there, and became involved in a multitudinous number of projects, including land development, which made him a millionaire several times over. He aided financially a number of institutions and individuals, perhaps even the Frémonts (HENDRICKS).

2. Lucy Sherman, who died at age ninety-one in 1942, would marry Eli P. Clark, who became associated with her brother in building the Los Angeles electric street railway system.

To Horatio Nelson Rust

Prescott, Arizona, Jany. 10, '79.

My dear Mr. Rust,

My daughter wrote explaining why your valuable box of Indian curiosities had not been opened until now when it reached us in San

Francisco. I could do no more than send you the line of acknowledgement of its arrival. But I had no idea of the value of its contents until now. I had not known our Indians had such decided idols in those you send me.

The one with arms turned upward—a female figure—is Asiatic in model and is the regular accepted type of the old Mother Earth of bountiful nature. And how aquiline all the features are! They are temporarily on shelves but will soon be in a glazed cabinet. To wish is not to have in this remote region and one waits their turn at the cabinet makers, although we are wonderfully comfortable and even elegant here.

I have been surprised and most agreeably so at the completeness of modern life up here in spite of remoteness and the difficulties of transportation of which you can gain some idea from the General's report to the government and his message to the Legislature, which I send you.

Here we are in the midst of evidences of a long past and crowded population. Remains of huge castles are used as sheep corrals—walls that have stood for centuries are taken down to build stone houses and the pottery is every where. I have begun an authentic collection which I shall be very happy to send you parts of. Just now the winter snows block our intended personal explorings but we are glad of the snows for that brings a great mining year. Thanking you very much for your beautiful and valuable collection and asking you to thank your daughter for the charming Indian bead work which is in such good, good taste of color, I am very sincerely yours,

Jessie B. Frémont

ALS (CSmH). The archeological interests of former Massachusettsan and abolitionist Horatio Nelson Rust (1828–1906) had led him to investigate Indian antiquities. He settled in Pasadena in 1881, engaged in the nursery business, and from 1890 to 1892 served as the U.S. Indian agent to the Mission Indians of Southern California.

To John Franklin Spalding

[c. Mar. 1879]

Dear Bishop Spalding:

Every one answers with willingness, and many with grateful eagerness, to the idea of an Episcopal church here. I enclose you a bit from a local paper, which sums up, in its own coarse way, the present condition.[1] The people here of the Roman Catholic faith have notified their clergyman that he does not suit them, and applied for a better. That, and the recent purchase of one of the best houses for a convent-school, show they are active, and understand the coming phase is not to be one of neglect and "let-alone," such as has prevailed here in Church matters.

You ask about the "undoubted permanence" of places. To this no answer could be made while the Legislature still sat. Tucson and this place have been the point of contention, and, as you know, they have alternately moved and removed and re-removed the capital. But things are quiet now until two years hence, as the Legislature fortunately meets only that often. Before the next meeting the railroads now building and to be built will have so increased and altered the nature of the population, and the development of mining regions decided values in location, that a fairer decision can be made as to the chief town. It was much trouble to ward off the change at present, but it was done. Then came up an unexpected order of reservation of about all the best lands, the best-watered certainly in the Territory, and the pretensions of Phoenix, the chief town of the locality, were, for the time, effectually laid aside, as it is now included in an Indian reservation.

Tucson is so well started and grounded in its Mexican trade, and will now have the South Pacific Railroad trade also, that it holds itself as the proper place. It is certainly a permanent town, and there will go naturally the first wave of railroad travel. This place, however, has a fresh and invigorating climate, and its mining neighborhood is claimed to be as good and perhaps of a more durable nature than that to the South. As you know, this makes the population. For myself, I want so much to have the Church here, it would be such a stay and relief to be able to hear the Service again, that I am afraid of over-stating the value of this town's prospects. And you will have to accept me and my want of logical information in place of the General's writing, for there was no breathing-time during the work of the Legislature, and immediately after its adjournment he had to leave for Washington, asking me to write and give you such information as he could gather.[2]

In brief, it about amounts to this: "A good Clergyman," meaning (to them) a good man, whose example bears out this teaching; a good mind, and, what they quite value here, good gentlemanly habits — such a man would command respect and support. An unfortunately rude young man did a great deal of mischief lately by forgetting St. Paul's maxim to be all things to all men, and telling a full congregation of the evils he had noticed among them. The people left the church in a body. You know, one must get the good will of people, and establish a habit of confidence in good will in return, before going the length of harsh public reprimand. The instinct of a well-bred man would have avoided this.

They are an odd people here, with an unusual number of men of education and of previous ease of life, who have come here to retrieve fortune. These, with their families, and the fort, with its officers and their families, give the key-note to a very different and a higher order of society than one could look for in a far-off frontier mining town. Just now the town is going through a depressing transition, and it shudders to find itself threatened with all the life and competiton of railroad transportation. By May we, here in Prescott, shall be only twenty-two hours from the terminus, Maricopa Wells. That means a great loss of business to the local merchants here, until the cross railroad is built connecting us with the Southern Pacific. So they are indisposed to any new expense. But if such a Clergyman as you can see would be a genuine Missionary of the Church militant comes here, he will make roots, and there will always be enough of us to keep him from feeling the beginning too heavy.

The school here is uncommonly good. The principal is a manly, Christian young man, as well as an enthusiast in his vocation: and the scholars of the older class are the typical American young people, to whom education is a right as well as an advantage. It has been a nucleus for good ideas and morals.

The place is nearly six thousand feet up, and the air is trying to many. "Strangers may be known by the blood-spots on their hand-kerchiefs," as Bayard Taylor said of Colorado.[3] But we are all well here, though the blood-spots do come sometimes. I question whether the battle-fields of life can be selected for their freedom from blood-stains, and this is neither easy nor pleasant duty for a man of sensibility and refinement to come to; and yet such a man can do more by his mere living and presence than the clearest head, unaided by such safeguards against wounding feeling or repelling a dawn of conscience.

In short, it is not only Missionary work, but representative Missionary work, that is needed here to begin. It would secure all that is genuine here, and soon the needed church and church endowments would follow. That much I feel warranted in saying; and with regrets that I cannot give you better and more compact information, I am, with great respect and regard, Sincerely yours,

Jessie Benton Frémont

Printed, *Spirit of Missions,* 54 (June 1879): 220–21. John Franklin Spalding (1828–1902) was missionary bishop of Colorado and Wyoming, with oversight of Arizona and New Mexico.

1. *Spirit of Missions* printed the contents of the article, which maintained that "the Churches seem to have given Arizona up to the devil," and predicted that "if they don't send some one soon, like 'the heathen in his blindness,' we shall all 'bow down to wood and stone.' " In St. Louis in Nov. 1880, after JBF had left Arizona, George K. Dunlop was consecrated bishop of Arizona and New Mexico. When he arrived in his diocese the following spring, he found no churches, no property, and only a handful of communicants.

2. JCF had left for Washington on Feb. 25, 1879, ostensibly to lobby for the recall of the presidential order that would resettle friendly Pima Indians from the Casa Grande Valley into the nearby Salt River Valley. White settlers upstream had diverted irrigation water that these Indians needed to feed themselves. The proposed resettlement, however, was very unpopular, since it would enlarge the Gila River Indian reservation and put the Pimas in the rich valley whose heart is now the city of Phoenix. The territorial legislature voted $2,000 for JCF's expenses, and he was successful in pleading the settlers' case with the federal authorities.

3. With respect to the altitude of Black Hawk and Central City, the Frémonts' old friend, Bayard Taylor, had noted that nosebleed "is a common complaint with newcomers, and the old settlers can always recognize such by their bloody pocket-hankerchiefs" (*Colorado: A Summer Trip* [1867], p. 57).

To Edward F. Beale

Prescott, Arizona
April 30th '79.

Dear Mr. Beale

Did you ever get a long letter from me—illustrated by my own remarkable pen sketches of mule teams and such—written about the end of October? Since the General has been in New York I learn some few to whom I wrote then did not get the letters—also some valuable mining letters from the General did not reach New York—and answers to other letters of his, answers of first importance were never received here. While telegrams concerning these came through. There have been no mail robberies since January I think as Genl. Willcox had the worst neighborhood guarded after an officer was robbed of govt. moneys when going to Yuma. But I begin to think from never hearing from you or Emily[1] that some of my letters must have been in the cut mail bags. And the General writes me he did not find you at home. Your four-leaved clovers brought good luck. I am sure before this the General must have succeeded in seeing you and you will know much from him personally.

I shall be sorry if my long letter never reached you for our eight days up from Yuma with the camps, the sunrise starts the searching for water and all the care for the mules and—oh the fearful bits of road at times!—were like the '49 time when Job and Picayune and the Indians' horses made my four in hand and you were whip and the General outrider—only no trees, no grass, no sweet sea winds, no fresh food—no comfortable old farms.[2] Major Lord had everything ready for us at Yuma and we were as comfortable as forethought and kind good will could make us. But climate and vegetation need more than that to influence them.

The newspapers say you are to put a colony on the Tejon—and from letters I learn Mamie is in Washington—well, "looking soft and content." That sounds well. I hope you are all well—Emily? Her pale blue and white gown that evening we dined with you gave her vague pre-Raphaelite effects. Tell her blue coupeés and white roses are things of memory only here—not a flower grows willingly here for forty to sixty degrees difference from day to night shock all their little lives out. But it is underground that the bouquet is to be found.

The girls will be amused to know that old Mary who came out with us is considered "fine looking" here (by herself also). We are charmed with our Chinese servants as we chanced on really good ones—altogether we are really comfortable and as Genl. Sherman will have told you this is an extraordinary little town for society. And the Fort has its pleasant people—among them Col. and Mrs. Biddle[3]—he is from Philadelphia, handsome and pleasant of the Biddle family.

When it grows hot—it is only 84° to 94° now—we shall retreat to Sta. Monica. Maybe if you are out we may meet up there? Anyway you shall know when the four-leaved clovers have done a finished work—unless the General can tell you before he returns. But that would be too quick. With remembrances to all—especially the girls. Yours,

Jessie B. Frémont

ALS (DLC—Beale Papers)

1. Beale's daughter Emily, with her quips and breezy manners, inspired the character of Victoria Dare in Henry Adams's novel *Democracy* (G. THOMPSON, 219). Adams and Beale were Lafayette Square neighbors. Emily (d. 1912) married wealthy John Roll McLean, owner of the Washington *Post* and the Washington Gas Light Company. Her older sister Mary (d. 1925), whom JBF calls "Mamie," married George Bahkmeteff of the Russian diplomatic corps. He was ambassador to the United States during the last five years of Czar Nicholas's reign.
2. JBF refers to a summer camping trip the Frémonts and Beale made between Monterey and San Francisco in a little carriage that had been built for her on the East Coast. They stopped at various ranches to visit old Californians, since JCF, in a subtle way, was campaigning for political office. Before coming to Arizona, JBF had recorded the memories of that pleasant time in *A Year of American Travel.*
3. Col. James Biddle (1832–1910) became involved in the mining claims of the Frémonts. On Oct. 28, 1879, he and Frank registered a claim to the Green Crystal, three-eighths mile northeast of Eureka, and two weeks later, he and JCF filed a claim on the Copper King. Both were in the Verde District (Yavapai County, Mines, 8: 303–4, 244–45). Ironically all three men had lost their claims before an important strike was made on the neighboring Eureka claim. A vein of rich copper ore, fifty-six feet wide, was discovered to run directly under the undeveloped Copper King. This later became the great Jerome operation, which was subsequently acquired by William A. Clark of Montana and still later was purchased by the Phelps Dodge Corporation (FIREMAN, 15).

The Colonel's wife, Ellen McGowan Biddle, devoted a great deal of space to Prescott in her *Reminiscences of a Soldier's Wife* (1907), but, strangely, did not mention the Frémonts.

To Richard C. Drum

Prescott, Arizona Territory.
May 6th '79.

My dear Sir

The class of '79 will soon be coming to you for vacancies and I write to remind you that the 3d vacancy after the class of '78 was allotted, was to be given to my son Frank. His health is absolutely good now and there are conditions of public affairs which make me absolutely agree with his intention to return to the army.[1]

I have written to Col. Rogers[2] asking him to see no hitch or delay comes to the confirmation of this appointment and I hope you will find it quite in your power to reach the promised vacancy as the six or eight months you thought needed are now past. The General intended seeing you in regard to this but as it is a matter I have at heart I give it my personal care also and hope to hear at an early day favorably from you. Sincerely yours,

Jessie Benton Frémont

ALS (DNA-94, Francis P. Fremont appointment file, 4922–ACP 1877). Col. Richard C. Drum (1825–1909) was assistant adjutant general.

1. In the fall of 1877, JBF had begun contacting politicians and military officials requesting that they use their influence to obtain an army commission for Frank. For example, see JBF to Nathaniel Banks, Nov. 2, 1877, with its enclosure to the secretary of war (DNA-94, Francis Preston Frémont appointment file, 4922–ACP 1877).

2. Rogers was President Hayes's private secretary. See JBF to Rogers, Nov. 9, 1879, below.

To Nelly Haskell Browne

Prescott June 29 [1879].

Dear Nell

A new lot of mail robbers have been successfully taking the mail on the new route. Judge Silent[1] had written three especially important and *private!* letters by that mail of the 20th. He has just sentenced a mail robber to ten years in the Yuma Penitentiary—fancy that in that climate! We asked him what he would do to this man if he were caught—I rather think however he would be thought "too" delicate for transportation like certain fruits, and get consumed on the spot. I think they got a letter from me to you. The babies on the children's birthday card have so much that recalls your boys that I wrote again of the pleasure they gave me. You are all around us in your needlework and your photographs. And now came Maida & Sheila[2] to complete the family (nothing at all of my Sally[3]—I have everything else—the old tintype of her is blurred). I am very glad GB was able to join them, it will add so much to their pleasure and please Mr. Browne and do him good. Your letter gives us glimpses of Betty. Judge Silent told us one thing kept impressing itself agreeably on him in New York and still more so in Boston—the fresh *clean* faces of the girls & women[4]— it is the rule to powder & daub in San Francisco, up here too—it is quite funny to see that smeared smooth white face, & red wrists emerging from one button pale gloves. But the crème de lis is sure to be on. Then a lot of crimped bang. Between the two a clean face and tidy hair are the exception so the judge was charmed with the absence of paste. Betty was in for it like everyone else—has she given it up? I want you to write me about her as you would talk to me. I know my sister will hate to leave St. Louis and our family there and all the large dignity of a wealthy and old position. But how to reconcile this being in New York with Major Hughes's duties? And it takes lots and lots of money to live in New York as Betty has done in San Francisco, with the best people.[5]

Please talk to me about all this as you see it.

We are expecting any hour the telegram to say the General has started. The Judge was very tired by the heat of the last part of the road—we made him eat here and now he is all well again. Chung is a master of the art of delicate and nourishng food—so many varieties of bread! and muffins and all sorts of flour things—and soups that are so light and refreshing and withal inexpensive. Lil is charmed with him. GB would make a big bracket & put him on it for a valuable curiosity. As for Frank he has grown out of his clothes—he is so soundly well now. He is tasting the sweets of well done work now. His answers to the letters sent to his Father vary from a few lines to several pages— sometimes he has mailed as many as nineteen answers in one day*— but it is an average of four or five. Sometimes a body of men with, each, small capital, write a lot of questions. To one such Frank's answer, and the printed statistics sent, have produced a return answer of thanks and their intention to come out in the autumn. The mines are beginning to shew the effect of new good machinery and methods—stock in one which was to be had for fifty cents a share in the winter now easily sells for fifty dollars a share.

We are all so well that we find ourselves taking a healthy interest in all things around us mining & marriages and marketing or whatever turns up.

Frank has written how Mr. Von Schraeder [Schrader][6] caught and killed the seven Indians who had been running off cattle and had killed a farmer. This involves so much—it is such a desperately rocky hiding place sort of a country that this is an immense feat, and is good for all interests. It is a feather in the army cap here and the post have so cordially made us one with them that we are very pleased for them— as well as for the settlers.

Good night dear Nell. I hope the robbers will be kind enough to forward this if they take it.

Did we tell you about our sister of charity who died?[7] And the

* Over three hundred have been answered.

Mother Basil, a french sister who returns tomorrow to Tucson after looking into matters here. A charming and sweet lady.[8] Lil has gone into friendship with one that remains—a Chicago woman—as nice as possible—she has taught for two years among the Papago Indians— she knows *well*, French German and Spanish as well as English. She is only about twenty-eight or thirty and Lil and herself are really good friends.[9] They have the County Hospital here and Lil keeps it in newspapers etc. and in bits of good things for the sick. Sally has a long letter from me with lots of things. I am so glad you and children make one family—squeeze my Jack and Georgie too for me—and always dear Nell the love of your Affectionate,

JBF.

It is midnight & cool—I cut off this bit of paper because it got under the drip of the lamp.

AL initialed (CU-B—Frémont Papers).

1. Charles Silent (1843–1918) was a German born lawyer who enjoyed a fine reputation as a promoter and railroad builder in California before his appointment as one of the three judges to the Arizona territorial bench. He had left his family in San José and resided alone in Prescott; Lily noted that he had a standing invitation to dine with the Frémonts. He literally became JCF's "silent" business partner. Like Moses Sherman, he, too, would prosper and move on to California.

2. The two dogs of the Brownes had belonged originally to the Frémonts. Thor seems to have been the sire of Maida.

3. A reference to Charley Frémont's wife.

4. Silent had gone east with JCF at the end of Feb. 1879 and returned to the territory before the governor.

5. When Maj. Hughes was transferred from San Francisco to St. Louis, his wife Betty and her mother, Jessie's sister Eliza Jones, had followed him. Betty was now on a month's visit to New York (Elizabeth Benton Frémont to Nelly Haskell Browne, Feb. 24, May 27, 1879, CU-B—Frémont Papers).

6. Frederick Von Schrader (1851–1916) of the Twelfth Infantry had trapped a remnant of Apaches in Tonto Basin, sparing only the life of a woman (Report of Gen. O. B. Willcox to the Assistant Adjutant General, Military Division of the Pacific, Presidio of San Francisco, as printed in Prescott *Daily Arizona Miner*, Nov. 19, 1879).

7. The "Sisters of Charity" were the Sisters of St. Joseph of Carondelet from the St. Louis House, who had come to Tucson in 1870, 1874, and 1876. Three—Mary Martha Dunne, Mary Rose Dorna (sometimes given as Doran), and M. John Berchmans Hartrich (the sister whose death occurred on June 14) had been sent to Prescott in 1878 to open St. Joseph's Hospital for miners (DOUGHERTY, 322).

Sister John, born in 1846 in Ste. Marie, Ill., had professed her vows on Sept. 8, 1868, and had served as superior at St. Joseph's Convent in Waterloo, Ill., from 1871 until 1876 when she came to Arizona with Mother Mary Basil Morris and Sisters Mary Rose Dorna and Eutichiana Piccini. A diary of that fifty-two day journey may be found in AMES.

8. Mother Basil had taken her final vows in 1861 in Moutiers, France, the year she came to America. She was provincial superior at Tucson when St. Mary's Hospital opened but was transferred in 1881 to Georgetown, Colo., where she became superior at St. Joseph Hospital (Archivist Sister Patricia J. Kelly, CSJ, of St. Joseph Carondelet, St. Louis, May 4, 1988, to Mary Lee Spence).

9. The sister with teaching experience among the Papago Indians was Mary Martha Dunne, who with two other sisters had traveled to Arizona with Bishop Salpointe, arriving in Tucson on Jan. 27, 1874. The Sisters of St. Joseph staffed the Papago Indian School at San Xavier only between 1873 and 1876, which rules out Sister Mary Rose Dorna (or Doran) as the teacher with two years of experience among the Papagos, since she did not arrive in the territory until 1876. For the initial hiring of the sisters, see R. A. Wilbur to John A. Tonner, June 30, 1873, DNA-75, Arizona Superintendency; and FLICK.

Sister Monica Corrigan (née Annie Taggert), who left an account of her trek to Arizona in 1870 with six other sisters, is prominently associated with Prescott and is mentioned by Lily Frémont in her letters and in her *Recollections*. She came to Prescott after the death of M. John Berchmans Hartrich (AMES; Prescott *Weekly Miner*, Sept. 6, 1879; information from Sister Alberta Cammack, Archivist, St. Mary's Hospital, Tucson).

To Nelly Haskell Browne

[Printed letterhead]
Territory of Arizona,
Executive Department
Prescott, Oct. 3d 1879.

Dear Nell

The General has gone to hunt an "equivalent" in the Dictionary. This gives me time to write a bit on my own account. We are very busy these days. The Report for the Government is getting written in the intervals of going to & fro to examine mines. Mr. Maynard is quite delightful as well as a man of such eminence in his profession that it is a pleasure to the General to talk with him.[1] He and Judge Silent meet up with us every day at our noon breakfast and at dinner and it is a great refreshment to Lil & I to have them as well as the General and Frank. We had a pretty solitary pull of it the six months of the General's absence—but all's well that ends well. Twelve big mines have been examined. They go off, wheels or horseback—cooked rations in small quantity, and such fare as the miners have while at the mines—"beans & things." If it is known they are coming "canned things" are got ready. Chung makes such good Maryland biscuit, that with them & potted ham & turkey etc. (and a canteen of fresh water, and some good apples) they get on well. Add to these small "turnovers" of different fruit pies. A convenient form to handle and keeps in the moisture of the contents (note for dry climate).

October 4. 11:30.

I will send this as it is. I get so tired writing that I can't see when to write good letters. At 7, the General and I have had our tea & are pegging away here until 11:30 when Mary clamors for her table. Then I do my hair & refresh for breakfast, which is a pleasant resting time. Then more work & people, &c. &c.

Jack is a darling—what lovely dimpled hands. The mean man cut off his right hand—save one full impression. We were so sorry for Hunt's death. How proud GB must have been of the babies on the Wedding Tour. I am glad for every pleasure that comes into your life. Tell Sally this mg's mail brought me the "log of the Cactus—Sept. 22" She is a dear child.

Give her my love and tell her I will write when I am my own owner. Now I am J.C.F.'s pen. Your loving,

Marraine

ALS (CU-B—Frémont Papers).

1. Earlier in the year, while in the East, JCF had begun organizing a syndicate to acquire and develop a group of twenty mining claims in Arizona. John Hoey and J. C. Babcock of Adams Express Company and their friends were interested. So also were Messrs. M. & S. Sternberger and their associates. The contract was to depend upon the reports of the experts sent out by the two parties. Tentatively, the capital was put at $10,000,000 represented by one million shares.

As examining expert, the Adams Express group chose Freiburg-trained George W. Maynard, an experienced mining engineer who was a friend and neighbor of Jack Howard and Rossiter Raymond in Brooklyn. Messrs. M. & S. Sternberger sent out R. Einhorn, likewise educated at Freiburg. Initially, both engineers dined with the territorial governor's family. Later the Frémonts came to view R. Einhorn as conspiring against their interests (JCF to Rogers, July 31, 1879, CU-B—Rogers Papers, and Elizabeth Benton Frémont to Nelly Browne, Sept. 7, 1879, CU-B—Frémont Papers; JBF to Rogers, Dec. 16 [1879], below).

To William J. Morton

[Printed letterhead]
Territory of Arizona,
Executive Department
Prescott, October 13th 1879.

Dear Dr. Morton

I am leaving here Thursday to go direct to New York with only a break of two days at San Francisco. Will you not be pleased to see me? and to hear my budget? I want a town address for telegrams and letters (I shall have a perch with my children at Staten Island) and we thought we would take permission to make it 33 E. 33d until I could settle for a town address. I shall be very busy and very useful and we think we have our foundation solid enough to see a home not far ahead.

It's hard to leave the General and Lil. But he will be busy and moving about and she says she is glad to be useful.

I am in a crowding hurry and interrupted all the time—until the 28th 29th or 30th. Affectionately your

JBF.

AL initialed (CU-B—Morton Papers). The primary reason for JBF's sudden departure from Prescott was JCF's need to have her in New York as his agent in the hawking of mining properties and as his personal lobbyist in Washington while he tended affairs in the territory.

To William K. Rogers

New Brighton Staten Island
Sunday, 9th Novr. [1879]

Dear Colonel Rogers

I reached here Tuesday but met a snowfall which astonished my throat and lungs and I am only today out of bed again.

I had intended going tomorrow to Washington as there are several things I would rather tell than write you. I will not delay however telling you of a fortunate turn for us, personally, which ends many years of care. The Syndicate[1] moves slowly but this is outside *and quite concluded.*[2]

Of some other matters I have that to shew you which makes the
General's letter to you about a thwarting official clear, and shews how
needed it is to replace him with one who acts, at least without malice
and treachery.[3]

I will either be in Washington very soon or write you fully—at
present I am thoroughly bruised and worn by my long journey and
the many changes in temperature and elevation—varying from 350
feet below the sea level to 8000 feet above—from desert sun and
sands to the snows at Sherman, and here the wet snow of this coast.
But "alls well that ends well" and I know it will please the President
when I tell him of my fortune restored—that magnolia was a fair
omen.[4]

Everything has turned into our working combination and if the
General had a decently fair man as his second in position all would
be complete. But this one thwarted his work in the most underhand
ways and in all sorts of ways makes trouble, and loss. Sincerely yours,

Jessie Benton Frémont

ALS (CU-B—Rogers Papers). Ohio-born William King Rogers (1828–93) had
been President Hayes's law partner and intimate friend before becoming his private
secretary. He did not get on well with either the press or the public, and Hayes
later noted that Rogers was "easily duped; trusts all men who profess friendship,"
and lacked "a sense of duty and responsibility" (HOOGENBOOM, 58). Rogers was
to have 10,000 shares in the syndicate that was being formulated.

1. For information on the syndicate, see JBF to Nelly Browne, Oct. 3, 1879, above.
2. This is a reference to the Silver Prince, which had been one of the mines examined
for the Syndicate but now in the hands of the Frémonts, Judge Silent, and the Shillabers
of San Francisco. JBF later explained: "Mr. Maynard examined this mine and reported
it, by telegraph, to the Syndicate as the richest mine he had ever examined, or seen.
They would not take it because it could only be had for cash, and their plan only
intended payment after his return and the full counsel & consent of the Syndicate. So
it lapsed, and Judge Silent and the General got the refusal for thirty days" (to Rogers,
Nov. 19, 1879, CU-B—Rogers Papers). For the Shillabers' connection with the mine,
see Andrew Curtin et al. to Cynthia H. Shillaber, Nov. 17, 1879, and Cynthia H.
Shillaber to Abram S. Hewitt, Jan. 5 and 6, 1880, in Yavapai County, Ariz., Recorder's
Office, Book 12 of Deeds, pp. 227–34.
3. JCF had written Rogers, Sept. 3, 1879, about the deficiencies of John J. Gosper,
the territorial secretary (AzTeS—Bert Fireman Collection, Box 3).
4. President Hayes had given JBF a magnolia blossom at the time of JCF's appointment as territorial governor (see JBF to Hayes, Mar. 29 [1880], below).

To William K. Rogers

Everett House, New York City
December 2d. 1879.
Private

Dear Colonel Rogers

It is decided the General should be here now to give his own impress to new work which I have been so fortunate as to start.[1]

This includes, among other properties, a mine proving itself to be the richest known in Arizona—in which I am a fourth owner, as my part for having placed it—or rather sold, one fourth for all the money needed to own it.[2] I am most happy and proud that I did this—it at once put independent power as well as fortune back into the General's hands. To work this mine and some others just by it, now bonded *personally* to the General and Judge Silent, requires capital which I am promised will be furnished by a strong House here which is placing English capital in Arizona mines.

I cannot well risk by mail business details—nor can I run down to Washington and see you just now as I wished for I am still warding off bronchitis. But you will see that it is very essential the General should be here himself. And now that the richest of the mines there is *sold & paid for and in our personal possession* the public voice has changed (as it always does with success when one can do without it) to entire approval of all the General may do.

It would best suit his interests to be quite foot loose—but to resign now would give the power next winter when the Legislature meets again, to unknown people and interests. And if he continues there he will prevent and veto any vexatious legislation regarding mines and railroads—both of which make openings for black-mail work in mining country legislatures.

We have everything arranged for the management and development of our own mine—first class mining engineer &c—and I go back early in the Spring. Meantime the General needs permission by telegraph in order to get here in good time to make his own arrangements for his own interests and for friends who have helped him wear through the dark eleventh hour. Dark enough it was! We are neither of us of the class of "friends remembering not."

Will you please have the permission telegraphed direct to Prescott,

A.[rizona] T.[erritory] and be so good as to let me know when it goes off, that I may tell the House here with which I am working. My warm regards to the President.

Jessie Benton Frémont

ALS (CU-B—Rogers Papers).

1. JBF wants JCF to be granted leave from his territorial post so that he might come east again to promote his business interests.

2. JBF is referring to the sale of the Silver Prince Mine and a group of claims surrounding it in the Bradshaw Mountains of Arizona (see JBF to Rogers, Nov. 9 [1879], above). The Frémont name is not in the public records, but JBF wrote Rogers that "the mine as it stands is now owned entirely by Judge Silent, myself and the San Francisco party, who owns one fourth" (Nov. 19, 1879, CU-B—Rogers Papers).

To William K. Rogers

[Dec. 7 (1879)]

Dear Mr. Rogers

I quite understand the obstacle and know that none exists in yours or the President's good will.[1]

The General was back at Prescott & on duty the 23 of *August* not *October*—but that would not affect the present situation.

For how long does this interdict hold good (or bad)? Will the 1st of January begin a new year?

Judge Silent could do almost equally well. Could he have a leave? and when? Pray excuse my applying to you so much but this is a question of great fortunes, and of remarkable advancement to Arizona. I have made one connection here which will—if satisfied with a first investment, now made, introduce over two millions of English capital. And this is calm, business work by personal agency and management of those investing.

No sitting on the nest and looking at the village can equal the work to be done by going to and fro.

I think it will be found of record that Govr. Hoyt left often. And he did absolutely nothing to advance the Territory.

Pray let me know if a leave can be granted Judge Silent? and when? and if the new year begins a fresh time for the General in which he can have a "ticket of leave."

With many thanks to you and the President for your good will and the attention you have given this, I am your friend,

Jessie Benton Frémont

Sunday mg. Dec. 7.

ALS (CU-B—Rogers Papers).

1. JCF had been refused leave as he had already been absent six months from his territorial post.

To William K. Rogers

Dec. 16. 4 P.M. [1879]
Everett House, New York City

Dear Mr. Rogers

Thanks for the trouble you have taken. Fortunately I am having success that goes beyond our hopes, and good friends doing all the real work.

I write now though just to say that I have been informed that Mr. Gosper, Secty. of State for Arizona, has gone to Washington and boasted to my informant that "he had blocked the Genl's work here" and would do him and Judge Silent a mischief in Washington. This with some information given the General early in November, substantiates the fact that the anonymous letters mailed in Prescott up to Oct. 10. and received here by Messrs. Hoey and Babcock were from him.[1]

Mr. Gosper, a man named Pinckham [Pinkham][2] and another named Einhorn planned all this in a room at the Hotel in Prescott, but the stovepipe hole led the sounds to the next room. And the man in it gave notice of all he heard to his lawyer Mr. Churchill[3] who told it to the General—with the man's offer to give evidence publicly if needed.

Mr. Gosper relies on Genl. Garfield[4] and Bishop Simpson![5] They cannot know much of him. I write this asking you to speak of it to Mr. Schurz. Mr. Gosper has told me he "was all right with a man in that Dept. who watched his interests."

You know we have been forbearing about Mr. Gosper. But when it comes to this underhand work I have to ask that whatever he says he may be required to communicate openly for reference to the General, and to Judge Silent—against whom he has a grievance on his divorce matter.[6]

You are very good in all your own overworked state to give me so much time. But I am too necessary here for two weeks yet to leave my post. Otherwise I would come down and give a few days to Mr. Gosper. Will you have me informed if that is desirable? I shall consider silence an answer that I am not needed. Sincerely,

J. B. Frémont

ALS (CU-B—Rogers Papers).

1. John Hoey and J. C. Babcock were associated with Adams Express Company and interested in the syndicate that the Frémonts hoped to put together in the East to work Arizona mines (see JBF to Nelly Browne, Oct. 3, 1879, note 1, above). The main office of Adams Express was at 59 Broadway, New York, and by 1881, perhaps earlier, Hoey was general manager and Babcock treasurer of the company.

2. The Prescott *Daily Arizona Miner,* Oct. 18, 1879, identified George M. Pinkham as the owner of the Lone Star Mine in Mohave. The same newspaper, Nov. 11, 1879, avowed that it had never entertained serious expectations of a purchase by the New York Syndicate of Yavapai mining properties, but thought Pinkham was a blackmailer and had formed with Einhorn an "unholy trinity of malice, ignorance and greed." Additional strictures on Pinkham were made by the pro-Frémont paper on June 21, 1880.

3. Clark Churchill was in legal practice with Thomas Fitch. He later moved to Phoenix and conceived and carried through to completion the great Arizona Canal ("General Clark Churchill of Phoenix," *Southwest Illustrated Magazine,* 1 (June 1895): 113.

4. James Abram Garfield (1831–81), later president of the United States, was currently a member of the House of Representatives.

5. An American Methodist Episcopal bishop, Matthew Simpson (1811–84) had delivered the eulogy at President Lincoln's burial in Springfield, Ill. He was sympathetic to Gosper, a Methodist, and ultimately intervened with President Hayes, also a Methodist, to prevent Gosper's removal as territorial secretary (CLARK, 295).

6. Earlier in 1879, the Arizona Territorial Legislature had passed the Omnibus Divorce bill, which released fifteen couples from the bonds of matrimony, among whom was John Jay Gosper (WAGONER, 60). Why Gosper was unhappy with Judge Silent has not been ascertained unless the judge had earlier refused to entertain a judicial action for divorce.

To William K. Rogers

Private
Everett House, January 8th. 1880.

Dear Colonel Rogers

I give to you and through you to the President, and please until I give you further notice keep this to yourselves, the first announcement of my great success here. Mr. Gosper with his clever cunning had the success treason can have over open work, and broke up the Hoey & Babcock Syndicate. Mr. Babcock reluctantly gave it up.

I would not see them or explain or in any way waste time on people who could be so influenced against the facts as submitted by their own selected expert. To say nothing of the General's opinions.

Now, a new arrangement has been made—the money telegraphed to Prescott to be paid over by the Bank of Arizona on Judge Silent's certificate of title, and more money to follow without stint to meet all the requirements of developing and working this first mine.

And it is not a freaky Company but a one-man power, and that man being Abram S. Hewitt you will see there is no failure in the work this time.[1]

Also two other mines have been arranged for with names equally good but less known to the general public.[2] In all six will be bought— bought by people who can pay cash and who do not have to go to the public first. Some of these will be put into a company after they have been worked so as to prove by actual testing under the Engineer and assayer (first starting out there) that they justify the statements made regarding them. One of these mines, that I have sold part of has no lower than 35 to 60$ the ton. The Comstock made its fortune on 50$ ore. With this is a great quantity at 3 to 400$ the ton, and much at 9, 11, and 1700$ the ton. You can judge the results from such ores worked by skill and abundant capital. It has been a battle here against influences chiefly hidden, but I begin to think well of my clairvoyante instinct for I have upset more than one clever plan by instinct of danger alone—afterwards proved by evidence. But I have won and now I report to the President and yourself—to you two only. For Mr. Hewitt likes to work quietly and I cannot, I do not at all wish even to trumpet success. In a few weeks it will be generally known. No one here but my immediate family and the admirable business friend through whom I acted know at all about this. In fact silence makes safety.

I am coming to Washington very soon—when I am through some needed work on the other mines. I have had acute bronchitis and a touch of pneumonia in the left lung and will be glad to get out of this damp sea air. But if I were well I would have gone down for a day or two to try and secure for Judge Silent the judgeship of Senator Farley's new bill.[3] He deserves it every way. Senator Farley knows him. Judge Silent has helped us get these mines and I have made his fortune also in getting them placed here. I never forget a friend any more than my Father did, and though it is troublesome yet I must punish some enemies as a little example. Will you not ask the President from me to be favorable to Judge Silent's appointment—unless indeed the place is promised?

I have just had a beautiful photograph of my son Frank. Thank you for remembering him. He says Ouray[4] is old & half civilized and wants peace, but the young chiefs are all for war. With remembering friendship, yours,

Jessie Benton Frémont

ALS (CU-B—Rogers Papers).

1. On Jan. 5 and 6, 1880, Cynthia H. Shillaber and her husband Theodore ceded their interests in the Silver Prince to Abram S. Hewitt (1822–1903), the first American manufacturer of steel and a former president of the American Institute of Mining Engineers. Active in the establishment and management of Cooper Union, Hewitt had just completed a service of four years in the U.S. House of Representatives. For the cession, see Yavapai County, Ariz., Records, Book 12 of Deeds, pp. 230–34.

The Silver Prince Mining Company was subsequently incorporated on Apr. 17, 1880, in New York with a capital stock of $2,000,000 divided into 200,000 shares of $10 each (see copy of Articles of Incorporation, AzTeS—Bert Fireman Collection, Box 3).

2. These two mines have not been identified; possibly they were two of the three mines mentioned in JCF's Mar. 10, 1880, letter to Rogers. "Our friends have purchased a cluster of mines in addition to the Silver Prince, the Black Warrior which is a continuation of the Prince and perhaps a richer mine and the Tuscumbia & Tuscarosa all of them showing very high grade ores" (CU-B—Rogers Papers).

3. The bill of Senator James T. Farley (1829–86), a Democrat from California, would reestablish a federal district court for southern California. It was never reported out of the Committee on the Judiciary to which it was referred, and it was not until 1886 that Congress gave back to southern California its district court (*Congressional Record*, 46th Cong., 2d sess., vol. 10:135; COSGRAVE, 63–64).

4. Within a few days of JBF's writing, Ouray (1833–80), designated as "Chief of the Colorado Utes" by white officials, led a delegation to Washington in an attempt to prevent removal of his people from Colorado as the result of an Indian-settler confrontation. Ouray had spent part of his youth with a well-to-do Spanish ranching family near Taos. He died later in 1880 of kidney failure (R. WILSON, 88–91).

To Henry [Altman?]

[Jan. 14, 1880]

Henry [Altman?] Esqre.
92 Broadway

In answer to your question about our old friend "Kit Carson" you can tell the artist that Carson's eyes were of a pale but clear blue—

very steady—kindly, and observing—the right eye always a little contracted—rather by the closing up of the eyelids—as in taking sight.

His hair was hardly "blonde"—rather, a sunburned very pale light
brown.

He had a most expressive face on which was marked the quiet
tenacity of his character as well as his keen observation and great
natural courtesy.

I like to hear of respect being paid to a man who was every way a
fine representative of the best qualities a brave open-air life (given in
its latter part to a noble devotion to his country) could develop in an
originally fine and genuinely American character.

I should like to see the picture when it is ready to shew. Yours truly,

Jessie Benton Frémont
January 14th 1880
Everett House, N. Y.

ALS (UHi). Henry Altman, or Alsman, has not been identified.

To John Greenleaf Whittier

[Jan. 21–22, 1880]

Dear Mr. Whittier

I have just received from the General in Arizona a copy (of a copy)
of the note sent by you to Mr. Merriam of New York who had given
you the authorship of the lines on Recrossing the Rocky Mountains.[1]

Often in these bitter years, colder and harder to wear through than
any snows of nature's sending—in the silence that falls around those
who are struggling with great calamities—I have thought of you and
asked myself whether your own single nature—your poet's insight too
would not make you feel how undeserved were the trials that came
upon the General. Now I know. Otherwise I would not write to thank
you for the words of that note, and to tell you that at last the tide
has turned for us.

To get a great road out of the hands of the General who had mapped
it out over years of explorations, fostered it, put into it his life and
friends and fortune, it was necessary to break him down both in fortune
and name. The evidence of this plan is well known to business people

here and political people in Washington. It was successful—thoroughly as regards our fortune, and for a time the cloud rested on the General's name even. About that time my youngest son, then at West Point had pneumonia, followed by hemorrhages from the lungs. The shadow of death lay over us also. I went with my beautiful [talented?] boy to Nassau—the General took his solitary way across the continent to look after some remaining property we had there and see how to rebuild a home for us all.

On the way, passing those deep chasms in the Sierra where he had struggled for life against cold and hunger he felt suddenly and keenly how much harder was man's ingratitude—for be sure the blow had come from within—from men he had benefitted greatly. The contrast of the old brave life with this state of things—the curiously unfair result of such a life was so clear to him, that at once he wrote me those lines. They came to me, in pencil, shaken a little in the writing by the motion of the train. The railway train crossing the country he had opened up to the coast he had added to his country—and where he had so largely made the difference for free labor over slave-state. We were a continent and part of an ocean apart. It was very uncertain whether even the soft climate of Nassau could keep life in my boy. We could not afford to be together in our mutual need of strength. It was the solitary agony of each of us. I have never known any one so dependent on home for outlet of feelings as the General is. Perhaps because we were so young when our lives came together and I have shared his life so much. This was a de profundis [desperate] cry from him to me.

I sent the lines to Littell without any name, only asking they should publish them where so many noble and comforting words had been read by me for many years. The General knew nothing of this until I gave him the number with the lines in print.

He was very pleased. But his is the most reserved and shy nature I ever met. Not that nor any other beautiful evidence of his inner life would ever be known but to those of us who have been his inner life.

I do not write of this time willingly—it was hard enough to wear through it—but I wanted you to have the background. Now it is all changed.

A great fire here destroyed our property in a Gold & Silver Refinery—or rather the General's interest in the refinery which was to work on a new process at which he had long labored and brought to a paying state. Then, when our ship was burned I said let us go back to the country where you were young and created fortunes for others, as well as yourself—this sets us free—it is not annihilation but a new birth.

So we went out to Arizona. First laying before the President and the Senate such judicial findings and various legal papers as proved "that five years research had failed to shew any but honorable work and motives" on the General's part regarding his railroad. Absolute judicial approval as well as acquittal—this we insisted should be read and understood when the General's name went before the jury of his peers, the U.S. Senate and the result was a unanimous confirmation.

There the General knew that his long experience of mines would bring him chances of fortune.

I have had the great happiness of succeeding in selling here a part of a mine we have proved to be of unusual value. It will be worked as a private property, the one buying into it here making only one of four owners. All in harmony with each other, and two having great wealth. This of itself is enough property. But we have more to dispose of and it is certain that nothing succeeds like success.

My dear boy has so completely regained his health that he is now a manly robust young officer—doing duty heartily and with enjoyment in Montana—the thermometer from 20° to 40° degrees below zero. Moose hunting, deer and other game. You see we were spared the grief of a broken household.

Your letter was written Christmas day. That day I was struggling against pneumonia and my physician had the disadvantage of acute bronchitis already loading my chest to fight against. But I had done my work here and the family was again independent—and so I was like a victorious chief after battle. Now I am quite well. The General, and my daughter who is with him in Prescott, Arizona are being renewed in that mountain-pine air. In fact, it is well with us.

They were so touched by your few words that they sent them copied to me.

It is a long time since you saw us but you are not of the forgetting kind. And you are among those I would not have think unfairly of my great and noble husband. More great in his silent acceptance of undeserved calamity than in the days men praised him for other endurance and other brave work.

I know you will quite understand and excuse this long personal letter. I do not feel the General is "personal" only. His good name is part of the country's record. To him that hath shall be given and I am already in the fair way to have more than one injustice redressed.

Thursday 22d

I wrote this yesterday (the General's birthday) in my first pleasure at your friendly words—then I thought it was putting too much of ourselves out to you. One of the clever and often true sayings of clever frenchmen is "Beware of your first impulse for it is generally good." I think I will revert to the first impulse and send this.

And you must not trouble yourself to answer except to let me know it *was* best to follow the first impulse. Sincerely yours,

Jessie Benton Frémont

Everett House, New York City,
Union Square, North.

ALS (MH).

1. See JBF to Black, Feb. 21 [1875], note 1, above.

To Rutherford B. Hayes

Easter Monday [Mar. 29, 1880]

My dear Mr. Hayes

You will not have forgotten I am sure the magnolia blossom you gave me—nearly two years ago—nor have I forgotten the good feeling for the General with which you added your good wishes.

It has proved indeed a fair omen for us, and following a revived old Italian fashion, I have had this "memorial platter" painted to keep you in mind that *we remember.*

It would have been more artistic to have the ground work a rich red—but red is the color of war and passion while blue is peace. The mixture of blue and red makes purple which is the emblem of struggle— and as violets are my flower and one must be in some sort or other of effort and unrest until we reach Heaven's blue I put my flowers by your magnolia flower. You see the blue is already predominating in them over the purple, for I think we are nearing peace in our home.

And when you notice the platter which I hope you will keep by you, remember it is to your appreciation of the General that we owe this return to peace—via Arizona it is true but our very long lane had its turning and no road is too hard or too long which leads to one's aim.

Very sincerely yours, and Mrs. Hayes's friend,

Jessie Benton Frémont

Bennett[1] feels his reputation as the South Kensington artist, impaired by the obscuring of the inscription, but I would not let him have another fortnight to prepare a new platter. I make this explanation for his professional pride.

The inscription should read

"President Hayes from Mrs. Frémont. June 8. '79"[2]

Monday evg.
106 East 25th Street

ALS (OFH).

1. John Bennett was associated with Joseph White in a china and earthenware decorating business at 18 White Street (between Church Street and West Broadway) in New York City.
2. The date should read "1878." JBF was in Arizona on June 8, 1879, and it would have been impossible for President Hayes to give her a magnolia. JCF's appointment as territorial governor of Arizona came on June 8, 1878.

To William K. Rogers

[July 10, 1880]

Dear Colonel Rogers

As you took so much time and trouble to get justice done Judge Silent, I send you some of the expressions of joy the success has caused in our mountain top. My daughter's letters made such a frontier-picture I thought perhaps it would interest the President to hear parts of them, as well as that really well summed up article "A Great Victory" in the paper I enclose.

Campbell[1] was entirely left out in the Convention—not getting one vote. "Grant Oury" being the new nominee for delegate.[2]

Our last despatch, sent through last night says "the Judge recovering."[3] But he had a fearfully prolonged mental strain. And he has cultivated as well as natural sensitivities—and has been aggrieved in every way. But we hope now he will regain strength from the affectionate friendship this trial has drawn out to him from all classes. "There is a vast deal of vital air in loving words" [Walter Savage] Landor says.

My Frank says with enough money and quinine a man can be the arbiter of his own destinies—I would add a third—affection. Sincerely yours,

Jessie Benton Frémont
Everett House July 10th

I told you those were *sincere* people out there—not a sham among them. What they say and do they mean.

ALS (CU-B—Rogers Papers). Enclosed was a clipping from the Prescott *Weekly Arizona Democrat,* June 25, 1880, with a mark by the column, "A Great Victory."

1. The Arizona territorial delegate to Congress, John G. Campbell (1827-1901), had attempted to have Silent removed as justice because of his business activities. Campbell was also antagonistic toward JCF.
2. Granville H. Oury (1825-91) had been in Arizona since 1856 and very active in politics, serving in various county and territorial offices (WAGONER, 81, 89, 91).
3. JBF had written Nelly Browne that Judge Silent had been dangerously ill—a combination of Brights' disease and strain. She herself had been so upset by his condition that she had taken *"the whole of* GB's good brandy—and it was very comforting" ([Apr.] 14 [1880], CU-B—Frémont Papers).

To William K. Rogers

[July 16, 1880]

Dear Colonel Rogers

You will remember I told you of the Consul at Guaymas (Sonora) Mr. Willard.[1] He has been ten or twelve years there, well liked and making harmony in many knotty cases—and now that the long exile is about ending and rapid communication about to make Guaymas a good post Mr. Willard's place is about to be asked for—for no reason except that it is a good one now and wanted, I am told, for an employee of the Atchison & Topeka road. One shall reap what another has sown, but sometimes this injustice can be prevented by knowing it in time, so as Mr. Willard wants to stay and reap the results of his long knowledge of local values now they *are* values, and as he has been especially useful and friendly to the General out there, we put him in your friendly care in case a new consul to Guaymas is asked for. With Mariscal[2] he was entirely friendly.

You see one good turn deserves another as the woman said when she asked for a load of hay because a cow had been given to her. You were good and successful for our friend Judge Silent, and now put in the hay for Mr. Willard! (This style of argument belongs rather to the Lincoln era, but it said itself). Sincerely yours,

Jessie B. Frémont
July 16th, Everett House

ALS (CU-B—Rogers Papers).

1. A native of Pennsylvania, Alexander Willard was living in California when he was appointed consul at Guaymas. He was helping JCF obtain coal property in Mexico, and a year after JBF's letter, he was still listed as consul, but it is impossible to say if she had any influence in his retention.
2. Ignacio Mariscal (1829–1910) had been Mexico's minister to the United States.

To William K. Rogers

[Aug. 1880]

Dear Mr. Rogers

Together with the letter already sent you this will explain, very briefly—but I fear to intrude too far on the President's time—why the General has to be here. It is so good for the Territory to have him over its mines and helping with its Indians as he has done (and we don't want them to be coaxed into fighting by the people who want war contracts and so damage mining) that for a little longer he ought to remain Governor. Otherwise it is hampering. But let him come and talk it over with the President. It is quite another post now from when we went out—and will only be given over on consultation and quietly—if he finds he cannot hold it consistently with his interests. But as I explained, he can be of reliable value next legislature (next January—'81). Mines in Arizona have at last made successful head against the Colorado people here. Mine is in first class hands. I would say whose, but for future work they prefer not yet appearing as taking any part in mining work.

I hope this will suffice to explain the real need of a leave by telegraph. Very sincerely yours,

Jessie Benton Frémont

You are very kind to take the trouble of the explanation—of course I comprehend but I had not thought of the official part. See the disadvantage of having grown up to grant rather than ask, but to this President asking is not hard.

May I have a line to say "Done."

ALS (CU-B—Rogers Papers).

To William K. Rogers

personal
Saturday, August 21st [1880]
Everett House

Dear Col. Rogers

I was very sorry to learn you had had that wearing low fever. You ought to come into sharp sea air if you had to be carried on a litter. You can't get rid of fever in Washington especially at the West End.

We see the President starts next week for the Pacific Coast. The General wishes him to know why he is still here. To go off would have been to leave uncompleted the large mining consolidation—delayed by the work against Judge Silent which was taken advantage of to make unreasonable demands. Everything has been completed now— the last part, the adding a mill (*not* the Peck)[1] only ended Thursday. And *for some local advantages* that is not made public yet.

Also the General has been asked to stay and assist in some political meetings about to take place here.

In Prescott, the best people are more than satisfied with his being here for it is sending a stream of ready money through there and giving value to all mining properties.

But some other representations may be made to Washington, in fact Mr. Delegate Campbell has gone to Washington to do all he can to have the General "removed for non-residence." The General wishes to know if the President intends going into Arizona? And if the President wishes he should drop matters here and go out at once, or would he approve of a little longer stay to complete other large work now nearly concluded.

One of these the General would prefer telling you of—today the papers are to be signed giving him the control. All previous examinations are satisfactorily ended.

Another, requiring but brief work now, is a body of land, 260,000 (two hundred & sixty thousand acres) near the Arizona line—S.E.— on the line of the R R. This morning is given to inspecting the maps & titles. These are said to be quite clear and final. And only a small sum now in cash is required—and a moderate amount altogether.[2] About this great property—(mines, cattle ranches in operation &c) the General wants very much to see you.

After going into the rough of things in Arizona, it would be hard not to have the use of the position now it is so changed in value. At the same time, the General feels he cannot leave these certain and immense openings to fortune. But I hope the President will see it as you would and accord his consent to delay. Sincerely yours,

Jessie B. Frémont

ALS (CU-B—Rogers Papers).

1. The Peck mine and mill were within a half mile of the Silver Prince and had been worked with great success until 1878, when operations ceased owing to legal controversies (Bureau of the Mint, *Report of the Director of the Mint Upon the Production of the Precious Metals in the United States* [for 1881] [Washington, 1882]:259).

2. JCF had written Rogers that "they," meaning himself, Rogers, Judge Silent, and James Blaine could control the "whole for a sum ranging from one hundred to a hundred and fifty thousand dollars. As a first step, we secure one hundred square miles for ten thousand dollars" (n. d., CU-B—Rogers Papers). This would involve the acquisition of the 18,000-acre San Rafael del Valle rancho, which extended to the town of Charleston (discontinued in 1888) and also surrounded the town of Hereford. It included coal as well as gold and silver mines, and by using the Atchison and Topeka Railroad, which ran nearby, they could supply that line as well as the Southern Pacific Railroad and all of southern Arizona with coal. He warned that Collis P. Huntington was already interested in the coal.

To Rutherford B. Hayes

"Wendover" near Sing Sing, N. Y.
July 7th [1881]

Dear Mr. Hayes

Col Rogers has I rather think in the press of his crowding business forgotten to write to you for a letter we value as part of the family record, and which he says was by mistake in the collection of such letters you took home with you. Will you take the trouble to look it up and send it to me here?

It is from the late Senator Chandler[1] of Michigan and records the fact that at a time when the General's attitude was making a difference against the success of the election (the second, in '64) of Mr. Lincoln. He Mr. Chandler together with Mr. Wade and Mr. Henry Winter Davis[2] came to Mr. Frémont and put before him the peril into which his continuing as a candidate put the success of our party. They were empowered to offer any terms in return for his withdrawing his name — among others the Blairs were not to be in any political position &c.

The General has as everyone knows a longer score of cruel wrongs than could be wiped out by later acts of that administration — but when he saw it as Mr. Chandler and Mr. Wade did, he not only withdrew his name but utterly refused any appointments patronage or retaliation. I think Mr. Chandler uses the words "in a critical moment your act was vital to the safety of the party."[3]

You see why we value this letter. It is so much to us that I risk giving you some trouble to find it for me. It was in May of '79[4] that it was shewn to you. Mrs. Hayes and yourself must have followed with deeper realization even than others the progress of the dreadful misfortune which has changed all ideas of the White House and made it a very mecca — in thought — for prayers. If a whole nation's good wishes and indignant tenderness could give life Garfield is safe.[5] Only individuals feel otherwise.

My address is just yet for the coming ten days — when I return to Arizona — with my son and his family here (Care J. C. Frémont, Jr., U.S. Navy, Sing Sing, N.Y.).

I hope you will not find it too much trouble to look me up the letter? And with remembrances to Mrs. Hayes and regards to yourself, I am always Sincerely yours,

Jessie Benton Frémont

ALS (OFH).

1. Zachariah Chandler (1813-79) had been prominent in the organization of the Republican party in 1854 and had served Michigan as a senator from 1857 to 1875 and then again in 1879 until his death later that year while JCF was in Arizona. In 1864 he was on terms of closest friendship with JCF, Henry Winter Davis, and Benjamin Wade, but wished to see Lincoln reelected and the Republican party unified. He had

no use for General McClellan, whom the Democrats had nominated for the presidency in 1864.

2. Several times a member of the House of Representatives and a strong Maryland Unionist, Henry Winter Davis (1817-65) was often in opposition to Lincoln and an unrelenting foe of Montgomery Blair.

3. JBF gave more details about this episode in "Great Events" and copied into that record JCF's June 4, 1864, letter accepting the nomination of the dissident faction of the Republican party for the presidency (pp. 383-92). See also W. E. SMITH, 2:279-88, and NEVINS [1], 471-582. At first the Lincoln Republicans did not take his candidacy very seriously, but he did have the widespread support of the German press, and many came to feel that he would pull a large vote and jeopardize the success of the Republican party. Some proposed that both Lincoln and Frémont withdraw in favor of a compromise candidate. Led by Zachariah Chandler, practical politicians and foes of Montgomery Blair won a pledge from the president that if Frémont would withdraw from the race, he would be given an active position and Montgomery Blair would leave the cabinet. In the interests of party harmony, JCF did withdraw, refusing both reward and patronage and, he said, even the resignation of Montgomery Blair. Lincoln, however, did ask for and accept Blair's resignation.

4. JBF probably means May 1878, which would be about a month before President Hayes nominated JCF for the territorial governorship.

5. President James Garfield had been shot by Charles A. Guiteau on July 3, 1881, but he did not die until Sept. 19 (PESKIN, 596).

To Julius E. Hilgard

Sing Sing on the Hudson
(Post Office Box No. 15)
September 13th 1881

My dear Sir,

Captain [Carlile P.] Patterson took great interest in the health of my son's wife, and had planned for him duty for the winter which should at the same time give her the warm dry air of Arizona and have her with us there, at Tucson.

I do not know if the death of our long-time friend [i.e., Patterson] changes this detail? And whether the Apache outbreak may not make the magnetic survey undesirable for this winter? You will excuse my writing you this personal letter, for at the first cold day the consumptive symptoms betrayed themselves again in Mrs. Frémont. She is very dear to me too — and I believe a dry warm winter together with a peaceful mind will make the chance she needs to outgrow this tendancy [sic].

And though the General goes immediately to Arizona I wait to know what my son's orders for the winter will be that I may adapt myself to them. He is now on the Bache. Of course as an officer he can ask no question. But my old relations with Captain Patterson and his family gave me a different footing from official life only. And without personal relations with yourself I think human and humane relations are always binding enough to quite excuse this personal application I make for information from you. Under Captain Patterson's arrangement my son was to have gone to the Coast Survey Office in Washington for some weeks' preparation for the work in Arizona.

It would be very kind (and aid me greatly in my care of my invalid) if we could have such certainities of my son's movements as would let us shape ours in time before cold weather.

And pray understand that though in war time or under necessity I can be a good imitation of a Spartan mother yet as it is not a natural role I greatly prefer this distinct modern way of asking directly for what I want.

And I shall feel quite sure your decisions are in accordance with duty even if they may not quite meet the plan that had been arranged by Captain Patterson.

Will you be good enough to let me have an answer to the address I give (P. O. Box 15—Sing Sing). Very sincerely yours,

Jessie Benton Frémont

ALS (ICHi). Julius E. Hilgard (1825–91) had succeeded Patterson as superintendent of the Coast and Geodetic Survey. JBF wrote this letter on behalf of her naval son, Charley.

To Richard C. Drum

New York, Sep. 13 [1881].

personal
Dear General Drum

As the General has asked for our son I want to ask your aid in having this done.[1] It will greatly help forward public work and what I am thinking of more—(I write this as the children say "out of my own head" and without even telling the General who might object to so unofficial an act) is that it will give the general some one he can trust, and who will not only be efficient but will spare him doubts as well as much fatigue.

Mr. Lincoln[2] has been so appreciative and considerate towards the General that I hope his absence will not make a difference. I trust I may count on your assistance?

There is more than one reason—more than any present reason why such a small request of the General's should be granted. Very sincerely yours,

Jessie Benton Frémont

(Mrs. Fremont, P. O. Box, Sing Sing-on-Hudson New York).

ALS (DNA-94, Francis P. Fremont appointment file, 4922–ACP 1877). Richard C. Drum was adjutant general.

1. JCF had requested that Frank be transferred to Arizona from his post at Fort Missoula, Mont.—allegedly to take charge of organizing home guard companies. If the requests for both Frank and Charley were successful, the immediate family would be gathered in Tucson. JBF intimated to Nelly Browne that the Frémont men would be involved in "big big cattle ranch work" (n. d., CU-B—Frémont Papers).
2. Abraham Lincoln's son, Robert Todd Lincoln (1843–1926), was secretary of war.

To William T. Sherman

Sunday, September 18th [1881]
Sing Sing P. O. Box 15

Dear General Sherman

You know Arizona travel and something of Arizona officials. The General will have horrid work in travel and in all the details of making the local Guard. He has asked for our son Frank to assist him in this work, and it seems your objection to such detail is about the only obstacle to his being ordered at once to Arizona to do that duty.

Can you not make an exception this time? It will be for the public good that is sure—and it will be of inestimable good as helping the General.

I know you would prefer to say Yes to any request I make to you—please think twice before you do *not* say it. I am going out by way of San Francisco taking with me my daughter-in-law and the baby. Even this first chill in the weather has told against her. I believe, however, Tucson will do for her what Monterey did for you and for me.[1]

The General has applied to the War Department for Frank, my son, if you can be so kind as to authorize his coming to do this work in Arizona, I will be very happy and very thankful to you. And I hope you will not be too "military" to this petition of mine but let yourself be personal and kind.[2] Sincerely yours,

Jessie Benton Frémont

I have taken permission to make you a figure on my [canvas?] in a (pen & ink) picture of the going into Arizona. I was asked to tell of some work I did in the schools there, and "make it interesting" with "personal points"—so as foreground I gave the travel up, and the meeting you as an incident. I will send it to you when it is printed.[3]

ALS (DLC—William T. Sherman Papers).

1. JBF had met Sherman in Monterey in 1849 when they were both recovering their health.
2. The Frémonts' attempts to have Frank transferred to Arizona failed, even though the appeal was carried over the heads of generals to the secretary of war. Within three weeks, JCF would resign the territorial governorship.
3. JBF's article on her "Arizona Class" first appeared in *Wide Awake* in 1883, was printed the next year in *How to Learn and Earn* (Boston: D. Lothrop Company, 1884), and then in *Autumn Leaves: A Pictorial Library of Prose, Poetry and Art*, ed. by Daphne Dale (National Book Mart, 1893).

Informal Will

Suffern, Rockland County
New York
April 21, 1882

I wish to make known as clearly and legally as I can, that such personal effects as remain to me after the uprooting of our home I desire to have belong to my only and dear and good daughter Elizabeth Benton Frémont. We two have many ideas connected with these things and they mean much to us. It is my daughter's wish that her brother Frank should have after her the silver tea set and all the table silver. The little coffee pot which I gave to the General when we were young together in Paris, and when our oldest (living) boy was a baby, I would like the General to leave to that son John Charles Frémont to be given through him, after, to "little Jack"—the General's namesake and my little darling grandson.[1]

My diamond-enamelled buttons and pin I wish to go to my three children. The pin to Lily, the buttons, one each, to Charley and Frank. And I would like Charley to leave his to my little new namesake now five days old.[2] I intend having attached to each piece on the reverse side a good miniature of myself with some of my hair between.

My seal ring I give to my dear Frank. He has been daughter and son both to his Father and myself during many trying times.

This is only putting into writing what the children and myself have agreed to verbally.

Jessie Benton Frémont

ALS (CU-B—Frémont Papers).

1. John Charles Fremont III had been born in Feb. 1880. Like his father, he pursued a naval career, reaching the rank of captain before his death in 1957 (New York *Times* obit., Oct. 14, 1957).

2. JBF's grandaughter, Jessie Benton Frémont, died in Washington, D.C. in 1979, having been a resident there for almost thirty-four years after retiring from a career as social secretary in New York City (Washington *Post* obit., Jan. 26, 1979).

To Dorothea Dix

Suffern
Rockland County
New York.
July 18 [1882].

My dear Miss Dix

A letter from your and my dear friend Dr. Eliot tells me he is going to Trenton to see you and it reminds him of the work of which I did (a very little) part under you two in '61.

Before that you had put some of your thoughts into me. You may forget but I do not, your coming up to see me in my room, as I was not well, the summer California came into the Union. I was at my Father's house. You told me some things I had not then thought of, and told me I must use the talents of position, fortune and such means as I had to secure attention for the good of those who could not help themselves.

My dear lady I have tried to do this. It had been home teaching in many forms, example as well as precept, but yours was a command to come forth and not live for self.

You have done so much good in your life that you do not know how far and spreading your influence has worked results.

My daughter asks me to say that she too wishes to be recalled to your memory—that she was your aid de camp for the days you inspected hospitals and camps at St. Louis, and she wishes to join me in warm remembrances to you.

The General is away just now quite far, in Sonora, in Mexico but my two grand children are here on a visit. Their father was not born when I first knew you. With us all (all of us but the babies) you are an honored name—they will know in time. Sincerely yours,

Jessie Benton Frémont

ALS (MH). Shortly before JBF wrote this letter, the noted reformer Dorothea Dix had retired to the Trenton, N.J., state hospital, which she had helped bring into existence thirty-five years earlier.

To John D. Townsend

Suffern, Rockland County, New York.
February 8th. 1883.

Dear Mr. Townsend

Sally cut this from the Tribune of the 5th and sent it to me asking if it was not "a sort of libel"?

It certainly is so far as facts go. I never had Hay Fever or Catarrh or any sort of recurring or smoldering complaint. I live or I die. I came nigh dying in your house but that was a sudden thing and you know how quickly and how thoroughly I recovered.

You know I am not fussy about print. But the General says this must be stopped and I too dislike this misuse of my name.

The General said he would go in and see you about it but I had best send the slip directly to you. Naturally this notice will be spread everywhere. I thought of you as having not only the knowledge how to stop it, but from your personal knowledge of me I do not need to prove I am a quite healthy person.

I left Arizona in October of '79 and I have not been back there.

I would like the authority for this notice, although it is possible the whole thing is an advertisement founded on imagination.

I am so very sorry about Lizzie and her mother's long anxious journey. As Frank is not to be at home until tonight I do not know news later than Mrs. Townsend's starting off.

I shall never forget the tender care and feeling you all gave me when I had that congestive chill at your house and, as I wrote Carrie, I feel nearer to you in illness and trouble than in your usual life. But, always, I am sincerely yours,

J. B. Frémont

[The clipping on catarrh and hay fever reads:

Johnston, Holloway & Co., wholesale druggists of Philadelphia report that some time ago a gentleman handed them a dollar with a request to send a good catarrh cure to two army officers in Arizona. Recently the same gentleman told them that both officers and the wife of Gen. John C. Fremont, Gov. of Arizona, had been *cured* of Catarrh by the two bottles of Ely's Cream Balm, 50 cents, by mail or of druggists.

ELY'S CREAM BALM CO.
Owego, N. Y.]

Is there no legal remedy against such absolutely false and unauthorized use of one's name?

ALS (IGK). Addressed to 343 West 34th Street, New York, N.Y. Author of *New York in Bondage,* John D. Townsend (1835–96) was a prominent attorney and the father of Carrie, whom Frank Frémont married on Nov. 14, 1883. John Townsend's wife, Caroline, mentioned later in the letter, had been born in Worcester, Mass., and wrote about the plight of New York "street children."

To William K. Rogers

Sunday. New York June 17th [1883].
218 West 59.

Dear Col. Rogers

When we unite in a campaign it has always been successful. Will you use your knowledge *who* to speak to, to get this matter of Miss Acker's put straight?[1]

I do not say anything of her very great fitness and skill or the intelligent requirements of the service in holding on to such, especially when it is had at half rates from a woman for you know even better than I that it is not justice but favor.

We have both been [angered?]—we need not blink facts about the deplorable misrule of official service in Washington. Only one gets more by not saying this out loud.

If I were younger I would go on a crusade against this white slavery—this turning of the screw on the worn nerves of educated poverty. But as it is "I speak fair." And you must do the same for this lady who has many strong friends but as you know the summer scatters everyone.

You must come here to see us when you are in town again. We are facing the Park and it is every way a comfortable place. Sincerely yours,

J. B. Frémont

I have mailed the original to the Secretary. Please, if you know the real motive power put your finger on him—and at once—to oblige the General as well as myself.

[Enclosure]
To Henry M. Teller

New York, June 15, 1883.
No. 218 West 59.

To the Honble. Secretary of the Interior
My dear Sir

I wish to ask your personal attention to the case of Miss Acker, a lady of unusual efficiency and skill, who has been for two years in the Draughtsman's Dept. of the Patent Office.

Because of some reductions Miss Acker's name was on the list of those dropped from service on the 15th of this month.

The General and myself have a hope that if you will see into this case yourself Miss Acker will be at once replaced.

We personally know her family and friends—we know that her skill is unusual, that both at the Cooper Institute where she studied, and in the department where for two years she has been employed, her capacity has been proved to be exceptional, and we know that as a recognition of good work faithfully done by a most deserving young woman her re-appointment will be gratefully felt by other friends than ourselves—persons of influence long connected with Mr. Cooper in his carrying out of his efforts to provide women with secure independence.[2]

If you would be so kind as to ask the officer in charge of the Draughtsman's Dept to give his opinion of Miss Acker's value, I think nothing more would be needed to secure what myself and all who know of her, hope will be done. Trusting to hear this is possible, I am sincerely yours,

Jessie Benton Frémont

[Enclosure]

Hon Mr. Teller
My dear Sir

I wish to add to what Mrs. Frémont has said that I am much interested in the family to which Miss Acker belongs, and that I will be glad to know that in consideration of her decided merit her case has been favorably reconsidered and her place given back to her. Yours truly,

(Signed) J. C. Frémont

ALS with copied enclosures (CU-B—Rogers Papers).

1. As noted in JBF's letter to Henry M. Teller, the secretary of the interior, Kate R. Acker was employed in the Patent Office. Since her employment is not listed in the *Official Register* of the United States Civil Service for 1881, she must have been employed after July 1, 1881, and then dropped before July 1, 1883, as her name does not appear in either year's *Register*. She is, however, listed as a "copyist of Drawings" in the Patent Office for 1885 and 1887.

2. Founded for the advancement of science and art by inventor and manufacturer Peter Cooper (1791–1883), Cooper Institute of New York City combined the ideal and the practical in education.

To Elizabeth Blair Lee

New York, 218 West 59th street
Sunday July 29th [1883].

Dear Lizzie

I did not know until you were gone what Mary Martin had told Lily of the sorrowful cause of your own ill health.

I was so sorry for my idle light talk about my babies and everything—so out of tune with the thoughts filling your mind.

But you understood it then? and you must feel now that in the many many memories of a dear past and gone life which all thronged over me in seeing you again, I should have recalled most those belonging with cares you shared with me and helped me bear.

It was so good of you to come and see me—every way. And I liked to tell you of the dear young lives that have brightened mine—and of my boys—your Father's and Mr. Lee's godsons.[1]

Since the newspapers have told us what you were really feeling, one among many memories of Silver Spring has kept before me—the night you watched with me until the morning came and my little Annie ceased to feel pain. I never never forget that time and your pitying care for her. I knew it, dimly, then—I know it surely now that for the death of a baby girl there should be no sorrow for life is hard on women but when one is still young it is hard to give up a baby.

I had written to Mrs. Barlow to ask her to take me in for the night—that I might go down and see you, when we saw the end had come[2] and you, I thought would no longer be with Mary [Martin]. Although for your own people to whom you are so dear and needed you should take every care of your hurt health and if sea air does you good keep in it.

I hope the coming here did not tire you? But it was such a happy surprise to me that you must not let that tell against the good it did me and thank you again for coming—there is no need to put such feelings in words—not in written words which are so feeble after all. Life narrows and grows chill when one is as transplanted as I have been time after time—it was more to me than you who have "lived among your own people" can realize, to have the earlier time of unbroken home and friends brought livingly to me.

Let your loving people take care of you and keep well, for them, for many and many a year to come—and whenever I am near you I will come and tell you better than a letter can that you did me good and that I am always your old friend,

Jessie Benton Frémont

ALS (NjP—Blair-Lee Papers).

1. Frank and Charley Frémont, respectively.
2. Montgomery Blair had died two days earlier, on July 27, 1883.

To John Sherman

Monday morning
April 14 [1884]

Dear Mr. Sherman

I called yesterday to make you the General's thanks—and mine—
for the kind way in which you have interested yourself in the matter
of putting him [JCF] on the Retired list. For several reasons this means
so much to him that it is not easy to express the feeling with which
we meet friendly help.

I wanted too to know when it would best suit you to introduce it
in the Senate?

Today? when Mr. Dorsheimer puts it before the House—or as you
prefer.

Mr. Dorsheimer was an adjt. to the General in Missouri, and is now
his lawyer in New York, and in '56 an active warm political friend—
it is a matter now in which he has strong feeling.

If the messenger brings your assent to putting in the same Bill today
I will have a copy of the House resolution go to you at once—or later
as you may judge best. And I would like at the time it least interferes
with your other duties, to see you about it and get your advice as to
what I ought or ought not to do.

For this is so much the one hope and effort of my life now that I
do not want to make mistakes.[1] Very sincerely yours,

Jessie Benton Frémont

ALS (DLC—John Sherman Papers). Formerly secretary of the treasury in the
Hayes administration, John Sherman (1823-1900) was serving Ohio in the Senate.

1. The movement to have Congress pass a bill to put JCF on the retired army list
as a major general, and thereby obtain some financial security for the Frémonts, would
finally be successful in Mar. 1890. There was much opposition, some stemming from
JCF's involvement in the Memphis and El Paso railroad scandal (See JBF to Sherman,
May 4 [1884], DLC).

To Simon Cameron

the Arlington, Washington, D. C.
June 11, 1884.

My dear Mr. Cameron

You may have forgotten, but I do not, the fine and appreciative
speech you made in a debate in the Senate toward the close of the

session in June of '70, in which you spoke of Mr. Frémont's services to the whole country—his later political-pioneer work, and the then recent war-record.

Remembering this—now that we need friends—I write to say that as your son is on the Military Committee of the Senate, and that Committee can by a favorable report insure the passage of the Bill now before it for placing the General on the Retired list—I so need the active good will of your son that I write to ask your influence with him.[1]

I do not know Senator Cameron. I would go to you if you were here. Perhaps this letter may do more than I could by seeing your son, for you, knowing me, knowing General Frémont personally—as well as understandingly—and your certainty that there would be no such request but for the need—will give to Senator Cameron your own friendly feeling and wish. And in that way secure his attention, and his assistance in getting the Bill at once before the Senate. There, it is certain of a large majority. Democrats as well as our own side have given—offered, me the most hearty manly American support. It only needs to come out of Committee. Of course a favorable report would greatly aid.

The Bill was presented by Senator Sherman *April 14*. Memorials from New York, San Francisco, Indiana and Kansas have been sent to the Senate asking immediate attention to it.

Will you be so kind as to let me know if this reached you? With the summer-travel I doubt your being at home. If you are I feel sure I can count upon your aid. Sincerely yours,

Jessie Benton Frémont

ALS (DLC—Simon Cameron Papers).

1. James Donald Cameron (1833–1918) had been elected to the Senate in 1877 to fill the vacancy caused by the resignation of his father and served Pennsylvania in that capacity until Mar. 3, 1897.

To Ella Farman Pratt

Tuesday 19th August [1884]
New Brighton, S[taten] I[sland]

Dear Mrs. Pratt

Your note of the 17th enclosing a check has come in this morning's mail. This is just a line of acknowledgment, and to say you are to have only comfortable feelings about me — every way — so drop any "regretfullys."

I too have been, and am, up to my heart in occupying thoughts. My dear baby of a son — always a loving child and sweet and childlike in tenderness to me, and indeed to us all, has gone, the 11th, on a "three years cruise" to what his little girl named for me calls "A Sout Pasikit."[1] She was the youngest yesterday — she may have a baby successor any hour now.[2] I have been up with the dear brave young mother who thought only how to lessen her husband's sorrow. And he, hers. [*Margin note:* He is the acknowledged champion athlete as well as naval officer of his date. Manly in the highest and best type — and for that, loving and gentle.]

I am going up again — we are but two hours apart. She has a lovely voice and this sea-foggy atmosphere which is life to me tells on her throat — and she is in the high hills back of the Hudson in dry air. A most charming family home surrounded by relations and friends and with nurse & physician of old date, and all congenial. And two such children for beauty, goodness, health and sound, *not* precocious, minds as I have no other knowledge of. But — all the more time for remembering. Still she has sense, and a sweet sense of constant surprise and gratitude for all her many blessings, and so she *makes* herself busy and content. And the new baby will fill her hands as well as her heart for she with all her beauty, her charm of wit and music, is a true mother and her babies are welcome and cared for from the first instants of their existence (& pre-existence). Consequently they are delights as they unfold.

One grieves to see separation or sorrow come into such lives. But could we ensure happiness if we had the full ordering of our lives? I have found submission, patience — thankfulness for the gift of feeling intensely the happiness when it can come — carry one on through *such* troubles. And when the let-up comes one goes into it *"without poisoning today with tomorrow,"* or yesterday — and "clear comfort" as the northern people say takes its blessed sway for the time.

I will write the fourth Virginia story. Let me know for "when" and the proof sheet of the other three would be most serviceable & guiding to me, if I can have it.

I have four numbers written — but not quite crushed flat enough yet. And the whole foreign series is nearly ready. I have profited by a lull. I think you will be pleased with them all though I cannot give you a "Bodisco wedding" each time.[3] That is a very misleading narrative of the rewards that come to the idle school-girl and therefore will be popular. Sincerely yours,

J. B. Frémont

ALS (MH). Ella Farman Pratt (d. 1907) and her husband, Charles Stuart Pratt, were the editors of the young people's magazine *Wide Awake* and later of *Little Folks*. Mrs. Pratt was also the author of many children's books, including *Good-for-Nothing Polly* and *A Little Woman.*

1. On June 7, John Charles Frémont, Jr., had been ordered to be ready for sea duty. He seems to have been assigned first to the *Lackawanna* and then transferred to the *Hartford* on Sept. 24, 1884, for Pacific duty (DNA-15, John C. Frémont, Admiral, XC-268 365 2).

2. The baby was a girl and named Juliet Van Wyck. She married Henry Hull, a star of stage and screen, and lived for many years at Old Lyme, Conn.

3. In "The Bodisco Wedding," which also appeared in *Souvenirs*, JBF recounts the splendor that accompanied the marriage of her sixteen-year-old schoolgirl friend, Harriet Williams, the daughter of a government clerk, to Baron Alexander Bodisco, the stout, aging, but very rich Russian ambassador. Jessie was a bridesmaid at the 1840 wedding, and looking back at it many years later, she saw it as a ceremonial exchange of youth and beauty for money and position ("Memoirs," 30–32). When a notice of Ben Perley Poore's forthcoming *Reminiscences* (1886) indicated that he would give an account of the Bodisco wedding and attribute the fine satin gowns of the bridesmaids to the generosity of the Russian ambassador, JBF wrote to correct the error. The gifts "could be permitted to some of them who were sister and cousins to his bride, but not possible towards myself and Helen Morris, a daughter of Commodore Morris" (to B. F. Poore, July 12 [1886], NN—Miscellaneous Papers).

To William Carey Jones, Jr.

October 14 [1884]
New Brighton Staten Island

Dear Carey

I had a rheumatic fever in August & this squeezed writing is the best I can do yet.

My physician Dr. Morton is back in town now & I am going up in the morning for treatment by electricity.[1] I will write you more fully then. Now it hurts my stiff fingers.

Your letter is of real value and interest. I have written to Mr. Royce[2] to say the General will be glad to arrange with him for a full talk as soon as he is back from Michigan (where he was specially urged to come by both the local Com[mittee] & Mr. Blaine).[3] Bancroft[4] is only a "joiner." We know him and his methods.

With a short hand man to record & with questions clearly submitted, the General could answer enough in an hour to make a book—and all true and with proof existing.

Wasn't it sweet the baby remembered you. I am so glad you have her. I think you are good and all the happiness that little life, and successful work can give you will I trust be yours. We all felt deeply interested by you, and for you.[5]

I have written to Mrs. Shillaber—(not telling how I heard) of "a return of her ill health." She had written me this Spring of it & of her recovery. I had seen she had gone to the Sandwich Islands for the winter. I am sorry for her. Let me know more of her please.

My stiff hand cuts off my writing but I see the gain of your friend's writing from facts especially after he has met the General. Thank you for the trouble you took. In your research about Father try Tennessee.

I will keep in mind any chance to add to your collection. Affectionately your aunt,

Jessie B. Frémont

ALS (courtesy of Mrs. Lincoln C. Reynolds, Corvallis, Oreg.). William Carey Jones, Jr. (1854–1923), JBF's nephew, was an instructor in U.S. history and constitutional law at the University of California, Berkeley. He later became a professor of jurisprudence and author of the *Illustrated History of the University of California* (1895).

1. While electric belts, corsets, even hairbrushes, were part of a popular form of medical quackery in the nineteenth century. Dr. William J. Morton was one of the nation's foremost neurologists and a leading scientific proponent of the use of electrotherapeutic treatment. For a general statement on nervous disease and electric medicine, see GREENWAY.

Two weeks after the letter to Carey, Elizabeth Benton Frémont wrote Nelly Haskell Browne, "Mother is building up on the Drs. Morton electrical & medical treatment—they say she has a touch of rheumatism mixed with gout, the latter brought on by improverishment of the blood & a general run down condition, so she has been put on cod liver oil (you can fancy how easy she finds it to take!) & other building up medicines, & her general health shows she is getting stronger" (Oct. 28 [1884], CU-B—Frémont Papers). Earlier in August, JBF's right knee and hand had been so painful that Lily had arranged her hair and done all her writing.

2. A native Californian and a philosopher, Josiah Royce (1855–1916) was a former classmate and faculty colleague of Carey Jones at the University of California, Berkeley. Royce had moved to Harvard in 1882, but since he was writing a book on California, he wished to interview the Frémonts, especially as to their assertions that JCF had secret instructions for his part in seizing California in 1846. After correspondence and

interviews, Royce concluded that JCF's actions had been open disobedience, irreconciliable with his official instructions. For letters to the Frémonts and reports to Henry L. Oak of his interviews with them, see ROYCE [2], 141–200 passim. After the publication in 1886 of his *California from the Conquest in 1846 to the Second Vigilance Committee in San Francisco: A Study of American Character*, with its strictures on JCF, the Royce-Jones friendship cooled. In the Oct. 1890 issue of the *Atlantic Monthly*, Royce further analyzed JCF's qualities, pronouncing him a baffling "enigma," "a creature of shadow-land," a fit subject for a student of psychology, and again returned to his theme that JCF had thwarted the Washington government's plans for a peaceful acquisition of California, thereby bringing confusion and sorrow to that land but glory to himself. The article aroused the "complete 'fight'" in JBF, as she wrote her nephew (to Carey Jones, Nov. 7, 1890, courtesy of Mrs. Lincoln C. Reynolds).

3. JCF was supporting James G. Blaine for the presidency of the United States. He and Blaine were speaking at various towns in Michigan from the rear platform of a train. The New York *Tribune* informed the public that JCF's efforts would no doubt result to his material advantage. "Senator Palmer intends to take charge of the bill to place Fremont upon the retired list of the army, and to make it his special business" (quoted by New York *Herald*, Oct. 19, 1884).

4. Hubert Howe Bancroft (1832–1918), American publisher and a prolific writer on the American West. Royce's correspondent, Henry Lebreus Oak (1844–1905), was superintendent of Bancroft's books and documents, which in 1905 became the Bancroft Library when the collection was sold to the University of California. Oak was the author of the first five of Bancroft's seven volumes on California.

5. Carey Jones's little daughter, Alice Benton Jones, had been born on Oct. 3, 1882. Her mother died two months later, and Jones and his infant daughter then made their home in Berkeley with the Whitcombs, Alice's maternal grandparents (information from Mrs. Lincoln C. Reynolds).

Statement Concerning Secret Affairs Relating to the Mexican War

[late Dec. 1884]

Mr. Buchanan often brought important papers in Spanish, from the confidential agent in Mexico (during the war) to my Father's for translation. My sister and myself would make the translations. Genl. Dix (N.Y.) was on the Military Com. & knew Spanish. He was a near neighbor & congenial friend. My Father too knew Spanish thoroughly, and he & Genl. Dix would read out a translation to Mr. Buchanan and after, we (who knew Spanish well) made out the written papers.

The Librarian and translator at the State Dept. Mr. Greenhough [Greenhow] of course knew Spanish. But his wife was in the pay of the English Legation as a spy & our private information reached them through her. Mr. Buchanan when he knew this thought best to cut off opportunities but not betray knowledge of being watched.

This is only one of many corroborating bits of circumstantial evidence of constant rivalry & counteraction by England regarding Mexico.

In the opening of our [Civil] war Genl. Scott had Mrs. Greenhough's house and papers seized as she was then (a widow) known to be a spy for the South and lots of proofs were found of her old & present and long continued service as spy to England.

This will not be dwelt on in Genl. Keyes's memoirs. I have not seen them, but as the seizure included the capture of his love letters to Mrs. Greenhough on which she based a large money demand, he was much laughed at as some were made public. As a U.S. officer she found him valuable for information—their old relations being "confidential."[1]

She was a while in the old capitol prison then she went to Halifax where she received a large sum in English gold. She was on a blockade runner making for Norfolk [Wilmington, N.C.] when she was drowned in the surf while landing from a small boat. She would keep her gold on her & it weighed her down.[2]

This is to to tell you how I was confidential translator often, listener oftener to military matters in my Father's library when Mr. Buchanan came for consultations and a [nerve?] power not in *his* nature.

For 20 years my Father was Chairman of the Military Com. He knew the personnel of the army and their wants in a way no passing Secretary could. Also he had been in the army and in addition to experience had a love for military matters. Our house—the "Library"—and my Father's com[mittee] room were the real war Dept.

(In the time of the Mexican War the Brussels stair carpet leading to the library, had to be renewed twice during the session of Congress such was the stream of "armed men" or rather men whose profession was arms who passed up & down from that room.)[3]

Mr. Buchanan had no fibre in him that responded to war—or combativeness in any form. It was a moral impossibility that *any* move towards gaining California should have been made without my Father's knowledge.[4]

And this idea of a secret mission given to Mr. Larkin has simply *never* been heard of by me before.[5] And it is an absurd idea that it would have availed against well known English intentions and Californian preferences.

AD (CSmH). JBF prepared this document for Josiah Royce following his first interview with the Frémonts in early Dec. 1884.

1. General Erasmus D. Keyes (1810–95) had been romantically entangled with the widow Greenhow, but her biographer maintains that nothing appears in the Pinkerton or War Department records to substantiate JBF's claim that Keyes's letters were found in Rose Greenhow's correspondence at the time of her arrest as a spy (ROSS, 81–82).

2. Mrs. Greenhow was released from the Old Capitol prison in June 1862 and went south pledging not to return to the north. The next year she went to Europe to act as unofficial agent for the Confederacy and to have her prison diary published. Her book, *My Imprisonment and the First Year of Abolition Rule at Washington,* made a great deal of money for her. It was the gold from her book, sewn into her clothing and about her neck in a leather reticule—not a late payment from the British government for her services during the Mexican War as JBF implies—that so weighted her down that she sank at once. The *Condor* had called at Halifax before attempting its almost successful run to the Confederate port of Wilmington.

3. With respect to JBF's statement on the "Brussels carpet," Royce wrote sarcastically to Henry L. Oak, "You have probably never considered what grand evidence an old carpet can furnish.—Talk of the *dusty* tomes of history!!" (ROYCE [2], 146).

4. See JBF to Torrey, Mar. 21, 1847, above, wherein she implies that JCF had known nothing of the impending war with Mexico and that he and she had felt no sympathy for it. In 1885, when Royce submitted the summary of his interview with the Frémonts for their perusal, she took exception to the mild wording of a sentence. Royce had written that in pre-1846 conversations between JCF and Benton the possibility of a transfer of California "was often mentioned." " 'Mentioned' is not the word," she wrote, "for what was earnestly planned discussed and *intended.*"

5. Elsewhere in Royce's summary, JBF lined out her negative comments on Larkin, but maintained the ridiculousness of his being entrusted with the work of a confidential agent. In reality he had received secret instructions from Secretary of State Buchanan to work for the peaceful transfer of California to the United States; a copy of Larkin's instructions had also gone to JCF. The Frémonts insisted, however, that John had been designated to take and hold possession of California in the event of any occurrence that would justify it, so as to prevent its falling into the hands of England. JBF explained that the private letters from herself and Benton that Lt. Archibald Gillespie carried to JCF in the Oregon wilderness "were in a manner in family cypher—so full were they of reference to talks & agreements known only at home" (J. Royce notes on Frémont interview with JBF marginalia, CU-B—Oak Papers). For a detailed discussion of JCF's controversial role in California and documents pertaining thereto, see SPENCE & JACKSON.

To [William A. Croffut]

[Nov. 30, 1885]

In Wide-Awake you will find under "Saint Louis" and "California"[1] the central idea indicated—the part had by my Father and Mr. Frémont in shaping and carrying forward the growth of the *West.* From the Mississippi to the Pacific Ocean. An outlet planned for and worked for by my Father from the time he went to Missouri in 1817. There was made later "Geographical explorations to the sources of the Mississippi" (a part of his plan) during Mr. Van Buren's administration; Mr. Nicollet a french astronomer and savant being in charge and having assigned to him as topographical engineer Mr. Frémont—then a 2d Lt. and quite unknown to us. But known to the Secretary of War Mr. Poinsett of S.C.—on their return to Washington in '39–40 after three years work in the upper Missi. Mr. Frémont was introduced to my Father. And in that way came about the combination that brought such results to the West, and the whole country. For the long thought and planning of my Father found active and expanding expression in the nature, the cultivated special capacities, and the powerful inner motive of Mr. Frémont.

It was my great good fortune to blend these lives and no one knows as I do the fire-side history, so to speak, of the growth of our western empire.

Without my Father's position of power and his powerful compelling will, Mr. Frémont could not have carried out their plans. There is much inside history to this.

Without Mr. Frémont's own perception, will, and singular endurance, the work could not have been carried out. It was an Empire they planned to open up and expand—with a sea coast on the Pacific to equal that on the Atlantic. It was done in spite of Washington.

And when acquired it was made free territory. And the building of the railroads which lead there formed part of the design. All of this I saw grow and become a fixed condition. Leading to free labor everywhere.

It has been the letting in of light in many ways. An old hunter said to me "Before his (Mr. Frémont's) time all that country was as a book sealed with seven seals—now, it is as open as the palm of my hand," unrolling his large hand as he spoke.

Of physical obstacles—of cold and hunger and incessant danger you know. You do not know of the ignorance, the jealousy, the constant underhand thwarting, but there was a great watchman on guard for Mr. Frémont in Washington and they won against all the odds.

Please read in Wide Awake, the St. Louis and California numbers, to feel something of this atmosphere of far reaching insight and thought and plan—it explains how the two lives supplemented and complemented each other. One life was neither long enough nor able for the separated but united action to the common end.

I had my part. It was renunciation—for the first eight years of married life, not three of them were shared together—brief stays of a few months in Washington to report, then renew work—made here and there a home time—if hard writing and work on maps left any other thought—but the absences were long; eighteen months, once *two years and five months,* and no letters or knowledge of each other but by fitful chances of hunters or kindly Indians. *Eleven months* we have been without any break to silence.

That is only personal but I think it counts under "endurance."

The records of all the journeys, the steel plates, wood cuts and photogravures of likenesses, to accompany this noble record I have in charge.

Mr. Childs was to have published the General's explorations written by himself in '55. For this much work was done. Buttre[2] engraved on steel large plates. Frank Howard Key,[3] the artist made the wood engravings (they are fine) and Hamilton[4] painted in oil and Darley in india ink the most noteworthy of the scenes. These were all taken from Daguerreotype views made by Mr. Frémont—the first application of any truthful process to nature in any record of travel.[5] They were naturally blotched and imperfect. He had them all made into photographs by Brady, and under his own superintendence and explanations & notes touched with india ink into completeness by a clever artist. Then Buttre engraved many on steel. Only one set of proofs was made. Everything has been kept boxed securely—of course '56 ended all personal work—Mr. Childs became impatient (the result of the election brought another aspect you see) and the General took back all the material—maps, plates, &c. &c.—and paid Mr. Child's "bill of expenses," 10,000$. With some after thoughts fetching it up to 16,000$. Then through our lawyer Coles Morris who had attended to it all, *all* that belonged with the book—*everything* was given to me by Deed.

I have deeds & all complete. That was in '57. Nearly thirty years ago.

I have kept on accumulating what fits into this. At times I have written on special points. My plan is clearly blocked out, and with the General I have made what can be used—a little condensed—as a full index. Also an introduction.

I think there is enough for one book and two monographs. No two men could be less alike in method and tastes than my Father and the General. While each had in common not only tenacity but staying power and the courage of their opinions as well as the common form of courage. Each had a consideration for the weak and helpless that was only equalled by their aggression and daring against power. Each while fronting and not sparing a public foe was gentle and tender and of utmost simplicity and refinement in home life. They have been the two most agreeable companions, the most elevating and strong friends I have known. And I have known well some exceptional friends during my life. It has been my pride and grateful happiness to have shared their lives. And if I on occasions have been of use and aided in large moments I can say like Portia

> Being so fathered and so husbanded
> Should I not be stronger than my sex.

I am now exactly in the mind and position to make up this record and give it to the public. Except in purely personal matters there will be no assertion. All outside matters rest on proved recorded statements. It is the putting them in line and leading up to the noble success that crowned these lives that makes it necessary to have the careful long well sifted records I have gathered. And only myself can do it with truth and the whole truth. While I know how to suppress personality and what would appear over estimate. That will be for my own special unhampered monographs.

Also *I* can condense without omitting necessary links. This has been my governing idea all these years since '56. Earlier, a part of it. For in '48 my Father put together many pamplets, speeches, reports of committees, odds & ends on the acquisition of California, had them bound together and started me on that chapter.

He scorned reward, but he prized fame. In St. Louis they have put in their Park his bronze statue which faces to the *West* and on the pedestal are his words

> *There* is the *East.*
> There is the road to India.

Words he had spoken to them years before and for which men smiled and touched their foreheads, saying he has the Eastern trade on the brain.

"Then men said he was mad. Now they ask hath he a God." And my Father was alone as St. Paul was in far sightedness.

To do this writing properly I must have my frame. If I were able to publish and print & bind and sell it all by myself I would go at it my own way. But the writing it is my limit. And I want to discuss with those whose experience gives them a dictating position as to the *available form* and general tone. Otherwise there would be much to alter or do twice.

Mr. Samuel Hall,[6] 8th & Broadway, had all this well in his [mind?] and would have been most agreeable to me as publisher, but when he found death was in him, he had to give it up. *He* knew the West too. He told me he could guarantee 25,000 copies sold from Chicago out, to the northwest and into the southwest and Oregon and California. His idea was one large volume at 5$. The expense of getting up the splendidly illustrated book would be so light—because of all the plates being ready—except a few photogravures, that the profits would be out of all usual proportion large.

I have now everything arranged for my writing. I will be in Washington in the house of a friend where I have taken the whole Library floor. Three south windows and a wood fire in a *real* Library. And all the government records at my disposal. I shall not be keeping house and my bronchitis and my daughter's hurt lung make enough alibi from the cruel waste of time of the common kind in visits & such.

I am very well and I shall be surrounded by the homes of members of my family who are agreeable to me, and I have most agreeable friends there, so that my life will be refreshed and varied while not intruded on.

As the mediums say "the conditions are favorable."

Nor the least of them is my having all my children near me again—including dear grandchildren.

It is le bon moment de repos [the right time to rest] after many agitations and I want to use it for my labor of love. And you will help me find the best channel? Sincerely yours,

                                        Jessie Benton Frémont

ALS (DLC—Jessie Benton Frémont Misc. Ms. Collection). William A. Croffut (1835–1915), to whom JBF appealed for advice, was a journalist and versatile author. JBF also gave Croffut a separate memorandum on the growth of the West, ending with the lament: "And as yet, not one public expression of notice or thanks has been given to the General—not even a vote of thanks from Congress." Croffut claimed in *An American Possession,* 272–73, that he had introduced the Frémonts to his publisher, Belford, Clarke & Co., who subsequently published JCF's *Memoirs.*

1. The *Wide Awake* articles on St. Louis and California also appeared later in her *Souvenirs of My Time*.

2. John Chester Buttre (1821–1893), wood engraver and portrait painter, was best known for his three-volume *American Portrait Gallery* (1880–81).

3. JBF has scrambled the name of Francis Scott Key's grandson. He was Frank Key Howard (1826–72), but his cousin, John Ross Key (1832–1920), seems to have been the artist. Young Howard had a brief legal career before becoming one of the proprietors and the managing editor of the Baltimore *Daily Exchange,* whereas John Ross had a career as illustrator and landscape painter. He was the only artist-grandson of Francis Scott Key.

4. Irish born James Hamilton (1819–78) was a marine and landscape painter who had also illustrated Elisha Kane's *Arctic Explorations* (1856).

5. The daguerreotypes of Solomon Nunes Carvalho, artist on the fifth expedition, formed the basis for much of the art work in the *Memoirs.*

6. About fifty-four at the time of his death of lung trouble in Feb. 1885, Samuel L. Hall was primarily an art publisher in New York, with a branch in Chicago (TEBBEL, 2:430; *Publishers' Weekly,* 27 [Feb. 28, 1885]: 252, obit.).

To George Browne

Washington, March 18th 1886
No. 1310, 19th St. N. W.

Dear Mr. Browne

The enclosed note from Mrs. Shaw[1] spares my writing more at length which you will excuse as my rheumatic hand begins to feel the steady work on our Book. A first part of which is now in the hands of the printer.

The General is splendidly well and happy in his work. We are in an atmosphere of appreciation and respect to him which, added to our happy change of fortune makes even his vitality greater. Except a tired hand & shoulder I too am admirably well and Lil has gone through the winter without further hurt to her lung but she has not gone out after dark or in bad weather.

For the first part of the work a younger head of myself was wanted to accompany those of my Father at 40 and the General at 35. But for Miss Charlotte, the head you have would have been used. It is the only youngish head we know. I wrote to Mrs. Shaw & had not time for a letter to you and answer, and I cannot yet afford explanatory cablegrams.

So I took permission for granted, and explaining to her the need for haste (that the engraver might work at once to meet the early April use of the likeness), I asked she would have it copied by Almsteadt [Almstaedt][2] in photograph and that my publisher Mr. Belford would personally see to it all and the safe return of the picture.

The prospectus, which will be a foretaste of the book, is to have the early head of my Father and the General and should have had mine. This we must lose for the prospectus. But I write now to ask your permission to use it—to have photograph copy by Almsteadt then return it to your representative—a day's absence perhaps from its usual place—that we may have it for the Book?

It was made in '56 by Buchanan Read and has souvenirs of time & associations which fit it in with that period.

I know it will trouble you that it was refused for you would not only forward what would be for my advantage, but as the portrait is to come back to me when I can pay for it, it seemed doubly hard. Until I have no debts I cannot indulge myself in buying it back. First I must stand clear.

It will be a most beautiful book. Over a hundred illustrations all original—all fine—and with *meaning,* and the publishers mean it to be, they say, "*the* American book of the 19th Century." Paper, size, type, illustrations—all will be of the best order.

As we had the costly work of steel engraving, and fine wood cuts, all ready, & *mine,* that takes away the chief expense. They credit me with that as my property and increased our proportion of return in accordance. As I told you the contract was most liberal and has been recorded—passed through to Lil—so we work on certainties.

The purchase of Louisiana in 1804 gave opportunity to use my finest head of Bonaparte and Mr. Barlow lends me an equally fine head of Jefferson. Until you come to do such work you can't think how hedged in by copyrights even Jefferson's head is.

Each portrait in our book is *new.* Mr. Beale gives me a charming one of himself—photographed on his reaching New York, then colored—now photographed (he had it done for me) from the painting.[3] He came through Mexico in September '48 with the first gold—and to cross Mexico from Mazatlan to Vera Cruz with such news just after the Mexican war and their loss of California would have cost his life. So as he was dark & spoke Spanish he disguised himself in Mexican dress and it is a very picturesque picture. The dear old Rocky Mountain flag is reproduced, full page, in color [*Margin note:* dimmed & tattered—and a sight to move men who had carried a flag through dangers]—the swords & medals in gold—the order of merit in its blue enamel & gold with its ribbon of black and silver—Carson's head is genuine and new.

There will be 40 illustrations (I should have said 41) published in the Prospectus with fifty pages of letter press. Among the illustrations is a full page facsimile, written out expressly by Whittier for this purpose—with a charming note—"I am glad to know thee is writing" &c.—A facsimile of a letter to me by my Father "Senate Chamber May 14 1848—The Flag—with descriptive letter press—The Charleston sword rattlesnake & all—The order of merit—full size with its German ribbon of black and silver—and maps of 1803—1843—1883—portraits of our nation's growth.[4] Did it ever occur to you that the Columbia and the Mississippi were french rivers when my Father was a man grown? How small was *our* country then—now!

It is most exciting writing to compact all this growth with its chief helpers into one smooth narrative. Most delightful to produce proof on proof that but for Mr. Frémont's action California would have been english. Now we hold "from sea to sea—the whole temperate zone on this continent."

You who helped maintain this grand nationality will feel "I too am a Roman"[5] when you read *the* Book, the dear book that secures fame and brings fortune. I am writing too much—for my time—but I wanted you to see it was no idle wish that made me take the liberty of assuming your permission to copy my head for this prospectus—the forerunner of the book—to be part of it after. It will be an album d'Amerique in itself. And I am right sorry to be left out.

Especially as I know that no care has been taken of that picture which was removed upstairs to a sewing room. Where your mother found it on the floor and had it at once hung up. In her absence—who knows?

Anyway you will give me the permit for a photograph to be taken—better late than never—but I lost my place.

Tell Nelly the first gap I see in my wall of work I will tell her what a lovely time our life here is. The President has been most gracious—sending the Marshal Col. Wilson[6] with personal messages of invitation to his receiving of the Diplomatic Corps, then again the Army & Navy. The General went to these and I too—the only places I have been at night. [*Margin note:* The President was emphatic in his welcoming the

General—telling him a second time that he was gratified that he had come.]

Genl. Sheridan[7] at once granted the General's asking to have Frank here longer, and *suggested* an extension of two months to his leave until he could think up a detail of duty here.[8] And everyone shows a consideration and respect, which is most comforting and gratifying.

We have a little house but very pretty and in the best part of the town. By taking it for a year we get it much lower and it gives us time to get in our money, and at our leisure look up one to buy. For this is our right place. It is now "the winter Newport" and the town is beautiful in itself and well lived in.

Tell Nelly her gloves went to the President's and that when I can I will tell her lots. Meantime she must not "count letters" with me. Sally, with her mother & the children is near by. The children come to me often. Frank & Carrie were here a month—all of us here but dear far away Charley. But a little later I can manage for him. "To him that hath shall be given."[9] Affectionately to you both,

J. B. Frémont

ALS (CU-B—Frémont Papers).

1. The Mar. 16, 1886, note from Caro B. Gallaudet Shaw of 38 Brighton, Staten Island, indicates that Miss Nichols, who had been left responsible for things in the house where the picture was located, would gladly lend the T. Buchanan Read portrait of JBF for copying, but could not do so "without an order" from George Browne. Browne had apparently acquired the portrait during the financial troubles of the Frémonts.

2. Isaac Almstaedt (1851–1921) of Staten Island photographed hundreds of obscure and prominent people, including Buffalo Bill and Cornelius Vanderbilt, copied and enlarged pictures, and made innumerable stereoscopic pictures of the Island landscape. The *Staten Island Historian,* 5 (Winter/Spring 1988): 26–27, gives a sketch of his life.

3. Writing to Mrs. Beale on Mar. 12, 1886, to acknowledge receipt of the photograph, JBF noted that she had "mailed it at once to our publishers who will be charmed by such a variation to the ordinary costume of men's portraits. I am so sorry I have none of Mr. Frémont in the same rig. Even Carson is in 'store clothes' " (DLC—Beale Papers).

4. The facsimile of the Benton letter and the picture of the sword did not appear in the elaborate *Prospectus* (CSmH).

5. A reference to St. Paul, who, when about to be scourged by the Romans, let it be known that he, too, was a Roman and freeborn. See Acts 22:24–30. It is also an allusion to Benton whom some called "the noblest Roman," and, of course, as his daughter, JBF would be a Roman, too.

6. Bvt. Col. John M. Wilson (1837–1919) was superintendent of public buildings and grounds.

7. General Philip H. Sheridan (1831–88), Indian fighter and Union general, had succeeded William T. Sherman as commander-in-chief of the army in 1884.

8. On Feb. 6, 1886, JBF had asked the president for a staff promotion for Frank (DLC—Cleveland Papers).

9. See Mark 4:25, and also Matthew 25:29.

To George Bancroft

Washington D.C
1310—19th N.W.
[late June 1886]

Dear Mr. Bancroft,

I have no roses[1] to send you but this geranium is of my own growing and its name—the stag-horn—fits it to go to you with my thanks for your precious letter about "our" Book.[2] It is so full of wild country and hills and deer that the leaf is appropriate. *You* can feel that the delight of this writing is too keen for the heat to tell on us, though I am sure the sea winds that bring nerve and strength would be greatly beneficial.

Still over everything dominates the great content—the surprise always to me that when all is so changing and transitory this long time together has been granted to Mr. Frémont and myself. And as you will notice he speaks of his life as in reality the life of three. My Father was so vitalizing that his ceasing to live did not end his power over our lives. He seems very present these days as we talk of him and write of him, here where we were all together. I know you will appreciate all we say of his unwearied work for Oregon when it had no existance in the public mind. That will come more fully in Part II.

These are not yet to be given to the public. The publishers are not contented with some hasty work, too hastily done, to retrieve time after the fire and are having some portraits &c. remade.[3] But I wished you to read what we had written. Later, the critical examination of [finish?] can be made on the completed work. The first volume we will finish in August. Meantime I bring my first venture of serious writing[4] to you knowing none are so kindly indulgent as the Masters—it is the prentice-hand that is quick to see faults. And when the Master is a friend also I have no fears. You name it rightly a tribute to my Father. Very few knew him as you did, as the Father, the friend, the charming instructive companion of his daughters. For you this will not be merely a pamphlet but a doorway opening upon a great past—in your life as well as my Father's. California and Oregon are your work so largely that it is personal history you will read.

It was very good of you to write yourself but you must not take the trouble again. I want an "again"—after you have read us.

The good sea air will send you back fresh and well, and with one volume off my hands I can indulge myself sometime in a visit to you then. We shall be here through August—then a rest in sea air for awhile.

With thanks for your letter which I have put away in rose leaves. I am dear Mr. Bancroft your old friend's attached daughter,

Jessie Benton Frémont

ALS (MHi—Bancroft Papers). Endorsed: "Rec'd 7 July [1886]." George Bancroft (1800–91) had been secretary of the navy during the conquest of California in 1846, and JBF had sought information from the aging statesman and historian as to the government's orders to JCF in 1845 and 1846.

1. Bancroft summered at "Roseclyffe," his home in Newport, R.I., where his gardens contained 500 varieties of roses (NYE, 282–83).

2. Bancroft had graciously thanked the Messrs. Belford and Clarke for sending him a copy of the first part of JCF's *Memoirs,* noting that he could bear testimony to the correctness of the sketch of Benton, "in private life, a most devoted husband and father, in public life, resolute and even aggressive." He went on to add, "It is well that [the country] should renew the memory of the victorious adventures which broke down the Rocky Mountains as barriers to our progress" (July 9, 1886, copy in JBF, "Memoirs," 76 [first draft]).

3. A fire on May 26 at the publishers, Belford, Clarke & Company, which had offices in both Chicago and New York, delayed publication until early in 1887.

4. JBF refers to her "Biographical Sketch of Senator Benton," which was eventually included in the *Memoirs.*

To Nelly Haskell Browne

2422 Craven Terrace[1]
Sunday [Dec. 1887]

Dear Nelly,

We could not get to you to say goodbye but a day's rest here has put us each in travelling order and at 5 P.M. we go on, via New Orleans to Los Angeles for the winter. The General took a heavy, bronchial cold about Thanksgiving—threatening pneumonia. As soon as he could safely leave the warm rooms we got off—and as you see we are outrunning the snow.

Lil has been going down ever since the first cold—a steady hacking cough. *I*! have been the active one, getting the tickets! Seeing business people and making all ready. I stayed over two nights with the Townsends but had not a leisure breath so it is only this written goodbye.

The General is fairly well and comfortable. This is a dear lovely home of Charley's and Sally is a first class housekeeper and we are so at home, so welcome and in such an atmosphere of content and lovely home living and dear children that we start all happy. Goodbye and a happy Xmas homecoming for G. B. Even Frank and Carrie are here to be with us in the shape of their Xmas gifts to the children and photographs and letters from themselves.[2]

Write to us sometimes, just Los Angeles, California.[3] Affectionately,

JBF

AL initialed (CU-B—Frémont Papers).

1. The Fremonts were on their way to California and had stopped in Washington, D.C., to visit Charley and his family.
2. Frank was with his regiment at Fort Missoula, Mont.
3. JBF did not return east again.

"AN EARTHLY PARADISE"
LOS ANGELES, 1888–1902

"The General is 'perfectly well,' " Jessie wrote enthusiastically to a correspondent four months after the Frémonts reached Los Angeles. "How can one fail to regain health here. . . . Open windows, sunshine, orange blossoms, clover knee-deep, that makes an earthly Paradise."[1] The Frémonts had arrived on Christmas Eve, 1887, welcomed at the train station by a crowd of well-wishers who included their old Prescott friend, Charles Silent, now a successful Los Angeles businessman. The Los Angeles *Times* recorded their arrival, noting that John retained his "firm, erect military bearing" while Jessie was "a perfect woman, whose massive coils of snow-white hair are a veritable crown."[2]

They settled at the Marlborough, a residential hotel crowded with eastern health seekers. John's bronchitis and Jessie's own aching joints, which she attributed to rheumatism, soon vanished, and by February she reported that they were walking three to five miles a day in the springlike weather, through "lovely green hills and blossoming orchards" or along stretches of sandy beach.[3]

Jessie's enchantment with California would remain a persistent theme in her letters of this last period of her life and underline a state of mind that more often approximated contentment than resignation. Even poverty seemed less oppressive in balmy Los Angeles: street children, with their sunburned faces, were "round full fed," showing little of the hopeless distress she had seen in New York City. "It rests one not to see doomed children."[4]

They were also nourished by the warmth of their reception. Less aware of the stains on his reputation, many Angelenos seemed eager to accept John Frémont as the hero he still looked to be. Introduced to the struggling young artist John Gutzon Borglum, later renowned for his presidential heads at Mount Rushmore, Jessie, with her quick recognition of talent, arranged that he paint her husband's portrait. "Fremont always came in on the arm of his wife who seemed the one person he wanted to please," a friend of Borglum's recalled. "She brought with her a military coat adorned with gold fringe and epaulets, a garment the great Indian fighter wore with dignity. . . . it was a good picture . . . day after day it assumed more life and grandeur."[5]

The Frémonts had been lured to Los Angeles not only by the possibility of improved health but also by the hope of profiting from the real estate boom that swept southern California in the late 1880s. Silent was among the developers of the new town of Inglewood, in the southwest environs of Los Angeles, and it was doubtless he who promised that the Frémonts would receive a house there in exchange for the use of their name in promoting the ambitious development. But within months of the Frémonts' arrival, the boom began to collapse, and Inglewood failed.[6] The Frémonts were forced to turn again to well-worn hopes: a pension for John's army service and compensation for Black Point. Jessie also continued her own writing, vital income during the next several years. Invigorated by her return to California, she began to write about her experiences at remote Las Mariposas. Published as a series of articles in *Wide Awake* and then as the volume *Far West Sketches* (1890), it was one of her most appealing books. Meanwhile, in the fall of 1888, John returned east to persuade Congress to pass the needed legislation for his pension and to drum up investors for his California real estate schemes. Jessie and Lily remained in Los Angeles.

While Jessie had returned to California for good, John, of his remaining nearly two years of life, would spend only six more weeks, in the summer of 1889, in California.[7] At first it was his pension that kept him in New York and Washington. But when he was finally granted a generous $6,000 a year by Congress in the spring of 1890, he nonetheless stayed on, ostensibly to complete an article for *Century* magazine and to pursue several unfinished business ventures.

In a July 7, 1890, letter to her husband, written just before his sudden and unexpected death in a New York City boardinghouse, Jessie implied that money alone kept them apart. This was clearly the myth the Frémonts chose to tell each other. But the pattern of separation, begun when John's western explorations kept him away for three of the first five years of their marriage, was now an essential part of their complex relationship and would not change in this last phase of their married life.

Nonetheless, John's death on July 13, 1890, devastated Jessie. The Frémont children exchanged anxious letters about her ability to survive the blow. Indeed, looking back, Jessie remembered the long mourning process as "nervous prostration—annihilation it seemed to me."[8]

But she did not allow herself to grieve immediately. John had left unfinished the article he was writing for *Century* magazine on his part in the conquest of California. Within weeks of his death, Jessie sat down to complete it by the September 1 deadline.

The resulting article, and the correspondence surrounding it, show Jessie at her weakest and most poignant. In a letter to *Century* editor Robert Underwood Johnson, she was both pleading and imperative, asserting that he publish the article unchanged "for justice to the General. And for consolation to me."[9] Ignoring the complexities of the American conquest of California and the needling questions Josiah Royce and others had asked about her husband's role, she proclaimed John Frémont's heroic part with lofty assurance. When Johnson asked her to revise, she agreed, then reconsidered, telling her nephew, University of California professor Carey Jones, "I had a full day's hard and angry thinking—restoring the General's own words, ideas, and punctuation."[10]

Meanwhile, admirers had begun a campaign to bring John's body to California for burial overlooking the Golden Gate. Jessie was enthusiastic. "It has taken hold of Mother's heart and its accomplishment would bring her sustaining strength," Lily confided to Carey Jones.[11] But several of the assessments of John's life that appeared soon after his death were harshly critical. A writer in the *Overland Monthly* claimed that Frémont was no pathfinder but followed a "plainly marked road." In the *Atlantic*, Royce himself twisted the knife in a bitter attack on Frémont as a "literary figment" who accomplished "absolutely no one significant thing."[12] When the controversy threatened to extend to the California legislature, where funding for a Frémont memorial was to be debated, Jessie abruptly decided to accept the offer of a gravesite at Rockland Cemetery in New York State, overlooking the Hudson opposite Pocaho. "I would not bring him from such loving memory . . . to be subjected to discussion," she wrote Carey Jones.[13]

As Jessie struggled to defend her husband's image, she faced a precarious financial situation. John's military pension had ceased with his death, and she was forced to borrow money from Los Angeles friends. Charley assumed that she and Lily would return east to live with him, but Jessie was determined to remain in Los Angeles. News of her predicament leaked out and received national publicity.[14] On September 24, amid supportive newspaper editorials, Congress granted her a widow's pension of $2,000 a year. At the same time, a group of women, spearheaded by her friend, Los Angeles civic leader Caroline Severance, organized a campaign to buy a house for her. Tactfully the group persuaded her to accept what could have been humiliating charity as "a gift from the women of California and a memorial of our regard for General Frémont."[15]

The house, designed by young architect Sumner Hunt with Jessie's stipulation to avoid Victorian "gingerbread," reflected the emerging California craftsman style with its emphasis on simplicity, natural and handmade materials, and the integration of the house with its outdoor setting.[16] Set in a grove of thirty-two orange trees, it was constructed of redwood with generous verandas facing north and south. Inside, western motifs dominated the decoration, including a collection of Indian baskets and a frieze of stylized oranges on the sitting room walls. Describing her new home in lavish detail to artist Gutzon Borglum, she delighted in the "artistic unconventionality" of it all.[17]

Settled with Lily in her final home by July 1891, Jessie summoned her latent strength for a last sustained effort to restore John's battered reputation. The project she undertook was the long postponed second volume of his memoirs, covering the most controversial periods of his life, including the court-martial, the 1856 election campaign, the Civil War, and his postwar business ventures. Jessie planned her campaign carefully. Long convinced that a woman must be indirect if she hoped to be effective, she decided to use lighter stories from her own life as "an entering wedge" to soften her audience for the "facts" of her husband's career.[18]

Frank Frémont arranged leave from the army to help with the project, and within six months they had completed an exhaustive 400-manuscript-page defense of John Frémont's career. Jessie had secured a publishing contract, but the firm was on shaky financial grounds and failed in 1894. "Great Events during the Life of Major General John

C. Frémont . . . and of Jessie Benton Frémont" would never be published.[19]

It was her last sustained effort for John Frémont. The next years, as she recovered from his death, were increasingly contented. As she sat on her veranda, shaded by climbing roses and wisteria, her bitterness at past injustices faded. Before John's death, Jessie had been actively involved in the Los Angeles community. As her grief diminished, she resumed a part, drawn in by her closest friend during these last years, Caroline Severance, a national leader in the woman's rights movement. Four years older than Jessie, she was a vital, active woman who had been a strong abolitionist during her eastern years and in 1868 had founded, with Julia Ward Howe, the first woman's club in America. In 1875 she and her husband, Theodoric, who suffered from tuberculosis, moved to Los Angeles, where she continued her reform activities.[20]

Caroline Severance found Jessie "brilliant, spontaneous, and original."[21] Loyally she adopted the myth of the Frémont marriage, describing John in a memorial poem published in the *Overland Monthly* as a "soldier statesman" and "lover-husband, to his latest day."[22] When Caroline Severance's own husband died in 1892, the two widows drew closer. Living only a few blocks apart, they often saw each other daily. In a Thanksgiving greeting in 1894, Jessie wrote with typical warmth, "Just a word to say you are a constant 'Thanksgiving' to be grateful for—such a true affectionate friend."[23]

In 1891, Severance had founded the Friday Morning Club, a woman's organization with a focus on civic reform. Jessie was invigorated by the openness and optimism of this community of active women. Both she and Lily became members, and Lily served a term as first vice-president. Club members advocated women's suffrage, promoted public kindergartens, backed women for such public positions as school board member and county supervisor of education, and established a women's work exchange. At club meetings, discussion topics ranged from socialism and international disarmament to dress reform, with a sizeable group admitting they no longer wore corsets.[24]

Jessie was also enlivened by her friendship with Charles Fletcher Lummis, the flamboyant Harvard-educated journalist, amateur ethnologist, and California booster who made his magazine, *Land of Sunshine* (later *Out West*), the center of a flourishing regional culture. Lummis pronounced Jessie "the most interesting woman I ever met"[25] and defended John Frémont's centrality in California history. Jessie shared Lummis's vision of southern California as a Mediterrean rather than puritan culture, as well as his enthusiasm for Theodore Roosevelt. She also supported Lummis's efforts to restore the California missions, to preserve the redwoods, and to encourage local artists like Gutzon Borglum.

In Borglum, Jessie found another young talent to nurture, encourage, and cajole. When he and his wife went to study in Europe, she sent him a barrage of warmly maternal advice, while using her influence to acquaint potential patrons like Leland Stanford and M. H. de Young with his work.

Through the mid-1890s, Jessie continued to thrive. "Sunday is my seventy-second birthday, & it is not reasonable to be so thoroughly unconsciously well as I am," she wrote Borglum.[26] But growing deafness made her increasingly reclusive. Except for an occasional piece for Charles Lummis's *Land of Sunshine,* she ceased writing for publication. Lily became more dominant in regulating her mother's life. Over the years they had grown deeply dependent. "Lil and I need each other so much and are so knit together that neither can face the separation," Jessie had explained to a friend a year after John's death.[27]

In June 1900, Jessie fell and fractured her left hip. The next months were filled with pain. Confined to a wheelchair but with her mind preternaturally active, she began to write her personal memoirs. Focusing on her childhood, she wrote more openly than she had in earlier reminiscences about the same events. Miss English's Female Seminary now seemed more repressive than charming, and the life of her Virginia relations more confining and closed. She wrote affectionately about her father, but her energy seemed to fade as she reached her married years. Eventually, she put away the manuscript "for compelling reasons."[28] Possibly Lily discouraged her project.

Chafing in her pain and restricted in mobility to a "rolling chair," Jessie had moments of self-pity. "I am so tenderly and intelligently guarded that I never open a letter, or see a visitor, or am told anything thay may agitate me," she explained to *Ladies Home Journal* editor Edward Bok in Mar. 1901. "I try my best not to be a 'nervous invalid' but the shock to the nerves was very great and abides with me."[29]

Yet even her last letters reveal some of her old spirit. She could still be pleased when tourists "Kodacked" the Frémont house and grow indignant at a proposed statue of John that looked like "a short wellfed man, shading his eyes with his hand" rather than the gaunt hero of the expeditions.[30] Only in her last six months of life did she lapse into silence, evidently writing no more letters. Increasingly frail, she withdrew into herself. On Dec. 27, 1902, seventy-eight-year-old Jessie Benton Frémont died quietly in her sleep.

Notes

1. To Joseph L. Budd, Mar. 28, 1888 (IaHi).
2. Dec. 26, 1887.
3. To Charles De Arnaud, Feb. 13 [1888] (CSmH).
4. To Nelly Haskell Browne, July 5, 1890 (CU-B—Frémont Papers).
5. SHAFF & SHAFF, 33–34. The portrait is now at the Southwest Museum.
6. The failing Inglewood developers tried to renege on the promised house, but Silent evidently intervened to see that they received it. They never occupied the house, however; by the spring of 1889 they were renting it out and probably sold it soon thereafter (JBF to Nelly Haskell Browne, Apr. 28 [1889], CU-B—Fremont Papers). For information on the Inglewood development, see Los Angeles *Times*, Jan. 1, 1888; DUMKE, 61–63; and JCF to Leland, Jan. 5, 1888 (NN—L. Kohns Collection). Another concurrent JCF land scheme involved the sale of southern California acreage for a Belgian colony (see JCF to Charles De Arnaud, Feb. 15, 1888, NNPM, and Mar. 12, 1888, MB).
7. See JCF to Charles De Arnaud, June 4, 1889 (CSmH).
8. To William A. Croffut, Sept. 22, 1894 (DLC—Croffut Papers).
9. Aug. 28, 1890, below.
10. Nov. 7, 1890 (courtesy of Mrs. Lincoln Reynolds, Corvallis, Oreg.).
11. Aug. 6, 1890 (courtesy of Mrs. Lincoln Reynolds).
12. See WELLS, 249; ROYCE [1], 550.
13. Dec. 8 [1890] (courtesy of Mrs. Lincoln Reynolds).
14. See, for example, San Francisco *Morning Call*, Sept. 17, 20, 24–26, 1890; New York *Times*, Sept. 18, 1890.
15. Statement, CU-B—Frémont Papers.
16. To John Gutzon Borglum, Jan. 3, 1891[92], below. On the California craftsman style, see ANDERSEN ET AL.
17. To Gutzon Borglum, Jan. 17, 1891[92], below.
18. To William Carey Jones, Jr., Oct. 28, 1890, below.
19. The manuscript is in the Frémont Papers, CU-B.
20. On Severance in Los Angeles, see JENSEN.
21. RUDDY, 127.
22. Quoted in RUDDY, 128–29.
23. Nov. 28, 1894 (CSmH—Severance Papers).

24. On the activities of Los Angeles women during this period, see APOSTAL, HUBBELL & LOTHROP, and LOTHROP.

25. FISKE & LUMMIS, 157.

26. May 25, 1896 (DLC—Borglum Papers).

27. To Charlotte (LeMoyne) Wills, July 5, 1891 (NNC—Nevins Papers).

28. JBF to Edward William Bok, Apr. 4, 1901, below.

29. Mar. 28, 1901 (CLjC).

30. To John Burt Colton, Jan. 16, 1902, below.

To Collis P. Huntington

Los Angeles, March 30. 1888.
Marlborough Hotel.

Dear Mr. Huntington,

We were sorry, and disappointed, that we could not meet you when you came through this place. Especially I wanted you to see how health has returned to the General—thanks to your instant comprehension and friendly aid to me in getting him, at once, out of New York winter weather.

You are so busy a man that I am shy of intruding on your time, even to say our warmest thanks are all the time freshly given you.[1]

I hope we shall see you if you are in Los Angeles again. I was very unhappy when I saw you last—that is all changed now—and, we shall try again to tell you so in person, and it will please you to realize how much you go for in this changed new life of ours. Always, sincerely yours,

Jessie Benton Frémont

ALS (NSyU—Huntington Papers). A Connecticut peddler in his youth, Collis P. Huntington (1821-1900), like JBF, had set out for California via Panama on the *Crescent City* in 1849. Establishing a store in Sacramento with Mark Hopkins, he eventually joined with Hopkins, Charles Crocker, and Leland Stanford in building the transcontinental railroad, making his vast fortune as the Central Pacific's shrewd financier and lobbyist.

1. Less than a month later, JBF would write Huntington again, asking him to use his influence with Congress to help pass the bill that would put JCF on the retired list of the army with the rank of major general, thereby entitling him to a military pension. "We have good and efficient friends at work," she wrote, "but you in full active life must have many who could be of deciding value there" (Apr. 20 [1888], NSyU). Again the bill failed to pass.

To John Charles Frémont

Los Angeles 22d January 1889.

Dear heart

I would not send you this notice of Godey's death[1] on your birthday—we went Sunday morning to the Hospital[2] and saw the Sister who was with him most. He got into town Wednesday evening and died Saturday evening being barely conscious at any time. As the Sister told us, he looked no more dead after breathing ceased than when he arrived — he was swollen in the face and I fancy from her description comatose — as he slept heavily most of the time. Suddenly he began hiccuping and seemed nauseated and in a few minutes life was ended. Hammel and Denker[3] (cattlemen & ranchmen and his "millionaire-friends") had insisted on his coming to this really beautiful Hospital, but it was too late. They took charge of all things and he had already been taken to the place from where he was to be sent to Bakersfield. Craig, Genl. Beale's man, telegraphing his wishes. His two rooms were *beautiful*.

I had a surprise in meeting his *widow*.[4] Maybe you knew he was married again? This time to a really uncommonly pretty little thing — a genuine Californian but of a delicate variety. "She neither can read nor write," the Sister told me, "and knows no English. We had to talk with her through a patient — a lady." She is very childlike — says "he left her a good house and she has many silk dresses." I talked with her. She is so pretty — the loveliest silky soft clean black hair — a clear good color in her dusky skin — great soft dark eyes and exquisite, small, ivory teeth. Only 20 now but already six years "casada" [married]. I asked her name. She is from here, a "Jimenez" but will live in Bakersfield because there tengo muy buena casa. Hoy es el mio [I have a very good house. Today it is mine.]. That house is a great point evidently. She had on a swell little gown "boughten" of black satin and black velvet — quite a hundred dollar gown if not more — for mourning a large new black silk "mascara" [veil] loose around her throat — her little brown hands were firmly crossed over a large unlaundried new hankerchief — man's size with a black border — her gold comb and earrings were natural to her. She was prim and intending to be quite correctly "a mourner" but her eyes danced over mi casa [my house]. She knew — vaguely — of you — that, "es el Señor que tenga una casa nueva muy grande — siempre una cuarta alla por *el* — cuando vino en Los Angeles?" [He is the gentleman who has a very large new house — always a room there for *him* — when he came to Los Angeles]. I left it at that.

So you see Alexis felt sure that what was yours was his to command. There was no more I could do.

The Hospital is *grand*. A fine site where old grounds, with large trees on the plateau and hill slopes, give a look of time as well as elegance to the whole.

The Sisters knew all about you—and me. One was sent for who had served in your Dept. in '61. They were as happy to meet me, to shew their house, as women can be. I promised to bring you there to "see what is done in this country."

But Godey's little wife was the astonishment to me. Lil and I were glad he had had a kittenish young life around about his.

I am getting all right—the weather is *cold* and bracing. Your loving,

JBF

AL initialed (CLSM). Envelope addressed to "Genl. Frémont, Care of Col. H. M. Porter, American Banknote Co., Church Street, New York City, N.Y."

1. JBF enclosed a notice from the Los Angeles *Herald,* Jan. 20, 1889, announcing the death of Alexis (sometimes Alexander) Godey at age seventy-one. Of French-Canadian ancestry, Godey had been a stalwart of JCF's on three expeditions and worked for him on the Mariposas estate. In courage and professional skills, JCF viewed him as a formidable rival to Kit Carson. From the early 1860s, Godey was engaged in cattle and sheep ranching in Kern County, including a brief partnership with Edward F. Beale to raise sheep on Beale's immense El Tejon Ranch (G. THOMPSON, 151–53).

2. The Los Angeles Infirmary, commonly known as Sisters' Hospital, was established in 1859 and rebuilt on a new site in 1885. Run by the Sisters of Charity, it could care for 100 patients (Los Angeles *City Directory,* 1892).

3. German-born brothers-in-law Henry Hammel (1834–90) and Andrew H. Denker (1840–92) were longtime business partners involved in hotel management, cattle ranching, and real estate, including much of what would become Beverly Hills (MCGROARTY, 3:432; GUINN, 821–22).

4. Maria Jimenez, a daughter of Navor Jimenez, was Godey's fifth and last wife. She inherited his Bakersfield house and later married Edward Salcido (LATTA [1], 51).

To John Greenleaf Whittier

West Washington street, near Oak.
Los Angeles California
November 19. 1889.

Dear Mr. Whittier

You would have had many letters from me if I wrote each time you were brought up in my mind, for thoughts of yours have become part of my ruling motives. This time I write because I know it will try even your in-born and controlled patience to bear the injustice to the Emperor of Brazil[1]—a man who has felt and lived up to, the claims of humanity in all forms. And see his reward! "Oh *Republic* what crimes are committed in thy name."[2]

Among the words I remember from you are "there is a time to *do,* and a time to *stand—aside.*" I never forget your saying this to me at our Nahant cottage, (in 1864) where you had come to say them to Mr. Frémont. Wendell Phillips who saw the "Do" more clearly than the "Stand—aside" insisted I had dreamed your visit. "Whittier goes nowhere—he *never* visits—his health does not let him" and other laughing arguments against your wise and necessary view of what the time demanded of Mr. Frémont—to renounce self for the good of the greater number. Do you not remember it too? It was a deciding word, coming from *you.*[3]

And how we have outlived all of that time! Here on this far shore where the serene climate gentles even hard memories I seem to look back into another life—its strifes ended—only its results in good cherished.

I have my daughter with me; my other children and the dear young grandchildren I have not seen for two years. It is much that they are well and write me fully and often but your Angel of Patience is more than ever part of my life. You may remember my telling you I read it in a newspaper when I was young—only twenty four—and pasted it in my prayer book of which it has all that time been part in its teachings.

The General had to return to New York this fall but will soon be back now. Your cousins will know the loveliness of this season here. I am writing by an open window, a La Marque rose wreathing all the gallery in deep green foliage and white roses but kept well trimmed back to pillars and balustrade to let in the sweet sweet sunshine. We are established here—in our "own hired house" as St. Paul puts it,[4] and the climate has brought health to my daughter & to me too after I got over my transplanting but it was a hard bout of home-sickness. We have many pleasant friends, and take our part in some of the good works of the town for there are many uprooted families here. My daughter does far more than I can now. And I write—hoping often that I too may find place in some tired heart and lead to new courage. Your cousins will let me know if you receive this? With our affectionate regards to you and your household I am your always-remembering friend,

Jessie Benton Frémont

ALS (NHi—Misc. Jessie Benton Frémont).

1. Pedro II (1825–91), the enlightened emperor of Brazil, had been overthrown by a military coup on Nov. 15. JBF was doubtless upset because Pedro, despite opposition from the planter class, had outlawed slavery. Although the coup established a republic, the government would be controlled by a series of military presidents who disregarded the constitution.
2. JBF probably refers to Jeanne-Marie (Philipon) Roland's celebrated last words before she was guillotined during the French Revolution: "O liberty! O liberty! What crimes are committed in thy name."
3. JBF more fully describes JCF's withdrawal from the 1864 presidential campaign in JBF to Samuel T. Pickard, May 28, 1893, below. See also JBF to Rutherford B. Hayes, July 7 [1881], above.
4. Acts 28:30.

To John Charles Frémont

Monday 4 p.m. July 7. 1890.

I have a chance to send this into town dear and I am going to direct [it] to your house for you may get it sooner. Not that there is anything to say beyond repeating the thanks for your telegram and its comforting promise and hope of a cable. I hope it will come. Mr. Merrill—if he comes again today, may make use of Dr. Morton's "hope."[1]

It is so slow this writing—"if" I could I would telegraph all the time. But then we could be together so there would be no need for telegrams. I was very glad to hear from Charley that Sally was strong enough to be moved out to their house. Has not Charley a good billet?[2] You must visit his ship before you leave. He seems sure of its being there off and on for half a year yet (not that *you* can stay that long). I think I am very bereft already. I like you—and it makes such a happy difference to see you.

Your JBF

AL initialed (CU-B—Frémont Papers).

1. In the spring, Congress had at last granted JCF a military pension, but he remained in a New York City boardinghouse at 49 West 25th Street to complete an article for *Century* magazine and to pursue several business ventures. He and longtime family physician William James Morton were involved in one scheme with some London investors, from whom he was expecting the cable JBF mentions (see JCF to Elizabeth Benton Frémont, July 9 [1890], NNC—Nevins Papers; to Morton, [Dec. 14, 1889] and Dec. 16, 1889, CU-B—Morton Papers; and to JBF, July 11, 1890, CU-B—Frémont

Papers). Merrill was probably John Alexander Merrill (1849–1927), a former Presbyterian minister who had begun to invest in southern California real estate. It was Merrill
who would deliver the news of JCF's unexpected death on July 13 to JBF (PRESS
REFERENCE, 1:579; New York *Times,* July 15, 1890).

2. John Charles Frémont, Jr., had just been assigned to the new cruiser *Philadelphia*
at the Brooklyn Navy Yard (JBF to Henry Brace, Aug. 18, 1890, DLC—Borglum
Papers). His wife, Sally, had been seriously ill for three months.

To Robert Underwood Johnson

Los Angeles, August 28. 1890.

Dear Mr. Johnson

The California paper has gone to you by Wells Fargo's Express. With
it the war paper and one of Mr. Bancroft's little letters.[1] These are all
so personal and warmly friendly I do not know if it is quite right to
print any. But this is a "voucher" and so many are of the doubting
école de Saint Thomas that they must see and touch to believe—they
have their functions in life. "Conservatives are intended to preserve
what enthusiasts created." They cannot help being born inadequate.

I did not count the words. A rough calculation shewed I must go
a little beyond your limit. But there is not a fact—I think not even a
wording that can be altered without injury to the whole. And the whole
is the *final speaking* of the General. I beg you to keep this in mind
and feel this as, not so much regulation copy, but as you felt that
sacred silence in the church.

I ask this for justice to the General. And for consolation to me. At
times this writing has been torture. To stumble alone over what had
been our delightful work together but it was all I could now do for
him and I alone could do it. Now it is done. Will you protect it dear
Mr. Johnson. It is the truth, nothing but the truth but not the whole
truth for there was only space for bare facts.

The first part is *exactly* as Mr. Frémont *wrote it to stand*—up to
the first expedition. Then, as he had briefed it for his final shaping,
roughly outlined. I had to condense even that. The Klamath Lake
episode—Gillespie's arrival,[2] the nature of Indian dangers—he said
must be retained in full as he wrote it. It fits in, necessarily, to the
later part also.

I condensed all I dared of the remaining facts of the intervening facts until Monterey and Sloat[3] are reached. The grant to McNamara[4] and Seymour's orders to English consuls[5] are indispensable as evidence.

The offered resignation of Mr. Frémont's commission has never before been told—in print.[6] It too *must* be kept to justify what he told Sloat. That, with all the letters of that time from 1842 to 1854, the last of the five expeditions, were lost when my Father's house was burned. He had intended publishing them—and much unwritten western history—a joint editing by himself and Mr. Frémont. Many letters had however been used by my Father—many printed in Niles Register, Congressional speeches, and Washington and Western papers. I looked up these from the Library of Congress and other sources, and my daughter typed copies.

Mr. Bancroft has an admirably kept library. He took much trouble, with the friendly aid of his Secretary Mr. A. Lyon, to verify fully his own and Mr. Frémont's memories.

In short all is *essential* and all is *proved*. Nothing can be spared from this condensed record just sent you.

The note by me must be kept also.

Back to back, on the same leaf with the General's noble head—is an editorial in Harper's Weekly of July 26th ('90). It shews the old venom that was so long successful against Mr. Frémont. As it says he had no anti-slavery record, nothing to identify him with the free soil feeling, it is just to shew how Mr. Frémont *voluntarily* renounced actual millions to keep secure this State to free labor.[7]

For their part as Senators in helping to keep California free soil both my Father and Mr. Frémont were defeated by the slavery power. That ended my Father's thirty years in the Senate.

"Reformers die but reforms live on." From my father's state of Missouri Mr. Frémont launched the key word *Emancipation*—and the people forced it to become the law of the land. Let these reasons explain why the unabridged writing should stand.

I have to ask you to put up with my writing. My daughter broke down when her type writing for her father was done. We go in the morning for a week of rest to a friend who lives on the sea shore.

But when I am back I hope to hear from you that what I have sent will be published without change.

We come back to another house, 517, West 23d street. This is full of pain to us, and now too large.

Dear Mr. Johnson protect the General's memory. Relying on you &
yours sincerely,

Jessie Benton Frémont

ALS (CLjC). Robert Underwood Johnson (1853–1937) was the associate editor
of *Century* magazine.

1. Despite her grief, JBF had managed to complete "The Conquest of California,"
the article her husband had been writing for *Century* magazine just before he died
(published in *Century,* 41 [Apr. 1891]: 917–28). She had also enclosed her own "Origin
of the Frémont Explorations" (*Century,* 41 [Mar. 1891]: 766–71). JBF's article includes
a July 2, 1886, note lauding Benton and Frémont's parts in western expansion from
the distinguished historian George Bancroft, James Polk's secretary of the navy during
the California conquest. Three additional letters from Bancroft relating to the conquest,
dated Sept. 2, 3, and 6, 1886, appear in JCF's *Century* article.

2. The letters and messages Marine Lt. Archibald Gillespie (1812–73) brought JCF
at Upper Klamath Lake in southern Oregon were at the heart of the controversy over
JCF's role in the California conquest. Traveling to California at the behest of President
Polk, who both coveted California and feared a British takeover, Gillespie carried a
secret dispatch for American consul Thomas Larkin, urging him to use extreme vigilence
in discovering and defeating any foreign attempt to seize California and, by peaceful
means, to encourage the Californians to join the United States. Gillespie also brought
news that war with Mexico was imminent. Gillespie carried the same news and instructions to JCF at Klamath Lake and also gave him a personal letter from Benton,
which, JCF claimed in his *Century* article, conveyed the message that "England must
not get a foothold; that we *must be first.* I was to *act,* discreetly but positively" (p.
923). Although Josiah Royce and others asserted that JCF went far beyond any instructions Gillespie carried, it was on this basis that JCF claimed he had joined the
Bear Flag revolt.

3. Commodore John Drake Sloat (1781–1867), commander of the U.S. Pacific fleet,
delayed six weeks after he learned fighting had broken out between Mexico and the
United States before acting on long-standing instructions from Navy Secretary Bancroft
to occupy California ports once war was declared. Bancroft later reprimanded Sloat
for his hesitation and replaced him with the more aggressive Robert Stockton. In a
note in JCF's *Century* article, JBF claimed that it was "the prompt decisive action
taken by Frémont" in joining the Bear Flag revolt that finally forced Sloat to act (p.
927). On this issue see HARLOW, 118–23.

4. Father Eugene McNamara, an Irish priest who reached Monterey in June 1846,
had successfully negotiated with the Mexican-California authorities for a large grant
of land in the San Joaquin Valley on which he planned to settle thousands of Irish
emigrants, a scheme JCF viewed as a veiled British attempt to appropriate California.
JCF later acquired documents relating to the McNamara plan and sent them to Secretary
of State Buchanan (HARLOW, 132–33).

5. Unknown to the Americans at the time and to JBF when she wrote this letter,
Rear Admiral George Seymour (1787–1870), commander of the British squadron in
the Pacific, had orders not to intervene in California. However, after the American
takeover, Seymour did write the British consul in California, with a copy to Sloat,
questioning the permanency of the American occupation (ibid., 132–34).

6. JCF had submitted his resignation from the army to Benton, to use if the Polk
administration chose to disavow his participation in the Bear Flag revolt.

7. The belittling editorial claimed that JCF was "an intrepid adventurer, who, happening upon California at a doubtful moment, had acquired by doubtful means, a sudden prominence . . . while the romance of his career was heightened by his elopement with the brilliant daughter of [Benton]." Moreover, having no antislavery record when he was nominated for the presidency in 1856, he was "merely a symbol, never a leader." In answer, JBF pointed out that he had opposed slavery in California during the 1849 constitutional convention, even though he could have made more money from his Mariposas mines if he had been able to use slave labor (see J. B. FRÉMONT [3], 95).

To William Carey Jones, Jr.

Tuesday morning October 28, 1890.
Los Angeles, 517, West 23d.

Dear Carey

I sent off a little avant courier of a pencil note to you yesterday to let you know *I fully agreed* with Mr. Johnson's wish to have every point made clear and plain to the average public, regarding the General's part in acquiring California.[1] You too, have a knowledge of the special blankness, or prejudice, of minds needing to be informed. Myself I do not feel the wisdom of trying to change prejudice. I would distinctly give the truth so that any mind preferring truth could not fail to adopt it but there are minds which think it fine not to believe what is plain but to distort things with some theory of their own. Let them go. But until I read Mr. Johnson's criticisms I do not try to think what he needed. He is uncommonly kind to take so much trouble to have the paper *quite* fair to the General. For a busy editor in that most complacent prosperous New York atmosphere he is remarkable—and I shall meet him all I can.

I only wonder I did *anything* at the time—August—that was intelligible. All September was a blur of bodily and mental suffering. I am coming back, surely, to strength and nerve. I can walk—not yet alone for I need Lily's arm, dear good child—a quarter of a mile. And daily I take an hour or two hours sometimes on the cable cars[2]—they glide so smoothly they tire me less than a carriage. And then I am not obliged to speak, or say thank you as I must even to Mrs. Severance who is the only one I have seen. I get home tired, but wholesomely tired now. At first it was depressing. But there are unexplored depths in us that only solitude of heart can find—a weary exploration but leading nearer to Divine strength.

"Lead Thou my feet."

Do you know well, Cardinal Newman's[3] hymn of self-renunciation, "Lead Kindly Light." To the General it was a revealing of his own later growth. Nina knew of it and it was chanted when friends gathered to look their last in the church. He had repeated it to me, by starlight, as we walked beyond our cottage—

> "I was not ever thus, nor prayed that Thou
> Shouldst lead me on.
> I loved to choose and see my path, but now
> Lead Thou me on."

You love us so truly dear Carey that what makes our necessary comfort will greatly interest you to know of. The dear women here who love Lily, as well as myself, have combined to give us a comfortable homestead—to us *both*. With my pension this secures every comfort but above all independence now, and a corner stone for Lily afterward.[4] And I have—*this is yet only known to Lil and myself*—the Websters[5] as my publishers for Memoirs of myself. This they *offered*—telling me they *could make money* for me. They are honest and rich, and have their reputation. Of course there can be no such money as they made for Grant or even will make for Mrs. Grant who is writing her memoirs, but *any* money is good and it is inspiring to write with the certainty of gathering a part of the gains. I owe this to the friendly action of Senator and Mrs Jones (Nevada).[6] Mark Twain (Mr. Clemens) is intimate with them. I told Mrs. Jones I wanted to make money this way and if I were in New York I would see the Websters—when she answered leave that to me and to Mr. Jones. Then came the Websters' good letter of offer—and telling *me* to fix the time after I was again well, when they could write me fully of the business arrangements. I am getting surely strong again and my work calls me on. I think I can now fix December the 1st as my time for beginning—I am so afraid of delays. I put it *my* memoirs to avoid all complications with the Belfords.[7] But my life from my fifteenth year was the General's. And always Father's until his life ended. So it is their lives I tell. And of mine only enough to make the lighter reading for general interest. I want to make this book *an entering wedge*. I think I know the public. And I want it with me. I want it to find me *interesting*. Then, well established, I can say more; sharply to facts.

But now I am Sixtus the 5th.[8] Feminine courtesy, and deference, are the crutches the public expects a woman to use. I must be firmly on my seat of authority before I drop them.

Our friends leave to us the choice of a house, all ready and furnished (in which we are now) or to build one to suit us exactly. I think they agree with me that Time is a great element in deciding. This is a charming house, among them close, and with a car line and a cable on either street adjoining. And its spare room is yours whenever you come dear Carey. Mary is our only servant but she is fully capable, with a supplement at times. So we see peace and useful busy work ahead. And health is returning. I will write you as often as is needed. I am trying to get through answering all the kind letters I could not answer as they came. Affectionately your

Aunt Jessie

ALS (Courtesy of Mrs. Lincoln C. Reynolds, Corvallis, Oreg.).

1. Robert Underwood Johnson had informed JBF that the article by JCF she had edited for *Century* was "exceedingly scrappy" and "vague, halting, colorless, unskillful" (Oct. 13, 1890, copy, CU-B—Jones Papers). He had sent the manuscript to her nephew, University of California professor William Carey Jones, Jr., for review (Oct. 15, 1890, ibid).

2. JBF would remain enthusiastic about Los Angeles's growing network of electric streetcars, which encompassed 1,164 miles of track at its peak in 1926. Early developers included Prescott, Ariz., friends Moses H. Sherman and Eli P. Clark, who in 1891 presented her with a lifetime pass. (CRUMP, 32–38, 173).

3. English cardinal and writer John Henry Newman (1801–90).

4. California women spearheaded a successful drive to raise money to purchase a lot and build a $3,500 house for JBF and Lily (Committee statement, n.d. CU-B—Frémont Papers; New York *Times*, July 26, 1891). The house was important as a "corner stone" for Lily because JBF's widow's pension of $2,000 a year, granted by Congress on Sept. 24, would cease at her death (San Francisco *Morning Call*, Sept. 25, 1890).

5. Charles L. Webster & Company had been established by Samuel Clemens to publish *Huckleberry Finn*. Clemens had also arranged for Webster to publish Ulysses S. Grant's *Personal Memoirs* (1885), which earned nearly half a million dollars in royalties. Julia Grant's *Memoirs*, however, would remain unpublished until 1975 (MCFEELY, 501, 504, 518). Webster & Company failed in 1894, and JBF's manuscript was never published (WEBSTER, 396).

6. John Percival Jones (1829–1912), a Comstock millionaire, served as Nevada senator, 1873–1903. In 1875, he had founded Santa Monica, Calif., as a real estate development, and JBF often stayed with his family there. His wife, Georgina Frances (Sullivan) Jones, was chair of the committee of California women who raised money for JBF's house.

7. Belford, Clarke & Company of Chicago had published the first volume of JCF's memoirs in 1887.

8. JBF makes a similar reference to Pope Sixtus V and his crutches in her letter to Frederick Billings, Feb. 7, 1862, above.

To James R. Gilmore

Los Angeles January 5. 1891.

My dear Sir

I am very troubled that your two letters, and the admirable and just notice of General Frémont have been so long unnoticed. It is only today that I know of their being here. My daughter has been so anxious about my slow recovery from a long illness that she, too faithfully, obeyed the peremptory order of our physician to let me do no more writing until certain bad conditions were past. I have had to complete for the Century a paper left incomplete by Genl. Frémont—it required so much selecting, abridging, verifying, that not being in right condition for such a strain of brain work, I broke down when it was finished— and my physician told my daughter *I must not think* under penalty of lasting injury.

I trust this will explain satisfactorily to you the delay. And I hope the returned paper is in time.

I find so little to alter, so much to be gratefully pleased with for the large and intelligent grasp of condensations, that I only send a few notes for your personal information. You have reached the truth *in essence* where some lesser points are slightly incorrect, but by and large it is wonderfully just. There were some points on which the General was sensitively anxious to stand clearly right before our people. That the honor and happiness to be always his trusted secretary from my eighteenth year and in listening to my Father and himself, and recording and having charge of preserving papers and records, and with clear memories of both these who served their country well, I think I can in larger measure than any other person give to the young men of the country the best portraits of these combined lives. When my health is firmly re-established *I* intend doing this—in my own way.

I wish you would let me introduce to you my youngest son who is, for a short leave, in New York. I sent to him a duplicate of the paper for the Century, and as I am not safely well yet, I would like you to see in that certain facts about the conquest of California which it would tire me too much to copy. You have the essence of the truth—

it *was* entirely the unhesitating action of Mr. Frémont which decided the situation, though some details are in error in your paper—only details however. The Century of course has the only right to see this until it is printed—which may be in March—but my son will shew it to you in confidence, for the full truth is given there for the first time—and above all else we protect the General. And I wish you to see there is reason for the faith you have had in Mr. Frémont's being the determining force in acquiring California. The paper for the Century will be a valuable historical document—*if* they publish it as written— one which could only come from Mr. Frémont—except the concluding sentences (by myself) the whole is in his own words; and those of the Hon. George Bancroft, who, alone, directed all military work on that coast until 1847. When it passed into the hands of Mr. Marcy[1] and a late arrival of U.S. dragoons.[2] The real work was done in 1846 in June and July and quite terminated by treaty in January of 1847. Mr. Bancroft was before that gone as minister to England, and the new hands all round made a muddle of what had been smooth and complete.

With many thanks for the unusual fairness, and insight, of the paper you sent me I am very sincerely yours,

Jessie Benton Frémont

My address remains Los Angeles though I shall be for the next few months at the seaside—Santa Monica—but it is but an hour by rail from here and I return here when I feel quite firm in health again. JBF.

Typed ms. returned by same mail. JBF.

I have spoiled but little of your copy. It has been a most pleasant duty to go over it carefully. I write by this mail to Miss Seward.[3] And my son to have him call on you—unless he is ordered to join for the Sioux troubles. JBF.

ALS (MdBJ). Writer and lecturer James Roberts Gilmore (1822–1903) had asked JBF to review an entry on Frémont prepared for his projected *Gilmore's Cyclopaedia of American Biography*. A prospectus and specimen pages for the *Cyclopaedia* appeared in 1891, but the work was apparently never published.

1. William Learned Marcy (1786–1857), a three-time New York governor, was James Polk's secretary of war.

2. Gen. Stephen Watts Kearny and his hundred dragoons reached California in Dec. 1846, in time to participate only in the last two battles of the conquest.

3. In an earlier letter, Gilmore had evidently asked JBF to write the Frémont entry; declining, she suggested her "dear friend" Olive Risley Seward (JBF to Gilmore, Oct. 22, 1890, MdBJ). It appears, however, that Gilmore wrote the entry himself.

To John Greenleaf Whittier

Santa Monica
near Los Angeles
February 8th 1891.

Dear Mr. Whittier

It was a surprise of the most pleasing kind to get your remembrance —
here by the Sundown Sea it came to me most fitly.[1] And I value the
words you added, fully as much as you must have known I would.

My daughter, who has the name you love, Elizabeth — is here with
me; we two make our home in Los Angeles but I am here for a few
months to regain health. We have a cottage on the bluff and I can sit
there and feel the enchanting soft freshness of this blue ocean and get
that stilled feeling the sea always brings me. There is nothing crude or
newly raw about this lovely spot for it was well planted nearly twenty
years ago — equal to fifty elsewhere — and the broad terrace on the
bluff has its wide double avenues of old wind-swept cypress and eucalyptus trees, where a long mile of firm grass-grown walk can be had.
And a hundred feet below the long rollers break on a firm sand beach
on which one can drive for many many miles.

To you, SnowBound[2] at this season, it is hard to realize the June-
like beauty of the roses and heliotrope and honeysuckle and fuschias
that cover the cottages to the roof, while beds of violets are in full
bloom. And yet morning and evening we have wood fires, for beauty
and companionship more than necessity. Not drift wood, but the
fragrant eucalyptus and cypress, and the loppings from orange and fruit
orchards. I think it will please you even to read of such beauty and
sweetness in natural surroundings. We have what is more beautiful
still — true loving friends. Real, heartfelt sympathy *does* bring healing
and helps to give strength for the inevitable endurance of what seems
unendurable.

I told you how, so long ago, I was but twenty two, Mr. Frémont
gave me a prayer book into which I pasted your Angel of Patience. It
grew into my life and I have long known its full meaning, now, more
than ever.

I cannot go to my sons and the dear young ones in their eastern
homes, both my daughter and myself need this even serene gentle

climate, but I feel very near to the older life when I am remembered as you remembered me.

I have work to finish when I get quiet health again, and dear friends, women who love us both, have made for us a home in the lovely neighborhood your nieces will remember—where the velvety cypress hedges and curtains of roses were so beautiful. We stay here until May when the house will be quite finished and there I will write and have I hope good use of my life until my sun goes down. It is so good to know of your continued beautiful writing, and you have the privilege of being in familiar scenes and near friends of long standing. I do trust as much peaceful health and its great helping power to use life may remain with you.

I have been out in the garden to get you a fresh violet. It will be withered when it has made the long journey but it will have with it some perfume still. I wish I could send you many, and the pale pink Duchesse roses I had to bring in, for today there is a sea wind that scorches their delicate petals. Is it not a charming legacy to us from Spanish times that the two stations of health giving in the South are the turbulent St. Augustine on the stormy Atlantic and here on the placid Pacific Santa Monica—his loving hoping patient Mother—who had her great reward in seeing her son turn all his impassioned energy to doing right.

Dear Mr. Whittier I have been back to Nahant, to Amesbury, to many memories as I wrote to you. Thank you for the warming softening influence.

And remember me to the nieces who gave me a pleasant day in Los Angeles—and who make your days more pleasant to you.

With affectionate friendship I am as always sincerely yours,

Jessie Benton Frémont

ALS (MiMtpT).

1. Whittier had sent JBF a copy of his newest book of poems, *At Sundown* (1890).
2. A reference to "Snow-Bound," perhaps Whittier's finest poem.

To John Gutzon Borglum

Los Angeles January 3d, 1891[92].

Dear Mr. Borglum

I have your letter of December 15 from Paris and answer at once that my thanks and affectionate good wishes may reach Mrs. Borglum and yourself before your next move.

This will be a brief letter because I am crowded with writing but I want to answer the business points—first I must tell you both how truly delightful Mrs. Borlgum's long letter was—it was so good to see into your interieur, to go bycycling with you and the dogs, to know of Phil Rollins's[1] most lovable behaviour. When it came, my son, Frank, and myself were finishing up, *on contract time,* the writing out of the General's memoirs. To do this we had to examine, sift, verify and read up masses of collateral writings and records—to condense without losing a point or becoming diffuse either; and I was still so near to my long illness—nervous prostration—that too much thinking or feeling brought back old bad conditions and of six days three at least had to be absolute idleness—in bed or at best in a hammock where I would fall asleep in the open air. Fever, loss of sleep and appetite came almost certainly after even agreeable exertion. [*Margin note:* We finished our book *within* time—it will make 500 printed pages but it was hard on me.] Now, I can walk a mile, and write all morning—that is from nine to one but I feel better when I just dawdle. I have lots and lots to say to you both but you will know from what I have told you that it was work to keep alive. Lily would miss me too much—and I want to keep with her, and keep for her my pension. It is only two thousand but that and this lovely home give us our comforts and we brought on enough of the old home in books and china and pictures and home ideas—things that were packed away nearly six years ago. We furnished our house ourselves and if you ever see it you will say it is artistic. The architect Sumner Hunt[2] is a New York and Boston man with the best large ideas and we agreed entirely on *no pettiness*—no gingerbread, so the house is simplicity and comfort combined. I will mail to the care of Monroe [Munroe] a packet for you with photographs. I am about discouraged by my losses in the foreign mails. My sister [Eliza Benton Jones] in Florence had not heard from me in eighteen months, and I had written rather often. If mailing is not *very* sure I will try Wells Fargo for I want you to have the photographs I send. That of your mare and colt came safely.

I don't know who the present minister to Spain is but I will learn and write to him at once. Senator Palmer[3] who was his immediate predecessor is a warm personal [friend] of ours and was really attached to the General but I will do as you ask, and send the letter to Monroe's care. I knew Johnny Monroe as a baby.[4]

About Lininger.[5] It is both trying and mortifying to be put in a false position by him. But he is on the ground and would defend himself for his business sake and you could not keep pace with him. The public *hate* a controversy. Nobody cares so much about us as we care for ourselves and nobody wants to "take sides"—especially where one man may possibly be of advantage to them and the other is not in the show business but is merely in the right.

You can, and ought, to write a careful statement to be used in case of real need for it—but that is different from *beginning* a controversy. Lininger will say black is white where his interests are at stake—then who would you send it to to *use* or *not?* That is a delicate point and would need tact, both business and social tact. There is no real harm done unless Lininger renews his assertions of useful patronage and is offensively public about it. The very best way to do is to go on to independent success, *then* expose him. That is hard counsel to follow but it is good I think. *He* will be the first to offer his services if you no longer need him. Then, you have your opportunity.

I think you should secure as early as possible some friendly ally at the Fair.[6] I can, and will write about you to its President, Palmer (the late minister to Spain). I am so out of the current nowadays, but I sometimes know people, and you must always let me know where I could, would or might be of use.

Mr. Friend[7] has made me an interieur where my writing desk with myself and above the desk the dear noble face I owe to you are given. You will see they are not yet developed—but in sending one to Mr. and Mrs. Palmer I will speak for you and your picture for the Fair. I will get you Mr. Eastman's address. All the family are in Chicago. Barrett has married very well—family and fortune and agreeable girl—it pleases them.[8]

This is my stint for tonight. Mrs. Severance has grippe. I go to see her daily. She was pleased by your message. I have not had a line from the Rollins until yesterday—then a lovely water color of sea beach—solitary as your tree.[9] Affectionately yours and Mrs. Borglum's friend,

Jessie Benton Frémont

[*Margin note:* Some leaves of the red roses you liked.]

ALS (DLC—Borglum Papers). The son of Danish immigrants, John Gutzon Borglum (1867–1941) attended primary school in Frémont, Neb., which delighted JBF. He moved to Los Angeles in 1884, where he worked as a lithographer and began to paint. In 1888 he painted JCF's portrait, and JBF became an enthusiastic supporter, providing both advice and introductions to potential patrons. In 1889 Borglum married his art teacher, Elizabeth (Jaynes) Putnam (1848-1922); in late 1890, the couple set out for France and Spain, selling paintings en route to pay their way. In Paris, much influenced by Rodin, Borglum turned to sculpture. Returning to Los Angeles, he did a small delicate head of JBF. In 1896, as he achieved national recognition, he left Los Angeles permanently. His most famous works are the presidential heads at Mount Rushmore, which occupied the last fourteen years of his life (*Land of Sunshine,* 4 (Dec. 1895): 34-37; STARR, 121-22; SHAFF & SHAFF).

1. In earlier letters, JBF had advised Borglum on securing the patronage of wealthy young Princeton graduate Philip Ashton Rollins (1869-1950), who had wintered in California with his sisters two years before (see JBF to Borglum, Mar. 15 [1890], DLC—Borglum Papers). The heir to western cattle ranches, Rollins would devote much of his life to amassing an important collection of western Americana, which he left to Princeton (New York *Times* obit., Sept. 12, 1950).

2. New York-trained architect Sumner P. Hunt (1865-1938) began practice in Los Angeles in 1889 in the new California craftsman style. His most noted work, built in 1912 for Charles Lummis, is the Southwest Museum (PRESS REFERENCE, 1:66; New York *Times* obit., Nov. 21, 1938).

3. Former Michigan senator Thomas Witherell Palmer (1830-1913), an advocate of woman's suffrage, served as ambassador to Spain, 1889-91.

4. "Johnny" Munroe (d. 1904, age 54) was the son and successor to John Munroe (d. 1871), founder of John Munroe and Company, for many years the Frémonts' Paris bankers (New York *Times* obit., Dec. 2, 1904).

5. George Washington Lininger (1834-1907), owner of an agricultural equipment firm, maintained a private art gallery in Omaha and made frequent trips to Europe to supplement his collection. When the Borglums stopped in Omaha en route to Europe, Lininger exhibited their paintings and evidently agreed to finance their European trip, but JBF's letter suggests he reneged on the arrangement (MORTON, 2:386; SHAFF & SHAFF, 35-38; Los Angeles *Times,* June 30, 1890).

6. The World's Columbian Exposition would be held in Chicago in 1893. When Borglum returned to California, he worked on a mural, *Noche Triste,* depicting the conflict between Cortés and the Aztecs, for the fair but did not complete it in time (SHAFF & SHAFF, 43, 45).

7. Herve Friend (1842-1907) was a Boston-born photographer and photoengraver active in Los Angeles, 1887-95 (information courtesy of Peter Palmquist, ed., *The Daguerreian Annual;* C—California Death Index).

8. Barrett Eastman (1869-1910) was a Chicago journalist. His wife, Sophia (b. 1873), was the daughter of five-time Chicago mayor Carter H. Harrison, who was assassinated in office in 1893. JBF particularly liked the beautiful Sophia Eastman, to whom she was related through the Preston family of Virginia (JBF to Caroline Severance, Mar. 16, 1897, CSmH). The Eastmans' marriage ended in divorce; Barrett remarried but committed suicide a year later (Chicago *Record Herald* obit., Jan. 16, 1910).

9. Borglum had given JBF several paintings, including one of a cypress tree entitled *Windswept,* which at one point Philip Rollins had been interested in buying (JBF to Borglum, Mar. 15 [1890], DLC—Borglum Papers). It was probably similar to an 1889 Borglum work, *Solitude,* which depicted a lone cypress against a dark sky and pounding surf (SHAFF & SHAFF, 34).

To John Gutzon Borglum

Sunday night, 17th January 1891[92].

Dear Mr. Borglum

I send you a note of introduction which will I am sure be a pass key for you to the best things you may wish to study. The unfortunate minister is named GRUBB[1] — and he has recently married an English woman — that is all I know of him — read my letter and go by it.

I send you a rumpled first proof of an interieur just made for me by Mr. Friend. I will send you finished proofs, mounted, of each of the four he made. Each has some points you and Mrs. Borglum will appreciate. *The* feature is your head of the General. I wish you would shew that to the Minister for in all the Velasquez heads there is not one more noble, more knightly than this portrait you made so like, so true to the General's inner nature.

I am writing now at the old Nantucket desk you will remember — a shaded lamp throws up light with life like effect on the dear face — how grateful I am to you for it I can never express. It is our true shrine. There are violets before it now — we keep flowers there always — the candlesticks were for many years on my writing table, and on the General's in our adjoining rooms. The portrait of myself was painted in 1856 by Buchanan Read — the General especially liked the eyes and mouth. I turned my back because the hair is lovely and because it shews me actually writing — it is only for my own chosen people I had it made. You will see we have an artistic boudoir-parlor. Your tree hangs on the same wall with the General, only a south window intervening — no other pictures on that side. The opposite wall has a low bookcase its whole unbroken length and above it many pictures, and much china, bronze &c — wreckage from our old days as are the books there and in the hall. A large beautiful fire place, dignified — of oiled redwood with maroon brown freize tiles, brass fender and irons &c and *wood fire* faces the sliding doors. You see the portières. They, and the walls (of cartridge paper) are of pale olive green, with greyish white and golden brown touches in the portières and in the freize — the freize is perfect — papering but with a good idea oranges, in brownish green, drab green just hinted golden green and equally good treatment of the leaves — the whole [intelligently?] brightened by here and there gilding outlines. We furnished the house ourselves and the papering I paid for with a check for Xmas writing. Rugs, table covers, chairs all harmonize and some few appreciate and delight in the artistic unconventionality while all think it "very fine." The dining room, across the little hall, is equally charming with corner fire place and a corner china cupboard whose glass doors keep dust off lovely old china—but you will see and what is more sit and eat there often I hope.

Goodbye to both of you for to-night. Affectionately your friend

Jessie Benton Frémont

ALS (DLC—Borglum Papers).

1. Edward Burd Grubb (1841–1913), a Civil War hero and wealthy Pennsylvania businessman, had been appointed minister to Spain in 1889 (New York *Times* obit., July 8, 1913).

To Caroline Severance

[June 28, 1892]

My dear Mrs. Severance

I am truly sorry I can't be with you today at the Kindergarten meeting[1]—as you *know,* I *cannot,* and as you know *equally well*—, I wish, literally from my heart, to be of use in that most wise, most patriotic, and benevolent care for young children. The care of our future citizens and law makers—or law breakers—is in our hands *more* while they are very young than is possible to catch up with, if they are left to the "education of the street." In our day of intelligence, prevention has displaced cure, wherever the best thought prevails. It is our *national fault* if Reform schools have to be provided, to meet the omission of *care* for the very young & the *Kindergarten* is the prevention, while the cure (?) becomes a doubtful problem after neglected childhood. This brings the Kindergarten to the front as wise *economy.*

While to the average working mother it is a rest for mind and body to know her little ones are in safe keeping, and their busy young instincts are assimilating good and not evil, it also doubles her working energy. And it is twice blessed in making the *children, instructors* in *turn,* for we all need to learn the instincts, the curious outreachings and unforeseen grasp of those groping young creatures.

It is a fortunate thing for Los Angeles that it has the experience, the large knowledge and rare training of Mrs. Mayhew[2]—who is in such apostolic succession of educating by kindness, with the dear Dr. Eliot of St. Louis, and Susie Blow[3] who had his great help in her devoting her youth, her fortune, her uncommon talents, and personal advanatages of family and beauty, all to this great womanly work.

I am proud of St. Louis when I remember its noble advance work in education, *progressive* education, not building on nelgect but on wise and gentle care. Over the first of the public schools is cut, in great stone letters, "*Benton* School"—in memory of my Father's earnest work for education. The Kindergarten was not known in his day, but its need and its future bearing was felt by him; for he fully believed with the laws of Ancient Rome, that even the unborn child, was the care of the State, as the coming citizen.

Rising above human law is the enduring command "Suffer little children to come unto me."[4] To prevent the best care for them—either through neglect or apathy or ignorance—is sinning against that Divine order. For those who have given thought to the subject there is no possibility of neglect. Each of us *is* our brother's keeper—most of all, when he is in the helpless stage of early childhood. Chances may retard universal acknowledgement of the peremptory value of Kindergartens but it is Truth, as well as wisdom and kindness, and must prevail, over all our country—where American feeling governs—as it does in the West—and has not yet in New York City.

But the subject leads too far,—it is the sowing what the country is to reap. Shall it be Wheat or Tares? Sincerely yours—and all children's friend,—

Jessie Benton Frémont.

June 28th 1892
Los Angeles.

ALS (CSmH—Severance Papers). A devoted advocate of early childhood education, Severance had launched California's first kindergarten and teacher-training program in 1876 under the noted educator Emma Marwedel. In 1884, Severance founded the Free Kindergarten Association, which financed kindergartens for underprivileged children and eventually persuaded the Los Angeles school system to inaugurate a public kindergarten program. By 1895, 1,314 children would be enrolled in Los Angeles public kindergartens (SPLITTER, 232–34; RUDDY, 87–88).

1. JBF refers to the June 28 commencement of the first training class for kindergarten

teachers established in the Los Angeles public school system. An audience of six or seven hundred attended the ceremony, which included demonstrations of the kindergarten program (Los Angeles *Times,* June 28, 29, 1892).

2. Nora Dorn Mayhew, the director of the new teacher training class in Los Angeles, had studied under noted kindergarten educator Susan Blow in St. Louis (ASSOC. CHILDHOOD, 21).

3. Susan Blow (1843–1916) was the brilliant and idealistic daughter of Henry Blow of St. Louis, a civic-minded, antislavery Republican who had been both a Benton and Frémont political ally. A disciple of Friedrich Froebel and Elizabeth Peabody, Susan Blow became a distinguished leader in the kindergarten movement. In 1873, in the progressive atmosphere of post–Civil War St. Louis, she directed the first public kindergarten in America; by 1880, there were fifty-eight kindergartens in the St. Louis public school system. See SNYDER, 59–85, on her life and influence.

4. Mark 10:14.

To Samuel T. Pickard

Los Angeles, May 28th 1893.

Dear Mr. Pickard

I return you my letter to Mr. Whittier and give you permission to use it—in full, or in part as you see fit.[1] We did indeed have friendly, assured relations, not depending on much personal seeing for that was not in the line of our lives, but some things are once for always.

Mr. Whittier did come to Nahant to speak those words to Mr. Frémont—who was in New York just that week. Wendell Phillips refused to believe Whittier had actually "made a visit"—"you are imaginative" he laughed "and saw a vision—Whittier goes *nowhere.*"

Yet he did come to us impelled by the seriousness of the election condition—a condition Lincoln's biographers Hay & Nicolay have agreed to say was only laughed at.[2] About the time of Whittier's coming the General had a visit, in New York, at the law office of David Dudley Field, from Senator Z. Chandler, Chairman National Com. Republican, representing a decision made in the President's (Lincoln) cabinet room at Washington. Henry Winter Davis and others of the governing Republicans were the council. My papers are in New York in the care of my son Lt. Frank Frémont (who has the whole recorded, typed, and to be published) so that I do not venture to be as exact as even *my* memory justifies but in sum, Chandler, *from President Lincoln, asked the General to withdraw* as division of votes would peril the Republican party, as *"a vital service to the party."*

Accustomed to a different nature of men, Mr. Lincoln with this offered political power; the *giving office to Frémont's friends; and, the removal of the Blairs* from their positions of office.

Mr. Frémont refused all offers of political position or *any personal* considerations. The safety of the Republican party was his one and only reason for accepting, or now, for withdrawing from the nomination.[3] When it was first planned, Gov. Andrew was to have been named—as representing the true, vigorous, actions and intentions of the party. The leading men of the party were agreed this was needed. Genl. Frémont was to act with the leading Germans of the West and Northwest—the East also—who were gravely dissatisfied. Before the renomination of President Lincoln events changed somewhat. From various causes many fell off, and ultimately fell into line. [lines missing?] the General's *motives* at that time. He acted with the best thought of some of the truest men of the country but *they* fell back and left him to lead.

Mr. Lincoln's cruel death silenced much truth, and since then he has been shaped and exalted into such "a faultless monster as the world ne'er saw"[4]—not content with his real greatness he has been made to appear incapable of error—and in short viewed in all ways from the altered conditions of a generation later, and the great "Ifs" of historical *possibilities,* together with often small minds in judgment.

That the General *did* act with "singular magnanimity" is perfectly true. He was incapable of putting self before duty. And he did feel— all his life—his duty to the noble Republican party that had so honored him. And for which he always worked with heart and faith. Whittier was a poet and *felt* this. Did you ever see some lines by Genl. Frémont, "On re-crossing the Rocky mountains after many years"? Mr. Whittier included them in his Songs of Three Centuries,[5] with a note, regretting they were anonymous. A New York friend of ours sent him the fact that they were by Mr. Frémont (I do not know if this is given in later editions). Read the lines and you will see how greatly charmed Mr. Frémont, a poet himself, was by Whittier's message to him—"there is a time to act, and a time to Stand Aside"—as before, Whittier spoke the right and fitting word at the time of test. There ought to be a letter to him, telling that the General had decided to "Stand Aside."[6]

I have no papers here belonging back of our arrival here six years ago. My son brought on, and took back, all belonging with our six months work over a completed memoir of his Father—to be published.

There is a time for each thing. The General's name will grow to mean much more to our people as time clears away interested writers who mystify simple facts for their own ends.

Your book dealing with the kindest, gentlest of men, whose righteous wrath was impersonal, and pitying while condemning, may not, must not have, any political question. So in its limited scope you cannot very well—not fairly to Genl. Frémont—give only *partial* allusion to that "stand aside" visit. The request—not any way so [single?] in meaning of large duty—had already come from the President, through the Chairman of the Republican National Committee, on consultation with men who foresaw McClellan's success from the division in the Republican party. The letters and facts my son holds. Sincerely yours,

Jessie Benton Frémont

[*Margin note:* This letter is *not* private though you may not decide to use its facts. JBF]

ALS (MH). Samuel T. Pickard (1828–1915), longtime editor of the influential Portland (Maine) *Transcript,* was married to John Greenleaf Whittier's niece, Elizabeth Hussey Whittier. When Whittier died in 1892, Pickard became his literary executor and biographer.

1. JBF's account of her friendship with Whittier, with excerpts from their correspondence, appears in PICKARD, 2:460–66, 487.
2. In their ten-volume 1890 biography of Abraham Lincoln, his two former secretaries, John G. Nicolay (1832–1901) and John Hay, claimed that Lincoln had viewed Frémont's 1864 presidential bid "with amusement" (NICOLAY & HAY, 9:40). In reality, Lincoln was seriously concerned (see, for example, KOERNER, 2:432).
3. For further information about this episode, in which Chandler and Davis, speaking for Lincoln, offered to remove Montgomery Blair from the Cabinet in exchange for JCF's withdrawal, see JBF to Rutherford B. Hayes, July 7 [1881], above.
4. *Essay on Poetry* by John Sheffield, Duke of Buckingham (1648–1721).
5. *Song of Three Centuries* (Boston: J. R. Osgood, 1876) and numerous subsequent editions.
6. No letter immediately after Whittier's 1864 visit has been found; PICKARD (2:487) quotes from JBF to Whittier, Nov. 19, 1889, above.

To Nelly Haskell Browne

Los Angeles, March 18th 1895.

Dear Nell

Your friend has not yet put in an appearance. I hope to be in when she does come but I am out a great deal. In this loveliest fresh season

it is good to breathe open air all day, if one can. Lil and I are rarely
in (except for meals) and always for our good home evenings which
she too finds pleasant with books and nice people often until nearly
eleven. We are both wonderfully well and one of my nicest neighbors,
a Boston woman who has lived long in Egypt, Syria, and such, has a
comfortable carriage with a civilized step and her husband loves driving
and he and the horses are safe so I go with them almost every afternoon
for real long country drives from two to five o'clock. The orchards
are in bloom and the natural growth of flowers and grass make hills
and dales in green plush embroidered with violet, pink, yellow, white—
lovely air, lovely scenery all framed in by the sudden mountains. It is
not your Fusiama,[1] and we miss the body of water but it is very lovely
and brings one sleep and appetite. Though I can, and do, walk my
daily mile or mile and a half in the morning. Consequently I am really
well. You see I hold to living until we get Black Point, after that my
pension will not be needed.

Lil too is exceptionally well. You go so often to the East that you
know more of my people's home there than I do—except from letters.

Jack* is doing finely at the school—academy I beg its pardon—that
George Curtis so approved of.[2] [*Margin note:* *Jack/just fifteen/ had
been named "Frémont's Peak" by the school boys—he is now five-
feet ten inches]. Sally sang a composition (music by someone else but
words by Curtis) at the annual fête-day held in his memory on his
birthday. Mrs. Curtis there, and warmly thanking Sally. Sally made a
real success in the Mikado as Yum-Yum—both her acting and singing
were *good*. And Carrie is having *her* successes as singer in Minneapolis
as well as at the Fort.[3] She is in demand for small charities out there.
They are all well—all "content" and busy.

We are all in great peace every way. We *could* do with more money,
and I think we will have it but where I have so much to fill my heart
with thanks I am—as our prayer book puts it "afraid and ashamed"
to ask for more. We always are glad to hear from you, affectionately,

J. B. Frémont

ALS (CU-B—Frémont Papers).

1. Nelly and her husband had moved to Tacoma, Wash., about 1887-88, where
their Fujiyama was, of course, Mount Rainier. George Browne prospered as a real
estate and streetcar promoter; in June 1888, he became a founding officer of the St.

Paul and Tacoma Lumber Company, the world's largest sawmill operation (MORGAN, 257–59; HUNT, 2:20–24).

2. JBF's grandson Jack (John C. Frémont III) was attending the Staten Island Academy, where longtime *Harper's* editor George William Curtis had been a trustee. After his 1892 death, Curtis's birthday was celebrated annually at the school (MILNE, 131, 190). In advance of the 1895 festivities, the New York *Times* had announced that "Mrs. John C. Fremont [Sally] will render several of [Curtis's] poems, which had been set to music" (Feb. 25, 1895). Mrs. Curtis was Anna (Shaw) Curtis (1836–1923), a daughter of JBF's friends Francis and Sarah (Sturgis) Shaw.

3. JBF's son Frank and family were stationed at Fort Snelling, Minn., where all was not as well as JBF supposed. Over the next fourteen years, Frank would divorce and remarry, declare bankruptcy, and be court-martialed three times on various charges, including financial irregularities and insubordination, for which he would be dismissed from the army in 1909. Included in Frank's army file are a number of letters on his behalf from JBF, including an Oct. 30, 1901, plea to Theodore Roosevelt for "justice" for Frank during his first court-martial (DNA-153, General Courts-Martial 26308, Francis P. Fremont). For his military career, see DNA-94, Francis P. Fremont appointment file, 4922-ACP 1877; New York *Times,* Apr. 8, 11–13, 24, 26, 1907, Jan. 4, Mar. 25, 1909.

To Theodore Roosevelt

Los Angeles, August 21st, 1899.

Dear Governor Roosevelt

Dining last evening with Judge Charles Silent he spoke to me of a letter he had written you regarding an Arch to be raised for Dewey.[1] As Judge Silent cannot well say just who he is, I thought I would— (quite unknown to him). He is a reserved, very forceful, man who is foremost here in initiating good work and having put the more demonstrative people at it, remains in the background but *always working.* He is our closest friend here.

The beautiful entrance—an eagle poised high on a column over a cluster of electric lights—marking the chief entrance to the great park here is of *his* thought—it is called "the Frémont Gate."[2] Consider him introduced by me, I know I am among the more favored of nations.

I am so glad of everything that brings my son into relations with you. He wrote me of the charming dinner they had at Oyster Bay and sent me a cutting from the Sun of his Report on the dumping in the Harbor and that pall of smoke from the cremation works at its mouth.[3]

I know he will work with more faith in success from being with you in these measures. You are an inspiration. I am very, *very* much pleased with you, if you will allow me to say so—at seventy six one speaks. You are my typical American in everything. With sincere respect, yours truly,

Jessie Benton Frémont

ALS (DLC—Theodore Roosevelt Papers). JBF was enthusiastic about conservationist, western aficionado, civic reformer, and Rough Rider Theodore Roosevelt (1858-1919), no doubt in part because he had also written an appreciative biography of Thomas Hart Benton, with whom he clearly identified. At the time of this letter, Roosevelt was governor of New York. In 1901 he became vice-president and assumed the presidency when William McKinley was shot on Sept. 14.

Roosevelt responded to JBF's letter in his usual brief, enthusiastic style: "It is always a pleasure to hear from you. You know I think your son one of the finest officers in our navy, and I have unlimited faith in him . . . I am glad to hear about the Judge. Anything I can do I will most gladly" (Sept. 2, 1899, DLC—Theodore Roosevelt Papers).

1. On May 1, 1898, Commodore George Dewey (1837-1917) had seized Manila Bay; on Aug. 14, Spain surrendered the Philippine Islands to the United States. In 1900 a Spanish American War Memorial, featuring a statue of a war veteran rather than Dewey specifically, would be placed in Central Park, now Pershing Square, in downtown Los Angeles (FED. WRITERS, 157).

2. The Frémont Gate, battered and without the eagle, still stands in Los Angeles's Elysian Park.

3. As supervisor of New York harbor, John Charles Frémont, Jr., had alerted Governor Roosevelt of pollution in the bay. In response Roosevelt requested a report and a tour of the "abuse." After the tour, Roosevelt invited Charley and his wife to dinner at his Oyster Bay home (see Roosevelt to John Charles Frémont, Jr., Mar. 16, July 15, 25, 1899, DLC—Theodore Roosevelt Papers).

To Edward William Bok

[Apr. 4, 1901]

My dear Mr. Bok

You *may* condense this. *I cannot.*

It cost me two sleepless nights to think it out. *I feel every word needed.*

Regarding *The Memoir,*[1] I would like your advice, but not now. Sincerely yours,

Jessie Benton Frémont

Los Angeles
April 4th 1901.

Your request calls for what resumes itself into a record of illness.

We hurried out here twelve years ago to save the life of Genl. Frémont, who was sinking under acute bronchitis. A year restored his health so completely that he went to New York and was returning here, successful in his business, when in his place there came a telegram saying his life had ended.

I have never opened a telegram since that one. Nervous prostration held me—as one paralyzed—for three years. With dawning strength rheumatism set in. In a sharp attack I had a fall. There was nothing to catch within reach, and my effort to save myself only resulted in badly fracturing the left hip joint. This being just over the *sciatic nerve* gave me its added "nerve pain." For six weeks I knew nothing but torture. This was ten months ago. I cannot yet stand alone. Though the bone has knit—a miracle of vitality at my age, seventy seven, but the *nerve shock* remains.

I never open a letter first nor am told anything which can agitate me. My daughter watches over me tenderly and I do try to be braver—but there are so many hours in ten months!

At first my sight felt the shock. My eyes seemed *awry*. Now, however thanks to patience and rigid abstaining from using them I can read all day. People are so kind. Books are brought to me and friends send me them by mail. Memoirs, travel, novels. I owe much to the "Sky Pilot"[2] with its lesson in cheerful resignation.

This amazing winter climate lets me go for long drives in my rolling-chair whose solid rubber tires enable me to cross streets. Or I sit in my garden with a bed-side table for desk and write there where the roses are in thousands. Both my sons are in the Phillipines and writing to them exhausts my little store of strength.

I had at heart a Memoir I wanted to write. Notwithstanding drawbacks I have written it—finished to the last word. Then, for compelling reasons I put away indefinitely.

My house is charming. To tourists it is always pointed out as the "Frémont House" and often Kodacked.

At night when we are shut in and a wood fire is needed I often think gratefully how cheerful it is—my good nurse and my daughter with their laughing rival games of solitaire (I never could learn it, *dominoes* are my one game) I with my book—a cripple for life—but that life is not long.

Jessie Benton Frémont

Los Angeles, April 4th, 1901.

ALS (DLC—Bok Papers). Named editor of the *Ladies' Home Journal* in 1889, civic-minded and practical Edward Bok (1863–1930) was in the process of making it the most popular woman's magazine in America. An article on JBF had been submitted to the magazine, and Bok requested a photograph. He ultimately rejected the article but queried JBF about her own literary activities, probably with a contribution to his magazine in mind (see JBF to Bok, Mar. 13, 18, 28, 1901, CLjC)

1. JBF refers not to "Great Events," the unpublished second volume of JCF's memoirs, which she and her son Frank completed in 1891, but her own personal "Memoirs," written while she was convalescing from a fractured hip, as described in this letter (both CU-B—Frémont Papers).

2. *The Sky Pilot* (1899) was a best-selling novel by Ralph Connor, a pseudonym for Canadian author Charles William Gordon (1860–1937), a Presbyterian minister. Set in the frontier West, it had a strong Christian message (TOYE, 306–8).

To John Burt Colton

Los Angeles, January 16th 1902.

My dear Mr. Colton

I answer your letter at once for it interests me greatly, although this is one of my bad days from rheumatism in my hurt leg. I must write briefly therefore and ask your kind excuses for seeming abruptness.

First I thank you heartily for your most kind letter to the President.[1]

As to Mrs. Bracken[2]—I have *not* heard from her *not now*—*nor ever.* She thought, apparently, that her genius could construct a man who would meet the requirements of a *portrait statue,* entirely unbiased by any evidence. She has not seen even a photograph I should judge. My old friend, Mr. Whiton,[3] sent me a photograph of what *she calls* a statue. A short, wellfed man, shading his eyes with his hand.

For a man of five feet ten, meeting all sorts of privations—until he looked *disembowelled* as my Mother said, this is a cardinal deviation from truth.

Mrs. Bracken has *never, in any way,* consulted me. St. Gaudens was a long after-thought as a "teacher."

Myself I should be really sorry to have her concerned *in any way* with the memory of the General.

I understand his grave is quite overgrown with weeds and brambles. You saw my helpless state last year. I am as helpless now as then and need a skilled nurse. I have no money to attend to this grave. The General would be the last person to allow me to neglect the living for the dead. But, if I get repayment for my property, *then* I intend placing there a simple slab with

The Pathfinder
Born January 21st, 1813
Died June [July] 13th, 1890.

and fence in the enclosure which was deeded to me as a burial plot. But no Mrs. Bracken.

Any telegraph office—the New York Post office could have given her my address. Let her go.

I will send you a letter to your addressed envelope. Also a photograph of myself to your Kansas City address. You are very kind to take so much trouble for me and I feel it. Sincerely yours,

Jessie Benton Frémont

John B. Colton, Esqre.
Kansas City.

ALS (CSmH—Jayhawkers of '49 Papers). At age seventeen, John B. Colton (1831–1919) had journeyed west with the famous Jayhawker party of Galesburg, Ill., which suffered so terribly in crossing Death Valley. Colton became the historian of the group and arranged annual meetings of the survivors; his extensive collection of Jayhawker material is now at the Huntington Library (LATTA [2], 161–63).

1. Colton had written Theodore Roosevelt to urge passage of JBF's Black Point claim bill. On Jan. 26, Colton wrote JBF that Roosevelt had replied positively (CSmH—Jayhawkers of '49 Papers).
2. Clio Hinton Bracken (d. 1925, age 55) was a New York City sculptor who had studied with Saint-Gaudens and Rodin. In 1895, the Associated Pioneers of the Territorial Days of California, based in New York, had commissioned her to create a heroic-size bronze statue of Frémont, to be placed at his Rockland Cemetery gravesite, overlooking the Hudson near Piermont, N.Y. The Bracken statue was evidently never completed, probably for lack of funds. In 1906, the state of New York placed a simple inscribed monument on the Frémonts' grave, where JBF's ashes had by then also been placed (New York *Herald,* Apr. 14, 28, 1895, May 20, 1900; New York *Times* obit., Feb. 13, 1925).
3. William H. Whiton of Piermont, N.Y., a longtime family friend, had helped

secure JCF's gravesite at Rockland Cemetery, of which he was a trustee (New York *Times,* Nov. 23, Dec. 16, 1894).

To Emma Hill (Hadley) Ballard

Los Angeles, June 26th, 1902.

My dear Mrs. Ballard

Your kind remembrance[1] of me came to me safely on my birthday, but I have been so constantly ill that until now I could not acknowledge them to you myself. I had forgotten the bronze of the Free Slave.[2] The bronze is from the gun buried with young Shaw who raised and led his negro troops, the 54th Massachusetts, to their death—and his— at Fort Wagner, S.C. You remember the answer of the opposing Genl. when young Shaw's body was asked for? "*No.* Let him lie among his niggers." The Shaws met this by saying in answer, "Let him lie among the people committed to his care—to rise with them at the last."[3]

Now, with the softening of time "*What does not man live down for he is conquered by the mighty hours*"[4]—now a memorial school, the Shaw school, rises where the beautiful boy rode to his death.

The statue is by Ward*—the books below it are Schoolcraft's History of the American Indians.[5] It is all a part of our old home—as it was a part of the life we had lived together. [*Margin note:* *You should see the Memorial bronze by St. Gaudens in Boston.[6] It is noble.]

It tires me to write or I would write you, now, the story of that cross given Mr. Frémont by the King of Prussia and the beautiful story of that beautiful sword.

The sword my youngest son has, the cross my daughter has—other swords my eldest son keeps,—so now you have the (nearly) full story of your picture.

With many thanks and much love to you I am yours most sincerely,

Jessie Benton Frémont

Written with much pain. J.B.F.

ALS (MoSHi—Benton Papers). Emma Hill (Hadley) Ballard was the wife of James F. Ballard (1851-1931), a wealthy St. Louis drug manufacturer, who by 1900 had begun to amass a noteworthy collection of oriental rugs, paintings, and other art objects. The Ballards had recently purchased an 1867 portrait of JCF painted by Giuseppe Fagnani. When Emma Ballard informed JBF, she replied that she was "glad to know that picture is again in honorable hands. When everything else was lost to us, this too was sold—for *120$*. It cost *1500$*. . . . It was to have been returned to me for the amount paid for it at the auction. A companion portrait of myself, same size, same framing of red velvet, and heavy outer frame of dark wood, was sold for 100$ and bought in by a friend who has given it to my youngest son." The purchaser of the JCF portrait, however, had asked "*400$* for the picture—then interest on the whole for all the time; I could not pay more than the 150$—that makes me very thankful you have it" (Feb. 10, 1902, MoSHi—Benton Papers). In 1909, the Ballards donated the JCF portrait to the Missouri Historical Society.

1. At JBF's request, Emma Ballard had sent her photographs of the JCF portrait, which showed him, in military uniform with a medal around his neck and a sword in his left hand, leaning against a bookshelf with a bronze sculpture on it.
2. Sculptor John Quincy Adams Ward (1830–1910) had incorporated a piece of the iron gun, given JBF by Robert Gould Shaw's second-in-command, Edward N. Hallowell, in a copy of his celebrated sculpture, *The Freedman*, which he cast for her in 1865 (see JBF to Ward, Dec. 23, 1865, and two undated letters [Dec.-Jan. 1865–66], NAll).
3. When Shaw's parents, Francis and Sarah Shaw, learned of Union efforts to retrieve their son's body from Fort Wagner, they stated that they wanted him to remain with the fallen black troops he had commanded (BURCHARD, 142–43).
4. Friedrich von Schiller, *The Death of Wallenstein*, act 5, sc. 3.
5. A reference to the six-volume work, *Historical and Statistical Information Respecting the History, Condition, and Prospects of the Indian Tribes of the United States* (1851–57), by pioneer ethnologist Henry Rowe Schoolcraft (1793–1864).
6. The monument to Shaw and his regiment by Augustus Saint-Gaudens (1848–1907) was unveiled in Boston in 1897 (BURCHARD, 15).

BIBLIOGRAPHY

The notes to the various letters contain full citations to government documents, legal cases, statutes, and newspapers, and they are not listed here. Nor are sources cited for information to be found in standard biographical dictionaries or guides to literature, although a few should be mentioned, such as the *Dictionary of American Biography* with its eight supplements, *The National Cyclopedia of American Biography* (63 vols. as of 1984), Dan L. Thrapp's *Encyclopedia of Frontier Biography* (3 vols., 1990), *Notable American Women* (4 vols., 1971–80), and the American Biographical Archive [microform], which collects information from several hundred English-language biographical reference works in the United States and Canada. While it does not give much information, the *Official Register of the United States, Containing a List of Officers and Employees in the Civil, Military, and Naval Service* (90 vols., 1830–1920) can be a validating tool for obscure government figures.

Lengthy Manuscripts Cited

"Great Events." "Great Events during the Life of Major General John C. Frémont . . . and of Jessie Benton Frémont," 1891. An unpublished manuscript prepared by JBF and her son, Francis Preston Frémont, following the death of John C. Frémont. It was intended as a sequel to his *Memoirs of My Life.* Bancroft Library, University of California, Berkeley.

JBF, "Memoirs." Jessie Benton Frémont, "Memoirs" in two drafts, partially in typescript and partially in handwriting, with some pages of additions. They were prepared late in life, perhaps as late as 1901–2. Generally, the

citations in this volume are to the second of the two versions. Bancroft
Library, University of California, Berkeley.

Books, Articles, and Theses Cited

ABBOTT   Abbott, John S. C. *The History of Hortense.* New York: Harper
& Brothers, 1870.

ALAMEDA   *Alameda County, The Eden of the Pacific: A History of Alameda County from Its Formation to the Present.* Oakland, Calif.: Tribune
Publishing, 1898.

AMES   Ames, Sister Aloysia, C. S. J. *The St. Mary's I Knew.* Tucson, Ariz.:
privately printed, 1970.

ANDERSEN ET AL.   Andersen, Timothy J., Eudorah M. Moore, and Robert
M. Winter, eds. *California Design, 1910.* Salt Lake City: Peregrine Smith
Books, 1974.

ANDREWS   Andrews, J. Cutler. *The North Reports the Civil War.* Pittsburgh: University of Pittsburgh Press, 1955.

APOSTOL   Apostol, Jane. "They Said It with Flowers: The Los Angeles
Flower Festival Society," *Southern California Quarterly,* 62 (Spring 1980):
67–76.

ASSOC. CHILDHOOD   Association for Childhood Education. *History of
the Kindergarten Movement in the Western States, Hawaii and Alaska.*
Compiled by Barbara Greenwood. Washington, D.C.: Association for Childhood Education, 1940.

BACON & HOWLAND   Bacon, Georgeanna Woolsey, and Eliza Woolsey
Howland. *Letters of a Family during the War for the Union, 1861–1865.*
2 vols. Privately printed, 1899.

BANCROFT   Bancroft, Hubert Howe. *History of California.* 7 vols. San
Francisco: History Company, 1884–90.

BARNARD   Barnard, Harry. *Rutherford B. Hayes and His America.* Indianapolis: Bobbs-Merrill, 1954.

BARTLETT   Bartlett, Ruhl J. *John C. Frémont and the Republican Party.*
1930. Reprint. New York: Da Capo Press, 1970.

BARTRAM   Bartram, R. Conover, ed. "The Diary of John Hamilton Cornish,
1846–1860," *South Carolina Historical Magazine,* 64 (Apr. 1963): 73–85.

BASSAN   Bassan, Maurice. *Hawthorne's Son: The Life and Literary Career
of Julian Hawthorne.* Columbus: Ohio State University Press, 1970.

BATES   Bates, Edward. *The Diary of Edward Bates, 1859–1866.* Ed. by
Howard K. Beale. Annual Report of the American Historical Association
for the Year 1930. Vol. 4. Washington, D.C.: U.S. Government Printing
Office, 1933.

BELL   Bell, Virginia. "Trenor Park: A New Englander in California," *California History*, 60 (Summer 1981): 158-71.

BENTON   Benton, Thomas Hart. *Thirty Years' View.* . . . 2 vols. New York: D. Appleton, 1854-56.

BIGELOW [1]   Bigelow, John. *Memoir of the Life and Public Services of John Charles Fremont.* New York: Derby & Jackson, 1856.

BIGELOW [2]   ———. *Retrospections of an Active Life.* 5 vols. New York: Baker & Taylor, 1909-13.

BLACK   Black, Jeremiah S. "The Character of Mr. Seward.—A Reply to C. F. Adams, Sr.," *Galaxy*, 17 (Jan.-June 1874): 107-21.

BLAIR & TARSHIS   Blair, Harry C., and Rebecca Tarshis, *Lincoln's Constant Ally: The Life of Colonel Edward D. Baker.* Portland, Oreg.: Oregon Historical Society, 1960.

BOATNER   Boatner, Mark Mayo. *The Civil War Dictionary.* New York: David McKay, 1962.

BOSQUI   Bosqui, Edward. *Memoirs.* Oakland, Calif.: Holmes Book Company, 1952.

BRAY   Bray, Martha. *Joseph Nicollet and His Map.* Philadelphia: American Philosophical Society, 1980.

BRADFORD   Bradford, Gamaliel. *Wives.* New York: Harper & Brothers, 1925.

BREMNER   Bremner, Robert H. *The Public Good: Philanthropy and Welfare in the Civil War Era.* New York: Alfred A. Knopf, 1980.

BRIGANCE   Brigance, William N. *Jeremiah Sullivan Black, a Defender of the Constitution and the Ten Commandants.* New York: Da Capo Press, 1971.

BROCK   Brock, R. A. *Virginia and Virginians.* Vol. 2. Richmond: H. H. Hardesty, 1888.

BROWNE   Browne, J. Ross. *J. Ross Browne: His Letters, Journals, and Writings.* Ed. by Lina F. Browne. Albuquerque: University of New Mexico Press, 1969.

BRUNNINGS   Brunnings, Florence E. *Folk Song Index.* New York: Garland, 1981.

BUCHANAN   Buchanan, Albert Russell. *David S. Terry of California, Dueling Judge.* San Marino, Calif.: Huntington Library, 1956.

BURCHARD   Burchard, Peter. *One Gallant Rush: Robert Gould Shaw and His Brave Black Regiment.* New York: St. Martin's Press, 1965.

BUTLER   Butler, Benjamin F. *Private and Official Correspondence of Gen. Benjamin F. Butler during the Period of the Civil War.* 5 vols. Norwood, Mass.: Plimpton Press, 1917.

CALLAHAN   Callahan, Edward W., ed. *List of Officers of the Navy of the*

United States and of the Marine Corps from 1775 to 1900. New York: L. R. Hamersly, 1901.

CARMAN & LUTHIN   Carman, Harry J., and Reinhard H. Luthin. *Lincoln and the Patronage.* New York: Columbia University Press, 1943.

C. CARPENTER   Carpenter, Charles. *History of American Schoolbooks.* Philadelphia: University of Pennsylvania Press, 1963.

J. A. CARPENTER   Carpenter, John A. *Sword and Olive Branch: Oliver Otis Howard.* Pittsburgh: University of Pittsburgh Press, 1964.

CASTEL   Castel, Albert F. *General Sterling Price and the Civil War in the West.* Baton Rouge: Louisiana State University Press, 1968.

CHAMBERS   Chambers, William N. *Old Bullion Benton, Senator from the New West: Thomas Hart Benton, 1782-1858.* Boston: Little, Brown, 1956.

F. J. CHILD   Child, Francis James, ed. *The English and Scottish Popular Ballads.* 5 vols. New York: The Folklore Press, 1956.

L. M. CHILD   Child, Lydia Maria. *Lydia Maria Child: Selected Letters, 1817-1880.* Ed. by Milton Meltzer and Patricia G. Holland. Amherst: University of Massachusetts Press, 1982.

CLAPP   Clapp, Margaret. *Forgotten First Citizen: John Bigelow.* Boston: Little, Brown, 1947.

CLARK   Clark, Robert D. *The Life of Matthew Simpson.* New York: Macmillan, 1956.

C. COLLINS   Collins, Carvel, ed. *Sam Ward in the Gold Rush.* Stanford: Stanford University Press, 1949.

L. COLLINS   Collins, Lewis. *Collins' Historical Sketches of Kentucky: History of Kentucky.* 2 vols. Covington, Ky.: Collins & Company, 1882.

CORNISH & LAAS   Cornish, Dudley Taylor, and Virginia Jeans Laas. *Lincoln's Lee: The Life of Samuel Phillips Lee, United States Navy, 1812-1897.* Lawrence: University Press of Kansas, 1986.

COSGRAVE   Cosgrave, George. *Early California Justice: The History of the United States District Court for the Southern District of California, 1849-1944.* Ed. by Roy Vernon Sowers. San Francisco: Grabhorn Press, 1948.

CRAMPTON   Crampton, C. Gregory. "The Opening of the Mariposa Mining Region, 1849-1859, with Particular Reference to the Mexican Land Grant of John Charles Frémont." Ph.D. dissertation, University of California, Berkeley, 1941.

CRANDALL   Crandall, Andrew W. *The Early History of the Republican Party, 1854-1856.* Boston: Richard G. Badger, 1930.

CROSBY   Crosby, Elisha O. *Memoirs . . . 1849 to 1864.* Ed. by Charles Albro Barker. San Marino, Calif.: Huntington Library, 1945.

CROUTHAMEL   Crouthamel, James L. *James Watson Webb, a Biography.* Middletown, Conn.: Wesleyan University Press, 1969.

CRUMP   Crump, Spencer. *Ride the Big Red Cars: How Trolleys Helped*

Build Southern California. Corona del Mar, Calif.: Trans-Anglo Books, 1977.

CULLUM   Cullum, George W. *Biographical Register of the Officers and Graduates of the U. S. Military Academy . . . 1802, to 1890,* 3d ed. 3 vols. Boston: Houghton Mifflin, 1891.

DALY   Daly, Maria. *Diary of a Union Lady, 1861–1865.* Ed. by Harold Earl Hammond. New York: Funk & Wagnalls, 1962.

DANA   Dana, Richard Henry. "Twenty-Four Years After," in *Two Years Before the Mast.* Boston: Houghton Mifflin, 1887.

DAVIS   Davis, Rebecca Harding. *Bits of Gossip.* Boston: Houghton Mifflin, 1904.

DOBSON   Dobson, Austin. *Four French Women.* London: Chatto & Windus, 1890.

DORMAN   Dorman, John Frederick. *The Prestons of Smithfield and Greenfield in Virginia: Descendants of John and Elizabeth (Patton) Preston through Five Generations.* Louisville, Ky.: Filson Club, 1982.

DOUGHERTY   Dougherty, Sister Dolorita, et al. *Sisters of St. Joseph of Carondolet.* St. Louis: B. Herder Book Company, 1966.

DUMKE   Dumke, Glenn S. *The Boom of the Eighties in Southern California.* San Marino, Calif.: Huntington Library, 1944.

DUNNING   Dunning, Charles (with Edward H. Peplow, Jr.). *Rocks to Riches: The Story of American Mining . . . as Reflected in the Colorful History of Mining in Arizona.* Phoenix: Southwest Publishing, 1959.

ELIOT   Eliot, William G. "Western Sanitary Commission," *North American Review,* 98 (Apr. 1864): 519–30.

FAUST   Faust, Patricia L, ed. *Historical Times Illustrated Encyclopedia of the Civil War.* New York: Harper & Row, 1986.

FED. WRITERS   Federal Writers' Project. *California: A Guide to the Golden State.* American Guide Series. New York: Hastings House, 1939.

FERMER   Fermer, Douglas. *James Gordon Bennett and the New York Herald: A Study of Editorial Opinion in the Civil War Era, 1854–1867.* Woodbridge, Suffolk, England: Royal Historical Society, 1986.

FIREMAN   Fireman, Bert M. "Frémont's Arizona Adventure," *The American West,* 1 (Winter 1964): 8–19.

FISH   Fish, Stuyvesant. *Ancestors of Hamilton Fish and Julia Ursin Niemcewicz Kean, His Wife.* New York: Evening Post Job Printing Office, 1929.

FISKE & LUMMIS   Fiske, Turbesé Lummis, and Keith Lummis. *Charles F. Lummis: The Man and His West.* Norman: University of Oklahoma Press, 1975.

FLICK   Flick, Lawrence F. "The Papago Indians and Their Church," *American Catholic Historical Society Records,* 5 (Dec. 1894): 385–415.

FRAZER   Frazer, Robert W. "The Ochoa Bond Negotiations of 1865–67," *Pacific Historical Review,* 11 (Dec. 1942): 397–414.

FREDRICKSON   Fredrickson, George M. *The Inner Civil War: Northern Intellectuals and the Crisis of the Union.* Harper & Row: New York, 1965.

E. B. FRÉMONT   Frémont, Elizabeth Benton. *Recollections of Elizabeth Benton Frémont.* Compiled by I. T. Martin. New York: F. H. Hitchcock, 1912.

J. B. FRÉMONT [1]   Frémont, Jessie Benton. *Souvenirs of My Time.* Boston: D. Lothrop, 1887.

J. B. FRÉMONT [2]   ———. *The Story of the Guard.* Boston: Ticknor and Fields, 1863.

J. B. FRÉMONT [3]   ———. *A Year of American Travel.* 1878. New ed. Introduction by Patrice Manahan. San Francisco: Book Club of California, 1960.

FROST   Frost, O. W. *Joaquin Miller.* New York: Twayne Publishers, 1967.

GAER   Gaer, Joseph, ed. *Bret Harte: Bibliography and Biographical Data.* New York: Burt Franklin, 1968.

GARRISON   Garrison, William Lloyd. *The Letters of William Lloyd Garrison.* Ed. by Walter M. Merrill. 6 vols. Cambridge: Belknap Press of Harvard University, 1971–81.

GATES   Gates, Paul W. "The Frémont-Jones Scramble for California Land Claims," *Southern California Quarterly,* 56 (Spring 1974): 13–44.

GIENAPP   Gienapp, William E. *The Origins of the Republican Party, 1852–1856.* New York: Oxford University Press, 1987.

GOFF   Goff, John S. *Arizona Territorial Officials: The Governors, 1863–1912.* Cave Creek, Ariz.: Black Mountain Press, 1975.

GRANT   Grant, Ulysses S. *The Papers of Ulysses S. Grant.* Ed. by John Y. Simon. 16 vols. Carbondale: Southern Illinois University Press, 1967–88.

GREENWAY   Greenway, John L. " 'Nervous Disease' and Electric Medicine," in *Pseudo-Science and Society in Nineteenth Century America.* Ed. by Arthur Wrobel. Lexington: University Press of Kentucky, 1987.

GROCE & WALLACE   Groce, George C., and David H. Wallace. *The New-York Historical Society's Dictionary of Artists in America, 1564–1860.* New Haven: Yale University Press, 1957.

GUILD & CARTER   Guild, Thelma S., and Harvey L. Carter. *Kit Carson: A Pattern for Heroes.* Lincoln: University of Nebraska Press, 1984.

GUINN   Guinn, J. M. *Historical and Biographical Record of Los Angeles and Vicinity.* Chicago: Chapman Publishing, 1901.

HAFEN & HAFEN   Hafen, LeRoy R., and Ann W. Hafen, eds. *Central Route to the Pacific by Gwinn Harris Heap.* Glendale, Calif.: Arthur H. Clark, 1957.

HALE   Hale, Sarah Josepha. *Woman's Record; or Sketches of All Distin-*

guished Women from the Creation to A. D. 1854. 1855. Reprint. New York: Source Books, 1970.

HALLOWELL   Hallowell, Anna Davis. *James and Lucretia Mott. Life and Letters.* Boston: Houghton Mifflin, 1884.

HALSTEAD   Halstead, Murat. *Trimmers, Trucklers and Temporizers: Notes of Murat Halstead from the Political Conventions of 1856.* Ed. by William B. Hesseltine and Rex G. Fisher. Madison: State Historical Society of Wisconsin, 1961.

HARLOW   Harlow, Neal. *California Conquered: War and Peace on the Pacific, 1846-1850.* Berkeley: University of California Press, 1982.

HARPER   Harper, Ida Husted. *The Life and Work of Susan B. Anthony.* 3 vols. Indianapolis: Bowen-Merrill, 1899-1908.

HARRINGTON   Harrington, Fred Harvey. *Fighting Politician: Major General N. P. Banks.* Philadelphia: University of Pennsylvania Press, 1948.

HARTE   Harte, Bret. *The Writings of Bret Harte.* Roaring Camp Edition. 20 vols. Boston: Houghton Mifflin, 1897-1914.

HASTINGS   Hastings, Robert P. "Rufus Allen Lockwood," *California Historical Society Quarterly,* 34 (June, Sept., Dec. 1955): 97-110, 239-63, 333-40.

HAY   Hay, John. *Lincoln and the Civil War in the Diaries and Letters of John Hay.* Ed. by Tyler Dennett. New York: Dodd, Mead, 1939.

HAYES   Hayes, Rutherford B. *Diary and Letters of Rutherford Birchard Hayes.* Ed. by Charles R. Williams. 2 vols. Columbus: Ohio State Archaeological and Historical Society, 1922.

HEITMAN   Heitman, Francis B. *Historical Register and Dictionary of the United States Army . . . 1789 . . . 1903.* 2 vols. Washington, D.C.: U.S. Government Printing Office, 1903.

HENDRICKS   Hendricks, William D. *M. H. Sherman: A Pioneer Developer of the Pacific Southwest.* Corona del Mar, Calif.: Sherman Foundation, 1973.

HERR   Herr, Pamela. *Jessie Benton Frémont.* New York: Franklin Watts, 1987.

HOLLI & JONES   Holli, Melvin G., and Peter d'A. Jones. *Biographical Dictionary of American Mayors, 1820-1980.* Westport, Conn.: Greenwood Press, 1981.

HOLLISTER.   Hollister, O. J. *Life of Schuyler Colfax.* New York: Funk & Wagnalls, 1886.

HOOGENBOOM   Hoogenboom, Ari A. *President Rutherford B. Hayes.* Lawrence: University Press of Kansas, 1988.

HOWARD   Howard, John Raymond. *Remembrance of Things Past.* New York: Thomas Y. Crowell, 1925.

HOWE   Howe, Henry. *Historical Collections. Virginia.* Charleston, S.C.: W. R. Babcock, 1849.

HUBBELL & LOTHROP   Hubbell, Thelma Lee, and Gloria Ricci Lothrop. "The Friday Morning Club: A Los Angeles Legacy," *Southern California Quarterly,* 50 (Mar. 1968): 59–90.

HUNT   Hunt, Herbert. *Tacoma: Its History and Its Builders.* 3 vols. Chicago: S. J. Clarke Publishing, 1916.

ISELY   Isely, Jeter A. *Horace Greeley and the Republican Party, 1853–1861.* Princeton: Princeton University Press, 1947.

JACKSON [1]   Jackson, Donald. "The Myth of the Frémont Howitzer," *Bulletin* of the Missouri Historical Society, 12 (Apr. 1967): 205–14.

JACKSON [2]   Jackson, Donald. *Voyages of the Steamship Yellow Stone.* New York: Ticknor & Fields, 1985.

JACKSON & SPENCE   Jackson, Donald, and Mary Lee Spence, eds. *The Expeditions of John Charles Frémont.* Vol. 1, *Travels from 1838 to 1844.* Urbana: University of Illinois Press, 1970.

JAMES   James, Marquis. *The Life of Andrew Jackson.* Indianapolis: Bobbs-Merrill, 1938.

JENSEN   Jensen, Joan. "After Slavery: Caroline Severance in Los Angeles," *Southern California Quarterly,* 48 (June 1966): 175–86.

JOHANNSEN   Johannsen, Robert W. *To the Halls of the Montezumas: The Mexican War in the American Imagination.* New York: Oxford University Press, 1985.

JOHNSTON   Johnston, William Preston. *The Life of Gen. Albert Sidney Johnston.* New York: D. Appleton, 1878.

JULIAN   Julian, George. "George Julian's Journal: The Assassination of Lincoln," *Indiana Magazine of History,* 11 (Dec. 1915): 324–37.

KASSON   Kasson, Mrs. John A. "An Iowa Woman in Washington, D.C., 1861–65," *Iowa Journal of History,* 52 (Jan. 1954): 61–90.

KELLY   Kelly, Howard A. *A Cyclopedia of American Medical Biography.* 2 vols. Philadelphia: W. B. Saunders, 1912.

KIRWIN   Kirwin, Albert D. *John J. Crittenden.* Lexington: University of Kentucky Press, 1962.

KLEIN   Klein, Philip Shriver. *President James Buchanan.* University Park: Pennsylvania State University Press, 1962.

KOERNER   Koerner, Gustave. *Memoirs of Gustave Koerner, 1809–1896.* Ed. by Thomas J. McCormack. 2 vols. Cedar Rapids, Ia.: Torch Press, 1909.

LAMB   Lamb, Martha J. *History of the City of New York.* 2 vols. New York: A. S. Barnes, 1877–80.

LANE   Lane, Mrs. Julien C. *Key and Allied Families.* Macon, Ga.: Press of J. W. Burke, 1931.

LARKIN   Larkin, Thomas. *The Larkin Papers.* Ed. by George P. Hammond. 10 vols. Berkeley: University of California Press for the Bancroft Library, 1951–64.

LATTA [1]   Latta, Frank F. "Alexis Godey in Kern County," *Kern County Historical Society Fifth Annual Publication* (Nov. 1939): 23–52.

LATTA [2]   ———. *Death Valley '49ers.* Santa Cruz, Calif.: Bear State Books, 1979.

LAVENDER   Lavender, David. *Bent's Fort.* Garden City, N.Y.: Doubleday, 1954.

LECOMPTE   Lecompte, Janet. "A Letter from Jessie to Kit," *Bulletin* of the Missouri Historical Society, 29 (July 1973): 260–63.

LINCOLN   Lincoln, Abraham. *The Collected Works of Abraham Lincoln.* Ed. by Roy P. Basler. 8 vols. New Brunswick: Rutgers University Press, 1953–55.

LONG   Long, E. B. *The Civil War Day by Day.* Garden City, N.Y.: Doubleday, 1971.

LONGACRE   Longacre, Edward G. "A Profile of General Justus McKinstry," *Civil War Times Illustrated,* 17 (July 1978): 14–21.

LONGFELLOW   Longfellow, Henry Wadsworth. *The Letters of Henry Wadsworth Longfellow.* Ed. by Andrew Hilen. 6 vols. Cambridge: Belknap Press of Harvard University, 1966–82.

LOTHROP   Lothrop, Gloria Ricci. "Westering Women and the Ladies of Los Angeles: Some Similarities and Differences," *South Dakota Review,* 19 (Spring/Summer 1981): 41–67.

MCCLELLAN   McClellan, George B. *The Civil War Papers of George B. McClellan: Selected Correspondence, 1860–1865.* Ed. by Stephen W. Sears. New York: Ticknor & Fields, 1989.

MCFEELY   McFeely, William S. *Grant: A Biography.* New York: W. W. Norton, 1981.

MCGROARTY   McGroarty, John Steven, ed. *History of Los Angeles County.* 3 vols. Chicago: American Historical Society, 1923.

MCKELVEY   McKelvey, Susan D. *Botanical Exploration of the Trans-Mississippi West, 1790–1850.* Jamaica Plain, Mass.: Arnold Aboretum of Harvard University, 1955.

MCLANE   Monaghan, Jay. *The Private Journal of Louis McLane, U.S.N., 1844–48.* Los Angeles: Santa Barbara Historical Society, 1971.

MCPHERSON   McPherson, James M. *Battle Cry of Freedom: The Civil War Era.* New York: Oxford University Press, 1988.

MAXWELL   Maxwell, William Quentin. *Lincoln's Fifth Wheel: The Political History of the United States Sanitary Commission.* New York: Longmans, Green, 1956.

MELENDY & GILBERT   Melendy, H. Brett, and Benjamin F. Gilbert. *The Governors of California*. Georgetown, Calif.: Talisman Press, 1965.

MEMOIRS   Frémont, John C. *Memoirs of My Life . . . Including in the Narrative Five Journeys of Western Exploration during the Years 1842, 1843-4, 1845-7, 1848-9, 1853-4. Together with a Sketch of the Life of Senator Benton in Connection with Western Expansion by Jessie Benton Frémont*. Chicago: Belford, Clarke, 1887.

R. MILLER   Miller, Robert E. "Zagonyi," *Missouri Historical Review*, 76 (Jan. 1982): 174-92.

S. MILLER   Miller, Sally C. P. "James McDowell," *Washington and Lee Historical Papers*, 5 (1895): 37-210.

MILNE   Milne, Gordon. *George William Curtis and the Genteel Tradition*. Bloomington: Indiana University Press, 1956.

MINER   Miner, H. Craig. *The St. Louis–San Francisco Transcontinental Railroad: The Thirty-fifth Parallel Project, 1853-1890*. Lawrence: University Press of Kansas, 1972.

MONTAGUE   Montague, William L. *The Saint Louis Business Directory for 1853-54*. St. Louis: E. A. Lewis, 1853.

MOODY   Moody, Eric N., ed. *Western Carpetbagger: The Extraordinary Memoirs of "Senator" Thomas Fitch*. Reno: University of Nevada Press, 1978.

MOORE   Moore, Frank, ed. *The Rebellion Record: A Diary of American Events, with Documents*. 11 vols. New York: G. P. Putnam/D. Van Nostrand, 1861-68.

MORAN   Moran, Benjamin. *The Journal of Benjamin Moran, 1857-1865*. Ed. by Sarah A. Wallace and Frances E. Gillespie. 2 vols. Chicago: University of Chicago Press, 1948-49.

MORGAN   Morgan, Murray. *Puget's Sound: A Narrative of Early Tacoma and the Southern Sound*. Seattle: University of Washington Press, 1979.

MORRIS & MORRIS   Morris, Dan, and Inez Morris. *Who Was Who in American Politics*. New York: Hawthorn Books, 1974.

MORTON   Morton, J. Sterling. *Illustrated History of Nebraska*. 3 vols. Lincoln: Jacob North, 1905-13.

NEVINS [1]   Nevins, Allan. *Frémont: Pathmarker of the West*. New York: Longmans, Green, 1955.

NEVINS [2]   ———. *Hamilton Fish: The Inner History of the Grant Administration*. New York: Dodd, Mead, 1936.

NEVINS [3]   ———. *The War for the Union*. 4 vols. New York: Charles Scribner's Sons, 1959-71.

NICOLAY & HAY   Nicolay, John G., and John Hay. *Abraham Lincoln: A History*. 10 vols. New York: Century Company, 1890.

NYE   Nye, Russel B. *George Bancroft: Brahmin Rebel.* New York: Alfred A. Knopf, 1944.

OED   *The Oxford English Dictionary.* 2d ed. 20 vols. Prepared by J. A. Simpson and E. S. C. Weiner. Oxford: Clarendon Press, 1989.

OFFICIAL RECORDS   *The War of the Rebellion: A Compilation of the Official Records of the Union and Confederate Armies.* 129 vols. Washington, D.C.: U.S. Government Printing Office, 1880–1902.

OLMSTED   Olmsted, Frederick Law. *The Papers of Frederick Law Olmsted.* Vol. 5., *The California Frontier, 1863–1865.* Ed. by Victoria Post Ranney, Gerard J. Rauluk, and Carolyn F. Hoffman. Baltimore: Johns Hopkins University Press, 1990.

OLSEN   Olsen, Tillie. "A Biographical Interpretation," in *Life in the Iron Mills and Other Stories* by Rebecca Harding Davis. Old Westbury, N.Y.: Feminist Press, 1985.

OWSLEY   Owsley, Frank Lawrence. *King Cotton Diplomacy: Foreign Relations of the Confederate States of America.* 2d ed. Revised by Harriet Chappell Owsley. Chicago: University of Chicago Press, 1959.

PALMQUIST   Palmquist, Peter E. *Carleton E. Watkins: Photographer of the American West.* Albuquerque: University of New Mexico Press for the Amon Carter Museum, 1983.

PARRISH   Parrish, William Earl. *Turbulent Partnership: Missouri and the Union, 1861–1865.* Columbia: University of Missouri Press, 1963.

PAULSEN   Paulsen, George E. "The Legal Battle for the Candelaria Mine in Durango, Mexico, 1890–1917," *Arizona and the West,* 23 (Autumn 1981): 243–66.

PEARSON   Pearson, Henry Greenleaf. *The Life of John A. Andrew.* 2 vols. Boston: Houghton Mifflin, 1904.

PESKIN   Peskin, Allan. *Garfield.* Kent: Kent State University Press, 1978.

PHILLIPS   Phillips, Catherine Coffin. *Jessie Benton Frémont: A Woman Who Made History.* San Francisco: John Henry Nash, 1935.

PICKARD   Pickard, Samuel T. *The Life and Letters of John Greenleaf Whittier.* 2 vols. Boston: Houghton Mifflin, 1895.

PIONEER REGISTER   Bancroft, Hubert Howe. *Register of Pioneer Inhabitants of California, 1542 to 1848.* Los Angeles: Dawson's Book Shop, 1964.

POLK   Quaife, M. M., ed. *The Diary of James K. Polk during His Presidency, 1845–1849.* 4 vols. Chicago: A. C. McClurg, 1910.

POORE   Poore, Ben Perley. *The Political Register and Congressional Directory . . . 1776–1878.* Boston: Houghton, Osgood, 1878.

PORTER & DAVENPORT   Porter, Mae Reed, and Odessa Davenport. *Scotsman in Buckskin: Sir William Drummond Stewart and the Rocky Mountain Fur Trade.* New York: Hastings House, 1963.

POSNER   Posner, Russell M. "Thomas Starr King and the Mercy Million," *California Historical Society Quarterly*, 43 (Dec. 1964): 291–307.

PRESS REFERENCE   *Press Reference Library. Notables of the West.* 2 vols. International News Service: New York, 1913.

PREUSS   Preuss, Charles. *Exploring with Frémont: The Private Diaries of Charles Preuss.* Trans. and ed. by Erwin G. and Elisabeth K. Gudde. Norman: University of Oklahoma Press, 1958.

PRYOR   Pryor, Elizabeth Brown. *Clara Barton: Professional Angel.* Philadelphia: University of Pennsylvania Press, 1987.

RATHER   Rather, Lois. *Jessie Frémont at Black Point.* Oakland, Calif.: Rather Press, 1974.

RAWLEY   Rawley, James A. *Edwin D. Morgan, 1811–1883: Merchant in Politics.* New York: Columbia University Press, 1955.

RIDD   Ridd, Jay Donald. "Almon Whiting Babbitt, Mormon Emissary." M.A. thesis, University of Utah, 1953.

ROBBINS   Robbins, Christine Chapman. "John Torrey: His Life and Times," *Bulletin of the Torrey Botanical Club*, 95 (Nov.-Dec. 1968): 519–65

ROBERT   Robert, Joseph Clarke. *The Road from Monticello: A Study of the Virginia Slavery Debate of 1832.* Durham, N.C.: Duke University Press, 1941.

RODGERS   Rodgers, Andrew Denny. *John Torrey: A Story of North American Botany.* Princeton: Princeton University Press, 1942.

ROLAND   Roland, Charles P. *Albert Sidney Johnston: Soldier of Three Republics.* Austin: University of Texas Press, 1964.

ROPER   Roper, Laura Wood. *F. L. O.: A Biography of Frederick Law Olmsted.* Baltimore: Johns Hopkins University Press, 1973.

ROSIN   Rosin, Wilbert Henry. "Hamilton Rowan Gamble, Missouri's Civil War Governor." Ph.D. dissertation, University of Missouri, 1960; Ann Arbor: University Microfilms, 1969.

ROSS   Ross, Ishbel. *Rebel Rose: Life of Rose O'Neal, Confederate Spy.* New York: Harper & Brothers, 1954.

ROWAN & PRIMM   Rowan, Steven, and James Neal Primm. *Germans for a Free Missouri: Translations from the St. Louis Radical Press, 1857–1862.* Columbia: University of Missouri Press, 1983.

ROYCE [1]   Royce, Josiah. "Frémont," *Atlantic Monthly*, 66 (Oct. 1890): 548–57.

ROYCE [2]   Clendenning, John, ed. *The Letters of Josiah Royce.* Chicago: University of Chicago Press, 1970.

RUDDY   Ruddy, Ella Giles. *The Mother of Clubs: Caroline M. Seymour Severance.* Los Angeles: Baumgardt Publishing, 1906.

SARGENT   Sargent, Shirley, ed. *Mother Lode Narratives* by Jessie Benton Frémont. Ashland, Oreg.: Lewis Osborne, 1970.

SCHARF [1]   Scharf, J. Thomas. *The Chronicles of Baltimore.* Baltimore, Md.: Turnbull Brothers, 1874.

SCHARF [2]   ———. *History of Saint Louis City and County.* 2 vols. Philadelphia: Louis H. Everts, 1883.

SCHLESINGER   Schlesinger, Arthur M., Jr. *The Age of Jackson.* Boston: Little, Brown, 1945.

SCHOFIELD   Schofield, John M. *Forty-Six Years in the Army.* New York: Century Company, 1897.

SCHURZ   Schurz, Carl. *The Reminiscences of Carl Schurz, 1852-1863.* 3 vols. New York: McClure, 1907-8.

SEWARD   Seward, Frederick. *Seward at Washington . . . 1846-1861.* New York: Derby and Miller, 1891.

SHAFF & SHAFF   Shaff, Howard, and Audrey Karl Shaff. *Six Wars at a Time: The Life and Times of Gutzon Borglum, Sculptor of Mount Rushmore.* Sioux Falls, S.D.: Center for Western Studies, Augusta College, 1985.

SHALHOPE   Shalhope, Robert E. *Sterling Price.* Columbia: University of Missouri Press, 1971.

E. B. SMITH [1]   Smith, Elbert B. *Francis Preston Blair.* New York: Free Press, 1980.

E. B. SMITH [2]   ———. *Magnificent Missourian: The Life of Thomas Hart Benton.* Philadelphia: J. B. Lippincott, 1958.

F. B. SMITH   Smith, F. B. *The Making of the Second Reform Bill.* Melbourne, Australia: Melbourne University Press, 1966.

W. E. SMITH   Smith, William Ernest. *The Francis Preston Blair Family in Politics.* 2 vols. New York: Macmillan, 1933.

SNYDER   Snyder, Agnes. *Dauntless Women in Childhood Education, 1856-1931.* Washington, D.C.: Association for Childhood Education International, 1972.

SPARKS   Sparks, Jared. *The Life of Washington.* Boston: Ferdinand Andrews, 1839.

C. SPENCE   Spence, Clark C. *British Investments and the American Mining Frontier, 1860-1901.* Ithaca: Cornell University Press for the American Historical Association, 1958.

M. L. SPENCE [1]   Spence, Mary Lee. "David Hoffman: Frémont's Mariposa Agent in London," *Southern California Quarterly,* 60 (Winter 1978): 379-403.

M. L. SPENCE [2]   ———, ed. *The Expeditions of John Charles Frémont.* Vol. 3, *Travels from 1848 to 1854.* Urbana: University of Illinois Press, 1984.

M. L. SPENCE [3]   ———. "George W. Wright: Politician, Lobbyist, Entrepreneur," *Pacific Historical Review,* 58 (Aug. 1989): 345-59

SPENCE & JACKSON   Spence, Mary Lee, and Donald Jackson, eds. *The*

Expeditions of John Charles Frémont. Vol. 2, *The Bear Flag Revolt and the Court-Martial.* Urbana: University of Illinois Press, 1973.

SPIESS Spiess, Lincoln Bunce. "Carl Wimar: The Missouri Historical Society's Collection," *Gateway Heritage,* 3 (Winter, 1982–83): 16–29.

SPLITTER Splitter, Henry Winfred. "Education in Los Angeles, 1850–1900," pt. 2, *Historical Society of Southern California Quarterly,* 33 (Sept. 1951): 226–44.

STANTON Stanton, Elizabeth Cady. *Elizabeth Cady Stanton as Revealed in Her Letters, Diary, and Reminiscences.* Ed. by Theodore Stanton and Harriet Stanton Blatch. 2 vols. New York: Harper & Brothers, 1922.

STANTON ET AL. Stanton, Elizabeth Cady, Susan B. Anthony, and Matilda J. Gage. *History of Woman Suffrage.* Vols. 1–2 (1848–76). New York: Fowler & Wells, 1881–82.

STARR Starr, Kevin. *Inventing the Dream: California through the Progressive Era.* New York: Oxford University Press, 1985.

STEWART Stewart, James Brewer. *Wendell Phillips: Liberty's Hero.* Baton Rouge: Louisiana State University Press, 1986.

STRONG Strong, George Templeton. *The Diary of George Templeton Strong.* Ed. by Allan Nevins and Milton Halsey Thomas. 4 vols. New York: Macmillan, 1952.

STURHAHN Sturhahn, Joan. *Carvalho: Portrait of a Forgotten American.* New York: Richwood Publishing, 1976.

SWANBERG Swanberg, W. A. *Sickles the Incredible.* New York: Charles Scribner's Sons, 1956.

TALBOT Hine, Robert V., and Savoie Lottinville, eds. *Soldier in the West: Letters of Theodore Talbot during His Services in California, Mexico, and Oregon, 1845–53.* Norman: University of Oklahoma Press, 1972.

TANSILL Tansill, Charles Callan. *The Purchase of the Danish West Indies.* Baltimore: Johns Hopkins University Press, 1932.

G. TAYLOR Taylor, George Rogers. "The Beginnings of Mass Transportation in Urban America," pt. 2, *Smithsonian Journal of History,* 1 (Autumn 1966): 39–52.

V. TAYLOR Taylor, Virginia H. *The Franco-Texan Land Company.* Austin: University of Texas Press, 1969.

TEBBEL Tebbel, John A. *A History of Book Publishing in the United States.* 2 vols. New York: R. R. Bowker, 1975.

THARP Tharp, Louise Hall. *The Peabody Sisters of Salem.* Boston: Little, Brown, 1950.

G. THOMPSON Thompson, Gerald. *Edward F. Beale and the American West.* Albuquerque: University of New Mexico Press, 1983.

O. THOMPSON Thompson, Oscar, ed. *The International Cyclopedia of Music and Musicians.* 11th ed. New York: Dodd, Mead, 1895.

TOYE   Toye, William, ed. *The Oxford Companion to Canadian Literature.* Toronto: Oxford University Press, 1983.

TRACY   Tracy, Albert. "Frémont's Pursuit of Jackson ... The Journal of Colonel Albert Tracy, March-July 1862," ed. by Francis F. Wayland, *Virginia Magazine of History and Biography,* 70 (1962): 165–93, 332–54.

TRAPIER   Trapier, Paul. "Private Register of the Rev. Paul Trapier," *South Carolina Historical Magazine,* 58 (Apr.-Oct. 1957): 94–113, 163–82, 246–65.

UPHAM   Upham, Charles Wentworth. *Life, Explorations and Public Services of John Charles Fremont.* Boston: Ticknor and Fields, 1856.

VAN DEUSEN [1]   Van Deusen, Glyndon. *Thurlow Weed: Wizard of the Lobby.* Boston: Little, Brown, 1947.

VAN DEUSEN [2]   Van Deusen, Glyndon. *William Henry Seward.* New York: Oxford University Press, 1967.

VASVARY   Vasvary, Edmund. *Lincoln's Hungarian Heroes: The Participation of Hungarians in the Civil War, 1861-1865.* Washington, D.C.: Hungarian Reformed Federation of America, 1939.

WAGONER   Wagoner, Jay J. *Arizona Territory, 1863-1912.* Tucson: University of Arizona Press, 1970.

A. WALLACE   Wallace, Andrew. *Gen. August V. Kautz and the Southwestern Frontier.* Tucson: privately published, 1967.

D. H. WALLACE   Wallace, David H. *John Rogers: The People's Sculptor.* Middletown, Conn.: Wesleyan University Press, 1967.

WARD   Ward, George Kemp. *Andrew Warde and His Descendants, 1597-1910.* New York: A. T. De La Mare, 1910.

WARNER   Warner, Ezra J. *Generals in Blue: Lives of the Union Commanders.* Baton Rouge: Louisiana State University Press, 1964.

WASSON   Wasson, R. Gordon. *The Hall Carbine Affair.* New York: Pandick Press, 1948.

WEBSTER   Webster, Samuel Charles, ed. *Mark Twain, Business Man.* Boston: Little, Brown, 1946.

WEIGLEY   Weigley, Russell F. *Quartermaster General of the Union Army: A Biography of M. C. Meigs.* New York: Columbia University Press, 1959.

WEISS   Weiss, John. *Life and Correspondence of Theodore Parker.* 2 vols. New York: D. Appleton, 1864.

WELLS   Wells, Harry L. "Who Was the Pathfinder," *Overland Monthly,* 16 (Sept. 1890): 242–50.

WENDTE   Wendte, Charles W. *Thomas Starr King, Patriot and Preacher.* Boston: Beacon Press, 1921.

WHITTIER [1]   Whittier, John Greenleaf. *The Complete Poetical Works of John Greenleaf Whittier.* Boston: Houghton Mifflin, 1894.

WHITTIER [2]   ———. *The Letters of John Greenleaf Whittier.* Ed. by John B. Pickard. 3 vols. Cambridge: Belknap Press of Harvard University, 1975.

WILBERFORCE   Wilberforce, Reginald G. *Life of the Right Reverend Samuel Wilberforce.* . . . Vol. 3. London: John Murray, 1882.

D. WILSON   Wilson, Dorothy Clarke. *Stranger and Traveler: The Story of Dorothea Dix.* Boston: Little, Brown, 1975.

R. WILSON   Wilson, Rockwell. *The Utes: A Forgotten People.* Denver: Sage Books, 1956.

WOODFORD   Woodford, Frank B. *Lewis Cass.* New Brunswick, N.J.: Rutgers University Press, 1950.

WRIGHT   Wright, Carol von Pressentin. *New York* (Blue Guide). London: Ernest Benn, 1983.

WULFECK   Wulfeck, Dorothy Ford. *Marriages of Some Virginia Residents, 1607–1800.* 2 vols. Baltimore, Md.: Genealogical Publishing, 1986.

INDEX

The following abbreviations are used:

JBF   Jessie Benton Frémont
JCF   John Charles Frémont
EBF   Elizabeth Benton Frémont
Charley   John Charles Frémont, Jr.
Frank   Francis Preston Frémont